Lecture Notes in Computer Science   9610

Commenced Publication in 1973
Founding and Former Series Editors:
Gerhard Goos, Juris Hartmanis, and Jan van Leeuwen

Editorial Board

More information about this series at http://www.springer.com/series/7410

Kazue Sako (Ed.)

Topics in Cryptology – CT-RSA 2016

The Cryptographers' Track at the RSA Conference 2016
San Francisco, CA, USA, February 29 – March 4, 2016
Proceedings

 Springer

Editor
Kazue Sako
NEC Cloud Systems Research Laboratories
Kawasaki
Japan

ISSN 0302-9743   ISSN 1611-3349   (electronic)
Lecture Notes in Computer Science
ISBN 978-3-319-29484-1   ISBN 978-3-319-29485-8   (eBook)
DOI 10.1007/978-3-319-29485-8

Library of Congress Control Number: 2016930536

LNCS Sublibrary: SL4 – Security and Cryptology

Printed on acid-free paper

This Springer imprint is published by SpringerNature
The registered company is Springer International Publishing AG Switzerland

Preface

The RSA conference has been a major international event for information security experts since its inception in 1991. It is an annual event that attracts hundreds of vendors and thousands of participants from industry, government, and academia.

Since 2001, the RSA conference has included the Cryptographers' Track (CT-RSA), which provides a forum for current research in cryptography.

CT-RSA has become a major publication venue in cryptography. It covers a wide variety of topics from public-key to symmetric-key cryptography and from cryptographic protocols to primitives and their implementation security.

This volume represents the proceedings of the 2016 RSA Conference Cryptographers' Track, which was held in San Francisco, California, from February 29 to March 4, 2016.

A total of 76 full papers were submitted for review, out of which 26 papers were selected for presentation. As chair of the Program Committee, I deeply thank all the authors who contributed the results of their innovative research. My appreciation also goes to all the members of the Program Committee and the designated external reviewers who carefully reviewed the submissions. Each submission had at least three independent reviewers, and those authored/co-authored by a member of the Program Committee had six reviewers. The process of selection was very difficult, as each submission had different aspects in its contribution. It was carried out with enthusiastic discussion among the members of the Program Committee in a transparent manner.

In addition to the contributed talks, the program included a panel discussion moderated by Bart Preneel on "The Future of Bitcoin and Cryptocurrencies."

December 2015   Kazue Sako

Organization

The RSA Cryptographers' Track is an independently managed component of the annual RSA conference.

Steering Committee

Josh Benaloh	Microsoft Research, USA
Kaisa Nyberg	Aalto University School of Science, Finland
Ron Rivest	Massachusetts Institute of Technology, USA
Kazue Sako	NEC, Japan
Moti Yung	Google, USA

Program Chair

Kazue Sako	NEC, Japan

Program Committee

Frederik Armknecht	University of Mannheim, Germany
Nuttapong Attrapadung	AIST, Japan
Josh Benaloh	Microsoft Research, USA
Melissa Chase	Microsoft Research, USA
Chen-Mou Cheng	National Taiwan University, Taiwan
Jung Hee Cheon	Seoul National University, Korea
Jean-Sebastien Coron	University of Luxembourg, Luxembourg
Pooya Farshim	Queen's University Belfast, UK
Shai Halevi	IBM T.J. Watson Research Center, USA
Helena Handschuh	Cryptography Research, Inc., USA
Hüseyin Hışıl	Yasar University, Turkey
Thomas Johansson	Lund University, Sweden
Marc Joye	Technicolor, USA
Ghassan Karame	NEC Laboratories Europe, Germany
Nathan Keller	Bar-Ilan University, Israel
Vladimir Kolesnikov	Bell Labs Alcatel-Lucent, USA
Susan Langford	Hewlett-Packard Company, USA
Dongdai Lin	Chinese Academy of Sciences, China
Stefan Mangard	Graz University of Technology, Austria
Tal Moran	IDC Herzliya, Israel
Maria Naya-Plasencia	Inria, France
Kaisa Nyberg	Aalto University School of Science, Finland
Satoshi Obana	Hosei University, Japan
Kazue Sako (Chair)	NEC, Japan
Palash Sarkar	Indian Statistical Institute, India

Yu Sasaki	NTT, Japan
Ali Aydin Selcuk	TOBB University of Economics and Technology, Turkey
Abhi Shelet	University of Virginia, USA
Nigel Smart	University of Bristol, UK
Marc Stevens	CWI, The Netherlands
Willy Susilo	University of Wollongong, Australia
Dominique Unruh	University of Tartu, Estonia
Huaxiong Wang	Nanyang Technological University, Singapore

External Reviewers

Masayuki Abe	Mike Hutter	Khoa Nguyen
Murat Ak	Toshiyuki Isshiki	Valtteri Niemi
Achiya Bar-On	Christian Janson	Dan Page
Manuel Barbosa	Jinhyuck Jeong	Ludovic Perret
Asli Bay	Shaoquan Jiang	Sami Saab
Sonia Belaid	Kimmo Järvinen	Yusuke Sakai
Jens-Matthias Bohli	Miran Kim	Alexander Schlösser
Florian Bourse	Sungwook Kim	Jyh-Ren Shieh
Billy Brumley	Taechan Kim	Seonghan Shin
Anne Canteaut	Mehmet Sabir Kiraz	Shashank Singh
Jie Chen	Ilya Kizhvatov	Daniel Slamanig
Jiun-Peng Chen	Thomas Korak	Yongsoo Song
Rongmao Chen	Po-Chun Kuo	Claudio Soriente
Elke De Mulder	Virginie Lallemand	Martin Strand
Fabrizio De Santis	Hyung Tae Lee	Halil Kemal Taskin
Murat Demircioglu	Joo Hee Lee	Isamu Teranishi
David Derler	Yoohyeon Lee	Yosuke Todo
Itai Dinur	Wenting Li	Mike Tunstall
Nadia El Mrabet	Kaitai Liang	David Vigilant
Keita Emura	Zhen Liu	Lei Wang
Anne-Maria	Jake Longo Galea	Shota Yamada
Ernvall-Hytönen	Mark Marson	Guomin Yang
Daniel Gruss	Dan Martin	Shang-Yi Yang
Fuchun Guo	Takahiro Matsuda	Ramazan Yilmaz
Mike Hamburg	Amir Moradi	Yu Yu
Jinguang Han	Steven Myers	Emre Yüce
Xinyi Huang	Yusuke Naito	Rina Zeitoun

Contents

Lattice Cryptography

Cryptanalysis of Symmetric Key Encryption

Message Authentication Code and PRF-Security

Security of Public Key Encryption

Secure Key Exchange Schemes

Mitigating Server Breaches in Password-Based Authentication: Secure and Efficient Solutions

Olivier Blazy[1], Céline Chevalier[2]([✉]), and Damien Vergnaud[3]

[1] Université de Limoges, XLim, Limoges, France
[2] Université Panthéon-Assas, Paris, France
celine.chevalier@ens.fr
[3] ENS, CNRS, INRIA and PSL Research University, Paris, France

Abstract. *Password-Authenticated Key Exchange* allows users to generate a strong cryptographic key based on a shared "human-memorable" password without requiring a public-key infrastructure. It is one of the most widely used and fundamental cryptographic primitives. Unfortunately, mass password theft from organizations is continually in the news and, even if passwords are salted and hashed, brute force breaking of password hashing is usually very successful in practice.

In this paper, we propose two efficient protocols where the password database is somehow shared among two servers (or more), and authentication requires a distributed computation involving the client and the servers. In this scenario, even if a server compromise is doable, the secret exposure is not valuable to the adversary since it reveals only a share of the password database and does not permit to brute force guess a password without further interactions with the parties for each guess. Our protocols rely on *smooth projective hash functions* and are proven secure under classical assumption in the standard model (*i.e.* do not require idealized assumption, such as random oracles).

Keywords: Password-authenticated key exchange · Distributed computation · Decision diffie-hellman · Smooth projective hashing

1 Introduction

Authenticated Key Exchange protocols enable two parties to establish a shared cryptographically strong key over an insecure network under the complete control of an adversary. This primitive is one of the most widely used and fundamental cryptographic primitives and it obviously requires the parties to have authentication means, *e.g.* (public or secret) cryptographic keys or short (*i.e.*, low-entropy) secret keys.

PAKE, for *Password-Authenticated Key Exchange*, allows users to generate a strong cryptographic key based on a shared "human-memorable" password without requiring a public-key infrastructure. In this setting, an adversary controlling all communication in the network should not be able to mount an *offline dictionary attack*. More precisely, an eavesdropper should not obtain enough

© Springer International Publishing Switzerland 2016
K. Sako (Ed.): CT-RSA 2016, LNCS 9610, pp. 3–18, 2016.
DOI: 10.1007/978-3-319-29485-8_1

information to be able to brute force guess a password without further interactions with the parties for each guess. Note that *online dictionary attacks* in which an adversary simply attempts to log-in repeatedly, trying each possible low-entropy password can be dealt with using other computer security methods (such as limiting the number of attempts). In particular, strong security can be obtained even using passwords chosen from a small set of possible values (a four-digit pin, for example).

Incidents of sensitive customer information "hacking" (including leaking of passwords) in e-commerce systems are frequently revealed in the newspaper. In addition to major reputational damage, a company with a significant data breach may be sued by its clients for the breach and may be suspended or disqualified from future public sector or government work.

To alleviate the threat that stored passwords are revealed immediately in case of a server compromise, many servers adopt the approach for storing passwords in a hashed form with a random salt. When the database of hashed password is compromised, the offline dictionary attack requires a more important computational effort but remains usually possible. The notion of *Verifier-based PAKE*, where the client owns a password pw and the server knows a one-way transformation v of the password only were proposed by Bellovin and Merritt [BM92]. The two players eventually agree on a common high entropy secret if and only if pw and v match together. It prevents massive password recovering in case of server corruption and it forces the attacker who breaks into the server and is willing to recover passwords to perform an additional costly offline dictionary attack.

We consider an alternative approach inspired by the multi-party computation paradigm (and first suggested by Ford and Kaliski [FK00]). The password database on the server side is somehow shared among two servers (or more, but we focus here on two for sake of simplicity), and authentication requires a distributed computation involving the client – who still does not need an additional cryptographic device capable of storing high-entropy secret keys – and the two servers who will use some additional shared secret information. The interaction is performed using a *gateway* that does not know any secret information and ends up in the gateway and the client sharing a common key. The lifetime of the protocol is divided into distinct periods (for simplicity, one may think of these time periods as being of equal length; e.g. one day) and at the beginning of each period, the two servers interact and update their sharing of the password database. Similarly to proactive schemes in multi-party computation, we allow the adversary multiple corruptions of each server, limiting only the corruptions to one server for each period. The user does not need to update his password nor to perform any kind of computations and its interaction with the two servers (performed using the gateway) remains the same for the lifetime of the protocol. In this scenario, even if a server compromise is doable, the secret exposure is not valuable to the adversary since it reveals only a share of the password database and does not permit to run an offline dictionary attack.

The goal of our paper is to present practical realizations based on classical cryptographic assumptions in the standard security model.

Related Work. EKE (Encrypted Key Exchange) is the most famous instantiation of *Password-Authenticated Key Exchange*. It has been proposed by Bellovin and Merritt [BM92] and consists of a Diffie-Hellman key exchange [DH76], where the flows are symmetrically encrypted under the shared password.

A first formal security model was proposed by Bellare, Pointcheval and Rogaway [BPR00] (the BPR model), to deal with offline dictionary attacks. It essentially says that the best attack should be the online exhaustive search, consisting in trying all the passwords by successive executions of the protocol with the server. Several variants of EKE with BPR-security proofs have been proposed in the ideal-cipher model or the random-oracle model (see the survey [Poi12] for details). Katz, Ostrovsky and Yung [KOY01] proposed the first practical scheme, provably secure in the standard model under the Decision Diffie-Hellman assumption (DDH). It has been generalized by Gennaro and Lindell [GL03], making use of smooth projective hash functions.

As mentioned above, Ford and Kaliski [FK00] were the first to propose to distribute the capability to test passwords over multiple servers. Building on this approach, several such protocols were subsequently proposed in various settings (*e.g.* [Jab01, MSJ02, BJKS03, DG06, SK05, KMTG12, ACFP05, KM14]) and it is worth noting that the protocol from [BJKS03] is commercially available as EMC's *RSA Distributed Credential Protection*. Recently, Camenisch, Enderlein and Neven [CEN15] revisited this approach and proposed a scheme in the universal composability framework [Can01] (which has obvious advantages for password-based protocols since users often use related passwords for many providers). Camenisch *et al.* gave interesting details about the steps that need to be taken when a compromise actually occurs. Unfortunately, due to the inherent difficulties of construction of the simulator in the universal composability framework, their scheme is inefficient since users and servers have to perform a few hundred exponentiations each.

Our Contributions. In order to achieve practical constructions in the standard security model, we consider the variant of the BPR model[1] in the distributed setting proposed by Katz, MacKenzie, Taban and Gligor in [KMTG12]. In this security model, we assume that the communication between the client and the authentication servers, is carried on a basically insecure network. Messages can be tapped and modified by an adversary and the communication between the clients and the servers is asynchronous. The adversary should not be able to brute force guess a password without further interactions with the client for each guess even if he corrupts and impersonates a server in an active way.

Our first construction uses a similar approach to the schemes from [Jab01, MSJ02, BJKS03, DG06, SK05, KMTG12, ACFP05, KM14]: the user generates information theoretic shares of his password and sends them to the servers. In the authentication phase, the parties run a dedicated protocol to verify that

---

[1] Our schemes can be adapted to achieve security in universal composability framework using techniques similar to those used in [CEN15]. The resulting schemes are slightly more efficient but are unfortunately still not practical.

the provided password equals the priorly shared one. Our solution then consists in some sort of three-party PAKE, in which (1) the user implicitly checks (using a smooth projective hash function) that its password is indeed the sum of the shares owned by the two servers, and (2) each server implicitly checks that its share is the difference of the password owned by the user and the share owned by the other server. Contrary to the popular approach initiated in [KOY01, GL03] for PAKE, we cannot use two smooth projective hash functions (one for the client and one for the server) so we propose a technique in order to combine in a secure way six smooth projective hash functions. This new method (which may be of independent interest) allows us to prove the security of this construction under classical cryptographic assumptions (namely the DDH assumption) in the standard security model from [KMTG12] (without any idealized assumptions).

The main weakness of this first solution is that at each time period, the servers have to refresh the information-theoretic sharing of the password of all users. This can be handled easily using well-known techniques from proactive multi-party computation but if the number of users is large, this can be really time-consuming (in particular if the time period is very short). Our second construction (which is the main contribution of the paper) is built on the ideas from the first one but passwords are now encrypted using a public-key encryption scheme where the corresponding secret key is shared among the servers. At the beginning of each time period, the servers only need to refresh the sharing of this secret key but the password database is not modified (and can actually be public). Password verification and the authenticated key exchange is then carried out without ever decrypting the database. A secure protocol is run to verify that the password sent by the user matches the encrypted password. It is similar to the protocol we design for the first construction except that the user encrypts its password and the parties implicitly check (using in this case five smooth projective hash functions) that the message encrypted in this ciphertext is the same as the message encrypted in the database (using the secret key shared upon the servers). Both constructions consist in only two flows (one from the client and one from the servers) and a (private) flow from the servers to the gateway.

2   Preliminaries

In this section we recall various classical definitions, tools used throughout this paper. We use classical notions and notations and the familiar reader may skip this section.

Public-Key Encryption Scheme. An encryption scheme $\mathcal{E}$ is described by four algorithms (Setup, KeyGen, Encrypt, Decrypt):

– Setup($1^{\mathfrak{K}}$), where $\mathfrak{K}$ is the security parameter, generates the global parameters param of the scheme;
– KeyGen(param) outputs a pair of keys, a (public) encryption key ek and a (private) decryption key dk;

- Encrypt(ek, M; ρ) outputs a ciphertext C, on the message M, under the encryption key ek, with randomness ρ;
- Decrypt(dk, C) outputs the plaintext M, encrypted in the ciphertext C or $\perp$.

Such encryption scheme is required to have the classical properties, *Correctness* and *Indistinguishability under Chosen Plaintext Attack* IND-CPA [GM84]: One might want to increase the requirements on the security of an encryption, in this case the IND-CPA notion can be strengthened into Indistinguishability under Adaptive Chosen Ciphertext Attack IND-CCA (see the full version [BCV16] for formal definitions).

Smooth Projective Hash Functions. SPHF [CS02] were introduced by Cramer and Shoup. A projective hashing family is a family of hash functions that can be evaluated in two ways: using the (secret) hashing key, one can compute the function on every point in its domain, whereas using the (public) *projected* key one can only compute the function on a special subset of its domain. Such a family is deemed *smooth* if the value of the hash function on any point outside the special subset is independent of the projected key.

Smooth Projective Hashing System: A Smooth Projective Hash Function over a language $\mathcal{L} \subset X$, onto a set $\mathbb{G}$, is defined by five algorithms (Setup, HashKG, ProjKG, Hash, ProjHash):

- Setup($1^{\mathfrak{K}}$) where $\mathfrak{K}$ is the security parameter, generates the global parameters param of the scheme, and the description of an $\mathcal{NP}$ language $\mathcal{L}$;
- HashKG($\mathcal{L}$, param), outputs a hashing key hk for the language $\mathcal{L}$;
- ProjKG(hk, $(\mathcal{L}, \text{param}), W$), derives the projection key hp, possibly depending on the word W [GL03, ACP09] thanks to the hashing key hk.
- Hash(hk, $(\mathcal{L}, \text{param}), W$), outputs a hash value $v \in \mathbb{G}$, thanks to the hashing key hk, and W
- ProjHash(hp, $(\mathcal{L}, \text{param}), W, w$), outputs the hash value $v' \in \mathbb{G}$, thanks to the projection key hp and the witness w that $W \in \mathcal{L}$.

In the following, we consider $\mathcal{L}$ as a hard-partitioned subset of X, *i.e.* it is computationally hard to distinguish a random element in $\mathcal{L}$ from a random element in $X \setminus \mathcal{L}$. A Smooth Projective Hash Function SPHF should satisfy the following properties:

- *Correctness*: Let $W \in \mathcal{L}$ and w a witness of this membership. For all hashing keys hk and associated projection keys hp we have Hash(hk, $(\mathcal{L}, \text{param}), W$) = ProjHash(hp, $(\mathcal{L}, \text{param}), W, w$).
- *Smoothness*: For all $W \in X \setminus \mathcal{L}$ the following distributions are statistically indistinguishable:

$$\left\{ (\mathcal{L}, \text{param}, W, \text{hp}, v) \;\middle|\; \begin{array}{l} \text{param} = \text{Setup}(1^{\mathfrak{K}}), \text{hk} = \text{HashKG}(\mathcal{L}, \text{param}), \\ \text{hp} = \text{ProjKG}(\text{hk}, (\mathcal{L}, \text{param}), W), \\ v = \text{Hash}(\text{hk}, (\mathcal{L}, \text{param}), W) \end{array} \right\}$$

$$\simeq \left\{ (\mathcal{L}, \text{param}, W, \text{hp}, v) \;\middle|\; \begin{array}{l} \text{param} = \text{Setup}(1^{\mathfrak{K}}), \text{hk} = \text{HashKG}(\mathcal{L}, \text{param}), \\ \text{hp} = \text{ProjKG}(\text{hk}, (\mathcal{L}, \text{param}), W), v \xleftarrow{\$} \mathbb{G} \end{array} \right\}.$$

– *Pseudo-Randomness*: If $W \in \mathcal{L}$, then without a witness of membership the two previous distributions should remain computationally indistinguishable.

Classical Instantiations. For our needs, we consider discrete-logarithm based encryption schemes and related smooth projective hash functions. The underlying setting is a group $\mathbb{G}$ (denoted multiplicatively) of prime order p and we denote g a random generator of $\mathbb{G} = \langle g \rangle$. The security of our constructions will rely on the standard Decisional Diffie Hellman problems in $\mathbb{G}$:

Decisional Diffie Hellman (DDH) [Bon98]: The Decisional Diffie-Hellman hypothesis states that in a group $(p, \mathbb{G}, g)$ (written in multiplicative notation), given (g^μ, g^ν, g^ψ) for unknown $\mu, \nu \xleftarrow{\$} \mathbb{Z}_p$, it is hard to decide whether $\psi = \mu\nu$.

ElGamal encryption [ElG84] is defined by the following four algorithms:

– Setup($1^\mathfrak{K}$): The scheme needs a multiplicative group $(p, \mathbb{G}, g)$. The global parameters param consist of these elements $(p, \mathbb{G}, g)$.
– KeyGen(param): Chooses one random scalar $\alpha \xleftarrow{\$} \mathbb{Z}_p$, which define the secret key dk $= \alpha$, and the public key pk $= h = g^\alpha$.
– Encrypt(pk $= h, M; r$): For a message $M \in \mathbb{G}$ and a random scalar $r \xleftarrow{\$} \mathbb{Z}_p$, computes the ciphertext as $C = (c_1 = h^r M, c_2 = g^r)$.
– Decrypt(dk $= \alpha, C = (c_1, c_2)$): One computes $M = c_1/(c_2^\alpha)$.

As shown by Boneh [Bon98], this scheme is IND-CPA under the hardness of DDH.

Cramer-Shoup encryption scheme [CS98] is an IND-CCA version of the ElGamal Encryption.

– Setup($1^\mathfrak{K}$) generates a group $\mathbb{G}$ of order p, with a generator g
– KeyGen(param) generates $(g_1, g_2) \xleftarrow{\$} \mathbb{G}^2$, dk $= (x_1, x_2, y_1, y_2, z) \xleftarrow{\$} \mathbb{Z}_p^5$, and sets, $c = g_1^{x_1} g_2^{x_2}$, $d = g_1^{y_1} g_2^{y_2}$, and $h = g_1^z$. It also chooses a Collision-Resistant hash function $\mathfrak{H}_K$ in a hash family $\mathcal{H}$ (or simply a Universal One-Way Hash Function). The encryption key is ek $= (g_1, g_2, c, d, h, \mathfrak{H}_K)$.
– Encrypt(ek, $M; r$), for a message $M \in \mathbb{G}$ and a random scalar $r \in \mathbb{Z}_p$, the ciphertext is $C = (\mathbf{u} = (g_1^r, g_2^r), e = M \cdot h^r, v = (cd^\xi)^r)$, where v is computed afterwards with $\xi = \mathfrak{H}_K(\mathbf{u}, e)$.
– Decrypt(ℓ, dk, C): one computes $\xi = \mathfrak{H}_K(\mathbf{u}, e)$ and checks whether $u_1^{x_1 + \xi y_1} \cdot u_2^{x_2 + \xi y_2} \stackrel{?}{=} v$. If the equality holds, one computes $M = e/(u_1^z)$ and outputs M. Otherwise, one outputs $\perp$.

The security of the scheme is proven under the DDH assumption and the fact the hash function used is a Universal One-Way Hash Function (see [CS98]).

3   Security Model

Distributed PAKE. In a distributed PAKE system, we consider as usual a client (owning a password) willing to interact with a gateway, such as a website.

The difference compared to a non-distributed system is that the gateway itself interacts with two servers, and none of the three owns enough information to be able to recover the passwords of the clients on its own[2]. Such a scheme is correct if the interaction between a client with a correct password and the gateway succeeds. An honest execution of a distributed PAKE protocol should result in the client holding a session key K_U and the gateway holding a session key $K_G = K_U$.

We propose in this paper two settings that describe well this situation. In a first setting, we consider that the passwords of the clients are shared information-theoretically between the servers, such as $\pi = \pi_1 + \pi_2$ (if the password π belongs to an appropriate group) or with the help of any secret sharing protocol. At the beginning of each time period, the shares are updated, in a probabilistic way, using a public function Refresh, depending on the sharing protocol used.

In a second setting, we consider that the gateway owns a database of encrypted passwords (which can be considered public), and the servers each own a share of the corresponding private keys (obtained by a secret sharing protocol). At the beginning of each time period, the shares are updated, in a probabilistic way, using a public function Refresh, depending on the sharing protocol used.

Since the security of our schemes is not analyzed in the universal composability framework (contrary to the recent paper [CEN15]), the Refresh procedure can be handled easily using classical techniques from computational proactive secret sharing (see [OY91,HJKY95] for instance).

Security Model. We consider the classical model [BPR00] for authenticated key-exchange, adapted to the two-server setting by [ACFP05,KMTG12]. In the latter model, the authors assume that every client in the system shares its password with exactly two servers. We loosen this requirement here, depending on the setting considered, as described above. We refer the interested reader to these articles for the details and we give the high-level ideas in [BCV16].

4   Our Simple Protocol

In this first setting, we consider a client U owning a password π and willing to interact with a gateway G. The gateway interacts with two servers S_1 (owning π_1) and S_2 (owning π_2), such that $\pi = \pi_1 + \pi_2$. It should be noted that only the client's password is assumed to be small and human-memorable. The two "passwords" owned by the servers can be arbitrarily big. The aim of the protocol is to establish a shared session key between the client and the gateway.

A simple solution to this problem consists in considering some sort of three-party PAKE, in which the client implicitly checks (using an SPHF) whether its password is the sum of the shares owned by the two servers, and the servers implicitly check (also using an SPHF) whether their share is the difference of the

---

[2] Note that the gateway can be merged with one server.

password owned by the client and the share owned by the other server. For sake of simplicity, we denote the client U as S_0 and its password π as π_0.

4.1 Building Blocks

Cramer-Shoup Encryption and SPHF. We consider Cramer-Shoup encryption as described in Sect. 2. The public key is denoted by $\mathsf{ek} = (g_1, g_2, c, d, h, \mathfrak{H}_K)$ and the private key by $\mathsf{dk} = (x_1, x_2, y_1, y_2, z) \xleftarrow{\$} \mathbb{Z}_p^5$. The public parameters $(\mathbb{G}, p, g, \mathsf{ek})$ are given as a common reference string.

We denote the ciphertext of a message $M \in \mathbb{G}$ with the scalar $r \in \mathbb{Z}_p$ by $\mathcal{C} = \mathsf{CS}_{\mathsf{ek}}(M; r) = (u_1, u_2, e, v)$, with $v = cd^\xi$ and $\xi = \mathfrak{H}_K(u_1, u_2, e)$.

We use the SPHF described in [BBC+13] for the language of the valid ciphertexts of M under the public key ek. Its main advantage is that it can be computed without using the associated ciphertext, and in particular before having seen it. This allows all the participants to send their ciphertext and their projected keys in only one flow. The classical use of this SPHF is as follows: user U (owning a message M) and V (owning a message M') are supposed to share a common message, so that $M = M'$. User U wants to implicitly check this equality. To this aim, user V sends an encryption $\mathcal{C}$ of M' under randomness r. In order for U to implicitly check that $\mathcal{C}$ is a valid encryption of M, it chooses a hash key hk and computes and sends a projection key hp to V. If $M = M'$ and if the encryption was computed correctly, then the hash value H computed by U using the private value hk is the same as the projected hash value H' computed by V using the public value hp and its private witness r. The SPHF is described by the following algorithms.

$$\mathsf{Setup}(1^\Re): \mathsf{param} = (\mathsf{ek}, M)$$
$$\mathcal{L} = \{\mathcal{C} = (u_1, u_2, e, v) \in \mathbb{G}^4 \mid \exists r \in \mathbb{Z}_p \text{ s. t.}$$
$$\mathcal{C} = \mathsf{CS}_{\mathsf{ek}}(M; r)\}$$
$$\mathsf{HashKG}(\mathcal{L}, (\mathsf{ek}, M)): \mathsf{hk} = (\eta, \gamma, \theta, \lambda, \kappa) \xleftarrow{\$} \mathbb{Z}_p^5$$
$$\mathsf{ProjKG}(\mathsf{hk}, (\mathcal{L}, (\mathsf{ek}, M))): \mathsf{hp} = (\mathsf{hp}_1 = g_1^\eta g_2^\theta h^\lambda c^\kappa, \mathsf{hp}_2 = g_1^\gamma d^\kappa) \in \mathbb{G}^2$$
$$\mathsf{Hash}(\mathsf{hk}, (\mathcal{L}, (\mathsf{ek}, M)), \mathcal{C}): H = \mathsf{Hash}(\mathsf{hk}, (\mathsf{ek}, M), \mathcal{C}) = u_1^{(\eta+\xi\gamma)} u_2^\theta (e/M)^\lambda v^\kappa$$
$$\mathsf{ProjHash}(\mathsf{hp}, (\mathcal{L}, (\mathsf{ek}, M')), \mathcal{C}, r): H' = (\mathsf{hp}_1 \mathsf{hp}_2^\xi)^r$$

It has been known to be correct, smooth and pseudo-random since [BBC+13].

Main Idea of the Construction. In our setting, we denote by $\mathsf{pw}_b = g^{\pi_b}$. The main idea of the protocol is depicted on Fig. 1. For sake of readability, the participants which have a real role in the computations are directly linked by arrows in the picture, but one should keep in mind that all the participants (U, S_1 and S_2) only communicate with G, which then broadcasts all the messages.

In a classical SPHF-based two-party key-exchange between U and G, the client and the gateway would compute a Cramer-Shoup encryption of their password: $\mathcal{C}_0 = \mathsf{CS}_{\mathsf{ek}}(\mathsf{pw}_0; r_0)$ and $\mathcal{C}_G = \mathsf{CS}_{\mathsf{ek}}(\mathsf{pw}_G; r_G)$. The gateway would then send a projection key $\mathsf{hp}_{G,0}$ in order to implicitly check via an SPHF whether $\mathcal{C}_0$ is a valid Cramer-Shoup encryption of pw_G, and the client would send a projection key $\mathsf{hp}_{0,G}$ in order to implicitly check via an SPHF whether $\mathcal{C}_G$ is a valid Cramer-Shoup encryption of pw_0.

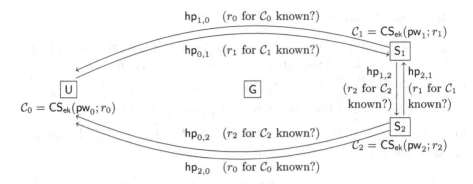

Fig. 1. Main idea of the construction

Here, since S_0 owns $\mathsf{pw}_0 = \mathsf{pw}_1 \cdot \mathsf{pw}_2$, so that the players do not share the same password, we consider an SPHF between each pair of players (S_i, S_j), in which player S_i computes the ciphertext $C_i = \mathsf{CS}_{\mathsf{ek}}(\mathsf{pw}_i; r_i)$, the keys $\mathsf{hk}_{i,j}$ and $\mathsf{hp}_{i,j}$ and sends $(C_i, \mathsf{hp}_{i,j})$ to S_j. It also computes the hash value $H_{i,j} = \mathsf{Hash}(\mathsf{hk}_{i,j}, (\mathsf{ek}, \mathsf{pw}_i), C_j)$ and the projected hash value $H'_{j,i} = \mathsf{ProjHash}(\mathsf{hp}_{j,i}, (\mathsf{ek}, M_i), C_i, r_i)$. Formally, for each pair of users (S_i, S_j), the language checked on S_j by S_i is defined as follows: $C_j \in \mathcal{L}_{i,j} = \{C = (u_1, u_2, e, v) \in \mathbb{G}^4 \mid \exists r \in \mathbb{Z}_p \text{ such that } C = \mathsf{CS}_{\mathsf{ek}}(\mathsf{pw}_j; r)\}$ but it cannot be checked directly by a unique SPHF since the passwords are different (and thus S_i does not know pw_j). Rather, we combine in the protocol the six SPHF described to globally ensure the correctness (each one remaining smooth and pseudo-random), as described in the next part. The correctness of the SPHF for the pair (S_i, S_j) implies that if everything was computed honestly, then one gets the equalities $H_{i,j}(\mathsf{pw}_i/\mathsf{pw}_j)^{\lambda_i} = H'_{i,j}$ and $H_{j,i}(\mathsf{pw}_j/\mathsf{pw}_i)^{\lambda_j} = H'_{j,i}$.

4.2 Login Procedure

– Each participant S_b picks r_b at random and computes a Cramer-Shoup encryption of its password $C_b = \mathsf{CS}_{\mathsf{ek}}(\mathsf{pw}_b; r_b)$, with $v_b = cd^{\xi_b}$.
  It also chooses, for $i \in \{0, 1, 2\} \setminus \{b\}$, a random hash key $\mathsf{hk}_{b,i} = (\eta_{b,i}, \gamma_{b,i}, \theta_{b,i}, \lambda_b, \kappa_{b,i})$ and sets $\mathsf{hp}_{b,i} = (\mathsf{hp}_{b,i;1}, \mathsf{hp}_{b,i;2}) = (g_1^{\eta_{b,i}} g_2^{\theta_{b,i}} h^{\lambda_b} c^{\kappa_{b,i}}, g_1^{\gamma_{b,i}} d^{\kappa_{b,i}})$ as the projection key intended to the participant S_i.
  It sends $(C_b, (\mathsf{hp}_{b,i})_{i \in \{0,1,2\} \setminus \{b\}})$ to the gateway G, which broadcasts these values to the other participants.
– After receiving the first flow from the servers, the client computes, for $i \in \{1, 2\}$, $H'_{i,0} = \mathsf{hp}_{i,0;1}{}^{r_0} \mathsf{hp}_{i,0;2}{}^{\xi_0 r_0}$. It also computes $H_0 = H_{0,1} \cdot H_{0,2} \cdot \mathsf{pw}_0^{\lambda_0}$, and sets its session key K_U as $K_\mathsf{U} = K_0 = H'_{1,0} \cdot H'_{2,0} \cdot H_0$.
  After receiving the first flow from the other server and the client, the server S_b computes, for $i \in \{0, 3 - b\}$, $H'_{i,b} = \mathsf{hp}_{i,b;1}{}^{r_b} \mathsf{hp}_{i,b;2}{}^{\xi_b r_b}$. It also computes $H_b = H_{b,0}/(H_{b,3-b} \cdot \mathsf{pw}_b^{\lambda_b})$, and sets its partial key K_b as $K_b = H'_{0,b} \cdot H'_{3-b,b} \cdot H_b$. It privately sends this value K_b to the gateway G.

- The gateway finally sets $K_G = K_1 \cdot K_2$.

Correctness. Recall that $H'_{i,j} = H_{i,j}(\mathsf{pw}_i/\mathsf{pw}_j)^{\lambda_i}$ for all pairs $(i,j) \in \{0,1,2\}^2$, so that the session key of the gateway is equal to $K_G = K_1 \cdot K_2$, *i.e.*

$$K_G = \frac{H'_{0,1}H'_{2,1}H_{1,0}}{H_{1,2}\mathsf{pw}_1^{\lambda_1}} \frac{H'_{0,2}H'_{1,2}H_{2,0}}{H_{2,1}\mathsf{pw}_2^{\lambda_2}} = H_{0,1}H_{1,0}H_{0,2}H_{2,0}\left(\frac{1}{\mathsf{pw}_2}\right)^{\lambda_1}\left(\frac{1}{\mathsf{pw}_1}\right)^{\lambda_2}\left(\frac{(\mathsf{pw}_0)^2}{\mathsf{pw}_1\mathsf{pw}_2}\right)^{\lambda_0}$$

while the session key of the client is $K_U = H'_{1,0} \cdot H'_{2,0} \cdot H_0$, *i.e.*

$$K_U = H'_{1,0} \cdot H'_{2,0} \cdot H_{0,1} \cdot H_{0,2} \cdot \mathsf{pw}_0^{\lambda_0} = H_{0,1}H_{1,0}H_{0,2}H_{2,0}\left(\frac{\mathsf{pw}_1}{\mathsf{pw}_0}\right)^{\lambda_1}\left(\frac{\mathsf{pw}_2}{\mathsf{pw}_0}\right)^{\lambda_2}(\mathsf{pw}_0)^{\lambda_0}$$

and these two values are equal as soon as $\mathsf{pw}_0 = \mathsf{pw}_1 \cdot \mathsf{pw}_2$.

Complexity. The following table sums up the number of group elements needed for each participant. It should be noted that in case one of the servers is the gateway, its communication costs are reduced.

	Ciphertext (Broadcast)	Projection Keys (Overall)	To the Gateway
Client	4	4	0
Server (each)	4	4	1

Proof of Security. The proof follows the spirit of the proofs given in [KV11, BBC+13]. For lack of space, a sketch is given in [BCV16].

5   Our Efficient Protocol

In this second setting, we consider again a client U owning a password π and willing to interact with a gateway G. The gateway owns a public database of encrypted passwords, and it interacts with two servers S_1 and S_2, each owning a share of the secret key of the encryption scheme. The aim of the protocol is to establish a shared session key between the client and the gateway.

The idea is similar to the protocol described in the former section, except that only the client needs to compute a ciphertext, the other ciphertext being publicly available from the database. The participants implicitly check (using several SPHF) that the message encrypted in the ciphertext of the client is the same as the message encrypted in the database (using the secret key shared upon the servers).

5.1   Building Blocks

Cramer-Shoup Encryption and SPHF. We consider Cramer-Shoup encryption as the previous construction. We use here the simpler SPHF described in [GL03] for the language of the valid ciphertexts of M under the public key ek, in which the participants need to see the ciphertext before being able to compute their projection keys. The SPHF is described by the following algorithms.

$$\mathsf{Setup}(1^\Re): \mathsf{param} = (\mathsf{ek}, M)$$
$$\mathcal{L} = \{\mathcal{C} = (u_1, u_2, e, v) \in \mathbb{G}^4 \mid \exists r \in \mathbb{Z}_p \text{ s. t.}$$
$$\mathcal{C} = \mathsf{CS}_{\mathsf{ek}}(M; r)\}$$
$$\mathsf{HashKG}(\mathcal{L}, (\mathsf{ek}, M)): \mathsf{hk} = (\eta, \theta, \lambda, \kappa) \xleftarrow{\$} \mathbb{Z}_p^4$$
$$\mathsf{ProjKG}(\mathsf{hk}, (\mathcal{L}, (\mathsf{ek}, M)), \mathcal{C}): \mathsf{hp} = g_1^\eta g_2^\theta h^\lambda (cd^\xi)^\kappa \in \mathbb{G}$$
$$\mathsf{Hash}(\mathsf{hk}, (\mathcal{L}, (\mathsf{ek}, M)), \mathcal{C}): H = u_1^\eta u_2^\theta (e/M)^\lambda v^\kappa$$
$$\mathsf{ProjHash}(\mathsf{hp}, (\mathcal{L}, (\mathsf{ek}, M')), \mathcal{C}, r): H' = \mathsf{hp}^r$$

It has been known to be correct, smooth and pseudo-random since [GL03].

El Gamal Encryption and SPHF. We consider El Gamal encryption as described in Sect. 2. The public key is denoted by $\mathsf{pk} = h = g^\alpha$ and the private key by $\mathsf{sk} = \alpha \xleftarrow{\$} \mathbb{Z}_p$. The public parameters $(\mathbb{G}, p, g, \mathsf{pk})$ are given as a common reference string. We denote the ciphertext of a message $M \in \mathbb{G}$ with the scalar $r \in \mathbb{Z}_p$ by $\mathcal{C} = \mathsf{EG}_{\mathsf{pk}}(M; r) = (e, u) = (h^r M, g^r)$.

The regular SPHF used throughout the literature [CS02] on the language $\{\mathcal{C} = (e, u) \in \mathbb{G}^2 \mid \exists r \in \mathbb{Z}_p \text{ such that } \mathcal{C} = \mathsf{EG}_{\mathsf{pk}}(M; r)\}$ of the valid encryptions of M, with r being the witness of the word $\mathcal{C}$, usually allows a server to check whether the ciphertext was honestly computed on the value M by a client, by generating a pair of keys $(\mathsf{hk}, \mathsf{hp})$ and sending hp to the client.

Here, on the contrary, we now want a client to implicitly check that a server knows the decryption key of the encryption scheme. This means that the client computes both the ciphertext (or the ciphertext is publicly available in a database, as here) and the pair of keys $(\mathsf{hk}, \mathsf{hp})$ and sends the ciphertext as well as hp to the server, which now uses the decryption key as a witness. This implies the following modifications to the algorithms of the SPHF:

$$\mathsf{Setup}(1^\Re): \mathsf{param} = (\mathsf{pk}, M)$$
$$\mathcal{L} = \{\mathcal{C} = (e, u) \in \mathbb{G}^2 \mid \exists \alpha \in \mathbb{Z}_p \text{ such that}$$
$$h = g^\alpha \text{ and } e/u^\alpha = M\}$$
$$\mathsf{HashKG}(\mathcal{L}, (\mathsf{pk}, M)): \mathsf{hk} = (\lambda, \mu) \xleftarrow{\$} \mathbb{Z}_p^2$$
$$\mathsf{ProjKG}(\mathsf{hk}, (\mathcal{L}, (\mathsf{pk}, M)), \mathcal{C}): \mathsf{hp} = u^\lambda g^\mu \in \mathbb{G}$$
$$\mathsf{Hash}(\mathsf{hk}, (\mathcal{L}, (\mathsf{pk}, M)), \mathcal{C}): H = h^\mu (e/M)^\lambda$$
$$\mathsf{ProjHash}(\mathsf{hp}, (\mathcal{L}, (\mathsf{pk}, M')), \mathcal{C}, \alpha): H' = \mathsf{hp}^\alpha$$

and we show that this SPHF satisfies the usual properties:

- *Correctness*: if $\mathcal{C} \in \mathcal{L}$ with witness α, one directly gets $H = H'$;
- *Smoothness*: assume $\mathcal{C} \notin \mathcal{L}$. It can then be parsed as $\mathcal{C} = (e, u)$ with $u = g^r$ and $e = h^r M' = g^{\alpha r} M g^{\delta_M}$ (with $M' \neq M$ and thus $\delta_M \neq 0$), so that $\mathsf{hp} = u^\lambda g^\mu = g^{r\lambda + \mu}$ and $H = h^\mu (e/M)^\lambda = g^{\alpha\mu} g^{(\alpha r + \delta_M)\lambda}$.

The smoothness is then easy to see by considering the following equality of matrices:
$$\begin{pmatrix} \log_g(\mathsf{hp}) \\ \log_g(H) \end{pmatrix} = \begin{pmatrix} r & 1 \\ \alpha r + \delta_M \& \alpha \end{pmatrix} \cdot \begin{pmatrix} \lambda \\ \mu \end{pmatrix}$$

which shows that as soon as the word is not a valid encryption of M, and so δ_M is not equal to 0, the Hash value H is not in the span of the projection key hp so that the two distributions described in Sect. 2 are indistinguishable.

- *Pseudo-Randomness.* Since El Gamal encryption is IND-CPA, it is impossible to distinguish between a real encryption and a random value without knowing the decryption key. Since the decryption key is the witness of the SPHF, without knowing the witness, the two distributions remain indistinguishable.

Main Idea of the Construction. Again, we denote the client U as S_0 and its password π as π_0. In our setting, we denote by $\mathsf{pw}_k = g^{\pi_k}$ for all k. The database contains El Gamal encryptions of each ciphertext pw_{U_i}, under randomness s_{U_i}: $\mathcal{C}_{U_i}^{db} = \mathsf{EG}_{\mathsf{pk}}(\mathsf{pw}_{U_i}; s_{U_i}) = (h^{s_{U_i}}\mathsf{pw}_{U_i}, g^{s_{U_i}})$, so that here, $\mathcal{C}_U^{db} = \mathsf{EG}_{\mathsf{pk}}(\mathsf{pw}_U; s_U) = (h^{s_U}\mathsf{pw}_U, g^{s_U})$. The client computes a Cramer-Shoup encryption of its password: $\mathcal{C}_0 = \mathsf{CS}_{\mathsf{ek}}(\mathsf{pw}_0; r_0) = (u_1, u_2, e, v)$ with $v = cd^\xi$. The execution of the protocol should succeed if these encryptions are correct and $\mathsf{pw}_0 = \mathsf{pw}_U$. Recall that the server $\mathcal{S}_i$ knows α_i such that $\alpha = \alpha_1 + \alpha_2$ is the decryption key of the El Gamal encryption.

The main idea is depicted on Fig. 2. For sake of readability, the participants which have a real role in the computations are directly linked by arrows in the picture, but one should keep in mind that all the participants (U, S_1 and S_2) only communicate with G, which then broadcasts all the messages.

In a classical SPHF-based two-party key-exchange between U and G, the gateway would check whether $\mathcal{C}_0$ is a valid Cramer-Shoup encryption of pw_U. Since here the password pw_U is unknown to the servers S_1 and S_2, this is done in our setting by two SPHF, using $\mathsf{hp}_1^{\mathsf{CS}}$ (sent by S_1) and $\mathsf{hp}_2^{\mathsf{CS}}$ (sent by S_2), where the servers use the first term of the public encryption $\mathcal{C}_U^{\mathsf{DB}}$ ($h^{s_U}\mathsf{pw}_U$) in order to cancel the unknown pw_U.

In a classical SPHF-based two-party key-exchange between U and G, the client would also check whether $\mathcal{C}_U^{\mathsf{DB}}$ is a valid El Gamal encryption of its password pw_0, *i.e.* whether the gateway knows a witness for its ciphertext $\mathcal{C}_U^{\mathsf{DB}}$ (s_U in the usual constructions, α here). Since α is unknown to the gateway, this is done in our setting by the combination of three SPHF, using $\mathsf{hp}_0^{\mathsf{EG}}$ (sent by the client), $\mathsf{hp}_1^{\mathsf{EG}}$ (sent by S_1) and $\mathsf{hp}_2^{\mathsf{EG}}$ (sent by S_2). These three SPHF allow the client and the servers to implicitly check that the servers know α_1 and α_2 such that $\mathcal{C}_U^{\mathsf{DB}}$ can be decrypted (using the decryption key $\alpha = \alpha_1 + \alpha_2$) to the same password pw_0 than the one encrypted in $\mathcal{C}_0$ sent by the client. Formally, the languages checked are as follows:

- by the client:
  $\mathcal{C}_U^{\mathsf{DB}} \in \mathcal{L}_0 = \{\mathcal{C} = (e, u) \in \mathbb{G}^2 \mid \exists \alpha \in \mathbb{Z}_p \text{ such that } h = g^\alpha \text{ and } e/u^\alpha = \mathsf{pw}_0\}$
- by server $\mathcal{S}_i$ (with respect to the client S_0 and server $\mathcal{S}_j$):
  $\mathcal{C}_0 \in \mathcal{L}_{i,0} = \{\mathcal{C} = (u_1, u_2, e, v) \in \mathbb{G}^4 \mid \exists r \in \mathbb{Z}_p \text{ such that } \mathcal{C} = \mathsf{CS}_{\mathsf{ek}}(\mathsf{pw}_U; r)\}$
  and $\mathcal{C}_U^{\mathsf{DB}} \in \mathcal{L}_{i,j} = \{\mathcal{C} = (e, u) \in \mathbb{G}^2 \mid \exists \alpha_j \in \mathbb{Z}_p \text{ such that } h = g^{\alpha_i + \alpha_j}\}$ and $e/u^{\alpha_i + \alpha_j} = \mathsf{pw}_U\}$

but they cannot be checked directly by a unique SPHF since the value pw_U appearing in the languages is unknown to the verifier $\mathcal{S}_i$. Rather, the server $\mathcal{S}_i$ will use the first term of the public encryption $\mathcal{C}_U^{\mathsf{DB}}$ ($h^{s_U}\mathsf{pw}_U$) in order to cancel this unknown pw_U. To achieve this goal, we combine the five SPHF described

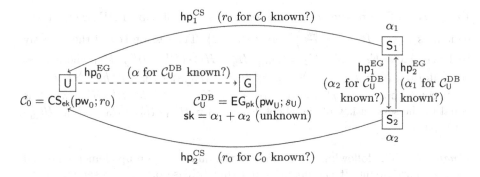

Fig. 2. Main idea of the construction

to globally ensure the correctness (each one remaining smooth and pseudo-randomness), as described in the next part.

5.2 Login Procedure

- The client $U = S_0$ chooses r_0 at random and computes a Cramer-Shoup encryption of its password $C_0 = CS_{ek}(pw_0; r_0) = (u_1, u_2, e, v)$ with $v = cd^\xi$.
  It also chooses a random (El Gamal) hash key $hk_0^{EG} = (\lambda_0, \mu_0)$ and computes the corresponding projected key on the ciphertext $C_U^{DB} = EG_{pk}(pw_U; s_U) = (h^{s_U} pw_U, g^{s_U})$ contained in the database: $hp_0^{EG} = g^{s_U \lambda_0} g^{\mu_0}$.
  It sends (C_0, hp_0^{EG}) to the gateway, which broadcasts these values to the servers.
- After receiving this flow from the client, the servers S_1 and S_2 also choose a random (El Gamal) hash key $hk_b^{EG} = (\lambda_b, \mu_b)$ and compute the corresponding projected key on the ciphertext C_U^{DB} contained in the database: $hp_b^{EG} = g^{s_U \lambda_b} g^{\mu_b}$.
  The servers S_1 and S_2 also choose a random (Cramer-Shoup) hash key $hk_b^{CS} = (\eta_b, \theta_b, \lambda_b, \kappa_b)$ (with the same value λ_b) and compute the corresponding projected key on the ciphertext C_0 sent by the client: $hp_b^{CS} = (g_1^{\eta_b} g_2^{\theta_b} h^{\lambda_b} (cd^\xi)^{\kappa_b})$.
  Each server sends (hp_b^{EG}, hp_b^{CS}) to the gateway G, which broadcasts these values to the other participants.
- After receiving the projected keys from the servers, the client computes, for $i \in \{1, 2\}$, $H'_{i,0} = (hp_i^{CS})^{r_0}$. It also computes $H_0 = (h^{s_U} pw_U / pw_0)^{\lambda_0} h^{\mu_0}$ by dividing the first term of the ciphertext C_U^{DB} contained in the database by its password pw_0. It finally sets its session key K_U as $K_U = K_0 = H'_{1,0} \cdot H'_{2,0} \cdot H_0$.
  After receiving the first flow from the other server and the client, the server S_b computes, for $i \in \{0, 3-b\}$, $H'_{i,b} = (hp_i^{EG})^{\alpha_b}$.
  It also computes $H_{b,0} = (u_1)^{\eta_b} (u_2)^{\theta_b} [e/(h^{s_U} pw_U)]^{\lambda_b} v^{\kappa_b}$ and $H_b = H_{b,0} \cdot (hp_b^{EG})^{\alpha_b} / h^{\mu_b}$, and sets its partial key K_b as $K_b = H'_{0,b} \cdot H'_{3-b,b} \cdot H_b$. It privately sends this value K_b to the gateway G.
- The gateway finally sets $K_G = K_1 \cdot K_2$.

Correctness. Due to the correctness of the Cramer-Shoup SPHF, we have the equalities $H'_{b,0} = H_{b,0} \left(\frac{h^{s_U} \text{pw}_U}{\text{pw}_0} \right)^{\lambda_b}$ for $b \in \{1, 2\}$. The session key of the gateway is thus equal to $K_G = K_1 \cdot K_2 = (H'_{0,1} \cdot H'_{2,1} \cdot H_1) \cdot (H'_{0,2} \cdot H'_{1,2} \cdot H_2)$ where, after computation, $K_b = h^{(\lambda_0 + \lambda_1 + \lambda_2)\alpha_b} g^{(\mu_0 + \mu_1 + \mu_2)\alpha_b} H'_{b,0} (\text{pw}_0 / \text{pw}_U)^{\lambda_b} h^{-s_U \lambda_b} h^{-\mu_b}$.

If $\text{pw}_0 = \text{pw}_U$, $h = g^\alpha$ and $\alpha = \alpha_1 + \alpha_2$, $K_G = h^{s_U \lambda_0} h^{\mu_0} H'_{1,0} H'_{2,0}$, which is equal to the session key of the client $K_U = K_0 = H'_{1,0} \cdot H'_{2,0} \cdot H_0 = H'_{1,0} \cdot H'_{2,0} \cdot h^{s_U \lambda_0} h^{\mu_0}$.

Complexity. The following table sums up the number of group elements needed for each participant. It should be noted that in case one of the servers is the gateway, its communication costs are reduced.

	Ciphertext (Broadcast)	Projection Keys (Overall)	Keys To the Gateway
Client	4	2	0
Server (each)	0	2	1

Compared to [KMTG12], the communication complexity of our protocol is decreased by more than 50 % (9 group elements instead of 20 group elements). For efficiency, as in [KMTG12], we count exponentiations only, and assume a multi-exponentiation with up to 5 bases can be computed at the cost of at most 1.5 exponentiations. The client performs the equivalent of 8 full exponentiations, while each server performs 7 exponentiations (instead of 15 and 13 respectively in [KMTG12]).

Proof of Security. The proof follows the idea of the former one. For lack of space, a sketch is given in [BCV16].

6   Conclusion

We presented two constructions of distributed Password-Authenticated Key Exchange between a user and several servers. We focused on presenting them in a classical group setting (with only two servers). Very efficient implementations of our protocols can be readily obtained using standard cryptographic libraries and do not require pairings.

Our methods can be generalized to the setting where n servers share the (encryption of the) password. SPHF can further handle polynomials of variables and the use of secret sharing techniques *à la* Shamir, allows to share polynomials evaluation between n servers and to provide a threshold distributed PAKE such that security is ensured as long as less than a certain arbitrary threshold $t \in \{1, \ldots, n\}$ of servers are compromised (contrary to the protocol from [DG06] which requires an honest majority of the servers).

Smooth projective hashing is mostly used in a classical discrete-logarithm-based setting (or pairing-based setting) but constructions were also proposed for Paillier encryption [CS02] and for LWE encryption [KV09]. These SPHF would allow a readily adaptation of our techniques to other classical settings of cryptography.

Acknowledgements. This work was supported in part by the French ANR Project ANR-14-CE28-0003 EnBiD.

References

[ACFP05] Abdalla, M., Chevassut, O., Fouque, P.-A., Pointcheval, D.: A simple threshold authenticated key exchange from short secrets. In: Roy, B. (ed.) ASIACRYPT 2005. LNCS, vol. 3788, pp. 566–584. Springer, Heidelberg (2005)

[ACP09] Abdalla, M., Chevalier, C., Pointcheval, D.: Smooth projective hashing for conditionally extractable commitments. In: Halevi, S. (ed.) CRYPTO 2009. LNCS, vol. 5677, pp. 671–689. Springer, Heidelberg (2009)

[BBC+13] Benhamouda, F., Blazy, O., Chevalier, C., Pointcheval, D., Vergnaud, D.: New techniques for SPHFs and efficient one-round PAKE protocols. In: Canetti, R., Garay, J.A. (eds.) CRYPTO 2013, Part I. LNCS, vol. 8042, pp. 449–475. Springer, Heidelberg (2013)

[BCV16] Blazy, O., Chevalier, C., Vergnaud, D.: Mitigating server breaches in password-based authentication: secure and efficient solutions. In: Sako, K. (eds.) Topics in Cryptology, CT-RSA 2016, pp. 3–18. Springer, Heidelberg (2016)

[BJKS03] Brainard, J.G., Juels, A., Kaliski, B., Szydlo, M.: A new two-server approach for authentication with short secrets. In: Proceedings of the 12th USENIX Security Symposium, Washington, D.C., USA, 4–8 August 2003 (2003)

[BM92] Bellovin, S.M., Merritt, M.: Encrypted key exchange: password-based protocols secure against dictionary attacks. In: 1992 IEEE Symposium on Security and Privacy, pp. 72–84. IEEE Computer Society Press, May 1992

[Bon98] Boneh, D.: The decision Diffie-Hellman problem. In: Buhler, J.P. (ed.) ANTS 1998. LNCS, vol. 1423, pp. 48–63. Springer, Heidelberg (1998)

[BPR00] Bellare, M., Pointcheval, D., Rogaway, P.: Authenticated key exchange secure against dictionary attacks. In: Preneel, B. (ed.) EUROCRYPT 2000. LNCS, vol. 1807, pp. 139–155. Springer, Heidelberg (2000)

[Can01] Canetti, R.: Universally composable security: a new paradigm for cryptographic protocols. In: 42nd FOCS, pp. 136–145. IEEE Computer Society Press, October 2001

[CEN15] Camenisch, J., Enderlein, R.R., Neven, G.: Two-server password-authenticated secret sharing UC-secure against transient corruptions. In: Katz, J. (ed.) PKC 2015. LNCS, vol. 9020, pp. 283–307. Springer, Heidelberg (2015)

[CS98] Cramer, R., Shoup, V.: A practical public key cryptosystem provably secure against adaptive chosen ciphertext attack. In: Krawczyk, H. (ed.) CRYPTO 1998. LNCS, vol. 1462, pp. 13–25. Springer, Heidelberg (1998)

[CS02] Cramer, R., Shoup, V.: Universal hash proofs and a paradigm for adaptive chosen ciphertext secure public-key encryption. In: Knudsen, L.R. (ed.) EUROCRYPT 2002. LNCS, vol. 2332, pp. 45–64. Springer, Heidelberg (2002)

[DG06] Di Raimondo, M., Gennaro, R.: Provably secure threshold password-authenticated key exchange. J. Comput. Syst. Sci. **72**(6), 978–1001 (2006)

[DH76] Diffie, W., Hellman, M.E.: New directions in cryptography. IEEE Trans. Inf. Theo. **22**(6), 644–654 (1976)

[ElG84] El Gamal, T.: A public key cryptosystem and a signature scheme based on discrete logarithms. In: Blakely, G.R., Chaum, D. (eds.) CRYPTO 1984. LNCS, vol. 196, pp. 10–18. Springer, Heidelberg (1985)

[FK00] Ford, W., Kaliski Jr., B.S.: Server-assisted generation of a strong secret from a password. In: 9th IEEE International Workshops on Enabling Technologies: Infrastructure for Collaborative Enterprises (WETICE 2000), Gaithersburg, MD, USA, 4–16 June 2000, pp. 176–180 (2000)

[GL03] Gennaro, R., Lindell, Y.: A framework for password-based authenticated key exchange. In: Biham, E. (ed.) EUROCRYPT 2003. LNCS, vol. 2656, pp. 524–543. Springer, Heidelberg (2003)

[GM84] Goldwasser, S., Micali, S.: Probabilistic encryption. J. Comput. Syst. Sci. $28(2)$, 270–299 (1984)

[HJKY95] Herzberg, A., Jarecki, S., Krawczyk, H., Yung, M.: Proactive secret sharing or: how to cope with perpetual leakage. In: Coppersmith, D. (ed.) CRYPTO 1995. LNCS, vol. 963, pp. 339–352. Springer, Heidelberg (1995)

[Jab01] Jablon, D.P.: Password authentication using multiple servers. In: Naccache, D. (ed.) CT-RSA 2001. LNCS, vol. 2020, pp. 344–360. Springer, Heidelberg (2001)

[KM14] Kiefer, F., Manulis, M.: Distributed smooth projective hashing and its application to two-server password authenticated key exchange. In: Boureanu, I., Owesarski, P., Vaudenay, S. (eds.) ACNS 2014. LNCS, vol. 8479, pp. 199–216. Springer, Heidelberg (2014)

[KMTG12] Katz, J., MacKenzie, P.D., Taban, G., Virgil, D.: Two-server password-only authenticated key exchange. J. Comput. Syst. Sci. $78(2)$, 651–669 (2012)

[KOY01] Katz, J., Ostrovsky, R., Yung, M.: Efficient password-authenticated key exchange using human-memorable passwords. In: Pfitzmann, B. (ed.) EUROCRYPT 2001. LNCS, vol. 2045, pp. 475–494. Springer, Heidelberg (2001)

[KV09] Katz, J., Vaikuntanathan, V.: Smooth projective hashing and password-based authenticated key exchange from lattices. In: Matsui, M. (ed.) ASIACRYPT 2009. LNCS, vol. 5912, pp. 636–652. Springer, Heidelberg (2009)

[KV11] Katz, J., Vaikuntanathan, V.: Round-optimal password-based authenticated key exchange. In: Ishai, Y. (ed.) TCC 2011. LNCS, vol. 6597, pp. 293–310. Springer, Heidelberg (2011)

[MSJ02] MacKenzie, P.D., Shrimpton, T., Jakobsson, M.: Threshold password-authenticated key exchange. In: Yung, M. (ed.) CRYPTO 2002. LNCS, vol. 2442, pp. 385–400. Springer, Heidelberg (2002)

[OY91] Ostrovsky, R., Yung, M.: How to withstand mobile virus attacks (extended abstract). In: 10th ACM PODC, pp. 51–59. ACM, August 1991

[Poi12] Pointcheval, D.: Password-based authenticated key exchange. In: Fischlin, M., Buchmann, J., Manulis, M. (eds.) PKC 2012. LNCS, vol. 7293, pp. 390–397. Springer, Heidelberg (2012)

[SK05] Szydlo, M., Kaliski, B.: Proofs for two-server password authentication. In: Menezes, A. (ed.) CT-RSA 2005. LNCS, vol. 3376, pp. 227–244. Springer, Heidelberg (2005)

Strongly Leakage-Resilient Authenticated Key Exchange

Rongmao Chen[1,2]($\boxtimes$), Yi Mu[1]($\boxtimes$), Guomin Yang[1],
Willy Susilo[1], and Fuchun Guo[1]

[1] School of Computing and Information Technology,
Centre for Computer and Information Security Research,
University of Wollongong, Wollongong, Australia
{rc517,ymu,gyang,wsusilo,fuchun}@uow.edu.au
[2] College of Computer, National University of Defense Technology,
Changsha, China

Abstract. Authenticated Key Exchange (AKE) protocols have been
widely deployed in many real-world applications for securing communication channels. In this paper, we make the following contributions. First,
we revisit the security modelling of leakage-resilient AKE protocols, and
show that the existing models either impose some unnatural restrictions
or do not sufficiently capture leakage attacks in reality. We then introduce
a new strong yet meaningful security model, named challenge-dependent
leakage-resilient eCK (CLR-eCK) model, to capture challenge-dependent
leakage attacks on both long-term secret key and ephemeral secret key
(i.e., randomness). Second, we propose a general framework for constructing one-round CLR-eCK-secure AKE protocols based on smooth projective hash functions (SPHFs). Finally, we present a practical instantiation
of the general framework based on the Decisional Diffie-Hellman assumption without random oracle. Our result shows that the instantiation is
efficient in terms of the communication and computation overhead and
captures more general leakage attacks.

Keywords: Authenticated key exchange · Challenge-dependent leakage · Strong randomness extractor · Smooth projective hash function

1 Introduction

Leakage-resilient cryptography, particularly leakage-resilient cryptographic primitives such as encryption, signature, and pseudo-random function, has been extensively studied in recent years. However, there are only very few works that have
been done on the modelling and construction of leakage-resilient authenticated
key exchange (AKE) protocols. This is somewhat surprising since AKE protocols
are among the most widely used cryptographic primitives. In particular, they form
a central component in many network standards, such as IPSec, SSL/TLS, SSH.
Many practical AKE protocols such as the ISO protocol (a.k.a. SIG-DH) [1,10]
and the Internet Key Exchange protocol (a.k.a. SIGMA) [22] have been proposed

© Springer International Publishing Switzerland 2016
K. Sako (Ed.): CT-RSA 2016, LNCS 9610, pp. 19–36, 2016.
DOI: 10.1007/978-3-319-29485-8_2

and deployed in the aforementioned network standards. In such an AKE protocol, each party holds a *long-term public key* and the corresponding *long-term secret key*, which are static in the establishment of different session keys for multiple communication sessions. In order to establish a unique session key for an individual session, each party also generates their own *ephemeral secret key* and exchanges the corresponding *ephemeral public key*. Both parties can derive a common session key based on their own secret keys and the public keys of the peer entity. We should note that in practice, an AKE protocol proven secure in the traditional model could be completely insecure in the presence of leakage attacks. For example, an attacker can launch a memory attack [2,19] to learn partial information about the long-term secret key, and also obtain partial information about the ephemeral secret key (i.e., randomness) of an AKE session (e.g., via poorly implemented PRNGs [24,29,33]).

1.1 Motivations of This Work

The general theme in formulating leakage resilience of cryptographic primitives is that in addition to the normal black-box interaction with an honest party, the adversary can also learn some partial information of the secret via an abstract leakage function f. This approach was applied to model leakage resilience of many cryptographic schemes [9,12,27,31]. One of the major problems of leakage resilient cryptography is to define a meaningful leakage function family $\mathcal{F}$ for a cryptographic primitive such that *the leakage functions in $\mathcal{F}$ can cover as many leakage attacks as possible while at the same time it is still feasible to construct a scheme that can be proven secure.*

Limitations in Existing Leakage-Resilient AKE Models. The above modelling approach has been applied to define leakage-resilient AKE protocols in [4,5,15,26]. However, we find that the existing leakage-resilient AKE models fail to fully capture general leakage attacks due to the following reasons.

UNNATURAL RESTRICTIONS. The *de facto* security definition of AKE requires that the real challenge session key should be indistinguishable from a randomly chosen key even when the adversary has obtained some information of the challenge session. However, such a definition will bring a problem when it comes to the leakage setting. During the execution of the challenge session, the adversary can access to the leakage oracle by encoding the available information about the challenge session into the leakage function and obtain partial information about the real session key. The previous security definitions for leakage-resilient AKE, e.g., [5,15,26,30], bypassed the definitional difficulty outlined above by only considering *challenge-independent leakage*. Namely, the adversary *cannot make a leakage query which involves a leakage function f that is related to the challenge session*. This approach indeed bypasses the technical problem, but it also puts some unnatural restrictions on the adversary by assuming leakage would not happen during the challenge AKE session. Such a definitional difficulty was also recognized in the prior work on leakage-resilient encryption schemes. For example, Naor and Segev wrote in [27] that "it will be very interesting to find an appropriate framework that allows a certain form of challenge-dependent leakage." We should note that there are some recent works on challenge-dependent leakage-resilient encryption schemes [20, 32], which addressed the problem by weakening the security notions.

INSUFFICIENT LEAKAGE CAPTURING. The notions proposed in [4, 5, 15, 26, 30] only focused on partial leakage of the long-term secret key. We should note that *the partial leakage here is independent from the (long-term/ephemeral) secret key reveal queries* in CK/eCK models. In reality, an attacker may completely reveal one (long-term/ephemeral) secret key and learn partial information about the other (ephemeral/long-term) secret key. Such an adversarial capability has never been considered in the previous models. In practice, as mentioned before, potential weakness of the randomness can be caused due to different reasons such as the poor implementation of pseudo-random number generators (PRNGs) [24, 29, 33]. Moreover, real leakage attacks (e.g., timing or power consumption analysis) can also be closely related to the randomness. The problem has been recognized in prior work on leakage-resilient encryption and signature schemes. For example, Halevi and Lin mentioned in [20] that "Another interesting question is to handle leakage from the encryption randomness, not just the secret key", which was later answered by the works in [8, 32]. In terms of the signature schemes, the notion of fully leakage-resilient signatures was also proposed by Katz and Vaikuntanathan [21]. However, to date there is no formal treatment on the randomness leakage in AKE.

On After-the-Fact Leakage. It is worth noting that Alawatugoda et al. [4] modelled after-the-fact leakage for AKE protocols. Their proposed model, named bounded after-the-fact leakage eCK model (BAFL-eCK), captures the leakage of long-term secret keys during the challenge session. However, the BAFL-eCK model has implicitly assumed that the long-term secret has split-state since otherwise their definition is unachievable in the eCK-model. Moreover, the central idea of their AKE construction is to utilize a split-state encryption scheme with a special property (i.e., pair generation indistinguishability), which is a strong assumption. We also note that the split-state approach seems not natural for dealing with ephemeral secret leakage. The work in [3] also introduced a continuous after-the-fact leakage eCK model which is a weaker variant of the one in [4] and hence also suffers from the aforementioned limitations.

Goal of This Work. In this work, we are interested in designing a more general and powerful leakage-resilient AKE model without the aforementioned limitations. Particularly, we ask two questions: *how to generally define a challenge-dependent leakage-resilient AKE security model capturing both long-term and ephemeral secret leakage*, and *how to construct an efficient AKE protocol proven secure under the proposed security model*. The motivation of this work is to solve these two outstanding problems which are of both practical and theoretical importance.

1.2   Related Work

Traditional AKE Security Notions. The Bellare-Rogaway (BR) model [7] gives the first formal security notion for AKE based on an indistinguishability game. Its variants are nowadays the *de facto* standard for AKE security analysis. In particular, the Canetti-Krawczyk (CK) model [10], which can be considered as the extension and combination of the BR model and the Bellare-Canetti-Krawczyk (BCK) model [6], has been used to prove the security of many widely used AKE protocols (e.g., SIG-DH). LaMacchia et al. [23] introduced an extension of the CK model, named eCK model, to consider stronger adversaries (in some aspects) who is allowed to access either the long-term secret key or the ephemeral secret key in the target session chosen by the adversary. We refer the readers to Choo et al. [11] for a detailed comparisons among the aforementioned AKE models, and to Cremers et al. [14] for a full analysis of these models.

Modelling Leakage Resilience. The method of protecting against leakage attacks by treating them in an abstract way was first proposed by Micali and Reyzin [25] based on the assumption that *only computation leaks information*. Inspired by the cold boot attack presented by Halderman et al. [19], Akavia et al. [2] formalized a general framework, namely, *Relative Leakage Model*, which implicitly assumes that, a leakage attack can reveal a fraction of the secret key, no matter what the secret key size is. The *Bounded-Retrieval Model* (BRM) [5] is a generalization of the relative leakage model. In BRM, the leakage-parameter forms an independent parameter of the system. The secret key-size is then chosen flexibly depending on the leakage parameter. Another relatively stronger leakage model is the *Auxiliary Input Model* [16] where the leakage is not necessarily bounded in length, but it is assumed to be computationally hard to recover the secret-key from the leakage.

Leakage-Resilient AKE. Alwen, Dodis and Wichs [5] presented an efficient leakage-resilient AKE protocol in the random oracle model. They considered a leakage-resilient security model (BRM-CK) and showed that a leakage-resilient AKE protocol can be constructed from an entropically-unforgeable digital signature scheme secure under chose-message attacks. The resulted AKE protocol, namely eSIG-DH, however, is at least 3-round and does not capture ephemeral secret key leakage. Also, the security model considered in [5] does not capture challenge-dependent leakage. In [15], Dodis et al. proposed new constructions of AKE protocols that are leakage-resilient in the CK security model (LR-CK). Similar to Alwen et al. [5], the security model given by Dodis et al. [15] is not challenge-dependent, and the proposed construction (i.e., Enc-DH) has 3-round and didn't consider randomness leakage. Another leakage-resilient model for AKE protocols is introduced by Moriyama and Okamoto [26]. Their notion, named λ-leakage resilient eCK (LR-eCK) security, is an extension of the eCK security model with the notion of λ-leakage resilience introduced in [2]. They also presented a 2-round AKE protocol that is λ-leakage resilient eCK secure without random oracles. However, they only considered the long-term secret key leakage (when the ephemeral secret key is revealed) but not the ephemeral secret key leakage (when the long-term secret key is revealed). Also, their model challenge-independent. Yang et al. [30] initiated the study on leakage resilient AKE in the auxiliary input model, which however, is based on the CK model and only captures the challenge-independent leakage of lone-term secret.

1.3   Our Results and Techniques

In this work, we address the aforementioned open problems by designing a strong yet meaningful AKE security model, namely *challenge-dependent leakage-resilient eCK* (CLR-eCK) model, to capture the challenge-dependent leakage attacks on both the long-term secret key and the ephemeral secret key; we then present a general framework for the construction of CLR-eCK-secure one-round AKE protocol as well as an efficient instantiation based on the DDH assumption. Below we give an overview of our results.

Overview of Our Model. As shown in Table 1, our model is the first *split-state-free* model that captures challenge-dependent leakage on both the long-term secret key and the ephemeral secret key (or randomness), which could occur in practice due to side-channel attacks and weak randomness implementations. In our proposed model, we consider the partial *Relative-Leakage* [2]. Our CLR-eCK security model addresses the limitations of the previous leakage-resilient models by allowing both long-term and ephemeral key leakage queries before, during and after the test (i.e., challenge) session. Nevertheless, we should prevent an adversary $\mathcal{M}$ from submitting a leakage function which encodes the session key derivation function of the test session since otherwise the adversary can trivially distinguish the real session key from a random key. To address this technical problem, instead of asking adversary $\mathcal{M}$ to specify the leakage functions before the system setup (i.e., non-adaptive leakage), we require $\mathcal{M}$ to commit a set of leakage functions before it obtains (via key reveal queries) all the inputs, except the to-be-leaked one, of the session key derivation function for the test session. Once $\mathcal{M}$ obtains all the other inputs, it can only use the leakage functions specified in the committed set to learn the partial information of the last unknown secret. To be more precise, in the CLR-eCK model, after $\mathcal{M}$ reveals the ephemeral secret key of the test session, it can only use any function $f_1 \in \mathcal{F}_1$ as the long-term secret key leakage function where $\mathcal{F}_1$ is the set of leakage functions committed by $\mathcal{M}$ before it reveals the ephemeral secret key. A similar treatment is done for the ephemeral secret key leakage function f_2. Under such a restriction, neither f_1 nor f_2 can be embedded with the session key derivation function of the test session and $\mathcal{M}$ cannot launch a trivial attack against the AKE protocol. Therefore, the adversary can still make leakage queries during and after the test session, and if the long-term/ephemeral key is not revealed, then the adversary even doesn't need to commit the ephemeral/long-term key leakage functions $\mathcal{F}_1$ or $\mathcal{F}_2$. We can see that our approach still allows the adversary to adaptively choose leakage functions and meanwhile can capture challenge-dependent leakage under the minimum restriction.

Table 1. Comparison with existing leakage-resilient AKE security models

AKE models	Partial leakage setting				Basic models
	Challenge-Dependent	Long-Term Key	Ephemeral Key	Leakage Model	
BRM-CK [5]	No	✓	×	*Bounded-Retrieval*	CK
LR-CK [15]	No	✓	×	*Relative Leakage*	CK
LR-eCK [26]	No	✓	×	*Relative Leakage*	eCK
BAFL-eCK [4]	Yes (w/ split-state)	✓	×	*Relative Leakage*	eCK
CLR-eCK	Yes (w/o split-state)	✓	✓	*Relative Leakage*	eCK

Generic AKE Construction. To illustrate the practicality of the model, we present a general framework for the construction of AKE protocol secure in our newly proposed challenge-dependent leakage-resilient eCK model. The framework can be regarded as a variant of the AKE protocols proposed by Okamoto et al. [26,28]. Roughly speaking, we apply both pseudo-random functions (PRFs) and strong randomness extractors in the computation of ephemeral public key and session key to obtain the security in the presence of key leakage. Specifically, we employ an (extended) smooth projective hash function (SPHF) which is defined based on a domain $\mathcal{X}$ and an $\mathcal{NP}$ language $\mathcal{L} \subset \mathcal{X}$. During the session execution, both parties generate their ephemeral secret key and apply a strong extractor to extract a fresh seed for a PRF in order to derive a word in $\mathcal{L}$. They then exchange their words with the corresponding witness kept secret locally. Additionally, they also run an ephemeral Diffie-Hellman protocol using the exponent which is also output by the PRF. At the end of session, they derive the session key by computing the hash value of both words along with the Diffie-Hellman shared key. The correctness of the framework can be easily obtained due to the property of SPHF and Diffie-Hellman protocol while the security is guaranteed by the strong extractors, pseudo-random functions, along with the underlying (2-)smooth SPHF bulit on an $\mathcal{NP}$ language where the subgroup decision problem is hard.

An Efficient Instantiation. We show that the building blocks in our framework can be instantiated efficiently based on the DDH assumption. Precisely, we first introduce the Diffie-Hellman language $\mathcal{L}_{\mathsf{DH}} = \{(u_1, u_2) | \exists r \in \mathbb{Z}_p, s.t., u_1 = g_1^r, u_2 = g_2^r\}$ where $\mathbb{G}$ is a group of primer order p and $g_1, g_2 \in \mathbb{G}$ are generators. We then use it to construct a 2-smooth SPHF, denoted by $\mathcal{SPHF}_{\mathsf{DH}}$. A concrete protocol based on $\mathcal{SPHF}_{\mathsf{DH}}$ is then presented and proved to be CLR-eCK-secure. A comparison between our protocol and the previous ones is given in Table 2. We should note that the communication cost in eSIG-DH [5] and Enc-DH [15] is higher than our protocol due to the reason that they require their underlying primitive, i.e., signature or encryption scheme, to be leakage-resilient. For example, according to the result (**Theorem 5.2**) of [15], to obtain $(1 - \varepsilon)$-leakage resilience, the ciphertexts CT transferred in the Enc-DH protocol has the size of $O(1/\varepsilon)|\mathbb{G}|$. Due to the same reason, the computation overhead of those protocols is also higher than that of our protocol.

Table 2. Comparison with existing leakage-resilient AKE protocols

Protocols	Round	Communication[a]	Computation[a]	Relative leakage[b]		Security	AKEmodels
				lsk	esk		
eSIG-DH [5]	3	$3 \cdot |Cer| + 2 \cdot |G| + 2 \cdot |Sig|$	$4 \cdot Exp + 2 \cdot Sgn + 2 \cdot Ver$	$(1 - \varepsilon)$	0	w/ RO	BRM-CK [5]
Enc-DH [15]	3	$4 \cdot |Cer| + |G| + 2 \cdot |CT|$	$4 \cdot Exp + 2 \cdot Enc + 2 \cdot Dec$	$(1 - \varepsilon)$	0	w/o RO	LR-CK [15]
MO [26]	2	$4 \cdot |Cer| + 9 \cdot |G| + 3 \cdot |Exk|$	$20 \cdot Exp$	$(1/4 - \varepsilon)$	0	w/o RO	LR-eCK [26]
π [4]	2	$4 \cdot |Cer| + 2 \cdot |G| + 2 \cdot |Sig|$	$24 \cdot Exp$	$(1/n - \varepsilon)$	0	w/o RO	BAFL-eCK [4]
Our protocol	1	$4 \cdot |Cer| + 6 \cdot |G| + 2 \cdot |Exk|$	$16 \cdot Exp$	$(1/4 - \varepsilon)$	$(1 - \varepsilon)$	w/o RO	CLR-eCK

[a] We use Cer to denote the certificate of a long-term public key, G a group of primer order p, CT a ciphertext, Sig a signature and Exk the key of a randomness extractor. For the computation cost, we use Exp to denote exponentiation, Sgn the signing operation, Ver the verification operation, Enc the encryption operation and Dec the decryption operation.
[b] The "Relative Leakage" column indicates the leakage ratio of a secret key. In [4], the secret key is split into n parts.

2   Preliminaries

2.1   Notation

For a finite set Ω, $\omega \xleftarrow{\$} \Omega$ denotes that ω is selected uniformly at random from Ω.

Statistical Indistinguishability. Let X and Y be two random variables over a finite domain Ω, the *statistical distance* between X and Y is defined as $SD(X, Y) = 1/2 \sum_{\omega \in \Omega} | \Pr[X = \omega] - \Pr[Y = \omega]|$. We say that X and Y are ϵ-*statistically indistinguishable* if $SD(X, Y) \leq \epsilon$ and for simplicity we denote it by $X \stackrel{s}{\equiv}_\epsilon Y$. If $\epsilon = 0$, we say that X and Y are *perfectly indistinguishable*.

Computational Indistinguishability. Let $\mathcal{V}_1$ and $\mathcal{V}_2$ be two probability distribution over a finite set Ω where $|\Omega| \geq 2^k$ and k is a security parameter. We then define a distinguisher $\widetilde{\mathcal{D}}$ as follows. In the game, $\widetilde{\mathcal{D}}$ takes as input $\mathcal{V}_1$ and $\mathcal{V}_2$, the challenger flips a coin $\gamma \xleftarrow{\$} \{0,1\}$. $\widetilde{\mathcal{D}}$ is then given an element $v_1 \xleftarrow{\$} \mathcal{V}_1$ if $\gamma = 1$, otherwise an element $v_2 \xleftarrow{\$} \mathcal{V}_2$. Finally, $\widetilde{\mathcal{D}}$ outputs a bit $\gamma' \in \{0,1\}$ as its guess on γ. We define the advantage of $\widetilde{\mathcal{D}}$ in this game as $\mathsf{Adv}_{\widetilde{\mathcal{D}}}^{\mathcal{V}_1, \mathcal{V}_2}(k) = \Pr[\gamma' = \gamma] - 1/2$. We say that $\mathcal{V}_1$ and $\mathcal{V}_2$ are *computationally indistinguishable* if for any polynomial-time distinguisher $\mathcal{D}$, $\mathsf{Adv}_{\widetilde{\mathcal{D}}}^{\mathcal{V}_1, \mathcal{V}_2}(k)$ is negligible, and we denote it by $\mathcal{V}_1 \stackrel{c}{\equiv} \mathcal{V}_2$.

2.2   Randomness Extractor

Average-Case Min-Entropy. The *min-entropy* of a random variable X is $\mathsf{H}_\infty(X) = -\log(\max_x \Pr[X = x])$. Dodis et al. [17] formalized the notion of average min-entropy that captures the unpredictability of a random variable X given the value of a random variable Y, formally defined as $\widetilde{\mathsf{H}}_\infty(X|Y) = -\log(\mathsf{E}_{y \leftarrow Y}[2^{-\mathsf{H}_\infty(X|Y=y)}])$. They also showed the following result on average min-entropy in [17].

Lemma 1 ([17]). *If Y has 2^λ possible values, then $\widetilde{\mathsf{H}}_\infty(X|Y) \geq \mathsf{H}_\infty(X) - \lambda$.*

Definition 1 (Average-Case Strong Extractor) [17]. *Let $k \in \mathbb{N}$ be a security parameter. A function* $\mathsf{Ext} : \{0,1\}^{n(k)} \times \{0,1\}^{t(k)} \to \{0,1\}^{l(k)}$ *is an average-case* (m, ϵ)-*strong extractor if for all pairs of random variables* (X, I) *such that* $X \in \{0,1\}^{n(k)}$ *and* $\widetilde{H}_\infty(X|I) \geq m$, *it holds that* $\mathsf{SD}((\mathsf{Ext}(X,S), S, I), (U, S, I)) \leq \epsilon$, *as long as* $l(k) \leq m - 2\log(1/\epsilon)$, *where* $S \xleftarrow{\$} \{0,1\}^{t(k)}$ *is the extraction key and* $U \xleftarrow{\$} \{0,1\}^{l(k)}$.

2.3   Pseudo-Random Function

Pseudo-Random Function [18]. Let $k \in \mathbb{N}$ be a security parameter. A function family F is associated with $\{\mathsf{Seed}_k\}_{k \in \mathbb{N}}$, $\{\mathsf{Dom}_k\}_{k \in \mathbb{N}}$ and $\{\mathsf{Rng}_k\}_{k \in \mathbb{N}}$. Formally, for any $\sum \xleftarrow{\$} \mathsf{Seed}_k$, $\sigma \xleftarrow{\$} \sum$, $\mathcal{D} \xleftarrow{\$} \mathsf{Dom}_k$ and $\mathcal{R} \xleftarrow{\$} \mathsf{Rng}_k$, $\mathsf{F}_\sigma^{k, \sum, \mathcal{D}, \mathcal{R}}$ defines a function which maps an element of $\mathcal{D}$ to an element of $\mathcal{R}$. That is, $\mathsf{F}_\sigma^{k, \sum, \mathcal{D}, \mathcal{R}}(\rho) \in \mathcal{R}$ for any $\rho \in \mathcal{D}$.

Definition 2 (PRF). F *is a pseudo-random function (PRF) family if* $\{\mathsf{F}_\sigma^{k, \sum, \mathcal{D}, \mathcal{R}}(\rho_i)\} \stackrel{c}{\equiv} \{RF(\rho_i)\}$ *for any* $\{\rho_i \in \mathcal{D}\}$ *adaptively chosen by any polynomial time distinguisher, where* RF *is a truly random function. That is, for any* $\rho \in \mathcal{D}, RF(\rho) \xleftarrow{\$} \mathcal{R}$.

π**PRF** [28]. Roughly speaking, πPRF refers to a pseudo-random function family that if a specific key σ is pairwise-independent from other keys, then the output of function with key σ is computationally indistinguishable from a random element.

Definition 3 (πPRF). *Define* $\widetilde{\mathsf{F}}(\rho_j) = \mathsf{F}_{\sigma_{i_j}}^{k, \sum, \mathcal{D}, \mathcal{R}}(\rho_j)$ *for* $i_j \in I_{\sum}$, $\rho_j \in \mathcal{D}$. *We say that* F *is a* πPRF *family if* $\{\widetilde{\mathsf{F}}(\rho_j)\} \stackrel{c}{\equiv} \{\widetilde{RF}(\rho_j)\}$ *for any* $\{i_j \in I_{\sum}, \rho_j \in \mathcal{D}\}$ $(j = 0, 1, ..., q(k))$ *adaptively chosen by any polynomial time distinguisher such that* σ_{i_0} *is pairwisely independent from* $\sigma_{i_j}(j > 0)$, *where* $\widetilde{RF}$ *is the same as* $\widetilde{\mathsf{F}}$ *except that* $\widetilde{RF}(\rho_0)$ *is replace by a truly random value in* $\mathcal{R}$.

2.4   Smooth Projective Hash Function

Smooth projective hash function (SPHF) is originally introduced by Cramer and Shoup [13] and extended for constructions of many cryptographic primitives.

Syntax. Roughly speaking, the definition of an SPHF requires the existence of a domain $\mathcal{X}$ and an underlying $\mathcal{NP}$ language $\mathcal{L}$, where elements of $\mathcal{L}$ form a subset $\mathcal{X}$, i.e., $\mathcal{L} \subset \mathcal{X}$. Formally, an SPHF over a language $\mathcal{L} \subset \mathcal{X}$, onto a set $\mathcal{Y}$, is defined as,

$\mathsf{SPHFSetup}(1^k)$: generates the parameters param and the description of language $\mathcal{L}$;

$\mathsf{HashKG}(\mathcal{L}, \mathsf{param})$: generates a hashing key hk for the language $\mathcal{L}$;

$\mathsf{ProjKG}(\mathsf{hk}, (\mathcal{L}, \mathsf{param}))$: derives the projection key hp from the hashing key hk;

$\mathsf{Hash}(\mathsf{hk}, (\mathcal{L}, \mathsf{param}), W)$: outputs the hash value $\mathsf{hv} \in \mathcal{Y}$ on the word W from hk;

ProjHash(hp, $(\mathcal{L}, \text{param}), W, w$): outputs the hash value hv$' \in \mathcal{Y}$, on the word W from the projection key hp, and the witness w for the fact that $W \in \mathcal{L}$.

Extension. In order to make the SPHF notion well applied for our work, similar to [13], we also need an extension of the SPHF in this paper. Precisely, we introduce the WordG algorithm and slightly modify the Hash, ProjHash algorithms for SPHF as follows.[1]

WordG($\mathcal{L}, \text{param}, w$): generates a word $W \in \mathcal{L}$ with w the witness;

Hash(hk, $(\mathcal{L}, \text{param}), W, aux$): outputs hv on W from hk and the auxiliary input aux;

ProjHash(hp, $(\mathcal{L}, \text{param}), W, w, aux$): outputs the hash value hv$' \in \mathcal{Y}$, on the word W from key hp, the witness w for the fact that $W \in \mathcal{L}$ and the auxiliary input aux.

Property. A smooth projective hash function should satisfy the following properties,

Correctness. Let $W = \text{WordG}(\mathcal{L}, \text{param}, w)$, then for all hashing key hk and projection key hp, Hash(hk, $(\mathcal{L}, \text{param}), W, aux$) = ProjHash(hp, $(\mathcal{L}, \text{param})$, W, w, aux).

Smoothness. For any $W \in \mathcal{X} \backslash \mathcal{L}$, the distribution $\mathcal{V}_1 = \{(\mathcal{L}, \text{param}, W, \text{hp}, aux, \text{hv}) | \text{hv} = \text{Hash}(\text{hk}, (\mathcal{L}, \text{param}), W, aux)\}$ is perfectly indistinguishable from the distribution $\mathcal{V}_2 = \{(\mathcal{L}, \text{param}, W, \text{hp}, aux, \text{hv}) | \text{hv} \xleftarrow{\$} \mathcal{Y}\}$.

Definition 4 (2-smooth SPHF). *For any* $W_1, W_2 \in \mathcal{X} \backslash \mathcal{L}$, *let* aux_1, aux_2 *be the auxiliary inputs such that* $(W_1, aux_1) \neq (W_2, aux_2)$, *we say an SPHF is 2-smooth if the distribution* $\mathcal{V}_1 = \{(\mathcal{L}, \text{param}, W_1, W_2, \text{hp}, aux_1, aux_2, \text{hv}_1, \text{hv}_2) | \text{hv}_2 = \text{Hash}(\text{hk}, (\mathcal{L}, \text{param}), W_2, aux_2)\}$ *is perfectly indistinguishable from* $\mathcal{V}_2 = \{(\mathcal{L}, \text{param}, W_1, W_2, \text{hp}, aux_1, aux_2, \text{hv}_1, \text{hv}_2) | \text{hv}_2 \xleftarrow{\$} \mathcal{Y}\}$, *where* $\text{hv}_1 = \text{Hash}(\text{hk}, (\mathcal{L}, \text{param}), W_1, aux_1)$.

Definition 5 (Hard Subset Membership Problem). *For a finite set* $\mathcal{X}$ *and an NP language* $\mathcal{L} \subset \mathcal{X}$, *we say the subset membership problem is hard if for any word* $W \xleftarrow{\$} \mathcal{L}$, W *is computationally indistinguishable from any random element chosen from* $\mathcal{X} \backslash \mathcal{L}$.

3 A New Strong Leakage-Resilient AKE Security Model

In this section, we assume that the reader is familiar with the details of AKE protocol and eCK model [23]. More details are referred to the full version.

---

[1] In the rest of paper, all the SPHFs are referred to as the extended SPHF and defined by algorithms (SPHFSetup, HashKG, ProjKG, WordG, Hash, ProjHash).

3.1   Challenge-Dependent Leakage-Resilient eCK Model

Our notion, named *Challenge-Dependent Leakage-Resilient eCK* (CLR-eCK) model is the first split-state-free security model that captures both long-term and ephemeral key leakage *and* allows the adversary to issue leakage queries even *after the activation of the test session*. Formally, adversary $\mathcal{M}$ is allowed to issue the following queries.

- Send($\mathcal{A}, \mathcal{B}, message$). Send *message* to party $\mathcal{A}$ on behalf of party $\mathcal{B}$, and obtain $\mathcal{A}$'s response for this message.
- EstablishParty(pid). Register a long-term public key on behalf of party pid, which is said to be *dishonest*.
- LongTermKeyReveal(pid). Query the long-term secret key of honest party pid.
- SessionKeyReveal(sid). Query the session key of the completed session sid.
- EphemeralKeyReveal(sid). Query the ephemeral secret key of session sid.
- LongTermKeyLeakage(f_1, pid). This query allows $\mathcal{M}$ to learn $f_1(lsk)$ where f_1 denotes the leakage function and lsk denotes the long-term secret key of party pid.
- EphemeralKeyLeakage(f_2, sid). This query allows $\mathcal{M}$ to learn $f_2(esk)$ where f_2 denotes the leakage function and esk denotes the ephemeral secret key used by an honest user in the session sid.
- Test(sid*). To answer this query, the challenger pick $b \xleftarrow{\$} \{0,1\}$. If $b = 1$, the challenger returns $SK^* \leftarrow$ SessionKeyReveal(sid*). Otherwise, the challenger sends the adversary a random key $R^* \xleftarrow{\$} \{0,1\}^{|SK^*|}$.

Note that the Test query can be issued only once but at any time during the game, and the game terminates as soon as $\mathcal{M}$ outputs its guess b' on b.

Restrictions on the Leakage Function. In our CLR-eCK security model, we consider several restrictions on the leakage function to prevent trivial attacks.

The first restriction is that the output size of the leakage function f_1 and f_2 must be less than $|lsk|$ and $|esk|$, respectively. Specifically, following the work in [27], we require the output size of a leakage function f is at most λ bits, which means the entropy loss of sk is at most λ bits upon observing $f(sk)$. Formally, we define two bounded leakage function families $\mathcal{F}_{\text{bbd-I}}$ and $\mathcal{F}_{\text{bbd-II}}$ as follows. $\mathcal{F}_{\text{bbd-I}}(k)$ is defined as the class of all polynomial-time computable functions: $f : \{0,1\}^{|lsk|} \rightarrow \{0,1\}^{\leq \lambda_1(k)}$, where $\lambda_1(k) < |lsk|$. $\mathcal{F}_{\text{bbd-II}}(k)$ is defined as the class of all polynomial-time computable functions: $f : \{0,1\}^{|esk|} \rightarrow \{0,1\}^{\leq \lambda_2(k)}$, where $\lambda_2(k) < |esk|$. We then require that the submitted leakage function should satisfy that $f_1 \in \mathcal{F}_{\text{bbd-I}}$ and $f_2 \in \mathcal{F}_{\text{bbd-II}}$.

Another restriction that must be enforced is related to the challenge-dependent leakage security of AKE protocols. Consider a test session sid* which is owned by party $\mathcal{A}$ with peer $\mathcal{B}$. Note that for a 2-pass AKE protocol, the session key of sid* is determined by $(\widehat{A}, \widehat{B}, lsk_{\mathcal{A}}, esk_{\mathcal{A}}^*, lpk_{\mathcal{B}}, epk_{\mathcal{B}}^*)$ which contains only two secret keys (i.e., $lsk_{\mathcal{A}}, esk_{\mathcal{A}}^*$). Since $\mathcal{M}$ is allowed to reveal $esk_{\mathcal{A}}^*$ ($lsk_{\mathcal{A}}$) in the eCK model, $\mathcal{M}$ can launch a trivial attack by encoding the session key derivation function into the leakage function of $lsk_{\mathcal{A}}$ ($esk_{\mathcal{A}}^*$) and hence wins the security game. Therefore, adversary $\mathcal{M}$ should not be allowed to adaptively issue leakage query after it obtains all the other (secret) information for session key computation, otherwise the security of AKE protocol is unachievable. More precisely, we describe the restrictions on LongTermKeyLeakage($f_1, \mathcal{A}$) and EphemeralKeyLeakage($f_2,$ sid*) as follows.

- $\mathcal{M}$ is allowed to ask for arbitrary leakage function $f_1 \in \mathcal{F}_{\text{bbd-I}}$ before it obtains the ephemeral secret key $esk_{\mathcal{A}}^*$, i.e., by issuing EphemeralKeyReveal(sid*) query; however, after obtaining $esk_{\mathcal{A}}^*$, $\mathcal{M}$ can only use the leakage functions $f_1 \in \mathcal{F}_1 \subset \mathcal{F}_{\text{bbd-I}}$ where $\mathcal{F}_1$ is a set of leakage functions chosen and submitted by $\mathcal{M}$ before it issues EphemeralKeyReveal(sid*).
- $\mathcal{M}$ is allowed to ask for arbitrary leakage function $f_2 \in \mathcal{F}_{\text{bbd-II}}$ before it obtains the long-term secret key $lsk_{\mathcal{A}}$, i.e., by issuing LongTermKeyReveal($\mathcal{A}$) query; however, after obtaining $lsk_{\mathcal{A}}$, $\mathcal{M}$ can only use the leakage functions $f_2 \in \mathcal{F}_2 \subset \mathcal{F}_{\text{bbd-II}}$ where $\mathcal{F}_2$ is a set of leakage functions chosen and submitted by $\mathcal{M}$ before it issues LongTermKeyReveal($\mathcal{A}$).

We should note that if $\overline{\text{sid}}^*$ exists, the above restriction must also be enforced for LongTermKeyLeakage($f_1, \mathcal{B}$) and EphemeralKeyLeakage($f_2, \overline{\text{sid}}^*$), since the session key of sid* is also determined by $(\widehat{A}, \widehat{B}, lpk_{\mathcal{A}}, epk_{\mathcal{A}}^*, lsk_{\mathcal{B}}, esk_{\mathcal{B}}^*)$.

Adaptive Leakage. One can see that our proposed model enables adversary $\mathcal{M}$ to choose $\mathcal{F}_1, \mathcal{F}_2$ adaptively and $\mathcal{M}$ can submit $\mathcal{F}_1, \mathcal{F}_2$ even after the challenge phase as long as the restriction holds. That is, $\mathcal{M}$ can specify function set $\mathcal{F}_1, \mathcal{F}_2$ after seeing $epk_{\mathcal{A}}^*$ and $epk_{\mathcal{B}}^*$. Also, if there is no long-term (ephemeral, respectively) key reveal query, then $\mathcal{F}_1$ ($\mathcal{F}_2$, respectively) is the same as $\mathcal{F}_{\text{bbd-I}}$ ($\mathcal{F}_{\text{bbd-II}}$, respectively). Implicitly, $\mathcal{M}$ is allowed to obtain $f_1(lsk_{\mathcal{A}}), f_1'(lsk_{\mathcal{B}}), f_2(esk_{\mathcal{A}}^*), f_2'(esk_{\mathcal{B}}^*)$ where $f_1, f_1' \in \mathcal{F}_{\text{bbd-I}}, f_2, f_2' \in \mathcal{F}_{\text{bbd-II}}$ can be dependent on $(lpk_{\mathcal{A}}, lpk_{\mathcal{B}}, epk_{\mathcal{A}}^*, epk_{\mathcal{B}}^*)$, or to obtain $f_1(lsk_{\mathcal{A}}), f_2(esk_{\mathcal{B}}^*)$ where $f_1 \in \mathcal{F}_1, f_2 \in \mathcal{F}_2$ can be dependent on $(lpk_{\mathcal{A}}, lpk_{\mathcal{B}}, lsk_{\mathcal{B}}, epk_{\mathcal{A}}^*, epk_{\mathcal{B}}^*)$ and $(lpk_{\mathcal{A}}, lpk_{\mathcal{B}}, epk_{\mathcal{A}}^*, esk_{\mathcal{A}}^*, epk_{\mathcal{B}}^*)$, respectively.

We define the notion of a *fresh session* in the CLR-eCK model as follows.

Definition 6 ((λ_1, λ_2)-Leakage Fresh Session in the CLR-eCK Model). *Let* sid *be a completed session owned by an honest party $\mathcal{A}$ with peer $\mathcal{B}$, who is also honest. Let* $\overline{\text{sid}}$ *denote the matching session of* sid*, if it exists. Session* sid *is said to be fresh in the* CLR-eCK *model if the following conditions hold:*

- sid *is a fresh session in the sense of eCK model.*
- $\mathcal{M}$ *only issues the queries* LongTermKeyLeakage($f_1, \mathcal{A}$), LongTermKeyLeakage ($f_1', \mathcal{B}$), EphemeralKeyLeakage($f_2,$ sid), EphemeralKeyLeakage($f_2', \overline{\text{sid}}$) *(if* $\overline{\text{sid}}$ *exists), such that* f_1, f_1', f_2, f_2' *satisfy the restrictions given above.*
- *The total output length of all the* LongTermKeyLeakage *queries to $\mathcal{A}$ ($\mathcal{B}$, respectively) is at most λ_1.*
- *The total output length of all the* EphemeralKeyLeakage *query to* sid *($\overline{\text{sid}}$, respectively, if it exists) is at most λ_2.*

We now describe the notion of CLR-eCK security.

Definition 7 (CLR-eCK **Security**). *Let the test session* sid* *be* (λ_1, λ_2)-*leakage fresh where adversary* $\mathcal{M}$ *issues* Test(sid*) *query. We define the advantage of* $\mathcal{M}$ *in the* CLR-eCK *game by* $\mathrm{Adv}_{\mathcal{M}}^{\mathsf{CLR\text{-}eCK}}(k) = \Pr[b' = b] - 1/2$, *where* k *is the security parameter of the AKE protocol. We say the AKE protocol is* (λ_1, λ_2)-*challenge-dependent leakage-resilient eCK-secure* $((\lambda_1, \lambda_2)$-CLR-eCK-*secure) if the matching session computes the same session key and for any probabilistic polynomial-time adversary* $\mathcal{M}$, $\mathrm{Adv}_{\mathcal{M}}^{\mathsf{CLR\text{-}eCK}}(k)$ *is negligible.*

4   One-Round CLR-eCK-Secure AKE

4.1   General Framework

Figure 1 describes a generic construction of the CLR-eCK secure AKE protocol. Suppose that k is the system security parameter. Let $\mathbb{G}$ be a group with prime order p and g is a random generator of $\mathbb{G}$. Let $\mathcal{SPHF}$ denote a 2-smooth SPHF over $\mathcal{L} \subset \mathcal{X}$ and onto the set $\mathcal{Y}$ such that the subset membership problem between $\mathcal{L}$ and $\mathcal{X}$ is hard. Denote the hashing key space by $\mathcal{HK}$, the projection

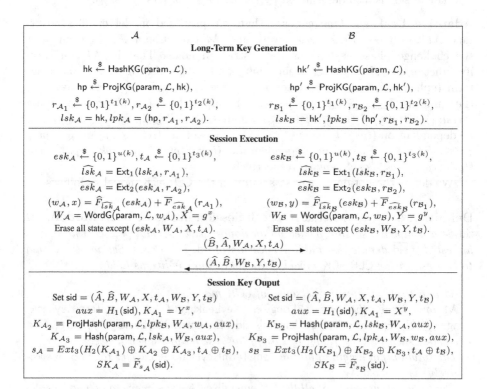

Fig. 1. Framework for CLR-eCK secure AKE

key space by $\mathcal{HP}$, the auxiliary input space by $\mathcal{AUX}$ and the witness space by $\mathcal{W}$. Pick two collision-resistant hash functions $H_1 : \{0,1\}^* \to \mathcal{AUX}, H_2 : \mathbb{G} \to \mathcal{Y}$.

Let $\lambda_1 = \lambda_1(k)$ be the bound on the amount of long-term secret key leakage and $\lambda_2 = \lambda_2(k)$ be that of the ephemeral secret key leakage. Let $\mathsf{Ext}_1, \mathsf{Ext}_2, \mathsf{Ext}_3$ be strong extractors as follows. $\mathsf{Ext}_1 : \mathcal{HK} \times \{0,1\}^{t_1(k)} \to \{0,1\}^{l_1(k)}$ is an average-case $(|\mathcal{HK}| - \lambda_1, \epsilon_1)$-strong extractor. $\mathsf{Ext}_2 : \{0,1\}^{u(k)} \times \{0,1\}^{t_2(k)} \to \{0,1\}^{l_2(k)}$ is an average-case $(k - \lambda_2, \epsilon_2)$-strong extractor. $\mathsf{Ext}_3 : \mathcal{Y} \times \{0,1\}^{t_3(k)} \to \{0,1\}^{l_3(k)}$ is an average-case $(|\mathcal{Y}| - \lambda_1, \epsilon_3)$-strong extractor. Here $\epsilon_1 = \epsilon_1(k), \epsilon_2 = \epsilon_2(k), \epsilon_3 = \epsilon_3(k)$ are negligible.

Let $\widehat{\mathsf{F}}$ and $\overline{\mathsf{F}}$ be PRF families and $\widetilde{\mathsf{F}}$ be a πPRF family as follows.

$\widehat{\mathsf{F}}^{k, \Sigma_{\widehat{\mathsf{F}}}, \mathcal{D}_{\widehat{\mathsf{F}}}, \mathcal{R}_{\widehat{\mathsf{F}}}} : \sum_{\widehat{\mathsf{F}}} = \{0,1\}^{l_1(k)}, \mathcal{D}_{\widehat{\mathsf{F}}} = \{0,1\}^{u(k)}, \mathcal{R}_{\widehat{\mathsf{F}}} = \mathcal{W} \times \mathbb{Z}_p,$

$\overline{\mathsf{F}}^{k, \Sigma_{\overline{\mathsf{F}}}, \mathcal{D}_{\overline{\mathsf{F}}}, \mathcal{R}_{\overline{\mathsf{F}}}} : \sum_{\overline{\mathsf{F}}} = \{0,1\}^{l_2(k)}, \mathcal{D}_{\overline{\mathsf{F}}} = \{0,1\}^{t_1(k)}, \mathcal{R}_{\overline{\mathsf{F}}} = \mathcal{W} \times \mathbb{Z}_p,$

$\widetilde{\mathsf{F}}^{k, \Sigma_{\widetilde{\mathsf{F}}}, \mathcal{D}_{\widetilde{\mathsf{F}}}, \mathcal{R}_{\widetilde{\mathsf{F}}}} : \sum_{\widetilde{\mathsf{F}}} = \{0,1\}^{l_3(k)}, \mathcal{D}_{\widetilde{\mathsf{F}}} = (\Lambda_k)^2 \times \mathcal{L}^2 \times \mathbb{G}^2 \times \{0,1\}^{2t_3(k)}, \mathcal{R}_{\widetilde{\mathsf{F}}} = \{0,1\}^{l_4(k)}.$[2]

Let $\widehat{F} \leftarrow \widehat{\mathsf{F}}^{k, \Sigma_{\widehat{\mathsf{F}}}, \mathcal{D}_{\widehat{\mathsf{F}}}, \mathcal{R}_{\widehat{\mathsf{F}}}}, \overline{F} \leftarrow \overline{\mathsf{F}}^{k, \Sigma_{\overline{\mathsf{F}}}, \mathcal{D}_{\overline{\mathsf{F}}}, \mathcal{R}_{\overline{\mathsf{F}}}}$ and $\widetilde{F} \leftarrow \widetilde{\mathsf{F}}^{k, \Sigma_{\widetilde{\mathsf{F}}}, \mathcal{D}_{\widetilde{\mathsf{F}}}, \mathcal{R}_{\widetilde{\mathsf{F}}}}$.

The system parameter is $(\mathsf{param}, \mathbb{G}, p, g, H_1, H_2, \mathsf{Ext}_1, \mathsf{Ext}_2, \mathsf{Ext}_3, \widehat{F}, \overline{F}, \widetilde{F})$ where $\mathsf{param} \leftarrow \mathsf{SPHFSetup}(1^k)$.

Correctness Analysis. One can note that $K_{A_1} = K_{B_1}$ as $K_{A_1} = Y^x = X^y = K_{B_1} = g^{xy}$. Due to the property of SPHF, we have $K_{A_2} = \mathsf{ProjHash}(\mathsf{param}, \mathcal{L}, lpk_B, W_A, w_A, aux) = \mathsf{Hash}(\mathsf{param}, \mathcal{L}, lsk_B, W_A, aux) = K_{B_2}, K_{A_3} = \mathsf{Hash}(\mathsf{param}, \mathcal{L}, lsk_A, W_B, aux) = \mathsf{ProjHash}(\mathsf{param}, \mathcal{L}, lpk_A, W_B, w_B, aux) = K_{B_3}$. Therefore, we can obtain that $s_A = Ext_3(H_2(K_{A_1}) \oplus K_{A_2} \oplus K_{A_3}, t_A \oplus t_B) = s_B = Ext_3(H_2(K_{B_1}) \oplus K_{B_2} \oplus K_{B_3}, t_A \oplus t_B)$, which guarantees that $SK_A = SK_B$.

4.2 Security Analysis

Theorem 1. *The AKE protocol following the general framework is (λ_1, λ_2)-CLR-eCK-secure if the underlying smooth projective hash function is 2-smooth, the DDH assumption holds in $\mathbb{G}$, H_1, H_2 are collision-resistant hash functions, $\widehat{F}$ and $\overline{F}$ are PRF families and $\widetilde{F}$ is a πPRF family. Here $\lambda_1 \leq \min\{|\mathcal{HK}| - 2\log(1/\epsilon_1) - l_1(k), |\mathcal{Y}| - 2\log(1/\epsilon_3) - l_3(k)\}, \lambda_2 \leq u(k) - 2\log(1/\epsilon_2) - l_2(k)$.*

Proof. Due to the space limitation, we just describe the proof sketch here. The full security proof will be given in the full paper.

Let session $\mathsf{sid}^* = (\widehat{A}, \widehat{B}, W_A^*, X^*, t_A^*, W_B^*, Y^*, t_B^*)$ be the target session chosen by adversary $\mathcal{M}$. $\mathcal{A}$ is the owner of the session sid^* and $\mathcal{B}$ is the peer. We then analyze the security of the AKE protocol in the following two disjoint cases.

Case I. *There exists a matching session, $\overline{\mathsf{sid}^*}$, of the target session sid^*.* Based on the definition, we can see that for each party, either long-term or ephemeral secret key remains unknown to the adversary. Without loss of generality, suppose that the adversary obtains at most λ_2-bits of the ephemeral secret key of target session

---

[2] In this paper, we denote the space of a certified long-term public key (such as $\widehat{A}$) by Λ_k.

sid*, we have that $\widehat{esk}_{\mathcal{A}}^* = \mathsf{Ext}_2(esk_{\mathcal{A}}^*, r_{\mathcal{A}_2}) \stackrel{s}{\equiv}_{\epsilon_2} \widehat{esk}_{\mathcal{A}}' \stackrel{\$}{\leftarrow} \{0,1\}^{l_2(k)}$. Therefore, $(w_{\mathcal{A}}^*, x^*) = \widehat{F}_{\widehat{lsk}_{\mathcal{A}}}(esk_{\mathcal{A}}^*) + \overline{F}_{\widehat{esk}_{\mathcal{A}}^*}(r_{\mathcal{A}_1}) \stackrel{c}{\equiv} (w_{\mathcal{A}}', x') \stackrel{\$}{\leftarrow} \mathcal{W} \times \mathbb{Z}_p$. Similarly, suppose that the adversary obtains at most λ_2-bits of the ephemeral secret key of matching session $\overline{\mathsf{sid}^*}$, we have that $\widehat{esk}_{\mathcal{B}}^* = \mathsf{Ext}_2(esk_{\mathcal{B}}^*, r_{\mathcal{B}_2}) \stackrel{s}{\equiv}_{\epsilon_2} \widehat{esk}_{\mathcal{B}}' \stackrel{\$}{\leftarrow} \{0,1\}^{l_2(k)}$, and thus $(w_{\mathcal{B}}^*, y^*) = \widehat{F}_{\widehat{lsk}_{\mathcal{B}}}(esk_{\mathcal{B}}^*) + \overline{F}_{\widehat{esk}_{\mathcal{B}}^*}(r_{\mathcal{B}_1}) \stackrel{c}{\equiv} (w_{\mathcal{B}}', y') \stackrel{\$}{\leftarrow} \mathcal{W} \times \mathbb{Z}_p$. Therefore, regardless of the type of the reveal query and leakage query, (x^*, y^*) are uniformly random elements in $\mathbb{Z}_p^2$ from the view of adversary $\mathcal{M}$. Therefore, $K_{\mathcal{A}_1}^* = K_{\mathcal{B}_1}^* = g^{x^* y^*}$ is computationally indistinguishable from a random element in $\mathbb{G}$ according to the DDH assumption and hence $H_2(K_{\mathcal{A}_1}^*)$ is a uniform random string from the view of $\mathcal{M}$ who is given $X^* = g^{x^*}, Y^* = g^{y^*}$. We then have that the seed $s_{\mathcal{A}}^*$ for the πPRF function is uniformly distributed and unknown to the adversary and thus the derived session key $SK_{\mathcal{A}}^*$ is computationally indistinguishable from a random string. It is worth noting that in this case we only require $\tilde{F}$ to be a normal PRF.

Case II. *There exists no matching session of the test session* sid*. In this case, the adversary cannot issue LongTermKeyReveal query to reveal the long-term secret key of $\mathcal{B}$ but may issue the leakage query LongTermKeyLeakage to learn some bit-information of $lsk_{\mathcal{B}}$. We prove the security of the AKE protocol as follows. In the simulation, we modify the security game via the following steps to obtain a new game. We first replace $K_{\mathcal{A}_2}^* = \mathsf{ProjHash}(\mathsf{param}, \mathcal{L}, lpk_{\mathcal{B}}, W_{\mathcal{A}}^*, w_{\mathcal{A}}^*, aux^*)$ by $K_{\mathcal{A}_2}^* = \mathsf{Hash}(\mathsf{param}, \mathcal{L}, lsk_{\mathcal{B}}, W_{\mathcal{A}}^*, aux^*)$, and then choose $W_{\mathcal{A}}^* \in \mathcal{X} \setminus \mathcal{L}$ instead of deriving it from $\mathcal{L}$ through the algorithm WordG. One can see that the new game is identical to the original game from the view of adversary $\mathcal{M}$ due to the fact that $\mathsf{ProjHash}(\mathsf{param}, \mathcal{L}, lpk_{\mathcal{B}}, W_{\mathcal{A}}^*, w_{\mathcal{A}}^*) = \mathsf{Hash}(\mathsf{param}, \mathcal{L}, lsk_{\mathcal{B}}, W_{\mathcal{A}}^*)$, and due to the difficulty of the subset membership problem which ensures that the distribution of $\mathcal{X} \setminus \mathcal{L}$ is indistinguishable from $\mathcal{L}$.

Note that adversary $\mathcal{M}$ may activate a session sid, which is not matching to session sid*, with $\mathcal{B}$. Precisely, $\mathcal{M}$ can choose $W \in \mathcal{X} \setminus \mathcal{L}$ (e.g., by replaying $W_{\mathcal{A}}^*$), send W to $\mathcal{B}$ and issue SessionKeyReveal(sid) query to learn the shared key. According to the property of 2-smooth of the underlying smooth projective hash function, we have that $K_{\mathcal{A}_2}^*$ is pairwisely independent from any other such key (denoted by $\tilde{K}$) and all public information (i.e., $\mathsf{param}, \mathcal{L}, lpk_{\mathcal{B}}, W_{\mathcal{A}}^*, aux^*$) and hence $\tilde{H}_\infty(K_{\mathcal{A}_2}^* | \tilde{K}, \mathsf{param}, \mathcal{L}, lpk_{\mathcal{B}}, W_{\mathcal{A}}^*, aux^*) = |\mathcal{Y}|$. Suppose that the leakage of $lsk_{\mathcal{B}}$ is at most λ_1-bits (denoted by $\widetilde{lsk}_{\mathcal{B}}$), and therefore (see *Lemma 1*), $\tilde{H}_\infty(K_{\mathcal{A}_2}^* | \tilde{K}, \mathsf{param}, \mathcal{L}, lpk_{\mathcal{B}}, W_{\mathcal{A}}^*, aux^*, \widetilde{lsk}_{\mathcal{B}}) \geq \tilde{H}_\infty(K_{\mathcal{A}_2}^* | \tilde{K}, \mathsf{param}, \mathcal{L}, lpk_{\mathcal{B}}, W_{\mathcal{A}}^*, aux^*) - \lambda_1 = |\mathcal{Y}| - \lambda_1$. Therefore, by using the strong extractor Ext_3, it holds that $s_{\mathcal{A}}^* = \mathsf{Ext}_3(H_2(K_{\mathcal{A}_1})^* \oplus K_{\mathcal{A}_2}^* \oplus K_{\mathcal{A}_3}^*, t_{\mathcal{A}}^* \oplus t_{\mathcal{B}}^*) \stackrel{s}{\equiv}_{\epsilon_3} s_{\mathcal{A}}' \stackrel{\$}{\leftarrow} \{0,1\}^{l_3(k)}$. One can see that $\mathcal{A}$ obtains a variable $s_{\mathcal{A}}^*$ which is pairwisely independent from any other such variables and thus the derived session key $SK_{\mathcal{A}}^*$ is computationally indistinguishable from a truly random element from $\mathcal{M}$'s view due to the application of πPRF, which completes the proof.

Simulation for Non-test Session. Note that for the two cases above, we have to simulate the non-test session correctly with the adversary. Specifically, when adversary $\mathcal{M}$ activates a non-test session with $\mathcal{A}$ or $\mathcal{B}$, the session execution simulated should be identical to the session run by $\mathcal{A}$ or $\mathcal{B}$ from the view of $\mathcal{M}$. One can note that this can be easily guaranteed when the query LongTermKeyReveal($\mathcal{A}$) or LongTermKeyReveal($\mathcal{B}$) is issued in the game. Since we know the long-term secret key of $\mathcal{A}$ or $\mathcal{B}$, we can just select an ephemeral secret key and compute the ephemeral public key correctly by using the long-term secret key and long-term public key. Nevertheless, if the query LongTermKeyReveal($\mathcal{A}$) or LongTermKeyReveal($\mathcal{B}$) is not issued, that is, without the long-term secret key of $\mathcal{A}$ or $\mathcal{B}$, the simulation of the non-test session owned by $\mathcal{A}$ or $\mathcal{B}$ can no longer be simulated as shown above. In this case, we simulate the session as follows. Suppose that we are to simulate the session owned by $\mathcal{A}$ without knowing $lsk_{\mathcal{A}}$, we pick $(r_1, r_2) \overset{\$}{\leftarrow} \mathcal{W} \times \mathbb{Z}_p$ and then compute $W_{\mathcal{A}} = \text{WordG}(\text{param}, \mathcal{L}, r_1), X = g^{r_2}$. We say that the session simulated in this way can be identical to the real session from $\mathcal{M}$'s view due to the pseudo-randomness of the PRF. To be more precise, even when $\mathcal{M}$ obtains at most λ_1-bits of $lsk_{\mathcal{A}}$ through LongTermKeyLeakage($\mathcal{A}$), the variable $\widehat{lsk}_{\mathcal{A}}$, which comes from $\text{Ext}_1(lsk_{\mathcal{A}}, r_{\mathcal{A}})$ and inputs to the pseudo-random function $\widehat{F}$, still remains unknown to adversary $\mathcal{M}$. Therefore, the value of $\widehat{F}_{\widehat{lsk}_{\mathcal{A}}}(esk_{\mathcal{A}})$ is computationally indistinguishable from a random element.

5 An Instantiation from DDH Assumption

In the following, we present the language we for the instantiation of our generic CLR-eCK-secure AKE protocol.

Diffie-Hellman Language. Let $\mathbb{G}$ be a group of prime order p and $g_1, g_2 \in \mathbb{G}$. The Diffie-Hellman Language is as $\mathcal{L}_{\text{DH}} = \{(u_1, u_2) | \exists r \in \mathbb{Z}_p, \text{s.t.}, u_1 = g_1^r, u_2 = g_2^r\}$. One can see that the witness space of $\mathcal{L}_{\text{DH}}$ is $\mathcal{W} = \mathbb{Z}_p$ and $\mathcal{L}_{\text{DH}} \subset \mathcal{X} = \mathbb{G}^2$. Due to the DDH assumption, we have that the subset membership problem over $\mathcal{L}_{\text{DH}}$ is hard.

SPHF on $\mathcal{L}_{\text{DH}}$. Here we show how to construct a 2-smooth SPHF (denoted by $\mathcal{SPHF}_{\text{DH}}$) over the language $\mathcal{L}_{\text{DH}} \subset \mathcal{X} = \mathbb{G}^2$ onto the group $\mathcal{Y} = \mathbb{G}$. Let $H_1 : \{0,1\}^* \to \mathbb{Z}_p$ denote a collision-resistant hash function. The concrete construction is as follows.

SPHFSetup(1^λ): param $= (\mathbb{G}, p, g_1, g_2)$;

HashKG($\mathcal{L}_{\text{DH}}$, param): hk $= (\alpha_1, \alpha_2, \beta_1, \beta_2) \overset{\$}{\leftarrow} \mathbb{Z}_p^4$;

ProjKG(hk, ($\mathcal{L}_{\text{DH}}$, param)): hp $= (\text{hp}_1, \text{hp}_2) = (g_1^{\alpha_1} g_2^{\alpha_2}, g_1^{\beta_1} g_2^{\beta_2}) \in \mathbb{G}_p^2$;

WordG(hk, ($\mathcal{L}_{\text{DH}}$, param), $w = r$): $W = (g_1^r, g_2^r)$;

Hash(hk, ($\mathcal{L}_{\text{DH}}$, param), $W = (u_1, u_2) = (g_1^r, g_2^r), aux = d = H_1(W, aux'))$: hv $= u_1^{\alpha_1 + d\beta_1} u_2^{\alpha_2 + d\beta_2}$;

ProjHash(hp, ($\mathcal{L}_{\text{DH}}$, param), $W = (u_1, u_2) = (g_1^r, g_2^r), w = r, aux = d = H_1(W, aux'))$: hv' $= \text{hp}_1^r \text{hp}_2^{dr}$.

Note that $\mathcal{Y} = \mathbb{G}, \mathcal{HK} = \mathbb{Z}_p^4, \mathcal{HP} = \mathbb{G}_p^2, \mathcal{AUX} = \mathbb{Z}_p, \mathcal{W} = \mathbb{Z}_p$. Then we have the following theorem. The proof is referred to the full version.

Theorem 2. $\mathcal{SPHF}_{\mathsf{DH}}$ *is a 2-smooth SPHF.*

The Concrete AKE Protocol. One can easily obtain the concrete AKE protocol using the instantiated $\mathcal{SPHF}_{\mathsf{DH}}$. Due to the space limitation, we postpone the details to the full version. Based on Theorems 1, 2 and 3, we have the following result for the concrete AKE protocol.

Theorem 3. *The concrete AKE protocol is* (λ_1, λ_2)-CLR-eCK-*secure, where* $\lambda_1 \leq \min\{4\log p - 2\log(1/\epsilon_1) - l_1(k), \log p - 2\log(1/\epsilon_3) - l_3(k)\}, \lambda_2 \leq u(k) - 2\log(1/\epsilon_2) - l_2(k)$.

Acknowledgements. We would like to thank Janaka Alawatugoda and the anonymous reviewers for their invaluable comments on a previous version of this paper. The work of Yi Mu is supported by the National Natural Science Foundation of China (Grant No. 61170298). The work of Guomin Yang is supported by the Australian Research Council Discovery Early Career Researcher Award (Grant No. DE150101116) and the National Natural Science Foundation of China (Grant No. 61472308).

References

1. Entity authentication mechanisms-part3: Entity authentication using asymmetric techniques. ISO/IEC IS 9789-3 (1993)
2. Akavia, A., Goldwasser, S., Vaikuntanathan, V.: Simultaneous hardcore bits and cryptography against memory attacks. In: Reingold, O. (ed.) TCC 2009. LNCS, vol. 5444, pp. 474–495. Springer, Heidelberg (2009)
3. Alawatugoda, J., Boyd, C., Stebila, D.: Continuous after-the-fact leakage-resilient key exchange. In: Susilo, W., Mu, Y. (eds.) ACISP 2014. LNCS, vol. 8544, pp. 258–273. Springer, Heidelberg (2014)
4. Alawatugoda, J., Stebila, D., Boyd, C.: Modelling after-the-fact leakage for key exchange. In: ASIACCS, pp. 207–216 (2014)
5. Alwen, J., Dodis, Y., Wichs, D.: Leakage-resilient public-key cryptography in the bounded-retrieval model. In: Halevi, S. (ed.) CRYPTO 2009. LNCS, vol. 5677, pp. 36–54. Springer, Heidelberg (2009)
6. Bellare, M., Canetti, R., Krawczyk, H.: A modular approach to the design and analysis of authentication and key exchange protocols (extended abstract). In: ACM Symposium on the Theory of Computing, pp. 419–428 (1998)
7. Bellare, M., Rogaway, P.: Entity authentication and key distribution. In: Stinson, D.R. (ed.) CRYPTO 1993. LNCS, vol. 773, pp. 232–249. Springer, Heidelberg (1994)
8. Bitansky, N., Canetti, R., Halevi, S.: Leakage-tolerant interactive protocols. In: Cramer, R. (ed.) TCC 2012. LNCS, vol. 7194, pp. 266–284. Springer, Heidelberg (2012)
9. Boyle, E., Segev, G., Wichs, D.: Fully leakage-resilient signatures. J. Cryptology **26**(3), 513–558 (2013)
10. Canetti, R., Krawczyk, H.: Analysis of key-exchange protocols and their use for building secure channels. In: Pfitzmann, B. (ed.) EUROCRYPT 2001. LNCS, vol. 2045, pp. 453–474. Springer, Heidelberg (2001)

11. Choo, K.-K.R., Boyd, C., Hitchcock, Y.: Examining indistinguishability-based proof models for key establishment protocols. In: Roy, B. (ed.) ASIACRYPT 2005. LNCS, vol. 3788, pp. 585–604. Springer, Heidelberg (2005)
12. Chow, S.S.M., Dodis, Y., Rouselakis, Y., Waters, B.: Practical leakage-resilient identity-based encryption from simple assumptions. In: CCS, pp. 152–161 (2010)
13. Cramer, R., Shoup, V.: Universal hash proofs and a paradigm for adaptive chosen ciphertext secure public-key encryption. In: Knudsen, L.R. (ed.) EUROCRYPT 2002. LNCS, vol. 2332, pp. 45–64. Springer, Heidelberg (2002)
14. Cremers, C.: Examining indistinguishability-based security models for key exchange protocols: the case of CK, CK-HMQV, and eCK. In: ASIACCS 2011, pp. 80–91 (2011)
15. Dodis, Y., Haralambiev, K., López-Alt, A., Wichs, D.: Efficient public-key cryptography in the presence of key leakage. In: Abe, M. (ed.) ASIACRYPT 2010. LNCS, vol. 6477, pp. 613–631. Springer, Heidelberg (2010)
16. Dodis, Y., Kalai, Y.T., Lovett, S.: On cryptography with auxiliary input. In: STOC, pp. 621–630 (2009)
17. Dodis, Y., Ostrovsky, R., Reyzin, L., Smith, A.: Fuzzy extractors: how to generate strong keys from biometrics and other noisy data. SIAM J. Comput. $38(1)$, 97–139 (2008)
18. Goldreich, O., Goldwasser, S., Micali, S.: How to construct random functions. J. ACM $33(4)$, 792–807 (1986)
19. Halderman, J.A., Schoen, S.D., Heninger, N., Clarkson, W., Paul, W., Calandrino, J.A., Feldman, A.J., Appelbaum, J., Felten, E.W.: Lest we remember: cold boot attacks on encryption keys. In: USENIX Security Symposium, pp. 45–60 (2008)
20. Halevi, S., Lin, H.: After-the-fact leakage in public-key encryption. In: Ishai, Y. (ed.) TCC 2011. LNCS, vol. 6597, pp. 107–124. Springer, Heidelberg (2011)
21. Katz, J., Vaikuntanathan, V.: Signature schemes with bounded leakage resilience. In: Matsui, M. (ed.) ASIACRYPT 2009. LNCS, vol. 5912, pp. 703–720. Springer, Heidelberg (2009)
22. Krawczyk, H.: SIGMA: the 'SIGn-and-MAc' approach to authenticated Diffie-Hellman and its use in the IKE protocols. In: Boneh, D. (ed.) CRYPTO 2003. LNCS, vol. 2729, pp. 400–425. Springer, Heidelberg (2003)
23. LaMacchia, B.A., Lauter, K., Mityagin, A.: Stronger security of authenticated key exchange. In: Susilo, W., Liu, J.K., Mu, Y. (eds.) ProvSec 2007. LNCS, vol. 4784, pp. 1–16. Springer, Heidelberg (2007)
24. Marvin, R.: Google admits an android crypto prng flaw led to bitcoin heist, August 2013. http://sdt.bz/64008
25. Micali, S., Reyzin, L.: Physically observable cryptography. In: Naor, M. (ed.) TCC 2004. LNCS, vol. 2951, pp. 278–296. Springer, Heidelberg (2004)
26. Moriyama, D., Okamoto, T.: Leakage resilient eCK-secure key exchange protocol without random oracles. In: ASIACCS, pp. 441–447 (2011)
27. Naor, M., Segev, G.: Public-Key cryptosystems resilient to key leakage. In: Halevi, S. (ed.) CRYPTO 2009. LNCS, vol. 5677, pp. 18–35. Springer, Heidelberg (2009)
28. Okamoto, T.: Authenticated key exchange and key encapsulation in the standard model. In: Kurosawa, K. (ed.) ASIACRYPT 2007. LNCS, vol. 4833, pp. 474–484. Springer, Heidelberg (2007)
29. Shumow, D., Ferguson, N.: On the possibility of a back door in the NIST SP800-90 dual Ec Prng. http://rump2007.cr.yp.to/15-shumow.pdf
30. Yang, G., Mu, Y., Susilo, W., Wong, D.S.: Leakage resilient authenticated key exchange secure in the auxiliary input model. In: Deng, R.H., Feng, T. (eds.) ISPEC 2013. LNCS, vol. 7863, pp. 204–217. Springer, Heidelberg (2013)

31. Yu, Y., Standaert, F., Pereira, O., Yung, M.: Practical leakage-resilient pseudorandom generators. In: CCS, pp. 141–151 (2010)
32. Yuen, T.H., Zhang, Y., Yiu, S.M., Liu, J.K.: Identity-based encryption with postchallenge auxiliary inputs for secure cloud applications and sensor networks. In: Kutyłowski, M., Vaidya, J. (eds.) ICAIS 2014, Part I. LNCS, vol. 8712, pp. 130–147. Springer, Heidelberg (2014)
33. Zetter, K.: How a crypto 'backdoor' pitted the tech world against the NSA. http://www.wired.com/threatlevel/2013/09/nsa-backdoor/all/

Authenticated Encryption

INT-RUP Analysis of Block-cipher Based Authenticated Encryption Schemes

Avik Chakraborti, Nilanjan Datta[✉], and Mridul Nandi

Indian Statistical Institute,
203, B.T. Road, Kolkata 700108, India
avikchkrbrti@gmail.com, nilanjan_isi_jrf@yahoo.com,
mridul.nandi@gmail.com

Abstract. Authenticated encryption (AE) is a mechanism to provide privacy as well as integrity of a plaintext. In the decryption phase of an AE scheme, the plaintext corresponding to a ciphertext is released if the tag is verified. As AE can be implemented in low end devices like smart cards, one may be forced to release plaintext before verification. Andreeva et al. address the issue of releasing unverified plaintext and formalize it by the notion called INT-RUP. In this paper, we consider "rate-1" block-cipher based affine authenticated encryption mode and show a generic INT-RUP attack on this mode. Using this attack idea, we also present an INT-RUP attack on CPFB (rate $\frac{3}{4}$). Then we present a variant of CPFB, called mCPFB (rate $\frac{3}{4}$) which achieves INT-RUP security.

Keywords: Authenticated encryption · Block cipher · Rate · INT-RUP

1 Introduction

The main application of cryptography is to implement a secure channel between two or more users to exchange information over that channel. The users initially have a shared key through an initial key set-up or key-exchange protocol. They use this key to authenticate and encrypt the transmitted information using efficient symmetric-key algorithms such as message authentication code (MAC) and (symmetric-key) encryption. The encryption provides privacy or confidentiality of the sensitive data, called plaintext or message, whereas a message authentication code provides data-integrity of the message. An authenticated encryption or AE is an integrated scheme which provides both privacy of plaintext and authenticity or data integrity of message or ciphertext. The decryption of an conventional AE scheme consists of two phases: plaintext computation and verification. If the verification is successful, then only the plaintext corresponding to the decryption, is released. But in practice, releasing plaintext after verification can be unavoidable at times. For example, when AE is implemented on low-end devices like smart cards, which has limited buffer, it is impossible to store entire plaintext. Also, there may be situations when a decrypted plaintext needs

© Springer International Publishing Switzerland 2016
K. Sako (Ed.): CT-RSA 2016, LNCS 9610, pp. 39–54, 2016.
DOI: 10.1007/978-3-319-29485-8_3

early processing due to real-time requirements, which may not be met if plaintext is released after verification. Moreover, if a scheme is secure under release of unverified plaintext, then one can increase efficiency of that scheme. For instance, one uses the two-pass Encrypt-then-MAC composition (first pass to verify the MAC and the second pass to decrypt the ciphertext) to avoid releasing unverified plaintext into a device with insecure memory [17]. If an AE construction is secure against the release of unverified plaintext, then a single pass would have been sufficient. Also, even if the attacker cannot observe the unverified plaintext directly, it could find interesting properties of the plaintext through side channel attacks. For example, in the padding oracle attacks introduced by Vaudenay [18], an error message or the lack of an acknowledgment indicates whether the unverified plaintext was correctly padded or not. In [4], Canvel et al. showed how to mount a padding oracle attack on a version of OpenSSL by exploiting timing differences in the decryption processing of TLS.

Note that, releasing unverified plaintext does not imply omitting verification, which remains essential to preventing incorrect plaintexts from being accepted. However, the scenario assumes that the attacker can observe the unverified plaintext, or any information relating to it, before verification is complete. This issue has been addressed and formalized by Andreeva et al. In the paper [2], Andreeva et al. address the issue of releasing unverified plaintext and formalize it by the two new notions called PA (Plaintext Awareness) and INT-RUP (INTegrity under Releasing Unverified Plaintext). To achieve privacy, they propose using plaintext awareness (PA) along with IND-CPA. An authenticated encryption scheme achieves PA if it has a plaintext extractor, which tries to fool adversaries by mimicking the decryption oracle without the secret key. Releasing unverified plaintext then becomes harmless as it is infeasible to distinguish the decryption oracle from the plaintext extractor. They introduce two notions of plaintext awareness in the symmetric-key setting - PA1 and PA2. The extractor is given access to the history of queries made to the encryption oracle in PA1, but not in PA2. Hence PA1 is used to take care of the RUP scenarios where the adversary has the goal to gain the additional knowledge from the query history. For situations in which the goal of the adversary is to decrypt one of the ciphertexts in the query history, PA2 is used. On the otherhand, an AE scheme is said to achieve INT-RUP security, if the adversary can generate a fresh valid ciphertext-tag pair given the additional power of access to a unverified decryption oracle, along with the encryption oracle.

In [2], Andreeva et al. also showed that most of the AE schemes using nonce IV (OCB [11], GCM [12] etc.) or arbitrary IV (COPA [3], McOE-G [6]) are not PA-1 secure where as schemes like CTR, CBC using random IV is PA1 secure. They also introduce two techniques called nonce-decoy and PRF-to-IV method to restore PA1 for nonce IV and arbitary IV schemes respectively. They also showed INT-RUP insecurity of schemes like OCB, COPA. The issue of releasing unverified plaintext has been acknowledged and explicitly discussed in the ongoing CAESAR competition [1] as well. It is of interest to investigate INT-RUP security of various schemes.

1.1   Our Contributions

In this paper, we consider the INT-RUP security of block-cipher based AE schemes. We call a block-cipher based AE scheme to be of "rate 1" if the no. of block-ciphers used to generate the ciphertext (without the tag) is exactly equal to the number of message blocks and the additional block-cipher calls, required to generate the tag is constant (doesn't depend on the number of message blocks). In this paper, we first consider weakness during the tag processing, which can be fixed with small modification in the tag generation. On the other hand, in this paper we describe an attack on the mode and hence can not be fixed with small modifications. In Sect. 3.3, using the similar idea as used in iFeed, we provide an INT-RUP attack on general feedback based AE mode. "rate-1" block-cipher based authenticated encryption mode. In Sects. 3.1 and 3.2, we describe this mode in details and provide some example of existing popular AE schemes that belong to this mode. Here we adopt the notations as used by Nandi [14] in the definition of linear mode authenticated encryption and extend it to define the generalized block-cipher based affine mode authenticated encryption scheme. Our main results are as follows:

(A). Generic INT-RUP attack on "rate-1" affine mode authenticated encryption. In Sect. 3.3, we describe a generic INT-RUP attack on this mode. Note that, in [14], Nandi gives a generalized PRP-SPRP attack (privacy attack) using similar idea that was used in the SPRP attack on XLS [15]. On the otherhand, our attack is a generalized INT-RUP attack (integrity attack in the RUP settings) and the attack technique used for our case is completely different from their approach. Our attack is similar to the one used in [2] during the INT-RUP attack on OCB. Note that, our attack doesn't depend on the type of IVs. One can fix the PA1 security by having random IVs but can not prevent the INT-RUP attack.

(B). INT-RUP attack on AES-CPFB [13]. In Sect. 4.1, we revisit the AE scheme AES-CPFB, submitted to the CAESAR competition. CPFB is an affine mode AE scheme whose rate is $\frac{3}{4}$. We show an INT-RUP attack on AES-CPFB by observing weaknesses in the construction design in AES-CPFB.

(C). mCPFB: A rate $\frac{3}{4}$ INT-RUP secure AE Scheme. In Sect. 4.3, we propose a modified version of CPFB named mCPFB and then prove the INT-RUP security of mCPFB in Sect. 4.4. This shows that, we can have INT-RUP secure affine mode AE constructions with rate $\frac{3}{4}$.

1.2   Significance of Our Results

The efficiency of a block-cipher based authenticated encryption improves as the number of block-cipher invocations per message block reduces. To have a secure authenticated encryption scheme, the no. of block-cipher calls required is atleast equal to the no. of blocks in the message. Our result shows that no "rate-1" block-cipher based authenticated encryption construction can be INT-RUP secure, meaning that in order to achieve INT-RUP security, one has to compromise the efficiency. Both efficiency and INT-RUP security can not come together for block-cipher based authenticated encryption schemes. On the other hand, by the INT-RUP security of mCPFB (rate $\frac{3}{4}$), we show that even with small decrease in the rate, the construction can achieve INT-RUP security. block-ciphers and hence the efficiency decreases.

2 Preliminaries

2.1 Rate of a Block-cipher Based AE Schemes

The rate of a block-cipher based encryption is defined as *the no. of message blocks processed per block-cipher call*. Consider an authenticated encryption scheme which requires $(s + c)$-many block-cipher calls (s many block-cipher calls to generate the ciphertext and additional c-many block-ciphers to generate the tag) to process l-block messages. The rate of the scheme is given by $\frac{l}{(s+c)}$. For any authenticated encryption scheme, s depends on the length of the message i.e. l. For most of the authenticated encryption schemes c is a very small constant (usually 1 or 2) and doesn't depend on l. For these schemes, we can ignore the c-term and consider the rate of the scheme as $\frac{l}{s}$. Here are the example of some block-cipher based authenticated encryption schemes and their rates:

- OCB [11], iFeed [19]: $s = l$, $c = 1$, rate = 1.
- COPA [3], ELmD [5]: $s = 2.l$, $c = 2$, rate = $\frac{1}{2}$.
- CPFB [13]: $s = \frac{4l}{3}$, $c = 2$, rate = $\frac{3}{4}$.
- CLOC [7], SILC [8]: $s = l$, $c = l$, rate = $\frac{1}{2}$.

2.2 Block Matrices and Its Properties

In this subsection, we discuss block matrices and its properties. We borrow some notations from [14]. A block is a n-bit field element. Denote $\mathbb{B} := \{0,1\}^n$. We represent a block in bold letters to distinguish it from an integer. For example $\mathbf{2}$ denotes a block (field element) where as 2 denotes an integer value. We denote both integer addition as well as field addition by $+$, which should be realized from the context. We call a matrix to be block-matrix if all the entries are blocks. Throughout the paper, we will consider any matrix as a block matrix. Let $\mathbb{M}_n(a,b)$ denote the set of all partitioned matrices $A_{a \times b}$ (of size $a \times b$ as a block partitioned matrix and of size $an \times bn$ as a binary matrix) whose $(i,j)^{\text{th}}$ entry, denoted $A[i,j]$, is a block-matrix for all $i \in [1..a] = \{1, \ldots, a\}$ and $j \in [1..b]$. The transpose of A, denoted A^{tr}, is applied as a binary matrix. Thus, $A^{tr}[i,j] = A[j,i]^{tr}$. where $A[i,*]$ and $A[*,j]$ denote i^{th} block-row and j^{th} block-column respectively. For $1 \le i \le j \le a$, we also write $A[i..j ; *]$ to mean the sub-matrix consisting of all rows in between i and j. We simply write $A[..j ; *]$ or $A[i.. ; *]$ to denote $A[1..j ; *]$ and $A[i..a ; *]$ respectively. We define similar notation for columns. By $(\mathbf{0})$ and $(\mathbf{1})$, we mean a matrix of appropriate size, whose all entries are 0 and 1 respectively.

A (square) matrix $A \in M_n(a, a)$ is called *(block-wise) diagonal* if for all $i \neq j$, $A[i, j] = \mathbf{0}$ and $A[i, i] = 1$. We represent it by $\mathbf{I}_a$. We call a (square) matrix $A \in M_n(a, a)$ *(block-wise) strictly lower triangular* if for all $1 \leq i \leq j \leq a$, $A[i, j] = \mathbf{0}$.

For all $X = (X_1, \ldots, X_l) \in \mathbb{B}^l$, we define an affine function mapping l blocks to b blocks as $A \cdot \begin{pmatrix} 1 \\ X \end{pmatrix} = (Y_1, \ldots, Y_b)$. Here, we consider X and Y as binary column vectors (we follow this convention which should be understood from the context). So *the block matrix $A[1, j]$ represents the constant term in Y_i and $A[i + 1, j]$ represents the contribution of X_j to define Y_i.* More formally,

$$Y_i = A[i, 1] + A[i, 2] \cdot X_1 + A[i, 3] \cdot X_2 + \cdots + A[i + 1, a] \cdot X_i, \quad 1 \leq i \leq b.$$

If $A[2..a, 2..b]$ is a strictly lower triangular matrix then Y_i is clearly functionally independent of $X_i, \ldots, X_l$, $1 \leq i \leq l$. So if we associate Y_i uniquely to each X_i (e.g., $Y_i = \rho(X_i)$ for some function ρ) then the choice of the vectors X and Y satisfying $A \cdot X = Y$ becomes unique. This observation is useful while we define intermediate inputs and outputs of a black-box based construction.

Useful Properties of Matrices. It is well known that the maximum number of linearly independent (binary) rows and columns of a matrix $A \in M_n(s, t)$ are same and this number is called rank of the matrix, denoted $\mathrm{rank}(A)$. So clearly we have $\mathrm{rank}(A) \leq \min\{ns, nt\}$.

Now, we briefly state two very important properties of matrices.

Lemma 1. *Let M and N be two matrices with same number of rows. If M doesn't have full rank but $[M : N]$ has full rank, then one can find a row vector R such that $R \cdot M = 0$ but $R \cdot N \neq 0$.*

Lemma 2. *Let $A \in M_n(s, t)$ and $r = rank(A)$. Then,*

If $s < t$, then we can find a solution (not necessarily unique) of $A \cdot x = 0$.

As the proofs are straightforward, we skip the proofs.

3 Generalized "rate-1" Affine Mode AE Schemes

3.1 Affine Query and Mode

A block matrix $J \in M_n(q, 1+l+q)$ is called (l, q)-**query function** if $J[*, l+1..]$ is block-wise strictly lower triangular. Here q represents the number of queries and l represents the number of blocks in the input. For any such *query function*, an input $M \in \mathbb{B}^l$, (and a tuple of q functions $\tilde{\rho} = (\rho_1, \ldots, \rho_q)$ over $\mathbb{B}$), we can *uniquely define* or associate U and V, called **intermediate input and output vector** respectively, satisfying

$$\text{(i) } J \cdot \begin{pmatrix} 1 \\ M \\ O \end{pmatrix} = I \text{ and (ii) } \tilde{\rho}(I) := (\rho_1(I_1), \ldots, \rho_q(I_q)) = O.$$

This can be easily shown by recursive definitions of I_i's and O_i's. More precisely, I_i is an affine function of $M, O_1, \ldots, O_{i-1}$ and O_i is uniquely determined by I_i through ρ_i, for all $1 \le i \le q$.

Informally, a (l, b, q)-affine mode is a mode which takes l blocks input and returns b blocks output based on executing block-functions building blocks. Formally, (l, b, q)-affine mode is defined by a block matrix $E \in \mathbb{M}_n(q + b, 1 + l + q)$ where $E[1..q, *]$ is a (l, q)-query function. For any q-tuple of functions $\tilde{\rho} \in \text{Func}^q$, the corresponding affine-mode function $E^{\tilde{\rho}} : \mathbb{B}^l \to \mathbb{B}^b$ is defined as $E^{\tilde{\rho}}(I) = O$ where

$$E \cdot \begin{pmatrix} 1 \\ M \\ O \end{pmatrix} = \begin{pmatrix} I \\ Z \end{pmatrix}, \quad \tilde{\rho}(I) = O.$$

So V is the intermediate output vector associated to the input I and the final output $Z := E[q + 1.., *] \cdot \begin{pmatrix} 1 \\ M \\ O \end{pmatrix}$, an affine function of O and M. Now observe that the functions of $\tilde{\rho}$ are non-linear and would be secret for the adversaries. So to obtain any information about the intermediate input and output, we only can equate intermediate outputs whenever two inputs collide for same function.

KEYED AFFINE MODE. Let $\mathcal{F} = \mathcal{F}_1 \times \cdots \times \mathcal{F}_f$ and k be a non-negative integer where $\mathcal{F}_i \subseteq \text{Func}$. A key-space $\mathcal{K}$ for any keyed function is of the form $\mathbb{B}^k \times \mathcal{F}$. We call $\mathcal{F}$ the function-key space and $\mathbb{B}^k$ masking-key space. Any function g is also written as g^{+1}.

Definition 1. *Let* $\mu : [1..q] \to [1..f]$, *called* key-assignment function, $\alpha := (\alpha_1, \ldots, \alpha_l) \in \{+1, -1\}^\ell$, *called* inverse-assignment tuple. *For any function-key* $\rho = (\rho_1, \ldots, \rho_f) \in \mathcal{F}$, *we define* $\rho_\mu^\alpha := (\rho_{\mu_1}^{\alpha_1}, \ldots, \rho_{\mu_q}^{\alpha_q})$. *We denote the set of all functions* ρ_μ^α *by* $\mathcal{F}_\mu^\alpha$.

Here we implicitly assume that whenever $\alpha_i = -1$, ρ_{μ_i} is a permutation. If $\alpha = +1^q$, we simply skip the notation α. In general, the presence of inverse call of building blocks may be required when we consider decryption of keyed function. For the encryption, or a keyed function where decryption is not defined, w.l.o.g. we may assume that $\alpha = 1^q$.

Definition 2. *A* (k, l, b, q) keyed affine mode *with key-space* $\mathcal{K}$, *key-assignment function* μ, *is a* $(k+l, b, q)$ linear mode E. *For each key* $\kappa := (L, \rho) \in \mathcal{K} := I_n^k \times \mathcal{F}$, *we define a keyed function* $E_\kappa(M) := E^{\rho_\mu}(K, M)$.

Observe that, given a key (K, ρ) and a key-assignment function μ, we can represent a (k, l, b, q) keyed affine function as follows:

$$E \cdot \begin{pmatrix} L \\ M \\ O \end{pmatrix} = \begin{pmatrix} I \\ Z \end{pmatrix}, \quad \rho_\mu(I) = O \qquad \text{where } L = \begin{pmatrix} 1 \\ K \end{pmatrix}$$

Definition 3 (Reordering of Vectors). *Let* $\alpha := (\alpha_1, \ldots, \alpha_q) \in \{1, -1\}^q$, *and* $\beta = (\beta_1, \ldots, \beta_q)$ *be a permutation over* $[1..q]$. *A pair of vectors* $(U, V) \in \mathbb{B}^{2q}$ *is* (α, β)*-reordering of a pair of vectors* $(X, Y) \in \mathbb{B}^{2q}$ *if*

$$(U_i, V_i) = \begin{cases} (X_{\beta_i}, Y_{\beta_i}) & \text{if } \alpha_i = 1, \\ (Y_{\beta_i}, X_{\beta_i}) & \text{if } \alpha_i = -1. \end{cases}$$

3.2   Affine Mode Authenticated Encryption Scheme

A (l, s, c) affine-mode authenticated encryption scheme takes an input $M \in \mathbb{B}^l$ and returns a tagged-ciphertext $(C, T) \in \mathbb{B}^l \times \mathbb{B}$ using $(s + c)$-many non-linear block computations. Moreover it requires exactly s-many non-linear block computations to compute C and additional c-many permutations for computing the tag T.

Definition 4. *A* $(k + l, l + 1, s + c)$*-affine mode* E, *is called* (l, s, c) *affine-mode authenticated encryption with key-space* $\mathcal{K} := \mathbb{B}^k \times \mathcal{F}$ *and key-assignment* π *if the corresponding decryption algorithm* D *is also a* $(k + l, l + 1, s + c)$*-linear mode with (1) an inverse assignment-tuple* $\alpha := (\alpha_1, \ldots, \alpha_{s+c}) \in \{1, -1\}$ *and (2) key-assignment* $\pi' := \beta \circ \pi$ *where* $\beta = (\beta_1, \ldots, \beta_{s+c})$ *is a permutation over* $[1..(s + c)]$. *Moreover,* $\forall M \in \mathbb{B}^l, L \in \mathbb{B}^k, \rho = (\rho_1, \ldots, \rho_f) \in \mathcal{F}$,

$$E. \begin{pmatrix} L \\ M \\ Y^* \end{pmatrix} = \begin{pmatrix} X^* \\ C \\ T \end{pmatrix}, \rho_{\pi_i}(U_i) = V_i$$

if and only if

$$D. \begin{pmatrix} L \\ C \\ V^* \end{pmatrix} = \begin{pmatrix} U^* \\ M \\ T \end{pmatrix}, \rho_{\pi'_i}^{\alpha_i}(X_i) = Y_i$$

where (U^*, V^*) *is* (α, β)*-reordering of* (X^*, Y^*). *Here* k, *no of keys used, is assumed to be a constant and doesn't depend on* l.

Rate-1 Affine Mode Authenticated Encryption Scheme. We call an affine (authenticated) encryption scheme to be "rate-1" if $s = l$ i.e. no of permutation calls to generate ciphertext (without the tag) of a message of length l is exactly l.

We represent a "rate-1" affine mode authenticated encryption as:

$$E. \begin{pmatrix} L \\ M \\ Y^* = \begin{pmatrix} Y \\ Y_{tag} \end{pmatrix} \end{pmatrix} = \begin{pmatrix} X^* = \begin{pmatrix} X \\ X_{tag} \end{pmatrix} \\ Z = \begin{pmatrix} C \\ T \end{pmatrix} \end{pmatrix}$$

where $X = X^*[1..l]$, $X_{tag} = X^*[(l + 1)..(l + c)]$, $Y = Y^*[1..l]$ and $Y_{tag} = Y^*[(l + 1)..(l + c)]$. It is easy to see that a "rate-1" affine mode AE scheme has the following structure of E:

$$E = \begin{pmatrix} (E_{11})_{l\times(k+1)} & (E_{12})_{l\times l} & (E_{13})_{l\times l} & (E_{14})_{l\times c} \\ (E_{21})_{c\times(k+1)} & (E_{22})_{c\times l} & (E_{23})_{c\times l} & (E_{24})_{c\times c} \\ (E_{31})_{l\times(k+1)} & (E_{32})_{l\times l} & (E_{33})_{l\times l} & (E_{34})_{l\times c} \\ (E_{41})_{1\times(k+1)} & (E_{42})_{1\times l} & (E_{43})_{1\times l} & (E_{44})_{1\times c} \end{pmatrix}$$

It is easy to check that E_{13} and E_{24} are strictly lower triangular matrices and $E_{14} = E_{34}$ are zero matrices.

For the decryption, we have identical representation as we replace E by D, X by U, Y by V, M by C and C by M.

Some popular examples of "rate-1" Affine Mode AE schemes are: iFeed, OCB etc. The E matrix corresponding to these constructions can be found in the full version.

Remark 1. It is easy to check that any feedback based "rate-1" AE construction, is a "rate-1" affine mode authenticated encryption. The detailed proof can be found in the full version.

Important Properties of the Decryption Matrix D

Lemma 3. *If $rank(D_{33}) < (l - (1 + k))n$, then the AE construction doesn't preserve privacy.*

Proof. We have the condition, $D_{31}.L + D_{32}.C + D_{33}.V = M$. As the combined rank of $[D_{31} : D_{32} : D_{33}]$ is full (otherwise scheme is not decryptable), we can find a row vector N s.t. $N.D_{32} \neq 0$ but $N.D_{31} = 0$ and $N.D_{33} = 0$. This gives a linear equation on C and P:

$$N.D_{32}.C = N.M.$$

Using, this equation, one can distinguish this scheme from a random function making a single query and checking whether the above equation holds or not. □

Lemma 4. *If $rank(D_{12}) < (l - c)n$, then the AE construction doesn't have integrity security.*

Proof. Let the decryption matrix for a AE Scheme is D, with $rank(D_{12}) < (l-c)n$. Now, we describe an integrity attack against the scheme using only one encryption query, as follows:

- Encryption Query: $(N, AD, M = (M_1, M_2, \ldots, M_l))$. Let, $C = (C_1, C_2, \ldots, C_l, T)$ be the tagged ciphertext.
- Find a non-zero $\Delta C = (\Delta C_1, \ldots, \Delta C_l)$ satisfying (i) $D_{12}\Delta C = 0$ and (ii) $D_{22}\Delta C = 0$. Rank of D_{12} ensures that we will find such a ΔC value for some l. Let it be ΔC^*
- Compute $\Delta T = D_{42}\Delta C^*$
- Forged Query: $(N, AD, C + \Delta C^*, T + \Delta T)$ □

3.3   INT-RUP Insecurity of "rate-1" Block-Cipher Based Affine Mode AE Schemes

In this section, we prove the following theorem:

Theorem 1. *Any "rate-1" block-cipher based Affine mode authenticated encryption scheme is INT-RUP insecure.*

Proof. Here we describe the generic INT-RUP attack on rate-1 affine domain authenticated encryption schemes. The attack consists of one encryption and one unverified plaintext query:

- Encryption Query: $(N, AD, M^0 = (M_1^0, M_2^0, \ldots, M_l^0))$. Let, $C^0 = (C_1^0, C_2^0, \ldots, C_l^0, T^0)$ be the tagged ciphertext.
- Unverified Plaintext Query: $(N, AD, C^1 = (C_1^1, C_2^1, \ldots, C_l^1))$. Let $M^1 = (M_1^1, M_2^1, \ldots, M_l^1)$ be the corresponding plaintext.
- Forged Query: $(N, AD, C^f = (C_1^f, C_2^f, \ldots, C_l^f), T^f)$, which realizes a $\delta = (\delta_1, \ldots, \delta_l)$ sequence. C^f realizes a δ-sequence if given a binary vector $\delta = (\delta_1, \ldots, \delta_l)$, $\forall i \leq l$, $U_i^f = U_i^{\delta_i}$ and $\forall i > l$, $U_i^f = U_i^0$.

Note that, as same nonce-associated data are used for all the queries, the keys will remain same for all the queries. Hence we have the following relations:

$$\begin{pmatrix} D_{12} & D_{13} \\ D_{32} & D_{33} \end{pmatrix} \cdot \begin{pmatrix} \Delta C^{ij} \\ \Delta V^{ij} \end{pmatrix} = \begin{pmatrix} \Delta U^{ij} \\ \Delta M^{ij} \end{pmatrix}, \quad i = 0, j \in \{1, f\}$$

$$\begin{pmatrix} D_{22} & D_{23} & D_{24} \\ D_{42} & D_{43} & D_{44} \end{pmatrix} \cdot \begin{pmatrix} \Delta C^{0f} \\ \Delta V^{0f} \\ \Delta V_{tag}^{0f} \end{pmatrix} = \begin{pmatrix} \Delta U_{tag}^{0f} \\ \Delta T^{0f} \end{pmatrix}$$

Now, our job is to find the value of $\Delta C^{0f} = (\Delta C_1^{0f}, \ldots, \Delta C_l^{0f})$ and T^{0f}. We find in the following steps:

- Step 1. Find ΔV_{01} from the equation, $D_{32}\Delta C^{01} + D_{33}\Delta V^{01} = \Delta M^{01}$:

$$\Delta V^{01} = D_{33}^{-1}(\Delta M^{01} + D_{32}\Delta C^{01})$$

- Step 2. Find ΔC^{0f} in terms of δ:

$$\Delta C^{0f} = D_{12}^{-1} \cdot (\Delta U^{0f} + D_{32}\Delta V^{0f})$$

As $\Delta U_i^{0f} = \delta_i \cdot \Delta U_i^{01}$ and $\Delta V_i^{0f} = \delta_i \cdot \Delta V_i^{01}$, one can write both ΔU^{0f} and V^{0f} as a linear combination of δ. So, we can write $(\Delta U^{0f} + D_{32}\Delta V^{0f}) = D^* \cdot \delta$, for some D^*. In fact we can find out D^* as follows:

$$D^* = \begin{pmatrix} \Delta U_1^{01} + D_{13}^{11} \cdot \Delta V_1^{01} & D_{13}^{12} \cdot \Delta V_2^{01} & \cdots & D_{13}^{1l} \cdot \Delta V_l^{01} \\ D_{13}^{21} \cdot \Delta V_1^{01} & \Delta U_2^{01} + D_{13}^{22} \cdot \Delta V_2^{01} & \cdots & D_{13}^{2l} \cdot \Delta V_l^{01} \\ \vdots & & & \\ D_{13}^{l1} \cdot \Delta V_1^{01} & D_{13}^{l2} \cdot \Delta V_2^{01} & \cdots & \Delta U_l^{01} + D_{13}^{ll} \cdot \Delta V_l^{01} \end{pmatrix}$$

So, we can write ΔC^{0f} as the following linear combination of δ:

$$\Delta C^{0f} = D_{12}^{-1}.D^*.\delta$$

- Step 3. Solve the following set of equations to find a δ that makes $\Delta U_{tag}^{0f} = 0$

$$D_{22}\Delta C^{0f} + D_{23}\Delta V^{0f} = 0$$

As ΔC_{0f} and ΔV^{0f} can be represented as linear combination of δ as mentioned already, the above equality implies $(D_{22}.D_{12}^{-1}.D^* + D_{23}.V^*).\delta = 0$. It is easy to see that this equation has at least one solution as long as $l > (c-1).n$. Let the solution be δ^*.

- Step 4. We find ΔC^{0f} and ΔT^{0f} as we put $\delta = \delta^*$ in the following equations:

$$\Delta C^{0f} = D_{12}^{-1}.D^*.\delta$$
$$\Delta T^{0f} = D_{42}\Delta C_{0f} + D_{43}\Delta V_{0f}$$

Thus we provide a generalized INT-RUP attack for any affine domain authenticated encryption schemes assuming D_{12} and D_{33} matrices are invertibles, which imply $rank(D_{12}) = rank(D_{33}) = l.n$.

CASE WHEN AT LEAST ONE OF D_{12} AND D_{33} DOESN'T HAVE FULL RANK. From Lemmas 3 and 4, we already know that $rank(D_{12})$ and $rank(D_{33})$ should be high. This ensures that if we set l appropriately to a high value, we will have a $(n \times n)$ submatrix which has full rank for both D_{12} as well as D_{33}. More formally, from Lemmas 3 and 4, we know that $rank(D_{12}) > (l - (k + 1))n$ and $rank(D_{33}) > (l - c)n$. It is easy to check that, we can find a value of l such that both the submatrix $D_{12}[l - n.., l - n..]$ and $D_{33}[l - n.., l - n..]$ both has full rank. As k and c are small constants, one can ensure that we will find such an l. Now one can easily modify the previous attack and apply here. $\square$

Corollary 1. *Any "rate-1" block-cipher based AE scheme is not integrity secure against Nonce-repeating adversaries.*

It is easy to verify it and can be found in the full version.

Remark 2 (Extension of the Attack for Any Number of Keys). In the definition of affine domain authenticated encryption, we have assumed k, number of keys to be constant. Some constructions like IACBC [9] and IAPM [10] use $\log l$ number of keys while encrypting l block messages. It is easy to see that our INT-RUP attack will be valid for these constructions as well. In general, this attack will be applicable for any "rate-1" authenticated encryption scheme for which D_{11} and D_{22} are invertible, even if the number of masking keys it use depends on the message length.

4   INT-RUP Analysis of CPFB, a Rate $\frac{3}{4}$ Block-cipher Based AE Scheme

4.1   Revisting CPFB

CPFB is a block-cipher based AE scheme which takes a nonce N, an associated data A (a blocks of 96 bits), a message M (l blocks of 96 bits), a secret key K (128-bit) as its input and outputs a ciphertext C (l blocks of 96 bits) and a 128 bit tag T. As one 128-bit block-cipher call is needed to process 96-bit message, the rate of the construction is $96/128 = 3/4$. Details of CPFB authenticated encryption is shown in Figure below (Fig. 1).

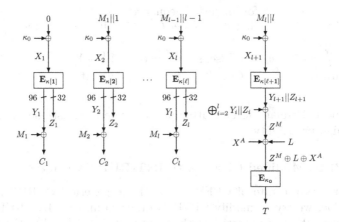

Fig. 1. Encryption and Tag Generation Phase of CPFB. Here $\kappa_i = E_K(N||i||l_N)$, $\kappa[i] = \kappa_j$ where $j = \lceil \frac{i}{2^{32}} \rceil$, $X^A := U_a$ where $U_i = U_{i-1} + E_{\kappa_0}(A_i||i)$ and $L = E_{\kappa_0}(a||l||0)$.

4.2   INT-RUP Attack on CPFB

The attack consists of one encryption and one unverified plaintext query. The attack steps are:

1. Make an encryption query: $(N, A, M^0 = (M_1^0, M_2^0, \ldots, M_l^0))$, where $l = 129$. Let $C^0 = (C_1^0, C_2^0 \ldots, C_l^0, T^0)$ be the tagged ciphertext. Let the corresponding X and Y vectors are, $X^0 = (X_1^0, \cdots, X_{l+1}^0)$ and $Y^0 = (Y_1^0, \cdots, Y_{l+1}^0)$ respectively.

2. Make an unverified plaintext decryption query: $(N, A, C^1 = (C_1^1, C_2^1, \cdots, C_l^1))$. Let, $M^1 = (M_1^1, M_2^1, \cdots, M_l^1)$ be the corresponding plaintext. Corresponding X and Y vectors are $X^1 = (X_1^1, \cdots, X_{l+1}^1)$ and $Y^1 = (Y_1^1, \cdots, Y_{l+1}^1)$ respectively.

3. Compute the first 96 bit Y values $Y_1^0, \cdots, Y_l^0$ and $Y_1^1, \cdots, Y_l^1$ from the two queries by XOR-ing the corresponding message and the ciphertext (by $M^0 + C^0$ and $M^1 + C^1$).

4. Find the δ-sequence $(\delta_1, \ldots, \delta_l)$, with $\delta_1 = 0$ such that, $\sum_{i=2}^{l}(Y_i^{\delta_i} || Z_i^{\delta_i}) = \sum_{i=2}^{l}(Y_i^0 || Z_i^0)$. One can expect 2^{32}-many such δ-sequences. This happens because with the help of first 96 bits in the expressions at both the sides of the above condition, we can form 128 linear equations on 128 unknowns $\delta_2, \ldots, \delta_{129}$ and with high probability we can get a solution. As, the last 32 bits in the expressions are assumed to be uniform and random, we expect 2^{32}-many such δ-sequences.

5. Perform the following for all such δ-sequence:
   (a) Set $C_1^f = C_1^0$. For all $1 < i < l$, set $C_i^f = C_i^{\delta_i}$ if $\delta_{i-1} = \delta_i$ and $C_i^{\delta_i} + Y_i^0 + Y_i^1$, otherwise.
   (b) Set $C_l^f = C_l^0$ if $\delta_l = 0$. Else, set $C_l^f = C_l^0 + Y_l^0 + Y_l^1$.
   (c) Return $(C_1^f, C_2^f, \cdots, C_l^f, T^0)$ as forged Ciphertext.

With the above 2^{32}-many forging attempts, we expect atleast one valid forgery with very high probability.

4.3   mCPFB: Modified CPFB with INT-RUP Security

Motivation. As the rate of CPFB is $\frac{3}{4}$ and the generic INT-RUP attack is not applicable, we try to modify CPFB in order to make it INT-RUP secure. We first observe that, a potential weakness of CPFB which led to the previous attack is that the Z_i values, computed during the message processing phase has no influence over the ciphertext C. However, all the 32-bit Z_i values are finally added during the computation of T. Thus, the entropy of the effect of the whole Z vector on the tag reduces to 32. Hence, computing a proper δ sequence is sufficient to forge a valid ciphertext tag pair as the attacker has access to the Y vector. So, injecting 32-bit Z_i values in a proper way during the process of generating ciphertext blocks may resist the previous attack. So, we tried to update CPFB by modifying X_i as follows $X_i = M_{i-1} || (i - 1) + \kappa_0 + Z_{i-1} || 0^{96}$, for $2 \le i \le l + 1$. This updated scheme resists the previous attack but with an additional 2^{24} unverified plaintext query, one can find a modified attack on this updated version as well as with 2^{32}-many forging attempts. The weakness of this updated version is that adversary can not observe only Z_i values and the final tag has only 32-bit entropy of the Z_i values. So, now we modify the construction such that final tag has full 128-bit entropy of the Z_i values and it comes out to be INT-RUP secure. We call the modified construction mCPFB and details of mCPFB is given below.

mCPFB Construction. The description of mCPFB construction is given below. Here, we use the notation $V_\alpha^{(d, \ell)}$ to denote a $(d \times l)$ vandermonde matrix whose $(i, j)^{th}$ entry is $\alpha^{(i-1)(l-j)}$.

Nonce Processing. The nonce N is used to generate the keys: $\kappa_i = E_K(N||i||l_N)$. This step is identical to that of CPFB.

AD Processing. The associated data A is partitioned into a-many 96 blocks. A_i, the ith associated data block is processed by $U_i = U_{i-1} + E_{\kappa_1}(A_i||i)$. $X^A := U_a$, is the final output. This step is also identical to that of CPFB except that we use the key κ_1 instead of κ_0.

Message Processing. mCPFB can process any message upto size $(2^{64} - 2^{32} - 4)$. In the message processing phase, we first expand $M = (M_1, \ldots, M_l)$ by a Distance 4 Error Correcting Code ECCode:

$$\mathsf{ECCode}(M) = (M_1, \ldots, M_l, M_{l+1}, M_{l+2}, M_{l+3})$$

where $(M_{l+1}, M_{l+2}, M_{l+3}) = V_\beta^{(3,l)} \cdot M$, with β as a primitive element of $\mathbb{F}_{2^{96}}$. In [16], it has been shown that ECCode for fixed length input has minimum distance 4. After the expansion, we process this expanded message in the same way as message is processed for CPFB. $C = (C_1, \ldots, C_l)$ is the ciphertext.

Tag Generation Phase. The tag T is calculated by $E_{\kappa_{-1}}(\tau)$ where $\tau = W_l \oplus X_A \oplus L$ and $\kappa_{-1} = \kappa_{2^{32}-1}$. Computation of W_l is done by as follows: $W_l = V_\alpha^{(4,l+3)} \cdot (Z_2, Z_3, \cdots, Z_{l+3}, Z_{l+4}) \oplus (0^{32}||V_l)$, where $V_l = Y_2 \oplus \cdots \oplus Y_{l+3}$ and α be a primitive element of $\mathbb{F}_{2^{32}}$. L is defined as $L = E_{\kappa_{-1}}(a||l||0)$.

4.4 INT-RUP Security for mCPFB

In this section, we prove the INT-RUP security of mCPFB in details. Consider the function f that takes N, I and i as input and outputs O such that $O = E_{\kappa[i]}(I||(i \bmod 2^{32}) + \kappa_0)$ where $\kappa[i] = E_K(N||j||l)$, $j = \lceil \frac{i}{2^{32}} \rceil$. f is assumed to have (q, ϵ)-PRF security where ϵ is believed to achieve beyond birthday security. Given this, we proof the following theorem:

Theorem 2. *Let f (defined as above) be $(q_e + q_r, \epsilon)$-PRF. Any adversary $\mathcal{A}$, making q_e many encryption query and q_r many unverified plaintext query, can break INT-RUP security (with single forgery attempt) of mCPFB has the following advantage: $Adv_{mCPFB}^{int\_rup}(\mathcal{A}) \leq \frac{5}{2^{128}} + \epsilon$*

Proof. First we consider the following important observations:

- As f $(q_e + q_r, \epsilon)$-PRF, we replace the f module by a random function. So for any two different(N, M_i, i), we consider $Y_i||Z_i$ to be uniform and random.
- Z-values have full 128-bit entropy on the tag T through the multiplication by Vandermonde matrix
- ECCode is a distance 4 error correcting code for fixed length inputs - thus for two different messages $M = (M_1, M_2, \cdots, M_l)$ and $M' = (M_1', M_2', \cdots, M_l')$, there are at least four indices for which the corresponding 32-bit Z-values are uniform and random
- For unverified plaintext queries the Z values are not known as the tag is not generated.

Now suppose the adversary makes encryption queries (N_i, A_i, M_i) and obtains (C_i, T_i) for $i = 1(1)q_e$, then makes unverified queries $(N_i^{rup}, A_i^{rup}, C_i^{rup})$ and obtains M_i^{rup} for $i = 1(1)q_r$ and then forges with (N^*, A^*, C^*, T^*). The view of the adversary is denoted by $View(\mathcal{A}) = \{(N_i, A_i, M_i, C_i, T_i)_{i=1(1)q_e};$ $(N_i^{rup}, A_i^{rup}, C_i^{rup}, M_i^{rup})_{i=1(1)q_r}\}$. Let Win be the event that an adversary $\mathcal{A}$ wins the INT-RUP security game. It is easy to check that,

$$Pr[\text{Win}] := max_v Pr[\text{Win}_v] = Pr[(N^*, A^*, C^*, T^*) \text{ is a valid}|View(\mathcal{A}) = v]$$

Now, for any v, if we can show that $Pr[\text{Win}_v] < \epsilon$, then we have $Pr[\text{Win}] < \epsilon$ and we will be done. Consider the following cases:

Case A. $\forall i, N^* \neq N_i$: As κ_{-1} is indepent with $\kappa_{-1}^1, \ldots, \kappa_{-1}^{q_e}$, we can bound the adversarial advantage by,

$$Pr[\text{Win}_v] = Pr[E_{\kappa_{-1}^*}(\tau^*) = T^*|View(\mathcal{A}) = v]$$

$$= (\frac{1}{2^{128}} \sum_{L^* \neq T^*} Pr[E_{\kappa_{-1}^*}(\tau^*)=T^*|E_{\kappa_{-1}^*}(a^*||l^*||0)=L^*]) + Pr[L^* = T^*]$$

$$\leq \frac{1}{2^{128}} + Pr[L^* = T^*]$$

$$\leq \frac{2}{2^{128}}$$

Case B. $\exists$ unique $i \ni N^* = N_i, T^* \neq T_i$: Here $\kappa_{-1}^* = \kappa_{-1}^i$. As T^* is a fresh block-cipher output, successful forging in this case is bounded as follows:

$$Pr[\text{Win}_v] = Pr[E_{\kappa_{-1}^*}(\tau^*) = T^*|View(\mathcal{A}) = v]$$

$$= \sum_{L^*, L_i \neq T^*} Pr[E_{\kappa_{-1}^*}(\tau^*) = T^*|E_{\kappa_{-1}^*}(\tau_i) = T_i, E_{\kappa_{-1}^*}(a^*||l^*||0) = L^*,$$

$$E_{\kappa_{-1}^*}(a_i||l_i||0) = L_i] + Pr[T^* \notin \{L_i, L^*\}]$$

$$\leq \frac{1}{2^{128} - 3} + Pr[T^* \notin \{L_i, L^*\}]$$

$$\leq \frac{1}{2^{128} - 3} + \frac{2}{2^{128}}$$

$$\leq \frac{5}{2^{128}}$$

Case C. $\exists$ unique $i \ni N^* = N_i$, $T^* = T_i$, $|C_i| = |C^*|$: Here also we have $\kappa_{-1}^* = \kappa_{-1}^i$. As $T^* = T_i$ here, we have to argue through the low collision probability of τ^* and τ_i. From observation (ii) and (iii), we found that there is atleast 4 non-zero entries in ΔZ for the ith encryption query and the forged query. With this entropy of Z, we bound the probability of Win for this case. More formally,

$$Pr[\text{Win}_v] = Pr[E_{\kappa_{-1}^*}(\tau^*) = T^*|View(\mathcal{A}) = v]$$

$$= Pr[E_{\kappa_{-1}^i}(\tau^*) = T_i|E_{\kappa_{-1}^i}(\tau_i) = T_i]$$

$$= Pr[W_l^* + X_m^* + L^* = W_l^i + X_m^i + L^i]$$

$$= Pr[W_l^* + W_l = c]$$
$$= Pr[V_\alpha^{(4,l+3)} \cdot \Delta Z = c']$$
$$\leq \frac{1}{2^{128}}$$

Case D. $\exists$ unique $i \ni N^* = N_i$, $T^* = T_i$, $|C_i| \neq |C^*|$: If the length of M_i and the forged ciphertext is different then we can't argue through the entropy of ΔZ as for two messages of different length ΔZ may vary in only one position. So, here we argue through the L-values for the two queries. In fact we show that in this case, we obtain a non-trivial equation on the corresponding L-values which can bounded by $\frac{1}{2^{128}}$. More formally,

$$Pr[\text{Win}_v] = Pr[E_{\kappa_{-1}^*}(\tau^*) = T^* | View(\mathcal{A}) = v]$$
$$= Pr[E_{\kappa_{-1}^*}(\tau^*) = T_i | E_{\kappa_{-1}^*}(\tau_i) = T_i]$$
$$= Pr[\tau^* = \tau_i]$$
$$= Pr[W_l^* + X_m^* + L^* = (W_l)_i + (X_m)_i + L_i]$$
$$= Pr[L^* + L_i = c]$$
$$= Pr[E_{\kappa_{-1}^*}(a^*||l^*||0) + E_{\kappa_{-1}^*}(a_i||l_i||0) = c]$$
$$\leq \frac{1}{2^{128}}. \qquad \square$$

5   Conclusion and Future Work

In this paper, we have provided a generic INT-RUP attack on any "rate-1" affine AE mode. This result signifies that, to achieve INT-RUP security, any block-cipher based AE scheme must use more block cipher calls than the number of message blocks. So, INT-RUP security of block cipher based AE schemes can be achieved at the cost of efficiency. We also extend this attack to attack CPFB whose rate is less than 1 but also shows a variant of CPFB, achieving INT-RUP security.

Analysis of the INT-RUP security for "rate< 1"-block cipher based AE constructions is a possible future work. We know that "rate-$\frac{1}{2}$" AE schemes like ELmD, SILC and CLOC are claimed to have INT-RUP security where as CoPA is not. So, it is of interest to find a property, that makes "rate-$\frac{1}{2}$" AE schemes INT-RUP secure. One can further extend it for any rate $r < 1$. Providing the upper bound of the rate of a block-cipher based AE scheme along with a construction would be an interesting problem.

Acknowledgement. This work has been supported by the Centre of Excellence in Cryptology and R. C. Bose Centre for Cryptology and Security, Indian Statistical Institute, Kolkata. We would like to thank the anonymous reviewers for their detailed comments and suggestions on our paper.

References

1. CAESAR Competition. http://competitions.cr.yp.to/caesar.html
2. Andreeva, E., Bogdanov, A., Luykx, A., Mennink, B., Mouha, N., Yasuda, K.: How to Securely Release Unverified Plaintext inAuthenticated Encryption (2014). http://eprint.iacr.org/2014/144
3. Andreeva, E., Bogdanov, A., Luykx, A., Mennink, B., Tischhauser, E., Yasuda, K.: AES-COPA v.1 (2014). http://competitions.cr.yp.to/round1/aescopav1.pdf
4. Canvel, B., Hiltgen, A.P., Vaudenay, S., Vuagnoux, M.: Password interception in a SSL/TLS channel. In: Boneh, D. (ed.) CRYPTO 2003. LNCS, vol. 2729, pp. 583–599. Springer, Heidelberg (2003)
5. Datta, N., Nandi, M.: ELmE: A misuse resistant parallel authenticated encryption. In: Susilo, W., Mu, Y. (eds.) ACISP 2014. LNCS, vol. 8544, pp. 306–321. Springer, Heidelberg (2014)
6. Fleischmann, E., Forler, C., Lucks, S.: McOE: A family of almost foolproof online authenticated encryption schemes. In: Canteaut, A. (ed.) FSE 2012. LNCS, vol. 7549, pp. 196–215. Springer, Heidelberg (2012)
7. Iwata, T., Minematsu, K., Guo, J., Morioka, S., Kobayashi, E.: CLOC: Compact Low-Overhead CFB (2014). http://competitions.cr.yp.to/round1/clocv1.pdf
8. Iwata, T., Minematsu, K., Guo, J., Morioka, S., Kobayashi, E.: SILC: SImple Lightweight CFB (2014). http://competitions.cr.yp.to/round1/silcv1.pdf
9. Jutla, C.: Encryption modes with almost free message integrity. J. Cryptology **21**, 547–578 (2008)
10. Jutla, C.: Parallelizable Encryption Mode with Almost Free Message Integrity (2000). http://csrc.nist.gov/CryptoToolkit/modes/proposedmodes/iapm/iapm-spec.pdf
11. Krovetz, T., Rogaway, P.: The OCB Authenticated-Encryption Algorithm (2013). http://datatracker.ietf.org/doc/draft-irtf-cfrg-ocb
12. McGrew, D.A., Viega, J.: The Galois/Counter Mode of Operation (GCM) (2005). http://csrc.nist.gov/groups/ST/toolkit/BCM/documents/proposedmodes/gcm/gcm-spec.pdf
13. Montes, M., Penazzi, D.: AES-CPFB v1 (2014). http://competitions.cr.yp.to/round1/aescpfbv1.pdf
14. Nandi, M.: On the Optimality of Non-Linear Computations of Length-PreservingEncryption Schemes (2015). https://eprint.iacr.org/2015/414.pdf
15. Nandi, M.: XLS is not a strong pseudorandom permutation. In: Sarkar, P., Iwata, T. (eds.) ASIACRYPT 2014. LNCS, vol. 8873, pp. 478–490. Springer, Heidelberg (2014)
16. Nandi, M.: On the minimum number of multiplications necessary for universal hash functions. In: Cid, C., Rechberger, C. (eds.) FSE 2014. LNCS, vol. 8540, pp. 489–507. Springer, Heidelberg (2015)
17. Tsang, P.P., Smith, S.W.: Secure cryptographic precomputation with insecure memory. In: Chen, L., Mu, Y., Susilo, W. (eds.) ISPEC 2008. LNCS, vol. 4991, pp. 146–160. Springer, Heidelberg (2008)
18. Vaudenay, S.: Security flaws induced by CBC padding - Applications to SSL, IPSEC, WTLS. In: Knudsen, L.R. (ed.) EUROCRYPT 2002. LNCS, vol. 2332, pp. 534–546. Springer, Heidelberg (2002)
19. Zhang, L., Wu, W., Sui, H., Wang, P.: iFeed[AES] v1 (2014). http://competitions.cr.yp.to/round1/ifeedaesv1.pdf

From Stateless to Stateful: Generic Authentication and Authenticated Encryption Constructions with Application to TLS

Colin Boyd[1], Britta Hale[1(✉)], Stig Frode Mjølsnes[1], and Douglas Stebila[2]

[1] Norwegian University of Science and Technology, NTNU, Trondheim, Norway
{colin.boyd,britta.hale,stig.mjolsnes}@item.ntnu.no
[2] Queensland University of Technology, Brisbane, Australia
stebila@qut.edu.au

Abstract. Authentication and authenticated encryption with associated data (AEAD) are applied in cryptographic protocols to provide message integrity. The definitions in the literature and the constructions used in practice all protect against forgeries, but offer varying levels of protection against replays, reordering, and drops. As a result of the lack of a systematic hierarchy of authentication and AEAD security notions, gaps have arisen in the literature, specifically in the provable security analysis of the Transport Layer Security (TLS) protocol. We present a hierarchy of authentication and AEAD security notions, interpolating between the lowest level of protection (against forgeries) and the highest level (against forgeries, replays, reordering, and drops). We show generically how to construct higher level schemes from a basic scheme and appropriate use of sequence numbers, and apply that to close the gap in the analysis of TLS record layer encryption.

Keywords: Authentication · Authenticated encryption with associated data (AEAD) · Transport Layer Security (TLS) protocol · Secure channels

1 Introduction

Message integrity is a vital security service demanded of cryptographic protocols, and is usually provided either by a message authentication code (MAC) or by a combined authenticated encryption scheme. The standard security property for a MAC is existential unforgeability under a chosen message attack.

There has been an extensive line of research on security notions and constructions for authenticated encryption schemes, with initial definitions given by Katz and Yung [14], Bellare and Namprempre [4], and Krawczyk [17]. For message confidentiality, an authenticated encryption scheme could achieve indistinguishability under either an adaptive chosen plaintext (IND-CPA) or an adaptive

D. Stebila—Supported by the Australian Research Council (ARC) Discovery Project, grant DP130104304.

chosen ciphertext (IND-CCA a.k.a. IND-CCA2) attack. For message integrity, an authenticated encryption scheme could achieve either integrity of plaintexts (INT-PTXT) or of ciphertexts (INT-CTXT). Shrimpton [28] combined the separate INT-CTXT and IND-CCA experiments into a single experiment which he called IND-CCA3.

Bellare and Namprempre [4] and Krawczyk [17] also investigated how to construct authenticated encryption schemes from MACs and symmetric encryption, evaluating three construction paradigms: encrypt-and-MAC, MAC-then-encrypt, and encrypt-then-MAC.

Rogaway [25] defined the notion of *authenticated encryption with associated data (AEAD)*, to capture the common real-world scenario in which some data (such as packet headers) needs to be sent authentically alongside a ciphertext, but need not be encrypted, and AEAD has taken prominence over plain authenticated encryption in recent years.

Despite the utility of authenticated encryption and AEAD, it is not enough to realize the secure channel property expected of cryptographic protocols for two reasons. First, secure channel protocols are often expected to perform an initial establishment of the encryption key using a key exchange protocol; see for example the original paper on secure channels by Canetti and Krawczyk [6] (and the follow-up by Namprempre [21]) as well as recent realizations such as the authenticated and confidential channel establishment (ACCE) model of Jager et al. [13]. (In this paper, we will not focus on the key exchange establishment phase of secure channels.) Second, and more important for this paper, applications often expect reliable delivery of a sequence of messages: that no attacker can replay messages, deliver them in a different order in which they were sent, or drop some messages without later detection.

To capture the notion of delivery of a sequence of messages, Bellare et al. [3] introduced *stateful authenticated encryption*, with two security properties: stateful integrity of ciphertexts (INT-SFCTXT) and stateful indistinguishability of ciphertexts (IND-SFCCA). Kohno et al. [16] extended the statefulness to AEAD schemes, and gave a hierarchy of 5 integrity notions: type (1) security against forgeries; type (2) type 1 plus security against replays; type (3) type 2 plus security against reordering; type (4) type 3 plus detection of previous drops but still accepting subsequent messages; type (5) type 4 plus but not accepting subsequent messages. The type 5 notion of Kohno et al. [16] is equivalent to the stateful authenticated encryption notion of Bellare et al. [3].

Paterson et al. [22] revisit AEAD definitions in the context of the Transport Layer Security (TLS) protocol. They present a combined AEAD security notion called *length-hiding authenticated encryption (LHAE)*, which provides message integrity and confidentiality similar to the type-5 security of Kohno et al. [16], even for messages of different length (hence "length-hiding"), and in a single combined security property (following Shrimpton [28]). Paterson et al. then go on to show that, under appropriate length conditions on the message authentication tag, a simplified form of the encode-then-MAC-then-encrypt form of encryption in the TLS record layer in ciphersuites that use a block cipher in CBC mode is a secure length-hiding authenticated encryption scheme. The simplification is that the statefulness aspects (sequence numbers) are not considered.

Jager et al. [13] and Krawczyk et al. [18], in their provable security analyses of the full TLS protocol (covering both the authenticated key exchange in the TLS handshake and the TLS record layer), rely on an extension of the work of Paterson et al. [22], namely a form of *stateful length-hiding authenticated encryption (sLHAE)*. Unfortunately, the work of Paterson et al. did not show that TLS encode-then-MAC-then-encrypt satisfies sLHAE, only LHAE. To our knowledge, this gap remains in the literature until now.

1.1 Our Contributions

In this work, we construct a hierarchy of authentication and AEAD security notions, show how to construct schemes with higher levels of security from a scheme with the lowest level of security combined with sequence numbers, and apply these techniques to TLS record layer encryption to bridge the gap between LHAE [22] and sLHAE [13].

First, we construct a hierarchy of authentication levels:

1. protection against forgeries,
2. protection against forgeries and replays,
3. protection against forgeries, replays, and reordering of messages, and
4. protection against forgeries, replays, reordering of messages, and dropped messages.

We give a similar hierarchy of definitions for AEAD, with single-experiment AEAD notions that combine integrity and indistinguishability, following Shrimpton [28]. In both cases, these hierarchy levels can be viewed as interpolating between existing *stateless* notions at our level 1 and existing *stateful* notions at our level 4.

Continuing, we show how to construct level 2, 3, and 4 schemes from level 1 schemes. The constructions are not surprising: by appropriate incorporation and checking of sequence numbers, the receiver can ensure it is receiving a valid sequence of sent messages. However, our constructions incorporate a degree of generality: rather than fixing how the sequence numbers are incorporated, we allow an *encoding scheme* to include them either *implicitly* or *explicitly*. For example, in an explicit encoding scheme, the sequence number might be authenticated and then transmitted alongside the ciphertext, in the manner of DTLS. Alternatively, in an implicit encoding scheme, the sequence number might be incorporated into the authentication calculation but not actually transmitted across the wire (since the receiving party ought to know what packet number to expect); this is how TLS works, for example.

We use this generic construction to close the gap in the provable security analysis of TLS record layer encryption. Paterson et al.'s analysis of a simplified form of TLS encode-then-MAC-then-encrypt (Π_{PRS}) shows that it satisfies the LHAE notion, equivalent to our level 1. We can formulate TLS's use of sequence numbers as an encoding scheme in our generic construction, and then see that the full form of TLS encode-then-MAC-then-encrypt (Π_{TLS}) is equivalent to our level-4 generic construction applied to Π_{PRS}, and thus Π_{TLS} achieves level-4 AEAD security, equivalent to sLHAE. Figure 1 illustrates the connection between our work and that of Paterson et al., Jager et al., and Krawczyk et al., depicting how the construction from level-1 AEAD to level-4 AEAD builds a missing and necessary bridge in the analysis of TLS.

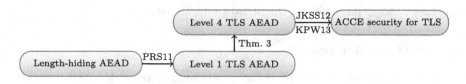

Fig. 1. TLS channel analysis.

Relation with Existing Work. The work most closely related to ours is the manuscript of Kohno et al. [16], who gave a hierarchy of AEAD notions. Our AEAD hierarchy maps on to theirs: our levels 1, 2, 3, and 4 correspond to their types 1, 2, 3, and 5, respectively. There are several differences with our work. They give constructions of higher level schemes directly from encryption and MAC schemes in the encrypt-and-MAC, MAC-then-encrypt, and encrypt-then-MAC paradigms, whereas we show how to construct higher levels generically from lower level schemes. Their AEAD hierarchy uses separate integrity and indistinguishability experiments at each level, whereas we use a single combined experiment at each level. We also give a hierarchy of authentication notions, not just AEAD notions, and thereby expand applicability to schemes outside of the AEAD context. Finally, we connect the hierarchy and our generic constructions with TLS record layer encryption.

Connection with Secure Channel Definitions. One motivation of our work was to understand the difference between the original CK01 secure channel definition of Canetti and Krawczyk [6] and the ACCE model of Jager et al. [13]. The confidentiality and integrity notions in CK01 and their NetAut protocol correspond with level 1 of our AEAD hierarchy – stateless authenticated encryption. A comment in their paper does require that the receiver "check for uniqueness of the incoming message", which would upgrade to level 2 in our hierarchy, and this is the notion that was used in a subsequent work by Namprempre [21]. In contrast, Jager et al.'s ACCE notion maps to level 4 of our AEAD hierarchy – sLHAE.

Application to Real-World Protocols. Each level of our AEAD hierarchy maps to the requirements expected in some real-world protocols:

- Level 1: DTLS [23,24]: Datagram TLS provides basic authentication, allows packets to be dropped, and will receive packets out of order, queuing them for future processing.

- Level 2: IPsec Authentication Header (AH) [15]: IPsec Authentication Header protocol provides similar replay detection using a window of recently received packets combined with dropping packets that are "too old".
- Level 2: DTLS with optional replay detection: Datagram TLS does allow optional replay detection [23,24, Sect. 3.3] using a similar technique to IPsec AH.
- Level 3: 802.11 [12] is designed to preventing reordering and to detect replays but allows for packet dropping.
- Level 4: TLS [7] is designed to receive a message sequence strictly as a sent, and will be discussed at greater length in Sect. 4.

A recent analysis [19] of the QUIC protocol [29] employed an AEAD level comparable to our level 1 AEAD; however, the replay-detection abilities of QUIC suggest that a higher authentication level should be achievable.

1.2 Additional Related Work

There are several additional lines of work on authenticated encryption.

One line of research views data "as a stream", rather than a discrete sequence of messages; practical implementations receive data byte-by-byte rather than as atomic messages in security definitions. Albrecht et al. [1] showed how to carry out a plaintext recovery attack against the Secure Shell (SSH) protocol as a result of byte-by-byte processing. This motivated the need for non-atomic authenticated encryption definitions [5,8]. The work of Fischlin et al. [8] in particular is motivated by protocols such as TLS, SSH, and QUIC, and describes checks that can again be correlated with our level-4 AEAD notion. It would be interesting to expand stream-based analysis in the direction of our hierarchical levels for protocols that allow packet dropping. For example, the QUIC protocol [29] runs over UDP and tolerates a degree of packet loss, making analysis under a level-4 stream-based notion inappropriate.

Another line of research focuses on the use of nonces in authenticated encryption [25,26], and more recently for the specific purposes of protecting implementations that misuse counters or nonces [9,11,27]. Meanwhile, Hoang et al. [10] define a notion of robust authenticated encryption which incorporates padding properties similar to the stateless form of LHAE of Paterson et al. [22]. Finally, additional recent work focuses on defining authenticated encryption results in the constructive cryptography framework [2,20].

2 Authentication Hierarchy

In this section, we formalize our 4-tier hierarchy of authentication notions, each level building on the previous, and show how to achieve higher level notions from level-1 combined with appropriate checks on sequence numbers.

2.1   Definitions

Definition 1. *A stateful authentication scheme Π for a message space $\mathcal{M}$, a key space $\mathcal{K}$, and an output space $\mathcal{C}$ is a tuple of algorithms:*

- *Kgn() $\xrightarrow{\$}$ k: A probabilistic key generation algorithm that outputs a key k.*
- *Snd$(k, m, st_E) \xrightarrow{\$} (c, st_E)$: A probabilistic authentication algorithm that takes as input a key $k \in \mathcal{K}$, a message $m \in \mathcal{M}$, and an authentication state st_E, and outputs a tagged message $c \in \mathcal{C}$ and updated state st_E.*
- *Rcv$(k, c, st_D) \rightarrow (m, \alpha, st_D)$: A deterministic verification algorithm that takes as input a key $k \in \mathcal{K}$, a tagged message $c \in \mathcal{C}$, and a verification state st_D, and outputs either a message $m \in \mathcal{M}$ or an error symbol $\perp$, a bit $\alpha \in \{0, 1\}$, and an updated state st_D.*

On first use, st_E and st_D are initialized to $\perp$.

Correctness is defined in the natural way: for all $m \in \mathcal{M}$, all $k \xleftarrow{\$} \text{Kgn}()$, all st_E and st_D defined in any sequence of encryptions and decryptions respectively, and all c such that $(c, st'_E) \leftarrow \text{Snd}(k, m, st_E)$, we have that $\text{Rcv}(k, c, st_D) = (m, 1, st'_D)$.

Note that in the case of a Rcv (message authentication check) failure, the receive algorithm outputs a failure symbol $\perp$, $\alpha = 0$ to denote a failed receipt, and an updated state st_D: $(\perp, 0, st_D) \leftarrow \text{Rcv}(k, c, st_D)$. Otherwise, the algorithm outputs the correctly received message m, $\alpha = 1$ to denote successful receipt, and an updated state st_D: $(m, 1, st_D) \leftarrow \text{Rcv}(k, c, st_D)$.

Formally we define a stateful authentication security experiment that can be *parameterized* with different authentication conditions to capture various levels of authentication. Four graded levels of authentication are defined for the experiment, correlated to different conditions, cond_i, under which an adversary $\mathcal{A}$ wins, as shown in Fig. 2. Note that cond_4 is strongly linked to authentication demands in analyses of TLS [13,22], a protocol with strict authentication requirements.

Definition 2. *Let Π be a stateful authentication scheme and let $\mathcal{A}$ be an adversary algorithm. Let $i \in \{1, \ldots, 4\}$. The stateful authentication experiment for Π with authentication condition cond_i is given by $\text{Exp}_{\Pi,\mathcal{A}}^{\text{auth}_i}$ in Fig. 2. We define*
$$\mathbf{Adv}_{\Pi}^{\text{auth}_i}(\mathcal{A}) = \Pr\left[\text{Exp}_{\Pi}^{\text{auth}_i}(\mathcal{A}) = 1\right].$$

Remark 1. If the authenticated message c takes the form of a ciphertext, then level-1 authentication is equivalent to INT-CTXT. If c is such that $c = (m, \text{MAC}(m))$, where MAC is a message authentication code, then level-1 authentication is equivalent to SUF-CMA. In order to maximize the application potential of our results, we provide the generality for either application.

2.2   Relations Among Authentication Notions

Each of the authentication notions sequentially implies the security of the levels below it. In the following theorem, the security implications between levels are formalized, with security at Level 2 implying security at Level 1, etc.

$\mathrm{Exp}_{\Pi,\mathcal{A}}^{\mathrm{auth}_i}()$:

1: $k \xleftarrow{\$} \mathrm{Kgn}()$
2: $st_{\mathrm{E}} \leftarrow \bot, st_{\mathrm{D}} \leftarrow \bot$
3: $u \leftarrow 0, v \leftarrow 0$
4: $r \leftarrow 0$
5: $\mathcal{A}^{\mathrm{Send}(\cdot),\mathrm{Recv}(\cdot)}()$
6: return r

Oracle $\mathrm{Send}(m)$:

1: $u \leftarrow u + 1$
2: $(sent_u, st_{\mathrm{E}}) \leftarrow \mathrm{Snd}(k, m, st_{\mathrm{E}})$
3: return $sent_u$ to $\mathcal{A}$

Oracle $\mathrm{Recv}(c)$:

1: $v \leftarrow v + 1$
2: $rcvd_v \leftarrow c$
3: $(m, \alpha, st_{\mathrm{D}}) \leftarrow \mathrm{Rcv}(k, c, st_{\mathrm{D}})$
4: if $(\alpha = 1) \wedge \mathsf{cond}_i$ then
5:     $r \leftarrow 1$
6:     return r from experiment
7: return $\bot$ to $\mathcal{A}$

1. **Basic authentication:**
   $\mathsf{cond}_1 = (\nexists w : c = sent_w)$
2. **Basic authentication, no replays:**
   $\mathsf{cond}_2 = (\nexists w : c = sent_w) \vee (\exists w < v : c = rcvd_w)$
3. **Basic authentication, no replays, strictly increasing:**
   $\mathsf{cond}_3 = (\nexists w : c = sent_w) \vee (\exists w, x, y : (w < v) \wedge (sent_x = rcvd_w) \wedge (sent_y = rcvd_v) \wedge (x \geq y))$
4. **Basic authentication, no replays, strictly increasing, no drops:**
   $\mathsf{cond}_4 = (u < v) \vee (c \neq sent_v)$

Fig. 2. Stateful authentication experiment auth_i with authentication condition cond_i for stateful authentication scheme $\Pi = (\mathrm{Kgn}, \mathrm{Snd}, \mathrm{Rcv})$ and adversary $\mathcal{A}$.

Theorem 1 (Level-$(i{+}1)$ authentication implies level-i authentication). *Let $\Pi = (\mathrm{Kgn}, \mathrm{Snd}, \mathrm{Rcv})$ be an authentication scheme and let $i \in \{1, 2, 3\}$. For any adversary $\mathcal{A}$, $\mathbf{Adv}_{\Pi}^{\mathrm{auth}_i}(\mathcal{A}) \leq \mathbf{Adv}_{\Pi}^{\mathrm{auth}_{i+1}}(\mathcal{A})$.*

The proof of Theorem 1 can be found in the full version and is omitted here due to space restrictions.

2.3 Constructing Higher Level Authentication Schemes

In this section, we generically show how to build higher level authentication schemes based on lower level authentication schemes and the inclusion of sequence numbers with appropriate checks. Since currently implemented protocols use both implicit and explicit sequence numbers, we generalize our model for an arbitrary *encoding scheme* which captures both implicit and explicit sequence numbers.

Definition 3 (Authentication encoding scheme). *An* (authentication) encoding scheme Coding *for a sequence number space S and message space $\mathcal{M}$ is a pair of algorithms:*

– Ecd$(\mathsf{sqn}, m) \rightarrow m_{\mathrm{ecd}}$: *A deterministic encoding algorithm that takes as input a sequence number* $\mathsf{sqn} \in \mathsf{S}$ *and a message* $m \in \mathcal{M}$, *and outputs an encoded message* $m_{\mathrm{ecd}} \in \mathcal{M}_{\mathrm{ecd}}$, *where* $\mathcal{M}_{\mathrm{ecd}}$ *is the encoded version of* $\mathcal{M}$.

– $\text{Dcd}(\text{sqnlist}, m_{\text{ecd}}) \rightarrow (\text{sqn}, m, \alpha)$: *A deterministic decoding algorithm that takes as input a sequence number list* $\text{sqnlist} \subset S$ *and an encoded message* $m_{\text{ecd}} \in \mathcal{M}_{\text{ecd}}$, *and outputs a sequence number* $\text{sqn} \in S$, *a message* $m \in \mathcal{M}$ *or an error symbol* $\perp$, *and a status variable* $\alpha = 1$ *if decoding was successful or* $\alpha = 0$ *otherwise.*

In our construction of higher level authentications, we will require that Ecd is collision-resistant.

We can construct schemes that use either implicit or explicit sequence numbers using Definition 3. For example, the scheme with $\text{Ecd}(\text{sqn}, m) := \text{sqn} \| m$ has an explicit sequence number, and may be very applicable in practice since sqn is sent explicitly with the message. An alternative scheme with implicit sequence numbers would be $\text{Ecd}(\text{sqn}, m) := m \| \text{MAC}(\text{sqn})$. Thus elements of the space $\mathcal{M}_{\text{ecd}}$ may take various forms, contingent on the properties desirable for Coding. We will see in Sect. 4.2 that the TLS record layer protocol uses an encoding scheme based on the second example above. We formally distinguish explicit and implicit sequence numbers as follows:

Definition 4. *We say that authentication encoding scheme* Coding *uses explicit sequence numbers if* $\text{Dcd}(\emptyset, \text{Ecd}(\text{sqn}, m)) = (\text{sqn}, m, 1)$ *for all* sqn *and all* m, *and that* Coding *uses implicit sequence numbers otherwise.*

We now present our generic constructions of level-i authentication schemes from a level-1 authentication scheme. The heart of our construction is a sequence number check $\text{TEST}i$ that will correspond to the authentication condition cond_i. Our constructions can accommodate any collision-resistant encoding scheme Coding, with either implicit or explicit sequence numbers; this requirement is specifically important in implicit authentication where the sequence number is not physically present on receipt. For conciseness, the notation Π_i' for $P(\Pi, \text{Ecd}, \text{TEST}i)$ will be generally employed.

Definition 5 (P construction). *Let* Π *be a (level-1) authentication scheme,* Coding *be an encoding scheme, and let* $\text{TEST}i$ *be one of the conditions specified in Fig. 3. Define* $\Pi_i' := P(\Pi, \text{Coding}, \text{TEST}i)$ *as the authentication scheme resulting from apply construction P in Fig. 3.*

In this construction, the check TEST2 corresponds to the condition for level-2 authentication. Basic level-1 authentication is assumed, so TEST2's protection against replays implies replay protection for condition cond_2. Namely, if $\exists w < v : c = rcvd_w$ then $\exists j : \text{sqn} = st_{\text{D}}.\text{sqnlist}_j$, since identical authenticated messages must contain identical sequence numbers. Similar connections exist between TEST3 and cond_3 and TEST4 and cond_4. Note that to check TEST2 it is necessary to maintain a record of all previously received sqn; thus $st_{\text{D}}.\text{sqnlist}$ must be a complete record. However, for TEST3 and TEST4, it is strictly only necessary for $st_{\text{D}}.\text{sqnlist}$ to contain the last received sqn.

The following theorem shows that the P construction with $\text{TEST}i$ achieves level-i authentication. Notably Theorem 2 depends on the collision-resistance of Ecd. For many encoding schemes, this follows immediately. For example, the

Π_i'.Kgn():
1: **return** Π.Kgn()

Π_i'.Snd(k, m, st_E'):
1: $(c, st_E'$.subst)
    $\leftarrow \Pi$.Snd(k, Ecd(st_E'.ctr, m), st_E'.subst)
2: st_E'.ctr $\leftarrow st_E'$.ctr $+ 1$
3: **return** (c, st_E')

Π_i'.Rcv(k, c, st_D'):
1: **if** st_D'.status = failed **then**
2:     **return** $(\bot, 0, st_D)$
3: $(m_\Pi, \alpha, st_D'$.subst)
    $\leftarrow \Pi$.Rcv(k, c, st_D'.subst)
4: **if** $\alpha = 1$ **then**
5:     (sqn, m, α) $\leftarrow$ Dcd(st_D'.sqnlist, m_Π)
6: **if** ($\alpha = 0$) $\lor$ TESTi **then**
7:     st_D'.status = failed
8:     **return** $(\bot, 0, st_D')$
9: st_D'.sqnlist $= st_D'$.sqnlist$\|$sqn
10: **return** (m, α, st_D')

Sequence number tests for building Π', correlated to authentication levels:

- **Basic authentication, no replays:**
  TEST2 $= (\exists j : $ sqn $= st_D'$.sqnlist$_j)$
- **Basic authentication, no replays, strictly increasing:**
  TEST3 $= (\exists j : $ sqn $\not> st_D'$.sqnlist$_j)$
- **Basic authentication, no replays, strictly increasing, no drops:**
  TEST4 $= (\exists j : $ sqn $\not> st_D'$.sqnlist$_j) \lor ($ sqn $\neq \max\{st_D'$.sqnlist$_j\} + 1)$

Description of states st_E' and st_D':

- st_E'.subst $:= st_E$, where st_E is the state in Π
- st_E'.ctr. When Π'.Snd is initialized, st_E'.ctr $\leftarrow 0$.
- st_D'.subst $:= st_D$, where st_D is the state in Π
- st_D'.status. Once st_D'.status = failed it is not reset and all subsequently received messages are also immediately aborted.
- st_D'.sqnlist, an ordered list of sequence numbers previously received. It is required that $|st_D'$.sqnlist$| \geq 1$ after the first received sqn; i.e. the size of the ordered set is maintained at 1 or greater. When Π'.Snd is initialized, st_D'.sqnlist $\leftarrow \bot$.

Fig. 3. Construction P of a level-i authentication scheme Π_i' from a level-1 authentication scheme Π and encoding scheme Coding = (Ecd, Dcd).

simple concatenation scheme Ecd(ctr, m) = ctr$\|m$ is clearly collision-resistant when assuming unambiguous concatenation. When such a scheme is used, the advantage of $\mathcal{A}$ is then directly reducible to the advantage of $\mathcal{F}$. Due to space restrictions, the proof of Theorem 2 can be found in the full version of this paper.

Theorem 2. *Let Π be a secure level-1 authentication scheme and Coding be an authentication encoding scheme with collision-resistant encoding. Let $i \in \{2, 3, 4\}$. Then $\Pi_i' = P(\Pi, \text{Coding}, \text{TEST}i)$, constructed as in Fig. 3, is a secure level-i authentication scheme. Specifically, let $\mathcal{A}$ be an adversary algorithm that runs in time t and asks q_s Send queries and q_r Recv queries, and let $q = q_s + q_r$. Then there exists an adversary $\mathcal{B}$ that runs in time $t_\mathcal{B} \approx t$ and asks no more than $q_\mathcal{B} = \frac{1}{2}q_s(q_s - 1)$ queries, and an adversary $\mathcal{F}$ that runs* *in time $t_{\mathcal{F}} \approx t$ and asks $q_{\mathcal{F}} = q$ queries, such that* $\mathbf{Adv}^{\mathsf{auth}_i}_{P(\Pi,\mathrm{Coding},\mathrm{TEST}i)}(\mathcal{A}) \leq$ $\mathbf{Adv}^{\mathsf{auth}_1}_{\Pi}(\mathcal{F}) + \mathbf{Adv}^{\mathrm{collision}}_{\mathrm{Ecd}}(\mathcal{B}).$

The time-cost for checking using implicit sequence numbers could be considerable when using a Level 2 or Level 3 authentication notion due to the need to check against all previously received messages. However, to our knowledge, there are no real-world implementations using implicit sequence numbers at these levels. Implicit sequence numbers have been used in instances where Level 4 authentication is desired, but explicit sequence numbers are usually employed at the lower levels. Logically, this also corresponds to desirable real-world instantiation formats; if a protocol allows packets to be dropped then it would be inconvenient to base authentication upon information that is not explicitly sent in each packet. Alternatively, if no drops are allowed, authentication can be checked against explicit or implicit information.

3   Authenticated Encryption Hierarchy

In this section, we build equivalent notions for *authenticated encryption with associated data (AEAD) schemes*. AEAD security is typically defined by extending the authentication notion with a type of *left-or-right* encryption game.

3.1   Definitions

Definition 6. *A stateful AEAD scheme Π for a message space $\mathcal{M}$, an associated data space $\mathcal{AD}$, a key space $\mathcal{K}$, and a ciphertext space $\mathcal{C}$, is a tuple of algorithms:*

- $\mathrm{Kgn}() \xrightarrow{\$} k$: *A probabilistic key generation algorithm that outputs a key k.*
- $\mathrm{E}(k, \ell, \mathsf{ad}, m, st_{\mathrm{E}}) \xrightarrow{\$} (c, st'_{\mathrm{E}})$: *A probabilistic encryption algorithm that takes as input a key $k \in \mathcal{K}$, a length $\ell \in \mathbb{Z}$, associated data $\mathsf{ad} \in \mathcal{AD}$, a message $m \in \mathcal{M}$, and an encryption state st_{E}, and outputs a ciphertext $c \in \mathcal{C}$ and updated state st'_{E}.*
- $\mathrm{D}(k, \mathsf{ad}, c, st_{\mathrm{D}}) \rightarrow (\mathsf{ad}, m, \alpha, st'_{\mathrm{D}})$: *A deterministic decryption algorithm that takes as input a key $k \in \mathcal{K}$, associated data $\mathsf{ad} \in \mathcal{AD}$, a ciphertext c, and a decryption state st_{D}, and outputs either associated data ad or an error symbol $\perp$, a message $m \in \mathcal{M}$ or an error symbol $\perp$, a bit $\alpha \in \{0, 1\}$, and an updated state st'_{D}.*

Compared with stateful authentication schemes in Definition 1, AEAD schemes utilize two further fields: ad, which is for associated data (such as authenticated but unencrypted header data), and an optional length field ℓ.

Correctness is defined in an analogous manner to that of stateful authentication schemes. Correspondingly we define 4 levels of stateful AEAD security.

Definition 7. *Let Π be a stateful AEAD scheme and let A be an PPT adversarial algorithm. Let $i \in \{1, \ldots, 4\}$ and let $b \in \{0, 1\}$. The stateful AEAD experiment for Π with condition cond_i and bit b is given by $\text{Exp}_{\Pi}^{\text{aead}_i - b}(A)$ in Fig. 4. We define $\mathbf{Adv}_{\Pi}^{\text{aead}_i}(A) = \left| \Pr\left[\text{Exp}_{\Pi}^{\text{aead}_i - 1}(A) = 1 \right] - \Pr\left[\text{Exp}_{\Pi}^{\text{aead}_i - 0}(A) = 1 \right] \right|$.*

The Encrypt and Decrypt oracles in Fig. 4 work together to provide both an authentication experiment and ciphertext indistinguishability experiment. When $b = 0$, the adversary always gets m_0 encrypted and never receives any decryption information. When $b = 1$, the adversary always gets m_1 encrypted and potentially receives decryption information. If the adversary makes an attempt to forge ciphertexts or violate the sequencing condition (modelled by the out-of-sync flag), then a secure stateful AEAD scheme should return $\perp$ in all subsequent decryption queries. If the adversary has caused the encryptor and decryptor to get out of sync (by forging a ciphertext or violating the sequencing condition) and ever receives non-$\perp$ from Decrypt, the adversary learns $b = 1$.

When ℓ is not used, the level-1 notion aead_1 corresponds to IND-CCA and INT-CTXT security of a stateless AEAD scheme.

When ℓ is used for length, the level-4 notion aead_4 corresponds to the stateful length-hiding authenticated encryption security notion of Krawczyk et al. [18] which is a slight modification of that of Jager et al. [13].

Analogously to Sect. 2.2, level-$(i + 1)$ AEAD security implies level-i AEAD security. The details are omitted due to space restrictions.

3.2 Constructing Higher Level AEAD Schemes

Similarly to Sect. 3, we can construct higher level AEAD schemes based on a level-1 AEAD scheme with the inclusion of sequence numbers with appropriate checks. We again generalize the approach using an encoding scheme that captures both implicit and explicit sequence numbers.

Definition 8 (AEAD encoding scheme). *An AEAD encoding scheme Coding for a sequence number space S, a message space $\mathcal{M}$, and an associated data space $\mathcal{AD}$ is a pair of algorithms:*

- *$\text{Ecd}(\text{sqn}, \text{ad}, m) \rightarrow (\text{ad}_{\text{ecd}}, m_{\text{ecd}})$: A deterministic encoding algorithm that takes as input a sequence number $\text{sqn} \in S$, associated data $\text{ad} \in \mathcal{AD}$, and a message $m \in \mathcal{M}$, and outputs an encoded associated data value $\text{ad}_{\text{ecd}} \in \mathcal{AD}_{\text{ecd}}$ and message $m_{\text{ecd}} \in \mathcal{M}_{\text{ecd}}$, where $\mathcal{AD}_{\text{ecd}}$ and $\mathcal{M}_{\text{ecd}}$ are the encoded versions of associated data space $\mathcal{AD}$ and message space $\mathcal{M}$, respectively.*
- *$\text{Dcd}(\text{sqnlist}, \text{ad}_{\text{ecd}}, m_{\text{ecd}}) \rightarrow (\text{sqn}, \text{ad}, m, \alpha)$: A deterministic decoding algorithm that takes as input a sequence number list $\text{sqnlist} \subset S$, an encoded associated data value ad_{ecd}, and an encoded message $m_{\text{ecd}} \in \mathcal{M}_{\text{ecd}}$, and outputs a sequence number $\text{sqn} \in S$, associated data $\text{ad} \in \mathcal{AD}$ or an error symbol $\perp$, a message $m \in \mathcal{M}$ or an error symbol $\perp$, and a status variable $\alpha = 1$ if decoding was successful or $\alpha = 0$ otherwise.*

$\mathsf{Exp}_{\Pi,\mathcal{A}}^{\mathsf{aead}_i - b}()$:

1: $k \xleftarrow{\$} \mathsf{Kgn}()$
2: $st_E \leftarrow \bot, st_D \leftarrow \bot$
3: $u \leftarrow 0, v \leftarrow 0$
4: $\mathsf{out\text{-}of\text{-}sync} \leftarrow 0$
5: $b' \xleftarrow{\$} \mathcal{A}^{\mathsf{Encrypt}(\cdot),\mathsf{Decrypt}(\cdot)}()$
6: **return** b'

Oracle $\mathsf{Encrypt}(\ell, \mathsf{ad}, m_0, m_1)$:

1: $u \leftarrow u + 1$
2: $(sent.c^{(0)}, st_E^{(0)}) \leftarrow E(k, \ell, \mathsf{ad}, m_0, st_E)$
3: $(sent.c^{(1)}, st_E^{(1)}) \leftarrow E(k, \ell, \mathsf{ad}, m_1, st_E)$
4: **if** $sent.c^{(0)} = \bot$ or $sent.c^{(1)} = \bot$ **then**
5:     **return** $\bot$
6: $(sent.ad_u, sent.c_u, st_E) := (\mathsf{ad}, sent.c^{(b)}, st_E^{(b)})$
7: **return** $sent.c_u$

Oracle $\mathsf{Decrypt}(\mathsf{ad}, c)$:

1: **if** $b = 0$ **then**
2:     **return** $\bot$
3: $v \leftarrow v + 1$
4: $rcvd.c_v \leftarrow c$
5: $(\mathsf{ad}, m, \alpha, st_D)$
    $\leftarrow D(k, \mathsf{ad}, c, st_D)$
6: **if** $(\alpha = 1) \wedge \mathsf{cond}_i$ **then**
7:     $\mathsf{out\text{-}of\text{-}sync} \leftarrow 1$
8: **if** $\mathsf{out\text{-}of\text{-}sync} = 1$ **then**
9:     **return** m
10: **return** $\bot$

---

1. **Basic authenticated encryption:**
   $\mathsf{cond}_1 = (\nexists w : (c = sent.c_w) \wedge (\mathsf{ad} = sent.ad_w))$
2. **Basic authenticated encryption, no replays:**
   $\mathsf{cond}_2 = (\nexists w : (c = sent.c_w) \wedge (\mathsf{ad} = sent.ad_w)) \vee (\exists w < v : c = rcvd.c_w)$
3. **Basic authenticated encryption, no replays, strictly increasing:**
   $\mathsf{cond}_3 = (\nexists w : (c = sent.c_w) \wedge (\mathsf{ad} = sent.ad_w)) \vee (\exists w, x, y : (w < v) \wedge (sent.c_x = rcvd.c_w) \wedge (sent.c_y = rcvd.c_v) \wedge (x \geq y))$
4. **Basic authenticated encryption, no replays, strictly increasing, no drops:**
   $\mathsf{cond}_4 = (u < v) \vee (c \neq sent.c_v) \vee (\mathsf{ad} \neq sent.ad_v)$

Fig. 4. Stateful AEAD experiment aead_i with authentication condition cond_i for stateful AEAD scheme $\Pi = (\mathsf{Kgn}, E, D)$ and adversary $\mathcal{A}$.

Definition 9. *We say that AEAD encoding scheme* Coding *uses* explicit *sequence numbers if, for all* sqn, ad, *and* m, *when* $\mathsf{Ecd}(\mathsf{sqn}, \mathsf{ad}, m) = (\mathsf{ad}_{\mathsf{ecd}}, m_{\mathsf{ecd}})$, *we have that* $\mathsf{Dcd}(\bot, \mathsf{ad}_{\mathsf{ecd}}, m_{\mathsf{ecd}}) = (\mathsf{sqn}, \mathsf{ad}, m, 1)$. *Otherwise, we say that* Coding *uses* implicit *sequence numbers.*

Definition 10 (P_{AEAD} construction). *Let Π be a (level-1) AEAD scheme,* Coding *be an AEAD encoding scheme, and let* TESTi *be a condition specified in Fig. 3. Define $\Pi_i' := P_{\mathrm{AEAD}}(\Pi, \mathsf{Ecd}, \mathsf{TEST}i)$ as the AEAD scheme resulting from applying construction P_{AEAD} in Fig. 5.*

Theorem 3. *Let Π be a secure level-1 AEAD scheme and* Coding *be an AEAD encoding scheme with collision-resistant encoding. Let* TESTi *be defined as in Fig. 3 and $i \in \{2, 3, 4\}$. Then $\Pi_i' = P_{\mathrm{AEAD}}(\Pi, \mathsf{Coding}, \mathsf{TEST}i)$, constructed as in Fig. 5, is a secure level-i AEAD scheme. Specifically, let $\mathcal{A}$ be an adversary algorithm that runs in time t and asks q_e* Encrypt *queries and q_d* Decrypt *queries, and let $q = q_e + q_d$. Then there exists an adversary $\mathcal{B}$ that runs in time $t_{\mathcal{B}} \approx t$*

$\Pi'_i.\mathrm{Kgn}()$:
1: **return** $\Pi.\mathrm{Kgn}()$

$\Pi'_i.\mathrm{E}(k, \ell, \mathsf{ad}, m, st'_\mathrm{E})$:
1: (ad_Π, m_Π)
   $\leftarrow \mathrm{Ecd}(st'_\mathrm{E}.\mathrm{ctr}, \mathsf{ad}, m)$
2: $(c, st'_\mathrm{E}.\mathrm{subst})$
   $\leftarrow \Pi.\mathrm{E}(k, m_\Pi, \mathsf{ad}_\Pi, l, st'_\mathrm{E}.\mathrm{subst})$
3: $st'_\mathrm{E}.\mathrm{ctr} \leftarrow st'_\mathrm{E}.\mathrm{ctr} + 1$
4: **return** (c, st'_E)

$\Pi'_i.\mathrm{D}(k, \mathsf{ad}, c, st'_\mathrm{D})$:
1: **if** $st'_\mathrm{D}.\mathrm{status} = \mathsf{failed}$ **then**
2:     **return** $(\bot, 0, st_\mathrm{D})$
3: $(\mathsf{ad}_\Pi, m_\Pi, \alpha, st'_\mathrm{D}.\mathrm{subst})$
   $\leftarrow \Pi.\mathrm{D}(k, \mathsf{ad}, c, st'_\mathrm{D}.\mathrm{subst})$
4: **if** $\alpha = 1$ **then**
5:     $(\mathrm{sqn}, \mathsf{ad}, m, \alpha)$
       $\leftarrow \mathrm{Dcd}(st'_\mathrm{D}.\mathrm{sqnlist}, \mathsf{ad}_\Pi, m_\Pi)$
6: **if** $(\alpha = 0) \vee \mathrm{TEST}i$ **then**
7:     $st'_\mathrm{D}.\mathrm{status} = \mathsf{failed}$
8:     **return** $(\bot, 0, st'_\mathrm{D})$
9: $st'_\mathrm{D}.\mathrm{sqnlist} = st'_\mathrm{D}.\mathrm{sqnlist}\|\mathrm{sqn}$
10: **return** $(m, \alpha, st'_\mathrm{D})$

Description of states st'_E and st'_D:

- $st'_\mathrm{E}.\mathrm{subst} := st_\mathrm{E}$, where st_E is the state in Π.
- $st'_\mathrm{E}.\mathrm{ctr}$. When $\Pi'.\mathrm{E}$ is initialized, $st'_\mathrm{E}.\mathrm{ctr} \leftarrow 0$.
- $st'_\mathrm{D}.\mathrm{subst} := st_\mathrm{D}$, where st_D is the state in Π.
- $st'_\mathrm{D}.\mathrm{status}$. Once $st'_\mathrm{D}.\mathrm{status} = \mathsf{failed}$ it is not reset and all subsequently received messages are also immediately aborted.
- $st'_\mathrm{D}.\mathrm{sqnlist}$, an ordered list of sequence numbers previously received. It is required that $|st'_\mathrm{D}.\mathrm{sqnlist}| \geq 1$ after the first received sqn; i.e. the size of the ordered set is maintained at 1 or greater. When $\Pi'.\mathrm{E}$ is initialized, $st'_\mathrm{D}.\mathrm{sqnlist} \leftarrow \bot$.

Fig. 5. Construction P_{AEAD} of a level-i AEAD scheme Π'_i from a level-1 AEAD scheme Π and AEAD encoding scheme $\mathrm{Coding} = (\mathrm{Ecd}, \mathrm{Dcd})$, with TEST$i$ as shown in Fig. 3.

and asks no more than $q_\mathcal{B} = \frac{1}{2}q_e(q_e - 1)$ queries, and an adversary $\mathcal{F}$ that runs in time $t_\mathcal{F} \approx t$ and asks $q_\mathcal{F} = q$ queries, such that $\mathbf{Adv}^{\mathrm{aead}_i}_{P_{\mathrm{AEAD}}(\Pi, \mathrm{Coding}, \mathrm{TEST}i)}(\mathcal{A}) \leq \mathbf{Adv}^{\mathrm{aead}_1}_{\Pi}(\mathcal{F}) + \mathbf{Adv}^{\mathrm{collision}}_{\mathrm{Ecd}}(\mathcal{B})$.

The proof of Theorem 3 is omitted due to space restrictions.

4 Authenticated Encryption in TLS

The work of Paterson et al. [18] showed that the MAC-then-encode-then-encrypt mode of CBC encryption in TLS 1.2 (with sufficiently long MAC tags) is a secure length-hiding authenticated encryption (LHAE) scheme, assuming the encryption function is a strong pseudorandom permutation and the MAC is a pseudorandom function. Their definition corresponds to level 1 of our AEAD hierarchy. Several subsequent work on the provable security of TLS, such as that of Jager et al. [13] and Krawczyk et al. [18], assume that the TLS record layer is a secure *stateful* length-hiding authenticated encryption (sLHAE) scheme, corresponding to level 4 of our AEAD hierarchy. To our knowledge, there has as of yet been no formal connection between the LHAE result of Paterson et al. and the sLHAE requirement of subsequent works; we address that gap in this section by bringing sequence numbers into the modeling using the framework in the previous sections.

4.1   TLS Sequence Numbers and Authentication Level

The TLS record layer utilizes sequence numbers to ensure detection of deleted or reordered records [7, p. 94]. Being 64-bits long, sequence number exhaustion for any given connection is unlikely and the specification demands renegotiation should it occur. Sequence numbers are sent implicitly by inclusion under the MAC (or AEAD). When instantiated, "the first record transmitted under a particular connection state MUST use sequence number 0" [7, Sect. 6.1] and each subsequent record increments the sequence number. Sequence numbers are continuous across record types (application and alert).

When the ciphersuite uses MAC-then-encode-then-encrypt, the MAC tag is computed as follows, where k is the MAC key (either MAC_write_key or MAC_read_key, depending on the direction), sqn is the 64-bit sequence number, and m is the (possibly compressed) TLS plaintext object (called TLSCompressed) [7]: MAC(k, sqn $\|$ m.type $\|$ m.version $\|$ m.length $\|$ m.fragment). Since the sequence number is implicit, a receiver will check the MAC verification using the expected sequence number. If the check fails, a bad_record_mac alert (type 20) will be generated – an alert that is always fatal [7, Sect. 7.2.2].

When the ciphersuite is uses a combined AEAD scheme, the sequence number, as well as several other values, are included in the additional data field [7]: ad = sqn $\|$ m.type $\|$ m.version $\|$ m.length. The ciphertext is then $c \leftarrow$ Encrypt(k, m.length, ad, m.fragment, st_E). The sequence number is not transmitted in the ciphertext. AEAD decryption is applied using the expected sequence number. Decryption failure must also result in a bad_record_mac fatal alert [7, Sect. 6.2.3.3].

4.2   From TLS Level-1 AEAD to Level-4 AEAD

Paterson et al. [22] show that a simplified version of TLS MAC-then-encode-then-encrypt, which we call Π_{PRS} and describe in the top half of Fig. 6, satisfies level-1 AEAD security. By design, Π_{PRS} includes the sequence number field in the ad, but never initializes it as Π_{PRS} is not stateful. However, the TLS record layer protocol as actually used is stateful and, as such, ought to achieve a higher level of AEAD; namely, it should satisfy level-4 AEAD. The bottom half of Fig. 6 shows the TLS MAC-then-encode-then-encrypt record layer with the use of sequence numbers as specified in the standard.

Our framework allows us to immediately show that Π_{TLS} satisfies level-4 AEAD security: we incorporate the sequence numbers in an implicit AEAD encoding scheme Coding$_{TLS}$, and then view Π_{TLS} as the result of applying the P_{AEAD} construction to Π_{PRS} and Coding$_{TLS}$.

Define AEAD encoding scheme Coding$_{TLS}$ = (Ecd$_{TLS}$, Dcd$_{TLS}$) as follows:

– Ecd$_{TLS}$(sqn, ad, m) = (sqn$\|$ad, m)
– Dcd$_{TLS}$(sqnlist, sqn$\|$ad, m) = (sqn, ad, m, α)

where $\alpha = 1$ if and only if sqn and sqnlist satisfy TEST4 in Fig. 3, ad $\neq \perp$, and $m \neq \perp$.

$\Pi_{PRS}.\mathrm{E}(k, \ell, \mathsf{ad}, m, \perp)$:
1: $(k_m, k_e) \leftarrow k$
2: $t \leftarrow \mathrm{MAC}(k_m, \mathsf{ad}, m)$
3: $c \leftarrow \mathrm{E}(k_e, \ell, m, t)$
4: **return** $(c, \perp)$

$\Pi_{PRS}.\mathrm{D}(k, \mathsf{ad}, c, \perp)$:
1: $(k_m, k_e) \leftarrow k$
2: $(m, t, \alpha) \leftarrow \mathrm{D}(k_e, c)$
3: **if** $\mathrm{MAC}(k_m, \mathsf{ad}, m) \neq t$ **then**
4:     **return** $(\perp, 0, \perp)$
5: **return** $(m, \alpha, \perp)$

$\Pi_{TLS}.\mathrm{E}(k, \ell, \mathsf{ad}, m, st_\mathrm{E})$:
1: $(k_m, k_e) \leftarrow k$
2: $t \leftarrow \mathrm{MAC}(k_m, st_\mathrm{E}.\mathsf{ctr}\|\mathsf{ad}, m)$
3: $c \leftarrow \mathrm{E}(k_e, \ell, m, t)$
4: $st_\mathrm{E}.\mathsf{ctr} \leftarrow st_\mathrm{E}.\mathsf{ctr} + 1$
5: **return** (c, st_E)

$\Pi_{TLS}.\mathrm{D}(k, \mathsf{ad}, c, st_\mathrm{D})$:
1: $(k_m, k_e) \leftarrow k$
2: **if** $st_\mathrm{D}.\mathsf{status} = \mathsf{failed}$ **then**
3:     **return** $(\perp, 0, st_\mathrm{D})$
4: $(m, t, \alpha) \leftarrow \mathrm{D}(k_e, c)$
5: **if** $\mathrm{MAC}(k_m, st_\mathrm{D}.\mathsf{ctr}\|\mathsf{ad}, m) \neq t$ **then**
6:     $\alpha \leftarrow 0$
7: **if** $\alpha = 0$ **then**
8:     $st_\mathrm{D}.\mathsf{status} \leftarrow \mathsf{failed}$
9:     **return** $(\perp, 0, st_\mathrm{D})$
10: $st_\mathrm{D}.\mathsf{ctr} \leftarrow st_\mathrm{D}.\mathsf{ctr} + 1$
11: **return** $(m, \alpha, st_\mathrm{D})$

Fig. 6. Construction of AEAD schemes Π_{PRS} (Paterson et al. [22] variant of TLS MAC-then-encode-then-encrypt) and Π_{TLS} (TLS MAC-then-encode-then-encrypt) from encode-then-encrypt scheme (E, D).

Theorem 4. $\Pi_{TLS} = P_{AEAD}(\Pi_{PRS}, \mathrm{Coding}_{TLS}, \mathrm{TEST4})$.

Theorem 4 follows semantically comparing Π_{TLS} and the scheme resulting from the construction $P_{AEAD}(\Pi_{PRS}, \mathrm{Coding}_{TLS}, \mathrm{TEST4})$.

Clearly, Ecd_{TLS} is collision-resistant due to the unambiguous parsing of sqn as a fixed-length 64-bit value. We can thus apply Theorem 3 to obtain Corollary 1.

Corollary 1. *The TLS record layer with MAC-then-encode-then-encrypt in CBC mode satisfies level-4 AEAD security. Specifically, let $\mathcal{A}$ be an adversary algorithm that runs in time t against Π_{TLS}. Then there exists an adversary $\mathcal{F}$ that runs in time $t_\mathcal{F} \approx t$ such that* $\mathbf{Adv}^{\mathsf{aead}_4}_{\Pi_{TLS}}(\mathcal{A}) \leq \mathbf{Adv}^{\mathsf{aead}_1}_{\Pi_{PRS}}(\mathcal{F})$.

From Paterson et al. [22] we know that the TLS record layer encryption in MAC-then-encode-then-encrypt CBC mode satisfies AEAD level-1 security when a secure cipher and message authentication code is used. Combined with Corollary 1, this means that the sLHAE security definition used by Jager et al. [13] and Krawczyk et al. [18] in their analyses of full TLS ciphersuites is achieved, and thus TLS is ACCE secure in this scenario.

References

1. Albrecht, M.R., Paterson, K.G., Watson, G.J.: Plaintext recovery attacks against SSH. In: 2009 IEEE Symposium on Security and Privacy, pp. 16–26. IEEE Computer Society Press, May 2009

2. Badertscher, C., Matt, C., Maurer, U., Rogaway, P., Tackmann, B.: Augmented secure channels and the goal of the TLS 1.3 record layer. Cryptology ePrint Archive, Report 2015/394 (2015). http://eprint.iacr.org/2015/394

3. Bellare, M., Kohno, T., Namprempre, C.: Authenticated encryption in SSH: provably fixing the SSH binary packet protocol. In: Atluri, V. (ed.) CCS 2002, pp. 1–11. ACM Press, November 2002

4. Bellare, M., Namprempre, C.: Authenticated encryption: relations among notions and analysis of the generic composition paradigm. In: Okamoto, T. (ed.) ASIACRYPT 2000. LNCS, vol. 1976, pp. 531–545. Springer, Heidelberg (2000)

5. Boldyreva, A., Degabriele, J.P., Paterson, K.G., Stam, M.: Security of symmetric encryption in the presence of ciphertext fragmentation. In: Pointcheval, D., Johansson, T. (eds.) EUROCRYPT 2012. LNCS, vol. 7237, pp. 682–699. Springer, Heidelberg (2012)

6. Canetti, R., Krawczyk, H.: Analysis of key-exchange protocols and their use for building secure channels. In: Pfitzmann, B. (ed.) EUROCRYPT 2001. LNCS, vol. 2045, pp. 453–474. Springer, Heidelberg (2001)

7. Dierks, T., Rescorla, E.: The Transport Layer Security (TLS) Protocol Version 1.2, RFC 5426 (2008). https://tools.ietf.org/html/rfc5426

8. Fischlin, M., Günther, F., Marson, G.A., Paterson, K.G.: Data is a stream: security of stream-based channels. In: Gennaro, R., Robshaw, M. (eds.) CRYPTO 2015. LNCS, vol. 9216, pp. 545–564. Springer, Heidelberg (2015)

9. Fleischmann, E., Forler, C., Lucks, S.: McOE: a family of almost foolproof on-line authenticated encryption schemes. In: Canteaut, A. (ed.) FSE 2012. LNCS, vol. 7549, pp. 196–215. Springer, Heidelberg (2012)

10. Hoang, V.T., Krovetz, T., Rogaway, P.: Robust authenticated-encryption: AEZ and the problem that it solves. Cryptology ePrint Archive, Report 2014/793 (2014). http://eprint.iacr.org/2014/793

11. Hoang, V.T., Reyhanitabar, R., Rogaway, P., Vizár, D.: Online authenticated-encryption and its nonce-reuse misuse-resistance. Cryptology ePrint Archive, Report 2015/189 (2015). http://eprint.iacr.org/2015/189

12. IEEE 802.11: Wireless LAN Medium Access Control (MAC) and Physical Layer (PHY) Specifications (2012). http://dx.org/10.1109/IEEESTD.2012.6178212

13. Jager, T., Kohlar, F., Schäge, S., Schwenk, J.: On the security of TLS-DHE in the standard model. In: Safavi-Naini, R., Canetti, R. (eds.) CRYPTO 2012. LNCS, vol. 7417, pp. 273–293. Springer, Heidelberg (2012)

14. Katz, J., Yung, M.: Unforgeable encryption and chosen ciphertext secure modes of operation. In: Schneier, B. (ed.) FSE 2000. LNCS, vol. 1978, pp. 284–299. Springer, Heidelberg (2001)

15. Kent, S.: IP Authentication Header, RFC 4302 (2005). https://tools.ietf.org/html/rfc4302

16. Kohno, T., Palacio, A., Black, J.: Building secure cryptographic transforms, or how to encrypt and MAC. Cryptology ePrint Archive, Report 2003/177 (2003). http://eprint.iacr.org/2003/177

17. Krawczyk, H.: The order of encryption and authentication for protecting communications (or: how secure is SSL?). In: Kilian, J. (ed.) CRYPTO 2001. LNCS, vol. 2139, pp. 310–331. Springer, Heidelberg (2001)

18. Krawczyk, H., Paterson, K.G., Wee, H.: On the security of the TLS protocol: a systematic analysis. In: Canetti, R., Garay, J.A. (eds.) CRYPTO 2013, Part I. LNCS, vol. 8042, pp. 429–448. Springer, Heidelberg (2013)

19. Lychev, R., Jero, S., Boldyreva, A., Nita-Rotaru, C.: How secure and quick is QUIC? Provable security and performance analyses. In: 2015 IEEE Symposium on Security and Privacy, pp. 214–231. IEEE Computer Society Press, May 2015
20. Maurer, U., Tackmann, B.: On the soundness of authenticate-then-encrypt: formalizing the malleability of symmetric encryption. In: Al-Shaer, E., Keromytis, A.D., Shmatikov, V. (eds.) CCS 2010, pp. 505–515. ACM Press, October 2010
21. Namprempre, C.: Secure channels based on authenticated encryption schemes: a simple characterization. In: Zheng, Y. (ed.) ASIACRYPT 2002. LNCS, vol. 2501, pp. 515–532. Springer, Heidelberg (2002)
22. Paterson, K.G., Ristenpart, T., Shrimpton, T.: Tag size *Does* matter: attacks and proofs for the TLS record protocol. In: Lee, D.H., Wang, X. (eds.) ASIACRYPT 2011. LNCS, vol. 7073, pp. 372–389. Springer, Heidelberg (2011)
23. Rescorla, E., Modadugu, N.: Datagram Transport Layer Security, RFC 4347 (2006). https://tools.ietf.org/html/rfc4347
24. Rescorla, E., Modadugu, N.: Datagram Transport Layer Security Version 1.2, RFC 6347 (2012). https://tools.ietf.org/html/rfc6347
25. Rogaway, P.: Authenticated-encryption with associated-data. In: Atluri, V. (ed.) CCS 2002, pp. 98–107. ACM Press, November 2002
26. Rogaway, P., Bellare, M., Black, J., Krovetz, T.: OCB: a block-cipher mode of operation for efficient authenticated encryption. In: CCS 2001, pp. 196–205. ACM Press, November 2001
27. Rogaway, P., Shrimpton, T.: A provable-security treatment of the key-wrap problem. In: Vaudenay, S. (ed.) EUROCRYPT 2006. LNCS, vol. 4004, pp. 373–390. Springer, Heidelberg (2006)
28. Shrimpton, T.: A characterization of authenticated-encryption as a form of chosen-ciphertext security. Cryptology ePrint Archive, Report 2004/272 (2004). http://eprint.iacr.org/2004/272
29. The Chromium Projects: QUIC, a multiplexed stream transport over UDP. https://www.chromium.org/quic. Accessed 2015

Searchable Symmetric Encryption

Dynamic Symmetric Searchable Encryption from Constrained Functional Encryption

Sebastian Gajek[1,2]([✉])

[1] NEC Research Laboratories Europe, Heidelberg, Germany
[2] Flensburg University of Applied Sciences, Flensburg, Germany
sebastian.gajek@gmail.com

Abstract. Searchable symmetric encryption allows a party to encrypt data while maintaining the ability to partially search for over it. We present a scheme that balances efficiency, privacy, and the set of admissible operations: Our scheme searches in time logarithmic in the size of the word dictionary (i.e., it is independent of the number of files), satisfies the strong security notion of search pattern privacy against adaptive attacks, supports complex search queries over a Boolean algebra (including conjunctions of multiple search words), provides the full functionality of addition and deletion of search words and identifiers, and is provably secure in the standard model.

At the heart of our system lies a novel cryptographic tool called constrained functional encryption (CFE) over the message plaintext. In a CFE system, the decryptability of ciphertexts is constrained to particular ciphertexts having been evaluated in a very concrete way. We give a definitional framework including a relaxed indistinguishability-based security notion. Our construction is proved secure based on the subgroup decision problem in bilinear groups for the class of inner products functions.

Keywords: Searchable encryption · Functional encryption · Pairings · Dual vector spaces

1 Introduction

A searchable encryption scheme (SSE) allows a party to encrypt a message, index the ciphertext, and at any point in time to efficiently look for the plaintext by issuing a search token encoding a search criterion. In addition, a searchable symmetric encryption scheme is dynamic, if it supports updates of the encrypted database. SSE is an ideal tool in settings where a party would like to outsource some data while it still wishes to maintain some privacy guarantees.

The best-possible notion of privacy hides the memory access during searches and updates. In particular, a server should not be able to tell whether a client retrieves a document which it already obtained from a previous query. One calls this property privacy of the *access pattern*. Satisfying access pattern privacy in its full generality requires oblivious RAMs introduced by Goldreich and

© Springer International Publishing Switzerland 2016
K. Sako (Ed.): CT-RSA 2016, LNCS 9610, pp. 75–89, 2016.
DOI: 10.1007/978-3-319-29485-8_5

Ostrovsky [6]. Unfortunately, as it is often the case, general-purpose solutions are inefficient and rather of theoretical interest (although significant steps have been made towards practical ORAMs [11]). A weaker notion, known as privacy of the *search pattern*, hides any information about the encoded keywords. In particular, a server should not be able to tell whether a client already has searched for the same word. Dynamic SSE schemes additionally ask for *update privacy*. The system shall leak no information about the documents and keywords through the execution of update protocols.

Apart from privacy, relevant design criteria for SSE systems include support of comprehensive search queries and scalability aspects measured in the communication and search complexity. Consider an encrypted version of a SQL-database. Search queries are typically formulated in a regular language, allowing for comprehensive expressions over multiple keywords. In file systems, such as Google's Drive and Amazon's S3, millions of users push, pull and delete files. Here, the desiderata is a low communication complexity for searches and updates. Ideally, the operation shall require a single round of communication, as most clients connect through high latency networks.

PREVIOUS WORK. The research community has proposed different SSE schemes, each one addressing different trade-offs between security, functionality and efficiency. While prior SSE schemes achieve sublinear search time that scales only with the number of documents matching the query [2–4,7,8], most of them lack of important properties usually required in practice like the ability to update the EDB, expressiveness in search queries and the capacity to run a search parallel searching. In Table 1 we give a comparison of the relevant schemes.

The exception is the ground-breaking work of Cash et al. [2,3]. In [3] they provide an SSE scheme with truly practical search capability and support of conjunctive search queries. Using techniques from multi-party computation they construct a scheme with search complexity $\mathcal{O}(r)$ where r is the number of documents matching a search word. They reduce the communication complexity with a clever pre-processing technique. Later Cash et al. [2] propose efficient SSE schemes that support updates to the encrypted database, i.e. dynamics. The protocols resemble previous techniques from [3].

OUR RESULTS. In this work we construct a searchable symmetric encryption system for searching on encrypted that is

1. *Search efficient.* Searching the encrypted database for all files containing a single keyword is independent of the number of files. It is bounded by the size of the word dictionary $\mathcal{W}$, i.e. $\mathcal{O}(\log |\mathcal{W}|)$ where the size of dictionary is fixed in advance.
2. *Communication efficient.* Communicating a search and update requires a single round of communication. A search queries is succinct. It contains $2\log |\mathcal{W}|$ elements of a pairing-friendly group $\mathbb{G}$.
3. *Private.* Searching for all files containing a word leaks no information about the searched word. Search tokens are probabilistic and indistinguishable from prior search queries.

Table 1. Comparison of SSE schemes for a single keyword [2, Fig. 1]. Notation: In security Ad means adaptive security in the standard model, Ad(ROM) means adaptive security in the random oracle model, NonAd means non-adaptive security; Leakage is leakage from encrypted database only; Search time is the complexity of the search algorithm while Comm. is the number of communication rounds; Update measures the communication complexity; Formula asks for support of Boolean expression; n = # documents, $m = |\mathcal{W}|$, $r = |\mathbf{DB}(w)|$, $N = \sum_w |\mathbf{DB}(w)|$, $M = max_w|\mathbf{DB}(w)|$, p = # processors, $|\mathcal{W}_{id}| = \#$ keyword changes in an update, $d_w = \#$ times the searched-for-keyword has been added/deleted.

Scheme	Security	Leakage	Dyn?	Index size	Search time/comm.	Update	Formula?
CGKO'06-1 [4]	NonAd	m, N	No	$\mathcal{O}(N + m)$	$\mathcal{O}(r)$, $\mathcal{O}(1)$	–	No
CGKO'06-2 [4]	Ad	Mn	No	$\mathcal{O}(Mn)$	$\mathcal{O}(r)$, $\mathcal{O}(r)$	–	No
KPR'12 [8]	Ad(ROM)	m,N	Yes	$\mathcal{O}(N + m)$	$\mathcal{O}(r)$, $\mathcal{O}(1)$	$\mathcal{O}(|\mathcal{W}_{id}|)$	No
KP'13 [7]	Ad(ROM)	m,n	Yes	$\mathcal{O}(mn)$	$\mathcal{O}((r \log n)/p)$, $\mathcal{O}(1)$	$\mathcal{O}(|\mathcal{W}_{id}| + m \log n)$	No
CJJJ+'14-1 [2]	NonAd, Ad(ROM)	N	No	$\mathcal{O}(N)$	$\mathcal{O}(r/p)$, $\mathcal{O}(1)$	–	Yes
CJJJ+'14-2 [2]	Ad	N	No	$\mathcal{O}(N)$	$\mathcal{O}(r/p)$, $\mathcal{O}(r)$	–	Yes
CJJJ+'14-3 [2]	NonAd, Ad(ROM)	N	Yes	$\mathcal{O}(N)$	$\mathcal{O}((r + d_w)/p)$, $\mathcal{O}(1)$	$\mathcal{O}(|\mathcal{W}_{id}| + m \log n)$	Yes
This work	Ad	N	Yes	$\mathcal{O}(m)$	$\mathcal{O}((\log m)/p)$, $\mathcal{O}(1)$	$\mathcal{O}((|\mathcal{W}_{id}| \log m)/p)$	Yes

4. *Dynamic.* Addition and deletion takes as much time and communication as searching for the file.
5. *Functional.* Searching for all files containing multiple keywords expressed as a Boolean formula of size $|\mathcal{W}_{id}|$ takes search time $\mathcal{O}(|\mathcal{W}_{id}| \cdot \log(|\mathcal{W}|))$.

Our scheme achieves the results by expressing the data structure as an *encrypted binary tree* (while prior work followed a linked list approach [2–4,7,8]). To traverse the encrypted tree, we construct a function-private secret-key functional encryption scheme for the inner product functionality. The system supports any arbitrary polynomial number of key queries and message queries with the property that the functional keys decrypt specific ciphertexts only. Our construction makes use of symmetric bilinear maps. The security notion we prove for our construction is a natural indistinguishability-based notion, and we establish it under the Subgroup Decision Assumption. To obtain correctness for our scheme, we assume that inner products will be contained in a polynomially-sized range. This assumption is sufficient for our application, as the tree is binary.

2 Preliminaries

2.1 Bilinear Groups

We recall some facts about bilinear groups and vector spaces.

Definition 1 (Bilinear Group). *A bilinear group is generated by a probabilistic algorithm $\mathcal{G}$ that takes as input a security parameter λ and outputs three abelian groups $\mathbb{G}, \mathbb{G}_1, \mathbb{G}_T$ with $\mathbb{G}_1 \subset \mathbb{G}$. The algorithm also computes an efficiently computable map $e : \mathbb{G} \times \mathbb{G} \to \mathbb{G}_T$ that is:*

– *bilinear: For all $g, h \in \mathbb{G}$, $x, y \in \mathbb{F}_p$ we have $e(g^x, h^y) = e(g, h)^{xy}$*
– *non-degenerate: For all $g, h \in \mathbb{G}$, we have $e(g, h) \neq 1$.*

We assume that group operations and random sampling in each group is efficiently computable and denote the output of $\mathcal{G}$ as $(\mathbb{G}, \mathbb{G}_1, \mathbb{G}_T, e)$.

In additive notation, a prime order bilinear group is closed under addition and scalar multiplication. It gives raise to a vector space over $\mathbb{G}$. To this end, we introduce some additional notation. Let $\mathbf{x} = (x_1, \ldots, x_n) \in \mathbb{F}_p^n$ be an exponent vector. We write $g^{\mathbf{x}} = (g^{x_1}, \ldots, g^{x_n})$ for the n-dimensional group vector in $\mathbb{G}$. For any "scalar" $\alpha \in \mathbb{F}_p$ we use the notation $(g^{\mathbf{x}})^\alpha$ to denote the scalar product $(g^{\alpha x_1}, \ldots, g^{\alpha x_n})$. If the context is clear, we use the term vector interchangeably for group elements and exponents.

Looking at bilinear groups as vector spaces allows us to express linear mappings between such spaces. One such linear mapping is the "dot" product (sometimes referred to as inner product in Euclidean spaces), defined as the sum of the products of the corresponding entries of two vectors. Geometrically, it is the product of the Euclidean magnitudes of the two vectors and the cosine of the angle between them. We define the analog of the dot product between two n-dimensional vectors in bilinear groups.

Definition 2 (Dot Product Group). *A dot product group is a bilinear group generated by the group generator $\mathcal{G}_*$. The generator also outputs an efficiently computable algorithm $d : \mathbb{G}^n \times \mathbb{G}^n \to \mathbb{G}_T$. The algorithm computes the "dot product" between two vectors $g^{\mathbf{x}}, h^{\mathbf{y}}$, written $g^{\mathbf{x}} * h^{\mathbf{y}}$, as*

$$d(g^{\mathbf{x}}, h^{\mathbf{y}}) = \prod_{i=1}^n e(g, h)^{x_i y_i} = e(g, h)^{\mathbf{x} * \mathbf{y}}$$

The dot product fulfils the following properties if $\mathbf{x}, \mathbf{y}$ and $\mathbf{z}$ are "vectors" in $\mathbb{F}_p^n$ and α, β are "scalars" in $\mathbb{F}_p$:

– *commutative: $g^{\mathbf{x}} * h^{\mathbf{y}} = h^{\mathbf{y}} * g^{\mathbf{x}}$*
– *distributive (over multiplication): $g^{\mathbf{x}} * (h^{\mathbf{y}} \ h^{\mathbf{z}}) = (g^{\mathbf{x}} * h^{\mathbf{y}}) (g^{\mathbf{x}} * h^{\mathbf{z}})$*
– *scalar multiplication: $g^{\alpha \mathbf{x}} * h^{\beta \mathbf{y}} = (g^{\mathbf{x}})^\alpha * (h^{\mathbf{y}})^\beta = (g^{\mathbf{x}} * h^{\mathbf{y}})^{\alpha \beta}$*
– *bilinear: $g^x * (h^{\alpha y} \ h^z) = (g^x * h^y)^\alpha \ (g^x * h^z)$.*

2.2 Dual Spaces

We will employ the concept of dual pairing vector spaces from [10]. We choose two random sets of vectors: $\mathbb{B} := \{\mathbf{b}_1, \ldots, \mathbf{b}_m\}$ and $\mathbb{B}^* := \{\mathbf{b}^*, \ldots, \mathbf{b}_m^*\}$ subject to the constraint that they are "dual orthonormal" in the following sense:

$$\langle \mathbf{b}_i, \mathbf{b}_i^* \rangle = 1 \bmod p \text{ for all } i$$
$$\langle \mathbf{b}_i, \mathbf{b}_j^* \rangle = 0 \bmod p \text{ for all } i \neq j$$

where $\langle \cdot, \cdot \rangle$ denotes the dot product.

We note that choosing sets $(\mathbb{B}, \mathbb{B}^*)$ at random from sets satisfying these dual orthonormality constraints can be realized by choosing a set of n vectors $\mathbb{B}$ uniformly at random from $\mathbb{F}_p^n$ (these vectors will be linearly independent with high probability), then determining each vector of $\mathbb{B}^*$ from its orthonormality constraints (these vectors will be close to the uniform distribution with high probability). We will denote choosing random dual orthonormal sets this way as: $(\mathbb{B}, \mathbb{B}^*) \leftarrow \mathcal{D}ual(\mathbb{F}_p^n)$.

2.3   Subset Membership Problem

The problem of deciding membership in a subset appears in various forms in cryptography. One canonical example is the decisional Diffie-Helman (DDH) problem in a group $\mathbb{G}$ of prime order p generated by g: Given $(g, g^x, g^y, T_b) \in \mathbb{G}$ the decisional Diffie-Hellman problem asks to decide if $T_0 = g^{xy}$ or $T_1 = g^z$ for random $x, y, z \leftarrow_R \mathbb{F}_p$. If we define the group G to be generated by (g, g) and the subgroup G_1 generated by (g, g^x), then the DDH problem asks to decide if (g^y, T_b) is a random member in G or G_1.

We recall Freeman's definition of the subgroup decision problem in the setting of symmetric pairing-friendly groups [5]. The assumption states that it is infeasible to distinguish a random sample from group G and a random sample from the subgroup $G_1 \subset G$. It has been used to prove security of the Boneh-Goh-Nissim encryption system and many other applications [1,5].

Definition 3 (Subgroup Decision Assumption). *Let $\mathcal{G}_*$ be a symmetric bilinear dot product group generator. We define the following distribution*

$$param := (\mathbb{G}, \mathbb{G}_1, \mathbb{G}_T, e, d) \leftarrow \mathcal{G}(1^\lambda)$$
$$G = \mathbb{G} \quad G_1 = \mathbb{G}_1$$
$$T_0 \leftarrow_R G_1 \quad T_1 \leftarrow_R G$$

We define the advantage of an algorithm $\mathcal{A}$ in solving the subgroup decision problem to be

$$\mathsf{Adv}^{\mathcal{A}}_{\mathsf{SDP}}(\lambda) = \left| Pr\left[\mathcal{A}(param, T_0) = 1\right] - Pr\left[\mathcal{A}(param, T_1) = 1\right] \right|$$

We say that $\mathcal{G}$ satisfies the subgroup decision assumption, if $\mathsf{Adv}^{\mathcal{A}}_{\mathsf{SDP}}(\lambda)$ is a negligible function of λ for any polynomial-time adversary $\mathcal{A}$.

Note, if the subgroup decision problem is infeasible in $\mathbb{G}$, then it is in $\mathbb{G}_T$ as well.

2.4   Cryptographic Building Blocks

Our searchable encryption will make use of pseudo-random objects. These can be efficiently generated with pseudo-random functions.

Definition 4 (Pseudo-random Function). *Let* $\mathsf{PRF} : \{0,1\}^* \times \{0,1\}^* \rightarrow \{0,1\}^*$ *be an efficient, length-preserving, keyed function. We define the advantage of distinguisher* $\mathcal{A}$ *as*

$$\mathsf{Adv}^{\mathcal{A}}_{\mathsf{PRF}}(\lambda) = \left| Pr[\mathcal{A}^{\mathsf{PRF}_s(\cdot)}(1^\lambda) = 1] - Pr[\mathcal{A}^{f(\cdot)}(1^\lambda) = 1] \right|$$

where the seed s *is chosen at random from* $\{0,1\}^*$ *and* f *is uniformly chosen at random from the set of functions mapping* λ *strings to* λ *strings. We say that* PRF *is a pseudorandom function, if* $\mathsf{Adv}^{\mathcal{A}}_{\mathsf{PRF}}(\lambda)$ *is a negligible function of* λ *for all probabilistic polynomial-time distinguishers* $\mathcal{A}$.

3 Constrained Functional Encryption over the Message Plaintext

3.1 Syntax

We will consider a specialization of the general definition of functional encryption to the particular functionality of computing dot products of n-length message plaintext vectors over a finite field $\mathbb{F}_p$ with one caveat. Whereas the functional encryption paradigm supports the generation of keys for the decryption of a particular function for any ciphertext, our notion additionally constraints the decryptability to a particular ciphertext.

To make the difference to functional encryption clear, we will refer to the scheme as constrained functional encryption. A private key functional encryption scheme for this functionality will have the following algorithms:

Definition 5 (Constrained Functional Encryption). *A constrained functional encryption system* CFE *consists of four algorithms* (Setup, KeyGen, Enc, Dec), *such that*

- *The* Setup *algorithm will take in the security parameter* λ *and the vector length a parameter* n *(a positive integer that is polynomial in* λ*). It will produce a master secret key* MSK.
- *The encryption algorithm* Enc *will take in the master secret key* MSK, *and a vector* $\boldsymbol{x} \in \mathbb{F}_p^n$. *It produces a ciphertext* $\boldsymbol{CT}_{x,q}$ *and an internal state* st_q *for the* q-*th ciphertext. (We will use counter* q *to point to a ciphertext.)*
- *The key generation algorithm* KeyGen *will take in the master secret key* MSK, *a vector* $\boldsymbol{y} \in \mathbb{F}_p^n$ *and the internal state* st_q. *It produces a secret key* $\boldsymbol{SK}_{y,q}$.
- *The decryption algorithm* Dec *will take in a secret key* $\boldsymbol{SK}_{y,q}$ *and a ciphertext* $\boldsymbol{CT}_{x,q}$. *It will output a value* $z \in \mathbb{F}_p$.

For correctness, we require that for all $\mathbf{x}, \mathbf{y} \in \mathbb{F}_p^n$, all MSK in the support of Setup$(1^\lambda, n)$, all pairs $(\mathbf{CT}_{\mathbf{x},q}, st_q)$ result of calling Enc$(MSK, \mathbf{x})$, all decryption keys $\mathbf{SK}_{\mathbf{y},q}$ result of calling KeyGen$(MSK, \mathbf{y}, st_q)$, we have

$$\mathsf{Dec}(\mathbf{SK}_{\mathbf{y},q}, \mathbf{CT}_{\mathbf{x},q}) = \langle \mathbf{x}, \mathbf{y} \rangle$$

3.2   Security

We will consider an indistinguishability-based security notion defined by a game between a challenger and an attacker. At the beginning of the game the challenger calls $\mathsf{Setup}(1^\lambda, n)$ to produce the master secret MSK. The challenger also selects a random bit b. Throughout the game, the attacker can (adaptively) interact with two oracles.

- To make a *ciphertext query*, the attacker submits two vectors $\mathbf{x}^0, \mathbf{x}^1 \in \mathbb{F}_p^n$ to the challenger, who then runs $\mathsf{Enc}(MSK, \mathbf{x}^b)$ and returns the resulting ciphertext $\mathbf{CT}_{\mathbf{x}^b, q}$ to the attacker. The challenger stores the state information st_q for the q-th query.
- To make a *key query*, it submits two vectors $\mathbf{y}^0, \mathbf{y}^1 \in \mathbb{F}_p^n$ along a pointer to the q-th ciphertext query to the challenger, who then runs $\mathsf{KeyGen}(MSK, \mathbf{y}^b, st_q)$ and returns the resulting $\mathbf{SK}_{\mathbf{y}^b}$ to the attacker.

The attacker can make any polynomial number of key and ciphertext queries throughout the game. Note, the result of each ciphertext query is the generation of a ciphertext plus some internal state. We denote by st_q the state information related to the q-th ciphertext. The challenger uses st_q to answer key queries linked to the q-th ciphertext. In other words, the decryption key only decrypts the inner product when applied to the q-th ciphertext. This captures the idea of constrained decryptability of ciphertexts. At the end of the game, the attacker must submit a guess b' for the bit b. We require that for all ciphertext queries $\mathbf{x}^0, \mathbf{x}^1$ and key queries $\mathbf{y}^0, \mathbf{y}^1$, it must hold that

$$\langle \mathbf{x}^0, \mathbf{y}^0 \rangle = \langle \mathbf{x}^1, \mathbf{y}^1 \rangle$$

The attacker's advantage is defined to be the $\left| \Pr[b = b'] - \frac{1}{2} \right|$.

Definition 6 *We say a private key functional encryption scheme for dot products over $\mathbb{F}_p^n$ has indistinguishable ciphertexts in presence of constrained decryption keys (or simply, is deemed secure), if any PPT attacker's advantage in the above game is negligible as a function of the security parameter λ.*

3.3   Construction

We now present our construction in symmetric bilinear groups. We will choose random dual orthonormal bases $(\mathbf{b}_1, \mathbf{b}_2) \in \mathbb{B}$ and $(\mathbf{b}_1^*, \mathbf{b}_2^*) \in \mathbb{B}^*$ that will be used in the exponent to encode the message and one-time key vectors respectively. Vectors will be encoded twice to create space for a hybrid security proof, resulting in a ciphertext $(A_i, B_i)_{i=1}^n$. A bit more concrete, the first bases $(\mathbf{b}_1, \mathbf{b}_1^*)$ encode the message vector $\mathbf{x}$ and $\mathbf{x}$, whereas the second bases $(\mathbf{b}_2, \mathbf{b}_2^*)$ encode the key vector $\mathbf{s}$ and $\mathbf{u}$.

We view it as a core feature of our construction that the structure of messages and keys in our scheme is perfectly symmetric, just on different sides of dual orthonormal bases. This gives raise to a scheme that is both homomorphic to the message plaintext and key with respect to addition and multiplication.

To generate a decryption key for an inner product function, we encrypt the vector $\mathbf{y}$ under the key vector $\mathbf{v}$ and $\mathbf{t}$, obtaining the "ciphertext" $(C_i, D_i)_{i=1}^n$, and add a cancellation term $E = e(g_2, h_2)^{\langle \mathbf{s}, \mathbf{t} \rangle}$ plus the base $F = e(g_1, h_1)$ for the discrete log computation. Decryption first "homomorphically" evaluates the inner product over the A and D elements. (The B and C elements are used in the proof.) The result is a ciphertext encoding the inner products of the message and key vectors. Next decryption just cancels out the key component E and computes the discrete log to the base F.

We will only require decryptions of $\langle \mathbf{x}, \mathbf{y} \rangle$ from a fixed polynomial range of values inside $\mathbb{F}_p$, as this will allow a decryption algorithm to compute it as a discrete log in a group where discrete log is generally hard. Hence, we expect the range of $\langle \mathbf{x}, \mathbf{y} \rangle$ to be small, say an integer in the set $\{0, \ldots, T\}$. Using Pollard's lambda method the computation of the discrete log takes expected time $\tilde{\mathcal{O}}(\sqrt{T})$ or alternatively space $\mathcal{O}(T)$ by storing a look up table for the T entries.

- Setup($1^\lambda, n$): On input the security parameter 1^λ and the dimension n, compute a symmetric bilinear dot product group $(\mathbb{G}, \mathbb{G}_1, \mathbb{G}_T, e, d) \leftarrow \mathcal{G}_*(1^\lambda)$ with $|\mathbb{G}| = p$. Choose generators $g_1, h_1 \in \mathbb{G}$ and $g_2, h_2 \in \mathbb{G}_1$. Sample at random orthonormal base $\mathbb{B}, \mathbb{B}^* \leftarrow \mathcal{D}ual(\mathbb{F}_p^2)$. The algorithm outputs the master secret MSK as $\mathbb{B}, \mathbb{B}^*, g_1, g_2, h_1, h_2, p, n$.
- Enc($MSK, \mathbf{x}$): To encrypt a message $\mathbf{x} \in \mathbb{F}_p^n$ under secret key MSK, choose random vectors $\mathbf{s}_q, \mathbf{u}_q \in \mathbb{F}_p^n$. Output ciphertext

$$\{A_i = (g_1^{\mathbf{b}_1})^{x_i}(g_2^{\mathbf{b}_2})^{s_i}, \ B_i = (h_1^{\mathbf{b}_1^*})^{x_i}(h_2^{\mathbf{b}_2^*})^{u_i}\}_{i=1}^n$$

and store the random vectors $st_q \leftarrow (\mathbf{s}_q, \mathbf{u}_q)$.
- KeyGen($MSK, \mathbf{y}, st_q$): To generate a decryption key for the q-th ciphertext under master secret MSK for vector $\mathbf{y} \in \mathbb{F}_p^n$, the algorithm chooses random vectors $\mathbf{t}, \mathbf{v} \in \mathbb{F}_p^n$ and sets the secret key $SK_{\mathbf{y}, q}$ as

$$\{C_i = (g_1^{\mathbf{b}_1})^{y_i}(g_2^{\mathbf{b}_2})^{v_i}, \ D_i = (h_1^{\mathbf{b}_1^*})^{y_i}(h_2^{\mathbf{b}_2^*})^{t_i}\}_{i=1}^n, \ E = e(g_2, h_2)^{\mathbf{s}_q \mathbf{t}}, \ F = e(g_1, h_1)$$

- Dec($SK_{\mathbf{y}, q}, CT$): To decrypt a ciphertext $\mathbf{CT}_{\mathbf{x}, q} = (A, B)$ with secret key $SK_{\mathbf{y}, q} = (C, D, E, F)$, compute

$$\prod_{i=1}^n \frac{d(A_i, D_i)}{E}$$

and return the discrete log to the base $F = e(g_1, h_1)$.

We would like to comment on the scheme:

- The above construction is *stateful*. It requires the encryptor to store the key vectors $st_q = (\mathbf{s}_q, \mathbf{u}_q)$ for every ciphertext. For efficient realizations of KeyGen one may reduce the storage complexity and re-compute the state using standard key derivation techniques. That is, instead of sampling vectors $\mathbf{s}_q, \mathbf{u}_q$ uniformly at random from $\mathbb{F}_p$, run a pseudorandom function $\mathsf{PRF}(k_i, q)$ for $i \in \{s, u\}$ where the k_i's are part of the master secret MSK and q is a pointer to the ciphertext.

- Some emerging applications ask to compute a predicate $P_{\mathbf{x}} : \mathbb{F}_p^n \rightarrow \{0, 1\}$ from the class of predicates $\mathcal{P} = \{P_{\mathbf{x}} | \mathbf{x} \in \mathbb{F}_p^n\}$ where $P_{\mathbf{x}}(\mathbf{y}) = 1$ if $\langle \mathbf{x}, \mathbf{y} \rangle = 0$ and $P_{\mathbf{x}}(\mathbf{y}) = 0$ otherwise. It has been shown that this way one can evaluate degree n polynomials and 2-CNF/DNF formuals [9]. Our scheme supports efficient predicate tests without computing the discrete log by comparing the output of the decryption to $F^0 = e(g_1, h_1)^0$.

We prove the following main theorem in the full version.

Theorem 1. *Assume the SDA assumption holds in $\mathcal{G}$, then the above scheme is secure.*

4   Dynamic Searchable Symmetric Encryption

A searchable encryption allows a client to encrypt data in such a way that it can later generate search tokens to send as queries to a storage server. Given a search token, the server can search over the encrypted data and return the appropriate encrypted files. Symmetric searchable encryption systems typically follow a blue print (at least when the system tolerates leakage of access patterns): One first encrypts the data with a scheme supporting pseudorandom ciphertexts[1] and tags ciphertexts with words. Next, one builds up a "cryptographic" data structure with word-identifier pairs. Each identifier points to a ciphertext (or set thereof). Then building a searchable encryption system boils down to designing search mechanisms for the data structure. Throughout the remainder of the paper, we implement the idea and define searchable encryption with respect to searching for identifiers in a data structure.

4.1   Syntax

We follow the notation of Cash et al. A database $\mathbf{DB} = ((id_i, \{w_j\}_{j \leq n})_{i \leq m})$ is represented as a list of identifier/word tuples where every (file) identifier $id_i \in \mathcal{I}$ taken form the index set $\mathcal{I}$ is associated with j words $\{w_j\}_{j \leq n}$ taken from a word dictionary $\mathcal{W}$. A search query $\psi(\mathbf{w}) = (\psi, \mathbf{w})$ is specified by a tuple of words $\mathbf{w} \subseteq \mathcal{W}$ and a boolean formula ψ on $\mathbf{w}$. We denote by $|\psi|$ the arity of the formula. We write $\mathbf{DB}(w_j)$ (resp. $\mathbf{DB}(\psi(\mathbf{w}))$) for the set of identifiers associated with the word w_j (resp. matching $\psi(\mathbf{w})$). An update query $\phi(\mathbf{u})$ is parameterized with an update operation $\mathbf{u}$. Updates of the form $(add, w, \mathbf{id})$, $(del, w, \mathbf{id})$ add or remove identifiers $\mathbf{id}$ assigned with word w; update operations of the form $(add, \mathbf{w}, id)$, $(del, \mathbf{w}, id)$ add or remove a list of words $\mathbf{w}$ from identifier id. We write $\mathbf{EDB}(\phi(\mathbf{u}))$ for the set of identifiers satisfying the update $\phi(\mathbf{u})$.

---

[1] Semantic security is not enough. The reason is that the notion leaks the length of messages.

Definition 7 (Searchable Encryption). *A dynamic searchable symmetric encryption scheme* DSSE *consists of three interactive algorithms* (Setup, Search, Update) *executed between the client and the server, such that*

- Setup(1^λ, $\textbf{\textit{DB}}$). *On input a security parameter λ and a data base $\textbf{\textit{DB}}$, the protocol outputs a secret key MSK and an encrypted database $\textbf{\textit{EDB}}$. The client stores the secret key MSK, whereas the server holds the encrypted database $\textbf{\textit{EDB}}$.*
- Search(MSK, $\psi(\textbf{\textit{w}})$, $\textbf{\textit{EDB}}$). *The protocol is between the client and server, where the client takes as input a secret key MSK and a search query $\psi(\textbf{\textit{w}})$ on words $\textbf{\textit{w}}$, and the server takes as input the encrypted database $\textbf{\textit{EDB}}$. The server outputs a set of identifiers $ID \subseteq \mathcal{I}$, the client has no output.*
- Update(MSK, $\phi(\textbf{\textit{u}})$, $\textbf{\textit{EDB}}$). *The protocol runs between the client and server, where the client input is a secret key MSK and an update query $\phi(\textbf{\textit{u}})$ on operation $\textbf{\textit{u}}$, and the server takes as input the encrypted database $\textbf{\textit{EDB}}$. At the end of the interaction, the client terminates with an updated state MSK' and the server with a modified database $\textbf{\textit{EDB}}'$.*

We say a DSSE system is non-interactive if Search and Update are two-round protocols.

Definition 8 (Correctness). *A dynamic symmetric searchable encryption* DSSE *system is correct, if for all databases $\textbf{\textit{DB}}$, all search queries $\psi(\textbf{\textit{w}})$, all update queries $\phi(\textbf{\textit{u}})$, and all $(MSK, \textbf{\textit{EDB}}) \leftarrow$ Setup(1^λ, $\textbf{\textit{DB}}$), it holds*

- *Search correctness: There exists a negligible function ε_s, s.t.*

$$Pr\big[\text{Search}(MSK, \psi(\textbf{\textit{w}}), \textbf{\textit{EDB}}) \neq \textbf{\textit{DB}}(\psi(\textbf{\textit{w}}))\big] = \varepsilon_s(\lambda)$$

- *Update correctness: There exists a negligible function ε_u, s.t.*

$$Pr\big[\text{Update}(MSK, \phi(\textbf{\textit{u}}), \textbf{\textit{EDB}}) \neq \textbf{\textit{EDB}}(\phi(\textbf{\textit{u}}))\big] = \varepsilon_u(\lambda)$$

4.2   Security

Our aim is to provide a strong notion of query privacy. In our model the server shall not tell apart search and update queries even if the same queries have been issued before. We allow the adversary to learn from the interaction with the system is the result of search and update queriers in terms of the associated identifiers. (Note, the server will learn the access pattern when asked to retrieve the ciphertexts as a consequence of the search and update.) To this end, we devise an experiment between the challenger and the adversary $\mathcal{A}$. The adversary chooses two databases $\textbf{DB}_0, \textbf{DB}_1$ and sends two queries q_0, q_1 (be it a search or be it an update query) to the challenger emulates the effect of the query q_b for a randomly chosen bit b on either of the two encrypted databases $\textbf{DB}_b$. The adversary $\mathcal{A}$ wins the experiment, if he guesses the database he interacts with. To avoid a trivial game, we must restrict the type of adversarial queries. Clearly, if the adversary defines a pair of queries which differ in their response, the adversary wins the experiment with overwhelming probability. Hence, for a meaning security notion, we require that for all search queries $\psi(\mathbf{w}) = (\psi, \mathbf{w})$, it holds that $\mathbf{DB}_0(\psi(\mathbf{w})_0) = \mathbf{DB}_1(\psi(\mathbf{w})_1)$; and for all update queries $\phi(\mathbf{u}) = (\phi, \mathbf{u})$, it holds that $\mathbf{EDB}_0(\phi(\mathbf{u})_0) = \mathbf{EDB}_1(\phi(\mathbf{u})_1)$. We summarize the above discussion in the following experiment:

Setup: Adversary $\mathcal{A}$ chooses two databases $\mathbf{DB}_0, \mathbf{DB}_1$. The challenger flips a bit $b \in \{0, 1\}$ and runs $\mathsf{Setup}(1^\lambda, \mathbf{DB}_b)$. It keeps the master secret MSK to itself and gives the encrypted database $\mathbf{EDB}_b$ to $\mathcal{A}$.

Challenge: Adversary $\mathcal{A}$ may additively send queries to oracles Search and Update:

– Search$(\cdot, \cdot)$: This oracle implements the search protocol. It expects two equally-sized search queries $(\psi(\mathbf{w})_b = (\psi_b, \mathbf{w}_b)$ subject to the restriction that

$$\mathbf{DB}_0(\psi(\mathbf{w})_0) = \mathbf{DB}_1(\psi(\mathbf{w})_1)$$

The purpose of the oracle is to emulate a client running the Search algorithm on input $(MSK, \psi(\mathbf{w})_b, \mathbf{EDB}_b)$.
– Update$(\cdot, \cdot)$: This oracle expects as input two equally-sized update queries $\phi(\mathbf{u})_0, \phi(\mathbf{u})_1$ subject to the restriction that

$$\mathbf{EDB}_0(\phi(\mathbf{u})_0) = \mathbf{EDB}_1(\phi(\mathbf{u})_1)$$

It emulates a client running the Update algorithm on input $(MSK, \phi(\mathbf{u})_b, \mathbf{EDB}_b)$.

Guess: At some point, the adversary $\mathcal{A}$ outputs a guess b'.
The advantage of an adversary $\mathcal{A}$ in this experiment is defined as $\Pr[b' = b] - \frac{1}{2}$.

Definition 9 (Full Security). *A dynamic symmetric searchable encryption system is fully secure, if all polynomial-time adversaries $\mathcal{A}$ have at most a negligible advantage in the above experiment.*

The above notion gives strong search query privacy guarantees in the sense that an adversary does not only learn the search words $\mathbf{w}$, but it neither learns the formula ψ. We also consider a relaxed version, where the scheme hides search words only. The experiment is identical to the above one except that we require $(\psi, \mathbf{w}_0) = (\psi, \mathbf{w}_1)$ to hold for all adversarial search queries $\psi(\mathbf{w}) = (\psi, \mathbf{w})$ and $(\phi, \mathbf{w}_0) = (\phi, \mathbf{w}_1)$ to hold for all adversarial update queries $\phi(\mathbf{u}) = (\phi, \mathbf{w})$.

Definition 10 (Weak Security). *A dynamic searchable symmetric encryption scheme is weakly secure, if all polynomial-time adversaries $\mathcal{A}$ have at most a negligible advantage in the modified experiment subject to the restriction that for all search and update queries, it holds that $(\psi, \boldsymbol{w}_0) = (\psi, \boldsymbol{w}_1)$ and $(\phi, \boldsymbol{w}_0) = (\phi, \boldsymbol{w}_1)$.*

4.3   A Note on the Blue-Print

The beginning of the section describes a blue print for searchable symmetric encryption systems. The fact that an index search scheme has indistinguishable search queriers allows us to construct a searchable symmetric encryption system against *outsider attackers* analyzing the frequency of (popular) search words given the client's and server's trace as follows: Before the server sends out the ciphertexts for the identified indexes, it re-randomises the ciphertexts.

4.4   High-Level Idea

For ease of explanation, we explain the main ideas behind searching for a *single* word. While a common ground of previous constructions has been a linked list data structure [2–4], our scheme implements a perfect binary tree data structure. The depth $d = \log |\mathcal{W}|$ of the binary tree is logarithmic in the total number of words (and a parameter fixed in advance).

We denote the k-th node at level l as $N_{k,l}$. The root is $N_{0,0}$. Every node has two children. Each edge connecting a parent node $N_{k,l}$ and a child $N_{k',l+1}$ is associated with a bit $b_l \in \{0,1\}$. Every leaf is randomly associated with a bucket b_j containing all indices $id_i \in \mathcal{ID}$ matching word $w_j \in \mathcal{W}$. Searching for a word $w = (w_0, \ldots, w_{d-1})$ means to traverse a path from the root $N_{0,0}$ to a leaf $N_{k,d-1}$ and read all identifiers in the bucket.

It remains to show how to implement a private decision mechanism for efficiently selecting the nodes. Here is where the constrained functional encryption comes into the game (for dimension $n = 1$). We generate a cryptographic binary tree where an encryption $(CT_{k,l}, q_{k,l}) \leftarrow \mathsf{Enc}(MSK, 1)$ represents node $N_{k,l}$.

To search for word $w = (w_0, \ldots, w_{d-1})$, we first compute the random encoding $b_j = (b_0, \ldots, b_{d-1})$ of word w_j with a pseudorandom function and next generate decryption keys $SK_{k,l} \leftarrow \mathsf{KeyGen}(MSK, b_l, q_{k,l})$ constrained to the set of nodes on the path from the root to the target leaf. Decrypting the node $N_{k,l}$ gives a hint to choose the child node $N_{k',l+1}$

$$\mathsf{Dec}(SK_{k,l}, CT_{k,l}) = \begin{cases} 0 & \text{if } b_l = 0 \\ 1 & \text{if } b_l = 1 \end{cases}$$

Applying this technique for all sequential nodes enables us to traverse the tree efficiently in $\mathcal{O}(\log |\mathcal{W}|)$. To search a formula over multiple words $\psi(\mathbf{w})$, one first searches for the buckets matching every word and then applies the formula over the indices of the buckets. Searching a compound expression of arity $|\psi|$ takes $\mathcal{O}(|\psi| \cdot \log |\mathcal{W}|)$. Updating the words in the encrypted database essentially requires to search for the bucket matching the word. One then adds a new index to the bucket, or deletes the bucket. The operation takes time $\mathcal{O}(\log |\mathcal{W}|)$.

Discussions and Generalizations. The use of the functional encryption scheme CFE has several advantages. First, it randomizes every search query. Without the probabilistic scheme the searchable encryption system would satisfy a weaker privacy notion, where the (outsider) adversary recognizes search queries previously sent. The scheme also makes sure that the server must traverse the tree before identifying the bucket and thereby does not deviate from the path. An adversary applying the search tokens to nodes other than the eligible ones or combining them with previous tokens receives random decryptions. These properties are the crux why the scheme leaks no more information other than the pattern to access the buckets. Third, the constrained functional encryption scheme grows in value, when one expresses a more comprehensive traversal policy. Recall, the CFE supports decryption of functions $f_{\mathbf{x}} : \mathbb{F}_p^n \to \mathbb{F}_p$ from the class of inner products $\mathcal{F} = \{f_{\mathbf{x}} | \mathbf{x} \in \mathbb{F}_p^n\}$ where $f_{\mathbf{x}}(\mathbf{y}) = \langle \mathbf{x}, \mathbf{y} \rangle$ is from a fixed polynomial range.

One may generalize the scheme to search on a directed acyclic graph in the following way:

- For each node $N_{k,l}$, encrypt a vector $\mathbf{x}_{k,l} \in \mathbb{F}_p^n$.
- For each edge connecting a parent node $N_{k,l}$ with a child $N_{k',l+1}$ assign a label $f_{\mathbf{x}_{k,l}}(\mathbf{y}_{k',l+1})$.
- To traverse from node $N_{k,l}$ to child $N_{k',l+1}$, decrypt node $N_{k,l}$ with a key for $\mathbf{y}_{k',l+1} \in \mathbb{F}_p^n$.

This way, the search conditions extend to inner product functions. These are particularly useful functions enabling the computation of conjunctions, disjunctions, CNF/DNF formulas, thresholds, Hadamard weights, and low range statistics. We leave details of the general scheme to search on directed acyclic graphs and other data structures to the full version. In the forthcoming section, we describe a searchable encryption scheme for the special case, where at node $N_{k,l}$ the inner product function computes a validity check by xor-ing $w_l \oplus 1$.

4.5   Description of the Construction

Let CFE $=$ (Setup, KeyGen, Enc, Dec) be constrained functional encryption scheme. Wlog, suppose $|\mathcal{W}| = 2^d$ is a power of 2. Let PRF $: \{0,1\}^\lambda \times \{0,1\}^d \to \{0,1\}^d$ be a pseudorandom function. Define a dynamic symmetric searchable encryption system DSSE $=$ (Setup, Search, Update) as follows:

- $Setup(1^\lambda, \mathbf{DB})$: On input a security parameter λ and database $\mathbf{DB} = ((id_i, \{w_j\}_{j \leq 2^d})_{i \leq m})$, build up an encrypted data structure as follows:
  1. Sample a random seed $s \leftarrow_R \{0,1\}^\lambda$ and generate a master secret key $msk \leftarrow$ CFE.Setup(1^λ) for the constrained functional encryption scheme for dimension $n = 1$.
  2. For every $w_j \in \mathbf{DB}$, add $\mathbf{DB}(w_j)$ to bucket $b_j \leftarrow$ PRF(s, w_j).
  3. Create the encrypted data structure by computing a set of $2^d - 1$ ciphertexts $CT_{k,l}, q_{k,l} \leftarrow$ Enc$(msk, 1)$ and assign each state $q_{k,l}$ with node $N_{k,l}$. Define M to be the set of all (k,l) pairs identifying the ciphertexts.
  4. Return the master secret $MSK = (s, q_{k,l})_{\forall (k,l) \in M}$ and the encrypted data structure $\mathbf{EDB} = (CT_{k,l})_{\forall (k,l) \in M}$.

- *Search*$(MSK, \psi(\mathbf{w}))$: To generate a search token $TK_{\psi(\mathbf{w})}$ for the query $\psi(\mathbf{w}) = (\psi, w_0, \ldots, w_{|\psi|})$, the client generates for every word $w_j = (w_0, \ldots, w_{d-1}$ a decryption key $\mathbf{SK}_j = (SK_{j,0}, \ldots, SK_{j,d-1})$ as follows:
    1. Recover the bucket $b_j = (b_{j,0}, \ldots, b_{j,d-1})$ for word w_j by computing $\mathsf{PRF}(s, w_j)$
    2. Compute for the kth node $N_{k,l}$ on the path to the bucket a decryption key $SK_{j,k} \leftarrow \mathsf{KeyGen}(MSK, b_{j,l}, q_{k,l})$.

  The client sends the search token $TK_{\psi(\mathbf{w})} = (\phi, \mathbf{SK}_1, \ldots \mathbf{SK}_{|\psi|})$ to the server. Upon receiving the token, the server searches for every decryption key $\mathbf{SK}_j = (SK_{j,0}, \ldots, SK_{j,d-1})$ the bucket b_j as follows:
    1. Decrypt for $0 \le l \le d - 1$ the bit $b_{j,l} \leftarrow \mathsf{Dec}(SK_{j,l}, CT_{k,l})$
    2. Traverse to the node at level $l + 1$ in the tree whose edge is associated with bit $b_{j,l}$.

  Once the server identified all buckets b_j, it applies the formula ϕ to retrieve the ciphertexts matching the identifiers $\psi(\mathbf{w})$.
- Update$(MSK, \phi(\mathbf{u}), \mathbf{EDB})$. To add files to the data structure, one needs to search for the bucket matching the word and store the file index in the bucket. Deletion of files matching a word requires to delete the bucket associated with the word. Deletion of a single file requires the client to decrypt the files and ask the server to delete the index associated with the corresponding ciphertext.

A careful inspection of our data structure reveals that buckets leak the number of stored words. The server may conduct a statistical analysis based on the sizes of buckets and use the extra information to break privacy. We note that prior work is susceptible the analysis as well. To prevent the server from learning words from the number of indices stored in a bucket, one may apply standard masking techniques to bias the size. One essentially adds "dummy" identifiers to normalize the bucket sizes.

4.6   Security Analysis

We are now ready to analyze the scheme.

Theorem 2. *Assume* PRF *is a secure pseudo-random function and* CFE *is a secure constrained functional encryption scheme. Then the above dynamic searchable encryption system is weakly secure.*

Proof (Sketch). The proof is trivial and therefor sketched. An adversary $\mathcal{A}$ breaking the security of the searchable encryption scheme can be used to construct a reduction against the pseudo-random function or constrained functional encryption scheme. To attack the pseudo-randomness, the reduction flips a bit b and simulates the searchable encryption scheme except that every invocation of PRF is forwarded to the pseudo-random oracle, implementing the PRF $(b = 0)$ or a random function with identical output range $(b = 1)$. When adversary $\mathcal{A}$ outputs a guess $b' = b$, then the reduction conjectures to deal with an oracle implementing the pseudo-random function PRF; otherwise, the reduction conjectures to interact with a random function. To attack the security of the constrained functional encryption scheme, the reduction emulates the generation of cryptographic binary tree by forwarding encryption requests to the challenge oracle. It simulates search and update queries by relaying the requests to its key generation oracle. When adversary $\mathcal{A}$ outputs a guess $b' = 0$, the reduction claims to interact with $\mathbf{EDB}_0$ searching for words $\psi(\mathbf{w})_0$ and making updates $\phi(\mathbf{u})_0$; otherwise, it claims to interact with $\mathbf{EDB}_1$ searching for words $\psi(\mathbf{w})_1$ and making updates $\phi(\mathbf{u})_1$.

Acknowledgment. This research was funded by the European Union within the FP7 AU2EU project.

References

1. Boneh, D., Goh, E.-J., Nissim, K.: Evaluating 2-DNF formulas on ciphertexts. In: Kilian, J. (ed.) TCC 2005. LNCS, vol. 3378, pp. 325–341. Springer, Heidelberg (2005)
2. Cash, D., Jaeger, J., Jarecki, S., Jutla, C., Krawczyk, H., Rosu, M.C., Steiner, M.: Dynamic searchable encryption in very large databases: data structures and implementation. In: Proceedings of NDSS 2014 (2014)
3. Cash, D., Jarecki, S., Jutla, C., Krawczyk, H., Roşu, M.-C., Steiner, M.: Highly-scalable searchable symmetric encryption with support for boolean queries. In: Canetti, R., Garay, J.A. (eds.) CRYPTO 2013, Part I. LNCS, vol. 8042, pp. 353–373. Springer, Heidelberg (2013)
4. Curtmola, R., Garay, J.A., Kamara, S., Ostrovsky, R.: Searchable symmetric encryption: improved definitions and efficient constructions. J. Comput. Secur. **19**(5), 895–934 (2011)
5. Freeman, D.M.: Converting pairing-based cryptosystems from composite-order groups to prime-order groups. In: Gilbert, H. (ed.) EUROCRYPT 2010. LNCS, vol. 6110, pp. 44–61. Springer, Heidelberg (2010)
6. Goldreich, O., Ostrovsky, R.: Software protection and simulation on oblivious RAMs. J. ACM **43**(3), 431–473 (1996)
7. Kamara, S., Papamanthou, C.: Parallel and dynamic searchable symmetric encryption. In: Sadeghi, A.-R. (ed.) FC 2013. LNCS, vol. 7859, pp. 258–274. Springer, Heidelberg (2013)
8. Kamara, S., Papamanthou, C., Roeder, T.: Dynamic searchable symmetric encryption. In: ACM Conference on Computer and Communications Security, pp. 965–976 (2012)
9. Katz, J., Sahai, A., Waters, B.: Predicate encryption supporting disjunctions, polynomial equations, and inner products. In: Smart, N.P. (ed.) EUROCRYPT 2008. LNCS, vol. 4965, pp. 146–162. Springer, Heidelberg (2008)
10. Okamoto, T., Takashima, K.: Dual pairing vector spaces and their applications. IEICE Trans. **98–A**(1), 3–15 (2015)
11. Stefanov, E., van Dijk, M., Shi, E., Fletcher, C.W., Ren, L., Yu, X., Devadas, S.: Path ORAM: an extremely simple oblivious RAM protocol. In: Sadeghi, A., Gligor, V.D., Yung, M. (eds.) 2013 ACM SIGSAC Conference on Computer and Communications Security, CCS 2013, Berlin, Germany, 4–8 November 2013, pp. 299–310. ACM (2013)

Private Large-Scale Databases with Distributed Searchable Symmetric Encryption

Yuval Ishai[1,3], Eyal Kushilevitz[1], Steve Lu[2]([✉]), and Rafail Ostrovsky[3]

[1] Technion, Haifa, Israel
{yuvali,eyalk}@cs.technion.ac.il
[2] Stealth Software Technologies, Inc., Los Angeles, USA
steve@stealthsoftwareinc.com
[3] UCLA, Los Angeles, USA
rafail@cs.ucla.edu

Abstract. With the growing popularity of remote storage, the ability to outsource a large private database yet be able to search on this encrypted data is critical. Searchable symmetric encryption (SSE) is a practical method of encrypting data so that natural operations such as searching can be performed on this data. It can be viewed as an efficient private-key alternative to powerful tools such as fully homomorphic encryption, oblivious RAM, or secure multiparty computation. The main drawbacks of existing SSE schemes are the limited types of search available to them and their leakage. In this paper, we present a construction of a private outsourced database in the two-server model (e.g. two cloud services) which can be thought of as an SSE scheme on a B-tree that allows for a wide variety of search features such as range queries, substring queries, and more. Our solution can hide all leakage due to access patterns ("metadata") between queries and features a tunable parameter that provides a smooth tradeoff between privacy and efficiency. This allows us to implement a solution that supports databases which are terabytes in size and contain millions of records with only a $5\times$ slowdown compared to MySQL when the query result size is around $10\,\%$ of the database, though the fixed costs dominate smaller queries resulting in over $100\times$ relative slowdown (under $1\,\mathrm{s}$ actual).

In addition, our solution also provides a mechanism for allowing data owners to set filters that prevent prohibited queries from returning any results, without revealing the filtering terms. Finally, we also present the benchmarks of our prototype implementation.

Y. Ishai, E. Kushilevitz, S. Lu and R. Ostrovsky—Work done while consulting for Stealth Software Technologies, Inc. Supported in part by the Intelligence Advanced Research Projects Activity (IARPA) via Department of Interior National Business Center (DoI/NBC) contract number D11PC20199 and ENTACT subcontract through MIT Lincoln Laboratory. The U.S. Government is authorized to reproduce and distribute reprints for Governmental purposes notwithstanding any copyright annotation therein. Disclaimer: The views and conclusions contained herein are those of the authors and should not be interpreted as necessarily representing the official policies or endorsement, either expressed or implied, of IARPA, DoI/NBC, or the U.S. Government.

© Springer International Publishing Switzerland 2016
K. Sako (Ed.): CT-RSA 2016, LNCS 9610, pp. 90–107, 2016.
DOI: 10.1007/978-3-319-29485-8_6

Keywords: Searchable symmetric encryption · Secure databases · Private cloud computing

1 Introduction

In order to protect a large database (e.g. for cloud storage), one would like to apply encryption on the database so that only those with the proper keys can decrypt. However, for ordinary semantically secure encryption, this precludes any ability to perform useful operations on this data other than decryption. The ability to perform limited searches or other operations on ciphertexts would greatly enhance the utility of the encrypted database. This topic has motivated researchers to study the problem from many different angles, and has lead to cryptographic solutions such as Private Information Retrieval (PIR) [10,23], Oblivious RAM [17,19,26,27], Encrypted Keyword Search [4,14,28], Deterministic and Order-preserving encryption [1–3], Fully Homomorphic Encryption [5,15], and more.

One of the promising approaches for searching on encrypted data is known as Searchable Symmetric Encryption (SSE). This approach has been the subject of a long line of research starting with Song et al. [29]. An SSE scheme allows the data to be encrypted using only private-key primitives that allow it to be searched upon at a very low cost, while attempting to minimize the correlation between queries. The latter information is commonly referred to as *query leakage* or *access pattern leakage*. An important improvement of obtaining a sublinear time solution was introduced in Curtmola et al. [11] and the notion of SSE was subsequently generalized to Structured Encryption by Chase and Kamara [9]. Recent works including that of Cash et al. [7] and Fisch et al. [13] present highly scalable SSE schemes supporting exact match queries and keyword searches, and also more complex Boolean formulas of these queries, and extended query types such as range queries.

Our motivation of building a large, scalable SSE scheme is similar to that of [7,13], but our approach and conclusions diverge from these works. Our aim is to build a light-weight solution that supports a variety of natural string-search queries. However, unlike their work, we insist on eliminating all leakage about the access pattern except an upper bound on the size of the individual matches, which must be leaked regardless of any efficiency requirements. Our solution builds on a B-tree data structure whose choice is natural as B-trees are ubiquitous, serve a variety of queries, and are more suitable for our cryptographic subprotocols compared to other string data structures like tries or n-grams.

We state a high level summary of our secure construction. At the heart of our construction is the ability for a client to privately search on a remotely held, encrypted B-tree such that (1) the client learns only the matching indices and nothing else about the entries in the tree, and (2) neither the client nor the remote parties learn which path was taken. Consider how a tree is travesed in the clear: starting from the root, a node is fetched, then the query is compared to the contents of the node which results in the pointer to a node in the next level, and this repeats until the leaf level is reached. We create cryptographic parallels to be able to perform this traversal while satisfying our security requirements.

In order to privately fetch a node from a level, PIR or even Symmetric PIR (SPIR, where the client does not learn anything beyond the query) does not fully guarantee our needs. There are two reasons for this: PIR still returns the node in the clear to the client, and the client must input a location to fetch. However, since the client should not learn which path was taken, nor the contents of the nodes, this information must be hidden. In order to account for this, we introduce a functionality known as shared-input-shared-output-SPIR or SisoSPIR that takes as input secret-shared values between the client and remote parties, and outputs a secret-shared node. This way, nodes can be fetched without out the client learning the location or contents of the node. We will see later that the construction is reminiscent of the "indirect indexing" techniques due to Naor and Nissim [25]. Then, in order to compute on the secret-shared node against the query, we employ lightweight MPC that effectively computes a b-way comparison gate, where b is the branching factor of the tree, and returns a secret-shared result.

With this idea in mind, we are then able to build securely queryable B-trees, which then leads to range queries, substring queries, and more. Our paper takes a formal treatment of these concepts as a composition of cryptographic functionalities, each of which is easy to analyze, and their combined security follows from standard secure composition theorems (e.g. Canetti [6]). We propose realiziations to these functionalities, and also implement them and benchmark our results. Our code has been independently tested to scale to terabytes in size and millions of records, and we present our own timings that show that our solution is around 5× slower compared to MySQL when querying around 10 % of the database, though the fixed costs dominate smaller queries resulting in over 100× relative slowdown (under 1 s actual).

1.1 Related Work

As noted above, the problem of searchable encryption, and that of private database management in general, can be solved using powerful general techniques such as Oblivious RAM, secure multiparty computation, and FHE. Our aim is to focus on practical solutions that have as little overhead as possible compared to an insecure solution. One of the interesting aspects of our construction is that we use highly efficient variants of Oblivious RAM, PIR, and MPC and apply them as sub-protocols only on *dramatically smaller portions* of the database.

There is a rich literature on searchable symmetric encryption (see for example [7–9,11,13,16,20–22,29]), and these works are highly relevant to the task at hand. Furthermore, recent works such as [12,24,32] have considered combining PIR with ORAM for efficiency reasons. While these schemes are more efficient than generic tools, they are limited in search functionality and possibly leak too much access pattern information. The most relevant work is that of Cash et al. [7], and we highlight the main differences between this work and ours. Indeed, our model uses two "servers" and a client, and the servers are assumed not to collude, as the two-server setting typically lends itself to more efficient instantiations. We also do not necessarily assume the data owner is the same as the client, which is the case for typical SSE schemes. This allows us to work in different settings, such as the example of a data owner delegating sensitive data to a semi-untrusted cloud, and still allowing a client (who is not the data owner themselves) to query against it while guaranteeing no unqueried information is leaked. If we assume that the client does own the data, then the client can play the role of both the client and the data owner, S1, in which case non-collusion is for free (of course, this would mean the client would have to store the index data that would have been held by the primary server, but this is less data than what is held by the "helper" server that has the encrypted payloads). We obtain different string-type searches as opposed to boolean formulas on exact matches obtained by [7], and our leakage definitions are similar to those of [7,9,11] (though the type of leakage allowed by our solution is much more limited).

We do pay a price in the non-collusion assumption and efficiency compared to existing schemes, but we believe this tradeoff provides an interesting contrast since we achieve less leakage and offer an alternative construction in achieving these types of search queries like those in existing SSE schemes while maintaining a practical level of efficiency.

1.2 Our Contributions

In this work, we introduce the notion of *distributed searchable symmetric encryption*. We define it in terms of an ideal three-party functionality, where there is a querying client, a data owner, and a helper server.

We outline our main result as follows: there is a data owner S1 that holds a database D that wants to outsource the bulk of the work of querying to a helper server S2 such that a client C can perform queries q against D by interacting with S1 and S2 (but mostly S2). The data owner wants the guarantee that only the results of the query is revealed to the C and no additional information about D, and only queries that satisfy the query policy list $\mathcal{P}$ will return any results. On the other hand, C does not want any additional information to be revealed about q to either S1 or S2. We can define a functionality $\mathcal{F}_{SSE}$ with two phases: Setup and Query such that during the setup phase, S1 inputs D and $\mathcal{P}$ to $\mathcal{F}_{SSE}$, which returns a leakage profile $\mathcal{L}_{Setup}^i$ to party $i \in$ S2, C, S1. During the query phase, C inputs a query q (range, substring, etc.) to $\mathcal{F}_{SSE}$ and the functionality checks that q satisfies $\mathcal{P}$ and returns the results to C if it conforms, while sending a leakage profile $\mathcal{L}_{Query}^i$ to player $i \in$ S2, C, S1.

Main Theorem (Informal). *There is a sublinear communication protocol realizing the above SSE functionality $\mathcal{F}_{SSE}$ where the leakage profiles only reveal minimal size information (no information about access patterns and intersection of queries or results across multiple queries). The protocol achieves 1-privacy in the semi-honest (honest-but-curious) model, i.e. any adversary corrupting a single party in the protocol can be simulated in the ideal model, and uses a logarithmic number of communication rounds in the size of the database.*

In order to construct an efficient realization of this ideal functionality, we define and construct a few intermediate sub-protocols that may be of independent interest. One new concept is that of privacy preserving data structures, which can be thought of as a more general variant of Oblivious Data Structures [30]. Other concepts include efficient realizations of shared-input-shared-output variants of cryptographic primitives such as pseudorandom functions and private information retrieval.

1.3 Roadmap

In Sect. 2 we describe background and our model. In Sect. 3 we provide a high-level overview of our new scheme and provide the detailed construction and proofs for our main technical functionality SisoSPIR in Sect. 4. We construct a full-fledged distributed SSE using this functionality in Sect. 5. We show how to reduce various query types into range queries in the full version. For the sake of brevity, we also defer our proofs to the full version.

We describe our benchmark results in Appendix A.

2 Background and Model

We consider a system of three parties: the client C, the server S1, and "helper server" S2. When considering adversarial behavior, we restrict our attention to the case of semi-honest (honest-but-curious) adversaries with the presence of an honest majority, i.e. only one party may be corrupted. Due to the low communication complexity, we automatically have some guarantees even against a malicious C. The assumption that the data owner server and the helper server are semi-honest and do not collude are reasonable if, for example, the helper server is a neutral cloud service.

We consider a simplified model of a database D, which we take to be a single table of records of the following form. D is a set of records indexed by t different fields $A_1, \ldots, A_t$, where each field A_i may take on some set of allowed values (e.g. string, date, enum, etc.). Each record $r \in D$ then takes the form $r = (x_1, \ldots, x_t, y)$ with each $x_i \in A_i$ denoting a searchable field value, and $y \in \{0,1\}^\ell$ (for some length parameter ℓ) being the payload. We make the simplifying assumptions that there is only one payload field (WLOG), the database schema is known to all parties, as well as the total number of records. All fields and records are padded up to the same length, and we assume A_1 to be a unique ID field, denoted by $id(r)$ for record r.

A *range* query q on a field A_i is of the form $x \prec b$ or $a \prec x$ or $a \prec x \prec b$, where $\prec$ can be either $<$ or $\leq$. The query returns all records r satisfying the inequality on field i. We focus on range queries and describe other query types and how to reduce them to range queries in the full version. We also consider simple query authorization policies p that take as input a query q and output 0 or 1. As long as p is efficiently computable via a Boolean formula, we can use general MPC to evaluate and enforce only queries satisfying p applied to q is 1 in our system. For example, our current implementation allows us to deny queries that are not of a particular query type, or column, or value.

3   Overview of Our Construction

In this section we include a high level overview of our solution. A formal description of the various sub-protocols and their security proofs will be given in Sects. 4 and 5. In this section only, for the sake of simplicity, we focus our description on just performing a range query on a binary tree. We first consider the scenario where we do not need to hide the data owner's information from the client C. Recall that protocols such as PIR or ORAM allow queries of the form "fetch location i" from a data array D to obtain $D[i]$ to be performed in a randomized fashion without leaking any access pattern information: even identical repeated queries look the same to everyone but the querier.

First, let us focus on a single column (say, 'Name') with entries $x_1, \ldots, x_n$ (with duplicity). During initialization, these are stored in a balanced B-tree T, and let T_i denote the i-th level of the tree, and $T_i[j]$ denote the j-th node on that level. On the leaves, we additionally store pointers (along with the x_i) that point back to the original rows of the DB. In order to perform a range query (say, fetch all records where 'Name'>'Bob'), the client C uses fetches the node in root T_0 of the tree. If the value in the node is larger than 'Bob' the client wants to go right, otherwise left. This determines which node j_1 to traverse to in level T_1 of the tree. C then uses a private fetching algorithm (such as PIR or ORAM) to fetch the node $T_1[j_1]$, and then determines whether to go left or right again, which will result in j_2 for level 2 of the tree. This proceeds until C reaches a leaf, whereupon it will also privately fetch all subsequent leaves (since this is a > query). Since these leaves contain pointers $i_1, \ldots, i_k$ to the original DB, C can also privately fetch these pointers.

In our full solution, much of the complexity arises when we do not want the client C to learn the contents of the database *not* returned by the query. We therefore introduce a secret-shared variant SisoSPIR to ensure the location and node are secret shared, and then apply secure multiparty computation to determine whether to go left or right, where the choice is also secret-shared. We explain at a high level how this is done. Whenever C is about to receive a result of privately fetching a node, the server S1 will mask it with a random value R_{node}. This renders the result node hidden, since now C cannot use this randomly masked value to determine whether to go left or right. Now, to determine which way to go, C invokes an MPC protocol with S1 that computes $query \geq value ? right : left$. We do not want C to know where it is exactly in the tree, so 'left' and 'right' are absolute pointers that are blinded. A common technique for this is to virtually shift the array by some random amount r, and offset the pointer by r. In order to handle policies, we incorporate a "killswitch" into the MPC where a non-compliant query will always lead the client down to a "no results found" leaf.

4   Formal Description

In this section we formally define and analyze the building blocks of our solution. All functionalities and protocols involve 3 parties: Server S1, Client C, and Helper Server S2.

Functionalities. We treat functionalities as picking their internal secret randomness. To model leakage, we use "leak x to P" to specify ideal functionality leakage which only affects the security requirement and not correctness, whereas "return y to P" is used to specify an actual output which affects both correctness and security. We treat the "Query phase" of functionalities as receiving a single query, with the implicit understanding that multiple queries are handled by repeating the Query phase sequentially for each query. We will sometimes invoke multiple sessions of the same protocol in parallel on different sets of inputs. Since we only consider security against semi-honest adversaries, parallel composition holds in general (we can run many simulators in parallel since the inputs cannot be modified by a semi-honest adversary to depend on the transcript). We define the main functionality we are trying to achieve, the distributed SSE functionality $\mathcal{F}_{SSE}$ in Fig. 1.

Functionality $\mathcal{F}_{\mathsf{SSE}}$

Setup. S1 inputs a database D and policy $\mathcal{P}$ to $\mathcal{F}_{SSE}$. Leak $\mathcal{L}^i_{Setup}$ (which is implementation defined) to party $i \in$ S2, C, S1.
Query. C inputs a query q. Checks that q satisfies $\mathcal{P}$ and returns the results of the query to C if it conforms. Leak a leakage profile $\mathcal{L}^i_{Query}$ to player $i \in$ S2, C, S1.

Fig. 1. The privacy preserving data structure functionality.

Protocols. To simplify the presentation of the protocols, we do not explicitly describe the authentication mechanism used for preventing attacks by the network. Security against the network is achieved via a standard use of encryption and MACs. This does not affect the security of the protocols against semi-honest insiders. We also simplify notation by letting parties pick their own randomness. We follow the standard convention of including in the *view* of each party only its internal randomness and the *incoming* messages. The outgoing messages are determined by the inputs, randomness, and incoming messages. Finally, we omit "Done" messages in the end of protocols, under the understanding that whenever a party finishes its role in a (sub)protocol, it sends a "Done" message to all other parties.

Security. We consider asymptotic (vs. concrete) security parameterized by a security parameter k. Security is defined with respect to families of polynomial-size circuits. Whenever we use a pseudorandom function (PRF) or a pseudorandom generator (PRG) we will instantiate these primitives using a standard block cipher such as AES with seed size equal to the standard key length of the block cipher. The correctness of some protocols assumes that the number of queries is smaller than 2^k. Concretely, the number of queries scheduled is polynomial in k, and the correctness requirement should hold for all sufficiently large k. We use the real/ideal simulation paradigm when discussing security of our protocols. Namely, we use the following standard definition for security (see e.g. Canetti [6] or Goldreich's Book [18]):

Definition 1. *We say a protocol* π *1-privately realizes* $\mathcal{F}$ *in the semi-honest model if for every semi-honest (honest-but-curious) PPT adversary A corrupting a party in a real protocol* π, *there exists a PPT simulator S playing the role of A that only interacts with the ideal* $\mathcal{F}$, *such that on all inputs, S produces a simulated transcript that is computationally indistinguishable from the view of A. The view of A includes the transcript of messages that A sees during the execution of the protocol as well as its internal randomness.*

We say that the protocol has perfect correctness if the output of π *always matches the output of* $\mathcal{F}$.

4.1 Technical Overview

We provide a technical overview of our construction at a high level. The goal of our construction is to build a protocol that 1-privately realizes the functionality $\mathcal{F}_{SSE}$. In order to build an efficient protocol, we look toward data structures that support fast evaluations of the queries we want (in particular, range queries). However, because the ideal functionality reveals nothing about the query except the so-called "leakage profile", we want to minimize this surface. If the data structure has vastly different number of lookups for best and worst-case queries, this would require our ideal functionality to reveal this information, otherwise no simulator could correctly guess how many lookups to simulate without knowledge of the data. Thus, as a tradeoff, we work only with privacy preserving data structures (which we introduce below) which roughly states that the access to the data structure is data independent. This is a very reasonable tradeoff as many real-world data structures already satisfy this property, in particular B-trees. After we introduce this notion, we focus just on the B-tree case, though our scheme extends to support any PPDS.

In our solution, the way a client performs a query is done roughly in two parts: first, the client interacts with S1 and S2 to traverse a B-tree to retrieve indexes matching the query, then interacts with S2 to retrieve the actual records at those indices. For the latter part, we introduce a primitive called weak distributed oblivious permutation Symmetric Private Information Retrieval or wSPIR for short, and its range-query variant rSPIR, that does the following: given a set of indices, the client can look them up from the S2 without revealing anything about the set of indices nor learning anything beyond that set of indices. This is accomplished by having the data randomly permuted and the client learning only the permuted indices.

The drawbacks of wSPIR is that once an element is looked up, it must be cached, and a more subtle point is that the indices must be known. During the traversal of the B-tree, we do not want any party to learn the path traversed by the query, and so this alone is insufficient. Therefore, we introduce another primitive, shared-input-shared-output SPIR, SisoSPIR which is a gadget that the input is a secret sharing of an index to an array (between the client and S2) and the output is a secret sharing of the indexed array element. We give two instantiations of SisoSPIR, a simple linear-time instantiation SisoLinSPIR and a more complex sublinear-time instantiation SisoSublinSPIR that we describe in the full version. The simplicity of the linear-time instantiation makes it faster than the sublinear-time version in the implementation for most realistic database sizes, though it is slower asymptotically.

Finally, the last ingredient is a general secure multiparty computation (MPC) scheme. The way we then combine all of our ingredients is as follows. The data owner S1 sets up a PPDS B-tree to store the index data, which points to the records of the actual database, then treats each level of the B-tree as an array to be used for SisoSPIR and the main database will be set up to be used for rSPIR. When the client wants to make a query, it starts at the root where it has a trivial secret sharing with S2 and invokes SisoSPIR to obtain a secret shared version of the root node (which is different each time a query is made). It then uses general MPC to compute comparisons to obtain a secret sharing of the index to the next level of the B-tree. With this, it can then invoke SisoSPIR for the next level, and continues down until the leaf level. Then S2 sends the leaf shares to the client whereupon it can reconstruct the index information, and then uses rSPIR to retrieve the records corresponding to the query.

4.2   Privacy Preserving Data Structures (PPDS)

We can think of a (static) data structure for some data set D (consisting of $(key, value)$ pairs) as being two algorithms $\mathcal{DS} = (\mathsf{Setup}, \mathsf{Query})$. The setup algorithm takes as input some dataset D and outputs the initial state and sizes of the memory arrays $M_1, \ldots, M_k$. The query algorithm takes as input some query x and produces a sequence of memory probes of the form $q_\ell = (i, j)$ and gets the j-th entry of M_i, i.e. $M_i[j]$. The sequence can be adaptive in the sense that $q_{\ell+1}$ may depend on $q_1, \ldots, q_\ell$ as well as all the $M_i[j]$ for all $q_k = (i, j)$.

We take a modular approach and say that since PIR can hide the actual j within a memory array M_i, a PPDS need only "hide" the access pattern across the memory arrays. That is to say, there exists a simulator that can simulate the sequence of memory arrays being accessed (though it need not simulate which element in that memory array). Note that in the extreme case where each memory array is treated as a single element, the definition flattens into that of oblivious data structures as defined in [30]. We formalize this concept as a functionality $\mathcal{F}_{\mathsf{PPDS}}^{\mathcal{DS}}$, relative to some data structure $\mathcal{DS} = (\mathsf{Setup}, \mathsf{Query})$, that leaks to S2 only the sizes of the memory arrays in Fig. 2.

Given a data structure, we define the three-party protocol $\pi^{\mathcal{DS}}$ to be: the server sets up the data structure, and the client sends its query to the server, the

---

Functionality $\mathcal{F}_{\mathsf{PPDS}}$

Setup. The functionality receives as input (SETUP, D), where D is some dataset, from
the server. The functionality runs Setup on D and outputs to the server a sequence
$M_1, \ldots, M_k$, where the length of the data stored in M_i is ℓ_i. It outputs $\{|M_i|\}, k, \{\ell_i\}$
to the client C and S2.

Query. The functionality receives from the client as input (QUERY, x), where x is a
query. The functionality runs Query and returns the probe results $M_i[j]$ and locations
$p_m = (i, j)$ to the client. It outputs to S2 only the is corresponding to the p_m probes.

Fig. 2. The privacy preserving data structure functionality.

server processes the query and sends back the result to the client and "leaks"
the memory array locations i to S2. We say that some data structure is privacy
preserving if $\pi^{\mathcal{DS}}$ is a 1-private (against a dishonest S2) implementation of the
functionality $\mathcal{F}_{\mathsf{PPDS}}^{\mathcal{DS}}$.

Observe that many data structures are well-suited for privacy-preserving data
structures. Hash tables, Bloom filters, trees, and sorted arrays with binary search
can all be converted to privacy-preserving ones. For the remainder of the paper,
we will fix balanced B-trees as our PPDS, and focus on building a secure way to
search on these B-trees.

4.3   General MPC

Some of our protocols will employ general secure multiparty computation (MPC)
for simple functionalities with short inputs. In particular, the circuit complexity
of functionalities we realize via general MPC will always be sublinear in the
database size N. To abstract away the details of the underlying general MPC
protocol we use, we will cast protocols that invoke it in the *MPC-hybrid model*.
That is, we will assume the availability of a trusted oracle which receives inputs
and delivers the outputs defined by the functionality. We will similarly use other
hybrid models that invoke specific functionalities which we have already shown
how to realize.

The implementation Π_{MPC} of an MPC oracle will use an efficient implementation of Yao's protocol [31] applied to a boolean circuit representing the functionality. To efficiently implement each 1–2 String OT in Yao's protocol, we use the
3 parties as follows: In an offline phase, S1 generates a random OT pair (s_0, s_1)
and (b, s_b), sends (s_0, s_1) to S2 (acting as OT sender) and (b, s_b) to C (acting as
OT receiver). In the online phase, we consume the precomputed random OTs
via a standard, perfectly secure reduction from OT to random OT. Thus, the
entire implementation of Π_{MPC} uses an arbitrary PRF as a black box, and does
not require the use of public-key primitives. We omit further details about the
implementation of Π_{MPC} and treat it from here on as a black box. Finally, we
will use sisoMPC to denote a shared-input-shared-output variant of MPC, where
the inputs and outputs are secret-shared between the parties (typically C and
S2).

4.4   Weak Distributed Oblivious Permutation SPIR

We define our lowest level ideal functionality, which we refer to as Weak-distributed-oblivious-permutation-SPIR (wSPIR). We summarize at a high level what the functionality does and how to implement it. It allows C to retrieve an indexed entry in an array generated by S1 using the help of S2. Define a protocol Π_{wSPIR} where S1 encrypts and permutes the array and sends it to S2 and gives the key and permutation to C so that later, C can fetch any location and decrypt. As long as C asks for each location once (caching the results), it is easy to see this hides access pattern from S2, and we do some additional work to ensure that C doesn't learn anything when performing a dummy query when there is a cache hit.

Lemma 1. *Protocol Π_{wSPIR} realizes wSPIR with perfect correctness (i.e. the output of the protocol always matches the output of the functionality) and with computational security against a single semi-honest party.*

4.5   Shared-Input Shared-Output SPIR

A disadvantage of wSPIR is that it requires C to know the query locations i_j, and in particular learn when a query is repeated. However, when these queries are obtained by traversing a data structure (rather than originating from C), it is desirable to hide the query locations and query results from C. To this end we define and implement a stronger primitive which receives the query locations i_j in a secret-shared form and produces the output in a secret-shared form. We refer to this functionality as *shared-input shared-output SPIR* (SisoSPIR).

For brevity, we present a linear implementation of SisoSPIR that we call SisoLinSPIR and describe the sublinear version in the full paper.

Both variants will use the following non-reactive *shared-input shared-output PRF* (SisoPRF) functionality. Loosely speaking, this functionality computes $f_r[x+y]$ and secret shares it as Q and $Q \oplus f_r[x+y]$, where r is a secret key to a PRF f and x and y are a secret sharing of an input, and Q is a random mask. We will use two different implementations of this functionality: in the linear solution we will realize it via a 2-server PIR protocol applied to a precomputed table of function values, and in the sublinear solution we will implement it via the general MPC protocol π_{MPC} applied to a circuit representation of F.

4.6   Linear Implementation

Figure 3 defines the functionality realized by the linear implementation of SisoSPIR, referred to as SisoLinSPIR, and Figs. 4 and 5 describe (respectively) the initialization phase and query phase of a protocol $\Pi_{SisoLinSPIR}$ realizing SisoLinSPIR. Note that the functionality leaks the input y of S2 to S1. This leakage is harmless, because in the higher level protocols y will always be random and independent of the inputs.

Functionality SisoLinSPIR

Init. Given an array $A \in (\{0,1\}^K)^N$ from S1:

1. Store N, K, A.
   The entries of A will be indexed by the elements of the cyclic group Z_N.
2. Leak N and K to C and S2.

Query. Given input $x \in Z_N$ from C and $y \in Z_N$ from S2 do the following:

1. Leak y to S1.
2. Pick a random $R \in \{0,1\}^K$.
3. Return R to C.
4. Return $R \oplus A[x+y]$ to S2.

Fig. 3. Ideal functionality for linear shared-input-shared-output-SPIR (SisoLinSPIR)

Protocol $\Pi_{\mathsf{SisoLinSPIR}}$.Init

Global parameters and functions.

- Computational security parameter 1^k.
- Pseudorandom function $F_r : \{0,1\}^* \rightarrow \{0,1\}^*$, where $r \in \{0,1\}^k$. The input and output length will be understood from the context.

Init.S1. On input (N, K, A), the Server S1 does the following:

1. Pick a random PRF key $r \in \{0,1\}^k$.
2. Generate the masked array B defined by $B[i] = A[i] \oplus F_r(i)$ for $i \in Z_N$.
3. Send N, K, B to S2 and N, K to C.

Init.C. Store the values N, K received from S1.
Init.S2. Store the values of N, K, B received from S1.

Fig. 4. The initialization phase $\Pi_{\mathsf{SisoLinSPIR}}$.Init for the functionality SisoLinSPIR

Protocol $\Pi_{\mathsf{SisoLinSPIR}}$.Query

1. S2 sends y to S1.
2. S2 and S1 locally generate a virtual database $B^{\leftarrow y}$ defined by $B^{\leftarrow y}[i] = B[i+y]$.
3. C picks a random $R \in \{0,1\}^K$.
4. C picks a random subset $T_{\mathsf{S1}} \subseteq Z_N$ and lets $T_{\mathsf{S2}} = T_{\mathsf{S1}} \oplus \{x\}$.
5. C sends R and T_{S1} to S1 and T_{S2} to S2.
6. S1 locally computes $Z_{\mathsf{S1}} = \bigoplus_{i \in T_{\mathsf{S1}}} B^{\leftarrow y}[i]$ and S2 computes $Z_{\mathsf{S2}} = \bigoplus_{i \in T_{\mathsf{S2}}} B^{\leftarrow y}[i]$.
7. S1 sends to S2 the string $Z'_{\mathsf{S1}} = Z_{\mathsf{S1}} \oplus R$.
8. Parties invoke the SisoPRF oracle with inputs (N, K, r) from S1, input x from C, and input y from S2. Let Y_{C} and Y_{S2} denote the outputs.
9. C outputs $R \oplus Y_{\mathsf{C}}$ and S2 outputs $Z_{\mathsf{S2}} \oplus Z'_{\mathsf{S1}} \oplus Y_{\mathsf{S2}}$.

Fig. 5. The query phase $\Pi_{\mathsf{SisoLinSPIR}}$.Query for the functionality SisoLinSPIR in the SisoPRF-hybrid model

Lemma 2 (Main Technical Construction of Linear SisoSPIR). *Protocol* $\Pi_{SisoLinSPIR}$ *realizes* SisoLinSPIR *in the* SisoPRF-*hybrid model with perfect correctness and computational security against any single semi-honest party.*

5   Full SSE and Range Queries

5.1   Weak Distributed Oblivious Permutation Range SPIR

In the full version, we give a simple extension from a single index weak SPIR (wSPIR) to a multi-index weak SPIR (rSPIR) that can support privately retrieving multiple locations at once, though remains "weak" in the sense that it relies on a permutation and must cache results.

5.2   FindEndpoints

Our goal will be to use the above protocols to retrieve a range of records, once we found the relevant endpoints. For this we use, for each searchable field and each type of query, a "helper" array which is sorted according to the field value (or, sometimes, tokens) and contain pointers to the actual records.

Figure 6 defines the ideal functionality FindEndpoints. This functionality allows C to find, given a query on field field of type type, the two endpoints of the range of matches inside an array $L^{\text{field,type}}$. The exact content of these arrays will be defined shortly.

Functionality FindEndpoints

Global parameters. List of pairs (field, type) such that S1 supports queries of type type to field field.

Init. For each pair (field, type) in the list, S1 provides an array $L^{\text{field,type}} \in (\{0,1\}^K)^N$.

1. Store each array $L^{\text{field,type}}$.
2. Leak the corresponding N and K to all parties.

Query. Given query q from C, do the following:

1. Let i_{left} be the minimal element of $L^{\text{field,type}}$ that matches q, or $i_{\text{left}} = +\infty$ if no such element exists.
2. Let i_{right} be the maximal element of $L^{\text{field,type}}$ that matches q, or $i_{\text{right}} = -\infty$ if no such element exists.
3. Return $i_{\text{left}}, i_{\text{right}}$ to C.

Fig. 6. Ideal functionality for FindEndpoints

The implementation of the FindEndpoints functionality is based on B-tree data-structures. S1, given each of the sorted arrays $L = L^{\text{field,type}}$ (for each supported pair (field,type)), builds a B-tree with branching factor b as follows: in the leaf layer, partition the elements of L into groups of b elements each (in order).

Protocol $\Pi_{\mathsf{FindEndpoints}}$.Init

Global parameters and functions. List of pairs (field, type) such that S1 supports queries of type type to field field.

Init.S1. For each pair (field, type) in the list, S1 is given an input array $L^{\mathsf{field,type}} \in (\{0,1\}^K)^{N^{\mathsf{field,type}}}$. It does the following:

1. Construct a B-tree $T^{\mathsf{field,type}}$, as described above, for the (field, type) pair.
2. Send $N^{\mathsf{field,type}}, K, T^{\mathsf{field,type}}$ to S2 and $N^{\mathsf{field,type}}, K$ to C.

Init.S2. Participate in SisoSublinSPIR.Init. Store the values $N^{\mathsf{field,type}}, K, T^{\mathsf{field,type}}$ received from S1.

Init.C. Participate in SisoSublinSPIR.Init. Store the values $N^{\mathsf{field,type}}, K$ received from S1.

Fig. 7. The initialization phase $\Pi_{\mathsf{FindEndpoints}}$.Init for the functionality FindEndpoints

---

Protocol $\Pi_{\mathsf{FindEndpoints}}$.Query

Global parameters and functions. MPC Protocols for the following functionalities:

– The functionality find-left gets as input (additive) shares for the content of the current node v in the B-tree (C-node and S2-node), a query q from C and a pointer left-trap for a trap node. It returns shares of a pointer (C-ptr, S2-ptr) to the leftmost (direct) child of v that satisfies the query q, or to left-trap if no such child exists. The functionality find-right is defined similarly for finding the rightmost child that satisfies q.

– The functionality ExtractEndpoints gets as input shares C-l-leaf, S2-l-leaf of the leftmost node satisfying q and C-r-leaf, S2-r-leaf of the rightmost node satisfying q. The first node is of the form $(x, i_{\text{left}}, i_{\text{realleft}})$ and the second is $(x', i_{\text{right}}, i_{\text{realright}})$. The functionality returns $i_{\text{left}}, i_{\text{right}}$ to C, except if $i_{\text{realleft}} = +\infty$ or $i_{\text{realright}} = -\infty$ or $i_{\text{realleft}} > i_{\text{realright}}$ or q does not satisfy the policy; in all of these cases return $i_{\text{left}} = +\infty, i_{\text{right}} = -\infty$.

Query. On input $q \in \{0,1\}^K$ for C:

1. $depth = \lceil \log_b N \rceil$, C-ptr $= root$, S2-ptr $= 0$
2. Do $depth$ times:
       Invoke $\Pi_{\mathsf{SisoLinSPIR}}$(C-ptr, S2-ptr) to obtain C-node, S2-node.
       Invoke MPC oracle for find-left(C-node, S2-node, q, left-trap) to obtain C-ptr, S2-ptr.
       End Do
3. Invoke $\Pi_{\mathsf{SisoSublinSPIR}}$(C-ptr, S2-ptr) to obtain shares of left leaf C-l-leaf, S2-l-leaf.
4. C-ptr $= root$, S2-ptr $= 0$
5. Do $depth$ times:
       Invoke $\Pi_{\mathsf{SisoLinSPIR}}$(C-ptr, S2-ptr) to obtain C-node, S2-node.
       Invoke MPC oracle for find-right(C-node, S2-node, q, right-trap). Obtain C-ptr, S2-ptr.
       End Do
6. Invoke $\Pi_{\mathsf{SisoSublinSPIR}}$(C-ptr, S2-ptr) to obtain shares of right leaf C-r-leaf, S2-r-leaf.

7. Invoke MPC oracle for ExtractEndpoints(C-l-leaf, S2-l-leaf, C-r-leaf, S2-r-leaf).

Fig. 8. The query phase $\Pi_{\mathsf{FindEndpoints}}$.Query for the functionality FindEndpoints in the (SisoPRF,MPC)-hybrid model

That is, for each such group, there is a leaf node (i.e., the i-th element of the array L belongs to the $\lfloor i/b \rfloor$) leaf node). We will also need to append the value

i to the i-th element in the leafs. Finally, we create a leftmost "trap" node that contains $-\infty$ and a rightmost "trap" node which contains $+\infty$ values. Non-leaf nodes will contain b elements of the form $(i_{\text{l-value}}, i_{\text{r-value}}, ptr)$, where the value of all elements inside the subtree pointed to by ptr is in the (closed) interval $[i_{\text{l-value}}, i_{\text{r-value}}]$. Again, each of these internal layers (excluding the root layer) will contain a leftmost and rightmost "trap" nodes. Finally, in the initialization we invoke SisoLinSPIR.Init for each such layer (which results in S2 having an "encrypted" form of the layer).

We take additional care in the leaf level and use SisoSublinSPIR padded with δ dummy entries.

Figure 7 describes the initialization phase of protocol $\Pi_{\text{FindEndpoints}}$ which realizes FindEndpoints with security against a single semi-honest party.

FindEndpoints. Query is implemented as described in the overview: the B-tree is privately traversed by invoking SisoSPIR and MPC on the node level by level. Figure 8 describes the query phase of protocol $\Pi_{\text{FindEndpoints}}$. Next, we consider the following outer protocol OuterFindEndpoints, that serves as an interface to FindEndpoints by applying a few additional permutations. The ideal functionality OuterFindEndpoints is described in Fig. 9. The implementation is straightforward as it is essentially obtained by replacing the various ideal functionalities by their actual implementations.

Functionality OuterFindEndpoints

Init. S1 is given database $D \in (\{0,1\}^K)^N$.
It picks a random permutation $\sigma : [N] \to [N]$. Then, for each field field and query type type that S1 supports, it does the following:

1. Compute arrays $L^{\text{field,type}}[i] = (x_i, i)$, $B^{\text{field,type}}[i] = ptr_i$ (of length $N^{\text{field,type}}$).
2. Pick a random permutation $\pi^{\text{field,type}} : [N^{\text{field,type}}] \to [N^{\text{field,type}}]$.
3. Let $L'^{\text{field,type}}[i] = (x_i, \pi^{\text{field,type}}(i))$ and $B'^{\text{field,type}}[i] = \sigma(ptr_i)$.
4. Invoke rSPIR.Init using $B'^{\text{field,type}}$ and $\pi^{\text{field,type}}$ as inputs.
5. Invoke FindEndpoints.Init using $L'^{\text{field,type}}$ as input.

Invoke wSPIR.Init using $D' = \sigma(D)$ (a randomly permuted version of database D) as input.
Query. Given query q of type type to field field from C, do the following:

1. Invoke FindEndpoints.Query using array $L'^{\text{field,type}}$ and query q.
   Obtain i_{left} and i_{right} which are equal $\pi^{\text{field,type}}(i_{\text{realleft}})$ and $\pi^{\text{field,type}}(i_{\text{realright}})$, respectively. If $i_{\text{left}} = +\infty$ then Return $\emptyset$ to C.
2. Invoke rSPIR.Query using i_{left} and i_{right} as inputs.
   Obtain all elements in $B'[(\pi^{\text{field,type}})^{-1}(i_{\text{left}}), \ldots, (\pi^{\text{field,type}})^{-1}(i_{\text{right}})]$ (that is, $B'[i_{\text{realleft}}, \ldots, i_{\text{realright}}]$).
3. Each of these values is of the form $\sigma(ptr_j)$, for some ptr_j which is a pointer to a record that actually matches the query q. C invokes the functionality Π_{wSPIR}.Query on each value $\sigma(ptr_j)$ to obtain the records $D'(\sigma(ptr_j)) = D[\sigma^{-1}(\sigma(ptr_j))] = D[ptr_j]$. Return records to C.

Fig. 9. Ideal functionality for OuterFindEndpoints

Remark. We discuss how to handle query policies: we augment the FindEndpoints functionality to take as input a policy from the server, and if it is not satisfied by the policy, it sets $i_{\text{left}} = +\infty$ and $i_{\text{right}} = -\infty$.

5.3   Putting it All Together

Theorem 1 (Main Theorem). *The OuterFindEndpoints protocol is a sublinear communication protocol realizing the distributed SSE functionality $\mathcal{F}_{SSE}$ where the leakage profiles only reveal the sizes of the objects (no information about access patterns and intersection of queries or results across multiple queries). The protocol achieves 1-privacy in the semi-honest model and uses a logarithmic number of communication rounds in the size of the database.*

6   Conclusion

In this paper, we presented a solution for large-scale private database outsourcing via an SSE-style construction on B-trees. We formalized a model for our two-server SSE, and provided an abstract scheme along with an efficient realization of the scheme as our solution. The solution has sublinear overhead and leaks no access pattern information up to δ queries. Finally, we implemented a prototype and provided benchmarked results for our solution, which is only 5× slower compared to MySQL when querying around 10 % of the database, with smaller queries resulting in over 100× relative slowdown due to fixed costs.

A   Implementation and Benchmarking

We implemented our protocol in C and C++ targeting a POSIX environment. In our implementation, we transmit all information over TLS, thus reducing the leakage to the network to just the *size* of communication. Our tests were run on a desktop machine running inside a Ubuntu 12.04 LTS virtual machine with

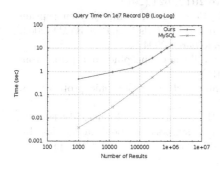

Fig. 10. Actual query times

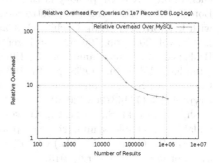

Fig. 11. Relative query times

8GB of RAM and 4 cores of an Intel i7-2600K 3.4GHz CPU assigned to it. Here, we give the results of tests compared to MySQL and defer component testing to the full version.

Actual Queries and Comparison to MySQL. We set up a database of 10 million records, where each record is roughly 0.5KB. We query the database using range queries that return roughly 1000, 10000, 50000, 100000, 250000, 500000, 750000, and 1 million records (which is 10 % of the database). The raw times are presented in Fig. 10. We consider the relative multiplicative overhead, which is presented in Fig. 11. We show a trend line in Fig. 12.

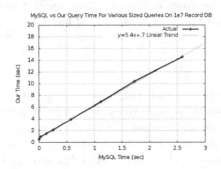

Fig. 12. Comparison to MySQL trendline

References

1. Agrawal, R., Kiernan, J., Srikant, R., Yirong, X.: Order-preserving encryption for numeric data. In: SIGMOD Conference, pp. 563–574 (2004)
2. Bellare, M., Boldyreva, A., O'Neill, A.: Deterministic and efficiently searchable encryption. In: Menezes, A. (ed.) CRYPTO 2007. LNCS, vol. 4622, pp. 535–552. Springer, Heidelberg (2007)
3. Boldyreva, A., Chenette, N., Lee, Y., O'Neill, A.: Order-preserving symmetric encryption. IACR Cryptology ePrint Archive **2012**, 624 (2012)
4. Boneh, D., Di Crescenzo, G., Ostrovsky, R., Persiano, G.: Public key encryption with keyword search. In: Cachin, C., Camenisch, J.L. (eds.) EUROCRYPT 2004. LNCS, vol. 3027, pp. 506–522. Springer, Heidelberg (2004)
5. Brakerski, Z., Vaikuntanathan, V.: Efficient fully homomorphic encryption from (standard) LWE. In: FOCS, pp. 97–106 (2011)
6. Canetti, R.: Security and composition of multiparty cryptographic protocols. J. Cryptol. **13**(1), 143–202 (2000)
7. Cash, D., Jarecki, S., Jutla, C., Krawczyk, H., Roşu, M.-C., Steiner, M.: Highly-scalable searchable symmetric encryption with support for boolean queries. In: Canetti, R., Garay, J.A. (eds.) CRYPTO 2013, Part I. LNCS, vol. 8042, pp. 353–373. Springer, Heidelberg (2013)
8. Chang, Y.-C., Mitzenmacher, M.: Privacy preserving keyword searches on remote encrypted data. In: Ioannidis, J., Keromytis, A.D., Yung, M. (eds.) ACNS 2005. LNCS, vol. 3531, pp. 442–455. Springer, Heidelberg (2005)

9. Chase, M., Kamara, S.: Structured encryption and controlled disclosure. In: Abe, M. (ed.) ASIACRYPT 2010. LNCS, vol. 6477, pp. 577–594. Springer, Heidelberg (2010)
10. Chor, B., Goldreich, O., Kushilevitz, E., Sudan, M.: Private information retrieval. In: FOCS, pp. 41–50 (1995)
11. Curtmola, R., Garay, J.A., Kamara, S., Ostrovsky, R.: Searchable symmetric encryption: improved definitions and efficient constructions. In: ACM CCS, pp. 79–88 (2006)
12. Dautrich, J., Ravishankar, C.: Combining ORAM with PIR to minimize bandwidth costs. In: ACM CODASPY, pp. 289–296 (2015)
13. Fisch, B., Vo, B., Krell, F., Kumarasubramanian, A., Kolesnikov, V., Malkin, T., Bellovin, S.M.: Malicious-client security in blind seer: a scalable private DBMS. IACR Cryptology ePrint Archive, vol. 963, p. 2014 (2014)
14. Freedman, M.J., Ishai, Y., Pinkas, B., Reingold, O.: Keyword search and oblivious pseudorandom functions. In: Kilian, J. (ed.) TCC 2005. LNCS, vol. 3378, pp. 303–324. Springer, Heidelberg (2005)
15. Gentry, C.: Fully homomorphic encryption using ideal lattices. In: STOC, pp. 169–178 (2009)
16. Goh, E.-J.: Secure indexes (2003)
17. Goldreich, O.: Towards a theory of software protection and simulation by oblivious RAMs. In: STOC, pp. 182–194 (1987)
18. Goldreich, O.: Foundations of Cryptography: Basic Tools. Cambridge University Press, Cambridge (2001)
19. Goldreich, O., Ostrovsky, R.: Software protection and simulation on oblivious RAMs. J. ACM **43**(3), 431–473 (1996)
20. Jarecki, S., Jutla, C.S., Krawczyk, H., Rosu, M.-C., Steiner, M.: Outsourced symmetric private information retrieval. In: ACM CCS, pp. 875–888 (2013)
21. Kamara, S., Papamanthou, C.: Parallel and dynamic searchable symmetric encryption. In: Financial Cryptography, pp. 258–274 (2013)
22. Kurosawa, K., Ohtaki, Y.: Uc-secure searchable symmetric encryption. In: Financial Cryptography, pp. 285–298 (2012)
23. Kushilevitz, E., Ostrovsky, R.: Replication is not needed: single database, computationally-private information retrieval. In: FOCS, pp. 364–373 (1997)
24. Mayberry, T., Blass, E.-O., Chan, A.H.: Efficient private file retrieval by combining ORAM and PIR. In: NDSS (2014)
25. Naor, M., Nissim, K.: Communication preserving protocols for secure function evaluation. In: STOC, pp. 590–599 (2001)
26. Ostrovsky, R.: Efficient computation on oblivious RAMs. In: STOC, pp. 514–523 (1990)
27. Ostrovsky, R.: Software protection and simulation on oblivious RAMs. Ph.D. thesis, Massachusetts Institute of Technology, Dept. of Electrical Engineering and Computer Science, June 1992
28. Ostrovsky, R., Skeith III, W.E.: Private searching on streaming data. In: Shoup, V. (ed.) CRYPTO 2005. LNCS, vol. 3621, pp. 223–240. Springer, Heidelberg (2005)
29. Song, D., Wagner, D., Perrig, A.: Practical techniques for searches on encrypted data. In: IEEE Symposium on Security and Privacy, pp. 44–55 (2000)
30. Wang, X.S., Nayak, K., Liu, C., T.-H., Chan, H., Shi, E., Stefanov, E., Huang, Y.: Oblivious data structures. In: ACM CCS, pp. 215–226 (2014)
31. Yao, A.C.C: Protocols for secure computations (extended abstract). In: FOCS, pp. 160–164 (1982)
32. Zhang, J., Ma, Q., Zhang, W., Qiao, D.: KT-ORAM: a bandwidth-efficient ORAM built on k-ary tree of PIR nodes. IACR Cryptology ePrint Archive **2014**, 624 (2014)

Digital Signatures with New Functionality

Short Randomizable Signatures

David Pointcheval[1]([⊠]) and Olivier Sanders[2]

[1] École Normale Supérieure, CNRS, INRIA, PSL Research University,
Paris, France
David.Pointcheval@ens.fr
[2] DGA-MI, Bruz, France

Abstract. Digital signature is a fundamental primitive with numerous applications. Following the development of pairing-based cryptography, several taking advantage of this setting have been proposed. Among them, the Camenisch-Lysyanskaya (CL) signature scheme is one of the most flexible and has been used as a building block for many other protocols. Unfortunately, this scheme suffers from a linear size in the number of messages to be signed which limits its use in many situations.

In this paper, we propose a new signature scheme with the same features as CL-signatures but without the linear-size drawback: our signature consists of only two elements, whatever the message length, and our algorithms are more efficient. This construction takes advantage of using type 3 pairings, that are already widely used for security and efficiency reasons.

We prove the security of our scheme without random oracles but in the generic group model. Finally, we show that protocols using CL-signatures can easily be instantiated with ours, leading to much more efficient constructions.

1 Introduction

Digital signature is one of the main cryptographic primitives which can be used in its own right, to provide the electronic version of handwritten signatures, but also as a building block for more complex primitives. Whereas efficiency is the main concern of the first case, the latter case usually requires a signature scheme with additional features. Indeed, when used as a building block, signatures must not just be efficient, they also have to be compatible with the goals and the other building blocks of the protocol. For example, privacy-preserving primitives usually require a signature scheme which allows signatures on committed secret values and compatible with zero-knowledge proofs.

1.1 Related Works

Constructing a versatile signature scheme that is both efficient and secure is not easy. One of the first construction specifically designed as a building block for other applications was proposed by Camenisch and Lysyanskaya [18].

O. Sanders—Work done while being at Orange Labs.

K. Sako (Ed.): CT-RSA 2016, LNCS 9610, pp. 111–126, 2016.
DOI: 10.1007/978-3-319-29485-8_7

Their construction, relying on the Strong RSA assumption [6], allows indeed signatures on committed values and proofs of knowledge of a signature.

The emergence of pairing-based cryptography [13,34] has created a need for such signature schemes compatible with this new setting. Indeed, many cryptographic protocols now use bilinear groups, *i.e.* a set of three groups $\mathbb{G}_1$, $\mathbb{G}_2$ and $\mathbb{G}_T$ along with a bilinear map $e : \mathbb{G}_1 \times \mathbb{G}_2 \to \mathbb{G}_T$. In 2004, Camenisch and Lysyanskaya proposed a new pairing-based signature scheme [19] whose flexibility has allowed it to be used in several applications, such as group signatures [10], direct anonymous attestations [9,25], aggregate signatures [35] or E-cash systems [21]. One of its most interesting features is probably the ability of its signatures to be randomized: given a valid CL-signature $\sigma = (a, b, c)$ on a message m, anyone can generate another valid signature on the same message by selecting a random scalar t and computing (a^t, b^t, c^t). The latter is indistinguishable from a fresh signature on m. Let us consider a typical situation for anonymous credentials [17], direct anonymous attestations [15], or group signatures [24]: a user first gets a signature σ on some secret value s and then has to prove, several times, that s is certified still keeping the proofs unlinkable. If σ were issued using a conventional signature scheme, it would have to be committed and the user would have to prove that the commitment opens to a valid signature on a secret value which is a rather complex statement to prove, even in the Random Oracle Model (ROM) [7]. Now, if σ is a CL-signature, then the user can simply compute a randomized version σ' of σ, sends it and proves that it is valid on the secret value. This idea underlies the efficiency of the constructions described in [9,10,25]. For these constructions, unlinkability relies on the DDH assumption in $\mathbb{G}_1$, and so requires the use of asymmetric pairings. But this is not a strong assumption, since they offer the best efficiency (see [29]).

One might have thought that the seminal work of Groth and Sahai [32], providing the first practical non-interactive zero-knowledge proofs (NIZKs) in the standard model, in conjunction with the recent structure-preserving signatures [1–3,23], has decreased interest for CL-signatures. However, that has not happened due to the huge performance gap between constructions in the standard model and constructions in the ROM: for example, the most efficient group signature in the standard model [31] consists of 50 group elements whereas [10], in the ROM, consists of only 3 group elements and two scalars. And for real-life applications, where time constraints are particularly challenging, constructions with NIZK proofs in the ROM seem unavoidable.

As a consequence, signatures schemes, such as the CL-signatures, compatible with NIZKs in the ROM still remain of huge practical interest.

Another primitive for which efficiency considerations are central is anonymous credentials. Unfortunately, even if they are one of the applications proposed for CL-signatures, most of these schemes [4,5,16,20] use other constructions, such as the one proposed by Boneh, Boyen and Shacham (BBS) [12]. This is due to a large extent to the size of CL-signatures, which is linear in the number of messages to be signed. Since a user of an anonymous credential system may have several attributes to be certified, this cost quickly becomes prohibitive. This is unfortunate because, here again, the randomizability of CL-signatures could lead to more efficient protocols.

1.2 Our Contribution

In this paper, we propose a new signature scheme, with the same features as CL-signatures, but with a remarkable efficiency. Indeed, whereas the original CL-signatures [19] on blocks of r messages consist of $1 + 2r$ elements of $\mathbb{G}_1$, ours only require 2 elements of $\mathbb{G}_1$, whatever r is. Moreover, as illustrated in Fig. 1 (see Sect. 7), our signature and verification algorithms are much more efficient.

Our work proceeds from the observation that most of the recent protocols [9,10,25] using CL-signatures require type 3 pairings for efficiency and security reasons (see [29]). However, CL-signatures, as most of the constructions from the beginnings of pairing-based cryptography, were designed for type 1 pairings. Unfortunately, this setting usually leads to more complex protocols since they cannot rely on assumptions which would have held with pairings of other types. This has been illustrated by the recent results [2,23] on structure-preserving signatures, which show that designing schemes specifically for type 3 pairings results in more efficient constructions.

Following the same rationale, we propose a signature scheme suited to such pairings: it can be seen as CL-signatures, but taking advantage of the full potential of type 3 pairings. The separation between the space of the signatures ($\mathbb{G}_1$) and the one of the public key ($\mathbb{G}_2$) allows indeed more efficient constructions since the elements of the latter can no longer be used to build forgeries in the former. Unfortunately, the security of our scheme does not rely on any standard assumption and so is proved in the generic group model, which does not provide the same guarantees. However, as illustrated by [2,11,19], relying on proofs in the generic group model or on non-standard assumptions (themselves proved in this model), allows more efficient constructions. For some applications with challenging time constraints, such as public transport where authentication must be performed in less than 300 ms [27,33], we argue that this trade-off, between efficiency and the security assumption, is reasonable. By providing short signatures with efficient algorithms, our solution may then contribute to make all features of modern cryptography more accessible.

Improving the efficiency of primitives with practical applications was also the concern of the authors of [22]. They proved, in the generic group model, the security of the MAC scheme introduced in [28] and used it to construct keyed-verification anonymous credentials (the secret-key analogue of standard anonymous credentials). Although our signature shares similarities with this scheme, it offers much more flexibility. Indeed, the construction described in [22,28] does not achieve public verifiability and so only fits the case where the verifier is also the issuer. Moreover, the protocols for obtaining or proving knowledge of a MAC on committed messages are more complex than the ones, for a signature, we describe in this paper.

Besides efficiency, one of the main advantages of our scheme is that it acts as a plug-in replacement for CL-signatures. Indeed, since they achieve the same properties than the latter, our signatures can be used to instantiate most of the protocols initially designed for CL ones. To illustrate this point, we convert our signature scheme into a sequential aggregate signature scheme [37] using an idea similar to the one of Lee, Lee and Yung [35]. The resulting aggregate signature only consists of 2 elements in $\mathbb{G}_1$ and so is shorter than theirs. Similar gains can be achieved for many other applications such as group signatures or anonymous credentials.

1.3   Organization

We review some definitions and notations in Sect. 2 and present new computational assumptions in Sect. 3. Section 4 describes our signature scheme whose conversion into a sequential aggregate signature scheme is described in Sect. 5. Section 6 describes a variant of our scheme allowing to sign committed values along with a protocol for proving knowledge of a signature. Section 7 provides a comparison with related works. Finally, we describe some applications and provide the security proofs in the appendices.

2   Preliminaries

2.1   Bilinear Groups

Bilinear groups are a set of three cyclic groups $\mathbb{G}_1$, $\mathbb{G}_2$, and $\mathbb{G}_T$ of prime order p along with a bilinear map $e : \mathbb{G}_1 \times \mathbb{G}_2 \to \mathbb{G}_T$ with the following properties:

1. for all $g \in \mathbb{G}_1, \widetilde{g} \in \mathbb{G}_2$ and $a, b \in \mathbb{Z}_p$, $e(g^a, \widetilde{g}^b) = e(g, \widetilde{g})^{a \cdot b}$;
2. for $g \neq 1_{\mathbb{G}_1}$ and $\widetilde{g} \neq 1_{\mathbb{G}_2}$, $e(g, \widetilde{g}) \neq 1_{\mathbb{G}_T}$;
3. the map e is efficiently computable.

Galbraith, Paterson, and Smart [29] defined three types of pairings: in type 1, $\mathbb{G}_1 = \mathbb{G}_2$; in type 2, $\mathbb{G}_1 \neq \mathbb{G}_2$ but there exists an efficient homomorphism $\phi : \mathbb{G}_2 \to \mathbb{G}_1$, while no efficient one exists in the other direction; in type 3, $\mathbb{G}_1 \neq \mathbb{G}_2$ and no efficiently computable homomorphism exists between $\mathbb{G}_1$ and $\mathbb{G}_2$, in either direction.

Although type 1 pairings were mostly used in the early-age of pairing-based cryptography, they have been gradually discarded in favour of type 3 pairings. Indeed, the latter offer a better efficiency and are compatible with several computational assumptions, such as the Decision Diffie-Hellman assumption in $\mathbb{G}_1$ or $\mathbb{G}_2$, also known as the XDH assumption, which does not hold in type 1 pairings.

In this work, we only consider type 3 pairings. We stress that using type 1 or type 2 pairings would make our signature scheme totally insecure.

2.2 Digital Signature Scheme

Syntax. A digital signature scheme Σ is defined by four algorithms:

- the Setup algorithm which, on input a security parameter k, outputs pp, a description of the public parameters;
- the key generation algorithm Keygen which, on input pp, outputs a pair of signing and verification keys (sk, pk) – we assume that sk contains pk, and that pk contains pp;
- the signing algorithm Sign which, on input the signing key sk and a message m, outputs a signature σ;
- the verification algorithm Verify which, on input m, σ and pk, outputs 1 if σ is a valid signature on m under pk, and 0 otherwise.

Security Notion. The standard security notion for a signature scheme is *existential unforgeability under chosen message attacks* (EUF-CMA) [30] which means that it is hard, even given access to a signing oracle, to output a valid pair (m, σ) for a message m never asked to the signing oracle. It is defined using the following game between a challenger $\mathcal{C}$ and an adversary $\mathcal{A}$:

- **Setup:** $\mathcal{C}$ runs the Setup and the Keygen algorithms to obtain sk and pk. The adversary is given the public key pk;
- **Queries:** $\mathcal{A}$ adaptively requests signatures on at most q messages $m_1, \ldots, m_q$. $\mathcal{C}$ answers each query by returning $\sigma_i \leftarrow \text{Sign}(\text{sk}, m_i)$;
- **Output:** $\mathcal{A}$ eventually outputs a message-signature pair (m^*, σ^*) and wins the game if $\text{Verify}(\text{pk}, m^*, \sigma^*) = 1$ and if $m^* \neq m_i \; \forall i \in [1, q]$.

A signature scheme is EUF-CMA secure if no probabilistic polynomial-time adversary $\mathcal{A}$ can win this game with non-negligible probability.

2.3 Sequential Aggregate Signature

Syntax. Sequential aggregate signature [37] is a special type of aggregate signature (introduced by Boneh *et al.* [14]) where the final signature on the list of messages is computed sequentially by each signer, who adds his signature on his message. It is defined by the four algorithms described below:

- the AS.Setup algorithm which, on input a security parameter k, outputs pp, a description of the public parameters;
- the key generation algorithm AS.Keygen which, on input pp, outputs a pair of signing and verification keys (sk, pk) – we assume that sk contains pk, and that pk contains pp;
- the signing algorithm AS.Sign which, on input an aggregate signature σ on messages $(m_1, \ldots, m_r)$ under public keys $(\text{pk}_1, \ldots, \text{pk}_r)$, a message m and a signing key sk such that $\text{pk} \notin \{\text{pk}_i\}_{i=1}^{r}$, outputs a new aggregate signature σ' on $(m_1, \ldots, m_r, m)$;
- the verification algorithm AS.Verify which, on input $(m_1, \ldots, m_r)$, σ and distinct public keys $(\text{pk}_1, \ldots, \text{pk}_r)$, outputs 1 if σ is a valid aggregate signature on $(m_1, \ldots, m_r)$ under $(\text{pk}_1, \ldots, \text{pk}_r)$, and 0 otherwise.

Security Model. The security property for a sequential aggregate signature scheme is *existential unforgeability under chosen message attacks* which requires that no adversary is able to forge an aggregate signature, on a set of messages of its choice, by a set of users whose secret keys are not all known to it. It is defined using the following game between a challenger $\mathcal{C}$ and an adversary $\mathcal{A}$:

- **Setup:** $\mathcal{C}$ first initializes a key list KeyList as empty. Next it runs the AS.Setup algorithm to get pp and the AS.Keygen algorithm to get the signing and verification keys $(\mathsf{sk}^*, \mathsf{pk}^*)$. The verification key pk^* is given to $\mathcal{A}$;
- **Join Queries:** $\mathcal{A}$ adaptively asks to add the public keys pk_i to KeyList;
- **Signature Query:** $\mathcal{A}$ adaptively requests aggregate signatures on at most q messages $m_1, \ldots, m_q$ under the challenge public key pk^*. For each query, it provides an aggregate signature σ_i on the messages $(m_{i,1}, \ldots, m_{i,r_i})$ under the public keys $(\mathsf{pk}_{i,1}, \ldots, \mathsf{pk}_{i,r_i})$, all in KeyList. Then $\mathcal{C}$ returns the aggregation AS.Sign$(\mathsf{sk}^*, \sigma_i, (m_{i,1}, \ldots, m_{i,r_i}), (\mathsf{pk}_{i,1}, \ldots, \mathsf{pk}_{i,r_i}), m_i)$;
- **Output:** $\mathcal{A}$ eventually outputs an aggregate signature σ on the messages $(m_1^*, \ldots, m_r^*)$ under the public keys $(\mathsf{pk}_1, \ldots, \mathsf{pk}_r)$ and wins the game if the following conditions are all satisfied:
  - AS.Verify$((\mathsf{pk}_1, \ldots, \mathsf{pk}_r), (m_1^*, \ldots, m_r^*), \sigma) = 1$;
  - For all $\mathsf{pk}_j \neq \mathsf{pk}^*$, $\mathsf{pk}_j \in$ KeyList ;
  - For some $j^* \in [1, r]$, $\mathsf{pk}^* = \mathsf{pk}_{j^*}$ and $m_{j^*}^*$ has not been queried to the signing oracle, *i.e.* $m_{j^*}^* \neq m_i$, for $i = 1, \ldots, q$.

A sequential aggregate signature scheme is EUF-CMA secure if no probabilistic polynomial-time adversary $\mathcal{A}$ can win this game with non-negligible probability.

Certified Keys. As in [35], we consider the setting proposed by Lu *et al.* [36] where users must prove knowledge of their signing key sk when they want to add a public key pk in KeyList. In the security proof, this enables the simulator to answer every signature query made by the adversary $\mathcal{A}$. As a consequence, in the **Join Query**, when $\mathcal{A}$ asks to add pk to KeyList, it additionally proves its knowledge of the corresponding secret key sk.

3 Assumption

A by-now classical assumption is the so-called LRSW [38], applied to many privacy-preserving protocols, such as the CL-signatures [19], that admit two protocols: an issuing protocol that allows a user to get a signature σ on a message x, just by sending a commitment of x to the signer, and a proving protocol that allows the user to prove, in a zero-knowledge way, his knowledge of a signature on a commitment of x. They lead to efficient anonymous credentials.

Definition 1 (LRSW Assumption). *Let $\mathbb{G}$ be a cyclic group of prime order p, with a generator g. For $X = g^x$ and $Y = g^y$, where x and y are random scalars in $\mathbb{Z}_p$, we define the oracle $\mathcal{O}(m)$ on input $m \in \mathbb{Z}_p$ that chooses a random $h \in \mathbb{G}$ and outputs the triple $T = (h, h^y, h^{x+mxy})$. Given (X, Y) and unlimited access to this oracle, no adversary can efficiently generate such a triple for a new scalar m^*, not asked to $\mathcal{O}$.*

This assumption has been introduced in [38] and proven in the generic group model, as modeled by Shoup [42].

We now propose two similar assumptions in bilinear groups of type 3 that will provide even more efficient protocols. We then prove them to hold in the bilinear generic group model.

Definition 2 (Assumption 1). *Let $(p, \mathbb{G}_1, \mathbb{G}_2, \mathbb{G}_T, e)$ a bilinear group setting of type 3, with g (resp. $\tilde{g}$) a generator of $\mathbb{G}_1$ (resp. $\mathbb{G}_2$). For $(X = g^x, Y = g^y)$ and $(\tilde{X} = \tilde{g}^x, \tilde{Y} = \tilde{g}^y)$, where x and y are random scalars in $\mathbb{Z}_p$, we define the oracle $\mathcal{O}(m)$ on input $m \in \mathbb{Z}_p$ that chooses a random $h \in \mathbb{G}_1$ and outputs the pair $P = (h, h^{x+my})$. Given $(g, Y, \tilde{g}, \tilde{X}, \tilde{Y})$ and unlimited access to this oracle, no adversary can efficiently generate such a pair, with $h \neq 1_{\mathbb{G}_1}$, for a new scalar m^*, not asked to $\mathcal{O}$.*

One can note that using pairings, an output of the adversary can be checked since the pair $P = (P_1, P_2)$ should satisfy $e(P_1, \tilde{X} \cdot \tilde{Y}^m) = e(P_2, \tilde{g})$. In addition, (X, Y) are enough to answer oracle queries: on a scalar $m \in \mathbb{Z}_p$, one computes $(g^r, (X \cdot Y^m)^r)$. This requires 3 exponentiations per query, while knowing (x, y) just requires a random sampling in $\mathbb{G}_1$ and one exponentiation.

In some situations, a weaker assumption will be enough, where Y is not given to the adversary:

Definition 3 (Assumption 2). *Let $(p, \mathbb{G}_1, \mathbb{G}_2, \mathbb{G}_T, e)$ a bilinear group setting of type 3, with g (resp. $\tilde{g}$) a generator of $\mathbb{G}_1$ (resp. $\mathbb{G}_2$). For $(\tilde{X} = \tilde{g}^x, \tilde{Y} = \tilde{g}^y)$ where x and y are random scalars in $\mathbb{Z}_p$, we define the oracle $\mathcal{O}(m)$ on input $m \in \mathbb{Z}_p$ that chooses a random $h \in \mathbb{G}$ and outputs the pair $P = (h, h^{x+my})$. Given $(\tilde{g}, \tilde{X}, \tilde{Y})$ and unlimited access to this oracle, no adversary can efficiently generate such a pair, with $h \neq 1_{\mathbb{G}_1}$, for a new scalar m^*, not asked to $\mathcal{O}$.*

Theorem 4. *The above Assumption 1 (and thus the Assumption 2) holds in the generic bilinear group model: after q oracle queries and q_G group-oracle queries, no adversary can generate a valid pair for a new scalar with probability greater than $6(q + q_G)^2/p$.*

The proof can be found in the full version [40].

4   Our Randomizable Digital Signature Scheme

For the sake of clarity, for our signature scheme, we first describe the specific case where only one message is signed. We then present an extension allowing to sign several messages and show that the security of the latter scheme holds under the security of the former (which holds under the weak Assumption 2).

4.1   A Single-Message Signature Scheme

Description. Our signature scheme to sign a message $m \in \mathbb{Z}_p$ consists of the following algorithms:

- Setup(1^k): Given a security parameter k, this algorithm outputs $pp \leftarrow$ $(p, \mathbb{G}_1, \mathbb{G}_2, \mathbb{G}_T, e)$. These bilinear groups must be of type 3. In the following, we denote $\mathbb{G}_1^* = \mathbb{G}_1 \backslash \{1_{\mathbb{G}_1}\}$;
- Keygen(pp): This algorithm selects $\tilde{g} \xleftarrow{\$} \mathbb{G}_2$ and $(x, y) \xleftarrow{\$} \mathbb{Z}_p^2$, computes $(\tilde{X}, \tilde{Y}) \leftarrow (\tilde{g}^x, \tilde{g}^y)$ and sets sk as (x, y) and pk as $(\tilde{g}, \tilde{X}, \tilde{Y})$;
- Sign(sk, m): This algorithm selects a random $h \xleftarrow{\$} \mathbb{G}_1^*$ and outputs $\sigma \leftarrow (h, h^{(x+y \cdot m)})$;
- Verify(pk, m, σ): This algorithm parses σ as (σ_1, σ_2) and checks whether $\sigma_1 \neq 1_{\mathbb{G}_1}$ and $e(\sigma_1, \tilde{X} \cdot \tilde{Y}^m) = e(\sigma_2, \tilde{g})$ are both satisfied. In the positive case, it outputs 1, and 0 otherwise.

Correctness: If $\sigma = (\sigma_1 = h, \sigma_2 = h^{(x+y \cdot m)})$, then

$$e(\sigma_1, \tilde{X} \cdot \tilde{Y}^m) = e(h, \tilde{X} \cdot \tilde{Y}^m) = e(h, \tilde{g})^{(x+y \cdot m)} = e(h^{(x+y \cdot m)}, \tilde{g}) = e(\sigma_2, \tilde{g}).$$

Remark 5. As already remarked above, the signature could be generated with the secret key being either (x, y) or $(X = g^x, Y = g^y)$. But the former leads a more efficient signature scheme.

Randomizability. As the CL-signatures, a signature $\sigma = (\sigma_1, \sigma_2)$ on a message m can be randomized by selecting a random $t \xleftarrow{\$} \mathbb{Z}_p^*$ and computing $\sigma' \leftarrow (\sigma_1^t, \sigma_2^t)$ which is still a valid signature on m: it corresponds to replace $h \in \mathbb{G}_1^*$ by $h' = h^t \in \mathbb{G}_1^*$.

Security Analysis. EUF-CMA is exactly the above Assumption 2, since a signing oracle is perfectly equivalent to the oracle $\mathcal{O}$.

4.2   A Multi-message Signature Scheme

Description. We now present a variant of the previous scheme to sign r-message vectors $(m_1, \ldots, m_r) \in \mathbb{Z}_p^r$ at once. Our signature scheme consists of the following algorithms, where all the sums and products are on j between 1 and r:

- Setup(1^k): Given a security parameter k, this algorithm outputs $pp \leftarrow$ $(p, \mathbb{G}_1, \mathbb{G}_2, \mathbb{G}_T, e)$. These bilinear groups must be of type 3. In the following, we denote $\mathbb{G}_1^* = \mathbb{G}_1 \backslash \{1_{\mathbb{G}_1}\}$;
- Keygen(pp): This algorithm selects $\tilde{g} \xleftarrow{\$} \mathbb{G}_2$ and $(x, y_1, \ldots, y_r) \xleftarrow{\$} \mathbb{Z}_p^{r+1}$, computes $(\tilde{X}, \tilde{Y}_1, \ldots, \tilde{Y}_r) \leftarrow (\tilde{g}^x, \tilde{g}^{y_1}, \ldots, \tilde{g}^{y_r})$ and sets sk as $(x, y_1, \ldots, y_r)$ and pk as $(\tilde{g}, \tilde{X}, \tilde{Y}_1, \ldots, \tilde{Y}_r)$.
- Sign(sk, $m_1, \ldots, m_r$): This algorithm selects a random $h \xleftarrow{\$} \mathbb{G}_1^*$ and outputs $\sigma \leftarrow (h, h^{(x+\sum y_j \cdot m_j)})$.
- Verify(pk, $(m_1, \ldots, m_r)$, σ): This algorithm parses σ as (σ_1, σ_2) and checks whether $\sigma_1 \neq 1_{\mathbb{G}_1}$ and $e(\sigma_1, \tilde{X} \cdot \prod \tilde{Y}_j^{m_j}) = e(\sigma_2, \tilde{g})$ are both satisfied. In the positive case, it outputs 1, and 0 otherwise.

Correctness: If $\sigma = (\sigma_1 = h, \sigma_2 = h^{(x + \sum y_j \cdot m_j)})$, then

$$e(\sigma_1, \widetilde{X} \cdot \prod \widetilde{Y}_j^{m_j}) = e(h, \widetilde{X} \cdot \prod \widetilde{Y}_j^{m_j}) = e(h, \widetilde{g})^{x + \sum y_j \cdot m_j}$$
$$= e(h^{x + \sum y_j \cdot m_j}, \widetilde{g}) = e(\sigma_2, \widetilde{g}).$$

Security Analysis. We now rely the security of this multiple-message signature scheme to the security of the single-message signature scheme, and so on Assumption 2. Due to space limitations, the proof of the following theorem is provided in in the full version [40].

Theorem 6. *The multiple-message signature scheme achieves the EUF-CMA security level under the above Assumption 2. More precisely, if an adversary can break the EUF-CMA of the multiple-message signature scheme with probability ε, then there exists an adversary against the EUF-CMA security of the single-message signature scheme, within the same running time and the same number of signing queries, succeeding with probability greater than $\varepsilon - q/p$.*

5   A Sequential Aggregate Signature

Our Construction. It is possible to slightly modify the scheme from Sect. 4.2 to convert it into a sequential aggregate signature scheme. The signer's secret key of the original scheme to sign r-message vector was $(x, y_1, \ldots, y_r)$. But now, let us assume one publishes a signature on the r-vector $(0, \ldots, 0)$: $(g, X) = (g, g^x) \in \mathbb{G}_1^2$ for some $g \in \mathbb{G}_1$. This additional knowledge does not help an adversary to produce forgeries on non-zero vectors, but the scalar value x is no longer useful in the secret key since one can sign a vector $(m_1, \ldots, m_r)$ by selecting a random $t \xleftarrow{\$} \mathbb{Z}_p$ and computing $(g^t, (X)^t \cdot (g^t)^{\sum y_j \cdot m_j})$. The correctness follows from the one of the original scheme.

On the other hand, we can use the public key sharing technique from [35] to construct an efficient sequential aggregate signature scheme in the standard model: each signer j (from 1 to r) generates his own signing and verification keys $(y_j, \widetilde{Y}_j)$ but uses the same element X from the public parameters. To sign a message $m_1 \in \mathbb{Z}_p^*$, the first selects a random $t_1 \xleftarrow{\$} \mathbb{Z}_p$ and outputs $(\sigma_1, \sigma_2) \leftarrow (g^{t_1}, (X)^{t_1} \cdot (g^{t_1})^{y_1 \cdot m_1})$. A subsequent signer 2 can generate an aggregate signature on m_2 by selecting a random t_2 and computing $(\sigma_1', \sigma_2') \leftarrow (\sigma_1^{t_2}, (\sigma_2 \cdot \sigma_1^{y_2 \cdot m_2})^{t_2})$. Therefore, $(\sigma_1', \sigma_2') = (g^{t_1 \cdot t_2}, g^{t_1 t_2 (x + m_1 \cdot y_1 + m_2 \cdot y_2)}) = (g^t, g^{t(x + m_1 \cdot y_1 + m_2 \cdot y_2)})$, for $t = t_1 t_2$, and so its validity can be verified using the Verify algorithm described in Sect. 4.2.

More formally, our sequential aggregate signature scheme is defined by the following algorithms.

- AS.Setup(1^k): Given a security parameter k, this algorithm selects a random $x \in \mathbb{Z}_p$ and outputs $pp \leftarrow (p, \mathbb{G}_1, \mathbb{G}_2, \mathbb{G}_T, e, g, X, \widetilde{g}, \widetilde{X})$, where $X = g^x$ and $\widetilde{X} = \widetilde{g}^x$ for some generators $(g, \widetilde{g}) \in \mathbb{G}_1 \times \mathbb{G}_2$.

- AS.Keygen(pp): This algorithm selects a random $y \overset{\$}{\leftarrow} \mathbb{Z}_p$, computes $\widetilde{Y} \leftarrow \widetilde{g}^y$ and sets sk as y and pk as $\widetilde{Y}$.
- AS.Sign(sk, σ, $(m_1, \ldots, m_r)$, $(\mathsf{pk}_1, \ldots, \mathsf{pk}_r)$, m) proceeds as follows:
    - If $r = 0$, then $\sigma \leftarrow (g, X)$;
    - If $r > 0$ but AS.Verify($(\mathsf{pk}_1, \ldots, \mathsf{pk}_r)$, σ, $(m_1, \ldots, m_r)$) = 0, then it halts;
    - If $m = 0$, then it halts;
    - If for some $j \in \{1, \ldots, r\}$ $\mathsf{pk}_j = \mathsf{pk}$, then it halts.

  If the algorithm did not halt, then it parses sk as y and σ as (σ_1, σ_2), selects $t \overset{\$}{\leftarrow} \mathbb{Z}_p$ and computes $\sigma' = (\sigma'_1, \sigma'_2) \leftarrow (\sigma_1^t, (\sigma_2 \cdot \sigma_1^{y \cdot m})^t)$. It eventually outputs σ'.
- AS.Verify($(\mathsf{pk}_1, \ldots, \mathsf{pk}_r)$, $(m_1, \ldots, m_r)$, σ) parses σ as (σ_1, σ_2) and pk_j as $\widetilde{Y}_j$, for $j = 1, \ldots, r$, and checks whether $\sigma_1 \neq 1_{\mathbb{G}_1}$ and $e(\sigma_1, \widetilde{X} \cdot \prod \widetilde{Y}_j^{m_j}) = e(\sigma_2, \widetilde{g})$ are both satisfied. In the positive case, it outputs 1, and 0 otherwise.

Correctness. If $r = 0$, then the algorithm AS.Sign outputs $(g^t, (X \cdot g^{y \cdot m})^t) = (g^t, g^{t(x+y \cdot m)})$. By induction, let us now assume that $\sigma = (g^s, g^{s(x+\sum y_j \cdot m_j)})$, then an aggregate signature σ' on m is equal to $(g^{t \cdot s}, g^{t \cdot s(x+m \cdot y+\sum y_j \cdot m_j)})$, which is equal to $(h, h^{x+\sum y_j \cdot m_j+y \cdot m})$ for some $h \in \mathbb{G}_1$. The correctness of our sequential aggregate signature scheme follows then from the signature scheme described in Sect. 4.2.

Security Analysis. We now rely the security of this aggregate signature scheme, in the certified public key setting, to the security of the single-message signature scheme, and so on Assumption 2:

Theorem 7. *The aggregate signature scheme achieves the EUF-CMA security level, in the certified public-key setting, under the above Assumption 2. More precisely, if an adversary can break the EUF-CMA of the aggregate signature scheme, then there exists an adversary against the EUF-CMA security of the single-message signature scheme, within the same running time and the same number of signing queries, succeeding with the same probability.*

The proof can be found in the in the full version [40].

6 Useful Features

6.1 Signing Committed Messages

Many cryptographic primitives require efficient protocols to obtain signatures on *committed* (or transformed) values. For example, in some group signature schemes [10,12,26], users must get a certificate on their secret key $m \in \mathbb{Z}_p$ to join the group. The non-frameability property [8] expected from such a primitive prevents the users to directly send the value m to the group manager. Instead, they rather send a public value g^m, for some public $g \in \mathbb{G}_1$, and start a protocol with the latter to get a signature on the secret value m.

Our signature scheme can be slightly modified to handle such a protocol: one can submit g^m to the signer and prove knowledge of m. If the proof is valid, the signer can return $\sigma = (\sigma_1, \sigma_2) \leftarrow (g^u, (g^x \cdot (g^m)^y)^u)$, for some $u \overset{\$}{\leftarrow} \mathbb{Z}_p$, which is a valid signature on m.

However, g^m is not hiding enough in some applications, and namely if information-theoretical security is required. For example, in anonymous credentials [17], the elements $g^{m_1}, \ldots, g^{m_r}$ may provide too much information on the attributes $(m_1, \ldots, m_r)$, if they belong to small sets.

The modified BBS signature scheme [12] described in [4] enables the signer to sign messages $(m_1, \ldots, m_r)$ from a Pedersen commitment [39] $C = g_0^t \cdot g_1^{m_1} \cdots g_r^{m_r}$ (where t is a random scalar). We need to slightly modify the scheme described in Sect. 4.2 to add such a feature. Indeed, the latter does not provide any element of $\mathbb{G}_1$ in the public key. The resulting protocol is described below, in the multi-message setting. But we first start with the single-message protocol.

A Single-Message Protocol. The signature scheme for signing one information-theoretically hidden message consists of the following algorithms:

- Setup(1^k): Given a security parameter k, this algorithm outputs $pp \leftarrow (p, \mathbb{G}_1, \mathbb{G}_2, \mathbb{G}_T, e)$. These bilinear groups must be of type 3. In the following, we denote $\mathbb{G}_1^* = \mathbb{G}_1 \backslash \{1_{\mathbb{G}_1}\}$ and $\mathbb{G}_2^* = \mathbb{G}_2 \backslash \{1_{\mathbb{G}_2}\}$, which are the sets of the generators.
- Keygen(pp): This algorithm selects $g \overset{\$}{\leftarrow} \mathbb{G}_1^*$, $\tilde{g} \overset{\$}{\leftarrow} \mathbb{G}_2^*$ and $(x, y) \overset{\$}{\leftarrow} \mathbb{Z}_p^2$, computes $(X, Y) \leftarrow (g^x, g^y)$ and $(\tilde{X}, \tilde{Y}) \leftarrow (\tilde{g}^x, \tilde{g}^y)$, and sets sk $\leftarrow X$ and pk $\leftarrow (g, Y, \tilde{g}, \tilde{X}, \tilde{Y})$.
- Protocol: A user who wishes to obtain a signature on the message $m \in \mathbb{Z}_p$ first selects a random $t \overset{\$}{\leftarrow} \mathbb{Z}_p$ and computes $C \leftarrow g^t Y^m$. He then sends C to the signer. They both run a proof of knowledge of the opening of the commitment. If the signer is convinced, he selects a random $u \overset{\$}{\leftarrow} \mathbb{Z}_p$ and returns $\sigma' \leftarrow (g^u, (XC)^u)$. The user can now unblind the signature by computing $\sigma \leftarrow (\sigma_1', \sigma_2'/\sigma_1'^t)$.

The element σ then satisfies $\sigma_1 = g^u$ and $\sigma_2 = (XC)^u/g^{ut} = (Xg^tY^m/g^t)^u = (XY^m)^u$, which is a valid signature on m for the single-message signature scheme described in Sect. 4.1. However, because of the additional elements in the public key, the EUF-CMA security of the underlying signature scheme now relies on the Assumption 1.

A Multi-message Protocol. The signature scheme for signing information-theoretically hidden messages consists of the following algorithms:

- Setup(1^k): Given a security parameter k, this algorithm outputs $pp \leftarrow (p, \mathbb{G}_1, \mathbb{G}_2, \mathbb{G}_T, e)$. These bilinear groups must be of type 3. In the following, we denote $\mathbb{G}_1^* = \mathbb{G}_1 \backslash \{1_{\mathbb{G}_1}\}$ and $\mathbb{G}_2^* = \mathbb{G}_2 \backslash \{1_{\mathbb{G}_2}\}$, which are the sets of the generators.

- **Keygen**(pp): This algorithm selects $g \xleftarrow{\$} \mathbb{G}_1^*$, $\tilde{g} \xleftarrow{\$} \mathbb{G}_2^*$ and $(x, y_1, \ldots, y_r) \xleftarrow{\$} \mathbb{Z}_p^{r+1}$, computes $(X, Y_1, \ldots, Y_r) \leftarrow (g^x, g^{y_1}, \ldots, g^{y_r})$ and $(\tilde{X}, \tilde{Y}_1, \ldots, \tilde{Y}_r) \leftarrow (\tilde{g}^x, \tilde{g}^{y_1}, \ldots, \tilde{g}^{y_r})$, and sets $\mathsf{sk} \leftarrow X$ and $\mathsf{pk} \leftarrow (g, Y_1, \ldots, Y_r, \tilde{g}, \tilde{X}, \tilde{Y}_1, \ldots, \tilde{Y}_r)$.
- **Protocol**: A user who wishes to obtain a signature on $(m_1, \ldots, m_r)$ first selects a random $t \xleftarrow{\$} \mathbb{Z}_p$ and computes $C \leftarrow g^t \prod_{i=1}^{r} Y_i^{m_i}$. He then sends C to the signer. They both run a proof of knowledge of the opening of the commitment. If the signer is convinced, he selects a random $u \xleftarrow{\$} \mathbb{Z}_p$ and returns $\sigma' \leftarrow (g^u, (XC)^u)$. The user can now unblind the signature by computing $\sigma \leftarrow (\sigma_1', \sigma_2'/\sigma_1'^t)$.

Again, the element σ satisfies $\sigma_1 = g^u$ and $\sigma_2 = (XC)^u/g^{ut}$. If one develops, $\sigma_2 = (Xg^t \prod_{i=1}^{r} Y_i^{m_i}/g^t)^u = (X \prod_{i=1}^{r} Y_i^{m_i})^u$, which is a valid signature on $(m_1, \ldots, m_r)$ for the multi-message signature scheme described in Sect. 4.2, but with additional elements in the public key: the EUF-CMA security of this multi-message signature scheme can also be shown equivalent to the one of the single-message signature scheme, with a similar proof as the one for Theorem 6, and thus relies on the Assumption 1.

6.2   Proving Knowledge of a Signature

If we still consider the example of anonymous credentials, the previous protocols have addressed the problem of their issuance. However, once a user has obtained his credential, he must also be able to use it to prove that its attributes are certified, while remaining anonymous. To do so, the protocols usually follow the framework described in [19] and so need an efficient way to prove knowledge of a signature.

Our scheme offers such functionality thanks to the ability of our signatures to be sequentially aggregated. Informally, to prove knowledge of a signature $\sigma = (\sigma_1, \sigma_2)$ on a message m, the user will aggregate a signature on some random message t under a dummy public key $\tilde{g}$ (which is part of the public parameters). The resulting signature σ' is then valid on the block (m, t) and does not reveal any information on m.

More formally, let $\mathsf{pk} \leftarrow (\tilde{g}, \tilde{X}, \tilde{Y}_1, \ldots, \tilde{Y}_r)$ be a public key for the signature scheme of Sect. 4.2 and $\sigma = (\sigma_1, \sigma_2)$ be a valid signature on a block $(m_1, \ldots, m_r)$ under it. To prove knowledge of σ, the prover does the following:

1. He selects random $r, t \xleftarrow{\$} \mathbb{Z}_p$ and computes $\sigma' \leftarrow (\sigma_1^r, (\sigma_2 \cdot \sigma_1^t)^r)$.
2. He sends $\sigma' = (\sigma_1', \sigma_2')$ to the verifier and carries out a zero-knowledge proof of knowledge π (such as the Schnorr's interactive protocol [41]) of $(m_1, \ldots, m_r)$ and t such that:

$$e(\sigma_1', \tilde{X}) \cdot \prod e(\sigma_1', \tilde{Y}_j)^{m_j} \cdot e(\sigma_1', \tilde{g})^t = e(\sigma_2', \tilde{g})$$

The verifier accepts if π is valid.

Theorem 8. *The protocol above is a zero-knowledge proof of knowledge of a signature σ on the block $(m_1, \ldots, m_r)$.*

The proof is provided in the in the full version [40].

7   Efficiency

We compare in Fig. 1 the efficiency of our scheme with the ones of CL-signatures [19] and BBS-signatures [4,12] since they are the most popular schemes used as building blocks for pairing-based protocols. As described in [4], to compute a BBS signature on a block of r messages $(m_1, \ldots, m_r)$, a signer whose secret key is $\gamma \in \mathbb{Z}_p$ first selects two random scalars e and s and then computes $A \leftarrow (g_0 g_1^s g_2^{m_1} \ldots g_{r+1}^{m_r})^{\frac{1}{e+\gamma}}$ for some public parameters $g_0, \ldots, g_{r+1}$. The signature is defined as (A, e, s). For proper comparison, we consider a variant of this scheme where the signer has generated the elements $g_i \leftarrow g_0^{y_i}$ for $i \in [1, r+1]$. Therefore, he can compute the element A more efficiently since
$$A = g_0^{\frac{1+\sum_{i=1}^{r+1} y_i \cdot m_i}{\gamma + e}}.$$

	Size of Sig.	Sig. Cost	Verif. Cost	Rand.	Pairings
Sign. Schemes					
BBS [12, 4]	$1\,\mathbb{G}_1 + 2\,\mathbb{Z}_p$	$2\,\mathsf{R}_{\mathbb{Z}_p} + 1\,\mathsf{E}_{\mathbb{G}_1}$	$2\,\mathsf{P} + 1\,\mathsf{E}_{\mathbb{G}_2} + (r+1)\,\mathsf{E}_{\mathbb{G}_1}$	No	All
CL [19]	$(1+2r)\,\mathbb{G}_1$	$1\,\mathsf{R}_{\mathbb{G}_1} + 2r\,\mathsf{E}_{\mathbb{G}_1}$	$4r\,\mathsf{P} + r\,\mathsf{E}_{\mathbb{G}_2}$	Yes	All
Ours [sect. 4.2]	$2\,\mathbb{G}_1$	$1\,\mathsf{R}_{\mathbb{G}_1} + 1\,\mathsf{E}_{\mathbb{G}_1}$	$2\,\mathsf{P} + r\,\mathsf{E}_{\mathbb{G}_2}$	Yes	type 3
Seq. Aggregate **Sign. Schemes**					
LLY [35]	$3\,\mathbb{G}_1$	$1\,\mathsf{Ver.} + 5\,\mathsf{E}_{\mathbb{G}_1}$	$5\,\mathsf{P} + r\,\mathsf{E}_{\mathbb{G}_2}$	Yes	All
Ours [sec. 5]	$2\,\mathbb{G}_1$	$1\mathsf{Ver.} + 3\,\mathsf{E}_{\mathbb{G}_1}$	$2\,\mathsf{P} + r\,\mathsf{E}_{\mathbb{G}_2}$	Yes	type 3

Fig. 1. Efficiency comparison between related works. Here, r refers to the number of messages, $\mathsf{R}_{\mathbb{G}_1}$ (resp. $\mathsf{R}_{\mathbb{Z}_p}$) to the cost of generating a random element of $\mathbb{G}_1$ (resp. $\mathbb{Z}_p$), $\mathsf{E}_{\mathbb{G}_i}$ to the cost of an exponentiation in $\mathbb{G}_i$ ($i \in \{1, 2\}$), P to the cost of a pairing computation and Ver to the cost of verifying an aggregate signature.

As illustrated in Fig. 1, our signature scheme (resp. sequential aggregate signature scheme) compares favourably with the one from [19] (resp. [35]). However, our scheme is only compatible with type 3 pairings but we argue that this is not a strong restriction since most of the recent cryptographic protocols already use them for efficiency and security reasons.

Although the efficiency of our scheme is similar to the one of BBS, we stress that the ability of our signatures to be randomized improves the efficiency of protocols using them. Indeed, as explained in Sect. 1.1, one cannot show several times a BBS signature while being unlinkable. One must then commit to the signature and then prove in a zero-knowledge way that the resulting commitment opens to a valid signature. This is not the case with our scheme since one can simply randomize the signature between each show. To illustrate this point, we provide some examples in in the full version [40].

8   Conclusion

In this work we have proposed a new signature scheme, suited for type 3 pairings, which achieves a remarkable efficiency. As CL-signatures, our signatures can be randomized and can be used as building blocks for many cryptographic primitives. In particular, they support efficient protocols for obtaining a signature on committed elements and can be efficiently combined with zero-knowledge proofs in the ROM. As illustrated in this paper, instantiating cryptographic constructions with our solution improves their efficiency and may therefore contribute to make them more accessible for real-life applications.

Acknowledgments. This work was supported in part by the European Research Council under the European Community's Seventh Framework Programme (FP7/2007-2013 Grant Agreement no. 339563 – CryptoCloud).

References

1. Abe, M., Fuchsbauer, G., Groth, J., Haralambiev, K., Ohkubo, M.: Structure-preserving signatures and commitments to group elements. In: Rabin, T. (ed.) CRYPTO 2010. LNCS, vol. 6223, pp. 209–236. Springer, Heidelberg (2010)
2. Abe, M., Groth, J., Haralambiev, K., Ohkubo, M.: Optimal structure-preserving signatures in asymmetric bilinear groups. In: Rogaway, P. (ed.) CRYPTO 2011. LNCS, vol. 6841, pp. 649–666. Springer, Heidelberg (2011)
3. Abe, M., Groth, J., Ohkubo, M., Tango, T.: Converting cryptographic schemes from symmetric to asymmetric bilinear groups. In: Garay, J.A., Gennaro, R. (eds.) CRYPTO 2014, Part I. LNCS, vol. 8616, pp. 241–260. Springer, Heidelberg (2014)
4. Au, M.H., Susilo, W., Mu, Y.: Constant-size dynamic k-TAA. In: De Prisco, R., Yung, M. (eds.) SCN 2006. LNCS, vol. 4116, pp. 111–125. Springer, Heidelberg (2006)
5. Baldimtsi, F., Lysyanskaya, A.: Anonymous credentials light. In: Sadeghi, A.R., Gligor, V.D., Yung, M. (eds.) ACM CCS 2013, pp. 1087–1098. ACM Press (2013)
6. Barić, N., Pfitzmann, B.: Collision-free accumulators and fail-stop signature schemes without trees. In: Fumy, W. (ed.) EUROCRYPT 1997. LNCS, vol. 1233, pp. 480–494. Springer, Heidelberg (1997)
7. Bellare, M., Rogaway, P.: Random oracles are practical: a paradigm for designing efficient protocols. In: Ashby, V. (ed.) ACM CCS 1993, pp. 62–73. ACM Press (1993)
8. Bellare, M., Shi, H., Zhang, C.: Foundations of group signatures: the case of dynamic groups. In: Menezes, A. (ed.) CT-RSA 2005. LNCS, vol. 3376, pp. 136–153. Springer, Heidelberg (2005)
9. Bernhard, D., Fuchsbauer, G., Ghadafi, E., Smart, N.P., Warinschi, B.: Anonymous attestation with user-controlled linkability. Int. J. Inf. Sec. **12**(3), 219–249 (2013)
10. Bichsel, P., Camenisch, J., Neven, G., Smart, N.P., Warinschi, B.: Get shorty via group signatures without encryption. In: Garay, J.A., De Prisco, R. (eds.) SCN 2010. LNCS, vol. 6280, pp. 381–398. Springer, Heidelberg (2010)
11. Boneh, D., Boyen, X.: Short signatures without random Oracles and the SDH assumption in bilinear groups. J. Cryptol. **21**(2), 149–177 (2008)

12. Boneh, D., Boyen, X., Shacham, H.: Short group signatures. In: Franklin, M. (ed.) CRYPTO 2004. LNCS, vol. 3152, pp. 41–55. Springer, Heidelberg (2004)
13. Boneh, D., Franklin, M.: Identity-based encryption from the weil pairing. In: Kilian, J. (ed.) CRYPTO 2001. LNCS, vol. 2139, pp. 213–229. Springer, Heidelberg (2001)
14. Boneh, D., Gentry, C., Lynn, B., Shacham, H.: Aggregate and verifiably encrypted. In: Biham, E. (ed.) EUROCRYPT 2003. LNCS, vol. 2656, pp. 416–432. Springer, Heidelberg (2003)
15. Brickell, E.F., Camenisch, J., Chen, L.: Direct anonymous attestation. In: Atluri, V., Pfitzmann, B., McDaniel, P. (eds.) ACM CCS 2004, pp. 132–145. ACM Press (2004)
16. Camenisch, J., Groß, T.: Efficient attributes for anonymous credentials. ACM Trans. Inf. Syst. Secur. 15(1), 4 (2012)
17. Camenisch, J.L., Lysyanskaya, A.: An efficient system for non-transferable anonymous credentials with optional anonymity revocation. In: Pfitzmann, B. (ed.) EUROCRYPT 2001. LNCS, vol. 2045, pp. 93–118. Springer, Heidelberg (2001)
18. Camenisch, J.L., Lysyanskaya, A.: A signature scheme with efficient protocols. In: Cimato, S., Galdi, C., Persiano, G. (eds.) SCN 2002. LNCS, vol. 2576, pp. 268–289. Springer, Heidelberg (2003)
19. Camenisch, J.L., Lysyanskaya, A.: Signature schemes and anonymous credentials from bilinear maps. In: Franklin, M. (ed.) CRYPTO 2004. LNCS, vol. 3152, pp. 56–72. Springer, Heidelberg (2004)
20. Canard, S., Lescuyer, R.: Protecting privacy by sanitizing personal data: a new approach to anonymous credentials. In: Chen, K., Xie, Q., Qiu, W., Li, N., Tzeng, W.G. (eds.) ASIACCS 2013, pp. 381–392. ACM Press (2013)
21. Canard, S., Pointcheval, D., Sanders, O., Traoré, J.: Divisible e-cash made practical. In: Katz, J. (ed.) PKC 2015. LNCS, vol. 9020, pp. 77–100. Springer, Heidelberg (2015)
22. Chase, M., Meiklejohn, S., Zaverucha, G.: Algebraic MACs and keyed-verification anonymous credentials. In: Ahn, G.J., Yung, M., Li, N. (eds.) ACM CCS 2014, pp. 1205–1216. ACM Press (2014)
23. Chatterjee, S., Menezes, A.: Typpe 2 structure-preserving signature schemes revisited. Cryptology ePrint Archive, Report 2014/635 (2014). http://eprint.iacr.org/2014/635
24. Chaum, D., van Heyst, E.: Group signatures. In: Davies, D.W. (ed.) EUROCRYPT 1991. LNCS, vol. 547, pp. 257–265. Springer, Heidelberg (1991)
25. Chen, L., Page, D., Smart, N.P.: On the design and implementation of an efficient DAA scheme. In: Gollmann, D., Lanet, J.-L., Iguchi-Cartigny, J. (eds.) CARDIS 2010. LNCS, vol. 6035, pp. 223–237. Springer, Heidelberg (2010)
26. Delerablée, C., Pointcheval, D.: Dynamic fully anonymous short group signatures. In: Nguyên, P.Q. (ed.) VIETCRYPT 2006. LNCS, vol. 4341, pp. 193–210. Springer, Heidelberg (2006)
27. Desmoulins, N., Lescuyer, R., Sanders, O., Traoré, J.: Direct anonymous attestations with dependent basename opening. In: Gritzalis, D., Kiayias, A., Askoxylakis, I. (eds.) CANS 2014. LNCS, vol. 8813, pp. 206–221. Springer, Heidelberg (2014)
28. Dodis, Y., Kiltz, E., Pietrzak, K., Wichs, D.: Message authentication, revisited. In: Pointcheval, D., Johansson, T. (eds.) EUROCRYPT 2012. LNCS, vol. 7237, pp. 355–374. Springer, Heidelberg (2012)
29. Galbraith, S.D., Paterson, K.G., Smart, N.P.: Pairings for cryptographers. Discrete Appl. Math. 156(16), 3113–3121 (2008)

30. Goldwasser, S., Micali, S., Rivest, R.L.: A digital signature scheme secure against adaptive chosen-message attacks. SIAM J. Comput. **17**(2), 281–308 (1988)
31. Groth, J.: Fully anonymous group signatures without random Oracles. In: Kurosawa, K. (ed.) ASIACRYPT 2007. LNCS, vol. 4833, pp. 164–180. Springer, Heidelberg (2007)
32. Groth, J., Sahai, A.: Efficient non-interactive proof systems for bilinear groups. In: Smart, N.P. (ed.) EUROCRYPT 2008. LNCS, vol. 4965, pp. 415–432. Springer, Heidelberg (2008)
33. Hinterwälder, G., Zenger, C.T., Baldimtsi, F., Lysyanskaya, A., Paar, C., Burleson, W.P.: Efficient e-cash in practice: NFC-based payments for public transportation systems. In: De Cristofaro, E., Wright, M. (eds.) PETS 2013. LNCS, vol. 7981, pp. 40–59. Springer, Heidelberg (2013)
34. Joux, A.: A one round protocol for tripartite Diffie-Hellman. In: Bosma, W. (ed.) ANTS 2000. LNCS, vol. 1838. Springer, Heidelberg (2000)
35. Lee, K., Lee, D.H., Yung, M.: Aggregating CL-signatures revisited: extended functionality and better efficiency. In: Sadeghi, A.-R. (ed.) FC 2013. LNCS, vol. 7859, pp. 171–188. Springer, Heidelberg (2013)
36. Lu, S., Ostrovsky, R., Sahai, A., Shacham, H., Waters, B.: Sequential aggregate signatures and multisignatures without random Oracles. In: Vaudenay, S. (ed.) EUROCRYPT 2006. LNCS, vol. 4004, pp. 465–485. Springer, Heidelberg (2006)
37. Lysyanskaya, A., Micali, S., Reyzin, L., Shacham, H.: Sequential aggregate signatures from trapdoor permutations. In: Cachin, C., Camenisch, J.L. (eds.) EUROCRYPT 2004. LNCS, vol. 3027, pp. 74–90. Springer, Heidelberg (2004)
38. Lysyanskaya, A., Rivest, R.L., Sahai, A., Wolf, S.: Pseudonym systems (extended abstract). In: Heys, H.M., Adams, C.M. (eds.) SAC 1999. LNCS, vol. 1758, pp. 184–199. Springer, Heidelberg (2000)
39. Pedersen, T.P.: Non-interactive and information-theoretic secure verifiable secret sharing. In: Feigenbaum, J. (ed.) CRYPTO 1991. LNCS, vol. 576, pp. 129–140. Springer, Heidelberg (1992)
40. Pointcheval, D., Sanders, O.: Short randomizable signatures. Cryptology ePrint Archive, Report 2015/525 (2015). http://eprint.iacr.org/2015/525
41. Schnorr, C.-P.: Efficient identification and signatures for smart cards. In: Brassard, G. (ed.) CRYPTO 1989. LNCS, vol. 435, pp. 239–252. Springer, Heidelberg (1990)
42. Shoup, V.: Lower bounds for discrete logarithms and related problems. In: Fumy, W. (ed.) EUROCRYPT 1997. LNCS, vol. 1233, pp. 256–266. Springer, Heidelberg (1997)

Non-Interactive Plaintext (In-)Equality Proofs and Group Signatures with Verifiable Controllable Linkability

Olivier Blazy[1], David Derler[2(✉)], Daniel Slamanig[2], and Raphael Spreitzer[2]

[1] XLim, Université de Limoges, Limoges, France
olivier.blazy@unilim.fr
[2] IAIK, Graz University of Technology, Graz, Austria
{david.derler,daniel.slamanig,raphael.spreitzer}@tugraz.at

Abstract. Group signatures are an important privacy-enhancing tool that allow to anonymously sign messages on behalf of a group. A recent feature for group signatures is controllable linkability, where a dedicated linking authority (LA) can determine whether two given signatures stem from the same signer without being able to identify the signer(s). Currently the linking authority is fully trusted, which is often not desirable.

In this paper, we firstly introduce a generic technique for non-interactive zero-knowledge plaintext equality and inequality proofs. In our setting, the prover is given two ciphertexts and some trapdoor information, but neither has access to the decryption key nor the randomness used to produce the respective ciphertexts. Thus, the prover performs these proofs on *unknown* plaintexts. Besides a generic technique, we also propose an efficient instantiation that adapts recent results from Blazy et al. (CT-RSA'15), and in particular a combination of Groth-Sahai (GS) proofs (or sigma proofs) and smooth projective hash functions (SPHFs).

While this result may be of independent interest, we use it to realize verifiable controllable linkability for group signatures. Here, the LA is required to non-interactively prove whether or not two signatures link (while it is not able to identify the signers). This significantly reduces the required trust in the linking authority. Moreover, we extend the model of group signatures to cover the feature of verifiable controllable linkability.

1 Introduction

Group signatures, introduced by Chaum and van Heyst [11], allow users to anonymously sign messages on behalf of a group. In case of dispute, a so-called opening authority is able to reveal the identity of the actual signer. While many popular group signature schemes (GSSs) (such as [2,8]) simply trust the output

The full version of this paper is available in the IACR Cryptology ePrint Archive.

D. Derler and D. Slamanig—Supported by EU H2020 project PRISMACLOUD, grant agreement n°644962.

R. Spreitzer—Supported by the Austrian Research Promotion Agency (FFG) and the Styrian Business Promotion Agency (SFG), grant agreement n°836628 (SeCoS).

K. Sako (Ed.): CT-RSA 2016, LNCS 9610, pp. 127–143, 2016.
DOI: 10.1007/978-3-319-29485-8_8

of the opening authority, Camenisch and Stadler [10] proposed to require a proof of the correctness of the opening mechanism. Later, Bellare et al. [3] introduced a model for dynamic group signatures (BSZ model) that incorporates this issue by requiring *publicly verifiable proofs of opening*, i.e., the opening authority provides a proof that the claimed signer indeed produced a given signature. Recently, Sakai et al. [33] identified an issue with this opening mechanism in the BSZ model and introduced an additional property called opening soundness. This property prevents signature hijacking, i.e., it prevents malicious group members (who cooperate with the opening authority) from claiming ownership of a signature produced by an honest group member. Over the years many other additional features for GSSs have been introduced (cf. Sect. 1.2).

One rather recent feature is called controllable linkability [21–23,34]. Here, a dedicated entity called linking authority (LA) can determine whether two given group signatures stem from the same signer, but the LA is *not* able to identify the signer(s). Consequently, the LA is strictly less powerful than the opening authority which can identify all signers by opening their signatures. Like early group signatures did not consider untrusted opening authorities, existing group signatures with controllable linkability [21–23,34] do *not* consider untrusted LAs. In particular, the LA simply provides a binary linking decision and thus has to be fully trusted. It is, however, desirable to reduce this trust. Ideally, in a way that the LA needs to provide verifiable evidence, i.e., a proof, of a correct decision. In this paper, we solve this open problem and introduce the novel concept of *verifiable controllable linkability* (VCL). Applications of VCL include different types of privacy-preserving data-mining scenarios in various fields such as online shopping, public transport, park- and road pricing. Essentially, whenever one requires to analyse customers' behavioural patterns in a privacy-respecting way and these computations are outsourced to a potentially untrusted party, e.g., a cloud provider, that needs to prove honest behaviour and must not be able to identify individuals. Moreover, their application to revocation mechanisms seems interesting to study.

1.1 Background and Motivation

Naive approaches to solve this problem, like abusing the opening-authority or requiring the LA to sign its decision, are not satisfactory and rather privacy intrusive. To give an idea of how we approach this problem, we have to look at the existing approaches to achieve controllable linkability without verifiability. This concept has been proposed for several GSSs by Hwang et al. [21–23]. As their approach to controllable linkability, however, is ad-hoc and always tailored to a specific GSS, Slamanig et al. [34] proposed a generic approach to add controllable linkability to pairing-based group signature schemes following the sign-and-encrypt-and-prove (SEP) paradigm (cf. Sect. 2.3), which covers a large class of practical group signatures in the ROM. We recall that a group signature in the SEP paradigm is an encryption of a per-user unique value (certificate) under the public key of the opening authority and a non-interactive zero-knowledge proof of a signature (on this certificate) from the group manager. This generic approach allows the LA to perform the linking operation on the encrypted membership certificates (which are used for opening group signatures) by means of a variant of the all-or-nothing public key encryption with equality tests (AoN-PKEET*) primitive. Basically, the LA obtains a *single* linking key (trapdoor) that allows plaintext equality tests on the membership certificates without being able to decrypt. Now, our idea is to require the LA to provide a proof that either two encrypted membership certificates contain the same or different unknown certificates (plaintexts). The particular challenge, however, is that the LA must not be able to identify the signers and thus needs to perform such proofs without knowing the plaintexts, the decryption key or the randomness used to produce the ciphertexts. Moreover, in contrast to opening proofs, we do not only need to provide a proof in case of a positive linking decision but also in case of a *negative* decision, i.e., when two ciphertexts contain different unknown plaintexts (certificates). This makes proving the correctness of a linking decision a much more challenging task.

1.2   Related Work

Group Signatures. In traceable signatures [13,26], the opening authority can compute a tracing trapdoor for a user, which allows the identification of all signatures generated by a particular user without violating the privacy of other users. In group signatures with message dependent opening [32], the opening authority cannot open any signature unless an additional authority (the admitter) admits to open signatures for specified messages and thus restricts the power of the opening authority. In deniable group signatures [24], the opener can, in addition to opening proofs, prove that a particular signature has not been generated by a particular signer. Apart from these opening capabilities, also linking capabilities have been investigated. For instance, the possibility to publicly link group signatures of users without identifying them [29] or to allow public tracing of signers who have produced a number of signatures above a certain threshold [37]. But also the linkability of signatures for a specified time frame (by fixing the randomness for a certain time [27] or by introducing specific time tokens [17]) have been considered. Another direction is to put the user in charge of controlling which signatures can be linked, as it is used in DAA [9] and related schemes [6]. These concepts are related to our work but do not help to realize our goals.

Plaintext Equality/Inequality Proofs. Zero-knowledge proofs of plaintext equality (under distinct public keys) are well known from the twin-encryption paradigm [30]. However, we require equality as well as inequality proofs and in our setting the prover neither has access to the decryption key nor the randomness used to produce the respective ciphertexts. Jakobsson and Juels [25] introduced the concept of distributed plaintext equality tests (PETs) within their approach to general secure multiparty computation. Basically, it allows $n > 1$ entities to determine whether two ElGamal ciphertexts encrypt the same or a different message without learning the message. However, this requires access to the decryption key. Choi et al. [12] provide zero-knowledge equality/inequality proofs for boolean ElGamal ciphertexts. Their approach requires the knowledge of the decryption key and the randomness used to produce the two ciphertexts. Parkes et al. [31] provide zero-knowledge equality/inequality proofs of plaintexts within Paillier ciphertexts, which however require either access to the randomness used to produce the ciphertexts or access to the plaintexts. Recently, Blazy et al. [7] introduced a generic approach to prove non-membership with respect to some language in non-interactive zero-knowledge. Among others, they show how to prove plaintext inequality of two ElGamal ciphertexts, where the verifier knows the plaintext and the randomness used to produce one of the ciphertexts. Therefore, none of these approaches directly fits our requirements.

1.3 Contribution

The contributions of this paper are as follows: (1) Based upon the idea of public key encryption with equality tests, we define a generic non-interactive proof system that allows to perform zero-knowledge proofs about plaintext equality and inequality with respect to any two ciphertexts under the same public key. Thereby, the prover is neither required to have access to the decryption key nor to the randomness used to produce the respective ciphertexts. (2) We show how Groth-Sahai (GS) proofs [20] and an adaptation of *non-interactive zero-knowledge proofs of non-membership* [7] can be combined to obtain an instantiation of our proof system. While an instantiation of such a proof system is of independent interest, it allows us to construct group signatures with *verifiable controllable linkability* (VCL-GS). (3) We adopt the model of GSSs with controllable linkability [21–23] to one for verifiable controllable linkability. In the vein of Sakai et al. [33], we introduce a property called *linking soundness*, which requires that even corrupted LAs (colluding with malicious users) cannot produce false linking proofs. (4) We show how to transform GSSs with controllable linkability following the SEP paradigm into GSSs with verifiable controllable linkability by using the proposed non-interactive zero-knowledge proof system.

2 Preliminaries

Subsequently, we discuss preliminaries and required tools.

Notation. Let $x \xleftarrow{R} X$ denote the operation that picks an element x uniformly at random from a set X. A function $\epsilon : \mathbb{N} \to \mathbb{R}^+$ is called negligible if for all $c > 0$ there is a k_0 such that $\epsilon(k) < 1/k^c$ for all $k > k_0$. In the remainder of this paper, we use ϵ to denote such a negligible function. We use boldface letters to denote vectors, e.g., $\mathbf{X} = (X_1, \dots X_n)$.

Let $\mathbb{G}_1 = \langle g \rangle$, $\mathbb{G}_2 = \langle \hat{g} \rangle$, and $\mathbb{G}_T$ be groups of prime order p. We write elements in $\mathbb{G}_2$ as $\hat{g}, \hat{h}$, etc. A bilinear map $e : \mathbb{G}_1 \times \mathbb{G}_2 \to \mathbb{G}_T$ is a map, where it holds for all $(u, \hat{v}, a, b) \in \mathbb{G}_1 \times \mathbb{G}_2 \times \mathbb{Z}_p^2$ that $e(u^a, \hat{v}^b) = e(u, \hat{v})^{ab}$, and $e(g, \hat{g}) \neq 1$, and e is efficiently computable. We assume the asymmetric setting where $\mathbb{G}_1 \neq \mathbb{G}_2$. The required hardness assumptions are provided in the full version.

2.1   Groth-Sahai (GS) Non-interactive Zero-Knowledge Proofs

Groth and Sahai [20] provide a framework for efficient non-interactive witness-indistinguishable (NIWI) and zero-knowledge (NIZK) proofs for languages defined over bilinear groups. It allows, among others, to prove statements about the satisfiability of so-called pairing product equations (PPEs). While the framework is quite independent of the underlying hardness assumption, we will use the instantiation based on the SXDH setting, and, thus, our further explanations are tailored to this setting. A PPE is of the form

$$\prod_{i=1}^{n} e(A_i, \hat{Y}_i) \cdot \prod_{i=1}^{m} e(X_i, \hat{B}_i) \cdot \prod_{i=1}^{m} \prod_{j=1}^{n} e(X_i, \hat{Y}_j)^{\gamma_{ij}} = t_T,$$

where $\mathbf{X} \in \mathbb{G}_1^m$, $\hat{\mathbf{Y}} \in \mathbb{G}_2^n$ are the secret vectors (to prove knowledge of) and $\mathbf{A} \in \mathbb{G}_1^n$, $\hat{\mathbf{B}} \in \mathbb{G}_2^m$, $\Gamma = (\gamma_{ij})_{i \in [m], j \in [n]} \in \mathbb{Z}_p^{n \cdot m}$, and $t_T \in \mathbb{G}_T$ are public constants. Informally, GS proofs use the following strategy. One commits to the vectors $\mathbf{X}$ and $\hat{\mathbf{Y}}$, and uses the commitments instead of the actual values in the PPE. The proof π is used to cancel out the randomness used in the commitments. As this does not directly work when using the groups $\mathbb{G}_1, \mathbb{G}_2$, and $\mathbb{G}_T$, one projects the involved elements to the vector spaces $\mathbb{G}_1^2, \mathbb{G}_2^2$, and $\mathbb{G}_T^4$ by using the defined projection maps and proves the satisfiability of the PPE using the projected elements and corresponding bilinear map $F : \mathbb{G}_1^2 \times \mathbb{G}_2^2 \to \mathbb{G}_T^4$.

More formally, a GS proof for a PPE allows to prove knowledge of a witness $w = (\mathbf{X}, \hat{\mathbf{Y}})$ such that the PPE, uniquely defined by the statement $x = (\mathbf{A}, \hat{\mathbf{B}}, \Gamma, t_T)$, is satisfied. Henceforth, let BG denote the description of the used bilinear group and let R be the relation such that $(\mathsf{BG}, x, w) \in R$ iff w is a satisfying witness for x with respect to BG. Further, let L_R be the corresponding language.

Formally, a non-interactive proof system in a bilinear group setting is defined as follows:

Definition 1. *A non-interactive proof system Π is a tuple of PPT algorithms* (BGGen, CRSGen, Proof, Verify), *which are defined as follows:*

BGGen(1^κ): Takes a security parameter κ as input, and outputs a bilinear group description BG.

CRSGen(BG): Takes a bilinear group description BG as input, and outputs a common reference string crs.

Proof(BG, crs, x, w): Takes a bilinear group description BG, a common reference string crs, a statement x, and a witness w as input, and outputs a proof π.

Verify(BG, crs, x, π): Takes a bilinear group description BG, a common reference string crs, a statement x, and a proof π as input, and outputs 1 if π is valid and 0 otherwise.

The security definitions for non-interactive proof systems are provided in the full version. GS proofs are perfectly complete, perfectly sound, and witness indistinguishable. Furthermore, they are composably zero-knowledge if $t_T = 1_{\mathbb{G}_T}$ and the PPE does not involve a pairing of two public constants.

Throughout this paper we use the GS-based commit-and-prove approach from [18], which allows to reuse the commitments in proofs for different statements. This allows us to prove statements with respect to commitments that are included in the CRS to obtain more efficient proofs. Moreover, the fact that the commitments are already contained in the CRS allows us to exclude the usage of trivial witnesses, i.e., $1_{\mathbb{G}_1}$ or $1_{\mathbb{G}_2}$.

2.2 Smooth Projective Hash Functions

Smooth projective hash functions (SPHF) [15] are families of pairs of functions (Hash, ProjHash) defined on a language L. They are indexed by a pair of associated keys (hk, hp), where the hashing key hk may be viewed as the private key and the projection key hp as the public key. On a word $W \in L$, both functions need to yield the same result, i.e., $\mathsf{Hash}(hk, L, W) = \mathsf{ProjHash}(hp, L, W, w)$, where the latter evaluation additionally requires a witness w that $W \in L$. Thus, they can be seen as a tool for implicit designated-verifier proofs of membership [1]. Formally SPHFs are defined as follows (cf. [5]).

Definition 2. *A SPHF for a language L is a tuple of PPT algorithms* (Setup, HashKG, ProjKG, Hash, ProjHash)*, which are defined as follows:*

Setup(1^κ): Takes a security parameter κ and generates the global parameters pp (we assume that all algorithms have access to pp).

HashKG(L): Takes a language L and outputs a hashing key hk for L.

ProjKG(hk, L, W): Takes a hashing key hk, a language L, and a word W and outputs a projection key hp, possibly depending on W.

Hash(hk, L, W): Takes a hashing key hk, a language L, and a word W and outputs a hash H'.

ProjHash(hp, L, W, w): Takes a projection key hp, a language L, a word W, and a witness w for $W \in L$ and outputs a hash H.

The security properties as well as the concrete ElGamal-based instantiation from [19] used in this paper are provided in the full version.

2.3 Sign-and-Encrypt-and-Prove Paradigm

Group signature schemes following the sign-and-encrypt-and-prove (SEP) paradigm are popular and there are various efficient constructions (in the ROM) following this paradigm. Such a scheme consist of the following three building blocks: (1) A secure signature scheme $\mathcal{DS} = (\mathsf{KeyGen_s}, \mathsf{Sign}, \mathsf{Vrfy})$, (2) an at least IND-CPA secure public key encryption scheme $\mathcal{AE} = (\mathsf{KeyGen_e}, \mathsf{Enc}, \mathsf{Dec})$ and (3) a non-interactive zero-knowledge proof of knowledge (NIZKPK) system, e.g., non-interactive versions of Σ-protocols obtained via the Fiat-Shamir transform in the ROM (denoted as signatures of knowledge (SoK) subsequently).

The group public key gpk consists of the public encryption key pk_e, and the signature verification key pk_s. The master opening key mok is the decryption key sk_e, and the master issuing key mik is the signing key sk_s. During the joining procedure a user i sends $f(x_i)$ to the issuer, where $f(\cdot)$ is a one-way function applied to a secret x_i. The issuer returns a signature cert $\leftarrow \mathsf{Sign}(\mathsf{sk}_s, f(x_i))$ which represents the user's certificate.

A group signature $\sigma = (T, \pi)$ for a message M consists of a ciphertext $T \leftarrow \mathsf{Enc}(\mathsf{pk}_e, \mathsf{cert})$ and the following SoK π:

$$\pi \leftarrow \mathsf{SoK}\{(x_i, \mathsf{cert}) : \mathsf{cert} = \mathsf{Sign}(\mathsf{sk}_s, f(x_i)) \;\wedge\; T = \mathsf{Enc}(\mathsf{pk}_e, \mathsf{cert})\}(M).$$

We note that there are slight deviations in instantiations of this paradigm (cf. [28,34]), e.g., sometimes cert is computed for x_i instead of $f(x_i)$ (which, however, does not yield constructions providing non-frameability), or T may represent an encryption of $f(x_i)$ or $g(x_i)$ for some one-way function $g(\cdot)$. We, however, stress that for our approach in this paper it does not matter how T is exactly constructed (beyond being the encryption of a per-user unique value).

2.4 All-or-Nothing Public Key Encryption with Equality Tests

Following the work of Tang [35,36], Slamanig et al. [34] modified the all-or-nothing public key encryption with equality tests (AON-PKEET*). The idea of AON-PKEET [35,36] is to allow specific entities in possession of a trapdoor to perform equality tests on ciphertexts without learning the underlying plaintext. Slamanig et al. additionally require this primitive to be compatible with efficient zero-knowledge proofs regarding the plaintexts, to ensure compatibility with group signature schemes following the SEP paradigm.

An AON-PKEET* scheme (KeyGen, Enc, Dec, Aut, Com) is a conventional (at least IND-CPA secure) public key encryption scheme (compatible with efficient zero-knowledge proofs) augmented by two additional algorithms Aut and Com (cf. [34] for a formal treatment).

Aut(sk_e): Takes the private decryption key sk_e of the public key encryption scheme and returns a trapdoor tk required for the equality test.

Com(T, T', tk): Takes two ciphertexts (T, T') and a trapdoor tk and returns 1 if both ciphertexts encrypt the same (unknown) message and 0 otherwise.

Definition 3 [34]. *An AON-PKEET* scheme is called secure if it is sound, provides OW-CPA security against Type-I adversaries (trapdoor holders) and if the underlying encryption scheme provides IND-CPA/IND-CCA security against Type-II adversaries (outsiders).*

Construction from ElGamal. In a bilinear group setting where the (S)XDH assumption is assumed to hold, one can rely on ElGamal encryption in $\mathbb{G}_1$. Let the private key be a random element $\xi \xleftarrow{R} \mathbb{Z}_p$ and the corresponding public key be $h \leftarrow g^\xi \in \mathbb{G}_1$, then the encryption of a message m is computed as $T = (T_1, T_2) = (g^\alpha, mh^\alpha)$ for a randomly chosen element $\alpha \xleftarrow{R} \mathbb{Z}_p$. The trapdoor generation and comparison algorithms are as follows:

Aut(ξ): Return the trapdoor $\mathsf{tk} \leftarrow (\hat{r}, \hat{t} = \hat{r}^\xi) \in \mathbb{G}_2^2$ for a random $\hat{r} \xleftarrow{R} \mathbb{G}_2$.

$\mathsf{Com}(T, T', \mathsf{tk})$: Given two ciphertexts $T = (T_1, T_2) = (g^\alpha, mh^\alpha)$ and $T' = (T'_1, T'_2) = (g^{\alpha'}, m'h^{\alpha'})$ and a trapdoor $\mathsf{tk} = (\hat{r}, \hat{t} = \hat{r}^\xi)$, return 1 if $e(T_2, \hat{r}) \cdot e(T_1, \hat{t})^{-1} = e(T'_2, \hat{r}) \cdot e(T'_1, \hat{t})^{-1}$ holds and 0 otherwise.

Lemma 1 [34]. *Under the co-CDH assumption* $\mathrm{AoN}\text{-}\mathrm{PKEET}^*$ *based on ElGamal in* $\mathbb{G}_1$ *in an (S)XDH setting is secure.*

3   Non-interactive Plaintext (In-)Equality Proofs

We are interested in plaintext equality and inequality proofs where the prover neither knows the randomness used for encryption, nor the decryption key and consequently also does *not* know the plaintexts. If we use the idea of AoN-PKEET* [34], the prover can use a trapdoor to determine whether two ciphertexts encrypt the same unknown plaintext, while not being able to decrypt. This, in turn, allows the prover to select which type of proof to conduct. Moreover, for AoN-PKEET* schemes in the pairing setting, we can use the pairing product equation that is used by the Com algorithm and a suitable proof framework to prove (1) knowledge of a trapdoor that is consistent with the respective public key, and (2) the satisfiability of the pairing product equation corresponding to Com when used with the non-revealed trapdoor on two ciphertexts in question. As we will see later, this allows us to prove plaintext equality in a straightforward way, while plaintext inequality requires a slightly more sophisticated approach.

3.1   A Generic Construction

Let $\mathcal{PKEQ} = (\mathsf{KeyGen}, \mathsf{Enc}, \mathsf{Dec}, \mathsf{Aut}, \mathsf{Com})$ be a secure AoN-PKEET* scheme. Building upon $\mathcal{PKEQ}$, we define a generic non-interactive proof system Π that—for two ciphertexts T and T' under some public key pk—allows to prove knowledge of a trapdoor tk, that either attests membership of (T, T', pk) in language $L_{R_\in}$ or in a language $L_{R_\notin}$. The corresponding NP-relations are defined as follows:

$$((T, T', \mathsf{pk}), \mathsf{tk}) \in R_\in \iff \mathsf{Com}(T, T', \mathsf{tk}) = 1 \ \wedge \ \mathsf{tk} \equiv \mathsf{pk},$$
$$((T, T', \mathsf{pk}), \mathsf{tk}) \in R_\notin \iff \mathsf{Com}(T, T', \mathsf{tk}) = 0 \ \wedge \ \mathsf{tk} \equiv \mathsf{pk},$$

where $\mathsf{tk} \equiv \mathsf{pk}$ denotes that tk corresponds to pk and we omit BG for simplicity. To obtain a non-interactive proof system Π with the desired expressiveness, we compose two non-interactive proof systems, namely $\Pi_\in$ and $\Pi_\notin$. Here, $\Pi_\in$ covers statements in $L_{R_\in}$, whereas $\Pi_\notin$ covers statements in $L_{R_\notin}$. It is easy to see that—by the soundness of $\mathcal{PKEQ}$—each tuple $((T, T', \mathsf{pk}), \mathsf{tk})$ is either in $R_\in$ or in $R_\notin$. Membership can be efficiently checked using the Com algorithm. The non-interactive proof system Π is presented in Scheme 1, where we assume that one can efficiently decide for which language a given proof π has been computed.[1] We call a non-interactive plaintext equality and inequality (NIPEI) proof system *secure* if it is perfectly complete, perfectly sound, and at least computationally zero-knowledge. The subsequent Lemma trivially follows from the fact that $L_{R_\in}$ and $L_{R_\notin}$ are disjoint.

---

[1] As $L_{R_\in}$ and $L_{R_\notin}$ are disjoint, one can otherwise just run Verify for both languages.

BGGen(1^κ) : Takes a security parameter κ as input, runs BG $\leftarrow \Pi_{\in,\notin}$.BGGen($1^\kappa$) and returns BG.[a]

CRSGen(BG) : Takes a bilinear group description BG as input, runs $\mathsf{crs}_\in \leftarrow \Pi_\in$.CRSGen(BG), and $\mathsf{crs}_{\notin} \leftarrow \Pi_{\notin}$.CRSGen(BG), and outputs a common reference string crs $\leftarrow (\mathsf{crs}_\in, \mathsf{crs}_{\notin})$.

Proof(BG, crs, (T, T', pk), tk) : Takes a bilinear group description BG, a common reference string crs, a statement (T, T', pk), and a witness tk. If $((T, T', \mathsf{pk}), \mathsf{tk}) \in R_\in$, return $\pi_\in \leftarrow \Pi_\in$.Proof(BG, $\mathsf{crs}_\in, (T, T', \mathsf{pk})$, tk). Otherwise, return $\pi_{\notin} \leftarrow \Pi_{\notin}$.Proof(BG, $\mathsf{crs}_{\notin}, (T, T', \mathsf{pk})$, tk).

Verify(BG, crs, (T, T', pk), π) : Takes a bilinear group description BG, a common reference string crs, a statement (T, T', pk) and a proof π. If π is for language $L_{R_\in}$ return $\Pi_\in$.Verify(BG, $\mathsf{crs}_\in, (T, T', \mathsf{pk})$, π) and if π is for language $L_{R_{\notin}}$ return $\Pi_{\notin}$.Verify(BG, $\mathsf{crs}_{\notin}, (T, T', \mathsf{pk})$, π).

---

[a] With $\Pi_{\in,\notin}$ we denote that both proof systems are with respect to the same bilinear group description.

Scheme 1. NIPEI Proof System

Lemma 2. *If $\Pi_\in$ and $\Pi_{\notin}$ are secure NIZK proof systems, then the resulting NIPEI proof system Π is also secure. Thereby, for every security property $p_\in$ of $\Pi_\in$ and corresponding security property $p_{\notin}$ of $\Pi_{\notin}$, Π inherits $p_\in$ if $p_\in$ is implied by $p_{\notin}$ and $p_{\notin}$ otherwise. That is, Π inherits the weaker security notion of both.*

3.2 Instantiation with $\mathcal{PKEQ}$ from ElGamal Encryption

We will now present a concrete instantiation of a NIPEI proof system in the SXDH setting where we base the $\mathcal{PKEQ}$ scheme on ElGamal encryption in $\mathbb{G}_1$. Recall, that $\mathsf{pk} = g^\xi$, the trapdoor is $\mathsf{tk} = (\hat{r}, \hat{t} = \hat{r}^\xi) \in \mathbb{G}_2^2$ and for two ciphertexts T and T', Com(T, T', tk) checks whether $e(T_2, \hat{r}) \cdot e(T_1, \hat{t})^{-1} = e(T_2', \hat{r}) \cdot e(T_1', \hat{t})^{-1}$ holds. If so, the ciphertexts encrypt the same plaintexts and different plaintexts otherwise. Subsequently, we present the relations $R_\in$ and $R_{\notin}$ for this $\mathcal{PKEQ}$ scheme. For membership in $R_\in$, the following PPEs need to be satisfied:

$$(((T_1, T_2), (T_1', T_2')), (\hat{r}, \hat{t})) \in R_\in \iff e(g^\xi, \hat{r}) \cdot e(g^{-1}, \hat{t}) = 1_{\mathbb{G}_T} \wedge$$
$$\hat{r} \neq 1_{\mathbb{G}_2} \wedge \hat{t} \neq 1_{\mathbb{G}_2} \wedge e(T_2 \cdot T_2'^{-1}, \hat{r}) \cdot e(T_1^{-1} \cdot T_1', \hat{t}) = 1_{\mathbb{G}_T}. \quad (1)$$

By the soundness of the underlying $\mathcal{PKEQ}$ scheme, the PPEs above deliver the desired soundness properties for membership in $R_\in$. For membership in $R_{\notin}$, we have to exchange the last literal in the conjunction of the PPEs above by $e(T_2 \cdot T_2'^{-1}, \hat{r}) \cdot e(T_1^{-1} \cdot T_1', \hat{t}) \neq 1_{\mathbb{G}_T}$. It is important to note that an inequality (as in the second part of the conjunction) cannot be proven using GS.

Instantiation of $\Pi_\in$. We use the GS-based commit-and-prove scheme from [18]. Thereby, the advantage is that it is possible to reach composable zero-knowledge even when reusing commitments in proofs for different statements.

Consequently, we can include commitments to $\hat{r}$ and $\hat{t}$ in the CRS and we can reuse these commitments to prove the satisfiability of the following PPE

$$\prod_{i=1}^{2} e(A_i, \hat{Y}_i) = e(T_2 \cdot T_2'^{-1}, \underline{\hat{r}}) \cdot e(T_1^{-1} \cdot T_1', \underline{\hat{t}}) = 1_{\mathbb{G}_T},$$

where the prover is given access to the openings of the commitments and the underlined values are not revealed to the verifier. The fact that the commitments are already contained in the CRS forces the prover to use commitments to the actual values which are consistent with the public key (instead of plugging in $\hat{r} = 1_{\mathbb{G}_2}, \hat{t} = 1_{\mathbb{G}_2}$ as the trivial solution).[2] The corresponding proof is very simple and can be communicated with two group elements in $\mathbb{G}_1$. Since our instantiation is a straightforward application of the GS-based commit-and-prove scheme, we obtain the following lemma:

Lemma 3. $\Pi_\in$ *provides perfect completeness, perfect soundness and—because of the form of the PPE—composable zero-knowledge.*[3]

Instantiation of $\Pi_\notin$. To construct a proof for plaintext inequality statements, we build upon a recent technique by Blazy et al. [7]. They show a generic way to (non-interactively) prove non-membership claims with respect to a language in zero-knowledge and provide multiple instantiations of their framework based on combinations of SPHFs and GS proofs. Informally, their generic technique for proving non-membership works as follows. They use a non-interactive proof system Π_1 that allows to prove possession of a witness demonstrating the membership of some statement in some language, where the respective proof fails. Then, they use a non-interactive proof system Π_2 that allows to prove that Π_1.Proof has been computed honestly. This way, it is possible to express non-membership statements by producing a proof such that Π_1.Verify returns 0 and proving that the proof itself was honestly computed (since otherwise such a faulty proof would be trivially computable).

We will build our instantiation upon a SPHF for Π_1 (where we can use the SPHF framework from [4], which allows to prove the required statements) and GS proofs for Π_2. However, in contrast to how this technique is used in [7], in our setting the verifier does not know the randomness of the commitments. This imposes an additional technicality to be discussed below. In particular, we additionally compute the hash value H using ProjHash on the prover side and prove that H was honestly computed using an additional non-interactive zero-knowledge proof system Π_3 (which we instantiate with GS proofs). In Scheme 2, we present our non-interactive proof system for membership in a language $L_{R_\notin}$ that contains all tuples $(T, T', \mathsf{pk}, \mathcal{C}_{\mathsf{tk}})$, where the trapdoor committed to in $\mathcal{C}_{\mathsf{tk}}$ allows to demonstrate plaintext inequality. For simplicity, crs is for Π_1 and Π_3.

---

[2] For the simulation we may still use $\hat{r} = 1_{\mathbb{G}_2}, \hat{t} = 1_{\mathbb{G}_2}$.

[3] We note that, due to using the commit-and-prove approach from [18], we also use their composable zero-knowledge notion for commit-and-prove schemes. This notion can be seen as a generalization of standard composable zero-knowledge.

$\mathbf{P} : L_{R_{\notin}}, (T, T', \mathsf{pk}, \boldsymbol{C}_{\mathsf{tk}}) \in L_{R_{\notin}}, \boldsymbol{R}_{\mathsf{tk}}, \mathsf{crs}$ $\mathbf{V} : L_R, (T, T', \mathsf{pk}, \boldsymbol{C}_{\mathsf{tk}}), \mathsf{crs}$

$hk \leftarrow \mathsf{HashKG}(L_R),$

$hp \leftarrow \mathsf{ProjKG}(hk, L_R, (T, T', \mathsf{pk}, \boldsymbol{C}_{\mathsf{tk}}))$

$H' \leftarrow \mathsf{Hash}(hk, L_R, (T, T', \mathsf{pk}, \boldsymbol{C}_{\mathsf{tk}}))$

$\phi \leftarrow \Pi_2.\mathsf{Proof}((H' \wedge hp), hk)$

$H \leftarrow \mathsf{ProjHash}(hp, L_R, (T, T', \mathsf{pk}, \boldsymbol{C}_{\mathsf{tk}}), \boldsymbol{R}_{\mathsf{tk}})$

$\psi \leftarrow \Pi_3.\mathsf{Proof}((hp, H, \boldsymbol{C}_{\mathsf{tk}}), (\boldsymbol{R}_{\mathsf{tk}}))$ $\xrightarrow{\quad hp, \phi, \psi, H, H' \quad}$ $\Pi_2.\mathsf{Verify}(\phi) \wedge$

$\Pi_3.\mathsf{Verify}(\psi) \overset{?}{=} 1 \wedge H \overset{?}{\neq} H'$

Scheme 2. NIPEI Proof System. **P** ... Prover, **V** ... Verifier.

A nice thing to note (which will allow us to improve the efficiency of $\Pi_{\notin}$) is that we do not need to simulate the proof ϕ. We will only require the proof to completely hide hk, i.e., to be witness indistinguishable.

Likewise to $\Pi_{\in}$, we can include the commitments $\boldsymbol{C}_{\mathsf{tk}}$ to tk in the CRS and use these commitments in the SPHF. Accordingly, the corresponding PPE simplifies to $e(T_2 \cdot T_2'^{-1}, \hat{r}) \cdot e(T_1^{-1} \cdot T_1', \hat{t}) \neq 1_{\mathbb{G}_T}$. We additionally include commitments $\boldsymbol{C}_R$ to the randomness $\boldsymbol{R}_{\mathsf{tk}}$ used to compute $\boldsymbol{C}_{\mathsf{tk}}$ in the CRS. Then we can use these commitments together with the GS-based commit-and-prove scheme from [18] to prove the honest computation of the projective hash value more efficiently. Likewise to the other commitments in the CRS, this ensures that the prover uses the correct values (while also ensuring the simulatability).

Since the instantiation of Π_1, Π_2, and Π_3 with the required properties is quite involved, we provide a detailed description in the full version. Finally, for Scheme 2 we can show the following:

Theorem 1. *If Π_1 is correct and the verifier cannot distinguish a failing proof (i.e., H) from random, Π_2 is complete, sound and witness indistinguishable, Π_3 is complete, sound and zero-knowledge, then $\Pi_{\notin}$ is also complete, sound and zero-knowledge.*

We prove Theorem 1 in the full version. By combining Lemmas 2, 3, and Theorem 1 we straightforwardly derive the following corollary for our instantiation of the proof system $\Pi = (\Pi_{\in}, \Pi_{\notin})$.

Corollary 1. *The NIPEI proof system Π obtained by combining the above instantiations of $\Pi_{\in}$ and $\Pi_{\notin}$ is secure, i.e., complete, sound, and zero-knowledge.*

Instantiations with Other Encryption Schemes. For simplicity, we have presented an instantiation in the SXDH setting using ElGamal, but it is straightforward to adapt to Cramer-Shoup [14] or twin-ElGamal [16]. Furthermore, it is easy to adapt it to the DLIN setting and the corresponding linear encryption schemes.

4 GSSs with Verifiable Controllable Linkability

Subsequently, we propose a model for group signatures that considers verifiable controllable linkability and builds upon the model of Hwang et al. [21–23] who formalized controllable linkability. Moreover, we consider the extension to the BSZ [3] model of Sakai et al. [33], i.e., opening soundness. The model involves three authorities: an issuing authority possessing the master issuing key (mik), an opening authority possessing the master opening key (mok), and a linking authority possessing the master linking key (mlk).

4.1   Model for GSSs with Verifiable Controllable Linkability

We now define GSSs with verifiable controllable linkability (VCL-GS).

Definition 4. *A VCL-GS is a tuple of efficient algorithms* $\mathcal{GS} =$ (GkGen, UkGen, Join, Issue, GSig, GVf, Open, Judge, Link, Judge$_{\mathsf{Link}}$), *defined as follows.*

GkGen(1^{κ}): On input a security parameter κ, this algorithm generates and outputs a tuple (gpk, mok, mik, mlk), representing the group public key, the master opening key, the master issuing key, and the master linking key.

UkGen(1^{κ}): On input a security parameter κ, this algorithm generates a user key pair (usk$_i$, upk$_i$).

Join(usk$_i$, upk$_i$): On input the user's key pair (usk$_i$, upk$_i$), this algorithm interacts with Issue and outputs the group signing key gsk$_i$ of user i.

Issue(gpk, mik, **reg**): On input of the group public key gpk, and the master issuing key mik and the registration table **reg**, this algorithm interacts with Join to add user i to the group.

GSig(gpk, M, gsk$_i$): On input of the group public key gpk, a message M, and a user's secret key gsk$_i$, this algorithm outputs a group signature σ.

GVf(gpk, M, σ): On input of the group public key gpk, a message M, and a signature σ, this algorithm verifies whether σ is valid with respect to M and gpk. If so, it outputs 1 and 0 otherwise.

Open(gpk, **reg**, M, σ, mok): On input of the group public key gpk, the registration table **reg**, a message M, a valid signature σ, and the master opening key mok, this algorithm returns the signer i together with a publicly verifiable proof τ attesting the validity of the claim and $\perp$ otherwise.

Judge(gpk, M, σ, i, upk$_i$, τ): On input of the group public key gpk, a message M, a valid signature σ, the claimed signer i, the public key upk$_i$ as well as a proof τ, this algorithm returns 1 if τ is a valid proof that i produced σ and 0 otherwise.

Link(gpk, M, σ, M', σ', mlk): On input of the group public key gpk, a message M, a corresponding valid signature σ, a message M', a corresponding valid signature σ' and the master linking key mlk, this algorithm determines whether σ and σ' have been produced by the same or different signers and returns the linking decision $b \in \{1, 0\}$ as well as a publicly verifiable proof ρ attesting the validity of this decision.

Judge$_{\mathsf{Link}}$(gpk, M, σ, M', σ', b, ρ): On input of the group public key gpk, a message M, a corresponding valid signature σ, a message M', a corresponding valid signature σ', a linking decision b as well as the corresponding linking proof ρ, this algorithm returns 1 if ρ is a valid proof for b with respect to σ and σ' and 0 otherwise.

Now we present the security properties for group signature schemes with verifiable controllable linkability. They are adopted from the model of Hwang et al. [21–23] for controllable linkability, which builds upon the BSZ [3] model.[4] In addition to the properties correctness, anonymity, non-frameability, and traceability defined in the BSZ model, Hwang et al. [21–23] introduced properties to cover controllable linkability, namely LO-linkability (link-only linkability), JP-unforgeability (judge-proof unforgeability), and E-linkability (enforced linkability). Additionally, we integrate the proposal of Sakai et al. [33] who introduced the additional property of (weak) opening soundness as an optional property.[5] We briefly sketch them below and present formal definitions in the full version.

- **Anonymity:** Signers remain anonymous for all entities except for the opening authority.
- **Traceability:** All valid signatures open correctly and allow to compute a valid opening proof.
- **Non-frameability:** No entity is able to produce a valid opening proof that falsely accuses an honest user as the signer.
- **JP-Unforgeability:** The linking key is not useful to generate valid opening proofs.
- **LO-Linkability:** The linking key is only useful to link signatures, but not to open signatures.
- **E-Linkability:** Colluding users, linkers, and openers are not able to generate two message-signature pairs yielding contradicting opening and linking decisions.
- **Opening Soundness:** Colluding issuers, users, linkers, and openers are not able to produce two different (contradicting) opening proofs, even when allowed to corrupt users and/or the opener.[6]

In addition to the above, in the vein of Sakai et al. we introduce the additional notion of *linking soundness*. We only consider a strong variant, where the adversary has access to all keys. Informally, linking soundness targets contradicting linking proofs, where the signatures as well as the proofs may be maliciously generated, yet accepted by GVf and Judge$_{\mathsf{Link}}$, respectively. In contrast, E-linkability targets contradicting results of Open and Link for maliciously generated signatures, where Open, Judge, and Link are honestly computed. Subsequently, we present a definition of linking soundness.

Definition 5 (Linking Soundness). *A group signature scheme $\mathcal{GS}$ with verifiable controllable linkability is said to provide linking soundness if for any adversary $\mathcal{A}$ and any $\kappa \in \mathbb{N}$, $\Pr[\mathsf{Exp}^{\mathsf{ls}}_{\mathcal{GS},\mathcal{A}}(\kappa) = 1] \leq \epsilon(\kappa)$.*

The experiment $\mathsf{Exp}^{\mathsf{ls}}_{\mathcal{GS},\mathcal{A}}$ is formally defined in the full version.

---

[4] Actually, it uses a weaker anonymity notion similar to CPA-full anonymity [8], where the challenge oracle can only be called once.

[5] We emphasize that this property is optional as there are no known GSSs with controllable linkability that have been shown to provide this property.

[6] Note that Sakai et al. [33] also introduced a weaker version of this property denoted as weak opening soundness.

4.2 Verifiable Controllable Linkability

Recall that in group signatures with controllable linkability the LA runs the Com algorithm of a $\mathcal{PKEQ}$ scheme to decide whether two ciphertexts contain the same unknown plaintext. Publishing the required trapdoor key tk would allow *any* party to link *any* two group signatures, which is clearly not desired. However, by means of our proposed NIPEI proof system we are able to allow the LA to verifiably prove whether or not any two signatures stem from the same signer without being able to identify the signer(s) and still only requiring tk.

Subsequently, we show how our generic construction for NIPEI proofs can be used to realize verifiable controllable linkability for group signatures following the SEP paradigm. Thereby, we assume that the used $\mathcal{PKEQ}$ is defined for bilinear groups, such that it is possible to set up the $\mathcal{PKEQ}$ and the proof systems in a compatible way. To this end, we assume that the group public key gpk contains a bilinear group description BG. Then, the modified group key generation algorithm GkGen' looks as follows:

GkGen'(1^κ): Run (gpk, mok, mik, mlk) $\leftarrow$ GkGen(1^κ) and obtain BG from gpk. Then, run crs $\leftarrow$ Π.CRSGen(BG), set gpk' $\leftarrow$ (gpk, crs) and return (gpk', mok, mik, mlk).

Furthermore, the algorithms Link and Link$_{\text{Judge}}$ operate as follows:

Link(gpk, M, σ, M', σ', mlk): Extract the ciphertexts T and T' from σ and σ', respectively. Obtain BG, pk$_e$ from gpk and tk from mlk. Compute $\rho \leftarrow$ Π.Prove(BG, crs, (T, T', pk_e), tk) and return the linking decision b and the corresponding proof ρ.

Link$_{\text{Judge}}$(gpk, $M, \sigma, M', \sigma', b, \rho$): Extract the ciphertexts T and T' from σ and σ'. Obtain BG, crs and pk$_e$ from gpk. If $b = 1$ and ρ is a proof for language $L_{R_{\notin}}$ or vice versa, return $\bot$. Otherwise, return Π.Verify(BG, crs, $(T, T', \text{pk}_e), \rho$).

Security Analysis. We investigate to which extent the extension of a group signature scheme with controllable linkability (i.e., the constructions in [21–23] and the generic conversion from [34]) to one with verifiable controllable linkability requires to re-evaluate the original security properties. Note that the proof of the subsequent theorem is quite independent of the concrete definition of anonymity and works for group signature schemes providing the weaker anonymity notion by Hwang et al. but also with stronger notions such as CPA-full or CCA2-full anonymity (cf. the discussion in the full version).

Theorem 2. *Let* $\mathcal{GS} = $ (GkGen, UkGen, Join, Issue, GSig, GVf, Open, Judge, Link) *be a secure group signature scheme with controllable linkability with or without (weak) opening soundness, let* Π *be a secure NIPEI proof system, and let* $\mathcal{PKEQ} = $ (KeyGen, Enc, Dec, Aut, Com) *be the used* AON-PKEET* *scheme, where* $\mathcal{PKEQ}$ *is compatible with* Π. *Then,* $\mathcal{GS}' = $ (GkGen, UkGen, Join, Issue, GSig, GVf, Open, Judge, Link, Judge$_{\text{Link}}$) *is a secure group signature scheme with verifiable controllable linkability with or without (weak) opening soundness.*

We prove Theorem 2 in the full version.

Instantiating $\Pi_{\not\in}$ for Group Signatures with Σ-Proofs. Many existing GSSs following the SEP paradigm are instantiated using the RO heuristic. Now, if one already relies on the ROM for the GSS, it might be an alternative to instantiate parts of $\Pi_{\not\in}$ (i.e., Π_2 and Π_3) using a non-interactive Σ protocol obtained via the Fiat-Shamir transform, which is specifically crafted for the application with verifiable controllable linkability and the used SPHF instantiation. In the full version, we illustrate such an instantiation of $\Pi_{\not\in}$.

References

1. Abdalla, M., Chevalier, C., Pointcheval, D.: Smooth projective hashing for conditionally extractable commitments. In: Halevi, S. (ed.) CRYPTO 2009. LNCS, vol. 5677, pp. 671–689. Springer, Heidelberg (2009)
2. Ateniese, G., Camenisch, J.L., Joye, M., Tsudik, G.: A practical and provably secure coalition-resistant group signature scheme. In: Bellare, M. (ed.) CRYPTO 2000. LNCS, vol. 1880, p. 255. Springer, Heidelberg (2000)
3. Bellare, M., Shi, H., Zhang, C.: Foundations of group signatures: the case of dynamic groups. In: Menezes, A. (ed.) CT-RSA 2005. LNCS, vol. 3376, pp. 136–153. Springer, Heidelberg (2005)
4. Benhamouda, F., Blazy, O., Chevalier, C., Pointcheval, D., Vergnaud, D.: Efficient UC-secure authenticated key-exchange for algebraic languages. In: Kurosawa, K., Hanaoka, G. (eds.) PKC 2013. LNCS, vol. 7778, pp. 272–291. Springer, Heidelberg (2013)
5. Benhamouda, F., Blazy, O., Chevalier, C., Pointcheval, D., Vergnaud, D.: New techniques for SPHFs and efficient one-round PAKE protocols. In: Canetti, R., Garay, J.A. (eds.) CRYPTO 2013, Part I. LNCS, vol. 8042, pp. 449–475. Springer, Heidelberg (2013)
6. Bernhard, D., Fuchsbauer, G., Ghadafi, E., Smart, N.P., Warinschi, B.: Anonymous attestation with user-controlled linkability. Int. J. Inf. Sec. **12**(3), 219–249 (2013)
7. Blazy, O., Chevalier, C., Vergnaud, D.: Non-interactive zero-knowledge proofs of non-membership. In: Nyberg, K. (ed.) CT-RSA 2015. LNCS, vol. 9048, pp. 145–164. Springer, Heidelberg (2015)
8. Boneh, D., Boyen, X., Shacham, H.: Short group signatures. In: Franklin, M. (ed.) CRYPTO 2004. LNCS, vol. 3152, pp. 41–55. Springer, Heidelberg (2004)
9. Brickell, E.F., Camenisch, J., Chen, L.: Direct anonymous attestation. In: ACM CCS. ACM (2004)
10. Camenisch, J.L., Stadler, M.A.: Efficient group signature schemes for large groups. In: Kaliski Jr., B.S. (ed.) CRYPTO 1997. LNCS, vol. 1294, pp. 410–424. Springer, Heidelberg (1997)
11. Chaum, D., van Heyst, E.: Group signatures. In: Davies, D.W. (ed.) EUROCRYPT 1991. LNCS, vol. 547, pp. 257–265. Springer, Heidelberg (1991)
12. Choi, S.G., Elbaz, A., Juels, A., Malkin, T., Yung, M.: Two-party computing with encrypted data. In: Kurosawa, K. (ed.) ASIACRYPT 2007. LNCS, vol. 4833, pp. 298–314. Springer, Heidelberg (2007)
13. Chow, S.S.M.: Real traceable signatures. In: Jacobson Jr., M.J., Rijmen, V., Safavi-Naini, R. (eds.) SAC 2009. LNCS, vol. 5867, pp. 92–107. Springer, Heidelberg (2009)

14. Cramer, R., Shoup, V.: A practical public key cryptosystem provably secure against adaptive chosen ciphertext attack. In: Krawczyk, H. (ed.) CRYPTO 1998. LNCS, vol. 1462, p. 13. Springer, Heidelberg (1998)

15. Cramer, R., Shoup, V.: Universal hash proofs and a paradigm for adaptive chosen ciphertext secure public-key encryption. In: Knudsen, L.R. (ed.) EUROCRYPT 2002. LNCS, vol. 2332, pp. 45–64. Springer, Heidelberg (2002)

16. Delerablée, C., Pointcheval, D.: Dynamic fully anonymous short group signatures. In: Nguyên, P.Q. (ed.) VIETCRYPT 2006. LNCS, vol. 4341, pp. 193–210. Springer, Heidelberg (2006)

17. Emura, K., Hayashi, T.: Road-to-vehicle communications with time-dependent anonymity: a light weight construction and its experimental results. Cryptology ePrint Archive, Report 2014/926 (2014)

18. Escala, A., Groth, J.: Fine-tuning Groth-Sahai proofs. In: Krawczyk, H. (ed.) PKC 2014. LNCS, vol. 8383, pp. 630–649. Springer, Heidelberg (2014)

19. Gennaro, R., Lindell, Y.: A framework for password-based authenticated key exchange. In: Biham, E. (ed.) EUROCRYPT 2003. LNCS, vol. 2656. Springer, Heidelberg (2003)

20. Groth, J., Sahai, A.: Efficient non-interactive proof systems for bilinear groups. In: Smart, N.P. (ed.) EUROCRYPT 2008. LNCS, vol. 4965, pp. 415–432. Springer, Heidelberg (2008)

21. Hwang, J.Y., Chen, L., Cho, H.S., Nyang, D.: Short dynamic group signature scheme supporting controllable linkability. IEEE Trans. Inf. Forensics Secur. **10**(6), 1109–1124 (2015)

22. Hwang, J.Y., Lee, S., Chung, B.-H., Cho, H.S., Nyang, D.: Short group signatures with controllable linkability. In: LightSec. IEEE (2011)

23. Hwang, J.Y., Lee, S., Chung, B.H., Cho, H.S., Nyang, D.: Group signatures with controllable linkability for dynamic membership. Inf. Sci. **222**, 761–778 (2013)

24. Ishida, A., Emura, K., Hanaoka, G., Sakai, Y., Tanaka, K.: Group signature with deniability: how to disavow a signature. Cryptology ePrint Archive, Report 2015/043 (2015)

25. Jakobsson, M., Juels, A.: Mix and match: secure function evaluation via cipher-texts. In: Okamoto, T. (ed.) ASIACRYPT 2000. LNCS, vol. 1976, pp. 162–177. Springer, Heidelberg (2000)

26. Kiayias, A., Tsiounis, Y., Yung, M.: Traceable signatures. In: Cachin, C., Camenisch, J.L. (eds.) EUROCRYPT 2004. LNCS, vol. 3027, pp. 571–589. Springer, Heidelberg (2004)

27. Malina, L., Castellà-Roca, J., Vives-Guasch, A., Hajny, J.: Short-term link-able group signatures with categorized batch verification. In: Garcia-Alfaro, J., Cuppens, F., Cuppens-Boulahia, N., Miri, A., Tawbi, N. (eds.) FPS 2012. LNCS, vol. 7743, pp. 244–260. Springer, Heidelberg (2013)

28. Nakanishi, T., Fujii, H., Hira, Y., Funabiki, N.: Revocable group signature schemes with constant costs for signing and verifying. In: Jarecki, S., Tsudik, G. (eds.) PKC 2009. LNCS, vol. 5443, pp. 463–480. Springer, Heidelberg (2009)

29. Nakanishi, T., Fujiwara, T., Watanabe, H.: A linkable group signature and its application to secret voting. Trans. IPSJ **40**(7), 3085–3096 (1999)

30. Naor, M., Yung, M.: Public-key cryptosystems provably secure against chosen ciphertext attacks. In: STOC 1990. ACM (1990)

31. Parkes, D.C., Rabin, M.O., Shieber, S.M., Thorpe, C.: Practical secrecy-preserving, verifiably correct and trustworthy auctions. Electron. Commer. Res. Appl. **7**(3), 294–312 (2008)

32. Sakai, Y., Emura, K., Hanaoka, G., Kawai, Y., Matsuda, T., Omote, K.: Group signatures with message-dependent opening. In: Abdalla, M., Lange, T. (eds.) Pairing 2012. LNCS, vol. 7708, pp. 270–294. Springer, Heidelberg (2013)

33. Sakai, Y., Schuldt, J.C.N., Emura, K., Hanaoka, G., Ohta, K.: On the security of dynamic group signatures: preventing signature hijacking. In: Fischlin, M., Buchmann, J., Manulis, M. (eds.) PKC 2012. LNCS, vol. 7293, pp. 715–732. Springer, Heidelberg (2012)

34. Slamanig, D., Spreitzer, R., Unterluggauer, T.: Adding controllable linkability to pairing-based group signatures for free. In: Chow, S.S.M., Camenisch, J., Hui, L.C.K., Yiu, S.M. (eds.) ISC 2014. LNCS, vol. 8783, pp. 388–400. Springer, Heidelberg (2014)

35. Tang, Q.: Public key encryption schemes supporting equality test with authorisation of different granularity. IJACT 2(4), 304–321 (2012)

36. Tang, Q.: Public key encryption supporting plaintext equality test and user-specified authorization. Secur. Commun. Netw. 5(12), 1351–1362 (2012)

37. Wei, V.K.: Tracing-by-linking group signatures. In: Zhou, J., López, J., Deng, R.H., Bao, F. (eds.) ISC 2005. LNCS, vol. 3650, pp. 149–163. Springer, Heidelberg (2005)

Secure Multi Party Computation

Hybrid Publicly Verifiable Computation

James Alderman$^{(\boxtimes)}$, Christian Janson, Carlos Cid, and Jason Crampton

Information Security Group, Royal Holloway, University of London, Egham,
Surrey TW20 0EX, UK
{James.Alderman,Carlos.Cid,Jason.Crampton}@rhul.ac.uk,
Christian.Janson.2012@live.rhul.ac.uk

Abstract. Publicly Verifiable Outsourced Computation (PVC) allows
weak devices to delegate computations to more powerful servers, and to
verify the correctness of results. Delegation and verification rely only on
public parameters, and thus PVC lends itself to large multi-user systems where entities need not be registered. In such settings, individual
user requirements may be diverse and cannot be realised with current
PVC solutions. In this paper, we introduce *Hybrid PVC* (HPVC) which,
with a single setup stage, provides a flexible solution to outsourced computation supporting multiple modes: (i) standard PVC, (ii) PVC with
cryptographically enforced access control policies restricting the servers
that may perform a given computation, and (iii) a reversed model of
PVC which we call *Verifiable Delegable Computation* (VDC) where data
is held remotely by servers. Entities may dynamically play the role of
delegators or servers as required.

Keywords: Publicly verifiable computation · Outsourced computation · Dual-Policy Attribute-based Encryption · Revocation · Access
control

1 Introduction

The trend towards cloud computing means that there is a growing trust dependency on remote servers and the functionality they provide. *Publicly Verifiable
Computation* (PVC) [20] allows *any* entity to use public information to delegate
or verify computations, and lends itself to large multi-user systems that are likely
to arise in practice (as delegators need not be individually registered).

However, in such a system, the individual user requirements may be diverse
and require different forms of outsourced computation, whereas current PVC
schemes support only a single form. Clients may wish to request computations
from a particular server or to issue a request to a large pool of servers; in the latter
case, they may wish to restrict the servers that can perform the computation to
only those possessing certain characteristics. Moreover, the data may be provided

---

J. Alderman—Partial funding by the European Commission under project H2020-
644024 "CLARUS", and support from BAE Systems Advanced Technology Centre
is gratefully acknowledged.

© Springer International Publishing Switzerland 2016
K. Sako (Ed.): CT-RSA 2016, LNCS 9610, pp. 147–163, 2016.
DOI: 10.1007/978-3-319-29485-8_9

by the client as part of the computation, or it may be stored by the server; and the role of servers and clients may be interchangeable depending on the context.

Consider the following scenarios: (i) employees with limited resources (e.g. using mobile devices when out of the office) need to delegate computations to more powerful servers. The workload of the employee may also involve responding to computation requests to perform tasks for other employees or to respond to inter-departmental queries over restricted databases; (ii) Entities that invest heavily in outsourced computations could find themselves with a valuable, processed dataset that is of interest to other parties, and hence want to selectively share this infor-mation by allowing others to query the dataset in a verifiable fashion; (iii) data-base servers that allow public queries may become overwhelmed with requests, and need to enlist additional servers to help (essentially the server acts as a del-egator to outsource queries with relevant data). Finally, (iv) consider a form of peer-to-peer network for sharing computational resources – as individual resource availability varies, entities can sell spare resources to perform computations for other users or make their own data available to others, whilst making computa-tion requests to other entities when resources run low.

Current PVC solutions do not handle these flexible requirements particu-larly well; although there are several different proposals in the literature that realise some of the requirements described above, each requires an independent (potentially expensive) setup stage. We introduce *Hybrid PVC* (HPVC) which is a single mechanism (with the associated costs of a single setup operation and a single set of system parameters to publish and maintain) which simultaneously satisfies all of the above requirements. Entities may play the role of both delega-tors and servers, in the following modes of operation, dynamically as required:

- **Revocable PVC** (RPVC) where clients with limited resources outsource computations on data of their choosing to more powerful, untrusted servers using only public information. Multiple servers can compute multiple func-tions. Servers may try to cheat to persuade verifiers of incorrect information or to avoid using their own resources. Misbehaving servers can be detected and revoked so that further results will be rejected and they will not be rewarded for their effort;
- **RPVC with access control** (RPVC-AC) which restricts the servers that may perform a given computation. Outsourced computations may be distrib-uted amongst a pool of available servers that are not individually authenti-cated and known by the delegator. Prior work [1] used symmetric primitives and required all entities to be registered in the system (including delegators) but we achieve a fully public system where only servers need be registered (as usual in PVC);
- **Verifiable Delegable Computation** (VDC) where servers are the data owners and make a static dataset available for verifiable querying. Clients request computations on subsets of the dataset using public, descriptive labels.

We begin, in Sect. 2, with a summary of related work and the KP-ABE-based PVC schemes [3, 20] on which we base our HPVC construction. In Sect. 3, we define the generic functionality and security properties of HPVC. We then, in Sect. 4.1, discuss each supported mode of computation, and how it fits our generic definition. To support user revocation [3], we introduce a new cryptographic primitive called Revocable-Key Dual-policy Attribute-based Encryption (rkDPABE) in Sect. 4.2, and finally, in Sect. 4.3, we instantiate HPVC using rkDPABE. Additional details, formal security games and proofs can be found in the full version online [2].

2 Background and Related Work

Verifiable computation [10,12,13,15,16,20,24] may be seen as a protocol between a (weak) client C and a server S, resulting in the provably correct computation of $F(x)$ by the server for the client's choice of F and x. The setup stage may be computationally expensive (amortised over multiple computations) but other operations should be efficient for the client. Some prior work used garbled circuits with fully homomorphic encryption [13,16] or targeted specific functions [10,12,15]. Chung et al. [14] introduced *memory delegation* which is similar to VDC; a client uploads his memory to a server who can update and compute a function F over the entire memory. Backes et al. [8] consider a client that outsources data and requests computations on a data portion. The client can efficiently verify the correctness of the result without holding the input data. Most work requires the client to know the data in order to verify [9,11,17,19]. *Verifiable oblivious storage* [5] ensures data confidentiality, access pattern privacy, integrity and freshness of data accesses. Work on authenticated data lends itself to verifiable outsourced computations, albeit for specific functions only. Backes et al. [7] use privacy-preserving proofs over authenticated data outsourced by a trusted client. Similar results are presented in [22] using public logs. It is notable that [7] and [11] achieve public verifiability. In independent and concurrent work, Shi et al. [21] use DP-ABE to combine keyword search on encrypted data with the enforcement of an access control policy.

Parno et al. [20] introduce *Publicly Verifiable Computation* (PVC) where multiple clients outsource computations of a single function to a single server, and verify the results. Alderman et al. [3] introduce a trusted Key Distribution Centre (KDC) to handle the expensive setup for all entities, to allow multiple servers to compute multiple functions, and to revoke misbehaving servers. Informally, the KDC acts as the root of trust to generate public parameters and delegation information, and to issue secret keys and evaluation keys to servers. To outsource the evaluation of $F(x)$, a delegator sends an encoded input $\sigma_{F(x)}$ to a server S, and publishes verification tokens. S uses an evaluation key for F to produce an encoded output $\theta_{F(x)}$. *Any* entity can verify correctness of $\theta_{F(x)}$ using a verification key and learn the value of $F(x)$. If S cheated they may be reported to the KDC for revocation.

The constructions of [3,20] to outsource a Boolean function, F, are based on Key-policy Attribute-based encryption (KP-ABE), which links ciphertexts with attribute sets and decryption keys with a policy; decryption only succeeds if the attributes satisfy the policy. For PVC, two random messages are encrypted and linked to the input data X (represented as attributes) to form the encoded input. The evaluation key is a pair of decryption keys linked to F and $\overline{F}$ (the complement function of F). Exactly *one* message can be recovered, implying whether F or $\overline{F}$ was satisfied, and hence if $F(X) = 1$ or 0. Ciphertext indistinguishability ensures S cannot return the other message to imply an incorrect result.

3   Hybrid Publicly Verifiable Computation

To accommodate different modes of computation, we define HPVC generically in terms of parameters ω, $\mathbb{O}$, ψ and $\mathbb{S}$. Depending on the mode (and which party provides the input data), $\mathbb{O}$ or $\mathbb{S}$ will encode functions, while ω or ψ encode input data, as detailed in Sect. 4.1. We retain the single, trusted key distribution centre (KDC) from RPVC [3] who initialises the system for a function family $\mathcal{F}$ resulting in a set of public parameters PP and a master secret key. For each function $F \in \mathcal{F}$, the KDC publishes a delegation key PK_F. It also registers each entity S_i that wants to act as a server by issuing a signing key SK_{S_i}. It may also update PP during any algorithm to reflect changes in the user population.

Depending on the mode, servers either compute functions $\mathbb{O}$ on behalf of clients, or make a dataset ψ available for public querying. The Certify algorithm is run by the KDC to produce an evaluation key $EK_{(\mathbb{O}, \psi), S_i}$ enabling S_i to perform these operations. S_i chooses a set of labels L_i – in RPVC or RPVC-AC modes, L_i uniquely represents the function F that S_i should be certified to compute; in VDC mode, L_i is a *set* of labels, each uniquely representing a data point contained in the dataset D_i owned by S_i[1]. In the VDC setting, the server is the data owner and so S_i also provides a list $\mathcal{F}_i$ advertising the functions that he is willing to evaluate on his data in accordance with his own data usage policies; in RPVC settings, $\mathcal{F}_i$ advertises the functions S_i is certified to compute.

To request a computation of $F(X)$ (encoded in ω or $\mathbb{S}$) from S_i, a delegator uses public information to run ProbGen. He provides labels $L_{F,X} \subseteq L_i$ describing the computation: in RPVC or RPVC-AC modes, the delegator provides the input data X and $L_{F,X}$ labels the function F to be applied; in VDC mode, the client uses the descriptive labels to choose a subset of data points $X \subseteq D_i, X \subseteq \mathrm{Dom}(F)$ held by S_i that should be computed on. ProbGen generates an encoded input $\sigma_{F,X}$ and a public verification key $VK_{F,X}$.

A server combines $\sigma_{F,X}$ with its evaluation key to compute $\theta_{F(X)}$ encoding the result $F(X)$. Any entity can verify the correctness of $\theta_{F(X)}$ using $VK_{F,X}$. Verification outputs the result $y = F(X)$ of the computation (if correct) and generates a token $\tau_{F(X)}$ which is sent to the KDC; if the token signifies that the result was incorrectly formed then the server is revoked from performing further evaluations. This prevents delegators wasting their (limited) resources outsourcing to a server known to be untrustworthy, and also acts as a deterrent, especially when servers are rewarded per computation.

---

[1] These descriptive labels (e.g. field names in a database) allow delegators to select data points to be used in a computation *without* knowing the data values.

Definition 1. A *Hybrid Publicly Verifiable Computation (HPVC) scheme* for a family of functions $\mathcal{F}$ comprises the following algorithms:

1. $(\text{PP}, \text{MK}) \xleftarrow{\$} \text{Setup}(1^\ell, \mathcal{F})$: run by the KDC to establish public parameters PP and a master secret key MK for the system. The inputs are the security parameter ℓ, and the family of functions $\mathcal{F}$ that may be computed;

2. $PK_F \xleftarrow{\$} \text{FnInit}(F, \text{MK}, \text{PP})$: run by the KDC to generate a public delegation key, PK_F, allowing entities to outsource, or request, computations of F;

3. $SK_{S_i} \xleftarrow{\$} \text{Register}(S_i, \text{MK}, \text{PP})$: run by the KDC to enrol an entity S_i within the system to act as a server. It generates a personalised signing key SK_{S_i};

4. $EK_{(\mathbb{O},\psi),S_i} \xleftarrow{\$} \text{Certify}(\text{mode}, S_i, (\mathbb{O}, \psi), L_i, \mathcal{F}_i, \text{MK}, \text{PP})$: run by the KDC to generate an evaluation key $EK_{(\mathbb{O},\psi),S_i}$ enabling the server S_i to compute on the pair $(\mathbb{O}, \psi)$. The algorithm also takes as input the mode in which it should operate, a set of labels L_i and a set of functions $\mathcal{F}_i$;

5. $(\sigma_{F,X}, VK_{F,X}) \xleftarrow{\$} \text{ProbGen}(\text{mode}, (\omega, \mathbb{S}), L_{F,X}, PK_F, \text{PP})$: run by an entity to request a computation of $F(X)$ from S_i. The inputs are the mode, the pair $(\omega, \mathbb{S})$ representing the computation, a set of labels $L_{F,X} \subseteq L_i$, the delegation key for F and the public parameters. The outputs are an encoded input $\sigma_{F,X}$ and a verification key $VK_{F,X}$;

6. $\theta_{F(X)} \xleftarrow{\$} \text{Compute}(\text{mode}, \sigma_{F,X}, EK_{(\mathbb{O},\psi),S_i}, SK_{S_i}, \text{PP})$: run by an entity S_i to compute $F(X)$. The inputs are the mode, an encoded input, and an evaluation key and signing key for S_i. The output, $\theta_{F(X)}$, encodes the result;

7. $(y, \tau_{F(X)}) \leftarrow \text{Verify}(\theta_{F(X)}, VK_{F,X}, \text{PP})$: run by any entity. The inputs are an encoded output produced by S_i and verification key; the outputs are the computation result $y = F(X)$ if the result was computed correctly, or else $y = \perp$, and a token $\tau_{F(X)}$ which is (accept, S_i) if $\theta_{F(X)}$ is correct, or (reject, S_i) otherwise;

8. $UM \xleftarrow{\$} \text{Revoke}(\tau_{F(X)}, \text{MK}, \text{PP})$: run by the KDC if a misbehaving server is reported. It returns $UM = \perp$ if $\tau_{F(X)} = $ (accept, S_i). Otherwise, all evaluation keys $EK_{(\cdot,\cdot),S_i}$ for S_i are rendered non-functional and the update material UM is a set of updated evaluation keys $\{EK_{(\mathbb{O},\psi),S'}\}$ for all servers.

3.1 Security Models

We now discuss desirable security properties for HPVC; additional formal models are found in the full paper [2][2]. Public verifiability, revocation and authorised computation are selective notions in line with our rkDPABE scheme introduced in Sect. 4.2.

Public Verifiability, presented in Game 1, ensures that a server that returns an incorrect result is detected by the verification algorithm so that they can be reported for revocation. The adversary, $\mathcal{A}$, may corrupt other servers, generate

---

[2] We do not consider input privacy here, but note that a revocable dual-policy predicate encryption scheme, if found, could easily replace our ABE scheme in Sect. 4.3. Security against vindictive servers and managers can also be adapted from [3].

Game 1. $\mathbf{Exp}_{\mathcal{A}}^{\mathrm{sPubVerif}}\left[\mathcal{HPVC}, 1^{\ell}, \mathcal{F}\right]$

1: $(\omega^{\star}, \mathbb{O}^{\star}, \psi^{\star}, \mathbb{S}^{\star}, L_{F,X^{\star}}, \mathrm{mode}) \xleftarrow{\$} \mathcal{A}(1^{\ell}, \mathcal{F})$
2: $(\mathrm{PP}, \mathrm{MK}) \xleftarrow{\$} \mathsf{Setup}(1^{\ell}, \mathcal{F})$
3: **if** $(\mathrm{mode} = VDC)$ **then** $(F \leftarrow \mathbb{S}^{\star}, X^{\star} \leftarrow \psi^{\star})$
4: **else** $(F \leftarrow \mathbb{O}^{\star}, X^{\star} \leftarrow \omega^{\star})$
5: $PK_F \xleftarrow{\$} \mathsf{FnInit}(F, \mathrm{MK}, \mathrm{PP})$
6: $(\sigma^{\star}, VK^{\star}) \xleftarrow{\$} \mathsf{ProbGen}(\mathrm{mode}, (\omega^{\star}, \mathbb{S}^{\star}), L_{F,X^{\star}}, PK_F, \mathrm{PP})$
7: $\theta^{\star} \xleftarrow{\$} \mathcal{A}^{\mathcal{O}}(\sigma^{\star}, VK^{\star}, PK_F, \mathrm{PP})$
8: $(y, \tau_{\theta^{\star}}) \leftarrow \mathsf{Verify}(\theta^{\star}, VK^{\star}, \mathrm{PP})$
9: **if** $(((y, \tau_{\theta^{\star}}) \neq (\bot, (\mathrm{reject}, \cdot)))$ **and** $(y \neq F(X^{\star})))$ **then**
10:     **return** 1
11: **else return** 0

arbitrary computations, and perform verification steps himself. $\mathcal{A}$ first selects its challenge parameters, including the mode it wishes its challenge to be generated in and the labels associated to its choice of inputs. We ask $\mathcal{A}$ to choose $\mathbb{O}^{\star}$ and $\psi^{\star}$, despite the challenge inputs being only $\omega^{\star}$ and $\mathbb{S}^{\star}$. This allows us to define the challenge in terms of F and $X^{\star}$ on line 3; note that $\mathbb{O}^{\star}$ and $\psi^{\star}$ can also be gleaned from the mode and labels, so this does not weaken the game – the adversary has already determined these values through its choices.

The challenger runs Setup and FnInit for the chosen function F. It then runs $\mathsf{ProbGen}$ to create the challenge parameters for the adversary, which are given to $\mathcal{A}$ along with the public information. The adversary is also given oracle access to the functions $\mathsf{FnInit}(\cdot, \mathrm{MK}, \mathrm{PP})$, $\mathsf{Register}(\cdot, \mathrm{MK}, \mathrm{PP})$, $\mathsf{Certify}(\cdot, \cdot, (\cdot, \cdot), \cdot, \cdot, \mathrm{MK}, \mathrm{PP})$ and $\mathsf{Revoke}(\cdot, \mathrm{MK}, \mathrm{PP})$, denoted by $\mathcal{O}$. $\mathcal{A}$ wins the game if it creates an encoded output that verifies correctly yet does not encode the correct value $F(x)$.

Definition 2. The *advantage* of a probabilistic polynomial time adversary $\mathcal{A}$ in the sPubVerif game for an HPVC construction, $\mathcal{HPVC}$, for a family of functions $\mathcal{F}$ is defined as:

$$Adv_{\mathcal{A}}^{\mathrm{sPubVerif}}(\mathcal{HPVC}, 1^{\ell}, \mathcal{F}) = \Pr\left[1 \xleftarrow{\$} \mathbf{Exp}_{\mathcal{A}}^{\mathrm{sPubVerif}}\left[\mathcal{HPVC}, 1^{\ell}, \mathcal{F}\right]\right].$$

$\mathcal{HPVC}$ is *secure with respect to selective public verifiability* if, for all PPT adversaries $\mathcal{A}$, $Adv_{\mathcal{A}}^{\mathrm{sPubVerif}}(\mathcal{HPVC}, 1^{\ell}, \mathcal{F})$ is negligible in ℓ.

– **Revocation** ensures that a server that has been detected as misbehaving cannot produce a result (even a correct result) that is accepted by a verifier – thus, the server cannot be rewarded for future work. To reflect the revocation mechanism of the rkDPABE primitive, we include a semi-static restriction whereby a list of entities to be revoked at the time of the challenge computation must be declared before the adversary receives oracle access[3].

---

[3] This restriction was also used in [6] for revocable KP-ABE, and could be removed if an adaptive, indirectly revocable ABE scheme is found.

– **Authorised Computation** extends the model of [1] to the public-key setting to ensure that an unauthorised server cannot produce acceptable results.

4 Instantiating HPVC

We construct an HPVC scheme for the class NC^1, which includes common arithmetic and matrix operations. Let $\mathcal{F}$ be the family of Boolean formulas closed under complement – for all $F \in \mathcal{F}$, $\overline{F}(x) = F(x) \oplus 1$ is also in $\mathcal{F}$. We construct our scheme from a novel use of Dual-policy Attribute-based Encryption (DP-ABE) which combines KP-ABE and Ciphertext-policy ABE (CP-ABE). Decryption keys are linked to an "objective" policy $\mathbb{O}$ and "subjective" attribute set ψ, and ciphertexts linked to an "objective" attribute set ω and "subjective" policy $\mathbb{S}$; decryption requires both policies to be satisfied – $\omega \in \mathbb{O}$ and $\psi \in \mathbb{S}$.

Following [20], we encrypt two random messages to form the encoded input, while decryption keys form evaluation keys; by linking these to F, $\overline{F}$ and X according to the mode, we ensure that exactly *one* message can be recovered, implying whether F or $\overline{F}$ was satisfied, and hence if $F(X) = 1$ or 0. DP-ABE security ensures a server cannot learn a message implying an invalid result.

The values of ω, $\mathbb{O}$, ψ and $\mathbb{S}$ depend upon the mode, as detailed in Table 1. Two additional parameters T_O and T_S "disable" modes when not required. Note that, trivially, $\psi \in \mathbb{S}$ when $\psi = \{T_S\}$ and $\mathbb{S} = \{\{T_S\}\}$, and similarly for T_O.

4.1 Supporting Different Modes

RPVC. In this mode, a delegator owns some input data X and wants to learn $F(X)$ but lacks the computational resources to do so itself; thus, the computation is outsourced. In this setting, only the parameters $\mathbb{O}$ and ω are required, and are set to be F and X respectively. The set X comprises a single datapoint: the input data to this particular computation. The remaining parameters $\mathbb{S}$ and ψ are defined in terms of the dummy parameter T_S. The set of functions $\mathcal{F}_i$ that a server is certified for during a single Certify operation is simply F, and the sets of labels L_i and $L_{F,X}$ both comprise a single element $l(F)$ uniquely labelling F.

Table 1. Parameter definitions for different modes

mode	$\mathbb{O}$	ψ	ω	$\mathbb{S}$
RPVC	F	$\{T_S\}$	X	$\{\{T_S\}\}$
RPVC-AC	F	s	X	P
VDC	$\{\{T_O\}\}$	D_i	$\{T_O\}$	F

mode	L_i	$L_{F,X}$	$\mathcal{F}_i$
RPVC	$\{l(F)\}$	$\{l(F)\}$	$\{F\}$
RPVC-AC	$\{l(F)\}$	$\{l(F)\}$	$\{F\}$
VDC	$\{l(x_{i,j})\}_{x_{i,j} \in D_i}$	$\{l(x_{i,j})\}_{x_{i,j} \in X}$	$\{(F, \{l(x_{i,j})\}_{x_{i,j} \in \mathsf{Dom}(F)})\}_{F \in \mathcal{F}}$

RPVC-AC. RPVC-AC [1] was introduced with the motivation that servers may be chosen from a pool based on resource availability, a bidding process etc. Delegators may not have previously authenticated the selected server, in contrast to prior models [20] where a client set up a PVC system with a single, known server.

The construction of [1] used a symmetric key assignment scheme allowing only authorised entities to derive the required keys. However, the KDC had to register all delegators and verifiers. This was due both to the policies being enforced (e.g. to restrict the computations delegators may outsource), and to the use of symmetric primitives – to encrypt inputs, delegators must know the secret symmetric key. Thus, the scheme is not strictly *publicly delegable* as delegation does not depend *only* on public information, and similarly for verification.

We retain public delegability and verifiability whilst restricting the servers that may perform a given computation. In some sense, servers are already authorised for functions by being issued evaluation keys. However, we believe that access control policies in this setting must consider additional factors than just functions. The semantic meaning and sensitivity of input data may affect the policy, or servers may need to possess specific resources or characteristics, or be geographically nearby to minimise latency. E.g. a government contractor may, due to the nature of its work, require servers to be within the same country.

One solution could be for the KDC to issue signed attributes to each server who attaches the required signatures to computation results for verification. In this case, a verifier must decide if the received attributes are sufficient. We consider the delegator that runs ProbGen to "own" the computation and, as such, it should specify the authorisation policy that a server must meet. As this is a publicly verifiable setting, any entity can verify and we believe (i) verifiers should not accept a result that the delegator itself would not accept, and (ii) it may be unreasonable to expect verifiers to have sufficient knowledge to determine the authorisation policy. Of course, the delegator could attach a signed authorisation policy to the verification key, but verifiers are not obliged to adhere to this policy and doing so creates additional work for the verifier – one of the key efficiency requirements for PVC is that verification is very cheap. Using DP-ABE to instantiate HPVC allows the delegator to specify the authorisation policy during ProbGen and requires no additional work on the part of the verifier compared to standard RPVC. Furthermore, an unauthorised server cannot actually perform the computation and hence verification will always fail.

We use the objective parameters ω and $\mathbb{O}$ to compute (as for RPVC) whilst the subjective parameters ψ and $\mathbb{S}$ enforce access control on the server. Servers are assigned both an evaluation key for a function F *and* a set of descriptive attributes describing their authorisation rights, $s \subseteq \mathcal{U}_S$, where $\mathcal{U}_S$ is a universe of attributes used solely to define authorisation. ProbGen operates on both the input data X *and* an authorisation policy $P \subseteq 2^{\mathcal{U}_S} \setminus \{\emptyset\}$ which defines the permissible sets of authorisation attributes to perform this computation. Servers may produce valid, acceptable outputs only if $s \in P$ i.e. they satisfy the authorisation policy. E.g. $P = (\texttt{Country} = \texttt{UK}) \vee ((\texttt{clearance} = \texttt{Secret}) \wedge (\texttt{Country} = \texttt{USA}))$ is satisfied by $s = \{\texttt{Country} = \texttt{UK}, \texttt{Capacity} = \texttt{3TB}\}$.

Table 2. Example database

User ID	Name	Age	Height
001	Alice	26	165
002	Bob	22	172

Table 3. Example list $\mathcal{F}_i$

F	Dom(F)
Average	Age of record 1, Height of record 1, Age of record 2, Height of record 2
Most common value	Name of record 1, Age of record 1, Height of record 1, Name of record 2, Age of record 2, Height of record 2

VDC. VDC reverses the role of the data owner – a server owns a static database and enables delegators to request computations/queries over the data. Hence, the user relationship is more akin to the traditional client-server model compared to PVC. Delegators learn nothing more than the result of the computation, and do not need the input data in order to verify. The *efficiency* requirement for VDC is also very different from PVC: outsourcing a computation is not merely an attempt to gain efficiency as the delegator never possesses the input data and so cannot execute the computation himself (even with the necessary resources). Thus, VDC does not have the stringent efficiency requirement present in PVC (that outsourcing and verifying computations be more efficient than performing the computation itself, for outsourcing to be worthwhile). Our solution behaves reasonably well, achieving constant time verification; the size of the query depends on the function F, while the size of the server's response depends only on the size of the result itself and *not* on the input size which may be large.

In VDC, each entity S_i that wants to act as a server owns a dataset $D_i = \{x_{i,j}\}_{j=1}^{m_i}$ comprising m_i data points. The KDC issues a single evaluation key EK_{D_i,S_i} enabling S_i to compute on subsets of D_i. S_i publishes a list L_i comprising a unique label $l(x_{i,j}) \in L_i$ for each data point $x_{i,j} \in D_i$, and a list of functions $\mathcal{F}_i \subseteq \mathcal{F}$ that are (i) meaningful on their dataset, and (ii) permissible according to their own access control policies. Furthermore, not all data points $x_{i,j} \in D_i$ may be appropriate for each function e.g. only numeric data should be input to an averaging function. $\mathcal{F}_i$ comprises elements $(F, \bigcup_{x_{i,j} \in \text{Dom}(F)} l(x_{i,j}))$ describing each function and the associated permissible inputs. Labels should *not* reveal the data values themselves to preserve the confidentiality of D_i.

Delegators may select servers and data using *only* these labels e.g. they may ask S_i to compute $F(X)$ for any function $F \in \mathcal{F}_i$ on a set of data points $X \subseteq \text{Dom}(F)$[4] by specifying labels $\{l(x_{i,j})\}_{x_{i,j} \in X}$. Although it may be tempting to suggest that S_i simply caches the results of computing each $F \in \mathcal{F}_i$, the number of input sets $X \subseteq \text{Dom}(F)$ could be large, making this an unattractive solution.

As an example, consider a server S_i that owns the database in Table 2. The dataset D_i represents this as a set of field values for each record in turn: $D_i = \{001, \text{Alice}, 26, 165, 002, \text{Bob}, 22, 172\}$. S_i publishes data labels $L_i = \{$User ID of record 1, Name of record 1, Age of record 1, Height of record 1, User ID of record 2, Name of record 2, Age of record 2, Height of record 2$\}$. In Table 3, $\mathcal{F}_i$ lists the functions and domains that S_i is willing to compute. To find the

---

[4] In contrast to prior modes where X was a single data point, F now takes $|X|$ inputs.

average age, a delegator queries "Average" on input $X = \{$Age of record 1, Age of record 2$\}$.

4.2   Revocable Dual-Policy Attribute-Based Encryption

Before instantiating HPVC, we first introduce a new cryptographic primitive which forms the basic building-block of our construction. If revocation is not required then a standard DP-ABE scheme can be used.

Definition 3. A *Revocable Key Dual-policy Attribute-based Encryption scheme* (rkDPABE) comprises five algorithms:

- $(PP, MK) \xleftarrow{\$} \mathsf{Setup}(1^\ell, \mathcal{U})$: takes the security parameter and attribute universe and generates public parameters PP and a master secret key MK;
- $CT_{(\omega,\mathbb{S}),t} \xleftarrow{\$} \mathsf{Encrypt}(m, (\omega, \mathbb{S}), t, PP)$: takes as input a message to be encrypted, an objective attribute set ω, a subjective policy $\mathbb{S}$, a time period t and the public parameters. It outputs a ciphertext that is valid for time t;
- $SK_{(\mathbb{O},\psi),\mathrm{ID}} \xleftarrow{\$} \mathsf{KeyGen}(\mathrm{ID}, (\mathbb{O}, \psi), MK, PP)$: takes an identity ID, an objective access structure $\mathbb{O}$, a subjective attribute set ψ, the master secret key and the public parameters. It outputs a secret decryption key $SK_{(\mathbb{O},\psi),\mathrm{ID}}$;
- $UK_{R,t} \xleftarrow{\$} \mathsf{KeyUpdate}(R, t, MK, PP)$: takes a revocation list R containing all revoked identities, the current time period, the master secret key and public parameters. It outputs updated key material $UK_{R,t}$ which makes the decryption keys $SK_{(\mathbb{O},\psi),\mathrm{ID}}$, for all non-revoked identities $\mathrm{ID} \notin R$, functional to decrypt ciphertexts encrypted for the time t;
- $PT \leftarrow \mathsf{Decrypt}(CT_{(\omega,\mathbb{S}),t}, (\omega, \mathbb{S}), SK_{(\mathbb{O},\psi),\mathrm{ID}}, (\mathbb{O}, \psi), UK_{R,t}, PP)$: takes as input a ciphertext formed for the time period t and the associated pair $(\omega,\mathbb{S})$, a decryption key for entity ID and the associated pair $(\mathbb{O}, \psi)$, an update key for the time t and the public parameters. It outputs a plaintext PT which is the encrypted message m, if and only if the objective attributes ω satisfies the objective access structure $\mathbb{O}$ *and* the subjective attributes ψ satisfies the subjective policy $\mathbb{S}$ *and* the value of t in the update key matches that specified during encryption. If not, PT is set to be a failure symbol $\perp$.

Definition 3 suffices to comprehend the remainder of this paper as we shall use an rkDPABE scheme in a black-box manner. For completeness, we give correctness and security definitions, a construction and a security proof in the full, online version of the paper [2].

4.3   Construction

As mentioned, we base our construction on rkDPABE by encoding inputs as attributes in a universe $\mathcal{U}_x$, and encoding Boolean functions as access structures over $\mathcal{U}_x$. Computations with n-bit outputs can be built from n Boolean functions returning each bit in turn. Negations can be handled by building rkDPABE from non-monotonic ABE [18] or, as here, by adding negated attributes to the universe [23]. For the ith bit of a binary input string $X = x_1 \ldots x_n$, define attributes $A_{X,i}^0$ and $A_{X,i}^1 \in \mathcal{U}_x$[5]; X is encoded as $A_X = \{A_{X,i}^j \in \mathcal{U}_x : x_i = j\}$.

Let $\mathcal{U}_l$ be a set of attributes (disjoint from $\mathcal{U}_x$) uniquely labelling each function and data item, and let $\mathcal{U}_{\mathrm{ID}}$ represent server identities. Let g be a one-way function and $\mathcal{DPABE}$ be a revocable key DP-ABE scheme for $\mathcal{F}$ with attribute universe $\mathcal{U} = \mathcal{U}_x \cup \mathcal{U}_l \cup \mathcal{U}_{\mathrm{ID}}$. We initialise two independent DP-ABE systems over $\mathcal{U}$, and define four additional "dummy" attributes to disable modes: T_O^0, T_S^0 for the first system, and T_O^1, T_S^1 for the second. We denote the complement functions as follows: in RPVC and RPVC-AC, recall $\mathbb{O} = F$ and $\mathbb{S} = \{\{T_S^0\}\}$; we define $\overline{\mathbb{O}} = \overline{F}$ and $\overline{\mathbb{S}} = \{\{T_S^1\}\}$. Similarly, for VDC, $\overline{\mathbb{O}} = \{\{T_0^1\}\}$ and $\overline{\mathbb{S}} = \overline{F}$.

1. Setup initialises two rkDPABE schemes over $\mathcal{U}$, an empty two-dimensional array L_{Reg} to list registered entities, a list of revoked entities L_{Rev} and a time source $\mathbb{T}$ (e.g. a networked clock or counter) to index update keys[6].

Algorithm 1. $(PP, MK) \xleftarrow{\$} \mathsf{HPVC.Setup}(1^\ell, \mathcal{F})$

1: $(MPK_{\mathrm{ABE}}^0, MSK_{\mathrm{ABE}}^0, T_O^0, T_S^0) \xleftarrow{\$} \mathsf{DPABE.Setup}(1^\ell, \mathcal{U})$
2: $(MPK_{\mathrm{ABE}}^1, MPK_{\mathrm{ABE}}^1, T_O^1, T_S^1) \xleftarrow{\$} \mathsf{DPABE.Setup}(1^\ell, \mathcal{U})$
3: **for** $S_i \in \mathcal{U}_{\mathrm{ID}}$ **do**
4: $\quad L_{\mathrm{Reg}}[S_i][0] \leftarrow \epsilon, L_{\mathrm{Reg}}[S_i][1] \leftarrow \{\epsilon\}$
5: Initialise $\mathbb{T}$
6: $L_{\mathrm{Rev}} \leftarrow \epsilon$
7: $\mathrm{PP} \leftarrow (MPK_{\mathrm{ABE}}^0, MPK_{\mathrm{ABE}}^1, L_{\mathrm{Reg}}, T_O^0, T_O^1, T_S^0, T_S^1, \mathbb{T})$
8: $\mathrm{MK} \leftarrow (MSK_{\mathrm{ABE}}^0, MSK_{\mathrm{ABE}}^1, L_{\mathrm{Rev}})$

---

2. FnInit sets the public delegation key PK_F (for all functions F) to be the public parameters for the system (since we use public key primitives).

Algorithm 2. $PK_F \xleftarrow{\$} \mathsf{HPVC.FnInit}(F, MK, PP)$

1: $PK_F \leftarrow \mathrm{PP}$

---

[5] Either by defining a large enough $\mathcal{U}_x$ or by hashing strings to elements of the attribute group. Unlike prior schemes [3,20], we include an identifier of the data X (based on the label $l(x_{i,j})$) in the attribute mapping to specify the data items to be used; alternatively, D_i could be a long bitstring formed by concatenating each data point, and the labels should identify the attributes corresponding to each data point.

[6] Our KDC will act as the trusted KeyGen authority already inherent in ABE schemes.

3. Register runs a signature KeyGen algorithm and adds the verification key to $L_{Reg}[S_i][0]$. These prevent servers being impersonated and wrongly revoked.

Algorithm 3. $SK_{S_i} \xleftarrow{\$} \mathsf{HPVC.Register}(S_i, \mathrm{MK}, \mathrm{PP})$

1: $(SK_{\mathrm{Sig}}, VK_{\mathrm{Sig}}) \xleftarrow{\$} \mathsf{Sig.KeyGen}(1^\ell)$
2: $SK_{S_i} \leftarrow SK_{\mathrm{Sig}}$
3: $L_{\mathrm{Reg}}[S_i][0] \leftarrow L_{\mathrm{Reg}}[S_i][0] \cup VK_{\mathrm{Sig}}$

---

4. Certify first adds an element $(F, \bigcup_{l \in L_i} l)$ to the list $L_{Reg}[S_i][1]$ for each $F \in \mathcal{F}_i$; this publicises the computations that S_i can perform (either functions in RPVC and RPVC-AC modes, or functions and data labels in VDC). The algorithm removes S_i from the revocation list, gets the current time from $\mathbb{T}$ and generates a decryption key for $(\mathbb{O}, A_\psi \cup \bigcup_{l \in L_i} l)$ (where A_ψ is the attribute set encoding ψ) in the first DP-ABE system. The additional attributes for the labels $l \in \mathcal{U}_l$ ensure that a key cannot be used to evaluate computations that do not correspond to these labels. In RPVC and RPVC-AC, this means that a key for function G cannot evaluate a computation request for $F(X)$. In VDC, it means that an evaluation key must be issued for a dataset D_i that includes (at least) the specified input data $X^\star$. It is sufficient to include labels only on the subjective attribute set; as these labels are a security measure against a misbehaving server, we amend the servers key but need not take similar measures against the delegator. Delegators can then specify, in the subjective policy that they create, the labels that are required; these must be in the server's key for successful evaluation (decryption). The KDC should check that the label corresponds to the input to ensure that a server does not advertise data he does not own. It also generates an update key for the current time period to prove that S_i is not currently revoked. In RPVC mode, another pair of keys is generated using the second DP-ABE system for the complement inputs.

Algorithm 4. $EK_{(\mathbb{O}, \psi), S_i} \xleftarrow{\$} \mathsf{HPVC.Certify}(\mathrm{mode}, S_i, (\mathbb{O}, \psi), L_i, \mathcal{F}_i, \mathrm{MK}, \mathrm{PP})$

1: **for** $F \in \mathcal{F}_i$ **do**
2:     $L_{\mathrm{Reg}}[S_i][1] \leftarrow L_{\mathrm{Reg}}[S_i][1] \cup (F, \bigcup_{l \in L_i} l)$
3: $L_{\mathrm{Rev}} \leftarrow L_{\mathrm{Rev}} \setminus S_i, \; t \leftarrow \mathbb{T}$
4: $SK_{\mathrm{ABE}}^0 \xleftarrow{\$} \mathsf{DPABE.KeyGen}(S_i, (\mathbb{O}, A_\psi \cup \bigcup_{l \in L_i} l), MSK_{\mathrm{ABE}}^0, MPK_{\mathrm{ABE}}^0)$
5: $UK_{L_{\mathrm{Rev}}, t}^0 \xleftarrow{\$} \mathsf{DPABE.KeyUpdate}(L_{\mathrm{Rev}}, t, MSK_{\mathrm{ABE}}^0, MPK_{\mathrm{ABE}}^0)$
6: **if** (mode =RPVC) **or** (mode =RPVC-AC) **then**
7:     $SK_{\mathrm{ABE}}^1 \xleftarrow{\$} \mathsf{DPABE.KeyGen}(S_i, (\overline{\mathbb{O}}, A_\psi \cup \bigcup_{l \in L_i} l), MSK_{\mathrm{ABE}}^1, MPK_{\mathrm{ABE}}^1)$
8:     $UK_{L_{\mathrm{Rev}}, t}^1 \xleftarrow{\$} \mathsf{DPABE.KeyUpdate}(L_{\mathrm{Rev}}, t, MSK_{\mathrm{ABE}}^1, MPK_{\mathrm{ABE}}^1)$
9: **else**
10:     $SK_{\mathrm{ABE}}^1 \leftarrow \perp, \; UK_{L_{\mathrm{Rev}}, t}^1 \leftarrow \perp$
11: $EK_{(\mathbb{O}, \psi), S_i} \leftarrow (SK_{\mathrm{ABE}}^0, SK_{\mathrm{ABE}}^1, UK_{L_{\mathrm{Rev}}, t}^0, UK_{L_{\mathrm{Rev}}, t}^1)$

5. ProbGen chooses messages m_0 and m_1 randomly from the message space. m_0 is encrypted with $(A_\omega, \mathbb{S} \wedge \bigwedge_{l \in L_{F,X}} l)$ in the first DPABE system, whilst m_1 is encrypted with the complement policy and either the first DPABE system for VDC or the second for RPVC (the attributes remain the same as it is the same attribute T_O^0 or input data X respectively). The verification key comprises g applied to each message; the one-wayness of g allows the key to be published.

Algorithm 5. $(\sigma_{F,X}, VK_{F,X}) \xleftarrow{\$} \mathsf{HPVC.ProbGen}(\mathtt{mode}, (\omega, \mathbb{S}), L_{F,X}, PK_F, \mathrm{PP})$

1: $(m_0, m_1) \xleftarrow{\$} \mathcal{M} \times \mathcal{M}$
2: $t \leftarrow \mathbb{T}$
3: $c_0 \xleftarrow{\$} \mathsf{DPABE.Encrypt}(m_0, (A_\omega, \mathbb{S} \wedge \bigwedge_{l \in L_{F,X}} l), t, MPK_{\mathrm{ABE}}^0)$
4: **if** $\mathtt{mode} = \mathrm{VDC}$ **then** $c_1 \xleftarrow{\$} \mathsf{DPABE.Encrypt}(m_1, (A_\omega, \bar{\mathbb{S}} \wedge \bigwedge_{l \in L_{F,X}} l), t, MPK_{\mathrm{ABE}}^0)$
5: **else** $c_1 \xleftarrow{\$} \mathsf{DPABE.Encrypt}(m_1, (A_\omega, \bar{\mathbb{S}} \wedge \bigwedge_{l \in L_{F,X}} l), t, MPK_{\mathrm{ABE}}^1)$
6: **return** $\sigma_{F,X} \leftarrow (c_0, c_1)$, $VK_{F,X} \leftarrow (g(m_0), g(m_1), L_{\mathrm{Reg}})$

---

6. Compute attempts to decrypt both ciphertexts, ensuring that different modes use the correct parameters. Decryption succeeds only if the function evaluates to 1 on the input data X i.e. the policy is satisfied. Since F and $\bar{F}$ output opposite results on X, exactly one plaintext will be a failure symbol $\perp$. The results are signed, along with the ID of the server S_i performing the computation.

Algorithm 6. $\theta_{F(X)} \xleftarrow{\$} \mathsf{HPVC.Compute}(\mathtt{mode}, \sigma_{F,X}, EK_{(\mathbb{O},\psi),S_i}, SK_{S_i}, \mathrm{PP})$

1: Parse $EK_{(\mathbb{O},\psi),S_i}$ as $(SK_{\mathrm{ABE}}^0, SK_{\mathrm{ABE}}^1, UK_{L_{\mathrm{Rev}},t}^0, UK_{L_{\mathrm{Rev}},t}^1)$ and $\sigma_{F,X}$ as (c_0, c_1)
2: $d_0 \leftarrow \mathsf{DPABE.Decrypt}(c_0, SK_{\mathrm{ABE}}^0, MPK_{\mathrm{ABE}}^0, UK_{L_{\mathrm{Rev}},t}^0)$
3: **if** $\mathtt{mode} = VDC$ **then** $d_1 \leftarrow \mathsf{DPABE.Decrypt}(c_1, SK_{\mathrm{ABE}}^0, MPK_{\mathrm{ABE}}^0, UK_{L_{\mathrm{Rev}},t}^0)$
4: **else** $d_1 \leftarrow \mathsf{DPABE.Decrypt}(c_1, SK_{\mathrm{ABE}}^1, MPK_{\mathrm{ABE}}^1, UK_{L_{\mathrm{Rev}},t}^1)$
5: $\gamma \xleftarrow{\$} \mathsf{Sig.Sign}((d_0, d_1, S_i), SK_{S_i})$
6: $\theta_{(\omega,\mathbb{S}),(\mathbb{O},\psi)} \leftarrow (d_0, d_1, S_i, \gamma)$

---

7. Verify verifies the signature using the verification key for S_i stored in L_{Reg}. If correct, it applies g to each plaintext in $\theta_{F(X)}$ and compares the results to the components of the verification key. If either comparison results in a match (i.e. the server successfully recovered a message), the output token is accept. Otherwise the result is rejected. If m_0 was returned then $F(X) = 1$ as m_0 was encrypted for the non-complemented inputs; if m_1 was returned then $F(X) = 0$.

Algorithm 7. $(y, \tau_{F(X)}) \leftarrow$ HPVC.Verify$(\theta_{F(X)}, VK_{F,X}, \mathrm{PP})$

1: Parse $VK_{F,X}$ as $(g(m_0), g(m_1), L_{\mathrm{Reg}})$ and $\theta_{F(X)}$ as (d_0, d_1, S_i, γ)
2: **if** accept $\leftarrow$ Sig.Verify$((d_0, d_1, S_i), \gamma, L_{\mathrm{Reg}}[S_i][0])$ **then**
3:    **if** $g(m_0) = g(d_0)$ **then return** $(y \leftarrow 1, \tau_{F(X)} \leftarrow (\mathrm{accept}, S_i))$
4:    **else if** $g(m_1) = g(d_1)$ **then return** $(y \leftarrow 0, \tau_{F(X)} \leftarrow (\mathrm{accept}, S_i))$
5:    **else return** $(y \leftarrow \perp, \tau_{F(X)} \leftarrow (\mathrm{reject}, S_i))$
6: **return** $(y \leftarrow \perp, \tau_{F(X)} \leftarrow (\mathrm{reject}, \perp))$

---

8. Revoke first checks whether a sever, S_i, should in fact be revoked. If so, it deletes the list $L_{\mathrm{Reg}}[S_i][1]$ of computations that S_i may perform. It also adds S_i to the revocation list, and refreshes the time source. It then generates new update keys for all non-revoked entities such that non-revoked keys are still functional in the new time period.

Algorithm 8. $UM \xleftarrow{\$}$ HPVC.Revoke$(\tau_{F(X)}, \mathrm{MK}, \mathrm{PP})$

1: **if** $(\tau_{F(X)} \neq (\mathrm{reject}, S_i))$ **then return** $UM \leftarrow \perp$
2: $L_{\mathrm{Reg}}[S_i][1] \leftarrow \{\epsilon\}$, $L_{\mathrm{Rev}} \leftarrow L_{\mathrm{Rev}} \cup S_i$
3: Refresh $\mathbb{T}$, $t \leftarrow \mathbb{T}$
4: $UK^0_{L_{\mathrm{Rev}}, t} \xleftarrow{\$}$ DPABE.KeyUpdate$(L_{\mathrm{Rev}}, t, MSK^0_{\mathrm{ABE}}, MPK^0_{\mathrm{ABE}})$
5: **if** (mode $=$RPVC) **or** (mode $=$ RPVC-AC) **then**
6:    $UK^1_{L_{\mathrm{Rev}}, t} \xleftarrow{\$}$ DPABE.KeyUpdate$(L_{\mathrm{Rev}}, t, MSK^1_{\mathrm{ABE}}, MPK^1_{\mathrm{ABE}})$
7: **for all** $S' \in \mathcal{U}_{\mathrm{ID}}$ **do**
8:    Parse $EK_{(\mathbb{O}, \psi), S'}$ as $(SK^0_{\mathrm{ABE}}, SK^1_{\mathrm{ABE}}, UK^0_{L_{\mathrm{Rev}}, t-1}, UK^1_{L_{\mathrm{Rev}}, t-1})$
9:    $EK_{(\mathbb{O}, \psi), S'} \leftarrow (SK^0_{\mathrm{ABE}}, SK^1_{\mathrm{ABE}}, UK^0_{L_{\mathrm{Rev}}, t}, UK^1_{L_{\mathrm{Rev}}, t})$
10: **return** $UM \leftarrow \{EK_{(\mathbb{O}, \psi), S'}\}_{S' \in \mathcal{U}_{\mathrm{ID}}}$

Theorem 1. *Given an* IND-sHRSS *secure rkDPABE scheme, a one-way function* g, *and an* EUF-CMA *signature scheme, this construction is secure in the sense of selective public verifiability, and selective semi-static revocation and selective authorised computation.*

Full proofs of security can be found in the full, online version of the paper [2]. Informally, to prove selective public verifiability, we show that we can replace the message encrypted under the *non-satisfied* function evaluation (i.e. the computation that evaluates to $F(x) \oplus 1$) with a randomly chosen message; due to the IND-CPA-style security of the rkDPABE scheme (implied by the IND-sHRSS property), an adversary cannot learn anything about a message for which the decryption policy is not satisfied. In particular, we can (implicitly) replace the message with the challenge message in an inversion game for the one-way function g and then the verification token for this message is the challenge input in that game. We therefore show that breaking the public verifiability of our construction (i.e. returning the message for the wrong computational result) will allow an adversary to invert the one-way function g.

5   Conclusion

We have introduced a hybrid model of publicly verifiable outsourced computation to support flexible and dynamic interactions between entities. Entities may request computations from other users, restrict which entities can perform computations on their behalf, perform computations for other users, and make data available for queries from other users, all in a verifiable manner.

Our instantiation, built from a novel use of DP-ABE, captures prior models of PVC [3, 20], extends RPVC-AC [1] to the public key setting to allow truly public delegability and verifiability, and introduces a novel form of ABE-based verifiable computation in the form of VDC. In follow up work, we have investigated VDC further with regards to searching on remote databases [4].

ABE was developed to enforce read-only access control policies, and the use of KP-ABE in PVC was a novel and surprising result [20]. A natural question to ask is whether other forms of ABE can similarly find use in this context. Our use of all possible modes of ABE provides an affirmative answer to this question.

DP-ABE has previously attracted relatively little attention, which we believe to be primarily due to its applications being less obvious than for the single-policy ABE schemes. Whilst KP- and CP-ABE are generally considered in the context of cryptographic access control, it is unclear that the policies enforced by DP-ABE are natural choices for access control. Thus an interesting side-effect of this work is to show that additional applications for DP-ABE do exist.

References

1. Alderman, J., Janson, C., Cid, C., Crampton, J.: Access control in publicly verifiable outsourced computation. In: Proceedings of the 10th ACM Symposium on Information, Computer and Communications Security, ASIA CCS 2015, New York, pp. 657–662. ACM (2015)
2. Alderman, J., Janson, C., Cid, C., Crampton, J.: Hybrid publicly verifiable computation. Cryptology ePrint Archive, Report/320, 2015 (2015)
3. Alderman, J., Janson, C., Cid, C., Crampton, J.: Revocation in publicly verifiable outsourced computation. In: Lin, D., Yung, M., Zhou, J. (eds.) Inscrypt 2014. LNCS, vol. 8957, pp. 51–71. Springer, Heidelberg (2015)
4. Pasalic, E., Knudsen, E.R. (eds.): Cryptography and Information Security in the Balkans. LNCS, vol. 9540. Springer, Switzerland (2016)
5. Apon, D., Katz, J., Shi, E., Thiruvengadam, A.: Verifiable oblivious storage. In: Krawczyk, H. (ed.) PKC 2014. LNCS, vol. 8383, pp. 131–148. Springer, Heidelberg (2014)
6. Attrapadung, N., Imai, H.: Attribute-based encryption supporting direct/indirect revocation modes. In: Parker, M.G. (ed.) Cryptography and Coding. LNCS, vol. 5921, pp. 278–300. Springer, Heidelberg (2009)
7. Backes, M., Barbosa, M., Fiore, D., Reischuk, R.M.: ADSNARK: nearly practical and privacy-preserving proofs on authenticated data. In: IEEE Symposium on Security and Privacy, SP 2015, San Jose, CA, USA, May 17–21, 2015, pp. 271–286. IEEE Computer Society (2015)

8. Backes, M., Fiore, D., Reischuk, R.M.: Verifiable delegation of computation on outsourced data. In: Proceedings of the ACM SIGSAC Conference on Computer & Communications Security, CCS 2013, New York, pp. 863–874. ACM (2013)
9. Ben-Sasson, E., Chiesa, A., Genkin, D., Tromer, E.: Fast reductions from rams to delegatable succinct constraint satisfaction problems: extended abstract. In: Proceedings of the 4th Conference on Innovations in Theoretical Computer Science, ITCS 2013, New York, pp. 401–414. ACM (2013)
10. Benabbas, S., Gennaro, R., Vahlis, Y.: Verifiable delegation of computation over large datasets. In: Rogaway, P. (ed.) CRYPTO 2011. LNCS, vol. 6841, pp. 111–131. Springer, Heidelberg (2011)
11. Bitansky, N., Canetti, R., Chiesa, A., Tromer, E.: From extractable collision resistance to succinct non-interactive arguments of knowledge, and back again. In: Proceedings of the 3rd Innovations in Theoretical Computer Science Conference, ITCS 2012, New York, pp. 326–349. ACM (2012)
12. Catalano, D., Fiore, D., Gennaro, R., Vamvourellis, K.: Algebraic (Trapdoor) one-way functions and their applications. In: Sahai, A. (ed.) TCC 2013. LNCS, vol. 7785, pp. 680–699. Springer, Heidelberg (2013)
13. Choi, S.G., Katz, J., Kumaresan, R., Cid, C.: Multi-client non-interactive verifiable computation. In: Sahai, A. (ed.) TCC 2013. LNCS, vol. 7785, pp. 499–518. Springer, Heidelberg (2013)
14. Chung, K.-M., Kalai, Y.T., Liu, F.-H., Raz, R.: Memory delegation. In: Rogaway, P. (ed.) CRYPTO 2011. LNCS, vol. 6841, pp. 151–168. Springer, Heidelberg (2011)
15. Fiore, D., Gennaro, R.: Publicly verifiable delegation of large polynomials and matrix computations, with applications. In: Yu, T., Danezis, G., Gligor, V.D. (eds.) The ACM Conference on Computer and Communications Security, CCS 2012, Raleigh, October 16–18, pp. 501–512. ACM (2012)
16. Gennaro, R., Gentry, C., Parno, B.: Non-interactive verifiable computing: outsourcing computation to untrusted workers. In: Rabin, T. (ed.) CRYPTO 2010. LNCS, vol. 6223, pp. 465–482. Springer, Heidelberg (2010)
17. Gennaro, R., Gentry, C., Parno, B., Raykova, M.: Quadratic span programs and succinct NIZKs without PCPs. In: Johansson, T., Nguyen, P.Q. (eds.) EUROCRYPT 2013. LNCS, vol. 7881, pp. 626–645. Springer, Heidelberg (2013)
18. Ostrovsky, R., Sahai, A., Waters, B.: Attribute-based encryption with non-monotonic access structures. In: Proceedings of the 14th ACM Conference on Computer and Communications Security, CCS 2007, New York, pp. 195–203. ACM (2007)
19. Papamanthou, C., Shi, E., Tamassia, R.: Signatures of correct computation. In: Sahai, A. (ed.) TCC 2013. LNCS, vol. 7785, pp. 222–242. Springer, Heidelberg (2013)
20. Parno, B., Raykova, M., Vaikuntanathan, V.: How to delegate and verify in public: verifiable computation from attribute-based encryption. In: Cramer, R. (ed.) TCC 2012. LNCS, vol. 7194, pp. 422–439. Springer, Heidelberg (2012)
21. Shi, J., Lai, J., Li, Y., Deng, R.H., Weng, J.: Authorized keyword search on encrypted data. In: Kutyłowski, M., Vaidya, J. (eds.) ICAIS 2014, Part I. LNCS, vol. 8712, pp. 419–435. Springer, Heidelberg (2014)
22. van den Hooff, J., Kaashoek, M.F., Zeldovich, N.: Versum: verifiable computations over large public logs. In: Ahn, G., Yung, M., Li, N. (eds.) Proceedings of the ACM SIGSAC Conference on Computer and Communications Security, Scottsdale, November 3–7, 2014, pp. 1304–1316. ACM (2014)

23. Waters, B.: Ciphertext-policy attribute-based encryption: an expressive, efficient, and provably secure realization. In: Catalano, D., Fazio, N., Gennaro, R., Nicolosi, A. (eds.) PKC 2011. LNCS, vol. 6571, pp. 53–70. Springer, Heidelberg (2011)
24. Zhang, L.F., Safavi-Naini, R.: Private outsourcing of polynomial evaluation and matrix multiplication using multilinear maps. In: Abdalla, M., Nita-Rotaru, C., Dahab, R. (eds.) CANS 2013. LNCS, vol. 8257, pp. 329–348. Springer, Heidelberg (2013)

Efficient Concurrent Covert Computation
of String Equality and Set Intersection

Chongwon Cho[1]([⊠]), Dana Dachman-Soled[2], and Stanisław Jarecki[3]

[1] Information and Systems Science Laboratory, HRL Laboratories, Malibu, USA
ccho@cs.ucla.edu
[2] Department of Computer Science, University of Maryland, College Park, USA
[3] Department of Computer Science, University of California, Irvine, USA

Abstract. The notion of covert computation, an enhanced form of secure multiparty computation, allows parties to jointly compute a function, while ensuring that *participating* parties cannot distinguish their counterparties from a random noise generator, until the end of the protocol, when the output of the function is revealed, if favorable to all parties. Previous works on covert computation achieved super-constant round protocols for general functionalities [5,16], with efficiency at least linear in the size of the circuit representation of the computed function. Indeed, [9] showed that constant-round covert computation of any non-trivial functionality with black-box simulation is impossible in the plain model.

In this work we construct the first practical constant-round covert protocol for a non-trivial functionality, namely the set-intersection functionality, in the Random Oracle Model. Our construction demonstrates the usefulness of covert subprotocols as building blocks in constructing larger protocols: We show how to compile a *concurrently* covert protocol for a single-input functionality, e.g. string equality, into an efficient secure and covert protocol for a corresponding multi-input functionality, e.g. set intersection.

Our main contributions are summarized as follows:

- We upgrade the notion of covert computation of [5] to *concurrent* covert computation.
- We provide a general compiler that converts *concurrent covert* protocols for single-input functionalities to *concurrent covert* protocols for corresponding multi-input counterparts of these functionalities, at linear cost, in the Random Oracle Model.
- To demonstrate the usefulness of our compiler, we construct a concurrently covert string equality protocol and then apply our compiler to achieve a two-message *concurrent covert* protocol for Set Intersection (SI) with a linear cost in the Random Oracle Model.

This work was done in part while the authors were visiting the Simons Institute for the Theory of Computing, supported by the Simons Foundation and by the DIMACS/Simons Collaboration in Cryptography through NSF award #CNS-1523467.

C. Cho—A part of work was performed while visiting University of California, Irvine

D. Dachman-Soled—Work supported in part by NSF CAREER award #CNS-1453045 and by a Ralph E. Powe Junior Faculty Enhancement Award.

S. Jarecki—Work supported in part by NSF CAREER award #CNS-0747541.

© Springer International Publishing Switzerland 2016
K. Sako (Ed.): CT-RSA 2016, LNCS 9610, pp. 164–179, 2016.
DOI: 10.1007/978-3-319-29485-8_10

1   Introduction

Steganography addresses a security question that is not usually considered in cryptography, namely how to make the very fact that a (secure) protocol is being executed, hidden from an eavesdropping adversary. Such hiding of a protocol instance is, in principle, possible if the public channels connecting the communicating parties are *steganographic* in the sense that they have intrinsic entropy. A protocol is steganographic, or *covert*, if its messages can be efficiently injected into such channels in a way that the resulting communication cannot be distinguished from the a priori behavior of these channels. A simple example of a steganographic channel is a *random channel*, which can be implemented e.g. using protocol nonces, random padding bits, lower bits of time stamps, and various other standard communication mechanisms which exhibit inherent entropy. Assuming such random communication channels, if protocol participants encode their protocol messages as binary strings which are indistinguishable from random, they can inject their out-going messages into the random channel, and interpret the information received on those channels as the protocol messages from other parties. The participants must synchronize the timing of using these channels, so they know which bits to interpret as protocol messages, but this can be public information, because the covertness of the protocol implies that the exchanged messages cannot be distinguished from the a priori behavior of these random channels.

Covert computation was formalized for the two-party setting by von Ahn et al. in [16] and in the multi-party setting by Chandran et al. in [5], as a protocol that lets the participants securely compute the desired functionality on their inputs, with the additional property that no *participating* party can distinguish the other participants from "random beacons" that send random binary strings of fixed length instead of proscribed protocol messages, until the end of the protocol, when the output of the function is revealed, if favorable to all parties. Both [5,16] show protocols for covert computation of any functionality which tolerates malicious adversaries, resp. in the two-party and the multi-party setting, but the costs of these protocols are linear in the size of the circuit representation of the computed function. Moreover, these protocols are not constant-round, and the subsequent work of [9] showed that this is a fundamental limitation on maliciously-secure covert computation (with black-box simulation) in the standard model, i.e., without access to trusted parameters or public keys. In a recent work, Jarecki [12] showed a constant-round covert *mutual-authentication* protocol, but that protocol satisfied only a game-based definition of an authentication problem. This leaves a natural open question whether useful two-party (or multi-party) tasks can be computed covertly in a more practical way, with constant-round protocols, in stronger but commonly assumed computational models, like the Random Oracle Model (ROM), or equivalently the Ideal Cipher Model [6,10].

Our Contributions: In this work we construct the first practical *two-message covert* protocol for the set-intersection functionality in the Ideal Cipher Model. That is, two parties, where each party holds a private set of size n, compute the intersection of their private sets. If the two input sets do not have an intersection, then no party can tell apart the following two cases: (1) the other party did not participate in the protocol execution, and (2) the other party did participate but the intersection was empty. Towards this goal, our contribution is three-fold:

(1) We introduce an upgraded version of the covert computation definition of [5], *concurrent covert* (*C-covert*) *computation*. We provide a definition of C-covert computation that enjoys advantages over the "single-shot" definition of covert computation in [5] because multiple instances of such protocols can execute concurrently, and the covertness and security properties are assured for each protocol instance.

(2) We show that covert protocols can serve as useful *tools* in constructing secure (and covert) protocols. Namely, we exhibit a general compiler which converts a *covert* protocol (supporting a concurrent composability) for a single-input functionality, e.g., a String Equality Test (SEQ) functionality which takes two strings and outputs 1 if they are equal and 0 (or $\perp$) otherwise, into a *covert* protocol computing a corresponding multi-input functionality, e.g. which in the case of SEQ would be a Set Intersection (SI) functionality. Our compiler is instantiated in the Ideal Cipher Model (equivalently the Random Oracle Model [6,10]) and it preserves the covertness and the round complexity of the underlying protocol for the single-input functionality, at the increase of the computational and bandwidth costs which is only linear in the number of inputs contributed by each party. (Technically, this compiler is slightly stronger because the covert protocol for the underlying single-input functionality must only satisfy a weaker version of the C-covert computation.) The construction of our compiler is rooted in the idea of the Index-Hiding Message Encoding (IHME) scheme of Manulis et al. [14]. While the security of IHME scheme is defined in terms of a game-based definition, the security of our compiler is generalized and defined in terms of simulation-based security, while the instantiation is provided in the Ideal Cipher Model.

(3) To make this general compiler result more concrete, we show an example of a two-party single-input functionality for the SEQ functionality (here presented in a one-sided output version), which on a pair of inputs (x, y) outputs $(b, \perp)$ where $b = 1$ if $x = y$ and 0 otherwise. The two-party multi-input functionality corresponding to the SEQ functionality is a Set Intersection (SI) functionality which takes a pair of *vectors* $((x_1, ..., x_n), (y_1, ..., y_n))$ as its inputs, and outputs $((b_1, ..., b_n), \perp)$ where $b_i = 1$ iff there exists j s.t. $x_i = y_j$. We construct a C-covert protocol for SEQ, and by applying the above compiler we obtain a C-covert protocol for the Set Intersection (SI) functionality. Since the C-covert protocol we show for SEQ takes 2 rounds and $O(1)$ group exponentiations, the resulting C-covert Set Intersection protocol takes 2 rounds and performs $O(n)$ group exponentiations. This compares well to existing standard, i.e. *non-covert*, Set Intersection protocols, e.g. [8,13]. Standard SI protocols have received lots of attention, and in particular there are multiple solutions which trade off public key operations for increased communication complexity, e.g. based on garbled circuits [11], Bloom Filters [7] or OT extensions [15] (see also the last reference for comparisons between various SI protocols). Still, we take our results as showing that covertness can be achieved for non-trivial functionalities of general interest, like the SI functionality, at the cost which is comparable to the non-covert protocols for the same functionality.

1.1   Technical Overview

Concurrent Covert Computation. We introduce a new notion of concurrent covert (C-covert) computation. Covert computation was first introduced by von Ahn et al. [16] in the two-party setting. Later, Chandran et al. [5] formulated the notion of covert multiparty computation based on the simulation paradigm. In this work, we initiate a study of composable covert computation by considering the case of concurrent self-composition. We give a formal definition of concurrent covert computation, which provides a framework for arguing whether a protocol remains covert while many instances of this protocol are executed concurrently in the system. In particular, our notion of C-covert computation follows the framework of universal composability (UC) by Canetti [4] although our notion has a limitation on its composability property compared to the notion of UC. Still, the notion we define upgrades the covert ("one-shot") computation notion of Chandran et al. by enabling concurrent and parallel self-composition of a covert protocol. Such a composability guarantee is at the crux of our application which compiles single-input (weakly) C-covert protocol to a C-covert protocol for the corresponding multi-input functionality. We note that our focus here is on concurrent composability and not full universal composability (UC) because only the former notion is required by the single-input to multi-input compiler: Our compiler executes multiple instances of the covert protocol for the single-input functionality, and hence its security requires that the underlying covert protocol is self-composable.

Intermediate Security Notions.   In the course of achieving concurrent covert security, we introduce a special class of functionalities that we call *indexed single-input* functionalities. Namely, we call a two-party functionality F indexed single-input (ISI) if there exists an *index function* I s.t. for all inputs (x, y) to F we have that $F(x, y) = \bot$ if $I(x) \neq I(y)$. We also introduce an intermediate security notion for ISI functionalities, called Weakly Concurrent Covert (in short, wC-covert) computation, which is a relaxation of C-covert computation. The high-level insight for this relaxation is that the simulator is allowed to possess additional advice which enables the simulation to go through. This relaxed notion of C-covert is sufficient in our compiler because the compiler construction ensures that the simulator has access to this advice, and hence it suffices that the underlying covert protocol is simulatable given this advice.

From wC-covert Single Input Protocol to C-covert Multi-input Protocol. We construct, in the Ideal Cipher Model, a compiler that converts any wC-covert protocol for ISI functionality to C-covert protocol for the indexed mult-input (IMI) version of the same functionality, where the IMI functionality on inputs $\boldsymbol{x} = (x^1, ..., x^n)$ and $\boldsymbol{y} = (y^1, ..., y^n)$ is defined, in short, as an $n \times n$ execution of the underlying ISI functionality on pairs of *matching* inputs, i.e. pairs (x^i, y^j) s.t. $I(x^i) = I(y^j)$. The compiler builds on the compiler idea proposed by Manulis et al. [14]. The compiler of [14] converts a particular protocol for single-input functionality, which in their case was a Secret Handshake protocol (see e.g. [1]), into a secure protocol for multi-input functionality, e.g. a multi-input version of a Secret Handshake, where each party puts a vector of credentials, which are then pair-wise matched by the functionality.

In this work, we give a general-purpose version of this compiler, where we show that *covertness* and *self-composability* are the crucial properties needed of the protocol for the single-input functionality to be compiled. And this shows, very interestingly, that covertness is not just an interesting goal in itself but also can be useful as a tool in building more efficient (e.g. linear time) two-party protocols for multi-input functionalities. We exemplify it with the construction of C-covert Set-Intersection protocol secure under Decisional Diffie-Hellman (DDH) assumption in the random oracle model, which uses $O(n)$ exponentiations and $O(n \text{ polylog } n)$ multiplications of group elements where n is the number of elements in the set contributed by each party. This compares quite well to the existing *non-covert* SI protocols (see the discussion of various SI protocols in [15], although that discussion concentrates on efficiency in the honest-but-curious setting).

Organization. In Sect. 2, we introduce the notions of C-covert computation, the indexed single-input and multi-input functionalities (ISI and IMI), and the related notions such as wC-covert computation, which will be utilized by our ISI-to-IMI compiler. In Sect. 3 we present the construction of compiler which converts a wC-covert protocol for a single-input (ISI) functionality into a C-covert protocol for the multi-input (IMI) version of this functionality, in the Ideal Cipher Model. In Sect. 4, we present an application of this compiler by exhibiting a wC-covert two-message $O(1)$-exponentiations covert protocol for the SEQ functionality in the Random Oracle Model.

2   Preliminaries

2.1   The Ideal Cipher Model

The ideal cipher model is an idealized model of computation in which entities (i.e., parties) has a public accessible to a ideal (random) block cipher. Such ideal cipher is a block cipher indexed by a key which is a k-bit string (or a field element) s.t. each key k defines a random permutation on l-bit strings. All entities in the ideal cipher model can make encryption and decryption queries to the cipher by specifying its index. In this work, we denote an ideal block cipher by $\Psi_k : \{0,1\}^l \to \{0,1\}^l$ and its inverse by $\Psi_k^{-1} : \{0,1\}^l \to \{0,1\}^l$. Coron et al. [6,10] showed that the ideal cipher model is equivalent to the Random Oracle Model (ROM), first formalized by Bellare and Rogaway [2]. Therefore, all results in this work can be translated into the same results in the Random Oracle Model. Throughout this work, we use these two names interchangeably.

2.2 Concurrent Covert Computation

We provide the definition of *concurrent covert* computation (C-covert) for a given functionality. Our definition of C-covert computation follows the framework of Universally composability (UC) by Canetti [4] as well as the definition of stand-alone (i.e. "single-shot") covert computation given by Chandran et al. [5]. Note that we provide the definition of concurrent covert computation for the multi-party case but in the remainder of the paper we will concentrate solely on the two-party functionalities and protocols, leaving general multi-party protocols to future work. Even though our definition builds upon the UC framework, its composability guarantee is restricted to concurrent self-composition. The main reason for this restrictiveness is that the definition guarantees only self-composability of covert computation for *functions*, i.e. not for general reactive functionalities as in the case of standard UC definition of Canetti [4]. We make this definitional choice because it is already sufficient in many applications, as exemplified e.g. by the compiler construction we present in this paper. Moreover, composing functionally distinct covert protocols is a challenge. Consider for example a protocol Π formed as a composition of protocols Π_1 and Π_2, where protocol Π_1 runs Π_2 as a subroutine, and note that an adversary might discover the participation of honest parties in the protocol from the outputs of subroutine Π_2 before the completion of protocol Π. In this work we concentrate on concurrent covertness and leave establishment of the framework of fully UC covert computation for future work.

Intuitively, the differences between the concurrent covert notion for functionality F we define below and the standard notion of concurrent computation for F is that (1) F's inputs and outputs are extended to include a special sign $\bot$ designating non-participation; (2) F is restricted to output a non-participation symbol $\bot$ to each party if *any* of these parties contributed $\bot$ as its input; and (3) the real-world protocol of an honest party on the non-participation input $\bot$ is fixed as a "random beacon", i.e. a protocol which sends out random bitstrings of fixed length independently of the messages it receives.

The Ideal Model. The definition of the ideal model is the UC analogue of the ideal model of Chandran et al. [5], except that composability guarantees are restricted to self-composition. The ideal process involves an ideal functionality $\mathcal{F}$, an ideal process adversary (simulator) Sim, an environment $\mathcal{Z}$ with input z, and a set of dummy parties $P_1, \ldots, P_n$. Parties may input a value $x \in \{0,1\}^k$ to the functionality or a special symbol $\bot$ to indicate that they do not participate in the protocol. Let $\overline{x}$ denote the vector of inputs (including $\bot$) of all parties.

Similarly to the stand-alone covert computation notion of [5], an ideal functionality $\mathcal{F}$ in the C-covert computation is defined by a pair of functions f, g, where $g : \{\{0,1\}^k \cup \{\bot\}\}^n \to \{0,1\}$ is a *favor function* where $g(\overline{x}) = 0$ if and only if $\overline{x}$ is either a non-favorable input (i.e. inputs on which parties want to hide their participation, e.g. two distinct strings in the case $\mathcal{F}$ is SEQ) or a subset of parties set their inputs to $\bot$ (which indicates that those parties do not partici-pates in the computation). The function $f : \{\{0,1\}^k \cup \{\bot\}\}^n \to \{\{0,1\}^k \cup \{\bot\}\}^n$ is the actual functionality to be jointly computed, and it is restricted so that

$f(\overline{x}) = \overline{y} \in \{\{0,1\}^k\}^n$ if $g(\overline{x}) = 1$, and $f(\overline{x}) = \{\perp\}^n$ if $g(\overline{x}) = 0$. In other words, function f outputs non-bot outputs if and only if the output of g on the inputs is favorable. We note that g and f can be randomized functions, in which case functionality $\mathcal{F}$ picks the randomness which is appended to input $\overline{x}$ before g and f execute.

Let $\mathsf{Ideal}_{\mathcal{F},\mathsf{Sim},\mathcal{Z}}(k,z,r)$ denote the output of environment $\mathcal{Z}$ after interacting in the ideal process with adversary S and ideal functionality $\mathcal{F}$, on security parameter k, input z, and random input $r = r_{\mathcal{Z}}, r_{\mathsf{Sim}}, r_{\mathcal{F}}$ as described above. Let $\mathsf{Ideal}_{\mathcal{F},\mathsf{Sim},\mathcal{Z}}(k;z)$ denote the random variable describing $\mathsf{Ideal}_{\mathcal{F},\mathsf{Sim},\mathcal{Z}}(k,z,r)$ when r is uniformly chosen. We denote the distribution ensemble of $\mathsf{Ideal}_{\mathcal{F},\mathsf{Sim},\mathcal{Z}}(k;z)$ by $\{\mathsf{Ideal}_{\mathcal{F},\mathsf{Sim},\mathcal{Z}}(k,z)\}_{k \in N; z \in \{0,1\}^*}$.

The Real Model. The definition of the real model is also the UC analogue of the real model of Chandran et al. [5]. It is as the real model in the standard UC security model, except that each honest party on the non-participation input $\perp$ is assumed to execute a "random beacon" protocol, i.e. to send out random bitstrings of lengths appropriate to a given protocol round. Let $\mathsf{Real}_{\Pi,\mathcal{A},\mathcal{Z}}(k,z,r)$ denote the output of environment $\mathcal{Z}$ after interacting in the ideal process with adversary $\mathcal{A}$ and parties running protocol Π on security parameter k, input z, and random tapes $r = r_{\mathcal{Z}}, r_{\mathcal{A}}, r_1, \ldots, r_n$ as described above. Let $\mathsf{Real}_{\Pi,\mathcal{A},\mathcal{Z}}(k;z)$ denote the random variable describing $\mathsf{Real}_{\Pi,\mathcal{A},\mathcal{Z}}(k,z,r)$ when r is uniformly chosen. Similar to the notations in the ideal model, we denote the distribution ensemble of $\mathsf{Real}_{\Pi,\mathcal{A},\mathcal{Z}}(k,z,r)$ by $\{\mathsf{Real}_{\Pi,\mathcal{A},\mathcal{F}}(k,z)\}_{k \in N; z \in \{0,1\}^*}$.

Definition 1. *Let $n \in N$. Let $\mathcal{F}$ be an ideal functionality and Π be an n-party protocol. We say that Π concurrently securely realizes $\mathcal{F}$ if for any adversary $\mathcal{A}$ there exists an ideal-process adversary Sim such that for any environment $\mathcal{Z}$,*

$$\{\mathsf{Ideal}_{\mathcal{F},\mathsf{Sim},\mathcal{Z}}(k,z)\}_{k \in N; z \in \{0,1\}^*} \stackrel{c}{\approx} \{\mathsf{Real}_{\Pi,\mathcal{A},\mathcal{Z}}(k,z)\}_{k \in N; z \in \{0,1\}^*}.$$

2.3 Indexed Functionalities

Below we define two special classes of functionalities, ISI and IMI, which specify syntactic requirements on the functionalities involved in the compiler described in Sect. 3. The first notion, of Indexed Single-Input (ISI) two-party functionality, is a syntactic constraint which makes such function subject to a compilation from a "single-input" to a "multi-input" functionality. The second notion, of Indexed Multi-Input (IMI) two-party functionality, describes the functionality that results from such compilation, as it is defined by the underlying ISI functionality and the numbers of inputs contributed by each party. Finally, in definition 4, we define a security requirement on a protocol for computing some ISI functionality F which is a *technical relaxation* of the C-covert notion of definition 1, and which turns out to suffice for the compilation procedure described in Sect. 3 to produce a C-covert protocol for the IMI functionality corresponding to F.

Definition 2 (Indexed single-input two-party functionalities). F *is said to be an indexed single-input (ISI) two-party functionality (over domain* D*), with* *an index function I, if on a pair of inputs $(x, y) \in D \times D$ it outputs $(\text{out}_A, \text{out}_B)$ where out_A and out_B are outputs to A and B respectively s.t. $\text{out}_A = \text{out}_B = \perp$ whenever $I(x) \neq I(y)$.*

Many natural functionalities are of the ISI type. The notion of an "index agreement" between parties' inputs appears natural especially in the case of functionalities which one would want to compute covertly. Note that the notion of covert computation for F involves an admission function g on inputs s.t. if $g(x, y) = 0$ then F outputs $\perp$ to all parties, in which case neither party can distinguish its counter-party from a random beacon. The notion of an index function I specializes this agreement function by requiring that $g(x, y) = 0$ whenever $I(x) \neq I(y)$. Consider the case of F being a PKI-based authentication policy verification, a Password Authenticated Key Exchange (PAKE), or a String Equality (SEQ) test. In each of these cases the inputs have to "match" for the function to return a positive output. In the case of PAKE and SEQ, the index function can be an identity, as both functionalities might want to return $\perp$ if $x \neq y$, while in the first case function I can output the hash of a public key, either the public key held by the verifier or the public key which issued the certificate held by the prover. Note that an ISI functionality models a computation where each party contributes a single such input, e.g. a string, a password, or a certificate, etc. Hence, a natural extension of any ISI functionality F is a multi-input version of this functionality, which we denote $\tilde{F}$, where each party can input a vector of n such inputs, and $\tilde{F}$ computes a pair-wise matching of these inputs (out of n^2 input pairs) and then runs F on input pairs which match successfully. In the following we present a relaxed version of such multi-input functionality where the number of inputs that a malicious party can enter into the functionality might deviate by some δ from the number of honest party's inputs.

Definition 3 (Indexed δ-relaxed multi-input two-party functionalities). *Let D be the domain of inputs, I be a function defined on D, and F be an indexed single-input two-party functionality over D with an index function I. Let $\tilde{F}$ be a two party functionality which for some integer $\delta \geq 0$, takes input $x = (x^1, \ldots, x^{n_1})$ from party A, and input $y = (y^1, \ldots, y^{n_2})$ from party B, where $n_1, n_2 \in [n, n + \delta]$ and $x^i, y^j \in D$ for every $i \in [n_1]$ and $j \in [n_2]$.*

$\tilde{F}$ is said to admit input x (resp. y) if $I(x^i) \neq I(x^j)$ (resp. $I(y^i) \neq I(y^j)$) for all $i, j \in [n_1]$ (resp. $i, j \in [n_2]$). Then, $\tilde{F}$ is said to be an indexed δ-relaxed multi-input (IMI) two-party functionality corresponding to F if $\tilde{F}(x, y)$ computes its output as follows:

1. *If $\tilde{F}$ does not admit inputs x or y, then it outputs $(\perp, \perp)$.*
2. *F computes output sets S_A and S_B as follows: It initializes S_A and S_B as empty sets, and then for each pair of inputs (x^i, y^j) for $(i, j) \in [n_1] \times [n_2]$ s.t. $z = I(x^i) = I(y^j)$, computes $(\text{out}_A, \text{out}_B)$ as an output of F on (x^i, y^j), and if out_A or $\text{out}_B \neq \perp$, then it adds (z, out_A) to S_A and (z, out_B) to S_B. Note that this computation invokes $O(n)$ instances of F because if x and y are admitted by $\tilde{F}$ then there can be at most $\min(n_1, n_2)$ pairs (x^i, y^j) s.t. $I(x^i) = I(y^j)$.*

Finally, if S_A and S_B are nonempty, then $\tilde{\mathsf{F}}$ outputs S_A to party A and S_B to party B. Otherwise it outputs $\perp$ to both parties.

When $\delta = 0$ where the size of inputs from both parties is equal, we simply call $\tilde{\mathsf{F}}$ an indexed multi-input two-party functionality corresponding to F.

2.4   Relaxed Covertness Notion for ISI Protocols

To utilize the full power of our ISI-to-IMI compiler construction we introduce a relaxed notion of C-covert security applicable to ISI functionalities, which we call "Weakly Concurrent Covert" (in short, wC-covert) security. The main difference from the definition of C-covert is that the simulator receives additional advice to simulate the view of environment. Namely, the simulator learns the index $I(x)$ (resp. $I(y)$) for an x (resp. y) input by an *honest* party A (resp. B). Intuitively, simulation of a protocol can only be easier if the simulator gets such advice on the honest party's input, and therefore a protocol that satisfies this relaxation is easier to achieve. (We will indeed see such construction in the Random Oracle Model (ROM) in Sect. 4.) The reason that we consider such a relaxed notion of C-covert security for a protocol computing an ISI functionality is that our compiler, shown in Sect. 3, compiling C-covert protocol for an ISI functionality F to a C-covert protocol for an IMI functionality $\tilde{\mathsf{F}}$ corresponding to F, is constructed in the ideal cipher model where each party encrypts its messages of an instance of the protocol for F such that if x is a party's input to an instance, then the party uses the ideal cipher $\Psi_a(\cdot)$ with key $a = I(x)$ to encode all messages belonging to the instance. The idea is that the simulator can embed a random output r for the honest party's ideal cipher queries. Only if the adversary then queries $\Psi_a^{-1}(r)$ will the simulator need to simulate the underlying message m of the protocol for F, using the *programmability* of the ideal cipher and the underlying simulator for F. Therefore, whenever the underlying simulator for F is instantiated, $a = I(x)$ is already known.

Definition 4 (wC-covert protocols for an ISI two-party functionality).
Let F be an ISI two-party functionality and let $\Pi = (A, B)$ be a two-party protocol that realizes F. Let x be the input of honest party and let x^* be the input of corrupted party. Protocol Π is a ρ-round wC-covert implementation of F if Π is C-covert computation of F with the following additional conditions:

1. *(Additional Advice). For all efficient environments $\mathcal{Z}$ and adversaries $\mathcal{A}$, there exists an PPT simulator Sim s.t. for all inputs x in the domain of inputs of F, the environment's output in the real world, $\mathrm{Real}_{\Pi,\mathcal{A},\mathcal{Z}}(k, z, r)$ is indistinguishable from the environment's output in the ideal world, $\mathrm{Ideal}_{\mathsf{F},\mathrm{Sim},\mathcal{Z}}(k, z, r)$, where the way messages are passed between $\mathcal{Z}$ and honest ideal players is identical to the one of definition of concurrent covert computation in the Sect. 2.2 except for the following change in the ideal world: When $\mathcal{Z}$ sends to an ideal honest party its input x to F, the security game gives an "advice" a to Sim where $a = I(x)$ if $x \neq \perp$ and $a = I(x^*)$ if $x = \perp$.*

2. *Consider a malicious strategy for party A (resp. B), where A chooses $s \leftarrow \{0,1\}^t$ such that t is the bit length of the message sent by A in protocol Π and sends s to (honest) B (resp. A) as its message in the j-th round of protocol Π for some $j \in [\rho]$. Then, with probability $1 - \mathsf{neg}(k)$ over choice of s, Sim, given the additional advice a as in Condition 1, queries the ideal functionality F with $\perp$ (and so the ideal party outputs $\perp$). Furthermore, with probability $1 - \mathsf{neg}(k)$, over choice of s for A's (resp. B's) j-th round message as above, Sim's subsequent messages, conditioned on s, are uniformly distributed.*

3   Compiling Single-Input TPCs to Multi-input TPCs

In this section, we present a compiler $\mathsf{Comp}(\Pi, n)$ which takes any wC-covert protocol Π for indexed single input two-party functionality F and converts it to a C-covert protocol $\tilde{\Pi}$ which securely implements the corresponding indexed multi-input two-party functionality $\tilde{\mathsf{F}}$. We first describe the compiler which results in a multi-input $\tilde{\mathsf{F}}$ which takes exactly n inputs from each party, and then we show how its efficiency can be improved if the resulting functionality $\tilde{\mathsf{F}}$ is relaxed to allow the dishonest parties to input $n + \delta$ inputs instead of n.

We first give some intuition for our compiler and the proof of security. For simple exposition in the following high-level intuition, we restrict ourselves to the case of the two-message protocols where each party sends a single message to each other (i.e., a single-round protocol). The formal construction of multi-round compiler is provided in Fig. 1. The very high-level intuition is that each party encodes n parallel messages (where n is the size of the party's input set) from n instantiations of the underlying protocol Π using an ideal cipher Ψ and a polynomial encoding. Specifically, A constructs a polynomial P_1^A such that for each input x^i of party A, $P_1^A(I(x^i)) = \Psi_{I(x^i)}(m_1^i)$ and sends P_1^A (i.e., its coefficients) to B as its message, where m_1^i is the corresponding first message of protocol Π. Due to the covertness of the underlying protocol Π, the party receiving the encoded message cannot tell which points of the polynomial were programmed. For each of its inputs y^i, party B recovers the value $m_1^i = \Psi_{I(y^i)}^{-1}(P_1^A(I(y^i)))$ and uses it to compute the corresponding second message m_2^i of protocol Π. Then, B encodes these messages in a similar fashion using polynomial P_2^B. B sends P_2^B to A who similarly recovers its output values.

There are several important points about the proof of security:

- **Using the Simulator for Π.** We note that the underlying simulator for Π, denoted by Sim_Π will be used to generate m_1^i when B is corrupt and m_2^i when A is corrupt. However, note that since the simulator Sim for the compiled protocol simulates the ideal cipher, Sim has the advantage that it can construct the polynomials P_1^A, P_2^B at random and then run the underlying simulator Sim_Π to generate m_1^i or m_2^i only when an inversion query is made to the ideal cipher. The advantage of this is that now Sim_Π can be given some auxiliary information about the ideal input $I(x^i)$ or $I(y^i)$. Specifically, when an adversary queries Ψ_a^{-1}, the simulator for the compiled program knows that the underyling message should be either a random message (corresponding to the element not being in the party's set) or it should be a protocol message for Π, computed using input x^i or y^i such that $I(x^i) = a$ or $I(y^i) = a$. Note that obtaining this auxiliary information is exactly the relaxation on Sim_Π is formalized in item (1) of Definition 4.

- **Ensuring Correctness.** We must account for the fact that a party may not query the ideal cipher but may simply embed a random message m in P_1^A or P_2^B with the hopes that it will be "valid". Specifically, in the case that a random message is embedded in P_2^B, we must ensure correctness. In other words, we must rule out the possibility that B embeds a random message, from which Sim_Π cannot extract a corresponding input y^i but which yields a valid output for the real party A. To address this issue, we assume that Π has the property that random messages will cause the other party to output $\perp$ with all but negligible probability. We note that this property of Π is formalized in item (2) of Definition 4.

See Fig. 1 for the formal description of the compiler $\text{Comp}(\Pi, n)$.

Theorem 1. *Let k be a security parameter. If Π is a wC-covert protocol for indexed single input two-party functionality F and $\Psi : \{0,1\}^* \to \{0,1\}^l$ is an ideal cipher with $l = n \cdot \omega(k)$, then $\text{Comp}(\Pi)$ is a secure, C-covert protocol for indexed multi-input two-party functionality $\tilde{F}$ corresponding to F, taking n inputs from each party.*

Remark 1. We note that our compiler does not require the parties to enter the same number of the inputs. An adversarial party's number of inputs to $Comp(\Pi, n)$ might be indeed differ from n even if the honest party's number of inputs is n. First consider the case that the number of inputs of an adversary is smaller than n. For this case, observe that the honest party given a degree-$n+1$ polynomial as a message from its adversary will extract only the messages m according to its own n indexes such that $I(x^i) = I(y^i)$ while automatically treating all the other messages as non-participating messages of adversary (even though the honest party does not notice it). For the case where adversary wants to enter inputs more than n encoded in a $n+1$-degree polynomial, we prove that no PPT adversary can do that if we choose appropriate parameters for random oracle. See the following Lemma 1.

Lemma 1. *Let k be a security parameter, let $q(k)$ be an arbitrary polynomial in k, and let $\delta \geq 1$ be a constant. Let A be any PPT adversary which runs in time $q(k)$, an arbitrary polynomial in k. Consider the following game $\text{Game}_{q,m,n,k,\delta}$ between adversary A and challenger C:*

1. *Repeat the following procedure q times:*
    (a) *A chooses a field element a from a field $F = GF(2^m)$. A sends it to C.*
    (b) *C responses with s uniformly sampled from field F.*
2. *Without loss of generality, assume that A chooses q distinct a's. Let T be the set of q pairs of (a, s) generated in the above procedure. A wins the game if there exists a degree n polynomial $f(x)$ such that there exist a subset $S \subset T$ where $|S| = n + \delta$ and $f(a) = s$ for all (a, s) in S.*

Compiler(Π, n)

Setup: Given a security parameter k, two parties A and B can utilize the following:
- a ρ-round protocol $\Pi = (A_\Pi, B_\Pi)$ for computing an indexed single-input two-party functionality F over domain D, with an index function $I : \mathsf{D} \to F$ where F is a field of order 2^k where A_Π and B_Π are message generators.
- an ideal cipher Ψ, and its inverse Ψ^{-1}, keyed by elements of F, where for all $v \in F$, $\Psi_v(\cdot) : \{0,1\}^l \to \{0,1\}^l$ and $\Psi_v^{-1}(\Psi_v(x)) = x$ for all $x \in \{0,1\}^l$.

Inputs: The inputs of parties A and B are respectively vectors $\boldsymbol{x} = \{x^1, x^2, \cdots, x^n\}$ and $\boldsymbol{y} = \{y^1, y^2, \cdots, y^n\}$ in D^n which are admitted by F, i.e. $I(x^i) \neq I(x^j)$ and $I(y^i) \neq I(y^j)$ for all $i \neq j$.

Protocol Execution: WLOG, party A first sends a message to party B which then responds back to A in each round.

To compute the messages, party A does the following:

For each j-th round such that $j \in [\rho]$,
- For each $i \in [n]$, do the following:
  - Choose random coins $r_{A,j}^i$.
  - Compute the message α_j^i of protocol Π on input x^i, protocol Π transcripts $\alpha_1^i, \beta_1^i, \cdots, \alpha_{i-1}^i, \beta_{i-1}^i$ and randomness $r_{A,1}^i, \cdots, r_{A,j}^i$ by using A_Π.
  - Query the ideal cipher $\Psi_{I(x^i)}(\cdot)$ to obtain $s_{A,j}^i = \Psi_{I(x^i)}(\alpha_j^i)$.
- Interpolate an n-degree polynomial P_j^A over F s.t. $P_j^A(0) = 0$ and $P_j^A(I(x^i)) = s_{A,j}^i$ for $i \in [n]$.
- Send P_j^A to B (i.e. a vector of coefficients of P_j^A or a vector of values of P_j^A on n fixed points).

To compute the messages (responses to A), party B does the following:

For each j-th round such that $j \in [\rho]$,
- For each $i \in [n]$, do the following:
  - Compute $\alpha_j^i = \Psi_{I(y^i)}^{-1}(P_j^A(I(y^i)))$.
  - Choose random coins $r_{B,j}^i$.
  - Compute the message β_j^i of protocol Π on input y^i, protocol Π transcripts $\alpha_1^i, \beta_1^i, \cdots, \alpha_{i-1}^i, \beta_{i-1}^i, \alpha_i^i$, randomness $r_{B,1}^i, \cdots, r_{B,j}^i$ by using B_Π.
  - Query the ideal cipher $\Psi_{I(y^i)}(\cdot)$ to obtain $s_{B,j}^i = \Psi_{I(y^i)}(\beta_j^i)$.
- Interpolate an n-degree polynomial P_j^B over F s.t. $P_j^B(0) = 0$ and $P_j^B(I(y^i)) = s_{B,j}^i$ for $i \in [n]$.
- Send P_j^B to A.

Output:
- For each $i \in [n]$, A does the following:
  - Compute $\alpha_\rho^i = \Psi_{I(x^i)}^{-1}(P_\rho^B(I(x^i)))$.
  - Choose random coins $r_{\rho+1}^i$.
  - Compute the i-th output $out^{I(x^i)}$ of protocol Π on input x^i, randomness $r_1^i, \cdots, r_{\rho+1}^i$, and protocol Π transcript $\alpha_1^i, \beta_1^i, \cdots, \alpha_\rho^i, \beta_\rho^i$ by using A_Π.
- Let S be the set of i's in $[n]$ such that $out^{I(x^i)} \neq \bot$.
- Output $S_{out} = \{(I(x^i), out^{I(x^i)}) \mid$ for $i \in S\}$ if $S \neq \emptyset$ and $\bot$ otherwise.
- B does the same as A by using B_Π on its own input and random coins.

Fig. 1. The compiler $\mathsf{Comp}(\Pi, n)$.

Then, for sufficiently large k, for all n and δ, if $m = n\omega(\log k)$, then for any PPT adversary $\mathcal{A}$ running in time q, $\mathcal{A}$ wins the above game except with negligible probability ϵ.

Proof. Towards contradiction, assume that the lemma is false. That is, there exists a PPT adversary $\mathcal{A}$ that runs in time $q = k^d$ for some constant d and wins the game with non-negligible probability: there exists some c such that

$$P := \Pr[\mathcal{A} \text{ wins Game}_{q,m,n,k,\delta}] \geq \frac{1}{k^c}$$

where the probability is taken over the coin toss of adversary $\mathcal{A}$.

Then, we have

$$P = \binom{q}{n+\delta}\frac{1}{|F|^\delta} = \binom{q}{n+\delta}\frac{1}{2^{m\delta}} \leq \frac{q^{n+\delta}}{2^{m\delta}}.$$

This means that

$$\frac{1}{k^c} \leq \frac{q^{n+\delta}}{2^{m\delta}} \Rightarrow \frac{2^{m\delta}}{q^{n+\delta}} \leq k^c \Rightarrow m\delta - (n+\delta)\log q^{n+\delta} \leq c\log k$$

$$\Rightarrow \frac{m\delta}{\log k} - dn - d\delta \leq c \Rightarrow \frac{\omega(\log k)n\delta}{\log k} - dn - d\delta \leq c \Rightarrow n(\omega(1)) \leq c.$$

Therefore, this completes the proof as we have a contradiction.   □

We provide the formal proof of Theorem 1 in the full version of this work due to the restriction of the space. One immediate consequence of Theorem 1 is that it compiles a wC-covert protocols for any ISI two-party functionality into a C-covert protocol for the same functionality in the ideal cipher model. That is, if we encode messages with a degree one polynomial (a linear function) vanishing at 0 where messages correspond to underlying weakly secure protocol Π for F, then the resulting compiled protocol $\mathsf{Comp}(\Pi)$ is a C-covert protocol for F.

Corollary 1. *If there is a wC-covert protocol for an ISI two-party functionality F then there is a C-covert protocol for F in the random oracle model.*

Improving Efficiency by Relaxing the Functionality. We note that Theorem 1 and its security proof rely on the fact that ideal cipher Ψ maps protocol messages into a string of length $m = n \cdot \omega(k)$, so the efficiency of protocol degrades linearly in n. To improve the compilation efficiency we can break this dependency between m and n by allowing (corrupted) parties to encode more than n messages into a polynomial. In particular, we relaxed the requirement of compiler that each party must put n inputs by allowing the parties to put $n + \delta$ inputs for $\delta \geq 0$. That is, if we allow $\delta = O(n)$ in the proof of Lemma 1 above, then it is easy to see $m = O(k)$, which is independent of the number of expected inputs. The simulator's strategy (provided in the full version) remains the same except that the simulator's time complexity increases by $O(n)$.

Theorem 2. *Let k be a security parameter and let $\delta = O(n)$. If Π is a* wC*-covert protocol for indexed single input two-party functionality* F *and* $\Psi : \{0,1\}^* \rightarrow \{0,1\}^l$ *is an ideal cipher with* $l = O(k)$, *then* Comp(Π) *is a secure,* C*-covert protocol for δ-relaxed indexed multi-input two-party functionality* $\tilde{\mathsf{F}}$ *corresponding to* F, *taking at most $n + \delta$ inputs from each party.*

4   Instantiation of **wC-covert** String Equality Protocol

In the following, we construct an efficient one-round C-covert set-intersection protocol in the random oracle model. Given the compiler presented in Sect. 3, the construction of wC-covert protocol for ISI two-party string equality protocol is sufficient for a C-covert set-intersection protocol.

At the very high-level, the main idea behind our construction is to utilize the Smooth Projective Hash Function (SPHF) for (Cramer-Shoup like, see [3] for more details) CCA-secure encryption defined in the Random Oracle Model. More specifically, let G be a cyclic group of prime q and H be a random oracle. Given a public key (g, h) where $h = g^\alpha$ for some $\alpha \in Z_q$, a party (called A) can encrypt its message p as $c = (g^r, h^r \cdot g^{H(p)})$ for some random $r \in Z_q$. Given the ciphertext c, another party (called B), if B possesses p, can extract a DDH tuple from the ciphertext c and create a hash value h and a projection key pk which is independent of message p. If A is given the projection key pk, then it may compute the same hash value h using its own witness r and pk. If B does not possess p, then B cannot extract a DDH tuple from the encryption and the hash value h becomes uniformly random in its range in the view of A even given projection key pk. For our wC-covert string equality protocol, we use this SPHF in both ways: from A to B and from B to A, where each direction checks if a party possess an identical string. The formal description of wC-covert string equality protocol is provided in Fig. 2.

Theorem 3. *Assume the DDH problem is hard in group G of order prime q and let H be a random oracle. Then, protocol Π is a one-round* wC*-covert protocol for the string-equality functionality.*

We prove Theorem 3 by proving two lemmas, Lemma 2 (correctness) and Lemma 3 (security). Due to the space constrain, we provide their proofs in the full version.

Lemma 2. *The protocol Π described in Fig. 2 is correct with overwhelming probability. That is, Π on input (p_A, p_B) outputs $(1, \perp)$ if and only if $p_A = p_B$ except with probability $1/2^q$.*

Lemma 3. *The protocol Π described in Fig. 2 is one-round* wC*-covert protocol as defined in Definition 4.*

Combining Theorem 1 (resp. Theorem 2) with Theorem 3 immediately yields two-pass C-covert set-intersection protocol (resp. with δ-relaxation). For the completeness, we provide the formal corollary as follows.

Covert Protocol $\Pi = \langle A, B \rangle$

Setup: A cyclic group G of prime order q, generator g, $h = g^\alpha$ for random α in Z_q. CRS $= (G, q, g, h)$ is published. Let H be a Random Oracle with outputs in Z_q. Random elements of G must be efficiently encodeable as random bitstrings of fixed length. (This is easy e.g. if G is a subgroup of residues mod p for $p-1 = q \cdot c$ s.t. $gcd(q, c) = 1$.)

Inputs: A has input p_A, B has input p_B.

Outputs: A outputs 1 if inputs p_A and p_B are equal. Otherwise, A outputs 0. B always outputs $\perp$. Inputs are favorable if $p_A = p_B$.

First Round:
- On input p_A, A does the following:
  1. Choose $e_A, d_A, r_A \leftarrow Z_q$.
  2. Set $\mathsf{pk}_A := g^{e_A} h^{d_A}$, $c_A^1 := g^{r_A}$, and $c_A^2 := h^{r_A} \cdot g^{H(p_A)}$.
  3. Send $(c_A^1, c_A^2, \mathsf{pk}_A)$ to B.

Second Round:
- B does the following:
  1. Choose $e_B, d_B, r_B \leftarrow Z_q$.
  2. Set $\mathsf{pk}_B := g^{e_B} h^{d_B}$, $c_B^1 := g^{r_B}$, and $c_B^2 := h^{r_B} \cdot g^{H(p_B)})$.
  3. Compute $k_{B1} := H((c_A^1)^{e_B} \cdot (c_A^2/g^{H(p_B)})^{d_B})$, $k_{B2} := H((\mathsf{pk}_A)^{r_B})$.
     Send $(c_B^1, c_B^2, \mathsf{pk}_B, k_B = k_{B1} \oplus k_{B2})$ to A.

Output:
- A computes $k_{A1} := H((\mathsf{pk}_B)^{r_A})$ and $k_{A2} := H((c_B^1)^{e_A} \cdot (c_B^2/g^{H(p_A)})^{d_A})$.
- A outputs 1 if $k_{A1} \oplus k_{A2} = k_B$, and 0 otherwise.

Fig. 2. A simple covert protocol Π for string equality functionality

Corollary 2. *Let k be a security parameter and let $\delta = 0$ (resp. $\delta = O(n)$). If Π is a wC-covert protocol for indexed single input two-party string equality functionality F and $\Psi : \{0,1\}^* \to \{0,1\}^l$ is an ideal cipher with $l = O(n\omega(\log k))$ (resp. $l = O(k)$), then $\mathsf{Comp}(\Pi, n)$ is a one-round C-covert protocol for (resp. δ-) relaxed set-intersection two-party functionality, taking a set of n (resp. at most $n + \delta$) elements from each party.*

References

1. Balfanz, D., Durfee, G., Shankar, N., Smetters, D., Staddon, J., Wong, H.C.: Secret handshakes from pairing-based key agreements. In: IEEE Symposium on Security and Privacy (2003)
2. Bellare, M., Rogaway, P.: Random oracles are practical: a paradigm for designing efficient protocols. In: Proceedings of the 1st ACM Conference on Computer and Communications Security, CCS 1993, pp. 62–73. ACM, New York (1993)
3. Benhamouda, F., Blazy, O., Chevalier, C., Pointcheval, D., Vergnaud, D.: New techniques for SPHFs and efficient one-round PAKE protocols. In: Canetti, R., Garay, J.A. (eds.) CRYPTO 2013, Part I. LNCS, vol. 8042, pp. 449–475. Springer, Heidelberg (2013)

4. Canetti, R.: Universally composable security: a new paradigm for cryptographic protocols. In: Proceedings of the 42Nd IEEE Symposium on Foundations of Computer Science, FOCS 2001, p. 136. IEEE Computer Society, Washington, DC (2001)
5. Chandran, N., Goyal, V., Ostrovsky, R., Sahai, A.: Covert multi-party computation. In: FOCS, pp. 238–248 (2007)
6. Coron, J.-S., Patarin, J., Seurin, Y.: The random oracle model and the ideal cipher model are equivalent. In: Wagner, D. (ed.) CRYPTO 2008. LNCS, vol. 5157, pp. 1–20. Springer, Heidelberg (2008)
7. Dong, C., Chen, L., Wen, Z.: When private set intersection meets big data: an efficient and scalable protocol. In: Computer and Communications Security (CCS), pp. 789–800 (2013)
8. Freedman, M.J., Hazay, C., Nissim, K., Pinkas, B.: Efficient set intersection with simulation-based security. J. Crypt., 1–41 (2014). doi:10.1007/s00145-014-9190-0
9. Goyal, V., Jain, A.: On the round complexity of covert computation. In: Proceedings of the Forty-second ACM Symposium on Theory of Computing, STOC 2010, pp. 191–200. ACM, New York (2010)
10. Holenstein, T., Künzler, R., Tessaro, S.: The equivalence of the random oracle model and the ideal cipher model, revisited. In: Proceedings of the 43rd ACM Symposium on Theory of Computing, STOC 2011, San Jose, CA, USA, 6–8 June 2011, pp. 89–98 (2011)
11. Huang, Y., Evans, D., Katz, J.: Private set intersection: are garbled circuits better than custom protocols? In: Network and Distributed System Security (NDSS) (2012)
12. Jarecki, S.: Practical covert authentication. In: Krawczyk, H. (ed.) PKC 2014. LNCS, vol. 8383, pp. 611–629. Springer, Heidelberg (2014)
13. Jarecki, S., Liu, X.: Fast secure computation of set intersection. In: Garay, J.A., De Prisco, R. (eds.) SCN 2010. LNCS, vol. 6280, pp. 418–435. Springer, Heidelberg (2010)
14. Manulis, M., Pinkas, B., Poettering, B.: Privacy-preserving group discovery with linear complexity. In: Zhou, J., Yung, M. (eds.) ACNS 2010. LNCS, vol. 6123, pp. 420–437. Springer, Heidelberg (2010)
15. Pinkas, B., Schneider, T., Zohner, M.: Faster private set intersection based on OT extension. In: Fu, K., Jung, J. (eds.) Proceedings of the 23rd USENIX Security Symposium, San Diego, CA, USA, 20–22 August 2014, pp. 797–812. USENIX Association (2014)
16. von Ahn, L., Hopper, N., Langford, J.: Covert two-party computation. In: Proceedings of the Thirty-seventh Annual ACM Symposium on Theory of Computing, STOC 2005, pp. 513–522. ACM, New York (2005)

How to Verify Procedures

Secure Audit Logs with Verifiable Excerpts

Gunnar Hartung[(✉)]

Karlsruhe Institute of Technology, Karlsruhe, Germany
gunnar.hartung@kit.edu

Abstract. Log files are the primary source of information when the past operation of a computing system needs to be determined. Keeping correct and accurate log files is important for after-the-fact forensics, as well as for system administration, maintenance, and auditing. Therefore, a line of research has emerged on how to cryptographically protect the integrity of log files even against intruders who gain control of the logging machine.

We contribute to this line of research by devising a scheme where one can verify integrity not only of the log file as a whole, but also of excerpts. This is helpful in various scenarios, including cloud provider auditing.

Keywords: Secure audit logs · Log files · Excerpts · Forward security

1 Introduction

Log files are append-only files recording information on events and actions within a computer system. They are essential for digital forensics, intrusion detection and for proving the correct operation of computers.

However, their evidentiary value can be severely impaired if it is unclear whether they have been tampered with. It is therefore imperative to protect log files from unauthorized modification. This need has been widely recognised, see for example [15, p.10], [19, Sects. 18.3 and 18.3.1], [9, Sect. 8.6].

However, to actually prove a claim e.g. in court with the help of a log file is problematic *even if* the log file's integrity is unharmed, since the log file may contain confidential information. Furthermore, a large fraction of log entries may be irrelevant. Filtering these out significantly facilitates the log file analysis.

In this work, we therefore propose a logging scheme that can support the *verification of excerpts* from a log file. Creating an excerpt naturally solves both problems: Log entries that contain confidential and/or irrelevant data can simply be omitted from the excerpt. Excerpts created with our scheme remain verifiable, and therefore retain their probative force. Let us illustrate their use with two examples.

Example 1 (Banking). Consider a bank B that provides financial services to its customers. In order to prove correct behaviour of its computer systems, the bank maintains log files on all transactions on customers' accounts.

K. Sako (Ed.): CT-RSA 2016, LNCS 9610, pp. 183–199, 2016.
DOI: 10.1007/978-3-319-29485-8_11

When a customer A accuses the bank of fraud or incorrect operation, the bank will want to use its log files to disprove A's allegations. However, submitting the entire log file as evidence to court is not an option, as this would compromise the confidentiality of all transactions recorded, including the ones of other customers. Besides, the log file may also be prohibitively large.

Alternative solutions might be handing the log file to an expert witness, who verifies the integrity of the log file, or to encrypt log entries under different keys and revealing keys selectively for verification. These solutions, however, are unsatisfactory, since both approaches do not solve the problem of the log file size. Moreover, the first one eliminates public verifiability.

Utilizing a logging scheme with verifiable excerpts, however, the problem at hand is simple: The bank B generates an excerpt from its log files, containing only information on the transactions on A's account and possibly general information, e.g. about the system state. This excerpt is then submitted to court, where it can be verified by the judge and everyone else. If the verification succeeds, the judge may safely consider the information from the excerpt in his/her deliberation.

Example 2 (Cloud Auditing). Imagine an organisation O that would like to use the services of a cloud provider, e.g. for storage. O may be legally required to pass regular audits, and must therefore be able to provide documentation of all relevant events in its computer systems. Therefore, the cloud provider C must be able to provide O with verifiable log files, which can then be included in O's audit report.

Now, if C was to hand over all its log files to O, this would reveal details about other customers' usage of C's services, which would most likely violate confidentiality constraints. Furthermore, once again, the entire log files may be too large for transmission by regular means.

Here, as above, audit logging schemes with verifiable excerpts can solve the problem at hand easily. With these, C could simply create an excerpt containing only information that is relevant for O from its log files. This would solve the confidentiality issue while simultaneously lightening the burden induced by the log file's size, while the excerpt can still be checked by the auditors.

Background. We consider a scenario where there is a single data logger (e.g. a server or a system of multiple servers), who is initially trusted to adhere to a specified protocol, but feared to be corrupted at some point in time. We would like to guarantee that after the logger has been corrupted, it cannot manipulate the log entries created before the corruption.

Preventing the modification of log data usually requires dedicated hardware, such as write-once read-many-times drives (WORM drives). Since employing such hardware may not always be a viable option, cryptographers and security researchers have taken on the task to create schemes or protocols to verify the integrity of log files, see e.g. [3,5,6,12,16,20,22,24,26]. These schemes cannot protect log data from actual modification, but they can be used to *detect* modifications, while being purely implemented in software. Knowing if and what log data has been tampered with is very valuable information for a forensic investigation.

In order to enable verification, the logger must create a verification key when the logging process is started. This verification key can then be distributed to a set of verifiers, or even published for everyone to see. Since the logger is trusted at the beginning of the process, the verification key is chosen honestly.

In our specific setting, we want the logger to be able to create excerpts from its log files. These excerpts should be verifiable by everyone in possession of the verification key. We demand that it be hard for the adversary to create an excerpt whose content deviates from the information logged honestly while the logger was uncorrupted, yet passes the verification.

Once the logger has been corrupted, it may surrender all cryptographic keys under its control to the adversary, rendering standard cryptographic schemes useless. To mitigate this problem, researchers have devised schemes (e.g. [1,2,4–6,8,13,14,17,21,27]) that guarantee "forward integrity" [6]. Such schemes use a *series* of secret keys $sk_0, \ldots, sk_{T-1}$, where each key sk_{i+1} can be computed from the previous key sk_i via a specified update procedure. Given $i \in \{0, \ldots, T-1\}$, the verification algorithm then checks whether the data at hand was indeed authenticated using key sk_i. Informally speaking, a scheme has forward integrity if obtaining one of these secret keys sk_i does not help in forging a proof of authenticity and integrity with respect to any previous key sk_j with $j < i$. Digital signature schemes as well as MACs that have forward integrity are also called *forward-secure*.

In this work, we will focus on logging systems that use digital signatures. These have two important advantages over MAC-based logging schemes: Firstly, anyone in possession of the public key pk can verify their integrity, i.e. log files can be verified publicly. Secondly, verifiers can not modify the log file without detection. Due to the symmetric nature of MACs, this *is* possible for MAC-based schemes. On the downside, signature-based logging schemes are usually less efficient than MAC-based schemes.

A secure log file, also called *secure audit log*, can be built from forward-secure signatures schemes as follows [6]. When a new log file is created, the scheme generates a key pair (sk_0, pk). The public key is copied and either published or distributed to a set of verifiers (e.g. auditors). When the logging system is put into operation, log entries are signed with key sk_0, and the resulting signatures are stored along with the log file. At some point in time, the signer updates the secret key sk_0 to sk_1, securely erases[1] sk_0 and continues signing log entries with sk_1 instead of sk_0. At a later point in time, the signer updates sk_1 to sk_2, deletes sk_1 and continues to work with sk_2, and so on. The time interval in which all log entries are signed using the secret key sk_i is called the *i-th epoch*.

When an attacker $\mathcal{A}$ takes control over the system during epoch i (and hence may obtain the secret key sk_i), the forward-security property guarantees that $\mathcal{A}$ cannot modify log entries signed in previous epochs without being detected. Note that $\mathcal{A}$ can trivially forge signatures for the current epoch i and all future

---

[1] Erasure of secret keys must be complete and irrecoverable to guarantee security, i.e., the secret keys must actually be overwritten or destroyed, instead of just removing (file) pointers or links to the secret key.

epochs by using the regular signing and updating procedures. When the log file needs to be verified later, everyone who is in possession of pk (or can securely retrieve a copy of it) can run the verification algorithm to see if the log file has been tampered with.

The scheme described above is highly simplified and has several weaknesses. Therefore, actual proposals in the literature as well as current implementations usually employ a combination of additional measures such as adding timestamps to log entries [6,16], numbering log entries with sequence numbers [6,16,24,26], chaining hash values [16,20], adding "epoch markers" that indicate the transition from one epoch to the next [6], adding "metronome entries" that just contain a current timestamp [12], and encryption of log entries to preserve confidentiality [12,20].

In our work, we abstract from most of these features. For our purposes, a (plain) log message is a string of bits $m \in \{0,1\}^*$. This bit string may contain timestamps and/or event types, may be formatted in any fashion and may be encrypted or not. We focus on the secure *storage* of log entries, instead of also considering the secure *transmission* of log entries to a logging server, since this problem is mostly orthogonal to the storage problem.

Previous and Related Work. Most of the older schemes for securing audit logs use hash chains and authenticate the hash values using forward-secure MACs [11,20]. The Logcrypt scheme by Holt [12] is similar in nature, but also supports (public-key) digital signatures for authentication. Marson and Poettering [18] devise a special type of one-way hash chain, where one can skip the computation of large parts of the chain, and directly compute each element without explicitly computing the previous ones. Ma and Tsudik [16] observed that such hash-chain-based approaches suffer from "truncation attacks", where the attacker deletes trailing log messages. They devised forward-secure sequential aggregate signatures based on e.g. [7] to deal with this issue. Yavuz, Peng and Reiter [24–26] devised two schemes tuned to very specific performance requirements. Waters et al. [23] focus on searchable encryption of log entries, but rely on other schemes to guarantee integrity.

The notion of excerpts from log files has not been explicitly considered before. We note, though, that LogFAS [26] can support the verification of *arbitrary* subsequences of log files. However, this is more an accidental property of the LogFAS construction than due to an explicit design goal, and furthermore, systems that can verify *every* subsequence are in general not suited for our example applications, as will be discussed in Sect. 3.

Closest to our work is the scheme by Crosby and Wallach [10], who devised a method for secure logging that allows for controlled deletion of certain log entries while keeping the remaining log entries verifiable. However, their scheme relies on frequent communication between the log server and one or more trusted auditors, whereas our scheme can be used non-interactively. Furthermore, they did not formulate a security notion and consequently did not give a proof of security for their scheme.

Finally, we point out a survey paper on secure logging by Accorsi [3], which gives an overview on some of the older schemes mentioned above.

Our Contribution. Our contribution is twofold: Firstly, we develop a model for secure logging with verifiable excerpts. The ability to verify excerpts can be useful (i) to provide full confidentiality and privacy of most of the log entries, even when a subset of the log entries needs to be disclosed, (ii) to save resources during transmission and storage of the excerpt, and (iii) to ease manual review of log files. We also develop a strong, formal security notion for such schemes.

Secondly, we propose a novel audit logging scheme that allows for verification of excerpts. Our scheme may be used to verify both the *correctness* of all log entries contained in an excerpt as well as the *completeness* of the excerpt, i.e. the presence of all relevant log entries in the excerpt. We rely on the application software to define which log entries are relevant for the excerpts. Our scheme makes efficient use of a forward-secure signature scheme, which is used in a black-box fashion. Therefore, our scheme can be tuned to meet specific performance goals, and be based on a variety of hardness assumptions. We analyse our scheme formally and give a perfectly tight reduction to the security of the underlying forward-secure signature scheme.

Outline. Section 2 introduces preliminary definitions and some notation. In Sect. 3, we develop a formal framework to reason about log files with excerpts, and give a security definition for such schemes. Section 4 presents our construction, proves that it fulfills the security notion from Sect. 3, and analyses the overhead imposed by our scheme. Finally, Sect. 5 concludes the paper.

2   Preliminaries, Notation and Conventions

Sequences. Let $S = \langle s_0, \ldots, s_{l-1} \rangle = \langle s_i \rangle_{i=0}^{l-1}$ be a finite sequence over some domain D. Then $|S| := l \in \mathbb{N}_0$ denotes the *length* of S. We write $v \in S$ to indicate that v is contained in S. The empty sequence is $\langle \rangle$. The concatenation of two finite sequences S_1, S_2 is denoted as $S_1 \parallel S_2$. If $s \in D$, we write $S_1 \parallel s$ as a shorthand for $S_1 \parallel \langle s \rangle$. If $S = \langle s_0, \ldots, s_{l-1} \rangle$ is a sequence and $P = \langle s_0, \ldots, s_{m-1} \rangle$ for some $m \le l$, then P is a *prefix* of S. If $I := \langle i_0, \ldots, i_{n-1} \rangle$ is a finite, strictly increasing sequence of numbers $i_j \in \{0, \ldots, l-1\}$ (for all $j \in \{0, \ldots, n-1\}$, with $n \in \mathbb{N}_0, n < l$), we call I an *index sequence for* S and $S' = \langle s_{i_0}, \ldots, s_{i_{n-1}} \rangle$ the *subsequence of S induced by I*.

Definition 1 (Operations on Subsequences). *Let* $S = \langle s_0, \ldots, s_{l-1} \rangle$*; let* $I = \langle i_0, \ldots, i_{v-1} \rangle$*,* $J = \langle j_0, \ldots, j_{w-1} \rangle$ *be two index sequences for* S*, and let* T, U *be the subsequences of* S *induced by* I *and* J*, respectively. Then:*

$T \cup U$ *is the subsequence of* S *that contains exactly those elements* s_k *for which*
    $k \in I$ *or* $k \in J$ *or both, in the order of increasing* $k \in \{0, \ldots, l-1\}$*,*
$T \cap U$ *is the subsequence of* S *that contains exactly those elements* s_k *for which*
    $k \in I$ *and* $k \in J$*, in the order of increasing* $k \in \{0, \ldots, l-1\}$*.*

Note that if S contains duplicates, then there may be different index sequences inducing the same subsequence. Therefore, the operations from Definition 1 are only well-defined if the index sequences I and J are given. In this work, we will omit specifying I and J when they are clear from the context.

General Notation. A log entry (log message, message) m is a bit string, i.e. $m \in \{0,1\}^*$. The concatenation operation on bit strings is also denoted by $\|$. A log file $M = \langle m_0, \ldots, m_{l-1} \rangle$ is a finite, possibly empty sequence of log entries.[2]

We write $X := V$ for a deterministic assignment operation. In contrast, $X \leftarrow V$ is used when V is a finite set and X is chosen uniformly at random from V, or V is a probabilistic algorithm and X is assigned the output of that algorithm. All random choices are considered to be independent. We write PPT for "probabilistic polynomial time". Throughout this paper, $\kappa \in \mathbb{N}_0$ is the security parameter. All algorithms are implicitly given 1^κ as an additional input. The set of all polynomials $p : \mathbb{N}_0 \to \mathbb{N}_0$ which are parameterized by κ is poly(κ).

Forward-Secure Signature Schemes

Definition 2 (Key-Evolving Signature Scheme, based on [4]). *A key-evolving digital signature scheme $\Sigma = $ (KeyGen, Update, Sign, Verify) is a tuple of PPT algorithms, which are described as follows.*

KeyGen(T) *receives an a priori upper bound T on the number of epochs as input. It generates and outputs a pair of keys, consisting of the initial private signing key sk_0 and the public verification key pk.*

Update(sk_i) *takes a secret key sk_i as input, evolves it to sk_{i+1} and outputs sk_{i+1}. The old signing key sk_i is then deleted in an unrecoverable fashion. If $i \geq T - 1$, the behaviour of Update may be undefined.*

Sign(sk_i, m) *computes and outputs a signature σ for a given message $m \in \{0,1\}^*$, using a secret key sk_i.*

Verify(pk, m, i, σ) *checks if σ is a valid signature under public key pk, created with the i-th secret key, for a given message m. If it deems the signature valid, it outputs 1, otherwise it outputs 0.*

We require correctness in the canonical sense. The reader is referred to the full version for a definition.

We assume without loss of generality that the message space of each signature scheme is $\{0,1\}^*$. We also assume that the algorithms Update and Sign have access to the public key and that the index i of a secret key sk_i can be extracted from sk_i efficiently.

Definition 3 (Forward-Secure Existential Unforgeability under Chosen Message Attacks). *Let $\Sigma = $ (KeyGen, Update, Sign, Verify) be a key-evolving signature scheme, $\mathcal{A}$ a PPT adversary and $T = T(\kappa)$ a polynomial. The experiment $FS\text{-}EUF\text{-}CMA\text{-}Exp_{\Sigma, \mathcal{A}, T}(\kappa)$ consists of the following three phases:*

---

[2] Note that $M = \langle m_0, \ldots, m_{l-1} \rangle \neq m_0 \| \ldots \| m_{l-1}$, i.e. we consider the log entries in M to be distinguishable.

Setup Phase. *The experiment begins by creating a pair of keys $(sk_0, pk) \leftarrow$ KeyGen(T), and initializing a counter $i := 0$. Afterwards $\mathcal{A}$ is called with inputs pk and T.*

Query Phase. *During the experiment, $\mathcal{A}$ may adaptively issue queries to the following three oracles:*

> **Signature Oracle.** *On input $m \in \{0,1\}^*$, the signature oracle computes the signature $\sigma = \text{Sign}(sk_i, m)$ for m using the current secret key sk_i. It returns σ to $\mathcal{A}$.*

> **Epoch Switching Oracle.** *Whenever $\mathcal{A}$ triggers the NextEpoch oracle, the experiment sets $sk_{i+1} \leftarrow \text{Update}(sk_i)$ and $i := i + 1$. The oracle returns the string "OK" to the adversary. $\mathcal{A}$ may invoke this oracle at most $T - 1$ times.*

> **Break In.** *Once in the experiment, the attacker may query a special BreakIn oracle that stores the current epoch number as $i_{\text{BreakIn}} := i$ and returns the current secret key sk_i to the adversary. After $\mathcal{A}$ has invoked this oracle, it is no longer allowed any oracle queries.[3]*

Forgery Phase. *Finally, the attacker outputs a forgery (m^*, i^*, σ^*). The experiment outputs 1 iff Verify$(pk, m^*, i^*, \sigma^*) = 1$, m^* was not submitted to the signature oracle during epoch i^*, and $i^* < i_{\text{BreakIn}}$. (Let $i_{\text{BreakIn}} := \infty$ if $\mathcal{A}$ did not use its BreakIn oracle.) Otherwise, the experiment outputs 0.*

We say that $\mathcal{A}$ wins an instance of this experiment iff the experiment outputs 1.

3   Secure Logging with Verifiable Excerpts

We now develop a formal model for log files with excerpts. Obviously, given a log file M, an excerpt E is a subsequence of M. However, a scheme where *each* subsequence of M can be verified[4] is not sufficient for our applications, since the provider of the excerpt could simply omit some critical log entries. Put differently, such a scheme may guarantee correctness of all log entries in the excerpt, but it does not guarantee that all relevant log entries are present.

To address this problem, we introduce *categories*. Each log entry is assigned to one or more categories, which may also overlap. Each category has a unique name $\nu \in \{0,1\}^*$. We require that when a new log entry m is appended to the log file, one must also specify the names of all categories that m is assigned to.

We return to our banking example from Sect. 1 to illustrate the use of such categories. The bank B introduces a category C_A for each customer A, and then adds each log entry concerning A's account to C_A. The problem of checking the completeness of the excerpt for A's account is thereby reduced to checking the

---

[3] This restriction is without loss of generality, since the adversary knows $sk_{i_{\text{BreakIn}}}$ after this query and can thus create signatures as well as all subsequent secret keys by itself. Also, triggering the NextEpoch oracle after the BreakIn oracle would have no consequences on the outcome of the game.

[4] LogFAS [26] offers such a capability.

presence of all log entries from the category C_A and possibly from other categories containing general information. Of course, categories may also be added based on other criteria, such as the event type (e.g. creation and termination of an account, deposition or withdrawal of funds, and many more). Note that the set of categories is not fixed in advance; rather the bank must be able to add new categories on-the-fly, as it gains new customers. The use of categories is similar in the cloud provider example.

3.1   Categorized Logging Schemes

Definition 4 (Categorized Messages and Log Files). *A categorized message (also categorized log entry) $m = (N, m')$ is a pair of a finite, non-empty set N^5 of category names $\nu \in \{0,1\}^*$ and a log entry $m' \in \{0,1\}^*$. A categorized log file $M = \langle m_0, \ldots, m_{l-1} \rangle$ is a finite sequence of categorized log entries m.*

When it is clear from the context that we mean categorized log entries or categorized log files, we will omit the term "categorized" for the sake of brevity.

Definition 5 (Categories). *A category with name $\nu \in \{0,1\}^*$ of a categorized log file $M = \langle (N_i, m'_i) \rangle_{i=0}^{l-1}$ is the (possibly empty) subsequence C of M that contains exactly those log entries $(N_i, m'_i) \in M$ where $\nu \in N_i$. C is denoted by $C(\nu, M)$. C's index sequence $I(\nu, M)$ is the (possibly empty, strictly increasing) sequence that contains all $i \in \{0, \ldots, l-1\}$ for which $\nu \in N_i$.*

Definition 6 (Excerpts). *Given a categorized log file $M = \langle m_i \rangle_{i=0}^{l-1}$ and a finite set N of category names, the excerpt for N is $E(N, M) = \bigcup_{\nu \in N} C(\nu, M)$. The index sequence $I(N, M)$ is the (possibly empty, strictly increasing) sequence of all i with $i \in I(\nu, M)$ for at least one $\nu \in N$.*

Clearly, $C(\nu, M)$ is induced by $I(\nu, M)$, and $E(N, M)$ is induced by $I(N, M)$. In the following, we will mostly omit the second parameter, since it will be clear from the context. Moreover, we make the convention that there is a category named "All" such that $C(\text{All}) = M$, i.e. All $\in N_0 \cap \ldots \cap N_{l-1}$. As a special case of excerpts, we obtain M as an excerpt for the categories $N = \{\text{All}\}$.

In the following, we adopt the convention that variables with two indices are an "aggregate" of values ranging from the first to the second index, i.e. $\sigma_{0,j}$ is the aggregate of $\sigma_0, \ldots, \sigma_j$. In our case, this aggregate is simply a sequence of the individual values, i.e. $\sigma_{0,j} := \langle \sigma_0, \ldots, \sigma_j \rangle$, $M_{0,j} := \langle m_0, \ldots, m_j \rangle$. However, $\sigma_{0,j}$ may in general also be an actual aggregate signature, as in [16].

Definition 7 (Categorized Key-Evolving Audit Log Scheme). *A categorized key-evolving audit log scheme is a quintuple of probabilistic polynomial time algorithms* (KeyGen, Update, Extract, AppendAndSign, Verify), *where:*

KeyGen(T) *outputs an initial signing key sk_0, a permanent verification key pk, and an initial signature $\sigma_{0,-1}$ for the empty log file. T is the number of supported epochs.*

---

[5] This is an upper case ν.

Update(sk_i, M, σ) *evolves the secret key sk_i for epoch i to the subsequent signing key sk_{i+1} and then outputs sk_{i+1}. sk_i is erased securely.* Update *may also use and modify the current log file M as well as the current signature σ, e.g. by adding epoch markers or metronome entries.*

Extract($sk_i, M_{0,j-1}, \sigma_{0,j-1}, N$) *takes a log file $M_{0,j-1}$ together with a signature $\sigma_{0,j-1}$ for $M_{0,j-1}$ and a set N of category names and outputs a signature σ for the excerpt $E(N)$, computed with the help of sk_i.*

AppendAndSign($sk_i, M_{0,j-1}, m_j, \sigma_{0,j-1}$) *takes as input the secret key sk_i, the current log file $M_{0,j-1}$, its signature $\sigma_{0,j-1}$ and a new log entry m_j and outputs a signature $\sigma_{0,j}$ for $M_{0,j} := M_{0,j-1} \parallel m_j$.*

Verify(pk, N, E, σ) *is given the verification key pk, a set $N = \{\nu_0, \ldots, \nu_{n-1}\}$ of category names, an excerpt E and a signature σ. It outputs 1 or 0, where 1 means $E = E(N, M)$, and 0 means $E \neq E(N, M)$.*

We require correctness as defined in full version of this work.

Note that we require Verify to validate E without actually knowing the complete log file M. This is the main difficulty that our construction must overcome.

3.2   Security Model

We now define our security notion for categorized key-evolving audit log schemes. It is similar to the above definition for key-evolving signature schemes, but adjusted to the append-only setting and to support extraction queries by the attacker.

Definition 8 (Forward-Secure Existential Unforgeability under Chosen Log Message Attacks). *For a categorized key-evolving audit log scheme Σ = (KeyGen, Update, Extract, AppendAndSign, Verify), a PPT adversary $\mathcal{A}$, the number of epochs $T := T(\kappa) \in \text{poly}(\kappa)$ and $\kappa \in \mathbb{N}_0$, the security experiment $FS\text{-}EUF\text{-}CLMA\text{-}Exp_{\Sigma,\mathcal{A},T}(\kappa)$ is defined as follows:*

Setup Phase. *The experiment generates the initial secret key, the public key and the initial signature as $(sk_0, pk, \sigma_{0,-1}) \leftarrow$ KeyGen(T). It initializes the epoch counter $i := 0$, the message counter $j := 0$, and the log file $M_{0,-1} := \langle\rangle$. It then starts $\mathcal{A}$ with inputs pk, T and $\sigma_{0,-1}$.*

Query Phase. *During the query phase, the adversary may adaptively issue queries to the following four oracles:*

  Signature Oracle. *Whenever $\mathcal{A}$ submits a message m_j to the signature oracle, the experiment appends that message to the log file by setting $M_{0,j} := M_{0,j-1} \parallel m_j$ and updates the signature to*

$$\sigma_{0,j} \leftarrow \text{AppendAndSign}(sk_i, M_{0,j-1}, m_j, \sigma_{0,j-1}) \ .$$

  It then sets $j := j + 1$. The oracle returns the new signature $\sigma_{0,j}$.

  Extraction Oracle. *On input of a set N of category names, the experiment creates a signature $\sigma \leftarrow$ Extract($sk_i, M_{0,j-1}, \sigma_{0,j-1}, N$) for the excerpt $E := E(N, M_{0,j-1})$ and gives (E, σ) to the adversary.*

Epoch Switching Oracle. *Upon a query to the* NextEpoch *oracle, the experiment updates the secret key (and possibly the log file and its signature) to* $sk_{i+1} \leftarrow \text{Update}(sk_i, M_{0,j-1}, \sigma_{0,j-1})$ *and increments the epoch counter* $i := i + 1$. *The oracle returns the updated log file* M' *and signature* σ' *to the attacker. This oracle may be queried at most* $T - 1$ *times.*

Break In. *Optionally, the adversary may use its* BreakIn *oracle to retrieve the current secret key* sk_i. *After this, it may no longer issue queries to any of its oracles.*[6] *The experiment sets* $i_{\text{BreakIn}} := i$. *(Let* $i_{\text{BreakIn}} := \infty$ *if* $\mathcal{A}$ *never queried this oracle.)*

Forgery Phase. *At the end of the experiment,* $\mathcal{A}$ *outputs a non-empty set* N^* *of categories, a forged excerpt* E^* *for* N^*, *and a forged signature* σ^* *of* E^*.

We say that $\mathcal{A}$ *wins the experiment, iff the following conditions hold.*

– *The signature is* valid, *i.e.* $\text{Verify}(pk, N^*, E^*, \sigma^*) = 1$.
– *The signature is* non-trivial, *i.e. it meets the following requirements:*
- *E^* has not been part of an answer of the extraction oracle to $\mathcal{A}$ for the categories N^*. More formally, if $N_0, \ldots, N_k$ are the sets of category names that $\mathcal{A}$ used to call its extraction oracle and $E_0, \ldots, E_k$ are the excerpts returned by the oracle, then we require $(N^*, E^*) \notin \{(N_0, E_0), \ldots, (N_k, E_k)\}$.*
- *If $\mathcal{A}$ used its BreakIn oracle to obtain a secret key sk_i, let $E_i = E(N^*, M_i)$, where M_i is the log file at the time of switching from epoch $i_{\text{BreakIn}} - 1$ to epoch i_{BreakIn}. (Formally, M_i is the log file returned by the most recent call to the NextEpoch oracle, so M_i includes all changes made by the Update algorithm. We let $M_i := \langle \rangle$ if $\mathcal{A}$ never called the NextEpoch oracle.) We require that E_i is not a prefix of E^*. Put differently, E^* must not just be a continuation/extension of E_i.*

Observe that our security model allows a log file to be truncated to the state of the most recent epoch switch, counting this as a trivial attack. In the full version, we argue that such attacks are inherent if $\mathcal{A}$ obtains a secret key.

4   Our Scheme

We now describe a scheme that realizes the above security notion. We call it SALVE, for "Secure Audit Log with Verifiable Excerpts". The main ingredient for SALVE is a forward-secure signature scheme. Let us briefly describe the basic ideas underlying our construction.

Sequence Numbers per Category. Instead of adding only global sequence numbers, we augment signatures with sequence numbers (counters) c_ν for *each* category ν. In particular, the sequence numbers for the category All work as global sequence numbers.

---

[6]   Again, this restriction is without loss of generality, see Footnote 3 on page 7.

Signing Counters. Each log entry is signed along with the sequence numbers belonging to the categories of the log entry. During verification, one checks if the counters of each category ν supposed to be present in the excerpt form the sequence $\langle 0, \ldots, c_\nu - 1 \rangle$.

Epoch Markers with Counters. Additionally, we sign all counters that have changed during an epoch i together with the epoch markers created at the end of epoch i. Epoch markers are added to an additional, reserved category named EM. By convention, EM is contained in all excerpts.

4.1   Formal Description

We introduce some additional notation. When signing multiple counter values, we will sign a partial map $f \colon \{0,1\}^* \to \mathbb{N}_0$, which is formally modelled as a *set f of pairs* $(\nu, c_\nu) \in \{0,1\}^* \times \mathbb{N}_0$, signifying $f(\nu) = c_\nu$. For each category name ν, there is at most one pair in f that has ν as the first component. We also write such partial maps as $\{\nu_0 \mapsto c_{\nu_0}, \ldots, \nu_n \mapsto c_{\nu_n}\}$. A *key* of f is a bit string $\nu \in \{0,1\}^*$ for which $f(\nu)$ is defined. The set of keys for f is $\mathrm{keys}(f) := \{\nu \in \{0,1\}^* \mid \exists c \in \mathbb{N}_0 : (\nu, c) \in f\}$.

We assume that SALVE uses an efficient encoding scheme to map pairs to bit strings. We require that there are no pairs (f, m') and (N, E) that are encoded to the same bit string.

SALVE. Let $\Sigma_{\mathrm{FS}} = (\mathrm{KeyGen}_{\mathrm{FS}}, \mathrm{Update}_{\mathrm{FS}}, \mathrm{Sign}_{\mathrm{FS}}, \mathrm{Verify}_{\mathrm{FS}})$ be a key-evolving signature scheme. The key-evolving categorized audit log scheme SALVE is given by the following algorithms:

$\mathrm{KeyGen}(T)$ creates a key pair by running $(sk_0, pk) \leftarrow \mathrm{KeyGen}_{\mathrm{FS}}(T+1)$. The initial signature is the empty sequence $\sigma_{0,-1} := \langle \rangle$. The output is $(sk_0, pk, \sigma_{0,-1})$.

$\mathrm{AppendAndSign}(sk_i, M_{0,j-1}, m_j = (N_j, m'_j), \sigma_{0,j-1})$ first determines the current counter values c_ν for all $\nu \in N_j$ (the total count of all log entries previously added to these categories). Let $c_\nu := 0$ for all categories ν that have never occurred before. We assume $\mathrm{EM} \notin N_j$, except when AppendAndSign is called from the Update algorithm (see below), and $\mathrm{All} \in N_j$.

Next, AppendAndSign creates the partial map $f_j = \{\nu \mapsto c_\nu \mid \nu \in N_j\}$, computes $\sigma'_j \leftarrow \mathrm{Sign}_{\mathrm{FS}}(sk_i, (f_j, m'_j))$, and appends $\sigma_j := (f_j, \sigma'_j)$ to $\sigma_{0,j-1}$ to obtain $\sigma_{0,j} := \langle \sigma_0, \ldots, \sigma_{j-1}, \sigma_j \rangle$. It outputs $\sigma_{0,j}$.

$\mathrm{Update}(sk_i, M_{0,j-1}, \sigma_{0,j-1})$ must append an epoch marker to $M_{0,j-1}$ (and its accompanying signature to $\sigma_{0,j-1}$) and update the secret key.

In order to create the epoch marker, it determines the set N of all categories that have received a new log entry during epoch i and the total number of log entries c_ν in each of these categories. It then creates $f'_j := \{\nu \mapsto c_\nu \mid \nu \in N\}$ and encodes ("End of epoch" $\| i, f'_j$) $=: m'_j$ as a bit string m'_j. The epoch marker is set to $m_j := (\{\mathrm{All}, \mathrm{EM}\}, m'_j)$ and appended to $M_{0,j-1}$. Next, the Update algorithm computes a signature $\sigma_{0,j} \leftarrow \mathrm{AppendAndSign}(sk_i, M_{0,j-1}, m_j, \sigma_{0,j-1})$ for the log file including the epoch marker m_j.

Finally, if $i < T$, Update computes $sk_{i+1} \leftarrow \text{Update}_{\text{FS}}(sk_i)$, securely erases sk_i and outputs sk_{i+1}. Otherwise it deletes sk_i and outputs $sk_{i+1} := \bot$.

Extract$(sk_i, M_{0,j}, \sigma_{0,j}, N)$ first determines $K := I(N, M_{0,j}) = \langle k_1, \ldots k_l \rangle$ and constructs the excerpt $E := E(N, M_{0,j})$. Then Extract computes $\sigma_E \leftarrow \text{Sign}_{\text{FS}}(sk_i, (N, E))$, and outputs $\sigma := \langle \sigma_{k_1}, \ldots, \sigma_{k_l}, \sigma_E \rangle$.

Verify(pk, N, E, σ) outputs 0 if EM $\notin N$. Otherwise, it initializes counters $c'_\nu := 0$ for all $\nu \in N \cup \{\text{All}\}$. In the following, let $E = \langle (N_0, m'_0), \ldots, (N_{l-1}, m'_{l-1}) \rangle$. Verify performs the following checks for each entry $m_j \in E$, in the order of increasing j:

1. It checks whether the signature for the individual log entry is valid: $\text{Verify}_{\text{FS}}(pk, (f_j, m'_j), c'_{\text{EM}}, \sigma'_j) = 1$,
2. whether m_j belongs to one of the requested categories: $N_j \cap N \neq \emptyset$,
3. whether m_j's set of category names N_j is unchanged: $\text{keys}(f_j) = N_j$, and
4. whether the counter values signed together with the message are as expected: $f_j(\nu) = c'_\nu$ for all $\nu \in N \cap N_j$.
5. If All $\notin N$, it checks whether $f_j(\text{All}) \geq c'_{\text{All}}$ and sets $c'_{\text{All}} := f_j(\text{All}) + 1$.
6. If m_j is an epoch marker, i.e. EM $\in N_j$, then Verify decodes m'_j to reconstruct f'_j. It then checks whether $f'_j(\nu) = c'_\nu$ for all $\nu \in \text{keys}(f'_j) \cap N$.

If any of these checks fail, Verify outputs 0. If they pass, Verify increments c'_ν by one for all $\nu \in N \cap N_j$. The verification procedure then continues with the next j, until (including) $j = l - 1$.

7. Finally, Verify checks whether $\text{Verify}_{\text{FS}}(pk, (N, E), c'_{\text{EM}}, \sigma_E) \overset{?}{=} 1$, and outputs 1 if so, and 0 otherwise.

A few notes are in order here:

1. For all log entries m_j, the number of epoch markers c_{EM} in the log file (or an excerpt) before m_j is identical to the number i of the epoch in which m_j was signed.
2. Excerpts created by SALVE are signed with the most recent secret key available. The verification algorithm implicitly checks for truncation attacks by using the number of epoch markers in the excerpt as the assumed epoch in which the excerpt has been created (see check 7). Thus, the final signature σ_E serves as an implicit proof that the signer knows the key of epoch c'_{EM}. Truncating a log file (or an excerpt) to an epoch before the break-in therefore requires forging a σ_E supposedly created with a previous secret key, and thus breaking the security of Σ_{FS}.

4.2   Security Analysis

We now analyse the security of our scheme above. The following theorem states our main result:

Theorem 1 (Security of SALVE). *If there exists a PPT attacker $\mathcal{A}$ that wins the FS-EUF-CLMA experiment against SALVE with probability $\varepsilon_{\mathcal{A}}$, then there exists a PPT attacker $\mathcal{B}$ that wins the FS-EUF-CMA game against Σ_{FS} with probability $\varepsilon_{\mathcal{B}} = \varepsilon_{\mathcal{A}}$.*

Proof. Let $\mathcal{A}$ be an attacker having success probability $\varepsilon_{\mathcal{A}}$ in the FS-EUF-CLMA experiment against SALVE. We construct an adversary $\mathcal{B}$ that tries to break the FS-EUF-CMA-security of the underlying scheme Σ_{FS}, using $\mathcal{A}$ as a component.

For this, $\mathcal{B}$ simulates the FS-EUF-CLMA experiment with SALVE for $\mathcal{A}$. The simulation is straightforward. (Nonetheless, a more detailed description can be found in the full version of this paper.) $\mathcal{B}$ (on input pk and T) starts $\mathcal{A}$ with inputs pk, $T-1$ and $\sigma_{0,-1} := \langle\rangle$. During the simulation, $\mathcal{B}$ keeps track of the log file M constructed so far, the signature σ for it, the sequence numbers c_{ν} for all categories ν, as well as the current epoch number i. When $\mathcal{A}$ calls its signature oracle, $\mathcal{B}$ executes the AppendAndSign algorithm, but uses its signature oracle in the FS-EUF-CMA-game instead of calling the Sign algorithm of Σ_{FS}. When $\mathcal{A}$ requests an excerpt, $\mathcal{B}$ similarly executes the Extract algorithm of SALVE, again replacing the call to the Sign algorithm of Σ_{FS} by a call to its signature oracle. When $\mathcal{A}$ makes a query to the NextEpoch oracle, $\mathcal{B}$ creates the epoch marker, appends it to M via the AppendAndSign algorithm as above, increments i and then triggers its own NextEpoch oracle in the FS-EUF-CMA-experiment. Finally, when $\mathcal{A}$ requests the current secret key via the BreakIn oracle, $\mathcal{B}$ obtains it using the BreakIn oracle in the FS-EUF-CMA experiment and returns it to $\mathcal{A}$.

At the end of the experiment, $\mathcal{A}$ outputs a forged excerpt E^*, a set of categories N^* and a forged signature σ^* for E^*. If $\mathcal{A}$ outputs an invalid or trivial forgery, then $\mathcal{B}$ outputs $\bot$ and aborts. Otherwise, $\mathcal{B}$ determines which of the following cases has occured and acts as described for each case. For this distinction, we let c_{EM}^* be the number of log entries $(N_j^*, m_j'^*)$ in E^* with $EM \in N_j^*$.

Case 1: E^* *contains* $c_{EM}^* < i_{\text{BreakIn}}$ *epoch markers.* In this case, $\mathcal{B}$ outputs $m^* := (N^*, E^*)$ as its message, the number $i^* := c_{EM}^*$ of epoch markers in E^* as the epoch number, and the last element σ_E^* of the sequence σ^* as its forged signature for m^*. σ_E^* must be a valid signature for (N^*, E^*), since otherwise Verify would have rejected the signature σ^* after check 7.

Furthermore, $\mathcal{B}$'s output is non-trivial, since firstly (N^*, E^*) can not be mixed up with $\mathcal{B}$'s signature queries for individual log entries because of the encoding, secondly, $\mathcal{B}$ never asked for a signature for (N^*, E^*) because $\mathcal{A}$'s output is non-trivial, and thirdly $i^* = c_{EM}^* < i_{\text{BreakIn}}$.

Hence, $\mathcal{B}$'s output is valid and non-trivial, so $\mathcal{B}$ wins the FS-EUF-CMA game.

Case 2: E^* *contains* $c_{EM}^* \geq i_{\text{BreakIn}}$ *epoch markers.* Let M_i and E_i be as in Definition 8. Observe that $i_{\text{BreakIn}} > 0$, because otherwise we had $E_i = M_i = \langle\rangle$, and then $\mathcal{A}$'s output were trivial.

Let E_i^* be the prefix of E^* up until (including) the i_{BreakIn}-th epoch marker (the i_{BreakIn}-th log message $(N_j^*, m_j'^*)$ with $EM \in N_j^*$). We know that E_i is not a prefix of E_i^*, since otherwise E_i would also be a prefix of E^* in contradiction to $\mathcal{A}$'s forgery not being trivial.

Let $E_i = \langle m_j \rangle_{j=0}^{l-1}$, $E_i^* = \langle m_j^* \rangle_{j=0}^{l^*-1}$, $m_j^* = (N_j^*, m_j'^*)$ for all $j \in \{0, \dots, l^* - 1\}$ and $m_j = (N_j, m_j')$ for all $j \in \{0, \dots, l-1\}$. $\mathcal{B}$ builds the sequences $S^* = \langle (f_0^*, m_0'^*), \dots, (f_{l^*-1}^*, m_{l^*-1}'^*) \rangle$ (taking the f_j^* from the signatures $\sigma_j^* \in \sigma^*$) and $S = \langle (f_0, m_0'), \dots, (f_{l-1}, m_{l-1}') \rangle$ (taking the f_j from the signatures σ_j it constructed during the simulation). Note that S contains exactly $\mathcal{B}$'s oracle queries during epochs 0 through $i_{\text{BreakIn}} - 1$, restricted to those messages that belong to at least one of the categories N^*. Also observe that $S^* \neq S$, since we otherwise had $E_i^* = E_i$ (by checks 2 and 3), in contradiction to E_i not being a prefix of E_i^*.

The key observation is that there must be a $(f_k^*, m_k'^*) \in S^*$ with $(f_k^*, m_k'^*) \notin S$ ($k \in \{0, \ldots, l^* - 1\}$). Suppose for the sake of a contradiction that there is no such pair. Then S^* consists entirely of pairs that also occur in S. Obviously, S^* can not contain duplicate pairs $(f_k^*, m_k'^*)$, since the verification algorithm would have rejected the excerpt when checking that counters always increase (checks 4 and/or 5). Since S^* contains only pairs also contained in S, contains no duplicates, and $S^* \neq S$, S^* is missing at least one tuple from S. S^* can not be missing an epoch marker, since it contains c_{EM}^* of them, exactly as S. So S^* is missing some regular log entry. But then Verify had failed when checking the counters in check 6, which is impossible if $\mathcal{A}$'s output was valid.

So we have established that S^* contains a pair $(f_k^*, m_k'^*) \notin S$. $\mathcal{B}$ searches for this pair, and outputs it as the message. It also outputs the number of epoch markers in S^* before $(f_k^*, m_k'^*)$ as the epoch number i^* and $\sigma_k'^*$ as the signature.

This is a valid signature, because of check 1. It remains to show that this is a non-trivial forgery. Firstly, the number of epoch markers before $(f_k^*, m_k'^*)$ is at most $i_{\text{BreakIn}} - 1$, so the signature $\sigma_k'^*$ is valid for an epoch $i^* < i_{\text{BreakIn}}$. Secondly, $\mathcal{B}$ has never requested $(f_k^*, m_k'^*)$ from its signature oracle, since $(f_k^*, m_k'^*) \notin S$, where S is exactly the set of $\mathcal{B}$'s signature queries for all messages belonging to at least one of the categories N^*, such as m_k^*. Hence, $\mathcal{B}$ wins the FS-EUF-CMA game in case 2, since it outputs a non-trivial and valid forgery.

Since $\mathcal{B}$'s simulation of the FS-EUF-CLMA game for $\mathcal{A}$ is perfect, $\mathcal{B}$ wins both in case 1 and in case 2, and one of these cases occurs whenever $\mathcal{A}$ outputs a valid and non-trivial signature, we have $\varepsilon_{\mathcal{B}} = \varepsilon_{\mathcal{A}}$. Also, $\mathcal{B}$ runs in polynomial time, as $\mathcal{A}$ does. □

4.3 Performance Analysis

In this section, we analyse the runtime and storage overhead of SALVE. Since SALVE can be instantiated with an arbitrary forward-secure signature scheme Σ_{FS}, we give our findings with regard to algorithm runtime in terms of calls to algorithms of Σ_{FS}, and our findings in regard to storage overhead in terms of key and signature sizes of Σ_{FS}, respectively.

Due to space restricitons, we can merely present the results; Table 1 summarizes our (conservatively simplified) findings. Our analysis is built on a few mild assumptions about the implementation, e.g. some simple caching. See the full version for a statement of these, the detailed analysis and a comparison with other schemes from the literature.

In Table 1, M refers to the current log file, i to the current epoch number, E to the excerpt being created or verified, N_{total} to the set of (the names of) all categories that have been used so far, N_{epoch} to the set of (the names of) the categories that have received a new log entry in the epoch being ended by the update procedure, and R to the total number of associations between log entries and categories (i.e. $R := \sum_{j=0}^{|M|-1} |N_j|$).

Table 1. Performance characteristics of SALVE in relation to Σ_{FS}. We use sets, sequences and bit strings instead of their size and length, respectively, to relieve notation.

Algorithm	Runtime
KeyGen	$1 \times \text{KeyGen}_{\text{FS}} + \mathcal{O}(1)$
AppendAndSign	$1 \times \text{Sign}_{\text{FS}} + \mathcal{O}(N_j(\log N_j + \log N_{\text{total}}) + m_j')$
Update	$1 \times \text{Update}_{\text{FS}} + 1 \times \text{Sign}_{\text{FS}} + \mathcal{O}(N_{\text{epoch}} \log N_{\text{total}})$
Extract	$1 \times \text{Sign}_{\text{FS}} + \mathcal{O}(R \log N)$
Verify	$(E + 1) \times \text{Verify}_{\text{FS}} + \mathcal{O}(R \log N)$

Datum	Size
Secret Key	$1 \times sk_{\text{FS}} + 0$
Public Key	$1 \times pk_{\text{FS}} + 0$
Log File Signature	$(M + i) \times \sigma_{\text{FS}} + \mathcal{O}(R)$
Excerpt Signature	$(E + i + 1) \times \sigma_{\text{FS}} + \mathcal{O}(R)$

5   Conclusion

It is a desirable feature of secure logging schemes to have verifiable excerpts. We have defined a security notion for such logging schemes, and proposed a new scheme that provably fulfills this notion. Our scheme can be instantiated with an arbitrary forward-secure signature scheme, and can therefore be tuned to specific performance requirements and based on a wide variety of computational assumptions.

Acknowledgements. I would like to thank Jörn Müller-Quade and my colleagues and friends Alexander Koch, Tobias Nilges and Bernhard Löwe for helpful discussions and remarks. I am also grateful to the anonymous reviewers for their comments. This work was supported by the German Federal Ministry of Education and Research (BMBF) as part of the MisPel program under grant no. 13N12063. The views expressed herein are the author's responsibility and do not necessarily reflect those of BMBF.

References

1. Abdalla, M., Miner, S.K., Namprempre, C.: Forward-secure threshold signature schemes. In: Naccache, D. (ed.) CT-RSA 2001. LNCS, vol. 2020, pp. 441–456. Springer, Heidelberg (2001). http://dx.doi.org/10.1007/3-540-45353-9_32
2. Abdalla, M., Reyzin, L.: A new forward-secure digital signature scheme. In: Okamoto, T. (ed.) ASIACRYPT 2000. LNCS, vol. 1976, pp. 116–129. Springer, Heidelberg (2000). http://dx.doi.org/10.1007/3-540-44448-3_10
3. Accorsi, R.: Safe-keeping digital evidence with secure logging protocols: state of the art and challenges. In: Fifth International Conference on IT Security Incident Management and IT Forensics, IMF 2009, pp. 94–110, September 2009. http://www2.informatik.uni-freiburg.de/accorsi/papers/imf09.pdf

4. Bellare, M., Miner, S.K.: A forward-secure digital signature scheme. In: Wiener, M. (ed.) CRYPTO 1999. LNCS, vol. 1666, pp. 431–448. Springer, Heidelberg (1999). http://dx.doi.org/10.1007/3-540-48405-1_28

5. Bellare, M., Yee, B.: Forward-security in private-key cryptography. In: Joye, M. (ed.) CT-RSA 2003. LNCS, vol. 2612, pp. 1–18. Springer, Heidelberg (2003). http://dx.doi.org/10.1007/3-540-36563-X_1

6. Bellare, M., Yee, B.S.: Forward integrity for secure audit logs. Technical report, University of California at San Diego (1997)

7. Boneh, D., Gentry, C., Lynn, B., Shacham, H.: Aggregate and verifiably encrypted signatures from bilinear maps. In: Biham, E. (ed.) EUROCRYPT 2003. LNCS, vol. 2656, pp. 416–432. Springer, Heidelberg (2003). http://dx.doi.org/10.1007/3-540-39200-9_26

8. Boyen, X., Shacham, H., Shen, E., Waters, B.: Forward-secure signatures with untrusted update. In: Proceedings of the 13th ACM Conference on Computer and Communications Security, CCS 2006, pp. 191–200. ACM, New York (2006). http://doi.acm.org/10.1145/1180405.1180430

9. Common criteria for information technology security evaluation, version 3.1 r4, part 2, September 2012. https://www.commoncriteriaportal.org/cc/

10. Crosby, S.A., Wallach, D.S.: Efficient data structures for tamper-evident logging. In: Proceedings of the 18th Conference on USENIX Security Symposium, SSYM 2009, pp. 317–334. USENIX Association, Berkeley, CA, USA (2009). http://dl.acm.org/citation.cfm?id=1855768.1855788

11. Futoransky, A., Kargieman, E.: VCR and PEO revised (1998). http://www.coresecurity.com/files/attachments/PEO.pdf. Accessed 18 February 2015

12. Holt, J.E.: Logcrypt: forward security and public verification for secure audit logs. In: Proceedings of the 2006 Australasian Workshops on Grid Computing and e-Research, ACSW Frontiers 2006, vol. 54, pp. 203–211. Australian Computer Society Inc., Darlinghurst, Australia (2006). http://dl.acm.org/citation.cfm?id=1151828.1151852

13. Hu, F., Wu, C.H., Irwin, J.D.: A new forward secure signature scheme using bilinear maps. Cryptology ePrint Archive, Report 2003/188 (2003). http://eprint.iacr.org/

14. Itkis, G., Reyzin, L.: Forward-secure signatures with optimal signing and verifying. In: Kilian, J. (ed.) CRYPTO 2001. LNCS, vol. 2139, pp. 332–354. Springer, Heidelberg (2001). http://dx.doi.org/10.1007/3-540-44647-8_20

15. Latham, D.C. (ed.): Department of Defense Trusted Computer System Evaluation Criteria. US Department of Defense, December 1985. http://csrc.nist.gov/publications/history/dod85.pdf

16. Ma, D., Tsudik, G.: A new approach to secure logging. In: Atluri, V. (ed.) DAS 2008. LNCS, vol. 5094, pp. 48–63. Springer, Heidelberg (2008). http://dx.doi.org/10.1007/978-3-540-70567-3_4

17. Malkin, T., Micciancio, D., Miner, S.: Efficient generic forward-secure signatures with an unbounded number of time periods. In: Knudsen, L.R. (ed.) EUROCRYPT 2002. LNCS, vol. 2332, pp. 400–417. Springer, Heidelberg (2002). http://dx.doi.org/10.1007/3-540-46035-7_27

18. Marson, G.A., Poettering, B.: Practical secure logging: seekable sequential key generators. In: Crampton, J., Jajodia, S., Mayes, K. (eds.) ESORICS 2013. LNCS, vol. 8134, pp. 111–128. Springer, Heidelberg (2013). http://dx.doi.org/10.1007/978-3-642-40203-6_7

19. An introduction to computer security: the NIST handbook. NIST Special Publication 800-12, October 1995. http://www.nist.gov/manuscript-publication-search.cfm?pub_id=890080

20. Schneier, B., Kelsey, J.: Cryptographic support for secure logs on untrusted machines. In: The Seventh USENIX Security Symposium Proceedings (1998)
21. Song, D.X.: Practical forward secure group signature schemes. In: Proceedings of the 8th ACM Conference on Computer and Communications Security, CCS 2001, pp. 225–234. ACM, New York (2001). http://doi.acm.org/10.1145/501983.502015
22. Stathopoulos, V., Kotzanikolaou, P., Magkos, E.: A framework for secure and verifiable logging in public communication networks. In: López, J. (ed.) CRITIS 2006. LNCS, vol. 4347, pp. 273–284. Springer, Heidelberg (2006). http://dx.doi.org/10.1007/11962977_22
23. Waters, B.R., Balfanz, D., Durfee, G., Smetters, D.K.: Building an encrypted and searchable audit log. In: The 11th Annual Network and Distributed System Security Symposium (2004)
24. Yavuz, A.A., Peng, N.: BAF: an efficient publicly verifiable secure audit logging scheme for distributed systems. In: Computer Security Applications Conference, ACSAC 2009, Annual, pp. 219–228, December 2009
25. Yavuz, A.A., Peng, N., Reiter, M.K.: BAF and FI-BAF: efficient and publicly verifiable cryptographic schemes for secure logging in resource-constrained systems. ACM Trans. Inf. Syst. Secur. 15(2), 9:1–9:28 (2012). http://doi.acm.org/10.1145/2240276.2240280
26. Yavuz, A.A., Ning, P., Reiter, M.K.: Efficient, compromise resilient and append-only cryptographic schemes for secure audit logging. In: Keromytis, A.D. (ed.) FC 2012. LNCS, vol. 7397, pp. 148–163. Springer, Heidelberg (2012). http://dx.doi.org/10.1007/978-3-642-32946-3_12
27. Zhang, J., Wu, Q., Wang, Y.: A novel efficient group signature scheme with forward security. In: Qing, S., Gollmann, D., Zhou, J. (eds.) ICICS 2003. LNCS, vol. 2836, pp. 292–300. Springer, Heidelberg (2003). http://dx.doi.org/10.1007/978-3-540-39927-8_27

Efficient Culpably Sound NIZK Shuffle Argument Without Random Oracles

Prastudy Fauzi and Helger Lipmaa[✉]

University of Tartu, Tartu, Estonia
helger.lipmaa@gmail.com

Abstract. One way to guarantee security against malicious voting servers is to use NIZK shuffle arguments. Up to now, only two NIZK shuffle arguments in the CRS model have been proposed. Both arguments are relatively inefficient compared to known random oracle based arguments. We propose a new, more efficient, shuffle argument in the CRS model. Importantly, its online prover's computational complexity is dominated by only two $(n+1)$-wide multi-exponentiations, where n is the number of ciphertexts. Compared to the previously fastest argument by Lipmaa and Zhang, it satisfies a stronger notion of soundness.

Keywords: Bilinear pairings · CRS model · Mix-net · Non-interactive zero knowledge · Shuffle argument

1 Introduction

A mix network, or mix-net, is a network of mix-servers designed to remove the link between ciphertexts and their senders. To achieve this goal, a mix-server of a mix-net initially obtains a list of ciphertexts $(z_i)_{i=1}^n$. It then re-randomizes and permutes this list, and outputs the new list $(z_i')_{i=1}^n$ together with a non-interactive zero knowledge (NIZK, [2]) shuffle argument [22] that proves the re-randomization and permutation was done correctly, without leaking any side information. If enc is a multiplicatively homomorphic public-key cryptosystem like Elgamal [7], a shuffle argument convinces the verifier that there exists a permutation ψ and a vector t of randomizers such that $z_i' = z_{\psi(i)} \cdot \mathsf{enc}_{\mathsf{pk}}(1; t_i)$, without revealing any information about ψ or t. Mix-nets improve security against malicious voting servers in e-voting. Other applications of mix-nets include anonymous web browsing, payment systems, and secure multiparty computation.

It is important to have a *non-interactive* shuffle argument outputting a short bit string that can be verified by anybody (possibly years later) without interacting with the prover. Many NIZK shuffle arguments are known in the random oracle model, see for example [9,10,13,20,23]. Since the random oracle model is only a heuristic, it is strongly recommended to construct NIZK arguments in

© Springer International Publishing Switzerland 2016
K. Sako (Ed.): CT-RSA 2016, LNCS 9610, pp. 200–216, 2016.
DOI: 10.1007/978-3-319-29485-8_12

the common reference string (CRS) model [2], without using random oracles.[1]
We note that the most efficient shuffle arguments in the random oracle model
like [13] also require a CRS.

Up to now, only two NIZK shuffle arguments in the CRS model have been
proposed, by Groth and Lu [15] and Lipmaa and Zhang [18,19], both of which
are significantly slower than the fastest arguments in the random oracle model
(see Table 1). The Groth-Lu shuffle argument only provides culpable soundness [15,16] in the sense that if a malicious prover can create an accepting shuffle
argument for an incorrect statement, then this prover *together* with a party that
knows the secret key can break the underlying security assumptions. Relaxation
of the soundness property is unavoidable, since [1] showed that only languages
in **P/poly** can have direct black-box adaptive perfect NIZK arguments under
a (polynomial) cryptographic hardness assumption. If the underlying cryptosystem is IND-CPA secure, then the shuffle language is *not* in **P/poly**, and thus it
is necessary to use knowledge assumptions [5] to prove its adaptive soundness.
Moreover, [15] argued that culpable soundness is a sufficient security notion for
shuffles, since in any real-life application of the shuffle argument there exists
some coalition of parties who knows the secret key.

Lipmaa and Zhang [18] proposed a more efficient NIZK shuffle argument by
using knowledge assumptions under which they also bypassed the impossibility
result of [1] and proved that their shuffle argument is sound. However, their
shuffle argument is sound only under the assumption that there is an extractor
that has access to the random coins of all encrypters, e.g., all voters, allowing her
to extract all plaintexts and randomizers. We say in this case that the argument
is *white-box sound*. White-box soundness is clearly a weaker security notion than
culpable soundness of [15], and it would be good to avoid it.

In addition, the use of knowledge assumptions in [18] forces the underlying
BBS [4] cryptosystem to include knowledge components (so ciphertexts are twice
as long) and be lifted (meaning that one has to solve discrete logarithm to
decrypt, so plaintexts must be small). Thus, one has to use a random oracle-less
range argument to guarantee that the plaintexts are small and thus to guarantee
the soundness of the *shuffle* argument (see [18] for a discussion). While range
proofs only have to be verified once (e.g., by only one mix-server), this still
means that the shuffle argument of [18] is somewhat slower than what is given
in Table 1. Moreover, in the case of e-voting, using only small plaintexts restricts
the applicability of a shuffle argument to only certain voting mechanisms like
majority. On the other hand, a mechanism such as Single Transferable Vote
would likely be unusable due to the length of the ballots.

Table 1 provides a brief comparison between known NIZK shuffle arguments
in the CRS model and the most computationally efficient known shuffle argument
in the random oracle model [13]. We emphasize that the values in parentheses

---

[1] In a practical implementation of a mix-net, one can use the random oracle model also
for other purposes, such as to construct a pseudo-number generator or a public-key
cryptosystem. In most of such cases, it is known how to avoid the random oracle
model, although this almost always incurs some additional cost.

Table 1. A comparison of different NIZK shuffle arguments, compared with the computationally most efficient known shuffle argument in the random oracle model [13].

	[15]	[19]	This work	[13]
|CRS|	$2n + 8$	$7n + 6$	$8n + 17$	$n + 1$
Communication	$15n + 120 \ (+3n)$	$6n + 11 \ (+6n)$	$7n + 2 \ (+2n)$	$480n$ bits
pro's comp.	$51n + 246 \ (+3n)$	$22n + 11 \ (+6n)$	$16n + 3 \ (+2n)$	$6n \ (+2n)$
ver's comp.	$75n + 282$	$28n + 18$	$18n + 6$	$6n$ exp.
Lifted	No	Yes	No	No
Soundness	Culp. sound	White-box sound	Culp. sound	Sound
Arg. of knowl.	no	yes	yes	yes
PKE (knowl. assm.)	no	yes	yes	no
Random oracle		no		yes

show the cost of computing and communicating the shuffled ciphertexts themselves, and must be added to the rest. Moreover, the cost of the shuffle argument from [18] should include the cost of a range argument. Unless written otherwise, the communication and the CRS length are given in group elements, the prover's computational complexity is given in exponentiations, and the verifier's computational complexity is given in bilinear pairings. In each row, highlighted cells denote the best efficiency or best security (e.g., not requiring the PKE assumption) among arguments in the CRS model. Of course, a full efficiency comparison can only be made after implementing the different shuffle arguments.

This brings us to the main question of the current paper:

> *Is it possible to construct an NIZK shuffle argument in the CRS model that is comparable in efficiency with existing random oracle model NIZK shuffle arguments? Moreover, can one do it while minimizing the use of knowledge assumptions (i.e., not requiring the knowledge extractor to have access to the random coins used by all encrypters) and using a standard, non-lifted, cryptosystem?*

Our Contributions. We give a partial answer to the main question. We propose a new pairing-based NIZK shuffle argument in the CRS model. Differently from [18], we prove the culpable soundness of the new argument instead of white-box soundness. Compared to [15], which also achieves culpable soundness, the new argument has 3 times faster proving and more than 4 times faster verification. Compared to [15,18], it is based on a more standard cryptosystem (Elgamal). While the new shuffle argument is still at least 2 times slower than the most efficient known random oracle based shuffle arguments, it has almost optimal *online* prover's computation. Of course, a full efficiency comparison can only be made after implementing the different shuffle arguments.

Our construction works as follows. We first commit to the permutation ψ (by committing separately to first $n - 1$ rows of the corresponding permutation matrix

$\boldsymbol{\Psi}$) and to the vector $\boldsymbol{t}$ of blinding randomizers. Here, we use the *polynomial commitment scheme* (see Sect. 2) with $\mathsf{com}(\mathsf{ck}; \boldsymbol{m}; r) = (g_1, g_2^\gamma)^{rP_0(\chi)+\sum_{i=1}^n m_i P_i(\chi)} \in \mathbb{G}_1 \times \mathbb{G}_2$, in pairing-based setting, where $\hat{e} : \mathbb{G}_1 \times \mathbb{G}_2 \to \mathbb{G}_T$ is a bilinear pairing, g_i is a generator of $\mathbb{G}_i$ for $i \in \{1, 2\}$, $(P_i(X))_{i=0}^n$ is a tuple of linearly independent polynomials, χ is a trapdoor, γ is a knowledge secret, and $\mathsf{ck} = ((g_1, g_2^\gamma)^{P_i(\chi)})_{i=0}^n$ is the CRS. For different values of $P_i(X)$, variants of this commitment scheme have been proposed before [12,14,17].

We show that $\boldsymbol{\Psi}$ is a correct permutation matrix by constructing n witness-indistinguishable succinct *unit vector arguments*, each of which guarantees that a row of $\boldsymbol{\Psi}$ is a unit vector, for implicitly constructed $\boldsymbol{\Psi}_n = \boldsymbol{1}_n - \sum_{i=1}^{n-1} \boldsymbol{\Psi}_i$. We use the recent square span programs (SSP, [6]) approach to choose the polynomials $P_i(X) = y_i(X)$ so that the unit vector argument is efficient. Since unit vectors are used in many contexts, we hope this argument is of independent interest.

After that, we postulate a natural concrete verification equation for shuffles, and construct the shuffle argument from this. If privacy were not an issue (and thus $z_i' = z_{\psi(i)}$ for every i), the verification equation would just be the tautology $\prod_{i=1}^n \hat{e}(z_i', g_2^{y_i(\chi)}) =^? \prod_{i=1}^n \hat{e}(z_i, g_2^{y_{\psi^{-1}(i)}(\chi)})$. Clearly, if the prover is honest, this equation holds. However, it does not yet guarantee soundness, since an adversary can use $g_1^{y_j(\chi)}$ (given in the CRS) to create $(z_i')_{i=1}^n$ in a malicious way. To eliminate this possibility, by roughly following an idea from [15], we also verify that $\prod_{i=1}^n \hat{e}(z_i', g_2^{\hat{y}_i(\chi)}) =^? \prod_{i=1}^n \hat{e}(z_i, g_2^{\hat{y}_{\psi^{-1}(i)}(\chi)})$ for some well-chosen polynomials $\hat{y}_i(X)$. (We note that instead of n univariate polynomials, [15] used n random variables χ_i, increasing the size of the secret key to $\Omega(n)$ bits.)

To show that the verifications are instantiated correctly, we also need a *same-message argument* that shows that commitments w.r.t. two tuples of polynomials $(y_i(X))_{i=1}^n$ and $(\hat{y}_i(X))_{i=1}^n$ commit to the same plaintext vectors. We construct an efficient same-message argument by using an approach that is (again, roughly) motivated by the QAP-based approach of [11]. This argument is an argument of knowledge, given that the polynomials $\hat{y}_i(X)$ satisfy an additional restriction.

Since we also require privacy, the actual verification equations are more complicated. In particular, $z_i' = z_{\psi(i)} \cdot \mathsf{enc}_{\mathsf{pk}}(1; t_i)$, and (say) $g_2^{y_{\psi^{-1}(i)}(\chi)}$ is replaced by the second element $g_2^{\gamma(r_i y_0(\chi)+y_{\psi^{-1}(i)}(\chi))}$ of a commitment to $\boldsymbol{\Psi}_i$. The resulting complication is minor (it requires one to include into the shuffle argument a single ciphertext $U \in \mathbb{G}_1^2$ that compensates for the added randomness). The full shuffle argument consists of commitments to $\boldsymbol{\Psi}$ and to $\boldsymbol{t}$ (both committed twice, w.r.t. the polynomials $(y_i(X))_{i=0}^n$ and $(\hat{y}_i(X))_{i=0}^n$), n unit vector arguments (one for each row of $\boldsymbol{\Psi}$), $n-1$ same-message arguments, and finally U.

If $\hat{y}_i(X)$ are well-chosen, then from the two verification equations and the soundness of the unit vector and same-message arguments it follows, under a new computational assumption PSP (*Power Simultaneous Product*, related to an assumption from [15]), that $z_i' = z_{\psi(i)}$ for every i.

We prove culpable soundness [15,16] of the new argument. Since the security of the new shuffle argument does not depend on the cryptosystem either having knowledge components or being lifted, we can use Elgamal encryption [7] instead of the non-standard knowledge BBS encryption introduced in [18]. Since the cryptosystem does not have to be lifted, one can use more complex voting mechanisms with more complex ballots. The use of knowledge assumptions means that the new argument is an argument of knowledge.

The new shuffle argument can be largely precomputed by the prover and forwarded to the verifier even before the common input (i.e., ciphertexts) arrive. Similarly, the verifier can perform a large part of verification before receiving the ciphertexts. (See [24] for motivation for precomputation.) The prover's computation in the online phase is dominated by just two $(n + 1)$-wide multi-exponentiations (the computation of U). The multi-exponentiations can be parallelized; this is important in practice due to the wide availability of highly parallel graphics processors.

Main Technical Challenges. While the main objective of the current work is efficiency, we emphasize that several steps of the new shuffle argument are technically involved. Throughout the paper, we use and combine very recent techniques from the design of efficient succinct non-interactive arguments of knowledge (SNARKs, [6,11,21], that are constructed with the main goal of achieving efficient verifiable computation) with quite unrelated techniques from the design of efficient shuffle arguments [15,18].

The security of the new shuffle argument relies on a new assumption, PSP. We prove that PSP holds in the generic bilinear group model, given that polynomials $\hat{y}_i(X)$ satisfy a very precise criterion. For the security of the SSP-based unit vector argument, we need $y_i(X)$ to satisfy another criterion, and for the security of the same-message argument, we need $y_i(X)$ and $\hat{y}_i(X)$ to satisfy a third criterion. The fact that polynomials $y_i(X)$ and $\hat{y}_i(X)$ that satisfy all three criteria exist is not a priori clear; $y_i(X)$ and $\hat{y}_i(X)$ (see Proposition 3) are also unlike any polynomials from the related literature on non-interactive zero knowledge.

Finally, the PSP assumption was carefully chosen so it will hold in the generic bilinear group model, and so the reduction from culpable soundness of the shuffle argument to the PSP assumption would work. While the PSP assumption is related to the SP assumption from [15], the situation in [15] was less fragile due to the use of independent random variables X_i and X_i^2 instead of polynomials $y_i(X)$ and $\hat{y}_i(X)$. In particular, the same-message argument is trivial in the case of using independent random variables.

Due to lack of space, several proofs and other details are given in the full version, [8].

2   Preliminaries

Let n be the number of ciphertexts to be shuffled. Let S_d be the symmetric group of d elements. Let $\mathbb{G}^*$ denote the group $\mathbb{G}$ without its identity element. For $a \leq b$, let $[a \mathinner{..} b] := \{c \in \mathbb{Z} : a \leq c \leq b\}$. Denote $(a, b)^c := (a^c, b^c)$. For a set of polynomials $\mathcal{F}$ that have the same domain, denote $g^{\mathcal{F}(a)} := (g^{f(a)})_{f \in \mathcal{F}}$.

A *permutation matrix* is a Boolean matrix with exactly one 1 in every row and column. If ψ is a permutation then the corresponding permutation matrix

$\boldsymbol{\Psi}_\psi$ is such that $(\boldsymbol{\Psi}_\psi)_{ij} = 1$ iff $j = \psi(i)$. Thus $(\boldsymbol{\Psi}_{\psi^{-1}})_{ij} = 1$ iff $i = \psi(j)$. Clearly, $\boldsymbol{\Psi}$ is a permutation matrix iff its every row is a unit vector, and the sum of all its row vectors is equal to the all-ones vector $\mathbf{1}_n$.

Let κ be the security parameter. We denote $f(\kappa) \approx_\kappa g(\kappa)$ if $|f(\kappa) - g(\kappa)|$ is negligible in κ. We abbreviate (non-uniform) probabilistic-polynomial time by (NU)PPT. On input 1^κ, a *bilinear map generator* BP returns $(p, \mathbb{G}_1, \mathbb{G}_2, \mathbb{G}_T, \hat{e})$, where $\mathbb{G}_1$, $\mathbb{G}_2$ and $\mathbb{G}_T$ are multiplicative cyclic groups of prime order p, and $\hat{e}$ is an efficient bilinear map $\hat{e} \colon \mathbb{G}_1 \times \mathbb{G}_2 \to \mathbb{G}_T$ that satisfies the following two properties, where g_1 (resp., g_2) is an arbitrary generator of $\mathbb{G}_1$ (resp., $\mathbb{G}_2$): (i) $\hat{e}(g_1, g_2) \neq 1$, and (ii) $\hat{e}(g_1^a, g_2^b) = \hat{e}(g_1, g_2)^{ab}$. Thus, $\hat{e}(g_1^a, g_2^b) = \hat{e}(g_1^c, g_2^d)$ iff $ab \equiv cd \pmod{p}$. We give BP another input, n (related to the input length), and allow p to depend on n. Finally, we assume that all algorithms that handle group elements reject if their inputs do not belong to corresponding groups.

We will now give short explanations of the main knowledge assumptions. Let $1 < d(n) < d^*(n) = \mathrm{poly}(\kappa)$ be two functions. We say that BP is

- $d(n)$-*PDL (Power Discrete Logarithm,* [17]) secure if any NUPPT adversary, given values $((g_1, g_2)^{\chi^i})_{i=0}^{d(n)}$, has negligible probability of producing χ.
- $(d(n), d^*(n))$-*PCDH (Power Computational Diffie-Hellman,* [11,12,14]) *secure* if any NUPPT adversary, given values $((g_1, g_2)^{\chi^i})_{i \in [0 \, .. \, d^*(n)] \setminus \{d(n)+1\}}$, has negligible probability of producing $g_1^{\chi^{d(n)+1}}$.
- $d(n)$-*TSDH (Target Strong Diffie-Hellman,* [3,21]) *secure* if any NUPPT adversary, given values $((g_1, g_2)^{\chi^i})_{i=0}^{d(n)}$, has negligible probability of producing a pair of values $\left(r, \hat{e}(g_1, g_2)^{1/(\chi - r)}\right)$ where $r \neq \chi$.

For algorithms A and X_{A}, we write $(y; y') \leftarrow (\mathsf{A} \| X_{\mathsf{A}})(\chi)$ if A on input χ outputs y, and X_{A} on the same input (including the random tape of A) outputs y' [1]. We will need knowledge assumptions w.r.t. up to 2 knowledge secrets γ_i. Let m be the number of different knowledge secrets in any concrete argument, in the current paper $m \leq 2$. Let $\mathcal{F} = (P_i)_{i=0}^n$ be a tuple of univariate polynomials, and $\mathcal{G}_1$ (resp., $\mathcal{G}_2$) be a tuple of univariate (resp., m-variate) polynomials. For $i \in [1 \, .. \, m]$, BP is $(\mathcal{F}, \mathcal{G}_1, \mathcal{G}_2, \gamma_i)$-*PKE (Power Knowledge of Exponent,* [14]) *secure* if for any NUPPT adversary A there exists a NUPPT extractor X_{A}, such that

$$
\Pr \left[
\begin{array}{l}
\mathsf{gk} \leftarrow \mathsf{BP}(1^\kappa, n), (g_1, g_2, \chi) \leftarrow_r \mathbb{G}_1^* \times \mathbb{G}_2^* \times \mathbb{Z}_p, \boldsymbol{\gamma} \leftarrow_r \mathbb{Z}_p^m, \\[4pt]
\boldsymbol{\gamma_{-i}} = (\gamma_1, \ldots, \gamma_{i-1}, \gamma_{i+1}, \ldots, \gamma_m), \mathsf{aux} \leftarrow \left(g_1^{\mathcal{G}_1(\chi)}, g_2^{\mathcal{G}_2(\chi, \boldsymbol{\gamma}_{-i})} \right), \\[4pt]
(h_1, h_2; (a_i)_{i=0}^n) \leftarrow (\mathsf{A} \| X_{\mathsf{A}})(\mathsf{gk}; (g_1, g_2^{\gamma_i})^{\mathcal{F}(\chi)}, \mathsf{aux}) : \\[4pt]
\hat{e}(h_1, g_2^{\gamma_i}) = \hat{e}(g_1, h_2) \wedge h_1 \neq g_1^{\sum_{i=0}^n a_i P_i(\chi)}
\end{array}
\right] \approx_\kappa 0 \ .
$$

The definition implies that aux may depend on $\boldsymbol{\gamma}_{-i}$ but not on γ_i. If $\mathcal{F} = (X^i)_{i=0}^d$ for some $d = d(n)$, then we replace the first argument in $(\mathcal{F}, \ldots)$-PKE with d. If $m = 1$, then we omit the last argument γ_i in $(\mathcal{F}, \ldots, \gamma_i)$-PKE.

We will use the Elgamal cryptosystem [7] $\Pi = (\mathsf{BP}, \mathsf{genpkc}, \mathsf{enc}, \mathsf{dec})$, defined as follows, in the bilinear setting.

Setup (1^κ)**:** Let $\mathsf{gk} \leftarrow (p, \mathbb{G}_1, \mathbb{G}_2, \mathbb{G}_T, \hat{e}) \leftarrow \mathsf{BP}(1^\kappa)$.

Key Generation $\mathsf{genpkc}(\mathsf{gk})$**:** Let $g_1 \leftarrow_r \mathbb{G}_1^*$. Set the secret key $\mathsf{sk} \leftarrow_r \mathbb{Z}_p$, and the public key $\mathsf{pk} \leftarrow (g_1, h = g_1^{\mathsf{sk}})$. Output $(\mathsf{pk}, \mathsf{sk})$.

Encryption $\mathsf{enc}_{\mathsf{pk}}(m; r)$**:** To encrypt a message $m \in \mathbb{G}_1$ with randomizer $r \in \mathbb{Z}_p$, output the ciphertext $\mathsf{enc}_{\mathsf{pk}}(m; r) = \mathsf{pk}^r \cdot (1, m) = (g^r, mh^r)$.

Decryption $\mathsf{dec}_{\mathsf{sk}}(c_1, c_2)$**:** $m = c_2/c_1^{\mathsf{sk}} = mh^r/h^r = m$.

Elgamal is clearly multiplicatively homomorphic. In particular, if $t \leftarrow_r \mathbb{Z}_p$, then for *any* m and r, $\mathsf{enc}_{\mathsf{pk}}(m; r) \cdot \mathsf{enc}_{\mathsf{pk}}(1; t) = \mathsf{enc}_{\mathsf{pk}}(m; r + t)$ is a random encryption of m. Elgamal is IND-CPA secure under the XDH assumption.

An extractable trapdoor commitment scheme consists of two efficient algorithms (that outputs a CRS and a trapdoor) and com (that, given a CRS, a message and a randomizer, outputs a commitment), and must satisfy the following four security properties. **Computational binding:** without access to the trapdoor, it is intractable to open a commitment to two different messages. **Trapdoor:** given access to the original message, the randomizer and the trapdoor, one can open the commitment to any other message. **Perfect hiding:** commitments of any two messages have the same distribution. **Extractable:** given access to the CRS, the commitment, and the random coins of the committer, one can obtain the value that the committer committed to.

We use the following extractable trapdoor *polynomial commitment scheme* that generalizes various earlier commitment schemes [12,14,17]. Let $n = \mathsf{poly}(\kappa)$, $n > 0$, be an integer. Let $P_i(X) \in \mathbb{Z}_p[X]$, for $i \in [0 .. n]$, be $n + 1$ linearly independent low-degree polynomials. First, $\mathsf{gencom}(1^\kappa, n)$ generates $\mathsf{gk} \leftarrow \mathsf{BP}(1^\kappa, n)$, picks $g_1 \leftarrow_r \mathbb{G}_1^*$, $g_2 \leftarrow_r \mathbb{G}_2^*$, and then outputs the CRS $\mathsf{ck} \leftarrow ((g_1^{P_i(\chi)}, g_2^{\gamma P_i(\chi)})_{i=0}^n)$ for $\chi \leftarrow_r \mathbb{Z}_p \setminus \{j : P_0(j) = 0\}$ and $\gamma \leftarrow_r \mathbb{Z}_p$. The trapdoor is equal to $\mathsf{td}_{\mathsf{com}} = \chi$.

The commitment of $\boldsymbol{a} \in \mathbb{Z}_p^n$, given a randomizer $r \leftarrow_r \mathbb{Z}_p$, is $\mathsf{com}(\mathsf{ck}; \boldsymbol{a}; r) := (g_1^{P_0(\chi)}, g_2^{\gamma P_0(\chi)})^r \cdot \prod_{i=1}^n (g_1^{P_i(\chi)}, g_2^{\gamma P_i(\chi)})^{a_i} \in \mathbb{G}_1 \times \mathbb{G}_2$. The validity of a commitment (A_1, A_2) can be checked by verifying that $\hat{e}(A_1, g_2^{\gamma P_0(\chi)}) = \hat{e}(g_1^{P_0(\chi)}, A_2)$. To open a commitment, the committer sends $(\boldsymbol{a}, r)$ to the verifier.

Theorem 1. *Denote* $\mathcal{F}_{\mathsf{com}} = (P_i(X))_{i=0}^n$. *The polynomial commitment scheme is perfectly hiding and trapdoor. Let* $d := \max_{f \in \mathcal{F}_{\mathsf{com}}}(\deg f)$. *If BP is d-PDL secure, then it is computationally binding. If BP is* $(\mathcal{F}_{\mathsf{com}}, \emptyset, \emptyset)$*-PKE secure, then it is extractable.*

Alternatively, we can think of com as being a commitment scheme that does not depend on the concrete polynomials at all, and the description of P_i is just given as a part of ck. We instantiate the polynomial commitment scheme with concrete polynomials later in Sects. 3 and 6.

An NIZK argument for a group-dependent language $\mathcal{L}$ consists of four algorithms, setup, gencrs, pro and ver. The setup algorithm setup takes as input 1^κ and n (the input length), and outputs the group description gk. The CRS generation algorithm gencrs takes as input gk and outputs the prover's CRS crs_p, the verifier's CRS crs_v, and a trapdoor td. (td is only required when the argument is zero-knowledge.) The distinction between crs_p and crs_v is only important for efficiency. The prover pro takes as input gk and crs_p, a statement u, and a witness w, and outputs an argument π. The verifier ver takes as input gk and crs_v, a statement u, and an argument π, and either accepts or rejects.

Some of the properties of an argument are: (i) *perfect completeness* (honest verifier always accepts honest prover's argument), (ii) *perfect witness-indistinguishability* (argument distributions corresponding to all allowable witnesses are equal), (iii) *perfect zero knowledge* (there exists an efficient simulator that can, given u, $(\mathsf{crs}_p, \mathsf{crs}_v)$ and td, output an argument that comes from the same distribution as the argument produced by the prover), (iv) *adaptive computational soundness* (if $u \notin \mathcal{L}$, then an arbitrary non-uniform probabilistic polynomial time prover has negligible success in creating a satisfying argument), and (v) *adaptive computational culpable soundness* [15,16] (if $u \notin \mathcal{L}$, then an arbitrary NUPPT prover has negligible success in creating a satisfying argument together with a witness that $u \notin \mathcal{L}$). An argument is an *argument of knowledge*, if from an accepting argument it follows that the prover knows the witness.

3   Unit Vector Argument

In a unit vector argument, the prover aims to convince the verifier that he knows how to open a commitment (A_1, A_2^γ) to *some* $(\boldsymbol{e}_I, r)$, where $\boldsymbol{e}_I$ denotes the Ith unit vector for $I \in [1 .. n]$. We construct the unit vector argument by using square span programs (SSP-s, [6], an especially efficient variant of the quadratic arithmetic programs of [11]).

Clearly, $\boldsymbol{a} \in \mathbb{Z}_p^n$ is a unit vector iff the following $n + 1$ conditions hold:

- $a_i \in \{0, 1\}$ for $i \in [1 .. n]$ (i.e., $\boldsymbol{a}$ is Boolean), and
- $\sum_{i=1}^n a_i = 1$.

We use the methodology of [6] to obtain an efficient NIZK argument out of these conditions. Let $\{0, 2\}^{n+1}$ denote the set of $(n + 1)$-dimensional vectors where every coefficient is from $\{0, 2\}$, let $\circ$ denote the Hadamard (entry-wise) product of two vectors, let $V := \begin{pmatrix} 2 \cdot I_{n \times n} \\ 1_n^\top \end{pmatrix} \in \mathbb{Z}_p^{(n+1) \times n}$ and $\boldsymbol{b} := \begin{pmatrix} \boldsymbol{0}_n \\ 1 \end{pmatrix} \in \mathbb{Z}_p^{n+1}$. Clearly, the above $n + 1$ conditions hold iff $V\boldsymbol{a} + \boldsymbol{b} \in \{0, 2\}^{n+1}$, i.e.,

$$(V\boldsymbol{a} + \boldsymbol{b} - 1_{n+1}) \circ (V\boldsymbol{a} + \boldsymbol{b} - 1_{n+1}) = 1_{n+1} . \tag{1}$$

Let ω_i, $i \in [1 .. n + 1]$ be $n + 1$ different values. Let $Z(X) := \prod_{i=1}^{n+1}(X - \omega_i)$ be the unique degree $n + 1$ monic polynomial, such that $Z(\omega_i) = 0$ for all $i \in [1 .. n+1]$. Let the ith Lagrange basis polynomial $\ell_i(X) := \prod_{i,j \in [1 .. n+1], j \neq i}((X - \omega_j)/(\omega_i - \omega_j))$ be the unique degree n polynomial, s.t. $\ell_i(\omega_i) = 1$ and $\ell_i(\omega_j) = 0$ for $j \neq i$. For a vector $\boldsymbol{x} \in \mathbb{Z}_p^{n+1}$, let $L_{\boldsymbol{x}}(X) = \sum_{i=1}^{n+1} x_i \ell_i(X)$ be a degree n polynomial that interpolates $\boldsymbol{x}$, i.e., $L_{\boldsymbol{x}}(\omega_i) = x_i$.

For $i \in [1 .. n]$, let $y_i(X)$ be the polynomial that interpolates the ith column of the matrix V. That is, $y_i(X) = 2\ell_i(X) + \ell_{n+1}(X)$ for $i \in [1 .. n]$. Let $y_0(X) = -1 + \ell_{n+1}(X)$ be the polynomial that interpolates $\boldsymbol{b} - 1_{n+1}$. We will use an instantiation of the polynomial commitment scheme with $\mathcal{F}_{\mathsf{com}} = (Z(X), (y_i(X))_{i=1}^n)$.

As in [6], we arrive at the polynomial $Q(X) = (\sum_{i=1}^{n} a_i y_i(X) + y_0(X))^2 - 1 = (y_I(X) + y_0(X))^2 - 1$ (here, we used the fact that $a = e_I$ for some $I \in [1..n]$), such that a is a unit vector iff $Z(X) \mid Q(X)$. As in [6,11], to obtain privacy, we now add randomness to $Q(X)$, arriving at the degree $2(n+1)$ polynomial $Q_{wi}(X) = (rZ(X) + y_I(X) + y_0(X))^2 - 1$. By [6,11], Eq. (1) holds iff

(i) $Q_{wi}(X) = (A(X) + y_0(X))^2 - 1$, where $A(X) = r_a Z(X) + \sum_{i=1}^{n} a_i y_i(X) \in$ span($\mathcal{F}_{com}$), and

(ii) $Z(X) \mid Q_{wi}(X)$.

An honest prover computes the degree $\leq n+1$ polynomial $\pi_{wi}(X) \leftarrow Q_{wi}(X)/Z(X) \in \mathbb{Z}_p[X]$, and sets the argument to be equal to $\pi_{uv}^* := g_1^{\pi_{wi}(\chi)}$ for a secret χ that instantiates X. If it exists, $\pi_{wi}(X) := Q_{wi}(X)/Z(X)$ is equal to $r^2 Z(X) + r \cdot 2(y_I(X) + y_0(X)) + \Pi_I(X)$, where for $i \in [1..n]$, $\Pi_i(X) := ((y_i(X) + y_0(X))^2 - 1)/Z(X)$ is a degree $\leq n-1$ polynomial and $Z(X) \mid ((y_i(X) + y_0(X))^2 - 1)$. Thus, computing π_{uv}^* uses two exponentiations.

We use a knowledge (PKE) assumption in a standard way to guarantee that $A(X)$ is in the span of $\{X^i\}_{i=0}^{n+1}$. As in [6,11], we then guarantee condition (i) by using a PCDH assumption and condition (ii) by using a TSDH assumption. Here, we use the same technique as in [11] and subsequent papers by introducing an additional secret, β, and adding one group element A_1^β to the argument.

System parameters: Let com be the polynomial commitment scheme and let
$\mathcal{F}_{com} = (Z(X), (y_i(X))_{i=1}^{n})$.

Setup $\mathsf{setup}_{uv}(1^\kappa, n)$: Let $\mathsf{gk} \leftarrow \mathsf{BP}(1^\kappa, n)$.

CRS generation $\mathsf{gencrs}_{uv}(\mathsf{gk})$: Let $(g_1, g_2, \chi, \beta, \gamma) \leftarrow_r \mathbb{G}_1^* \times \mathbb{G}_2^* \times \mathbb{Z}_p^3$, s.t. $Z(\chi) \neq 0$. Set $\mathsf{ck} \leftarrow (g_1, g_2^\gamma)^{\mathcal{F}_{com}(\chi)}$, $\mathsf{crs}_{uv,p} \leftarrow (\mathsf{ck}, (g_1^{2(y_i(\chi)+y_0(\chi))}, g_1^{\Pi_i(\chi)})_{i=1}^{n}, g_1^{\beta \cdot \mathcal{F}_{com}(\chi)})$, $\mathsf{crs}_{uv,v} \leftarrow (g_1, g_1^{y_0(\chi)}, g_2^\gamma, g_2^{\gamma y_0(\chi)}, g_2^{\gamma Z(\chi)}, g_2^{\gamma \beta}, \hat{e}(g_1, g_2^\gamma)^{-1})$. Return $\mathsf{crs}_{uv} = (\mathsf{crs}_{uv,p}, \mathsf{crs}_{uv,v})$.

Common input: $(A_1, A_2^\gamma) = ((g_1, g_2^\gamma)^{Z(\chi)})^r (g_1, g_2^\gamma)^{y_I(\chi)}$ where $I \in [1..n]$.

Proving $\mathsf{pro}_{uv}(\mathsf{gk}, \mathsf{crs}_{uv,p}; A_1, A_2^\gamma; w_{uv} = (a = e_I, r))$: Set $\pi_{uv}^* \leftarrow (g_1^{Z(\chi)})^{r^2} \cdot (g_1^{2(y_I(\chi)+y_0(\chi))})^r \cdot g_1^{\Pi_I(\chi)}$. Set $A_1^\beta \leftarrow (g_1^{\beta Z(\chi)})^r g_1^{\beta y_I(\chi)}$. Output $\pi_{uv} = (\pi_{uv}^*, A_1^\beta) \in \mathbb{G}_1^2$.

Verification $\mathsf{ver}_{uv}(\mathsf{gk}, \mathsf{crs}_{uv,v}; A_1, A_2^\gamma; \pi_{uv})$: Parse π_{uv} as $\pi_{uv} = (\pi_{uv}^*, A_1^\beta)$. Verify that (1) $\hat{e}(\pi_{uv}^*, g_2^{\gamma Z(\chi)}) = \hat{e}(A_1 \cdot g_1^{y_0(\chi)}, A_2^\gamma \cdot g_2^{\gamma y_0(\chi)}) \cdot \hat{e}(g_1, g_2^\gamma)^{-1}$, (2) $\hat{e}(g_1, A_2^\gamma) = \hat{e}(A_1, g_2^\gamma)$, and (3) $\hat{e}(A_1, g_2^{\gamma \beta}) = \hat{e}(A_1^\beta, g_2^\gamma)$.

Set $\mathcal{F}_{uv,1} = \{1\} \cup \mathcal{F}_{com} \cup X_\beta \mathcal{F}_{com}$ and $\mathcal{F}_{uv,2} = Y \mathcal{F}_{com} \cup \{Y, Y X_\beta\}$. The formal variable X_β (resp., Y) stands for the secret key β (resp., γ). Since other elements of crs_{uv} are only needed for optimization, crs_{uv} can be computed from $\mathsf{crs}_{uv}^* = (g_1^{\mathcal{F}_{uv,1}(\chi,\beta)}, g_2^{\mathcal{F}_{uv,2}(\chi,\beta,\gamma)})$. If $n > 2$ then $1 \notin \mathrm{span}(\{Z(X)\} \cup \{y_i(X)\}_{i=1}^n)$, and thus $\{1, Z(X)\} \cup \{y_i(X)\}_{i=1}^n$ is a basis of all polynomials of degree at most $n+1$. Thus, $\mathcal{F}_{uv,1}$ can be computed iff $\{X^i\}_{i=0}^{n+1} \cup \{X_\beta \mathcal{F}_{com}\}$ can be computed.

Theorem 2. *The new unit vector argument is perfectly complete and witness-indistinguishable. If* BP *is* $(n+1, 2n+3)$*-PCDH secure,* $(n+1)$*-TSDH secure, and*

$(n+1, X_\beta \mathcal{F}_{com}, \{YX_\beta\})$-PKE secure, then this argument is an adaptive argument of knowledge.

Proposition 1. The computation of (π^*_{uv}, A^β_1) takes one 2-wide multi-exponentiation and 1 exponentiation in $\mathbb{G}_1$. In addition, it takes 2 exponentiations (one in $\mathbb{G}_1$ and one in $\mathbb{G}_2$) in the master argument to compute (A_1, A^γ_2). The verifier computation is dominated by 6 pairings.

4 New Same-Message Argument

In a *same-message argument*, the prover aims to convince the verifier that he knows, given two commitment keys ck and $\widehat{ck}$ (that correspond to two tuples of polynomials $(P_i(X))^n_{i=0}$ and $(\hat{P}_i(X))^n_{i=0}$, respectively), how to open $(A_1, A^\gamma_2) = $ com(ck; $\boldsymbol{m}; r$) and $(\hat{A}_1, \hat{A}^\gamma_2) = $ com($\widehat{ck}; \boldsymbol{m}; \hat{r}$) as commitments (w.r.t. ck and $\widehat{ck}$) to the same plaintext vector $\boldsymbol{m}$ (but not necessarily to the same randomizer r).

We propose an efficient same-message argument using $\mathcal{F}_{com} = (Z(X), (y_i(X))^n_{i=1})$ as described in Sect. 3. In the shuffle argument, we need $(\hat{P}_i(X))^n_{i=0}$ to satisfy some specific requirements w.r.t. $\mathcal{F}_{com}$, see Sect. 5. We are free to choose $\hat{P}_i$ otherwise. We concentrate on a choice of $\hat{P}_i$ that satisfies those requirements yet enables us to construct an efficient same-message argument.

Denote $\hat{Z}(X) = \hat{P}_0(X)$. For the same-message argument to be an argument of knowledge *and* efficient, we choose $\hat{P}_i$ such that $(\hat{P}_i(\omega_j))^{n+1}_{j=1} = (y_i(\omega_j))^{n+1}_{j=1} = 2e_i + e_{n+1}$ for $i \in [1..n]$. Moreover, $(\hat{Z}(\omega_j))^{n+1}_{j=1} = (Z(\omega_j))^{n+1}_{j=1} = \boldsymbol{0}_{n+1}$.

Following similar methodology as in Sect. 3, define

$$Q_{wi}(X) := (\hat{r}\hat{Z}(X) + \textstyle\sum^n_{i=1} \hat{m}_i \hat{P}_i(X)) - (rZ(X) + \textstyle\sum^n_{i=1} m_i y_i(X)) \ .$$

Let $\hat{n}$ be the maximum degree of polynomials in $(y_i(X), \hat{P}_i(X))^n_{i=0}$, thus $\deg Q_{wi} \leq \hat{n}$. Since $Q_{wi}(\omega_j) = 2(\hat{m}_j - m_j)$ for $j \in [1..n]$, $Q_{wi}(\omega_j) = 0$ iff $m_j = \hat{m}_j$. Moreover, if $\boldsymbol{m} = \hat{\boldsymbol{m}}$ then $Q_{wi}(\omega_{n+1}) = \sum^n_{i=1} \hat{m}_i - \sum^n_{i=1} m_i = 0$. Hence, $\boldsymbol{m} = \hat{\boldsymbol{m}}$ iff

(i) $Q_{wi}(X) = \hat{A}(X) - A(X)$, where $A(X) \in$ span($\{Z(X)\} \cup \{y_i(X)\}^n_{i=1}$), and $\hat{A}(X) \in$ span($\{\hat{Z}(X)\} \cup \{\hat{P}_i(X)\}^n_{i=1}$), and
(ii) there exists a degree $\leq \hat{n} - (n+1)$ polynomial $\pi_{wi}(X) = Q_{wi}(X)/Z(X)$.

If the prover is honest, then $\pi_{wi}(X) = \hat{r}\hat{Z}(X)/Z(X) - r + \sum m_i \cdot ((\hat{P}_i(X) - y_i(X))/Z(X))$. Note that we do not need that $Q_{wi}(X) = 0$ as a polynomial, we just need that $Q_{wi}(\omega_i) = 0$, which is a deviation from the strategy usually used in QAP/QSP-based arguments [11].

We guarantee the conditions similarly to Sect. 3. The description of the argument follows. (Since it is derived as in Sect. 3, we omit further explanations.)

System parameters: Let $n = \text{poly}(\kappa)$. Let com be the polynomial commitment scheme and let $\mathcal{F}_{com} = (Z(X), (y_i)^n_{i=1})$ and $\hat{\mathcal{F}}_{com} = (\hat{Z}(X), (\hat{P}_i)^n_{i=1})$, where $\hat{P}_i(X)$ is such that $y_i(\omega_j) = \hat{P}_i(\omega_j)$ for $i \in [0..n+1]$ and $j \in [1..n+1]$.

Setup $\mathsf{setup}_{sm}(1^\kappa, n)$: Let $\mathsf{gk} \leftarrow \mathsf{BP}(1^\kappa, n)$.

CRS generation $\mathsf{gencrs}_{sm}(\mathsf{gk})$: Let $(g_1, g_2, \chi, \beta, \gamma, \hat{\gamma}) \leftarrow_r \mathbb{G}_1^* \times \mathbb{G}_2^* \times \mathbb{Z}_p^4$
with $Z(\chi) \neq 0$. Set $\mathsf{ck} \leftarrow (g_1, g_2^\gamma)^{\mathcal{F}_{com}(\chi)}$ and $\widehat{\mathsf{ck}} \leftarrow (g_1, g_2^{\hat{\gamma}})^{\hat{\mathcal{F}}_{com}(\chi)}$.
Let $\mathsf{crs}_{sm,p} \leftarrow (\mathsf{ck}, \widehat{\mathsf{ck}}, g_1^{\beta \cdot \mathcal{F}_{com}(\chi)}, g_1^{\hat{Z}(\chi)/Z(\chi)}, g_1, (g_1^{(\hat{P}_i(\chi) - y_i(\chi))/Z(\chi)})_{i=1}^n)$, and
$\mathsf{crs}_{sm,v} \leftarrow (g_1, g_2^\gamma, g_2^{\hat{\gamma}}, g_2^{\gamma\beta}, g_2^{\gamma Z(\chi)})$. Return $\mathsf{crs}_{sm} = (\mathsf{crs}_{sm,p}, \mathsf{crs}_{sm,v})$.

Common input: $(A_1, A_2^\gamma) = \mathsf{com}(\mathsf{ck}; \boldsymbol{m}; r)$, $(\hat{A}_1, \hat{A}_2^{\hat{\gamma}}) = \mathsf{com}(\widehat{\mathsf{ck}}; \boldsymbol{m}; \hat{r})$.

Argument generation $\mathsf{pro}_{sm}(\mathsf{gk}, \mathsf{crs}_{sm,p}; A_1, A_2^\gamma, \hat{A}_1, \hat{A}_2^{\hat{\gamma}}; \boldsymbol{m}, r, \hat{r})$: Set $\pi_{sm}^* \leftarrow$
$g_1^{\pi_{wi}(\chi)} = (g_1^{\hat{Z}(\chi)/Z(\chi)})^{\hat{r}} \cdot g_1^{-r} \cdot \prod_{i=1}^n (g_1^{(\hat{P}_i(\chi) - y_i(\chi))/Z(\chi)})^{m_i}$. Set $A_1^\beta \leftarrow$
$(g_1^{\beta Z(\chi)})^r \prod_{i=1}^n (g_1^{\beta y_i(\chi)})^{m_i}$. Output $\pi_{sm} = (\pi_{sm}^*, A_1^\beta) \in \mathbb{G}_1^2$.

Verification $\mathsf{ver}_{sm}(\mathsf{gk}, \mathsf{crs}_{sm,v}; (A_1, A_2^\gamma), (\hat{A}_1, \hat{A}_2^{\hat{\gamma}}); \pi_{sm})$:
Parse π_{sm} as $\pi_{sm} = (\pi_{sm}^*, A_1^\beta)$. Verify that (1) $\hat{e}(g_1, A_2^\gamma) = \hat{e}(A_1, g_2^\gamma)$, (2)
$\hat{e}(A_1, g_2^{\gamma\beta}) = \hat{e}(A_1^\beta, g_2^\gamma)$, (3) $\hat{e}(g_1, \hat{A}_2^{\hat{\gamma}}) = \hat{e}(\hat{A}_1, g_2^{\hat{\gamma}})$, and (4) $\hat{e}(\pi_{sm}^*, g_2^{\gamma Z(\chi)}) = \hat{e}(\hat{A}_1/A_1, g_2^\gamma)$.

Let $\hat{Y}$ be the formal variable corresponding to $\hat{\gamma}$. In the following theorem, it suffices to take $\mathsf{crs}^* = (g_1^{\mathcal{F}_{sm,1}(\chi, \beta)}, g_2^{\mathcal{F}_{sm,2}(\chi, \beta, \gamma, \hat{\gamma})})$, where $\mathcal{F}_{sm,1} = \{1\} \cup \mathcal{F}_{com} \cup \hat{\mathcal{F}}_{com} \cup X_\beta \mathcal{F}_{com} \cup \{\hat{Z}(X)/Z(X)\} \cup \{(\hat{P}_i(X) - y_i(X))/Z(X)\}_{i=1}^n$ and $\mathcal{F}_{sm,2} = Y \cdot (\{1, X_\beta\} \cup \mathcal{F}_{com}) \cup \hat{Y} \cdot (\{1\} \cup \hat{\mathcal{F}}_{com})$.

Theorem 3. *The same-message argument is perfectly complete and witness-indistinguishable. Let $\hat{n}$ be as above. If BP is $(\hat{n}, \hat{n} + n + 2)$-PCDH secure, $\hat{n}$-TSDH secure, $(n+1, \mathcal{F}_{sm,1} \setminus (\{1\} \cup \mathcal{F}_{com}), \mathcal{F}_{sm,2} \setminus Y \cdot (\{1\} \cup \mathcal{F}_{com}), \gamma)$-PKE secure, and $(\hat{\mathcal{F}}_{com}, \mathcal{F}_{sm,1} \setminus \hat{\mathcal{F}}_{com}, \mathcal{F}_{sm,2} \setminus \hat{Y}\hat{\mathcal{F}}_{com}, \hat{\gamma})$-PKE secure, then this argument is an adaptive argument of knowledge.*

Proposition 2. *The prover's computation is dominated by one $(W + 2)$-wide and one $(W + 1)$-wide multi-exponentiation in $\mathbb{G}_1$, where $0 \leq W \leq n$ is the number of elements in the vector $\boldsymbol{m}$ that are not in $\{0, 1\}$. The verifier's computation is dominated by 8 pairings.*

In the shuffle argument below, the prover uses $r = \hat{r}$, so prover's computation is $2W + 2$ exponentiations. For a unit vector $\boldsymbol{m}$, we additionally have $W = 0$ and computing A_1^β and the first two verification steps are already done in the unit vector argument anyway, so the argument only adds 1 exponentiation for the prover, and 4 pairings for the verifier.

5 New Assumption: PSP

We will next describe a new computational assumption (PSP) that is needed in the shuffle argument. The PSP assumption is related to but not equal to the SP assumption from [15]. Interestingly, the generic group proof of the PSP assumption relies on the Schwartz-Zippel lemma, while in most of the known interactive shuffle arguments (like [20]), the Schwartz-Zippel lemma is used in the reduction from the shuffle security to some underlying assumption.

Let $d(n) > n$ be a function. Let $\hat{\mathcal{F}} = (\hat{P}_i(X))_{i=0}^n$ be a tuple of polynomials. We say $(d(n), \hat{\mathcal{F}})$ is *PSP-friendly*, if the following set is linearly independent: $\hat{\mathcal{F}}_{d(n)} := \{X^i\}_{i=0}^{2d(n)} \cup \{X^i \cdot \hat{P}_j(X)\}_{0 \le i \le d(n), 0 \le j \le n} \cup \{\hat{P}_0(X)\hat{P}_j(X)\}_{j=0}^n$.

Let $(d(n), \hat{\mathcal{F}})$ be PSP-friendly. Let $\mathcal{F} = (P_i(X))_{i=0}^n$ be a tuple of polynomials of degree $\le d(n)$. The $(\mathcal{F}, \hat{\mathcal{F}})$-*Power Simultaneous Product (PSP) assumption* states that for any $n = \operatorname{poly}(\kappa)$ and any NUPPT adversary A,

$$\Pr\left[\begin{array}{l} \mathsf{gk} \leftarrow \mathsf{BP}(1^\kappa, n), (g_1, g_2, \chi) \leftarrow_r \mathbb{G}_1^* \times \mathbb{G}_2^* \times \mathbb{Z}_p, \\ \mathbb{G}_1^{n+2} \ni (t, \hat{t}, (s_i)_{i=1}^n) \leftarrow \mathsf{A}(\mathsf{gk}; ((g_1, g_2)^{\chi^i})_{i=0}^{d(n)}, (g_1, g_2)^{\hat{\mathcal{F}}(\chi)}) : \\ t^{P_0(\chi)} \cdot \prod_{i=1}^n s_i^{P_i(\chi)} = \hat{t}^{\hat{P}_0(\chi)} \cdot \prod_{i=1}^n s_i^{\hat{P}_i(\chi)} = 1 \wedge (\exists i \in [1 .. n] : s_i \ne 1) \end{array}\right] \approx_\kappa 0 .$$

In this section, we prove that the PSP assumption holds in the generic bilinear group model. PSP-friendliness and the PSP assumption are defined so that both the generic model proof and the reduction from the shuffle soundness to the PSP in Theorem 5 would go through. As in the case of SP, it is essential that two simultaneous products have to hold true; the simpler version of the PSP assumption with only one product (i.e., $t^{P_0(\chi)} \cdot \prod_{i=1}^n s_i^{P_i(\chi)} = 1$) does not hold in the generic bilinear group model. Differently from SP, the PSP assumption incorporates possibly distinct t and $\hat{t}$ since the same-message argument does not guarantee that the randomizers of two commitments are equal.

Generic Security of the PSP Assumption. We will briefly discuss the security of the PSP assumption in the generic bilinear group model. Similarly to [15], we start by picking a random asymmetric bilinear group $\mathsf{gk} := (p, \mathbb{G}_1, \mathbb{G}_2, \mathbb{G}_T, \hat{e}) \leftarrow \mathsf{BP}(1^\kappa)$. We now give a generic bilinear group model proof for the PSP assumption.

Theorem 4. *Let $\mathcal{F} = (P_i(X))_{i=0}^n$ be linearly independent with $1 \notin \operatorname{span}(\mathcal{F})$. Let $d = \max\{\deg P_i(X)\}$ and let $\hat{\mathcal{F}} = (\hat{P}_i(X))_{i=0}^n$ be such that $(d, \hat{\mathcal{F}})$ is PSP-friendly. The $(\mathcal{F}, \hat{\mathcal{F}})$-PSP assumption holds in the generic bilinear group model.*

Proof. Assume there exists a successful adversary A. In the generic bilinear group model, A acts obliviously to the actual representation of the group elements and only performs generic bilinear group operations such as multiplying elements in $\mathbb{G}_i$ for $i \in \{1, 2, T\}$, pairing elements in $\mathbb{G}_1$ and $\mathbb{G}_2$, and comparing elements to see if they are identical. Hence it can only produce new elements in $\mathbb{G}_1$ by multiplying existing group elements together.

Recall that the A's input is gk and $\mathsf{crs} = (((g_1, g_2)^{\chi^i})_{i=0}^d, (g_1, g_2)^{\hat{\mathcal{F}}(\chi)})$. Hence, keeping track of the group elements we get that A outputs $t, \hat{t}, s_i \in \mathbb{G}_1$, where $\log_{g_1} t = \sum_{j=0}^d t_j \chi^j + \sum_{j=0}^n t'_j \hat{P}_j(\chi)$, $\log_{g_1} \hat{t} = \sum_{j=0}^d \hat{t}_j \chi^j + \sum_{j=0}^n \hat{t}'_j \hat{P}_j(\chi)$, and $\log_{g_1} s_i = \sum_{j=0}^d s_{ij} \chi^j + \sum_{j=0}^n s'_{ij} \hat{P}_j(\chi)$, for *known* constants $t_j, t'_j, \hat{t}_j, \hat{t}'_j, s_{ij}, s'_{ij}$. Taking discrete logarithms of the PSP condition $t^{P_0(\chi)} \cdot \prod_{i=1}^n s_i^{P_i(\chi)} =$

$\hat{t}^{\hat{P}_0(x)} \cdot \prod_{i=1}^n s_i^{\hat{P}_i(x)} = 1$, we get that the two polynomials (for *known* coefficients) $d_1(X) := (\sum_{j=0}^d t_j X^j + \sum_{j=0}^n t'_j \hat{P}_j(X)) \cdot P_0(X) + \sum_{i=1}^n (\sum_{j=0}^d s_{ij} X^j + \sum_{j=0}^n s'_{ij} \hat{P}_j(X)) P_i(X)$, $d_2(X) := (\sum_{j=0}^d \hat{t}_j X^j + \sum_{j=0}^n \hat{t}'_j \hat{P}_j(X)) \cdot \hat{P}_0(X) + \sum_{i=1}^n (\sum_{j=0}^d s_{ij} X^j + \sum_{j=0}^n s'_{ij} \hat{P}_j(X)) \hat{P}_i(X)$ satisfy $d_1(\chi) = d_2(\chi) = 0$. Since the adversary is oblivious to the actual representation of the group elements it will do the same group operations no matter the actual value of $X(=\chi)$; so the values $t_j, \ldots, s'_{ij}$ are generated (almost[2]) independently of χ. By the Schwartz-Zippel lemma there is a negligible probability that $d_i(\chi) = 0$, for non-zero $d_i(X)$, when we choose χ randomly. Thus, with all but a negligible probability $d_1(X)$ and $d_2(X)$ are zero polynomials.

Since $\mathcal{F}$ and $\{X^i\}_{i=0}^{2d} \cup \{X^i \cdot \hat{P}_j(X)\}_{i \in [0 .. d], j \in [0 .. n]}$ are both linearly independent, $\{X^i\}_{i=0}^{2d} \cup \{P_i(X)\hat{P}_j(X)\}_{i,j \in [0 .. n]}$ is also linearly independent. We get from $d_1(X) = 0$ that $\sum_{j=0}^n t'_j P_0(X) \hat{P}_j(X) + \sum_{i=1}^n \sum_{j=0}^n s'_{ij} P_i(X) \hat{P}_j(X) = 0$, which implies $s'_{ij} = 0$ for $i \in [1 .. n], j \in [0 .. n]$. Substituting these values into $d_2(X) = 0$, we get that $\left(\sum_{j=0}^d \hat{t}_j X^j + \sum_{j=0}^n \hat{t}'_j \hat{P}_j(X) \right) \hat{P}_0(X) + \sum_{i=1}^n \sum_{j=0}^d s_{ij} X^j \hat{P}_i(X) = 0$. Since $\hat{\mathcal{F}}_d$ is linearly independent, we get that all coefficients in the above equation are zero, and in particular $s_{ij} = 0$ for $i \in [1 .. n], j \in [0 .. n]$. Thus $s_i = 1$ for $i \in [1 .. n]$. Contradiction to the fact that the adversary is successful.   □

6   New Shuffle Argument

Let Elgamal operate in $\mathbb{G}_1$ defined by gk. In a shuffle argument, the prover aims to convince the verifier that, given the description of a group, a public key, and two vectors of ciphertexts, the second vector of the ciphertexts is a permutation of rerandomized versions of the ciphertexts from the first vector. However, to achieve better efficiency, we construct a shuffle argument that is only culpably sound with respect to the next relation (i.e., $\mathcal{R}_{sh}^{\text{guilt}}$-sound:

$$\mathcal{R}_{sh,n}^{\text{guilt}} = \left\{ \begin{array}{l} (\text{gk}, (\text{pk}, (z_i)_{i=1}^n, (z'_i)_{i=1}^n), \text{sk}) : \text{gk} \in \text{BP}(1^\kappa, n) \wedge \\ (\text{pk}, \text{sk}) \in \text{genpkc}(\text{gk}) \wedge \left(\forall \psi \in S_n : \exists i : \text{dec}_{\text{sk}}(z'_i) \neq \text{dec}_{\text{sk}}(z_{\psi(i)}) \right) \end{array} \right\} .$$

The argument of [15] is proven to be $\mathcal{R}_{sh}^{\text{guilt}}$-sound with respect to the same relation. See [15] or the introduction for an explanation why $\mathcal{R}_{sh}^{\text{guilt}}$ is sufficient.

As noted in the introduction, we need to use same-message arguments and rely on the PSP assumption. Thus, we need polynomials $\hat{P}_j$ that satisfy two different requirements at once. First, to be able to use the same-message argument, we need that $y_j(\omega_k) = \hat{P}_j(\omega_k)$ for $k \in [1 .. n + 1]$. Second, to be able to use the PSP assumption, we need $(d, \hat{\mathcal{F}})$ to be PSP-friendly, and for this we need $\hat{P}_j(X)$ to have a sufficiently large degree. Recall that y_j are fixed by the unit vector argument. We now show that such a choice for $\hat{P}_j$ exists.

---

[2] A generic bilinear group adversary may learn a negligible amount of information about χ by comparing group elements; we skip this part in the proof.

Proposition 3. *Let* $\hat{y}_j(X) := (XZ(X) + 1)^{j-1}(X^2Z(X) + 1)y_j(X)$ *for* $j \in [1..n]$, *and* $\hat{Z}(X) = \hat{y}_0(X) := (XZ(X) + 1)^{n+1}Z(X)$. *Let* $\hat{\mathcal{F}}_{\mathsf{com}} = (\hat{y}_j(X))_{j=0}^n$. *Then* $\hat{y}_j(\omega_k) = y_j(\omega_k)$ *for all* j, k, *and* $(n+1, \hat{\mathcal{F}}_{\mathsf{com}})$ *is PSP-friendly.*

Next, we will provide the full description of the new shuffle argument. Note that $(c_i)_{i=1}^n$ are commitments to the rows of the permutation matrix $\boldsymbol{\Psi}$, proven by the n unit vector arguments $(\pi_{uv,i})_{i=1}^n$ and by the implicit computation of c_n. We denote $\hat{E}((a,b), c) := (\hat{e}(a,c), \hat{e}(b,c))$.

System parameters: Let $(\mathsf{genpkc}, \mathsf{enc}, \mathsf{dec})$ be the Elgamal cryptosystem. Let com be the polynomial commitment scheme. Consider polynomials $\mathcal{F}_{\mathsf{com}} = \{Z(X)\} \cup (y_i(X))_{i=1}^n$ from Sect. 3. Let $\hat{\mathcal{F}}_{\mathsf{com}} = (\hat{y}_i(X))_{i=0}^n$ be as in Proposition 3.

Setup $\mathsf{setup}_{sh}(1^\kappa, n)$: Let $\mathsf{gk} \leftarrow \mathsf{BP}(1^\kappa, n)$.

CRS generation $\mathsf{gencrs}_{sh}(\mathsf{gk})$: Let $(g_1, g_2, \chi, \beta, \gamma) \leftarrow_r \mathbb{G}_1^* \times \mathbb{G}_2^* \times \mathbb{Z}_p^3$ with $Z(\chi) \neq 0$. Let $(\mathsf{crs}_{uv,p}, \mathsf{crs}_{uv,v}) \leftarrow_r \mathsf{gencrs}_{uv}(\mathsf{gk}, n)$, $(\mathsf{crs}_{sm,p}, \mathsf{crs}_{sm,v}) \leftarrow_r \mathsf{gencrs}_{sm}(\mathsf{gk}, n)$, but by using the same $(g_1, g_2, \chi, \beta, \gamma)$ in both cases. Let $\mathsf{ck} \leftarrow (g_1, g_2^\gamma)^{\mathcal{F}_{\mathsf{com}}(\chi)}$ and $\widehat{\mathsf{ck}} \leftarrow (g_1, g_2^{\hat\gamma})^{\hat{\mathcal{F}}_{\mathsf{com}}(\chi)}$. Set $(D_1, D_2^\gamma) \leftarrow \mathsf{com}(\mathsf{ck}; \mathbf{1}_n; 0)$, $(\hat{D}_1, \hat{D}_2^{\hat\gamma}) \leftarrow \mathsf{com}(\widehat{\mathsf{ck}}; \mathbf{1}_n; 0)$. Set $\mathsf{crs}_{sh,p} \leftarrow (\mathsf{crs}_{uv,p}, \widehat{\mathsf{ck}}, g_1^{\hat{Z}(\chi)/Z(\chi)}, g_1, (g_1^{(\hat{y}_i(\chi) - y_i(\chi))/Z(\chi)})_{i=1}^n, D_1, D_2^\gamma, \hat{D}_1, \hat{D}_2^{\hat\gamma})$, $\mathsf{crs}_{sh,v} \leftarrow (\mathsf{crs}_{uv,v}, g_2^{\hat\gamma}, \{g_2^{\gamma y_i(\chi)}, g_2^{\hat\gamma \hat{y}_i(\chi)}\}_{i=0}^n, D_1, D_2^\gamma, \hat{D}_1, \hat{D}_2^{\hat\gamma})$, and $\mathsf{td}_{sh} \leftarrow \chi$. Return $((\mathsf{crs}_{sh,p}, \mathsf{crs}_{sh,v}), \mathsf{td}_{sh})$.

Common input: $(\mathsf{pk}, (z_i, z_i')_{i=1}^n)$, where $\mathsf{pk} = (g_1, h) \in \mathbb{G}_1^2$, $z_i \in \mathbb{G}_1^2$ and $z_i' = z_{\psi(i)} \cdot \mathsf{enc}_{\mathsf{pk}}(1; t_i) \in \mathbb{G}_1^2$.

Argument $\mathsf{pro}_{sh}(\mathsf{gk}, \mathsf{crs}_{sh,p}; \mathsf{pk}, (z_i, z_i')_{i=1}^n; \psi, (t_i)_{i=1}^n)$:

(1) Let $\boldsymbol{\Psi} = \boldsymbol{\Psi}_{\psi^{-1}}$ be the $n \times n$ permutation matrix corresponding to ψ^{-1}.

(2) For $i \in [1..n-1]$:
   Set $r_i \leftarrow \mathbb{Z}_p$, $(c_{i1}, c_{i2}^\gamma) \leftarrow \mathsf{com}(\mathsf{ck}; \boldsymbol{\Psi}_i; r_i)$, $(\hat{c}_{i1}, \hat{c}_{i2}^{\hat\gamma}) \leftarrow \mathsf{com}(\widehat{\mathsf{ck}}; \boldsymbol{\Psi}_i; r_i)$.

(3) Set $r_n \leftarrow -\sum_{i=1}^{n-1} r_i$, $(c_{n1}, c_{n2}^\gamma) \leftarrow (D_1, D_2^\gamma)/\prod_{i=1}^{n-1}(c_{i1}, c_{i2}^\gamma)$.

(4) Set $(\hat{c}_{n1}, \hat{c}_{n2}^{\hat\gamma}) \leftarrow (\hat{D}_1, \hat{D}_2^{\hat\gamma})/\prod_{i=1}^{n-1}(\hat{c}_{i1}, \hat{c}_{i2}^{\hat\gamma})$.

(5) For $i \in [1..n]$: set $\pi_{uv,i} = (\pi_{uv,i}^*, c_{i1}^\beta) \leftarrow \mathsf{pro}_{uv}(\mathsf{gk}, \mathsf{crs}_{uv,p}; c_{i1}, c_{i2}^\gamma; \boldsymbol{\Psi}_i, r_i)$.

(6) Set $r_t \leftarrow_r \mathbb{Z}_p$, $(d_1, d_2^\gamma) \leftarrow \mathsf{com}(\mathsf{ck}; \boldsymbol{t}; r_t)$, and $(\hat{d}_1, \hat{d}_2^{\hat\gamma}) \leftarrow \mathsf{com}(\widehat{\mathsf{ck}}; \boldsymbol{t}; r_t)$.

(7) For $i \in [1..n-1]$:
   Set $(\pi_{sm,i}^*, c_{i1}^\beta) \leftarrow \mathsf{pro}_{sm}(\mathsf{gk}, \mathsf{crs}_{sm,p}; c_{i1}, c_{i2}^\gamma, \hat{c}_{i1}, \hat{c}_{i2}^{\hat\gamma}; \boldsymbol{\Psi}_i, r_i, r_i)$.

(8) Set $\pi_{sm,d} \leftarrow \mathsf{pro}_{sm}(\mathsf{gk}, \mathsf{crs}_{sm,p}; d_1, d_2^\gamma, \hat{d}_1, \hat{d}_2^{\hat\gamma}; \boldsymbol{t}, r_t, r_t)$.

(9) Compute $U = (U_1, U_2) \leftarrow \mathsf{pk}^{r_t} \cdot \prod_{i=1}^n z_i^{r_i} \in \mathbb{G}_1^2$. // The only online step

(10) Output $\pi_{sh} \leftarrow ((c_{i1}, c_{i2}^\gamma, \hat{c}_{i1}, \hat{c}_{i2}^{\hat\gamma})_{i=1}^{n-1}, d_1, d_2^\gamma, \hat{d}_1, \hat{d}_2^{\hat\gamma}, (\pi_{uv,i})_{i=1}^n, (\pi_{sm,i}^*)_{i=1}^{n-1}, \pi_{sm,d}, U)$

Verification $\mathsf{ver}_{sh}(\mathsf{gk}, \mathsf{crs}_{sh,v}; \mathsf{pk}, (z_i, z_i')_{i=1}^n, \pi_{sh})$:

(1) Let $(c_{n1}, c_{n2}^\gamma) \leftarrow (D_1, D_2^\gamma)/\prod_{i=1}^{n-1}(c_{i1}, c_{i2}^\gamma)$.

(2) Let $(\hat{c}_{n1}, \hat{c}_{n2}^{\hat\gamma}) \leftarrow (\hat{D}_1, \hat{D}_2^{\hat\gamma})/\prod_{i=1}^{n-1}(\hat{c}_{i1}, \hat{c}_{i2}^{\hat\gamma})$.

(3) For $i \in [1..n]$: reject if $\mathsf{ver}_{uv}(\mathsf{gk}, \mathsf{crs}_{uv,v}; c_{i1}, c_{i2}^\gamma; \pi_{uv,i})$ rejects.

(4) For $i \in [1..n-1]$: reject if $\mathsf{ver}_{sm}(\mathsf{gk}; \mathsf{crs}_{sm,v}; c_{i1}, c_{i2}^\gamma, \hat{c}_{i1}, \hat{c}_{i2}^{\hat\gamma}; \pi_{sm,i})$ rejects.

(5) Reject if $\mathsf{ver}_{sm}(\mathsf{gk}, \mathsf{crs}_{sm,v}; d_1, d_2^\gamma, \hat{d}_1, \hat{d}_2^{\hat\gamma}; \pi_{sm,d})$ rejects.

(6) Check the PSP-related verification equations: // The only online step

  (a) $\prod_{i=1}^n \hat{E}(z_i', g_2^{\gamma y_i(\chi)}) / \prod_{i=1}^n \hat{E}(z_i, c_{i2}^\gamma) = \hat{E}((g_1, h), d_2^\gamma)/\hat{E}(U, g_2^{\gamma Z(\chi)})$,

  (b) $\prod_{i=1}^n \hat{E}(z_i', g_2^{\hat\gamma \hat{y}_i(\chi)}) / \prod_{i=1}^n \hat{E}(z_i, \hat{c}_{i2}^{\hat\gamma}) = \hat{E}((g_1, h), \hat{d}_2^{\hat\gamma})/\hat{E}(U, g_2^{\hat\gamma \hat{Z}(\chi)})$.

Since $\mathsf{ck}, \widehat{\mathsf{ck}} \subset \mathsf{crs}_{sh,p}$, $(D_1, D_2^\gamma) = \mathsf{com}(\mathsf{ck}; \mathbf{1}_n; 0)$ and $(\hat{D}_1, \hat{D}_2^{\hat\gamma}) = \mathsf{com}(\widehat{\mathsf{ck}}; \mathbf{1}_n; 0)$ can be computed from the rest of the CRS. (These four elements are only needed to optimize the computation of (c_{n1}, c_{n2}^γ) and $(\hat{c}_{n1}, \hat{c}_{n2}^{\hat\gamma})$.) For security, it suffices to take $\mathsf{crs}_{sh}^* = (g_1^{\mathcal{F}_{sh,1}(\chi,\beta)}, g_2^{\mathcal{F}_{sh,2}(\chi,\beta,\gamma,\hat\gamma)})$, where $\mathcal{F}_{sh,1} = \mathcal{F}_{uv,1} \cup \hat{\mathcal{F}}_{\mathsf{com}} \cup \{\hat{Z}(X)/Z(X)\} \cup \{(\hat{y}_i(X) - y_i(X))/Z(X)\}_{i=1}^n$ and $\mathcal{F}_{sh,2} = \mathcal{F}_{uv,2} \cup \hat{Y} \cdot (\{1\} \cup \hat{\mathcal{F}}_{\mathsf{com}})$.

Theorem 5. *The new shuffle argument is a non-interactive perfectly complete and perfectly zero-knowledge shuffle argument for Elgamal ciphertexts. If the $(n+1)$-TSDH, $(\hat{n}, \hat{n}+n+2)$-PCDH, $(\mathcal{F}_{\mathsf{com}}, \hat{\mathcal{F}}_{\mathsf{com}})$-PSP, $(n+1, \mathcal{F}_{sh,1} \setminus (\{1\} \cup \mathcal{F}_{\mathsf{com}}), \mathcal{F}_{sh,2} \setminus Y \cdot (\{1\} \cup \mathcal{F}_{\mathsf{com}}), \gamma)$-PKE, $(\hat{\mathcal{F}}_{\mathsf{com}}, \mathcal{F}_{sh,1} \setminus \hat{\mathcal{F}}_{\mathsf{com}}, \mathcal{F}_{sh,2} \setminus \hat{Y} \hat{\mathcal{F}}_{\mathsf{com}}, \hat\gamma)$-PKE assumptions hold, then the shuffle argument is adaptively computationally culpably sound w.r.t. the language $\mathcal{R}_{sh,n}^{\mathrm{guilt}}$ and an argument of knowledge.*

When using a Barreto-Naehrig curve, exponentiations in $\mathbb{G}_1$ are three times cheaper than in $\mathbb{G}_2$. Moreover, a single $(N+1)$-wide multi-exponentiations is considerably cheaper than $N+1$ exponentiations. Hence, we compute separately the number of exponentiations and multi-exponentiations in both $\mathbb{G}_1$ and $\mathbb{G}_2$. For the sake of the simplicity, Proposition 4 only summarizes those numbers.

Proposition 4. *The prover's CRS consists of $6n + 7$ elements of $\mathbb{G}_1$ and $2n + 4$ elements of $\mathbb{G}_2$. The verifier's CRS consists of 4 elements of $\mathbb{G}_1$, $2n + 8$ elements of $\mathbb{G}_2$, and 1 element of $\mathbb{G}_T$. The total CRS is $6n + 8$ elements of $\mathbb{G}_1$, $2n + 8$ elements of $\mathbb{G}_2$, and 1 element of $\mathbb{G}_T$, in total $8n + 17$ group elements. The communication complexity is $5n + 2$ elements of $\mathbb{G}_1$ and $2n$ elements of $\mathbb{G}_2$, in total $7n + 2$ group elements. The prover's and the verifier's computational complexity are as in Table 1.*

Importantly, both the proving and verification algorithm of the new shuffle argument can be divided into offline (independent of the common input $(\mathsf{pk}, (z_i, z_i')_{i=1}^n)$) and online (dependent on the common input) parts. The prover can precompute all elements of π_{sh} except U (i.e., execute all steps of the proving algorithm, except step (9)), and send them to the verifier before the inputs are fixed. The verifier can verify $\pi_{sh} \setminus \{U\}$ (i.e., execute all steps of the verification algorithm, except step (6)) in the precomputation step. Thus, the online computational complexity is dominated by two $(n+1)$-wide multi-exponentiations for the prover, and $8n + 4$ pairings for the verifier (note that $\hat{E}((g_1, h), d_2^\gamma)$ and $\hat{E}((g_1, h), \hat{d}_2^{\hat\gamma})$ can also be precomputed by the verifier).

Low online complexity is highly important in e-voting, where the online time (i.e., the time interval after the ballots are gathered and before the election results are announced) can be limited for legal reasons. In this case, the mix servers can execute all but step (9) of the proving algorithm and step (6) of the verification algorithm before the votes are even cast, assuming one is able to set a priori a reasonable upper bound on n, the number of votes. See [24] for additional motivation.

Acknowledgments. The authors were supported by the European Union's Horizon 2020 research and innovation programme under grant agreement No 653497 (project PANORAMIX), and the Estonian Research Council.

References

1. Abe, M., Fehr, S.: Perfect NIZK with adaptive soundness. In: Vadhan, S.P. (ed.) TCC 2007. LNCS, vol. 4392, pp. 118–136. Springer, Heidelberg (2007)
2. Blum, M., Feldman, P., Micali, S.: Non-interactive zero-knowledge and its applications. In: STOC 1998, pp. 103–112 (1988)
3. Boneh, D., Boyen, X.: Secure identity based encryption without random oracles. In: Franklin, M. (ed.) CRYPTO 2004. LNCS, vol. 3152, pp. 443–459. Springer, Heidelberg (2004)
4. Boneh, D., Boyen, X., Shacham, H.: Short group signatures. In: Franklin, M. (ed.) CRYPTO 2004. LNCS, vol. 3152, pp. 41–55. Springer, Heidelberg (2004)
5. Damgård, I.B.: Towards practical public key systems secure against chosen ciphertext attacks. In: Feigenbaum, J. (ed.) CRYPTO 1991. LNCS, vol. 576, pp. 445–456. Springer, Heidelberg (1992)
6. Danezis, G., Fournet, C., Groth, J., Kohlweiss, M.: Square span programs with applications to succinct NIZK arguments. In: Sarkar, P., Iwata, T. (eds.) ASIACRYPT 2014. LNCS, vol. 8873, pp. 532–550. Springer, Heidelberg (2014)
7. Elgamal, T.: A public key cryptosystem and a signature scheme based on discrete logarithms. IEEE Trans. Inf. Theory **31**(4), 469–472 (1985)
8. Fauzi, P., Lipmaa, H.: Efficient culpably sound NIZK shuffle argument without random oracles. Technical report 2015/1112, IACR (2015). http://eprint.iacr.org/2015/1112
9. Furukawa, J.: Efficient and verifiable shuffling and shuffle-decryption. IEICE Trans. **88–A**(1), 172–188 (2005)
10. Furukawa, J., Sako, K.: An efficient scheme for proving a shuffle. In: Kilian, J. (ed.) CRYPTO 2001. LNCS, vol. 2139, pp. 368–387. Springer, Heidelberg (2001)
11. Gennaro, R., Gentry, C., Parno, B., Raykova, M.: Quadratic span programs and succinct NIZKs without PCPs. In: Johansson, T., Nguyen, P.Q. (eds.) EUROCRYPT 2013. LNCS, vol. 7881, pp. 626–645. Springer, Heidelberg (2013)
12. Golle, P., Jarecki, S., Mironov, I.: Cryptographic primitives enforcing communication and storage complexity. In: Blaze, Matt (ed.) FC 2002. LNCS, vol. 2357, pp. 120–135. Springer, Heidelberg (2003)
13. Groth, J.: A verifiable secret shuffle of homomorphic encryptions. J. Cryptology **23**(4), 546–579 (2010)
14. Groth, J.: Short pairing-based non-interactive zero-knowledge arguments. In: Abe, M. (ed.) ASIACRYPT 2010. LNCS, vol. 6477, pp. 321–340. Springer, Heidelberg (2010)
15. Groth, J., Lu, S.: A non-interactive shuffle with pairing based verifiability. In: Kurosawa, K. (ed.) ASIACRYPT 2007. LNCS, vol. 4833, pp. 51–67. Springer, Heidelberg (2007)

16. Groth, J., Ostrovsky, R., Sahai, A.: New techniques for noninteractive zero-knowledge. J. ACM **59**(3), 1–35 (2012). Article No 11
17. Lipmaa, H.: Progression-free sets and sublinear pairing-based non-interactive zero-knowledge arguments. In: Cramer, R. (ed.) TCC 2012. LNCS, vol. 7194, pp. 169–189. Springer, Heidelberg (2012)
18. Lipmaa, H., Zhang, B.: A more efficient computationally sound non-interactive zero-knowledge shuffle argument. In: Visconti, I., De Prisco, R. (eds.) SCN 2012. LNCS, vol. 7485, pp. 477–502. Springer, Heidelberg (2012)
19. Lipmaa, H., Zhang, B.: A more efficient computationally sound non-interactive zero-knowledge shuffle argument. J. Comput. Secur. **21**(5), 685–719 (2013)
20. Neff, C.A.: A verifiable secret shuffle and its application to E-voting. In: ACM CCS 2001, pp. 116–125 (2001)
21. Parno, B., Gentry, C., Howell, J., Raykova, M.: Pinocchio: nearly practical verifiable computation. In: IEEE SP 2013, pp. 238–252 (2013)
22. Sako, K., Kilian, J.: Receipt-free mix-type voting scheme: a practical solution to the implementation of a voting booth. In: Guillou, L.C., Quisquater, J.-J. (eds.) EUROCRYPT 1995. LNCS, vol. 921, pp. 393–403. Springer, Heidelberg (1995)
23. Terelius, B., Wikström, D.: Proofs of restricted shuffles. In: Bernstein, D.J., Lange, T. (eds.) AFRICACRYPT 2010. LNCS, vol. 6055, pp. 100–113. Springer, Heidelberg (2010)
24. Wikström, D.: A commitment-consistent proof of a shuffle. In: Boyd, C., González Nieto, J. (eds.) ACISP 2009. LNCS, vol. 5594, pp. 407–421. Springer, Heidelberg (2009)

Side-Channel Attacks on Elliptic Curve Cryptography

ECDH Key-Extraction via Low-Bandwidth Electromagnetic Attacks on PCs

Daniel Genkin[1,2]([✉]), Lev Pachmanov[2], Itamar Pipman[2], and Eran Tromer[2]

[1] Technion, Haifa, Israel
danielg3@cs.technion.ac.il
[2] Tel Aviv University, Tel Aviv, Israel
{levp,itamarpi,tromer}@tau.ac.il

Abstract. We present the first physical side-channel attack on elliptic curve cryptography running on a PC. The attack targets the ECDH public-key encryption algorithm, as implemented in the latest version of GnuPG. By measuring the target's electromagnetic emanations, the attack extracts the secret decryption key within seconds, from a target located in an adjacent room across a wall. The attack utilizes a single carefully chosen ciphertext, and tailored time-frequency signal analysis techniques, to achieve full key extraction.

Keywords: Side-channel attack · Elliptic curve cryptography · Electromagnetic emanations

1 Introduction

Physical side-channel attacks exploit unintentional information leakage via low-level physical behavior of computing devices, such as electromagnetic radiation, power consumption, electric potential, acoustic emanations and thermal fluctuations. These have been used to break numerous cryptographic implementations; see [7, 28, 29] and the references therein.

Small devices, such as smartcards, RFID tags, FPGAs, microcontrollers, and simple embedded devices, have received much research attention with numerous published side-channel attacks. However, for more complex "PC" class devices (laptops, dekstops, servers etc.), there are few physical side-channel attacks demonstrated on cryptographic implementations: key extraction from RSA using acoustic attacks [24], and key extraction from RSA and ElGamal using the ground-potential and electromagnetic channels [22, 23]. As discussed in those works, attacks on PCs raise new and difficult challenges compared to attacking small devices: hardware and software complexity causing unpredictable behavior and noise; high clock speeds of several GHz; and attack scenarios that force non-invasive attacks and limit signal quality, bandwidth and acquisition time. In particular, the effective measurement bandwidth is much lower than the target CPU's clock rate, making it infeasible to distinguish individual instructions and necessitating new, algorithm-specific cryptanalytic techniques.

© Springer International Publishing Switzerland 2016
K. Sako (Ed.): CT-RSA 2016, LNCS 9610, pp. 219–235, 2016.
DOI: 10.1007/978-3-319-29485-8_13

This leaves open the question of what other cryptographic algorithm implementations on PCs are vulnerable to physical side-channel attacks, and with what range, duration and techniques.

1.1 Our Contribution

In this paper, we preset the first physical side-channel attack on elliptic curve cryptography running on a PC. Moreover, our attack is *non-adaptive*, requiring decryption of a single, non-adaptively chosen ciphertext in order to extract the whole secret key by monitoring the target's electromagnetic (EM) field for just a few seconds.

We empirically demonstrate our technique on the ECDH public-key encryption algorithm used in OpenPGP [13], as specified in RFC 6637 [27] and NIST-SP800-56A [8] and as implemented in Libgcrypt 1.6.3 (which is the latest version at the time of writing this paper). To extract the secret key from the observed electromagnetic leakage, we utilize intricate time-frequency analysis techniques.

We demonstrate the attack's effectiveness by extracting keys from unmodified laptops running GnuPG, using their EM emanations as measured from an adjacent room through a wall (see Fig. 6).

1.2 Attack Overview

The ECDH decryption consists primarily of multiplying the secret key (a scalar) by the curve point. The multiplication contains a sequence of point addition, doubling and inversion, and our approach utilizes the relation between the *operands* of these operations and the scalar. By asking for a decryption of a carefully-chosen ciphertext, we cause a specific curve point to appear as the operand in the elliptic curve additions. This point has a specific structure which causes an easy-to-observe effect on GnuPG's modular multiplication code. During the decryption of the chosen ciphertext, we measure the EM leakage of the target laptop, focusing on a narrow frequency band (frequencies in the range 1.5–2 MHz). After suitable signal processing, a clean trace is produced which reveals information about the operands used in the elliptic curve operations. This information, in turn, is used in order to reveal the secret key.

Our attacks *do not* assume any correlation between the sequence of elliptic curve double and add operations and the secret key. In particular, they work even if the scalar-by-point multiplication is implemented using only point additions.

1.3 Targeted Software and Hardware

Hardware. We target commodity laptop computers. During our experiments, we have tested numerous computes of various models and makes. The experiments described in this paper were conducted using a Lenovo 3000 N200 laptops, which exhibit a particularly clear signal. The attacks are completely non-intrusive: we did not modify the targets or open their chassis.

Software. We focus on Libgcrypt, which is popular cryptographic library that includes elliptic curve cryptography. Libgcrypt is used, in particular, by used in particular, by GnuPG 2.x [2], which is very popular implementation of the OpenPGP standard [13] used in applications such as encrypted mail and files. Concretely, we targeted Libgcrypt 1.6.3 (the latest versions at the time of writing), compiled using the MinGW GCC 4.6.2 [4].

Current Status. We are currently working with the developers of Libgcrypt and GnuPG to evaluate and deploy countermeasures preventing the attacks described in this paper (CVE 2015-7511). A new version of Libgcrypt will be released simultaneously with the publication of this paper.

Chosen Ciphertext Injection. Our attack requires decryption of chosen ciphertexts. Conveniently, GnuPG and Libgcrypt are used by various applications, where they are used to decrypt externally-controlled inputs (the list of GnuPG frontends [3] contains dozens of such applications). One concrete attack vector was observed in [24], where Enigmail [18], a plugin for the Mozilla Thunderbird e-mail client, automatically decrypts incoming emails by passing them to GnuPG. Thus, it is possible to close the attack loop by remotely injecting the chosen ciphertext required by our attack into GnuPG via PGP/MIME-encoded e-mail [17]. Similar observations hold for the GnuPG Outlook plugin, GpgOL.

1.4 Related Work

For small devices, side-channel attacks have been demonstrated, on numerous cryptographic implementations, using various channels, and in particular the EM channel starting with [5,21,35]. See [7,28,29] and the references therein.

Physical Attacks on ECC. Since the first attacks by Coron [16], there have been numerous physical side-channel attacks on implementations of Elliptic Curve Cryptography (ECC) on small devices; see the surveys [19,20] and the references therein. However, such attacks typically target small devices and either utilize subtle physical effects which are only visible at bandwidths exceeding the device's clock rate, or attack naive implementations (such as the double-and-add algorithm). Three notable exceptions to the above approach are the attacks of Okeya and Sakura [30] and Walter [38] attacking the Oswald-Aigner scalar randomization algorithm [33] assuming only the ability to distinguish between point addition and multiplication; the Refined Power Analysis attack of Goubin [26]; and the Zero-Value Point Attacks of Akishita and Takagi [6].

Unfortunately, all of the above approaches have significant drawbacks in the case of GnuPG executed on PCs. Recording clock-rate scale signals (required for most attacks) from a full-fledged PCs computer running a GHz-scale CPU is difficult and requires expensive, cumbersome, and delicate lab equipment. The attacks of Okeya and Sakura [30] and Walter [38] are only applicable to the Oswald-Aigner scalar randomization algorithm [33] (utilizing its non-determinism across various executions), which is not used by GnuPG. Finally, the attacks of Goubin [26] and Akishita and Takagi [6] utilize adaptive chosen ciphertexts, requiring hundreds of ciphertexts in order to extract the secret scalar. Since in order to obtain a noise-free aggregate-trace several traces are required per ciphertext, overall the attacks of [26] and [6] require the execution of several thousands of scalar-by-point multiplication operation, which is easily detectable.

Physical Side-Channel Attacks on PCs. Physical side-channel leakage from PCs have been demonstrated via voltage on USB ports [31] and power consumption [15]. Cryptographically, physical side-channels were exploited for extracting keys from GnuPG's RSA and ElGamal implementations, using the acoustic channel [24], the chassis-potential channel [23] and the electromagnetic channel [22,23] (across several GnuPG versions, including both square-and-always-multiply and windowed exponentiation). On a related class of devices, namely smartphones, Goller and Sigl [25] showed electromagnetic attacks on square-and-sometimes-multiply RSA.

Software Side-Cache Attacks on GnuPG. Software-based side-channel key-extraction attacks on PCs were demonstrated using timing differences [11,12] and contention for various microarchitectural resources, such as caches [10,32,34]. Recently such attacks were shown against GnuPG's implementation of RSA and ElGamal [39,40], as well as elliptic-curve DSA [9,37]. The latter attacks rely on the ability to distinguish between point doubling and point addition via cache access patterns, in order mount a lattice attack on DSA using partially known nonces. However, such types of attacks are not applicable for ECDH.

2 Cryptanalysis

2.1 GnuPG's Elliptic Curve Encryption Implementation

We attack OpenPGP's elliptic-curve public-key encryption scheme, called ECDH encryption, as specified in RFC 6637 [27] and defined as method C(1,1,ECC CDH) in NIST-SP800-56A [8]. In a nutshell, ECDH encryption is essentially Diffie-Hellman key exchange over a suitable elliptic curve, where one party's Diffie-Hellman message serves as that party's public key. The encryption operation runs the other party's part of the key exchange protocol against the public key, yielding a shared key. Decryption recomputes that shared key. Concretely, the ECDH encryption combines an elliptic-curve based Diffie-Hellman key exchange protocol and a symmetric-key cipher (typically AES), as follows. Given an elliptic curve group generator $\mathbb{G}$, key generation consists of generating a random scalar k. The secret key is then defined to be k while the public key is set to be $[k]\mathbb{G}$ (here and onward, we use additive group notation, and $[k]\mathbb{G}$ denotes scalar-by-point multiplication). Encryption of a message m is performed by generating a random scalar k', computing $[k']([k]\mathbb{G})$ and using the result in order to derive (using a key derivation function) a key x for the symmetric encryption algorithm. The message m is then symmetrically-encrypted using x, resulting in a ciphertext c'.

Algorithm 1. GnuPG's scalar-by-point multiplication operation (simplified).

Input: A positive scalar k and an elliptic-curve point $\mathbb{P}$, where $k_{n-1} \cdots k_0$ is the NAF representation of k, that is $k = \sum_{i=0}^{n-1} 2^i \cdot k_i$ and $k_i \in \{-1, 0, 1\}$ for all $i = 0, \cdots, n-1$.

Output: $[k]\mathbb{P}$.

```
 1: procedure POINT_MUL(k, ℙ)
 2:     A ← ℙ
 3:     for i ← n − 1 to 0 do
 4:         A ← [2]A
 5:         if k_i = 1 then
 6:             A ← A + ℙ
 7:         if k_i = −1 then
 8:             ℙ′ ← [−1]ℙ
 9:             A ← A + ℙ′
10:     return A
```

The overall ciphertext is set to be $c = (c', [k']\mathbb{G})$. Decryption of a ciphertext $c = (c', [k']\mathbb{G})$ is done by computing $[k]([k']\mathbb{G})$, applying the key derivation function on the result to obtain a key x' for the symmetric encryption algorithm, and decrypting c' using x', resulting in a message m'. Since $[k]([k']\mathbb{G}) = [k']([k]\mathbb{G})$, we obtain that $x' = x$, resulting in $m' = m$.

Our attack deduces the secret key k from the side-channel leakage during the scalar-by-point multiplication $[k]\mathbb{G}'$ in the decryption.

GnuPG's Scalar-by-Point Multiplication. We now review GnuPG's implementation of the scalar-by-point multiplication operation which is used during the ECDH encryption protocol. In order to perform the elliptic curve group operations as well as the large integer operations, GnuPG uses an internal mathematical library called MPI (based on GMP [1]). For Weierstrass curves, GnuPG performs the scalar-by-point multiplication operation using the standard double-and-add algorithm (Algorithm 1), maintaining the scalar in *non-adjacent form (NAF)* which we now discuss.

Non-Adjacent Form Representation. Introduced by Reitwiesner [36], the non-adjacent form is a common generalization of the standard binary representation of integers, allowing for both positive and negative bits. For example, the 4-digit NAF representation of 7 is $(1, 0, 0, -1)$ compared to its binary representation $(0, 1, 1, 1)$. The main advantage of using a NAF representation is that it minimizes the number of non-zero digits from about $1/2$ for the binary representation to about $1/3$. Since every non-zero digit requires a point addition operation, using a NAF representation minimizes the number of point additions. Thus, most modern representations of elliptic curve cryptography typically represent scalars in using NAF.

We proceed to describe GnuPG's point addition operation, used in lines 6 and 9. Later in Sect. 2.2 we will show how to exploit GnuPG's implementation of point addition in order to achieve key extraction.

Algorithm 2. GnuPG's point addition operation (simplified).

Input: Two points $\mathbb{P}_1 = (x_1, y_1, z_1)$ and $\mathbb{P}_2 = (x_2, y_2, z_2)$ in projective coordinates on an elliptic-curve based group of order p.

Output: A point $\mathbb{P}_3 = (x_3, y_3, z_3)$ in projective coordinates such that $\mathbb{P}_3 = \mathbb{P}_2 + \mathbb{P}_1$.

1: **procedure** POINT_ADD($\mathbb{P}_1, \mathbb{P}_2$)
2:     **if** $z_1 = 0$ **then**
3:         **return** $\mathbb{P}_2$ ▷ $\mathbb{P}_1$ is at infinity
4:     **if** $z_2 = 0$ **then**
5:         **return** $\mathbb{P}_1$ ▷ $\mathbb{P}_2$ is at infinity
6:     $l_1 \leftarrow x_1 z_2^2 \bmod p$
7:     $l_2 \leftarrow x_2 z_1^2 \bmod p$
8:     $l_3 \leftarrow l_1 - l_2 \bmod p$
9:     $l_4 \leftarrow y_1 z_2^3 \bmod p$
10:    $l_5 \leftarrow y_2 z_1^3 \bmod p$
11:    $l_6 \leftarrow l_4 - l_5 \bmod p$
12:    **if** $l_3 = 0$ and $l_6 = 0$ **then**
13:        **return** $(1,1,0)$ ▷ $\mathbb{P}_1$ is the inverse of $\mathbb{P}_2$ thus the result is infinity
14:    $l_7 \leftarrow l_1 + l_2 \bmod p$
15:    $l_8 \leftarrow l_4 + l_5 \bmod p$
16:    $z_3 \leftarrow z_1 z_2 l_3 \bmod p$
17:    $x_3 \leftarrow l_6^2 - l_7 l_3^2 \bmod p$
18:    $l_9 \leftarrow l_7 l_3^2 - 2x_3 \bmod p$
19:    $y_3 \leftarrow (l_9 l_6 - l_8 l_3^3)/2 \bmod p$
20:    **return** (x_3, y_3, z_3)

GnuPG's Point Addition. GnuPG stores elliptic curve points using projective coordinates. Each point is a tuple (x, y, z) where each element is a large integer stored using GnuPG's mathematical library, MPI. Large integers are stored by MPI as arrays of *limbs*, which are 32-bit words (on the x86 architecture used in our tests). Algorithm 2 is a pseudocode of GnuPG's point addition operation. Notice the multiplication by y_2 in line 10. We will now show how this multiplication can be exploited in order to distinguish between -1 and 1 valued NAF digits of k, resulting in a complete key extraction.

2.2 ECDH Attack Algorithm

Let *DA-sequence* denote the sequence of double and add operations performed in lines 4, 6 and 9 of Algorithm 1. Notice that it is possible to deduce all the locations of zero valued NAF digits of k by simply observing the DA sequence performed by Algorithm 1. However, since k is given in a NAF representation, recovering the DA-sequence alone is not enough for achieving key extraction: there remains an ambuguity between -1 and 1 valued NAF digits of k, since point addition is executed in both cases (in addition to point doubling).

Observing Point Inversions. An immediate approach for distinguishing between 1 and -1 valued NAF digits would consist of attempting to observe the point inversion operation performed in line 8. However, for Weierstrass curves, inverting a point $\mathbb{P} = (x, y)$ on an elliptic-curve group of order p, simply requires computing the inverse of y modulo p. This operation is too fast for us to observe in our low-bandwidth setting. Moreover, fact that point inversion is performed at every -1-valued digit of the NAF form of k constitutes a side-channel weakness in GnuPG's point multiplication code, which is unlikely to be present in a more robust implementation. We thus do not utilize this observation for our attack.

We proceed to describe how, by using a chosen ciphertext, an attacker can distinguish between the add operations performed by line 6 and the add operations performed by line 9. This information, together with the DA-sequence is enough to recover the secret scalar k.

Distinguishing Between the NAF Digits of k. Let $\mathbb{Q} = (x, y)$ be a point with small y (containing few limbs) and a random-looking (full-sized) x. Consider performing an ECDH encryption operation of a ciphertext $(c', \mathbb{Q})$ for some c'. Since GnuPG's internal representation uses projective coordinates, the point $\mathbb{Q}$ converted to a $\mathbb{P}$ in a projective representation $\mathbb{P} = (x, y, 1)$ and it is then passed to Algorithm 1. Next, $\mathbb{P}$ is used in lines 6 and 9 thereby affecting the leakage produced by each iteration of the main loop of Algorithm 1 as follows.

1. $k_i = 0$. In this case only a point doubling operation is performed by Algorithm 1. Thus, as mentioned before, these digits are immediately recoverable from the DA-sequence since any double operation which is not followed by an add operation corresponds to a zero valued digit of k.
2. $k_i = 1$. In this case $\mathbb{P}$ is passed as is to the point addition routine (Algorithm 2) as its second argument $\mathbb{P}_2$. Since y is small, the first operand, y_2, of the multiplication in line 10 is only a few limbs long.
3. $k_i = -1$. In this case the point $\mathbb{P}$ is first inverted by line 8. For Weierstrass curves, point inversion corresponds to computing the modular inverses of the y coordinate, so the y coordinate of $\mathbb{P}'$ is random looking. This $\mathbb{P}'$ is passed to the point addition routine (Algorithm 2) as its second argument $\mathbb{P}_2$. This makes the first operand, y_2, of the multiplication in line 10 be random looking and (likely) full length.

By observing the side-channel leakage produced by Algorithm 1, we will be able to recover the DA-sequence, and also distinguish, in each invocation the multiplication in line 10 of Algorithm 2, whether the first operand is short or full length. This information is enough in order to recover the secret scalar k.

2.3 Attacking the Always-Add Algorithm

In this section we generalize the above method for attacking a variant of Algorithm 1 where the point doubling operation is implemented using point addition. That is, we assume that line 4 is replaced by $\mathbb{A} \leftarrow \mathbb{A} + \mathbb{A}$. In particular, in this section, we do not assume that it is possible to immediately distinguish the point additions performed by lines 6 and 9 from the point doublings performed by line 4. As we show, it is possible to utilize two chosen ciphertexts in order to recover the DA-sequence as well as, for every addition operation, whether the corresponding NAF digit is 1 or −1.

Revealing the 1 Digits of k. As in Sect. 2.2, the attacker requests a decryption of a point $\mathbb{P}$ with small y coordinate. As discussed in Sect. 2.2, this creates a distinguishable leakage every time that $k_i = 1$ during the execution of the main loop of Algorithm 1, thereby revealing the locations in the DA-sequence of all such digits.

Revealing the −1 Digits of k. Next, the attacker selects a point $\mathbb{P}$ whose *inverse* has a small y coordinate, and requests an ECDH decryption of $(c, \mathbb{P})$ for some arbitrary value c. During the main loop of Algorithm 1 every time that $k_i = -1$ the inversion of $\mathbb{P}$, denoted by $\mathbb{P}'$, is passed to the point addition routine. Since $\mathbb{P}$ was chosen such that $\mathbb{P}'$ has a small y coordinate, as discussed in Sect. 2.2 this creates a distinguishable leakage every time that $k_i = -1$ during the main loop of Algorithm 1, thereby revealing the locations in the DA-sequence of all such digits.

Key Extraction. At this point the attacker has recovered the locations in the DA-sequence of all point additions as performed by lines 6 and 9 of Algorithm 1. Moreover, for each point addition, the attacker has recovered the corresponding value of k_i. Thus, all remaining operations in the DA-sequence are in fact points doublings. Using this information at hand, the scalar k can be recovered.

3   Signal Analysis and Experimental Results

3.1   Experimental Setup

This section describes the lab setup used for characterizing the EM leakage from target computers at frequencies of 0–5 MHz. We have also constructed a more realistic setup, described in see Sect. 3.3.

Probe. To measure the EM leakage from the target laptop with high spatial precision, we used a Langer LF-R 400 near field probe (a 25 mm loop probe, 0–50 MHz). The location of the probe relative to the laptop body greatly affects the measured signal. In our experiments, the best signal quality was obtained close to the CPU's voltage regulator, which on most laptops is located in the rear left corner. We thus placed the probe at that position, without any chassis intrusion or other modification to the target laptop.

Amplification and Digitization. To amplify the signal measured by the probe we used a (customized) Mini-Circuits ZPUL-30P amplifier, providing 40 dB of gain. The output of the amplifier was then low-pass filtered at 5 MHz and digitized using a National-Instruments PCI 6115 data acquisition device sampling at 10 Msample/s with 12 bits of ADC resolution.

3.2   Signal Analysis

Scalar-Dependant Leakage. As an initial confirmation of the existence of scalar-dependent leakage from the point multiplication, Fig. 1 shows five distinct leakage patterns, obtained by multiple invocation (in sequence) of Algorithm 1 using the same point $\mathbb{P}$ with small y coordinate and five different values of the scalar k. Such key-dependent leakage was observed on many target laptops, often in multiple frequency bands.

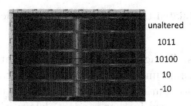

Fig. 1. EM measurement (0.5 s, 1.95-2.15 MHz) of five scalar-by-point multiplication operations using the NISTP-521 curve executed on a Lenovo 3000 N200 laptop. The scalar was overridden to be the 521-digit number obtained by repeating the pattern written to the right. In all cases, the curve point had the same random-looking x coordinate and a small y coordinate.

Observing Fig. 1, notice that for periodic scalars the spectral signature of the leakage signal has strong side-bands surrounding a central carrier frequency. This is a strong indication of a key-dependent modulation signal on a carrier frequency (analogously to modulations observed in [22,23])

Demodulation. We proceed to describe our signal processing methodology demodulating the acquired signal and deducing the DA-sequence, as well as for distinguishing between -1 and 1 NAF digits, for complete key extraction.

For each target, we manually scanned the spectrum and chose the carrier frequency exhibiting the clearest modulation side-bands. After analog filtering and sampling, we used a digital band pass filter to suppress all frequencies outside the band of interest. As in the case of [22,23], the key-dependent signal turned out to be frequency modulated (FM) on the carrier signal. Demodulation was performed using the digital Hilbert transform, followed by further filtering. Figure 2(a) shows an example of the resulting trace.

Obtaining a Clear Trace. Similarly to [22,23], parts of each demodulated decryption trace were occasionally corrupted by strong disturbances, e.g., due to timer interrupts in the target laptop. But even ignoring these, a simple visual inspection of the trace in Fig. 2(a) reveals no immediately obvious patterns or clues about the scalar k or the inner workings of Algorithm 1. In order to obtain a clearer trace and remove the interrupts, we used a multi-step procedure involving the aggregation of several dozen recorded decryption traces, as follows.

 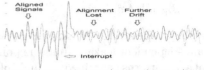

(a) Part of a trace obtained during a single decryption (after FM demodulation and filtering). Note the interrupt corrupting part of the signal.

(b) Two demodulated traces obtained during two decryption operations, using the same ciphertext and key. Note the loss of alignment due to the interrupt.

Fig. 2. Frequency demodulated traces obtained from a single decryption operation.

Interrupts and Drifts. To aggregate traces, we first attempted simple alignment via correlation. Unfortunately, the traces exhibited slow random drifts relative to each other, so that full alignment of entire traces proved difficult. In addition, interrupts induced further random delays in each trace relative to other traces, as well as signal distortion. See Fig. 2(b).

Initial Alignment. Despite the relative distortion between decryption traces, we did notice that a short trace segment immediately preceding each decryption operation was relatively similar across all measurements, rarely having any interrupts or drifts. We thus used this common segment to perform an initial alignment of all decryption traces, using simple correlation, as follows. We first, chose a reference trace at random and aligned the initial segment of all other traces relative to it. If the initial segment of the reference trace was corrupted due to noise or distortion, the current reference trace was discarded and a new one chosen. If the initial segment of one of the other traces did not align well with that of the reference trace, it was also discarded.

Gradual Alignment Correction. After achieving initial alignment of all decryption traces, we compensated for the gradual drifts of the traces relative to the reference trace by performing individual alignment correction as follows. Each trace was independently compared with the reference trace, by simultaneously inspecting it from beginning to end. Periodically, the relative phase lag between the two traces was estimated by cross-correlating a short local section in both traces. Any detected misalignment was immediately corrected. If an interrupt was detected in one of the traces during this process, the delay it induced was also corrected. Interrupts are easily detectable since they cause large frequency fluctuations. The above process was performed independently for each trace, always in respect to the original reference trace.

Trace Aggregation. Even after the alignment correction process described above, direct aggregation of the traces did not produce an aggregated trace with sufficient fidelity. In order to fine-tune the alignment and facilitate the aggregation process, we broke each trace down into shorter segments, each corresponding to roughly 20 double and add operations. These were in turn aligned

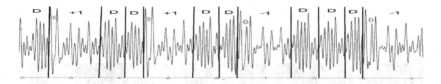

Fig. 3. Part of an aggregated trace obtained from several decryption operations during our attack. The double operations is marked with D and the add operations are marked with the corresponding bit of k_i (either 1 or -1). The red arrows mark the differences between additions performed by lines 6 and 9 of Algorithm 1. Notice that the difference occurs at the begining of each addition operation, as expected from Algorithm 2 (color figure online).

again across all traces via correlation with a corresponding randomly-chosen reference segment. After this final alignment step, segments were aggregated across all traces via a mean-median filter hybrid. For each segment and at each time point, the samples across all traces were sorted, and several lowest and highest values discarded. The rest of the samples were averaged, resulting in distortion-free aggregate trace segments. Figure 3 shows an example of such an aggregate segment. The individual double and add operations can now clearly be seen.

Key Extraction. For key extraction, we must deduce from each aggregated segment the partial DA-sequence it contains, as performed by Algorithm 1. Moreover, for each addition operation in the partial DA-sequence, we must also somehow distinguish whether the corresponding NAF digit is 1 or -1. Obtaining this information will result in several dozen sequences of trinary bits each representing a fragment of the NAF representation of the secret constant k. To facilitate the reconstruction of k from its fragments, we chose to take the aggregate trace segments mentioned in the previous section to be largely overlapping. In such a case, consecutive fragments of the NAF representation of k will have many overlapping bits, allowing for a unique reconstruction.

We now describe the process of extracting the partial DA-sequence from each aggregated segment as well as the process of determining whether the corresponding NAF digit is 1 or -1.

Extracting the Partial DA-Sequence. Although the sequence of double and add operations can be identified in Fig. 3 by careful observation, it is not clear how it can be extracted automatically and reliably. Attempting this in the (post-FM-demodulation) time domain appears difficult since both double and add operations are comprised of largely similar peaks. Instead, we utilize an alternative approach, utilizing the information present in the (post-FM-demodulation) frequency domain. The top and middle parts of Fig. 4 show an aggregated segment along with its corresponding spectrogram. It can be seen that the addition and doubling operations generate energy in two mostly separate frequency bands. We thus focus on the upper band which contains most of the energy of addition operations, and filter each aggregated segment around this frequency-band. Notice that each doubling operation also contributes some small amount

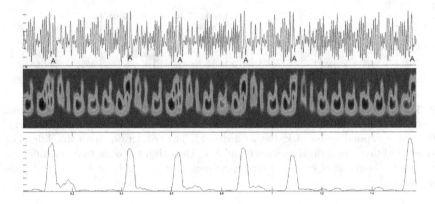

Fig. 4. Several stages of our approach for distinguishing between double and add operations. The topmost figure is the aggregated segment corresponding to the bottom two figures, with the locations of addition operations marked. The middle figure is the spectrogram of the aggregated segment with blue denotes frequencies with low-energy while red denotes frequencies with high energy. In this figure the horizontal frequency is time (0–1.6 ms) while the vertical axis is frequency (0–400 kHz). The bottom figure represents the final result of our approach clearly showing the locations of the addition operations, obtained by performing the procedure described above (color figure online).

of energy to this band, which may create false positives. In order to reliably extract the timings of all addition operations, we multiply the energy in the upper band with its own derivative with respect to time. In this manner we are able to enhance energy peaks that are already both strong and sharply-rising, and attenuate any other peaks. After additional smoothing and equalization, we obtain the trace in the bottom part of Fig. 4 in which the occurrences of addition operations are clearly visible. The timings of doubling operations are then inferred by the time-lapse between additions, thus recovering the partial DA-sequence present in each aggregated segment.

Distinguishing Between 1 and −1. While the spectrogram in Fig. 4 proved very useful in identifying sequences of double and add operations, it is far less effective in determining whether the NAF digit corresponding to an add operation is 1 or −1. The leakage induced by our chosen ciphertext is slight and only affects one of several modular multiplications performed by Algorithm 2. Since the leakage is so short lived, it is difficult to differentiate between the frequency signatures of the two cases. In order to overcome the issue we use the exact timings of the add operations (which are already known from the previous step). For each add operation we zoom in on each addition operation in the original aggregated trace using the timings obtained from the previous step. In this manner we discard anything unrelated to the addition operation itself. We then plot a spectrogram using a large time window, thereby increasing the frequency resolution at the price of time resolution. This reveals consistent differences between addition operations corresponding to 1 and −1 NAF digits, in two frequency

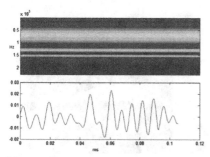

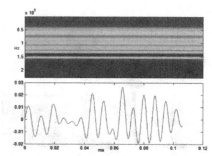

(a) An aggregated segment of an addition operations corresponding to a 1 NAF digit

(b) An aggregated segment of an addition operations corresponding to a −1 NAF digit

Fig. 5. Zoomed-in views (bottom) and spectrograms (top) of add operations corresponding to 1 and −1 NAF digits. Note the energy difference in the 50–125 kHz band between the two signals. This difference is consistent across all add operations, and can be used to differentiate between them.

bands, see Fig. 5. This difference allows us to consistently differentiate between the two add operations (corresponding to 1 and −1 NAF digits), resulting in a reliable key extraction.

Overall Attack Performance. Applying our attack to a randomly generated ECDH NISTP-521 key, by measuring the EM emanations of a Lenovo 3000 N200 target, we have extracted the secret scalar except its first 5 NAF digits, with an error of two digits. During the attack we have used traced obtained form 75 decryption operations, each lasting about 0.05 s, yielding a total measurement time of about $75 \cdot 0.05 = 3.75$ s.

3.3 Measuring the EM Leakage Through a Wall

In order to eavesdrop on the EM leakage of target computers in surrounding rooms, we constructed a more portable experimental setup which we now discuss.

Antenna. We have used an Aaronia Magnetic Direction Finder MDF 9400 antenna, designed for 9 kHz–400 MHz. This is essentially a tuned loop antenna.

Amplification and Digitization. The signals produced by the antenna were amplified first by a Mini-Circuits ZFL-1000 amplifier and then by a (customized) Mini-Circuits ZPUL-30P amplifier, providing a total of gain of approximately 60 dB (at the frequency of interest). The resulting signal was then low-pass filtered at 5 MHz and digitized using an Ettus Research USRP N200 software defined radio, equipped with a LFRX daughter board, at 10 Msample/s.

(a) Attacker's setup for capturing EM emanations. Left to right: power supply, antenna on stand, amplifiers, software defined radio (white box), analysis computer.

(b) Target (Lenovo 3000 N200), performing ECDH decryption operations, on the other side of the wall.

Fig. 6. Attacking a target computer in an adjacent room, across a wall.

Target Placement. The target laptop was placed in a room adjacent to the attacker's experimental setup, separated by a standard drywall (15 cm thick, reinforced with metal studs). The location and orientation of the antenna greatly affects the resulting signal. In our experiments, we have placed the antenna on the opposite side of the wall from the target computer's voltage regulator, with the antenna's loop plane parallel to the wall surface. See Fig. 6.

Attack Performance. Applying our attack and signal processing techniques to a target laptop (Lenovo 3000 N200) located in the adjacent room, we have successfully extracted the secret scalar of a randomly generated ECDH NISTP-521 key except its first 5 NAF digits and with an error of two digits. For the attack we have used traces collected by measuring the target's EM leakage during 66 decryptions, each lasting about 0.05 s. This yields a total measurement time of about 3.3 s.

4 Conclusion

This paper demonstrates the first side-channel attack on PC implementations of elliptic curve cryptology. Our techniques do not assume the leakage of secret-key material via the sequence of elliptic curve double and add operations. Instead our attacks rely on a strong correlation between the *operands* of elliptic curve addition operation and the secret key. By injecting chosen ciphertexts, we make the operands to GnuPG modular multiplication routine highly distinguishable, even by low-bandwidth measurements. Since the operands of the elliptic curve additions are highly correlated with the secret key, we are able to completely recover the key within only a few seconds of measurements.

Software Countermeasures. Our attacks extract the secret key by observing the leakage created during the decryption of a carefully chosen ciphertext (curve points) which creates some mathematical structure in the operands of the elliptic curve addition operation. We now review the common set of countermeasures for preventing such chosen ciphertext attacks, see [19, 20] for extended discussions.

Scalar Randomization and Splitting. Many side-channel attacks relay on averaging the leakage during several decryption operations on order to achieve key extraction. A scalar randomization countermeasure [16] prevents such averaging by adding to the scalar a random multiple of the group order before performing the scalar-by-point multiplication operation. This changes the sequence of elliptic curve double and add operations performed during different decryption operations, thus hindering the averaging operation. Another common and similar countermeasure splits the secret scalar k in into n parts $k_1, \cdots, k_n$ such that $k = \sum_{i=1}^{n} k_i$, performs the scalar-by-point multiplication operation separately on each k_i and them combines the result [14].

While such a countermeasure is indeed effective against our attack (since it requires traces obtained from several decryption operations), it will not stop chosen ciphertext attacks that only rely on a single trace for key extraction.

Point Blinding. This method protects the scalar k multiplied with a ciphertext point $\mathbb{P}$, by first generating a random point $\mathbb{R}$, computing $k(\mathbb{P} + \mathbb{R})$ and then subtracting $k\mathbb{R}$ from the result [16]. Such a countermeasure will completely block chosen ciphertext attacks since the attacker is no longer able to carefully chose a point $\mathbb{P}$ to be multiplied with k. However, the effect on performance of this countermeasure is often significant, since now two scalar-by-point multiplication operations have to be performed per decryption.

Future Work. While in the past few years there have been several physical key-extraction attacks on full fledged-PC computers [22–24], all of these attacks relied on a carefully chosen ciphertext and targeted various public key encryption schemes. We pose, as intriguing open problems, the challenges of non-chosen ciphertext attacks as well as attacking other cryptographic primitives (such as symmetric encryption). Finally, our attacks utilized traces obtained from about 70 decryption operations in order to extract the secret key. We pose the task of minimizing this number as another open problem.

References

1. GNU multiple precision arithmetic library. http://gmplib.org/
2. GNU Privacy Guard. https://www.gnupg.org
3. GnuPG Frontends. https://www.gnupg.org/related_software/frontends.html
4. Minimalist GNU for Windows. http://www.mingw.org
5. Agrawal, D., Archambeault, B., Rao, J.R., Rohatgi, P.: The EM side-channel(s). In: Kaliski Jr., B.S., Koç, Ç.K., Paar, C. (eds.) CHES 2002. LNCS, vol. 2523, pp. 29–45. Springer, Heidelberg (2003)

6. Akishita, T., Takagi, T.: Zero-value point attacks on elliptic curve cryptosystem. In: Boyd, C., Mao, W. (eds.) ISC 2003. LNCS, vol. 2851, pp. 218–233. Springer, Heidelberg (2003)

7. Anderson, R.J.: Security Engineering – A Guide to Building Dependable Distributed Systems, 2nd edn. Wiley, Hoboken (2008)

8. Barker, E., Johnson, D., Smid, M.: NIST SP 800–56a: recommendation for pairwise key establishment schemes using discrete logarithm cryptography (revised) (2007)

9. Benger, N., van de Pol, J., Smart, N.P., Yarom, Y.: "Ooh Aah.. Just a Little Bit": a small amount of side channel can go a long way. In: Batina, L., Robshaw, M. (eds.) CHES 2014. LNCS, vol. 8731, pp. 75–92. Springer, Heidelberg (2014)

10. Bernstein, D.J.: Cache-timing attacks on AES (2005). http://cr.yp.to/papers. html#cachetiming

11. Brumley, B.B., Tuveri, N.: Remote timing attacks are still practical. In: Atluri, V., Diaz, C. (eds.) ESORICS 2011. LNCS, vol. 6879, pp. 355–371. Springer, Heidelberg (2011)

12. Brumley, D., Boneh, D.: Remote timing attacks are practical. Comput. Netw. 48(5), 701–716 (2005)

13. Callas, J., Donnerhacke, L., Finney, H., Shaw, D., Thayer, R.: OpenPGP message format. RFC 4880, November 2007

14. Ciet, M., Joye, M.: (Virtually) Free randomization techniques for elliptic curve cryptography. In: Qing, S., Gollmann, D., Zhou, J. (eds.) ICICS 2003. LNCS, vol. 2836, pp. 348–359. Springer, Heidelberg (2003)

15. Clark, S.S., Mustafa, H.A., Ransford, B., Sorber, J., Fu, K., Xu, W.: Current events: identifying webpages by tapping the electrical outlet. In: Crampton, J., Jajodia, S., Mayes, K. (eds.) ESORICS 2013. LNCS, vol. 8134, pp. 700–717. Springer, Heidelberg (2013)

16. Coron, J.-S.: Resistance against differential power analysis for elliptic curve cryptosystems. In: Koç, Ç.K., Paar, C. (eds.) CHES 1999. LNCS, vol. 1717, pp. 292–302. Springer, Heidelberg (1999)

17. Elkins, M., Del Torto, D., Levien, R., Roessler, T.: MIME security with OpenPGP. RFC 3156 (2001). http://www.ietf.org/rfc/rfc3156.txt

18. The Enigmail Project: Enigmail: a simple interface for OpenPGP email security. https://www.enigmail.net

19. Fan, J., Guo, X., De Mulder, E., Schaumont, S., Preneel, B., Verbauwhede, I.: State-of-the-art of secure ECC implementations: a survey on known side-channel attacks and countermeasures. In: Proceedings of the IEEE International Symposium on Hardware-Oriented Security and Trust (HOST 2010), pp. 76–87 (2010)

20. Fan, J., Verbauwhede, I.: An updated survey on secure ECC implementations: attacks, countermeasures and cost. In: Naccache, D. (ed.) Cryptography and Security: From Theory to Applications. LNCS, vol. 6805, pp. 265–282. Springer, Heidelberg (2012)

21. Gandolfi, K., Mourtel, C., Olivier, F.: Electromagnetic analysis: concrete results. In: Koç, Ç.K., Naccache, D., Paar, C. (eds.) CHES 2001. LNCS, vol. 2162, pp. 251–261. Springer, Heidelberg (2001)

22. Genkin, D., Pachmanov, L., Pipman, I., Tromer, E.: Stealing keys from PCs using a radio: cheap electromagnetic attacks on windowed exponentiation. In: Güneysu, T., Handschuh, H. (eds.) CHES 2015. LNCS, vol. 9293, pp. 207–228. Springer, Heidelberg (2015). Extended version: Cryptology ePrint Archive, Report 2015/170

23. Genkin, D., Pipman, I., Tromer, E.: Get your hands off my laptop: physical side-channel key-extraction attacks on PCs. In: Batina, L., Robshaw, M. (eds.) CHES 2014. LNCS, vol. 8731, pp. 242–260. Springer, Heidelberg (2014)
24. Genkin, D., Shamir, A., Tromer, E.: RSA key extraction via low-bandwidth acoustic cryptanalysis. In: Garay, J.A., Gennaro, R. (eds.) CRYPTO 2014, Part I. LNCS, vol. 8616, pp. 444–461. Springer, Heidelberg (2014). Extended version: Cryptology ePrint Archive, Report 2013/857
25. Goller, G., Sigl, G.: Side Channel Attacks on Smartphones and Embedded Devices Using Standard Radio Equipment. In: Mangard, S., Poschmann, A.Y. (eds.) COSADE 2015. LNCS, vol. 9064, pp. 255–270. Springer, Heidelberg (2015)
26. Goubin, L.: A refined power-analysis attack on elliptic curve cryptosystems. In: Desmedt, Y.G. (ed.) PKC 2003. LNCS, vol. 2567, pp. 199–210. Springer, Heidelberg (2002)
27. Jivsov, A.: Elliptic curve cryptography (ECC) in OpenPGP. RFC 4880 (2012)
28. Kocher, P., Jaffe, J., Jun, B., Rohatgi, P.: Introduction to differential power analysis. J. Cryptographic Eng. 1(1), 5–27 (2011)
29. Mangard, S., Oswald, E., Popp, T.: Power Analysis Attacks – Revealing the Secrets of Smart Cards. Springer, Heidelberg (2007)
30. Okeya, K., Sakurai, K.: On insecurity of the side channel attack countermeasure using addition-subtraction chains under distinguishability between addition and doubling. In: Batten, L.M., Seberry, J. (eds.) ACISP 2002. LNCS, vol. 2384, pp. 420–435. Springer, Heidelberg (2002)
31. Oren, Y., Shamir, A.: How not to protect PCs from power analysis, presented at CRYPTO 2006 rump session (2006). http://iss.oy.ne.ro/HowNotToProtectPCsFromPowerAnalysis
32. Osvik, D.A., Shamir, A., Tromer, E.: Cache attacks and countermeasures: the case of AES. In: Pointcheval, D. (ed.) CT-RSA 2006. LNCS, vol. 3860, pp. 1–20. Springer, Heidelberg (2006)
33. Oswald, E., Aigner, M.: Randomized addition-subtraction chains as a countermeasure against power attacks. In: Koç, Ç.K., Naccache, D., Paar, C. (eds.) CHES 2001. LNCS, vol. 2162, pp. 39–50. Springer, Heidelberg (2001)
34. Percival, C.: Cache missing for fun and profit. Presented at BSDCan (2005). http://www.daemonology.net/hyperthreading-considered-harmful
35. Quisquater, J.-J., Samyde, D.: Electromagnetic analysis (EMA): measures and counter-measures for smart cards. In: Attali, S., Jensen, T. (eds.) E-smart 2001. LNCS, vol. 2140, pp. 200–210. Springer, Heidelberg (2001)
36. Reitwiesner, G.W.: Binary arithmetic. Adv. Comput. 1, 231–308 (1960)
37. van de Pol, J., Smart, N.P., Yarom, Y.: Just a little bit more. In: Nyberg, K. (ed.) CT-RSA 2015. LNCS, vol. 9048, pp. 3–21. Springer, Heidelberg (2015)
38. Walter, C.D.: Issues of security with the oswald-aigner exponentiation algorithm. In: Okamoto, T. (ed.) CT-RSA 2004. LNCS, vol. 2964, pp. 208–221. Springer, Heidelberg (2004)
39. Yarom, Y., Falkner, K.: FLUSH+RELOAD: a high resolution, lownoise, L3 cache side-channel attac. In: USENIX Security Symposium, pp. 719–732. USENIX Association (2014)
40. Yarom, Y., Liu, F., Ge, Q., Heiser, G., Lee, R.B.: Last-level cache side-channel attacks are practical. In: IEEE Symposium on Security and Privacy. IEEE (2015)

Side-Channel Analysis of Weierstrass and Koblitz Curve ECDSA on Android Smartphones

Pierre Belgarric[1,4]([✉]), Pierre-Alain Fouque[2],
Gilles Macario-Rat[1], and Mehdi Tibouchi[3]

[1] Orange Labs, Issy-les-Moulineaux, France
gilles.macariorat@orange.com, pierre.belgarric@hp.com
[2] Institut Universitaire de France, Université de Rennes 1, Rennes, France
pierre-alain.fouque@ens.fr
[3] NTT Secure Platform Laboratories, Tokyo, Japan
tibouchi.mehdi@lab.ntt.co.jp
[4] HP Labs, HP Inc., Bristol, UK

Abstract. In this paper, we study the side-channel resistance of the implementation of the ECDSA signature scheme in Android's standard cryptographic library. We show that, for elliptic curves over prime fields, one can recover the secret key very efficiently on smartphones using electromagnetic side-channel and well-known lattice reduction techniques. We experimentally show that elliptic curve operations (doublings and additions) can be distinguished in a multi-core CPU clocking over the giga-hertz. We then extend the standard lattice attack on ECDSA over prime fields to binary Koblitz curves. This is the first time that such an attack is described on Koblitz curves. These curves, which are also available in Bouncy Castle, allow very efficient implementations using the Frobenius operation. This leads to signal processing challenges since the number of available points are reduced. We investigate practical side-channel, showing the concrete vulnerability of such implementations. In comparison to previous works targeting smartphones, the attacks presented in the paper take benefit from discernible architectural features, like specific instructions computations or memory accesses.

1 Introduction

Side-Channel Analysis is an important set of techniques allowing to recover secret information. Isolation breaches are exploited during the execution of a sensitive algorithm [16,17]. Various sources of leakage can be used, such as physical ones (e.g., power consumption [17], electromagnetic emanations, or execution timing [16]), or microarchitectural ones (e.g., cache state or branch prediction).

Physical side-channels have been used for more than 15 years to assess the security of smartcards, ASIC and FPGA. Security vulnerabilities have been a real concern for embedded devices like smartcards that hold sensitive data and can be accessed by an adversary. These integrated circuits were thought to hold

© Springer International Publishing Switzerland 2016
K. Sako (Ed.): CT-RSA 2016, LNCS 9610, pp. 236–252, 2016.
DOI: 10.1007/978-3-319-29485-8_14

and protect only a few applications. But the upcoming of smartphones allowed all kinds of applications to be run on a unique mobile device, which was thought to be a mobile computer rather than a generalized smartcard. As a consequence, the hardware is not designed to be protected against physical attacks. This problem has been studied for many years by mobile operators to protect private data on these devices. Mobile operators standardized the SIM card which is used in many countries and is built to prevent any leakage of information. This chip is still used in today's phones. But the quantity of data processed nowadays is increasing exponentially, leading to a dead-end when considering the computing limitations of SIM cards and the latency of communication with smartphone hardware.

Sensitive applications are now developed on smartphones and software security vulnerability is an important issue. However, if the cryptographic library is not protected against physical attacks, the secret keys can be extracted and data protection becomes useless.

Our Contributions. With this evolution in mind we assess the security of Android smartphones against electromagnetic analysis. We show that the standard implementation of elliptic curve cryptography, which has been provided since the version 4.4 of the Android operating system, is not protected against these attacks and that the manipulated secret key can be extracted using a few hundreds of measurements. Many issues remained in the related literature [1,14,21,28] in order to mount a real and practical attack on mainstream libraries running on smartphones. No article address the security of widely used library such as Bouncy Castle and actual implementation. For instance, in [21], authors show that we can distinguish square and multiplication in the usual square-and-multiply algorithm. However, since in Bouncy Castle the implementation uses a sliding windows algorithm, this information is not sufficient to recover the secret key. Here, we show that on real implementation that calls this library we can recover the secret key.

On the hardware side, modern smartphone processors have interesting features which make physical attack harder: many cores, fast clock (GigaHertz, while smartcards are clocked at around 20 MHz), and the leaking parts of the circuit under focus are integrated into hundred millions of transistors. This makes the leaking signal much harder to acquire and interpret. Moreover, Android is a rich OS that use many threads running concurrently and the software is executed in an applicative virtual machine. Thus the abstraction layers induce many system activities and it is not really easy to get the full trace during cryptographic computation. Previous work mainly focused on simpler processors and OSes, with the noticeable exceptions of Genkin et al.'s works [10,11] and Zajic and Prvulovic's experiments [27]. Nevertheless, in the two first papers, exponentiations were not observed, and in the third paper, no cryptographic algorithm was evaluated. A more detailed review of related work, as well as of the Android smartphone architecture, is provided in the full version of this paper [6].

On a cryptanalytical viewpoint, implementations that were previously attacked on general-purpose devices, processed each bit independently. In order to have efficient cryptographic codes, sliding window algorithms are used in Bouncy Castle, and it is no more possible to mount the attacks described in related work. This explains the use of the lattice-based technique which only uses the last iterations of the trace. We can detect the last bits since we are able to identify a specific pattern that ends the computation. These attacks can be used even though we do not have the whole electromagnetic (EM) curve: with windowing algorithms, we cannot distinguish between the additions of different precomputed values and multi-threading can interrupt the double-and-add algorithm with different operations. Even in these difficult scenarios, we are able to identify the number of zero bits at the beginning or at the end of ECDSA nonces, leading to a successful lattice-based cryptanalysis.

Furthermore, the security of the windowing algorithm on Koblitz curves has not been investigated yet. Arithmetic on such curves is very efficient on hardware, and it has recently been shown that the new carryless vector instructions make these curves also appealing in software. It raises new signal processing challenge since the Frobenius endomorphism, which plays a role in the Koblitz curve setting analogous to doublings in standard scalar multiplications, is a very efficient operation, and is implemented through precomputed tables in Bouncy Castle. These operations are successfully monitored through EM side-channel. Lattice-based cryptanalysis has also been modified to address the specificities of these curves. In Bouncy Castle, the implementation of elliptic curves uses affine coordinates, but our attack can still be applied on other coordinates system such as Jacobian or lambda [19, 25] coordinates if the most significant bits of the nonces leak. Indeed, we learn these bits since we can distinguish the addition and double (frobenius in the case of binary curves) operations. Being able to distinguish them depends on their actual implementations, but in any coordinates systems, the internal operations are usually rather different and timing or power consumption are different if no careful protection are added.

We implement two EM side-channel attacks on smartphones running Android standard ECDSA implementations. We recover the private key using very few signatures either on prime field curves or on Koblitz ones. In the first attack, defined over prime field, we show that, even on systems as complex as smartphones, it is possible to distinguish exponentiation operations via EM side-channels. It allows to recover the least significant bits of the nonces during the execution of the sliding window exponentiation algorithm. Then, we conduct classical lattice-based cryptanalysis. The second attack is new and is an adaptation of the lattice-based attack in the case of Koblitz curves. In addition to this new technique, the efficient Frobenius operation is retrieved via EM side-channel. It allows to break these specific kind of curves even on complex devices.

Finally, as an application, we show that attacking Koblitz curves are interesting in order to mount an attack on Bitcoin. Indeed, Bitcoin uses a Koblitz curves and the cryptographic library uses Bouncy Castle. We propose a scenario which allows an attacker to stole the secret key of a user and spend his digital wallet.

Organization of the Paper. In Sect. 2, we describe some background on Android security and elliptic curve over prime field and binary field and their implementations in Bouncy Castle. In Sect. 3, we present how we acquire and process the signal. In Sect. 4, we show how we can recover the secret for prime field and binary curves and finally we address the possible countermeasures.

2 Background on Elliptic Curve Cryptography

The security of elliptic curve cryptography is based on the computational complexity of the discrete logarithm problem over the additive group of points of an elliptic curve. This problem is stated as follows: given P and Q two points such that $Q = k \cdot P$, finding k is difficult when the group order is a large prime. Let P be a publicly known generator point and a scalar k in the finite field. Efficient algorithms allow to compute a new point $Q = k \cdot P$. Here, we work with prime and binary curves. The arithmetic used to compute with Jacobian coordinates on prime field curves and affine coordinates for binary curve, and the exact implementations used in Bouncy Castle with NAF and TNAF representation is detailed in the full version of this paper [6]. Computations are done on large integers, using the *BigInteger* class. In Android, the class functions ultimately bind to native ones through the *JNI*. These native functions are implemented in an *OpenSSL* class.

Prime Field Elliptic Curve. An elliptic curve can be defined over some finite field $\mathbb{K}$ of characteristic different from 2 and 3 by its short Weierstrass equation $E(\mathbb{K})$ which is the set of points on:

$$E : y^2 = x^3 + ax + b, \tag{1}$$

where $a, b \in \mathbb{K}$ and the points $(x, y) \in \mathbb{K} \times \mathbb{K}$ are solution of Eq. (1). To serve as a neutral element, a point at infinity (∞) is added to the other points to form a group. The addition of two points, needed to efficiently compute $k \cdot P$, is defined for two points $P_1 = (x_1, y_1) \in E(\mathbb{K})$ and $P_2 = (x_2, y_2) \in E(\mathbb{K})$ by the new point $P_3 = (x_3, y_3) \in E(\mathbb{K})$ (see [12]): $P_3 = (\lambda^2 - x_1 - x_2, \lambda(x_1 - x_3) - y_1)$, where $\lambda = (y_1 - y_2)/(x_1 - x_2)$ if $P_1 \neq P_2$ and $\lambda = (3x_1^2 + a)/(2y_1)$ if $P_1 = P_2$.

The computation of these new coordinates requires to compute inversion which is time consuming. Consequently, the elliptic curve points are represented in Jacobian coordinates in Bouncy Castle. To reduce the number of additions, the nonces are represented in NAF and scalar multiplication is performed using a sliding window implementation.

Koblitz Curve. Koblitz curves are anomalous binary curves defined over $\mathbb{F}_2$ and considered over the extension field $\mathbb{F}_{2^m}$. The advantage of these curves is that scalar multiplication algorithms can avoid using point doublings and are very efficient on hardware. Recently, carryless instructions have been added to general processors which makes binary curves appealing as well for software [25]. In the case of Koblitz curve, it is shown in [3], that such curves are competitive. They have been discovered by Koblitz [15], efficient algorithms have been proposed by Solinas [26] and treated formally in [12]. Their equations have the following form $E_a(\mathbb{F}_{2^m})$:

$$y^2 + xy = x^3 + ax + 1, \text{ and } a = 0 \text{ or } 1. \tag{2}$$

The interest of these curves resides in some tricks in the arithmetic of point calculus. The Frobenius map $\tau : E_a(\mathbb{F}_{2^m}) \to E_a(\mathbb{F}_{2^m})$ is defined as

$$\tau(\infty) = \infty, \text{ and } \tau(x, y) = (x^2, y^2).$$

It can be efficiently computed because squaring in $\mathbb{F}_{2^m}$ is inexpensive since it consists in adding a bit to zero between each bit of the binary representation of an element and then reducing it modulo the polynomial defining the finite field. It is known that

$$(\tau^2 + 2)P = \mu\tau(P) \text{ for all } P \in E_a(\mathbb{F}_{2^m}),$$

where $\mu = (-1)^a$. Hence, the Frobenius map can be seen as a complex number τ satisfying $\tau^2 + 2 = \mu\tau$ so that $\tau = (\mu + \sqrt{-7})/2$. We can then consider $\mathbb{Z}[\tau]$ the ring of polynomials in τ and in order to multiply points in $E_a(\mathbb{F}_{2^m})$ by elements of the ring $\mathbb{Z}[\tau]$: $u_{l-1}\tau^{l-1} + \cdots + u_1\tau + u_0$. Consequently, we have very efficient computation if we are able to efficiently convert any integer k as $\sum_{i=0}^{l-1} k_i\tau^i$ where l is small and $k_i \in \{-1, 0, 1\}$. Such representation is called the $TNAF$ representation of the integer k. Moreover, there are efficient algorithms to compute it (see [12]). Finally, since $\tau^2 = \mu\tau - 2$, every element $\alpha \in \mathbb{Z}[\tau]$ can be written in canonical form as $\alpha = a_0 + a_1\tau$ where $a_0, a_1 \in \mathbb{Z}$. The implementation of Bouncy Castle in order to represent an integer in WTNAF representation (TNAF representation with window) is recalled in the full version of this paper [6].

ECDSA. The ECDSA signature scheme has been standardized by NIST in [24] and allows to sign any message m using two scalars (r, s) such that r is the abscissae of $k \cdot P$ and s is computed as $s = (rx + h)/k \mod q$, where q is a large prime, $h = H(m)$ and x is the signer's ECDSA secret key.

3   Signal Processing

In this section, we explain the experimental setup used to acquire the signal. The acquisition bench is described in details in the full version of this paper [6]. We present how we synchronize the signal and we show how to distinguish doubling and addition operations. We observe that the number of multiplications is different for doubling and addition, the time intervals between these multiplications being a characteristic of each operation. Then, we explain some particular issue according to the Bouncy Castle code. Finally, we show that the multiplications, corresponding to a decrease in signal energy, are used in a different CPU mode than the other executed instructions. It may possibly explain the observed leakage.

3.1   Synchronizing the Acquisitions

In [1], the oscilloscope is triggered at acquisition time through SD Card communication. The voltage of one of the data pins is monitored while a message is sent to the card. There are a few issues with that method. The SD Card is not used in all the smartphones. It is problematic to easily evaluate all devices. The mechanical base is not the same on all the platforms and much of them are difficult to access. The time is not very stable between the communication on the SD card and the beginning of the processing of interest. It is not an issue for so-called *horizontal* attacks (where the leakage patterns are a function of time) where only one trace is required, but for *vertical* attacks, it is important to have a stable and generic synchronizing signal. Finally, the phone is dismounted and a wire is melted on each evaluated phones.

To address these problems, we trigger on USB channel, which is the only standard I/O on smartphones. We send 120 bytes equal to 0 on the channel just before cryptographic computation. Low-pass filtering the USB physical signal gives a good approximation of a square signal, because the high frequencies of the succession of fronts are filtered. The pattern is clearly visible on Fig. 1, while sniffing the USB voltage signal. The oscilloscope triggers on a wide enough square pattern. Similarly a message can be sent just after the cryptographic processing to surround the interesting leakage in time. Other signals with the same values could transit on the channel triggering the oscilloscope on a wrong pattern. The probability of such an occurrence is low, and experimentally the problem did not occur during our experiments.

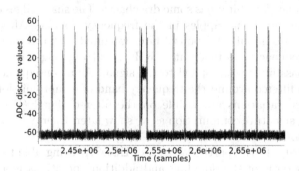

Fig. 1. USB voltage: synchronization message pattern sent on USB channel before the signature.

There is still significant jitter between oscilloscope triggering and the beginning of cryptographic computation. To improve the acquisitions, a "sleep" operation was added just before the sensitive computation. The CPU does not consume power during that period. It is easily detectable on EM signals as can be seen on Fig. 3(a). There are other time periods where the processor is idle. We forced this state to be long enough in order to discriminate it with other idle states between USB pattern and cryptographic computations.

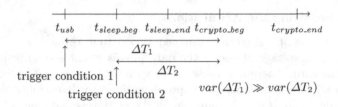

Fig. 2. Triggering sequence: first USB pattern (less false positives); second sleep state (less variance between adc triggering and algorithm start).

The coupling of USB channel pattern with CPU idle state (Fig. 2) leads to a precise synchronization stage. The jitter is only a few instructions long, which is very interesting, especially for investigations of *Differential Power Analysis*.

3.2 Energy Variations - Leakage Frequencies

Zooming on EM signal of Fig. 3(a), there are time locations when the AC absolute magnitude decreases, characteristic of signal energy variations. In signal processing, the energy of a signal is given by the integration over time of its squared absolute values: $E_s = \int_{-\infty}^{\infty} |x(t)|^2 dt$.

To locally evaluate the signal energy around a point in time, the integral is computed on a window centered on that point. It is equivalent to convoluting a square window centered on that point, and summing the values of the convoluted signal. Applied to all signal points, the output signal is a low-pass filtered signal of the original one. This filter has some drawbacks. The sharp edges of the square window involve important ripples in the frequency domain. Alternatively, we used a FIR (Finite Impulse Response) filter weighted with a Hamming window. The cutting frequency was taken at 50 KHz, a value giving a good SNR ratio. Then a high-pass filter was applied to the signal. As a consequence, the signal was band-pass filtered around the frequency band of compromission [2,9].

High energy variations are visible on the filtered signal (Fig. 3(b)). They happen during signature computation as we show later. Energy variations during the computation of sensitive values has long been of interest in the field of computer security. In the particular case of ECDSA, being able to differentiate the leakage patterns of the doubling and addition operations is a big security threat, because the flow of operations is directly linked to secret data.

Distinguishing EC Operations Patterns. The evaluation of a white box scalar multiplication, with a known scalar, and Bouncy Castle's doubling and addition implementations, allows the discrimination of the two operations patterns (Fig. 4(a)). Each operation is characterized by a specific set of low power peaks, defined by the number of peaks and the timing intervals between successive peaks.

If the number of operations to extract is low enough, a manual observation is possible, as is the case for the cryptanalysis presented in Sect. 4 where a few hundreds of operations are needed.

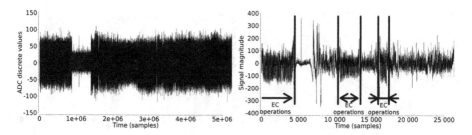

Fig. 3. (a) Measured signal: Noisy curve, visible period when processor is idle (*Qualcomm MSM 8225*) – (b) After signal filtering: higher energy variations during scalar multiplication (less time samples because of subsampling - *Qualcomm MSM 8225*)

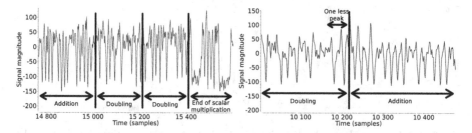

Fig. 4. (a) doubling and addition leakage patterns (*Qualcomm MSM 8225*) – (b) pattern of a doubling operation preceding an addition operation (*Qualcomm MSM 8225*)

The regularity of the peaks is compared to the code of both the doubling and the addition operations. Considering the doubling implementation (recalled in the full version of this paper [6]), the number of multiplications is the same as the number of peaks in the doubling leakage pattern. The number of additions and subtractions between successive multiplications ($\{3, 0, 1, 3, 6, 1, (1)\}$), which is plotted on Fig. 5(b), evolves similarly to the timing intervals on Fig. 4(b).

An interesting part of the doubling algorithm is the block condition (line 14 in the listing given in the full version [6]), which is executed if the operation is followed by another doubling. If it is followed by an addition, the block is not executed, and so, there is one less modular multiplication at the end of the function. This is clearly visible on the doubling pattern preceding the addition on Fig. 6(a). This explains the parentheses surrounding the last value of the list.

The addition sums a precomputed point to an intermediate one during exponentiation. The precomputed points have their coordinate Z set to one. It leads to computation simplifications since the field operations involving this value, its square, or its cubic value, do not need to be computed. If we consider the point P1 to be precomputed in addition algorithm (also listed in the full version [6]), the conditional blocks executed if the bit length of Z1 is different from one, are never computed. As a consequence, the number of additions and subtractions between successive multiplications gives the list $\{0, 0, 0, 2, 0, 0, 0, 4, 0, 1, 0, 0\}$, plotted on Fig. 6(b). It has the same look as the curve on Fig. 5(a). The same conclusions

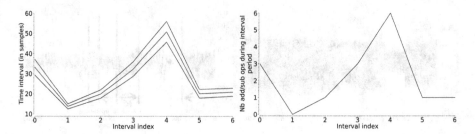

Fig. 5. (a) Mean and standard deviation of doubling operation time intervals – (b) Number of basic operations between multiplications in double BC source code

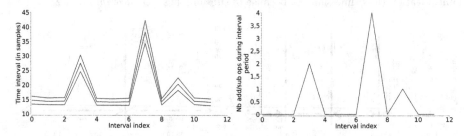

Fig. 6. (a) Mean and standard deviation of addition operation time intervals – (b) number of basic operations between multiplications in add BC source code

may be drawn from the Android debugger *DDMS* as described in the full version of this paper [6].

Attacker's Strength Considerations. The *Qualcomm MSM 8225* processor, clocked at 1.2 GHz, leaks in a frequency range which is under 50 KHz. This relatively low frequency can be explained by leaking operations executing during multiple clock ticks. An analog-to-digital converter with a sampling frequency of a few hundreds of kilo-hertz, allows to mount the attack with low investment costs. In the paper, the measurements were obtained by decreasing our oscilloscope bandpass cutting frequency to the minimum available one (20 MHz) and choosing a sampling frequency of 50 MHz. It is small in comparison to the smartphone's CPU clock frequency.

Contrary to the works of Genkin *et al.* [10,11], our attack is not subject to system interruptions (Fig. 3(b)). In fact in their paper, the frequency contents of exponentiation vary with computed values. If the OS cuts the processing in different chunks, the frequency spectrum of exponentiation will be greatly affected. Consequently, the specificities of the inputs will not be discernible with their method.

A Possible Explanation for the Leakages. Field multiplications are computed with the Java class *BigInteger*. These class functions ultimately bind to the native class *NativeBN* through the JNI. The native methods call binary code in shared library. Disassembling the library of interest, the machine code is executed in ARM mode during multiplication, contrarily to usual THUMB-2 mode for other instructions, e.g. addition instruction. Looking at the ARM reference manual for Thumb-2 [5], multiplication instructions are one of the few which have distinct features in ARM mode and in THUMB-2 mode. In particular, conditional flags can be modified in ARM mode, which is important for vectorial operations. It may explain this change of the CPU mode, and consequently the difference observed in the leakage. However, the impact on the leakage is difficult to establish.

One track that may be explored is the way integer pipelines are implemented. However, documentation is not always accessible. For example, the ARM Cortex-A8 architecture (which is not targeted in the paper) implements two ALUs, but only one implements a multiplier (see [4]). Consequently, depending on how the processor is able to fill both of the ALUs (e.g. because of data dependences or the number of successive multiplication in the program) may affect the amount of processing done at a given time. Similar design choices for the targeted processors may explain some leakage variations.

4   Lattice Attack on ECDSA

Monitoring EM radiation during EC scalar multiplication, it may be possible to recover the succession of doublings and additions. With Left-to-Right scalar multiplication, this information is sufficient to recover the private key from a single signature. However, this approach does not work against Bouncy Castle, which implements the efficient "window NAF" algorithm. A side-channel attacker cannot distinguish which of several precomputed points is added at each iteration. On the other hand, the number of zeros between successive additions (i.e. the number of doublings minus one) *can* be recovered using Simple Power Analysis. In particular, the number of doublings following the last addition reveals the number of zeros in the least significant bit positions (because the LSB of a window is always 1). Using that information, one can mount a full key-recovery attack using well-known lattice-based techniques.

Indeed, in ECDSA and other Schnorr-like signature schemes, an attacker who obtains sufficiently many signatures for which he knowns the least significant or most significant few bits of the random nonces k can recover the private signing key. Recovering this key from the signatures and the known bits of the nonces reduces to an instance of Boneh and Venkatesan's hidden number problem (HNP). The best-known variant of this attack is due to Howgrave-Graham and Smart (and was later revisited and made more precise by Nguyen and Shparlinski), and uses lattice reduction to solve the underlying HNP instance. It is recalled in the full version of this paper [6]. In particular, it yields a key-recovery attack against physical implementations of ECDSA signatures in which the side-channel leakage of scalar multiplication can be used to reveal the least or most significant bits of the nonce.

However, the side-channel attack does not typically apply to ECDSA signatures on Koblitz curves. The scalar multiplication on such curves is normally carried out using the τ-adic expansion of the nonce k. Therefore side-channel leakage can at best reveal the top or bottom bits of that τ-adic expansion, which do not determine the top or bottom bits of (the binary representation of) k itself.

In Sect. 4.2, we describe how a similar attack can be mounted in the setting of Koblitz curves nonetheless. More precisely, we show that the top (or bottom) bits of the τ-adic expansion of the nonce can also be used to recover the signing key. The problem it reduces to, can be seen as a higher-dimensional generalization of HNP that can also be solved using lattice reduction.

4.1 ECDSA over Prime Fields

From previous section, we have shown that we are able to visualize the inner structure of NAF representation of the secret nonce k involved in the computation of an ECDSA signature. Formally if $k = \sum_i \alpha_i 2^i$ is such a NAF representation of the secret k, then one can determine the positions i for which the NAF digit α_i is valid, otherwise said, is not zero. Although the values of the digits α_i are unknown, this gives us a large amount of information. In particular, it is sufficient to exploit the known position of the last digit: let ℓ be the position of the last digit in the NAF representation of k, then we know that the last ℓ digits in the *binary* representation of k, are a one, followed by $d - 1$ zeros.

Knowing the bits of the nonces, we can reduce the problem of recovering the secret key x to solving the HNP, which can be described as follows: given (t_i, u_i) pairs of integers such that

$$|xt_i - u_i|_q \leq q/2^{\ell+1},$$

where ℓ denotes the number of bits we recover, x denotes the hidden number we are looking for and $|\cdot|_q$ denotes the distance to $q\mathbb{Z}$, i.e. $|z|_q = \min_{a \in \mathbb{Z}} |z - aq|$. Such problem can be casted as a Closest Vector Problem (CVP) in a lattice and the LLL algorithm can be used to solve it in practice very efficiently. We recall the basic attack in the full version of this paper [6] and it can be found in [23]. The main advantage of this technique is that the number of signatures required is usually very small, but it cannot be used all the time when the number of bits becomes very small. Indeed, in this case for 160-bit modulus for instance, Liu and Nguyen used BKZ 2.0 to solve such lattice and the dimension becomes very high for lattice algorithms [18]. Following the steps used in [7,13,22] we are able to perform the recovery of the signer's ECDSA secret key. In our case we chose the elliptic curve P-256 of the NIST. Using the method described in [7], we choose to solve the HNP problem using the Shortest Vector Problem (SVP) on some lattice. Therefore by building an adequate matrix and reducing it using the BKZ algorithm, we find a vector, one of its coordinates being the secret key.

Experimental Results. To estimate how many signatures we need to process the attack with a high probability of success, we first performed simulated signatures and solved the problem with a Sage (version 6.2) BKZ algorithm implementation. We want to use as much information as we can and we use the technique developed in [7] to this end. Usually, the lattice takes only signatures that have at least ℓ bits and remove the other ones. Here, we want to extract as much information as it is possible and so we put on the diagonal the number of bits we recover. As in [7], we made experiments by varying the minimum value z of the parameter ℓ of the signatures selected to join the computation of the attack. And then we discovered as a rule of thumb, that for a 256-bit secret key, and a probability of success being nearly 100 %, the number of selected signatures should be above $\frac{200}{z}$, and therefore statistically, the total number of signatures to be processed should be above $\frac{200}{z}2^z$. As the complexity of the attack increases with the dimension of the matrix, we found that the best compromise was $z = 2$. Therefore, we processed approximately 500 signatures from which we selected only those for which ℓ was 2 or above, and they were 115 of such. As expected, the SVP attack gave us the secret key in less than five minutes on a common desktop.

4.2 New Attack on Koblitz ECDSA

Consider a Koblitz curve E with a subgroup $\mathbb{G}$ of large prime order q, and let τ be the eigenvalue of the Frobenius endomorphism of E acting on $\mathbb{G}$, seen as a quadratic integer (depending on E, we have $\tau = \frac{\pm 1 + \sqrt{-7}}{2}$). Suppose that we are given t ECDSA signatures (r_i, s_i) in $\mathbb{G}$, with random nonces k_i for which the top coefficients of some (signed) τ-adic expansion is known (the attack would work similarly for the bottom coefficients). Without loss of generality (up to the obvious affine transformation), we may assume that these known bits are all zero, so that the k_i's can be written in the form:

$$k_i = k_{i,0} + k_{i,1}\tau + \cdots + k_{i,\ell-1}\tau^{\ell-1} \in \mathbb{Z}[\tau]$$

where the coefficients $k_{i,j}$ belong to $\{-1, 0, 1\}$, and ℓ is some fixed integer length (the difference between the maximum length of the τ-adic expansions and the number of known zero nonce bits). Moreover, we can decompose k_i in the form $k_i = u_i + v_i\tau$ where u_i, v_i are the rational integers given by $v_i = (k_i - \overline{k_i})/\sqrt{-7}$ and $u_i = k_i - v_i\tau$. Due to the fact that $|\tau| = \sqrt{2}$ (which is crucial for our attack), it is easy to see that both u_i and v_i satisfy a bound of the form $O(\sqrt{2}^\ell)$, and in particular, there exists a constant $c > 0$ such that $u_i^2 + v_i^2 \leq c \cdot 2^\ell$ for all k_i. A discussion of how to estimate the constant c in cases of interest is provided in the full version of this paper [6].

Now for each signature (r_i, s_i), if we denote by h_i the hash value of the corresponding message, the ECDSA verification equation ensures that $k_i s_i \equiv h_i + x r_i \bmod q$, which we can rewrite as

$$x \equiv A_i u_i + \tau A_i v_i + B_i \mod q \tag{3}$$

in terms of the known constants $A_i = s_i/h_i$ and $B_i = -r_i/h_i$ in $\mathbb{Z}/q\mathbb{Z}$. Note that, in view of the bound on $u_i^2 + v_i^2$, (u_i, v_i) is contained in a disc of radius $\sqrt{c \cdot 2^\ell}$ centered at the origin, and the right-hand side of (3) can thus take $\big(1 + o(1)\big)\pi c \cdot 2^\ell$

distinct values at most. As a result, as soon as $\ell < \log_2(q/\pi c)$, each such equation should reveal some information about x, and we should be able to recover x when t is large enough, much in the same way as in the HNP setting.

We show how this can be done with lattice reduction (at least heuristically, although in principle the rigorous approach of Nguyen–Shparlinski can be extended to this setting as well). Let the vector $\boldsymbol{u} = (u_1, \ldots, u_t, v_1, \ldots, v_t, w) \in \mathbb{Z}^{2t+1}$, where w is chosen as $\lfloor \sqrt{c \cdot 2^{\ell-1}} \rfloor$. Since $\|\boldsymbol{u}\| \leq \sqrt{t \cdot c \cdot 2^\ell + w^2} \leq \sqrt{c(t+1/2)} \cdot 2^{\ell/2}$, its norm is bounded. Equation (3) can be rewritten in vector form as:

$$x \equiv \langle \boldsymbol{A}_i, \boldsymbol{u} \rangle \mod q$$

where $\boldsymbol{A}_i = (0, \ldots, 0, A_i, 0, \ldots, 0, \tau A_i, 0, \ldots, 0, B_i/w) \mod q \in \mathbb{Z}^{2t+1}$ has three nonzero components in positions i, $t+i$ and $2t+1$. In particular, $\boldsymbol{u}$ is orthogonal modulo q to each of the vectors $\boldsymbol{A}_1 - \boldsymbol{A}_2, \boldsymbol{A}_2 - \boldsymbol{A}_3, \ldots, \boldsymbol{A}_{t-1} - \boldsymbol{A}_t$ and it is short. We can therefore hope to recover it using lattice reduction.

More precisely, consider the lattice $L \subset \mathbb{Z}^{2t+1}$ of vectors that are orthogonal modulo q to each $\boldsymbol{A}_i - \boldsymbol{A}_{i+1}$, $i = 1, \ldots, t-1$, and whose last component is a multiple of w. L is the kernel of the obvious linear map $\mathbb{Z}^{2t+1} \to \mathbb{Z}/w\mathbb{Z} \times (\mathbb{Z}/q\mathbb{Z})^{t-1}$, and that map is surjective with overwhelming probability (since the vectors $\boldsymbol{A}_i$ themselves are linearly independent modulo q with overwhelming probability on the choice of the randomness in signature generation). Therefore, L is full rank and its volume is given by $\mathrm{vol}(L) = \#(\mathbb{Z}^{2t+1}/L) = \#\mathbb{Z}/w\mathbb{Z} \times (\mathbb{Z}/q\mathbb{Z})^{t-1} = wq^{t-1}$. If the vector $\boldsymbol{u} \in L$ is significantly shorter than the shortest vector length predicted by the Gaussian heuristic (namely $\sqrt{\frac{2t+1}{2\pi e}} \cdot \mathrm{vol}(L)^{1/(2t+1)}$), we should be able to recover $\boldsymbol{u}$ as the shortest vector in L (up to sign) using lattice reduction. This condition can be written as:

$$\sqrt{c(t+1/2)} \cdot 2^{\ell/2} \ll \sqrt{\frac{2t+1}{2\pi e}} \cdot \left(wq^{t-1}\right)^{1/(2t+1)}$$

or equivalently:

$$\ell \lesssim \log_2(q/c\pi e) - \frac{1}{t} \cdot \log_2\left(q\sqrt{2\pi e}\right)$$

which means that recovery is possible for t large enough when $\ell \lesssim \log_2(q/c\pi e)$ (which is quite close to the "information theoretic" bound mentioned above!), and in that case, the condition on t for recovery becomes:

$$t \gtrsim \frac{\log_2\left(q\sqrt{2\pi e}\right)}{\log_2(q/c\pi e) - \ell}. \tag{4}$$

We find that this condition is well-verified in practice, and once $\boldsymbol{u}$ is recovered, it is clearly straightforward to find the signing key x.

Finally, we mention that, to obtain a short basis of L in practice, we use standard orthogonal lattice techniques: we apply lattice reduction to the lattice generated by the rows of the matrix of dimension $3t$ written by blocks as:

$$\begin{pmatrix} \kappa q & & 0 & \mathbf{0} \\ & \ddots & & \vdots \\ 0 & & \kappa q & \mathbf{0} \\ \kappa(\mathbf{A}_1 - \mathbf{A}_2) & \cdots & \kappa(\mathbf{A}_{t-1} - \mathbf{A}_t) & \mathbf{I} \end{pmatrix} \mathbf{W}$$

where the $\mathbf{A}_i$'s are column vectors, $\mathbf{I}$ is the identity matrix of dimension $2t + 1$, κ is a suitably large constant, and $\mathbf{W}$ is the diagonal matrix $\mathrm{diag}(1, \ldots, 1, w)$ to account for the divisiblity condition on the last coefficient of vectors in L.

Experimental Results. We implemented our attack in Sage using BKZ-25 lattice reduction, and tested it against the NIST K-163 Koblitz curve, which has a group order of 162 bits, with random unsigned Koblitz expansions. Experimental results are collected in Table 1. As can be seen from that table, the condition on the number t of required signatures is very consistent with (4) with $c \approx 0.30$ (as discussed in the full version of this paper [6]). It is easy to attack up to 6 bits of bias.

Table 1. Implementation of our new attack against Koblitz curve K-163, using Sage's BKZ-25, run on single core of a Core i5-3570 CPU at 3.4 GHz.

Bits of bias ($\log_2 q - \ell$)	9	8	7	6
Predicted t (Eq. (4))	22	25	30	36
Experimental t	21	25	31	39
Lattice dimension	63	75	93	117
CPU time (s)	2.4	4.7	17	102

Practical SCA. We show on Fig. 7(a) and (b) that the Frobenius operation is distinguishable on *Qualcomm MSM 7225*. On Fig. 7(a), there are five Frobenius in the first succession of operations and four in the two others. Comparatively, there is one addition of points between each succession of Frobenius. The ratio of timing execution between addition and doubling is worse on prime field (see Fig. 4(a)). The Frobenius on Koblitz curves is implemented with pre-computed tables in *Bouncy Castle 1.50*. Thus, the leakage observed is different from the arithmetic implementations observed on prime field. The twofold repetition of pattern leakages in each Frobenius method is linked to the affine coordinate representation of elliptic curve points.

5   Use Case: Bitcoin Wallet

We present a significant use case, namely the Bitcoin crypto-currency [8,20], where our Koblitz cryptanalysis is of practical interest. A Bitcoin wallet is an Elliptic Curve key over the Koblitz curve Secp256k1. The knowledge of the private key allows to spend the money stored in the digital wallet. Therefore,

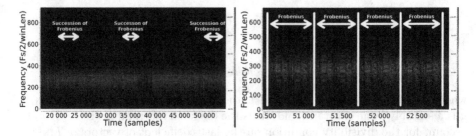

Fig. 7. (a) Succession of Frobenius and one addition between them (STFT, window length = 16000pts, Hamming window, *Qualcomm MSM 7225*) – (b) Zoom on a succession of four Frobenius operations (STFT, window length = 16000pts, Hamming window, *Qualcomm MSM 7225*)

eavesdropping some transactions may lead to the mathematical cryptanalysis presented in Sect. 4.2. Android wallet apps are generally lightweight clients based upon a Simplified Payement Verification (SPV) mode. These apps are usually developed upon *bitcoinj* which is a Java implementation of this lightweight mode. The core Cryptography of the library is based upon Bouncy Castle. Thus, the practical leakages observed in Sect. 4.2 make many Bitcoin users in danger.

To support our claim, a malicious NFC reader could be used by a shop where the Victim goes a few dozen of times and pays with Bitcoin stored in its smartphone. This reader could improve our lab synchronization through legitimate contactless channel. In addition, the reader would contain a hidden EM probe, thus monitoring a signature each time the Victim comes to the shop. The attack is still theoretical but the difficulty to catch the Attacker after theft evidence may motivate malevolent people. So, to become a sound technology in smartphone payement, crypto-currencies may integrate side-channel countermeasures, an overview of which is provided in the full version of this paper [6].

References

1. Aboulkassimi, D., Agoyan, M., Freund, L., Fournier, J., Robisson, B., Tria, A.: ElectroMagnetic analysis (EMA) of software AES on Java mobile phones. In: WIFS (2011)
2. Agrawal, D., Archambeault, B., Rao, J.R., Rohatgi, P.: The EM side-channel(s). CHES (2002). LNCS, vol. 2523, pp. 29–45. Springer, Heidelberg (2003)
3. Aranha, D.F., Faz-Hernández, A., López, J., Rodríguez-Henríquez, F.: Faster implementation of scalar multiplication on koblitz curves. In: Hevia, A., Neven, G. (eds.) LatinCrypt 2012. LNCS, vol. 7533, pp. 177–193. Springer, Heidelberg (2012)
4. ARM. The ARM architecture - with a focus on v7A and Cortex-A8. Presentation support
5. ARM. ARM Architecture Reference Manual - Thumb–2 supplement
6. Belgaric, P., Fouque, P.-A., Marcario-Rat, G., Tibouchi, M.: Side-channel analysis of Weierstrass and Koblitz curve ECDSA on Android smartphones. Cryptology ePrint Archive (2015). Full version of this paper. http://eprint.iacr.org/

7. Benger, N., van de Pol, J., Smart, N.P., Yarom, Y.: "Ooh Aah.. Just a Little Bit": a small amount of side channel can go a long way. In: Batina, L., Robshaw, M. (eds.) CHES 2014. LNCS, vol. 8731, pp. 75–92. Springer, Heidelberg (2014)

8. Bonneau, J., Miller, A., Clark, J., Narayanan, A., Kroll, J.A., Felten, E.W.: SoK: Research perspectives and challenges for bitcoin and cryptocurrencies. In: Security and Privacy (2015)

9. Gebotys, C.H., Ho, S., Tiu, C.C.: EM analysis of rijndael and ECC on a wireless java-based PDA. In: Rao, J.R., Sunar, B. (eds.) CHES 2005. LNCS, vol. 3659, pp. 250–264. Springer, Heidelberg (2005)

10. Genkin, D., Pipman, I., Tromer, E.: Get your hands off my laptop: physical side-channel key-extraction attacks on PCs. In: Batina, L., Robshaw, M. (eds.) CHES 2014. LNCS, vol. 8731, pp. 242–260. Springer, Heidelberg (2014)

11. Genkin, D., Shamir, A., Tromer, E.: RSA key extraction via low-bandwidth acoustic cryptanalysis. In: Garay, J.A., Gennaro, R. (eds.) CRYPTO 2014, Part I. LNCS, vol. 8616, pp. 444–461. Springer, Heidelberg (2014)

12. Hankerson, D., Vanstone, S., Menezes, A.: Guide to Elliptic Curve Cryptography. Springer Professional Computing. Springer, New York (2004)

13. Howgrave-Graham, N., Smart, N.P.: Lattice attacks on digital signature schemes. Des. Codes Crypt. 23(3), 283–290 (2001)

14. Kenworthy, G., Rohatgi, P.: Mobile device security: The case for side-channel resistance. Technical report, Cryptography Research Inc. (2012)

15. Koblitz, N.: CM-curves with good cryptographic properties. In: Feigenbaum, J. (ed.) CRYPTO 1991. LNCS, vol. 576, pp. 279–287. Springer, Heidelberg (1992)

16. Kocher, P.C.: Timing attacks on implementations of Diffie-Hellman, RSA, DSS, and other systems. In: Koblitz, N. (ed.) CRYPTO 1996. LNCS, vol. 1109, pp. 104–113. Springer, Heidelberg (1996)

17. Kocher, P.C., Jaffe, J., Jun, B.: Differential power analysis. In: Wiener, M. (ed.) CRYPTO 1999. LNCS, vol. 1666, pp. 388–397. Springer, Heidelberg (1999)

18. Liu, M., Nguyen, P.Q.: Solving BDD by enumeration: an update. In: Dawson, E. (ed.) CT-RSA 2013. LNCS, vol. 7779, pp. 293–309. Springer, Heidelberg (2013)

19. López, J., Dahab, R.: Improved algorithms for elliptic curve arithmetic in $GF(2^n)$. In: Tavares, S., Meijer, H. (eds.) SAC 1998. LNCS, vol. 1556, pp. 201–212. Springer, Heidelberg (1999)

20. Nakamoto, S.: Bitcoin: A peer-to-peer electronic cash system (2009)

21. Nakano, Y., Souissi, Y., Nguyen, R., Sauvage, L., Danger, J.-L., Guilley, S., Kiyomoto, S., Miyake, Y.: A pre-processing composition for secret key recovery on android smartphone. In: Naccache, D., Sauveron, D. (eds.) WISTP 2014. LNCS, vol. 8501, pp. 76–91. Springer, Heidelberg (2014)

22. Nguyen, P.Q., Shparlinski, I.: The insecurity of the elliptic curve digital signature algorithm with partially known nonces. Des. Codes Crypt. 30(2), 201–217 (2003)

23. Nguyen, P.Q., Tibouchi, M.: Lattice-based fault attacks on signatures. In: Joye, M., Tunstall, M. (eds.) Fault Analysis in Cryptography. Information Security and Cryptography. Springer, New York (2012)

24. NIST. Fips pub 186 - 3: Digital signature standard. Technical report, NIST, July 2013

25. Oliveira, T., López, J., Aranha, D.F., Rodríguez-Henríquez, F.: Lambda coordinates for binary elliptic curves. In: Bertoni, G., Coron, J.-S. (eds.) CHES 2013. LNCS, vol. 8086, pp. 311–330. Springer, Heidelberg (2013)

26. Solinas, J.A.: Efficient arithmetic on koblitz curves. Des. Codes Crypt. 19(2/3), 195–249 (2000)

27. Zajic, A., Prvulovic, M.: Experimental demonstration of electromagnetic information leakage from modern processor-memory systems. IEEE Trans. Electromagn. Compat. **56**(4), 885–893 (2014)
28. Zenger, C., Paar, C., Lemke-Rust, K., Kasper, T., Oswald, D.: Sema of rsa on a smartphone. Technical report, Ruhr-Universitat Bochum, October 2011

Hardware Attacks and Security

Enhancing Side-Channel Analysis
of Binary-Field Multiplication with Bit
Reliability

Peter Pessl[✉] and Stefan Mangard

Institute for Applied Information Processing and Communications (IAIK),
Graz University of Technology, Inffeldgasse 16a, 8010 Graz, Austria
{peter.pessl,stefan.mangard}@iaik.tugraz.at

Abstract. At Africacrypt 2010, Medwed et al. presented Fresh Re-
Keying as a countermeasure to protect low-cost devices against side-
channel analysis. They propose to use binary-field multiplication as a
re-keying function. In this paper, we present a new side-channel attack
on this construction (and multiplication in general). By using template
attacks and the simple algebraic structure of multiplication, the problem
of key recovery can be casted to the well known Learning Parity with
Noise problem (LPN). However, instead of using standard LPN solving
algorithms, we present a method which makes extensive use of bit reliabilities derived from side-channel information. It allows us to decrease
the attack runtime in cases with low-to-medium error probabilities. In a
practical experiment, we can successfully attack a protected 8-bit Fresh
Re-Keying implementation by Medwed et al. using only 512 traces.

Keywords: Side-channel analysis · Multiplication · LPN · Linear
decoding

1   Introduction

Binary-field multiplication, while not cryptographically strong in itself, offers
nice properties for the design of cryptographic systems. For instance, it provides
good diffusion and is, due to its linearity, very easy to mask and thus to protect
against side-channel analysis (SCA) attacks.

These properties led Medwed et al. [16] to use it as a re-keying function in
their *Fresh Re-Keying* scheme. The basic idea of Fresh Re-Keying is to combine
an encryption function f, such as the AES, with a re-keying function g - namely
said multiplication. For every invocation of f, first a *fresh* session key is derived
by using the re-keying function g with a master key and a public random nonce.

Since no such session key is used twice in the encryption function f, Medwed
et al. argue that it suffices to protect it against Simple Power Analysis (SPA)
type attacks. However, the definition of *SPA security* is relatively loose. Usually
it implies that a secret, in this case the session key, cannot be recovered when
using a single trace. Yet, due to the simple algebraic structure of the re-keying

© Springer International Publishing Switzerland 2016
K. Sako (Ed.): CT-RSA 2016, LNCS 9610, pp. 255–270, 2016.
DOI: 10.1007/978-3-319-29485-8_15

function, very limited information on this secret might be sufficient for master-key recovery.

In fact, leakage of a single session-key bit over multiple invocations allows to trivially reveal the master key. The remaining security of each session key however is still 127 bit, which can still be considered SPA secure in the classic definition. Thus, the required side-channel resistance of f still guaranteeing security of the master key is unclear.

The Attack of Belaïd et al. The above problem relates to the work of Belaïd et al. [1,2], where they present a side-channel attack on binary-field multiplications. Their attack applies to settings where a constant secret, i.e., a key, is multiplied with several known values. This is the case with Fresh Re-Keying and the AES-GCM, an authenticated encryption mode.

Belaïd et al. observe that a binary-field multiplication can be written as a matrix-vector product, or system of linear equations, over bits. If one can recover the right-hand side of this system, e.g., by using side-channel analysis, then it can be trivially solved for the key. Belaïd et al. assume that the side-channel adversary is able to observe a noisy Hamming weight of the n-bit multiplication result, but does not have access to leakage of intermediate or partial results. When observing a low or high Hamming weight, i.e., smaller or greater than $n/2$, they assume that all bits of the multiplication result are 0 or 1, respectively. The introduced errors in the system of linear equations do not allow solving by Gaussian elimination.

The problem of solving such erroneous systems is known as *Learning Parity with Noise* (LPN). The algorithms used to solve this problem tend to require a high amount of samples, which is a scarce resource in the side-channel context. In order to decrease this quantity, Belaïd et al. first discard observations with Hamming weight near $n/2$ to decrease the error probability. Then, they use a new LPN algorithm based on LF2 by Levieil and Fouque [13] to recover the key.

Our Contribution. In this work, we present a new side-channel attack on Fresh Re-Keying. Similarly though, our attack also applies to other scenarios using binary-field multiplication, such as AES-GCM.

Our attack makes use of side-channel templates, i.e., device profiling. These templates are used to derive reliability information on each of the session-key bits. We then present a new algorithm aimed at recovering the key when given an erroneous system of equations. This algorithm makes extensive use of the fact that, unlike in standard LPN, we possess said reliability information.

Our analysis suggests that, when compared the previous work, the presented attack can decrease runtime in practical settings. Namely, it performs well if the adversary is able to gather enough LPN samples exhibiting a low-to-medium error probability (e.g., up to 0.2). This makes it particularly well suited for adversaries having access to leakage of partial multiplication results, such as individual bytes.

We use our algorithm to mount an attack on an 8-bit software implementation of Fresh Re-Keying presented by Medwed et al. [15]. Their implementation uses shuffling as means to protect the AES against SPA and algebraic side-channel attacks. We use templates to circumvent this countermeasure without making any major assumptions on the implemented shuffling algorithm. We can successfully attack this implementation while only requiring a very small number of traces.

Outline. In Sect. 2, we describe Fresh Re-Keying and side-channel template attacks. Then, in Sect. 3 we define the Learning Parity with Noise problem and discuss algorithms aimed at solving this problem. After having introduced the groundwork, we give an attack outline and discuss the first steps in Sect. 4. In Sect. 5, we present our attack algorithm. Finally, in Sect. 6 we show an analysis of the attack performance by presenting outcomes of real and simulated experiments.

Notation. We now introduce some notation that is used throughout this paper. We denote bit vectors of length n as $GF(2^n)$, $\langle \cdot, \cdot \rangle$ denotes the binary inner product of the two such vectors.

We denote the probability of an event e as $P(e)$. For a random variable X, we use $\mathbb{E}(X)$ to denote its mean. In this paper, we use side-channel information to derive the probability that a bit b is set to 1. We write $p_b = P(b = 1)$. We use τ_b as the respective bias, i.e., $\tau_b = |p_b - 1/2|$. When performing a classification, we set $b = \lfloor p_b \rceil$, with $\lfloor \cdot \rceil$ the rounding operator. This classification has an error probability $\epsilon_i = 1/2 - \tau_i$.

The above is exactly the Bernoulli distribution with parameter p_b, we denote it as $Ber(p_b)$. We also make use of the so-called Poisson binomial distribution. This distribution describes the sum of N independent Bernoulli trials, where each trial has a possibly different Bernoulli parameter p_k. Given the vector $(p_1, \ldots, p_N)$, the respective density function can be computed by using the closed-form expression by Fernandez and Williams [10].

2 Fresh Re-Keying and Template Attacks

We now describe Fresh Re-Keying in more detail. Additionally, we recall side-channel template attacks. They will later allow us to derive probabilities for bits of the session key.

2.1 Fresh Re-Keying

Medwed et al. [16] introduced Fresh Re-Keying as a method to protect low-cost devices, such as RFID tags, against side-channel and fault attacks. The idea is to combine an encryption function f, e.g., the AES, with a re-keying function g. Every plaintext is encrypted using a fresh session key k^*. This k^* is obtained by invoking the re-keying function g with a fixed master key k and an on-tag generated public nonce r. This basic principle is shown in Fig. 1. Medwed et al. claim that this approach is particularly suited for challenge-response authentication protocols.

Medwed et al. claim that, as session keys k^* are never reused, it suffices to protect the encryption function f against Simple Power Analysis (SPA) type

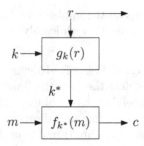

Fig. 1. Schematic of Fresh Re-Keying

attacks. The re-keying function g still requires protection against more powerful DPA-like attacks, but it does not need to be a cryptographically strong function. Instead, it should provide good diffusion and it should be easy to protect against DPA. They propose to use the following modular polynomial multiplication over $GF(2^8)$:

$$g : (GF(2^8)[y]/p(y))^2 \rightarrow GF(2^8)[y]/p(y) : (k, r) \rightarrow k * r \tag{1}$$

The polynomial $p(y) = y^d + 1$, with $d \in \{4, 8, 16\}$. We solely use $p(y) = y^{16} + 1$, as it is the most difficult to attack. For multiplication in $GF(2^8)$, we use the AES polynomial, i.e., $GF(2^8) = GF(2)[x]/(x^8 + x^4 + x^3 + x + 1)$.

The function g can be written as a matrix-vector product over $GF(2^8)$. With r_i and k_i ($0 \leq i < 16$) the bytes of the nonce and master key, respectively, the bytes of the session key k^* can be computed according to Eq. (2). Analogously, multiplications in $GF(2^8)$ can be written as matrix-vector products over $GF(2)$. Thus, g can be restated as a linear system over bits.

$$\begin{pmatrix} r_0 & r_{15} & r_{14} & \cdots & r_1 \\ r_1 & r_0 & r_{15} & \cdots & r_2 \\ r_2 & r_1 & r_0 & \cdots & r_3 \\ \vdots & \vdots & \vdots & \ddots & \vdots \\ r_{15} & r_{14} & r_{13} & \cdots & r_0 \end{pmatrix} \cdot \begin{pmatrix} k_0 \\ k_1 \\ k_2 \\ \vdots \\ k_{15} \end{pmatrix} = \begin{pmatrix} k_0^* \\ k_1^* \\ k_2^* \\ \vdots \\ k_{15}^* \end{pmatrix} \tag{2}$$

While this simple and regular structure makes implementation and masking easy, it is a potential risk when considering algebraic side-channel analysis. In fact, Medwed et al. were well aware of this threat, and they claim that cheap countermeasures are sufficient for protection. Concretely, they present a protected implementation of fresh re-keying running on an 8-bit microcontroller [15]. The re-keying function g is protected by means of masking and shuffling, whereas the encryption function f uses just the latter.

Fresh Re-Keying and Birthday-bound Security. Dobraunig et al. [8] showed that the Fresh Re-Keying scheme by Medwed et al. offers only birthday-bound security. They present a chosen-plaintext key-recovery attack having a time complexity of only $2 \cdot 2^{n/2}$ (instead of 2^n) for an n-bit key. However, their attack requires to pre-compute and store $2^{n/2}$ (key, ciphertext) pairs. Additionally, the attacked device, e.g., a low-cost tag featuring high execution times, needs to be queried $2^{n/2}$ times. These drawbacks make the attack impractical if, like in this paper, 128-bit AES is used. However, for weaker primitives, such as 80-bit PRESENT, the attack might be feasible.

In a follow-up work, Dobraunig et al. [9] proposed ways to provide higher security levels with Fresh Re-Keying. Yet, when using the same re-keying function g our attack still works. Thus, we omit the details of their work and focus on the original construction of Medwed et al.

2.2   Template Attacks and Leakage Model

Throughout this paper, we make extensive use of side-channel template attacks [6]. Instead of assuming a predetermined power model, such as Hamming-weight leakage, these attacks first profile the side-channel information of the attacked device. This requires possession of an identical device which is used for this profiling and whose key is already known.

When using an 8-bit device running the AES, an exemplary template attacks work as follows. One first profiles the side-channel information (on the profiling device) for each of the 256 possible inputs of the S-box. Then, templates typically following a multivariate Gaussian distribution are built. In the attack phase, each template is matched with the attack trace l coming from the attacked device. This results in a vector of conditional probabilities $p(s = v|l), 0 \leq v < 2^8$, with s the S-box input. Note that side-channel leakage can vary between otherwise identical devices. This might lead to inaccurate templates and conditional probabilities. We briefly discuss the impact on our attack later on.

For simulation of leakage, we use the common assumption that the device leaks a noisy Hamming weight of the processed data. The noise is assumed to be additive Gaussian with zero mean and variance σ_N^2. Thus, for a bit vector $\mathbf{z} \in \mathrm{GF}(2^n)$, we assume leakage $\mathcal{L}(\mathbf{z}) = \mathrm{HW}(\mathbf{z}) + \epsilon$, with $\epsilon \sim \mathcal{N}(0, \sigma_N)$. A common metric for the quality of the traces is the signal-to-noise ratio $\mathrm{SNR} = \sigma_S^2 / \sigma_N^2$ [14]. In the Hamming-weight leakage model, the signal variance $\sigma_S^2 = n/4$.

3   LPN and Solving Algorithms

Side-channel attacks on multiplication relate to the well known LPN problem. In this section, we restate its definition and give a brief overview of algorithms aimed at solving this problem. We then give a more in-depth explanation of LPN algorithms originating from coding theory.

3.1   Learning Parity with Noise

We now recall the formal definition of LPN (or more correctly of LPN's search version).

Definition 1 (Learning Parity with Noise). *Let* $\mathbf{k} \in GF(2^n)$ *and* $\epsilon \in (0, 0.5)$ *be a constant noise rate. Then, given* ν *vectors* $\mathbf{a}_i \in GF(2^n)$ *and noisy observations* $b_i = \langle \mathbf{a}_i, \mathbf{k} \rangle + e_i$, *the* $\mathbf{a}_i$ *sampled uniformly, and the* e_i *sampled from* $Ber(\epsilon)$, *find* $\mathbf{k}$.

The first algorithm to solve this problem in sub-exponential time was presented by Blum, Kalai, and Wassermann (BKW) [4]. Their algorithm was later improved by, e.g., Levieil and Fouque [13] and by Guo et al. [12]. A major drawback of BKW and its variants is the high number of required LPN samples ν. Especially in a side-channel context, this resource is somewhat scarce. This is even more so the case for Fresh Re-Keying, as it is targeted at low-resource devices typically featuring high execution times.

Connection to Random Linear Codes. The above LPN problem can be restated as decoding a random linear code over GF(2) [17]. Let $\mathbf{A} = [\mathbf{a}_i]_{0 \leq i < \nu}$ be the matrix whose rows are the $\mathbf{a}_i$. Further, let $\mathbf{b}$ and $\mathbf{e}$ be row vectors of the b_i and e_i, respectively. Then, one can think of $\mathbf{A}$ as generator matrix of a random linear code. Decoding requires to find the message $\mathbf{k}$ given a noisy word $\mathbf{b} = \mathbf{k}\mathbf{A} + \mathbf{e}$, which is exactly search LPN.

Linear codes are characterized by the three main parameters $[n, k, d]$, with n the code length, k the code dimension, and d the minimum Hamming distance between any two valid codewords. In the case of LPN, the dimension k is equal to the size of the secret. For random linear codes, the obtained code rate $R = k/n$ is, with very high probability, close to the Gilbert-Varshamov bound [7]. That is, $R \approx 1 - \mathrm{H}(d/n)$, with H the binary entropy function. The code length n is chosen according to this bound, with $d/n \approx \epsilon$.

Decoding random linear codes is an NP-hard problem, and decoding algorithms feature a runtime exponential in the code length. However, the sample requirements are much smaller when compared to BKW-style algorithms. We now give a brief introduction.

3.2   Algorithms for Decoding Random Linear Codes

The fastest algorithms for decoding random linear codes rely on *Information-Set Decoding* (ISD). First proposed by Prange in 1962 [18], these algorithms have quite a long history, with probably the most notable version being Stern's algorithm [19].

Syndrome Decoding. Before discussing decoding algorithms in detail, we briefly describe syndrome decoding. For a $(k \times n)$ generator matrix $\mathbf{G}$ in standard form, i.e., $\mathbf{G} = (I_k | Q)$, the so-called parity-check matrix $\mathbf{H}$ is given as $\mathbf{H} = (-Q^T | I_{n-k})$, with Q a $(k \times (n - k))$ matrix. The set of valid codewords C forms the kernel of the check matrix, i.e., $\mathbf{H}\mathbf{c} = 0, \forall \mathbf{c} \in C$. For a noisy word $\mathbf{y} = \mathbf{c} + \mathbf{e}$, we have $\mathbf{H}\mathbf{y} = \mathbf{H}\mathbf{e} = \mathbf{s}$. $\mathbf{s}$ is called the syndrome, it only depends on the error $\mathbf{e}$.

For decoding, we now want to find an error term $\mathbf{e}$ with some maximum weight w such that $\mathbf{H}\mathbf{e} = \mathbf{s}$. In other words, we are searching for at most w columns of $\mathbf{H}$ summing up to $\mathbf{s}$.

Stern's Attack (and Improvements). We now review Stern's algorithm. This algorithm takes as input a check matrix $\mathbf{H}$, a syndrome $\mathbf{s}$, and a maximum error weight w.

In a first step, Stern partitions the n columns of the parity-check matrix $\mathbf{H}$ into two distinct sets $\mathcal{I}, \mathcal{Q}$. $\mathcal{I}$ is made up of $(n - k)$ randomly selected columns which must form an invertible subset. $\mathcal{Q}$ is comprised of the remaining k columns. For simplicity, we assume that the columns of the check matrix are permuted such that $\mathbf{H}' = (\mathcal{Q}|\mathcal{I})$. Note that such a permutation also affects the syndrome and the position of error bits.

Next, he selects a size ℓ subset $\mathcal{Z}$ of $\mathcal{I}$, where ℓ is an algorithm parameter. $\mathcal{Q}$ is randomly split into two size $k/2$ subsets $\mathcal{X}, \mathcal{Y}$. The second part of $\mathbf{H}'$ is then transformed into identity form by applying elementary row operations. Stern then searches for (permuted) error terms $\mathbf{e}$ with a maximum weight w having exactly p nonzero bits in $\mathcal{X}$, p nonzero bits in $\mathcal{Y}$, no nonzero bits in $\mathcal{Z}$, and at most $w - 2p$ in the remaining columns. This is visualized in Eq. (3). This search uses a collision technique. If it fails, then the algorithm is restarted by selecting new $\mathcal{Q}$ and $\mathcal{I}$. For more details on the algorithm we refer to [3].

$$
\mathbf{H}' = (\mathcal{Q}|\mathcal{I}) =
\begin{pmatrix}
\overbrace{\begin{matrix}1 & 0 & 0\end{matrix}}^{k/2:\ p\ \text{err.}} \cdots & \cdots \overbrace{\begin{matrix}0 & 1 & 0\end{matrix}}^{k/2:\ p\ \text{err.}} & \overbrace{\begin{matrix}1\end{matrix}}^{\ell:\ 0\ \text{err.}} & & & \\
1 & 1 & 0 \cdots & \cdots 0 & 0 & 0 & 1 & & \\
0 & 1 & 1 \cdots & \cdots 1 & 1 & 1 & & 1 & \\
 & \vdots & & \vdots & & & & & \ddots \\
0 & 1 & 1 \cdots & \cdots 1 & 0 & 1 & & & & 1
\end{pmatrix}
\tag{3}
$$

Canteaut and Chabaud [5] proposed an improvement of this algorithm, which was later refined by Bernstein et al. [3]. Instead of choosing $\mathcal{Q}, \mathcal{I}$ randomly at each iteration and spending considerable time to transform $\mathbf{H}'$ to the desired form, one can use a simple column swapping. In each iteration, c elements of $\mathcal{Q}$ are exchanged with c from $\mathcal{I}$, where c is an algorithm parameter.

Stern and Reliability. The possibility of enhancing the performance of Stern's algorithm by using reliability information was briefly mentioned by Valembois [20]. However, thus far it was not used in a cryptographic or side-channel context. Also, it lacks proper description and an in-depth runtime analysis.

4   Attack Outline and Setup

In this section, we give a brief outline of our attack. Then, we describe in more detail the attack setup, i.e., how we compute bit probabilities from side-channel information. This is done for both the 8-bit leakage case and for the 128-bit case.

4.1   Outline

Before diving into the details, we now give a brief outline of our attack on Fresh Re-Keying. Here we focus on attacking the 8-bit software implementation by Medwed et al. [15].

In the very first step, we perform a template attack on the multiplication output k^*. Considering that the re-keying function g is (supposedly) implemented in a DPA-secure fashion, e.g., features masking and shuffling, attacking the multiplication result k^* directly seems unnecessarily difficult. Instead, we make use of the fact that k^* is used as (session) key in the following invocation of the AES. Thus, we use templates on the first-round S-box.

We then use the outcome of the template matching to derive a probability p_b for each session-key bit b. These probabilities are then used as input to our attack algorithm, which starts off by performing a filtering on the samples. Only those bits with low error probability are kept, while all others are discarded. The remaining equations are finally fed to a decoding algorithm, which solves the LPN problem and thus, allows master-key recovery. This algorithm is tweaked to use the reliability of the samples.

Why Decoding? Decoding is not the fastest way of solving LPN. However, in contrast to BKW-style algorithms it has very low sample requirements. In conjunction with filtering, this allows us to keep only the few best samples. Thus, we can reach a low average error rate. With BKW on the other hand, the higher number of required samples results in an increased expected error rate.

4.2   Fresh Re-Keying and 8-Bit Leakage

For the 8-bit implementation of Fresh Re-Keying, we perform a template attack on the first round of the AES. For each session key byte k_i^*, the vector of conditional probabilities $P(k_i^* = v|l)_{0 \le v < 2^8}$ is converted to bit-wise probabilities $p_{i,j} = \sum_{v:v[j]=1} P(k_i^* = v|l)$, with $v[j]$ the j-th bit of v.

Circumventing the Shuffling Countermeasure. As pointed out in Sect. 2.1, Medwed et al. [15] propose to use shuffling as a simple protection mechanism against algebraic attacks.

We circumvent this countermeasure by using a particular chosen constant plaintext $m = (00)||(FF)^{15}$, i.e., the first byte is set to 0 and all other bits are set to 1. Assuming a Hamming weight (or distance) leakage characteristic of the device, this particular choice maximizes the difference in power consumption during the initial AES key addition. By using templates on said key addition, it is possible to reveal the shuffled position of the 0 byte with probability significantly better than guessing.[1] In our attack, we use only the most likely position and thus can use 8 linear equations per trace. The bias of the corresponding S-box bits is multiplied with the probability of the classified shuffling position to obtain the final bias τ.[2]

The assumption of chosen plaintexts is reasonable in this context. The main proposed use case of Fresh Re-Keying is challenge-response authentication. In this setting, the attacked device chooses the nonce r, and the reader/attacker

---

[1] This method is only of limited use in a standard DPA, where the device uses a fixed key, as it strictly limits the number of observable plaintexts per key byte.

[2] This assumes that there is no reshuffling between key addition and S-box processing.

selects the challenge m. Observe that this attack technique does not make any assumptions on the implemented shuffling permutation-generation algorithm.

4.3   128-Bit Leakage

In the setting considered by Belaïd et al. [1], the attacker does not have access to partial results and can only observe the Hamming weight of the multiplication output. In this case, deriving bit probabilities is trivial. For an observed leakage $HW(\mathbf{z})$, with $\mathbf{z} \in GF(2^n)$, we have for each of the n bits $p_{i,0 \leq i < n} = HW(\mathbf{z})/n$.

5   Using Reliability to Increase Attack Performance

In this section, we explain our new attack algorithm and thus show how reliability information can be leveraged to reduce the computation time for the attack. First however, we introduce a new version of LPN which better describes the problem at hand.

5.1   LPVN: A New LPN Variant

In standard LPN (Definition 1), the error probability ϵ is constant for all samples. This, however, does not reflect the reality of the side-channel information, where every LPN sample can be assigned a possibly different error probability. We formalize this by introducing a new problem dubbed *Learning Parity with Variable Noise* (LPVN).

Definition 2 (Learning Parity with Variable Noise). *Let* $\mathbf{k} \in GF(2^n)$ *and* ψ *be a probability distribution over* $[0, 0.5]$. *Then, given* v *vectors* $\mathbf{a}_i \in GF(2^n)$, v *error probabilities* ϵ_i, *and noisy observations* $b_i = \langle \mathbf{a}_i, \mathbf{k} \rangle + e_i$, *the* $\mathbf{a}_i$ *sampled uniformly, the* ϵ_i *sampled from* ψ^3, *and the* e_i *sampled from* $Ber(\epsilon_i)$, *find* $\mathbf{k}$.

Casting LPVN to LPN is possible by simply setting $\epsilon = \mathbb{E}(\epsilon_i)$. However, the additional information in form of the ϵ_i allows to design more efficient algorithms. Also, it is easy to see that with a non-zero meta-probability distribution ψ in close vicinity of 0, the problem becomes trivial given enough samples.

5.2   Filtering

In the context of side-channel analysis, the overall average error rate $\mathbb{E}(\epsilon_i)$ can be expected to be high, i.e., beyond 0.25. The resulting large code length n (cf. Sect. 3.1) might lead to excruciating decoding runtimes.

In order to cut this time down drastically, we perform a filtering of the samples. When given a certain number v of LPVN samples, only the n with the lowest error probability are kept. All other samples are simply discarded. This

---

[3] This is not entirely correct for the attack of [1], in which each sampled error rate is applied to n samples instead of a single one. We neglect this minor difference.

approach differs from the filtering proposed by Belaïd et al. in that we can, at least in the 8-bit setting, filter individual bits. For 128-bit leakage however, the filtering methods are equivalent.

The number of available samples ν plays a crucial role in the expected attack runtime. By increasing ν, the quality of the best samples is also expected to rise. This in turn decreases the required code length n and the runtime of the decoding algorithm. Hence, a trade-off between the number of samples ν and computational complexity is possible. This is in stark contrast to standard LPN, where the decoding runtime is mostly independent of the number of samples.

Choosing the Code Length n. Thus far, we did not address the problem of selecting the code length n. In a heuristic approach, we choose the smallest n such that $R = k/n \geq 1 - H(d/n)$. We set d to the 75 % quantile of the error distribution function (computed using the Poisson binomial distribution) for the current n.

5.3   Using Reliability in Stern's Attack

After filtering, the n remaining samples are used as input for Stern's algorithm. More concretely, we use the improved version described by Bernstein et al. [3]. This algorithm does not directly cope with reliability information. Hence, by setting $b_i = \lfloor p_i \rceil$ a classification is performed.

Instead of discarding the reliability information at this point, we use it to further speed up the decoding process. Recall that the attack described in Sect. 3.2 involves a column-swapping step. We now tweak the algorithm by replacing the uniform selection of the swapped columns with a reliability-guided one. Goal is to minimize the expected error in $\mathcal{Q}$, while still assuring a high randomness in the chosen columns.

Column-Swapping Procedure. The probability that a column $t \in \mathcal{Q}$ is deselected in the next step is set to be directly proportional to its error probability ϵ_t, i.e., $P(t) = \epsilon_t / \sum_{t^* \in \mathcal{Q}} \epsilon_{t^*}$. Analogously, we use the *squared* bias to select the new column, i.e., for every $u \in \mathcal{I}$, $P(u) = \tau_u^2 / \sum_{u^* \in \mathcal{I}} \tau_{u^*}^2$. Experimentally we found that this combination gives the best performance.

We use rejection sampling in order to sample from these continuously changing probability density functions. Rejection sampling is a basic method to generate samples from a target probability distribution $f(x)$ when given samples from a different distribution $g(x)$. Concretely, we sample a $t \in \mathcal{Q}$ and a $u \in [0, \max_{0 \leq i < n}(\epsilon_i)]$ uniformly and accept t if $u < \epsilon_t$. Note that computation of the normalized probabilities $P(t)$ is not required for this method.

Runtime Analysis. The runtime of ISD algorithms is typically measured in the number of required bit operations. As the amount of operations per iteration of Stern's algorithm does not change when using our tweak, we refer to [3] for the calculation of this quantity. The number of required iterations however is expected to decrease. We now sketch our analysis.

In a first step, for each column t we retrieve $P(t \in \mathcal{Q})$, i.e., the average probability of t being part of $\mathcal{Q}$ when using above replacement rules. This is done by using a modified Markov-chain analysis. Then, we compute the probability density function for the error count for both $\mathcal{Q}$ and $\mathcal{I}$. For that we acquire the Poisson binomial PDF with $\epsilon_t \cdot P(t \in \mathcal{Q})$ and $\epsilon_t \cdot (1 - P(t \in \mathcal{Q}))$, respectively. Finally, a Markov-chain analysis similar to [3] is used to estimate the number of expected iterations. Due to space limitations, the detailed runtime analysis will appear in the full version of this paper.

The memory requirements of our decoding algorithm are negligible. They are limited to a single copy of the algorithm input per thread.

The Impact of Inaccurate Templates. As mentioned in Sect. 2.2, the leakage characteristic of the profiling device can slightly differ from that of the attacked device. This might lead to inaccurate templates and matching probabilities. As long as the profiling error is not too large, the attack will still work. However, the algorithm runtime and its analysis might suffer from inaccuracies.

6 Simulation and Practical Experiments

In order to show the real-world performance of our attack, we now present the outcome of our practical experiments. The focus is put upon the attack on 8-bit leakage, and more concretely on the software implementation of fresh re-keying proposed by Medwed et al. [15]. For completeness, the complexities for attacks on 128-bit leakage are also given.

6.1 Fresh Re-Keying on an 8-Bit Platform

We now report the outcome of both simulated and real attacks on the fresh re-keying implementation of [15]. We use the strategy described in Sect. 4.2, i.e., chosen plaintexts, to counter the proposed shuffling.

It is worth mentioning that both the simulated and real attack target only the block cipher f_{k^*}. Thus, it is independent of any countermeasures used to protect the re-keying function g. Also, we do not make any assumption on the generation of the permutation used for shuffling.

Simulation. For the simulated attack, traces according the Hamming-weight leakage model and some chosen SNR is generated. For each leaking S-box 3 samples (corresponding to the plaintext, the S-box input, and the S-box output) are generated. Due to the chosen plaintexts, the key is equivalent to the S-box input. Thus, it does not reveal any further information and was not included in simulation.

The $\mathrm{SNR_{PT}}$ for plaintext leakage was chosen to be smaller than $\mathrm{SNR_{SB}}$ used for S-box simulation. This was done in order to match the characteristic of the real device. Leakage and attack simulation was performed for two such SNR sets, namely for $(\mathrm{SNR_{SB}} = 1, \mathrm{SNR_{PT}} = 0.2)$ and for $(\mathrm{SNR_{SB}} = 0.5, \mathrm{SNR_{PT}} = 0.2)$. An estimation of the meta-probability distribution $\psi(\epsilon)$ is shown in Fig. 2.

Figure 3 depicts the expected attack runtime as a function of the available traces. Solid lines denote performed experiments, whereas dots show estimates.

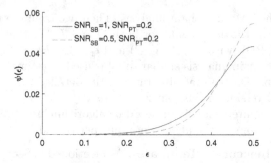

Fig. 2. Meta-probability ψ for simulated traces

We also compare the runtime of our tweaked decoding algorithm described with an untweaked version.[4] When using the parameters of Fig. 3b and 2^{12} traces, the attack requires approximately 2^{50} bit operations. Our attack implementation required, on average, 4 hours to recover the key, using 6 out of 8 virtual cores on a recent Intel Core i7 CPU.

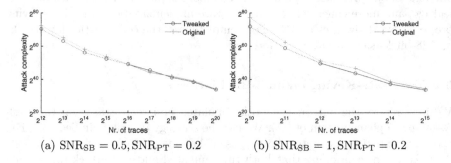

(a) $\text{SNR}_{\text{SB}} = 0.5, \text{SNR}_{\text{PT}} = 0.2$ (b) $\text{SNR}_{\text{SB}} = 1, \text{SNR}_{\text{PT}} = 0.2$

Fig. 3. Runtime complexity of the attack

Real Traces. We measured the power consumption of a shuffled AES software implementation running on an AVR ATxmega256A3. Using a separate set of 200.000 profiling traces, we built Gaussian templates for each of the 256 possible input values of the S-box and for the two chosen plaintext bytes.[5] The points of interest were chosen according to a student t-test, as proposed by Gierlichs et al. [11]. The attack was then performed on the same device.

Figure 4 depicts the outcome of the template attack. Figure 4b shows the estimated distribution of the confidence in the attack on the shuffling. The peak

---

[4] Beware that due to the strong dependency on the quality of the samples and the exponential complexity, the runtime can still vary greatly for a certain trace count.

[5] For the plaintext, we only consider leakage during the key addition. The initial operand fetching was ignored, as this can be implemented without leaking the shuffling position.

at 0 shows that there is an acceptable number of traces with high confidence in the identified shuffling position. The overall success rate is roughly 44 %.

Figure 4a shows the resulting $\psi(\epsilon)$. As it turns out, the density near 0 is relatively high. With a reasonable amount of traces, one can expect the 128 best equations to be error free. Thus, the system can be solved by using straightforward Gaussian elimination.[6] Still, the number of traces can be further reduced by using our attack. As shown in Fig. 5, 512 traces are sufficient to recover the master key in reasonable time.

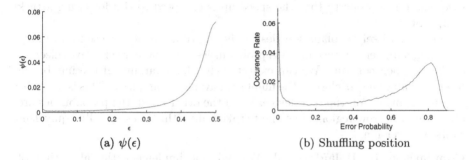

(a) $\psi(\epsilon)$ (b) Shuffling position

Fig. 4. Template attack on real traces

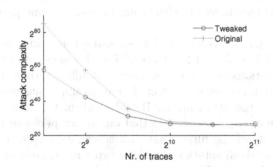

Fig. 5. Attack runtime for real traces

6.2 128-Bit Leakage

For completeness, we now give some runtime estimates for the setting of Belaïd et al. In their first example, they recover a 96-bit secret with the lowest error probability being 0.26. These numbers translate to a complexity of approximately 2^{55} for our attack. When comparing it to the above stated runtimes, this

---

[6] In fact, Belaïd et al. [15] present an attack on an 8-bit implementation using this approach. However, they do not consider the shuffling countermeasure and use Hamming-weight filtering instead of S-box templates.

is still well within the realms of feasibility. When attacking a 128-bit secret (with best error probability 0.28), the complexity rises to 2^{75}. Feasibility cannot be claimed anymore in this case.

6.3   Comparison of Algorithms

We now discuss the performance increase by using reliabilities in Stern's algorithm. As can be seen above, this speed-up varies greatly. In the attack on the real device it is substantial, whereas it becomes smaller in the simulations. All cases share the property that the speed-up is excepted to rise for rising attack complexity.

The most likely explanation lies in the distribution of the used ϵ_i. Simply speaking, a higher variance in these probabilities allows a more effective selection of the swapped columns. We can expect such a high variance if the number of filtered samples n gets close to the number of available samples ν. This is, e.g., the case in the attack on the real device. If, on the other hand, the probabilities are all within a narrow region, then the tweaked algorithm is essentially equivalent to its base version.

Comparison to Belaïd et al. We did not implement the algorithm of Belaïd et al., thus making a detailed and fair comparison difficult. Nonetheless, we now try to provide a point of reference. Belaïd et al. report that the attack on a 96-bit secret took 6.5 hours on a 32-core machine with 200 GB RAM. When using these parameters in their runtime analysis, one gets a complexity of roughly 2^{44}.

The same complexity is achieved when using their runtime analysis with the parameters of Fig. 3b and 2^{12} traces.[7] For this same attack, we require 4 hours for 2^{50} operations using 6 cores. Thus, the differing time constants in the exponential notation cannot be neglected. This example suggests that our new attack outperforms the algorithm by Belaïd et al. in this case. We performed further such evaluations. They suggest that our attack performs better for cases where the error rate of the filtered samples is low, e.g., up to 0.2, yet not low enough to allow a trivial solution. For high error rates, such as in the 128-bit leakage scenario, their algorithm performs clearly better.

7   Conclusion and Future Work

The results from the previous section clearly show that the simple structure of the re-keying function makes algebraic side-channel attacks a real threat. Also, it seems that shifting the task of DPA security to a dedicated re-keying function is not trivial. Leakage of its output must be considered in all subsequent operations

---

[7] Note that we already used our S-box templates and bit-wise filtering for this estimation. When using the extreme Hamming weight method proposed in [1] (on 8-bit data), then the expected error and thus runtime increases.

and simple protection mechanisms, such as shuffling, might not be sufficient for protection.

There exist multiple thinkable ways of protecting Fresh Re-Keying against the presented attacks. An obvious one is to add further countermeasures to the AES, which however increases protection overhead. Alternatively, one could change the re-keying function g, e.g., to polynomial multiplication over a prime field instead of $GF(2^8)$.

In future work, we intend to apply the idea of using reliability to BKW-style algorithms, such as LF1 [13]. Also, we would like to present an in-depth runtime comparison of solving algorithms.

Acknowledgements

 The research leading to these results has received funding from the European Union's Horizon 2020 research and innovation programme under grant agreement No 644052 (HECTOR). Furthermore, this work has been supported by the Austrian Research Promotion Agency (FFG) under grant number 845589 (SCALAS). We would also like to thank Benoît Gérard and Jean-Gabriel Kammerer for answering questions regarding their work and for providing the source code used for their runtime estimation.

References

1. Belaïd, S., Coron, J.-S., Fouque, P.-A., Gérard, B., Kammerer, J.-G., Prouff, E.: Improved side-channel analysis of finite-field multiplication. In: Güneysu, T., Handschuh, H. (eds.) CHES 2015. LNCS, vol. 9293, pp. 395–415. Springer, Heidelberg (2015)
2. Belaïd, S., Fouque, P.-A., Gérard, B.: Side-channel analysis of multiplications in $GF(2^{128})$. In: Sarkar, P., Iwata, T. (eds.) ASIACRYPT 2014, Part II. LNCS, vol. 8874, pp. 306–325. Springer, Heidelberg (2014)
3. Bernstein, D.J., Lange, T., Peters, C.: Attacking and defending the McEliece cryptosystem. In: Buchmann, J., Ding, J. (eds.) PQCrypto 2008. LNCS, vol. 5299, pp. 31–46. Springer, Heidelberg (2008)
4. Blum, A., Kalai, A., Wasserman, H.: Noise-tolerant learning, the parity problem, and the statistical query model. J. ACM **50**(4), 506–519 (2003)
5. Canteaut, A., Chabaud, F.: A new algorithm for finding minimum-weight words in a linear code: application to McEliece's cryptosystem and to narrow-sense BCH codes of length 511. IEEE Trans. Inf. Theor. **44**(1), 367–378 (1998)
6. Chari, S., Rao, J.R., Rohatgi, P.: Template attacks. In: Kaliski Jr, B.S., Koç, Ç.K., Paar, C. (eds.) CHES 2002. LNCS, vol. 2523, pp. 13–28. Springer, Heidelberg (2003)
7. Coffey, J., Goodman, R.: Any code of which we cannot think is good. IEEE Trans. Inf. Theor. **36**(6), 1453–1461 (1990)
8. Dobraunig, C., Eichlseder, M., Mangard, S., Mendel, F.: On the security of fresh re-keying to counteract side-channel and fault attacks. In: Joye, M., Moradi, A. (eds.) CARDIS 2014. LNCS, vol. 8968, pp. 233–244. Springer, Heidelberg (2015)
9. Dobraunig, C., Koeune, F., Mangard, S., Mendel, F., Standaert, F.: Towards fresh and hybrid re-keying schemes with beyond birthday security. In: 14th International Conference on Smart Card Research and Advanced Applications, CARDIS (2015, to appear)

10. Fernandez, M., Williams, S.: Closed-form expression for the poisson-binomial probability density function. IEEE Trans. Aerosp. Electron. Syst. **46**(2), 803–817 (2010)
11. Gierlichs, B., Lemke-Rust, K., Paar, C.: Templates vs. stochastic methods. In: Goubin, L., Matsui, M. (eds.) CHES 2006. LNCS, vol. 4249, pp. 15–29. Springer, Heidelberg (2006)
12. Guo, Q., Johansson, T., Löndahl, C.: Solving LPN using covering codes. In: Sarkar, P., Iwata, T. (eds.) ASIACRYPT 2014. LNCS, vol. 8873, pp. 1–20. Springer, Heidelberg (2014)
13. Levieil, É., Fouque, P.-A.: An improved LPN algorithm. In: De Prisco, R., Yung, M. (eds.) SCN 2006. LNCS, vol. 4116, pp. 348–359. Springer, Heidelberg (2006)
14. Mangard, S., Oswald, E., Popp, T.: Power Analysis Attacks - Revealing the Secrets of Smart Cards. Springer, USA (2007). 978-0-387-30857-9
15. Medwed, M., Petit, C., Regazzoni, F., Renauld, M., Standaert, F.-X.: Fresh re-keying II: securing multiple parties against side-channel and fault attacks. In: Prouff, E. (ed.) CARDIS 2011. LNCS, vol. 7079, pp. 115–132. Springer, Heidelberg (2011)
16. Medwed, M., Standaert, F.-X., Großschädl, J., Regazzoni, F.: Fresh re-keying: security against side-channel and fault attacks for low-cost devices. In: Bernstein, D.J., Lange, T. (eds.) AFRICACRYPT 2010. LNCS, vol. 6055, pp. 279–296. Springer, Heidelberg (2010)
17. Pietrzak, K.: Cryptography from learning parity with noise. In: Bieliková, M., Friedrich, G., Gottlob, G., Katzenbeisser, S., Turán, G. (eds.) SOFSEM 2012. LNCS, vol. 7147, pp. 99–114. Springer, Heidelberg (2012)
18. Prange, E.: The use of information sets in decoding cyclic codes. IRE Trans. Inf. Theor. **8**(5), 5–9 (1962)
19. Stern, J.: A method for finding codewords of small weight. In: Cohen, G., Godlewski, P. (eds.) Coding Theory 1986. LNCS, vol. 388, pp. 106–113. Springer, Heidelberg (1988)
20. Valembois, A.: Fast soft-decision decoding of linear codes, stochastic resonance in algorithms. In: Proceedings of the IEEE International Symposium on Information Theory, p. 91 (2000)

Towards a Unified Security Model for Physically Unclonable Functions

Frederik Armknecht[1], Daisuke Moriyama[2]([⊠]),
Ahmad-Reza Sadeghi[3], and Moti Yung[4]

[1] University of Mannheim, Mannheim, Germany
[2] NICT, Koganei, Japan
dmoriyam@nict.go.jp
[3] TU Darmstadt, Darmstadt, Germany
[4] Google and Columbia University, New York, USA

Abstract. The use of Physically Unclonable Functions (PUFs) in cryptographic protocols attracted an increased interest over recent years. Since sound security analysis requires a concise specification of the alleged properties of the PUF, there have been numerous trials to provide formal security models for PUFs. However, all these approaches have been tailored to specific types of applications or specific PUF instantiations. For the sake of applicability, composability, and comparability, however, there is a strong need for a unified security model for PUFs (to satisfy, for example, a need to answer whether a future protocol requirements match a new and coming PUF realization properties).

In this work, we propose a PUF model which generalizes various existing PUF models and includes security properties that have not been modeled so far. We prove the relation between some of the properties, and also discuss the relation of our model to existing ones.

Keywords: Physically unclonable function · Security model · Specifications

1 Introduction

Physically Unclonable Functions (PUFs) are functions represented by physical objects which are mainly provided by unavoidable arbitrary variations during the manufacturing process. PUFs can be used to secure secret key generation and key management as an alternative to achieving this by dedicated (more expensive) security processors, such as Trusted Platform Module (TPM) and employing random number generation. Currently, there are three major research topics regarding PUFs:

1. Hardware: Proposing a new construction of PUF or evaluating existing PUFs based on implementation (FPGA, ASIC, etc.) [12,13,18,19,22,26].
2. Protocol Design: Considering a PUF as an abstract building block and proposing new cryptographic primitives or protocols [4,6,7,14,21,23,29,31].

© Springer International Publishing Switzerland 2016
K. Sako (Ed.): CT-RSA 2016, LNCS 9610, pp. 271–287, 2016.
DOI: 10.1007/978-3-319-29485-8_16

3. Modeling: Investigating theoretical perspectives on PUFs and describing a security model [1, 2, 6, 12, 13, 25, 26].

In particular, we note that there have been, obviously, multiple attempts to come up with security models for PUFs, these often aimed for specific types of applications and/or PUF hardware types. This results in the very unsatisfying situation that, up to now, there is no one-for-all PUF model (or supermodel) which covers all desired properties. This deficiency has some serious consequences. For example, protocols where security has been shown under different models cannot be easily combined without requiring a new security analysis. In the worst case, formalizations may be even incompatible, which would demand a complete reevaluation of these parts. Another problem is that protocol designers face the challenge of choosing the "right" security model among the existing ones, and mapping models to devices is not often clear. In fact, as we will discuss, there exist PUF-based protocols which require a selection of security properties that are not covered by a single model yet.

Contribution

In this work, we aim at closing this gap, by comparing the various existing models, describing a new security model which unifies and extends them, and confront its properties against hardware devices and protocols in the field.

First, the new model covers the most relevant security properties of PUFs. The overall situation is depicted in Table 1. Here, the columns display the considered security properties. In the upper part of the table, we mark for a variety of security models, and which of these properties is covered by the respective model. Each model, indeed, covers some (or all) of the following notions: sufficient min-entropy of the outputs, one-wayness, unforgeability, and unclonability. To motivate the necessity of a unifying model, in the lower part we give examples of three previously published protocols, which security properties need to hold for these protocols to be secure. As one can observe, some models would not be suitable to analyze the security of some of the protocols. In fact only the model of Brzuska et al. [6] includes all four properties.

Unfortunately, even this model is not sufficiently comprehensive. For example, the RFID authentication scheme described in [29] requires that the PUF outputs are pseudorandom, a property not included into any of these models. Thus, our model does not only unify these models but formalizes three novel security properties: indistinguishability, pseudorandomness, and tamper resilience.

A further extension given by our model is the output distributions of PUFs. Due to the fact that PUF outputs are noisy, all models include the notion of *intra-distance* of outputs. This refers to the distance (with respect to an according metric) between several outputs of the same PUF on the same input. However, we argue that in addition two types of *inter-distance* should be part of a comprehensive security model. By *inter-distance I* we consider the variation of outputs of a *single* PUFs when queried on *multiple* input while *inter-distance II* is about the distance between the outputs of *multiple* PUFs on the *same* input.

Table 1. Comparison of several existing PUF security model and overview of required security properties for different protocol examples. One can analyze other PUF-based schemes or protocols so that which properties are required with this table.

Security model	Min-entropy	One-wayness	Unforge-ability	Unclon-ability	Indistin-guishability	Pseudo-randomness	Tamper-resilience
Pappu [26]	-	X	X	-	-	-	-
Gassend et al. [12]	-	-	X	-	-	-	-
Guajardo et al. [13]	-	-	X	-	-	-	-
Armknecht et al. [2]	X	-	-	X	-	-	-
Armknecht et al. [1]	X	-	X	X	-	-	-
Brzuska et al. [6]	X	X	X	X	-	-	-
Maes [20]	-	X	X	X	-	-	-
Ours	X	X	X	X	X	X	X
Example protocols	Min-entropy	One-wayness	Unforge-ability	Unclon-ability	Indistin-guishability	Pseudo-randomness	Tamper-resilience
Challenge-response [26]	-	-	X	-	-	-	-
PUF-PRF [2]	X	-	X	X	-	-	-
RFID Authentication [29]	-	-	-	X	-	X	-

So far, inter-distance I has been covered only by the model of Gassend et al. [12], while inter-distance II is only part of the model by Maes [20].

Since all these properties are covered by our model, it represents the most comprehensive model so far. We discuss the relation of our model to existing works in more detail at the end of this paper.

Important note: We have to stress that we do not claim that a single PUF should meet all these properties. This is clearly not the case. However, each of the properties covered in our model has been considered in previous work or is natural to be considered (e.g., tamper resilience). In that sense, we see our model as the most general (i.e., a super-model) and flexible one, that when given a PUF-based protocol requirements, allows to express the necessary security properties.

Outline. Section 2 summarizes the preliminaries. Section 3 describes our model in detail, and explains relations between the covered security properties. Section 4 compares our model to related work, while Sect. 5 concludes the paper.

2   Notations

For a probabilistic machine or algorithm A, the term $A(x)$ denotes the random variable of the output of A on input x. $a \leftarrow A(x)$ indicates the event that A outputs a on input x the value a. When A is a set, $y \xleftarrow{\cup} A$ means that y is uniformly selected from A. $|A| \leq \mathsf{poly}(x)$ indicates that the number of elements in A is polynomially bounded by x. When the parameter x is clear from the context, we omit it. When a is a value, $y := a$ denotes that y is set as a. For two values a, a', the expression $\mathsf{Dist}(a, a')$ denotes the distance between a and a' according to some metrics (e.g., Hamming distance, edit distance). $\tilde{H}_\infty(A)$ indicates the min-entropy of A and $\tilde{H}_\infty(A \mid B)$ evaluates the conditional min-entropy of A given B.

3   Security Model: Properties and Their Relationships

In this section, we describe our model. We start with a specification of the overall system and then formalize various properties of PUFs which are security relevant. A PUF is a probabilistic mapping $f : \mathcal{D} \to \mathcal{R}$ where $\mathcal{D}$ is a domain space and $\mathcal{R}$ is an output range of PUF f. The creation of a PUF is formally expressed by invoking a manufacturing process $\mathcal{MP}$. That is a $\mathcal{MP}$ is a randomized procedure which takes inputs from a range of parameters and outputs a new PUF. We do not specify the input range of $\mathcal{MP}$ in purpose as it strongly depends on the concrete PUF but also on the considered attacker model. For example, in the weakest attacker model the input range of $\mathcal{MP}$ is empty. This would model the case that there is one legitimate process for creating the PUF and an attacker can only invoke exactly this procedure. The other extreme is that $\mathcal{MP}$ is a kind of "universal creation process" where for any product an according parameter input does exist. In general, one may imagine that $\mathcal{MP}$ represents a class of creating processes which is parameterized. Next, we formalize the security properties with respect to a given security parameter λ and PPT attackers (polynomial in λ).

3.1   Output Distribution

Due to the fact that PUFs have noisy outputs, considering the output distribution is important. In the following, we specify four different requirements with respect to different aspects of the output distribution. Depending on the concrete application, one would have to choose a PUF where some or all of these conditions are met. We first give a formal definition and explain its rationale afterwards. The following definitions are parametrized by some thresholds δ_i, the number of iterations t, the number of inputs ℓ, the number of devices n, a negligible function $\epsilon(\cdot)$, and the security parameter λ.

Intra-Distance Requirement: Whenever a single PUF is repeatedly evaluated with a fixed input, the maximum distance between the corresponding outputs is at most δ_1. That is for any created PUF $f \leftarrow \mathcal{MP}(param)$ and any $y \in \mathcal{D}$, it holds that

$$\Pr\left[\max(\{\mathsf{Dist}(z_i, z_j)\}_{i \neq j}) \leq \delta_1 \mid y \in \mathcal{D}, \{z_i \leftarrow f(y)\}_{1 \leq i \leq t}\right] = 1 - \epsilon(\lambda).$$

Inter-Distance I Requirement: Whenever a single PUF is evaluated on different inputs, the minimum distance among them is at least δ_2. That is for a created PUF $f \leftarrow \mathcal{MP}(param)$ and for any $y_1, \ldots, y_\ell \in \mathcal{D}$, we have

$$\Pr\left[\min(\{\mathsf{Dist}(z_i, z_j)\}_{i \neq j}) \geq \delta_2 \,\middle|\, \begin{array}{l} y_1, \ldots, y_\ell \in \mathcal{D}, \\ \{z_i \leftarrow f(y_i)\}_{1 \leq i \leq \ell} \end{array}\right] = 1 - \epsilon(\lambda).$$

Inter-Distance II Requirement: Whenever multiple PUFs are evaluated on a single, fixed input, the minimum distance among them is at least δ_3. That is for any created PUF $f_i \leftarrow \mathcal{MP}(param)$ for $1 \leq i \leq n$ and any $y \in \mathcal{D}$, we have

$$\Pr\left[\min(\{\mathsf{Dist}(z_i, z_j)\}_{i \neq j}) \geq \delta_3 \mid y \in \mathcal{D}, \{z_i \leftarrow f_i(y)\}_{1 \leq i \leq n}\right] = 1 - \epsilon(\lambda).$$

Min-Entropy Requirement: Whenever multiple PUFs are evaluated on multiple inputs, the min-entropy of the outputs is at least δ_4, even if the other outputs are observed. Let $z_{i,j} \leftarrow f_i(y_j)$ be the output of a PUF f_i on input y_j where $f_i \leftarrow \mathcal{MP}(param)$. Then

$$\Pr\left[\tilde{H}_\infty(z_{i,j} \mid \mathcal{Z}_{i,j}) \geq \delta_4 \,\middle|\, \begin{array}{c} y_1,\ldots,y_\ell \in \mathcal{D}, \\ \mathcal{Z} := \{z_{i,j} \leftarrow f_i(y_j)\}_{1\leq i\leq n, 1\leq j\leq \ell}, \\ \mathcal{Z}_{i,j} := \mathcal{Z} \setminus \{z_{i,j}\} \end{array}\right] = 1 - \epsilon(\lambda)$$

holds for sufficiently large δ_4.

Definition 1. *A PUF $f : \mathcal{D} \to \mathcal{R}$ has $(\mathcal{MP}, t, n, \ell, \delta_1, \delta_2, \delta_3, \epsilon)$-variance if the PUF's output has inter and intra distances as described above, parameterized by $(\mathcal{MP}, t, n, \ell, \delta_1, \delta_2, \delta_3)$.*

Definition 2. *A PUF $f : \mathcal{D} \to \mathcal{R}$ has $(\mathcal{MP}, n, \ell, \delta_4, \epsilon)$-min-entropy if the PUF satisfies the min-entropy requirement explained above.*

The *intra-distance* and the two metrics of *inter-distance* are very important notions, crucial to ensure the correctness of schemes built on top of the PUF. For example, if $\delta_1 \geq \delta_2$ then outputs from the same inputs may exhibit a higher distance than outputs coming from different inputs. Similarly, $\delta_1 \geq \delta_3$ would result in the situation that outputs of the same PUF have a larger distance than outputs of other PUFs. This is, for example, critical when PUFs are used as authenticating devices. Therefore, $\delta_1 < \delta_2$ and $\delta_1 < \delta_3$ are necessary conditions to allow for a clear distinction between different inputs and different PUFs. These are fundamental issues to assure the *uniqueness* for each output.

One popular method to assert the uncertainty of the PUF's output is the notion of min-entropy. For example the min-entropy is an important aspects if combined with a *fuzzy extractor* [11] to ensure outputs with a sufficient level of randomness can be reconstructed nonetheless. Consequently, Bzruska et al. [6] included the notion of min-entropy in their model, but limited their definition to the case that the inputs have all a certain Hamming distance, which we omit in our model. Since the restriction of the inputs requires extra cost for the scheme layer itself, and correlated inputs may influence the min-entropy evaluation, we define the min-entropy for arbitrary chosen $y_i \in \mathcal{D}$. Furthermore, our min-entropy evaluation is more general than [6], so that outputs from other devices are also included to evaluate the conditional entropy. This is useful when we consider a multi-party setting where each party holds his own PUF.

Next, we provide formal security definitions for PUF properties that are based on security notions from "classical" cryptographic primitives. Throughout the rest of the paper, we assume that the number of PUFs created by a specific parameter via Create is polynomially bounded in λ and we simply denote the upper bound as n. Similarly, the Response query issued by a malicious adversary to obtain the PUF's response is also polynomially bounded. We also assume that intra-distance δ_1 is strictly smaller than any of the inter-distances (δ_2, δ_3) (except with negligible probability ϵ).

3.2 One-Wayness

One of the most basic security requirements in cryptography is one-wayness. This is formalized by the following game between a challenger and an adversary $\mathcal{A} = (\mathcal{A}_1, \mathcal{A}_2)$.

Setup. The challenger selects a manufacturing process $\mathcal{MP}$ and initial parameter $param$. The challenger sends $(1^\lambda, \mathcal{MP}, param)$ to adversary $\mathcal{A}_1$. In addition, the challenger creates a list List which is initially empty and initializes two counters (c_0, c_1).

Phase 1. $\mathcal{A}_1$ can adaptively issue the following oracle queries.
- When $\mathcal{A}_1$ issues Create($param'$), the challenger checks $param'$. If $param' = param$, the challenger increments c_0 and creates a new PUF $f_{c_0} \leftarrow \mathcal{MP}(param)$. If $param' \neq param$ and $param'$ is a valid input to the manufacturing process, the challenger increments c_1 and invokes $f'_{c_1} \leftarrow \mathcal{MP}(param')$. Otherwise, the challenger responds with $\perp$.
- When $\mathcal{A}_1$ sends Response(b, i, y_j) with $b \in \{0, 1\}$, the challenger proceeds as follows. If $b = 0$ (indicating that a correctly constructed PUF shall be queried) and if $i \leq c_0$, the challenger responds $z_{i,j} \leftarrow f_i(y_j)$. If $b = 1$ and $i \leq c_1$, the challenger responds $z'_{i,j} \leftarrow f'_i(y_j)$. Otherwise, the challenger outputs $\perp$.

Challenge. When $\mathcal{A}_1$ finishes Phase 1, $\mathcal{A}_1$ sends an index $i^* \leq c_0$ to the challenger and outputs state information st. Then the challenger selects $y^* \xleftarrow{U} \mathcal{D}$ and responds $z^* \leftarrow f_{i^*}(y^*)$ to $\mathcal{A}$.

Phase 2. Given z^* and st, $\mathcal{A}_2$ continuously issues the oracle query as Phase 1.

Guess. Finally, $\mathcal{A}_2$ outputs y_1^*.

The advantage of the adversary for the above game is defined by

$$\mathsf{Adv}_{\mathcal{A}}^{\mathsf{OW}}(\lambda, \delta_1) := \Pr[y^* = y_1^*] - (\ell + 1)/|\mathcal{D}|$$

where ℓ denotes the number of queries the adversary issued to the i^*-th PUF. The adversary wins the above game if $\mathsf{Adv}_{\mathcal{A}}^{\mathsf{OW}}(\lambda, \delta_1) > 0$ holds with non-negligible probability in λ.

In Phase 1 and 2, the adversary can submit Create($param'$) to create a new PUF. If $param' = param$, a PUF is created by the default parameter originally chosen by the challenger. Otherwise, a PUF is created with a different parameter specified by the adversary to generate a malicious PUF [8,25] or bad PUF [10,27]. A malicious PUF may leak extra information to the adversary. This is necessary as in general, one cannot exclude that an attacker could learn valuable information from evaluating PUF which are created with (possibly only slightly) different parameters. The adversary can obtain the output of PUFs via oracle query regardless of the parameter setting whenever the PUF has been created. We note that the attack target, chosen in the challenge phase and evaluated in the guess phase, is a PUF created by the default parameter $param$. As we will see later, the concept of malicious PUFs, i.e., PUFs being created by different parameters, are also useful to discuss the relationship to the notion of unclonability. $(\ell + 1)/|\mathcal{D}|$ gives the probability that the adversary trivially breaks the one-wayness with random guess when we faithfully cover the noise from the PUF; more detailed discussion is appeared in the full version of this paper.

Definition 3. *A PUF provides* $(\mathcal{MP}, n, \ell, \delta_1, \epsilon)$*-one-wayness if for any PPT adversary* $\mathcal{A}$*,* $\Pr[\mathsf{Adv}_{\mathcal{A}}^{\mathsf{OW}}(\lambda, \delta_1) > 0] \leq \epsilon(\lambda)$ *holds.*

3.3 Unforgeability

Many PUF-based protocols base their security on the assumption that estimating the output of a PUF should not be possible without having access to the device. While several previous works call this notion as *unpredictability*, we refer to this property as *unforgeability*. The main reason is that, as we will show, it shares many similarities with the typical security notions in the context of digital signature schemes or MACs, being Universal Unforgeability (UUF) and Existential Unforgeability (EUF). Both notions are considered in the context of different attack types: Key Only Attack (KOA), Known Message Attack (KMA), and Chosen Message Attack (CMA). In some cases, One Time (OT) security is also considered which refers to the case that the involved oracle can be queried only once.

In our model, we adopt these established security notions for PUFs. The EUF-CMA security game against a PUF is described by the following:

Setup. The challenger proceeds as the setup phase in the one-wayness game and sends $(1^\lambda, \mathcal{MP}, param)$ to adversary $\mathcal{A}$.

Learning. $\mathcal{A}$ can adaptively issue oracle queries (Create and Response) as defined in the one-wayness game.

Guess. After the learning phase, $\mathcal{A}$ outputs (i^*, y^*, z^*).

We disallow the adversary to submit Response$(param, i^*, y^*)$ in the learning phase. The advantage of the adversary is defined by

$$\mathsf{Adv}_{\mathcal{A}}^{\mathsf{EUF\text{-}CMA}}(\lambda, \delta_1) := \Pr[\mathsf{Dist}(z^*, f_{i^*}(y^*)) \leq \delta_1] - |\mathcal{Z}'|/|\mathcal{R}|$$

where f_i^* has been produced by a challenger in the learning phase and $\mathcal{Z}' := \{z \mid z_{i^*} \leftarrow f_{i^*}(y^*), \mathsf{Dist}(z_{i^*}, z) \leq \delta_1\}$. We say that the adversary wins the unforgeability game iff $\mathsf{Adv}_{\mathcal{A}}^{\mathsf{EUF\text{-}CMA}}(\lambda, \delta_1) > 0$ holds with non-negligible probability in λ.

A similar definition can be found in [1] but their security model considers only PUFs which are combined with a fuzzy extractor. We do not make any assumption on a post-processing mechanism and consider the security issue for the PUFs itself. Therefore, we do not evaluate the equality but (appropriate) distance between z^* and $f_{i^*}(y^*)$ (interestingly, the existing security models except [1] only consider the equality against the stand-alone PUFs). Since we adopt the intra-distance notion here, there are $|\mathcal{Z}'|$ candidates for $f_{i^*}(y^*)$ in $\mathcal{R}$. Hence, the advantage is defined as the probability to output a candidate minus the probability to simply pick a random element of this set.

Definition 4. *A PUF provides* $(\mathcal{MP}, n, \ell, \delta_1, \epsilon)$-*EUF-CMA security if for any PPT adversary* $\mathcal{A}$, $\Pr[\mathsf{Adv}_{\mathcal{A}}^{\mathsf{EUF\text{-}CMA}}(\lambda, \delta_1) > 0] \leq \epsilon(\lambda)$ *holds.*

3.4 Unclonability

As the name physically unclonable function indicates, an important assumption with respect to a PUF is that it should be hard for an adversary to come up with two PUFs that exhibit quite similar input-output behavior. We capture this by an unclonability game, formalized as follows:

Setup. The challenger proceeds as the setup phase in the one-wayness game and sends $(1^\lambda, \mathcal{MP}, param)$ to adversary $\mathcal{A}$.

Learning. $\mathcal{A}$ can adaptively issue the oracle queries (Create and Response) as defined in the one-wayness game.

Guess. After the learning phase, $\mathcal{A}$ outputs a triple of the form (i^*, b, j^*) with $b \in \{0, 1\}$ and $(b, i^*) \neq (b', j^*)$.

The goal of the attacker is to create a clone to a PUF which stems from the set of PUFs that have been created under the parameters *param*. We refer to these as the *original* parameters. The first entry i^* of the output refers to the i^*-th PUF within this set. The other two parameters (b, j^*) are interpreted as follows. If $b = 0$ then it refers to j^*-th PUF created under the original parameters *param* otherwise to the j^*-th PUF created under the modified parameters. Let f_{i^*} and f'_{j^*} denote these two PUFs. The adversary wins the unclonability game if PUF f'_{j^*} performs sufficiently similar to f_{i^*}. More formally, the advantage of the adversary is defined as

$$\mathsf{Adv}_{\mathcal{A}}^{\mathsf{Clone}}(\lambda, \delta_1) := \Pr[\forall y \in \mathcal{D}, \mathsf{Dist}(f_{i^*}(y), f'_{j^*}(y)) \leq \delta_1].$$

Definition 5. *A PUF provides* $(\mathcal{MP}, n, \ell, \delta_1, \epsilon)$-*unclonability if for any PPT adversary* $\mathcal{A}$, $\mathsf{Adv}_{\mathcal{A}}^{\mathsf{Clone}}(\lambda, \delta_1) \leq \epsilon(\lambda)$ *holds.*

Recall that an adversary may use parameters *param'* for the manufacturing process that are different to the originally used parameters *param*. However, she is only successful if she can clone a PUF that results from the original manufacturing process. On the other hand, the clone itself may result from different parameters *params'*. This has some fundamental consequences. For example, when $|\mathcal{D}| \in \mathsf{poly}(\lambda)$ holds, the adversary can learn all input-output pairs $\{(y_j, z_j)\}_j$ in the learning phase and select *param'* such that the input-output behavior includes the complete lookup table provided by $\{(y_j, z_j)\}_j$. This means $(\mathcal{MP}, n, |\mathcal{D}|, \delta_1, \epsilon)$-unclonability cannot be satisfied in such cases. Various memory-based PUFs belong to this class. We stress, however, that this does not mean that such PUFs are of no value, but rather that such PUFs need to be protected by additional measures.

The above definition aims to comprehensively capture the notion of unclonability. To this end, we have to consider two relaxed notions of unclonability. One approach is that the adversary may only create PUFs according to the original manufacturing process, i.e., $param' = param$ in all queries. We call this variant as *target unclonable*. Another way to cover a relaxed notion of unclonability is that we explicitly restrict the upper bound of oracle queries the adversary issues in the learning phase as $\ell < |\mathcal{D}|$. Since $|\mathcal{D}| \in \mathsf{poly}(\lambda)$ holds for memory-based PUFs, it is useful to consider this restriction. We call this variant as *restricted unclonable*.

Observe that our model covers scenarios like building attacks [28,30] and fault injection attacks [24]. The supervised learning in the machine learning attack analyzes a set of training data as input and estimates an unobserved output, so it is considered as an attack for the EUF-KMA security.

3.5 Indistinguishability

For many cryptographic schemes and protocols, the notion of indistinguishability is fundamental to providing security or privacy. Although it is useful for designers to capture the notion that a PUF's output is indistinguishable from another output, former models ignored this aspect and mainly concentrate on the unforgeability. Consider a simple challenge-response authentication performed by a PUF's input-output pair. The unforgeability against the PUF provides the security against impersonation attack, but the privacy aspect cannot be argued with this notion only. When a PUF satisfies indistinguishability, it means, in principle, that no one can deduce from observed output which PUF has been in use. Therefore, the notion of indistinguishability for PUFs is important with respect to *privacy-preserving* protocols. The indistinguishability game between a challenger and adversary $\mathcal{A} := (\mathcal{A}_1, \mathcal{A}_2)$ is defined as follows:

Setup. The challenger proceeds as the setup phase in the one-wayness game and sends $(1^\lambda, \mathcal{MP}, param)$ to adversary $\mathcal{A}$.

Phase 1. $\mathcal{A}_1$ can adaptively issue the oracle queries (Create and Response) as defined in the one-wayness game.

Challenge. The adversary submits two tuples (i_0^*, y_0^*) and (i_1^*, y_1^*) which are not issued as Response$(param, i_0^*, y_0^*)$, Response$(param, i_1^*, y_1^*)$ in Phase 1. Then the challenger flips a coin $b \xleftarrow{\mathsf{U}} \{0,1\}$ and responds $z_b^* \leftarrow f_{i_b^*}(y_b^*)$ to the adversary.

Phase 2. $\mathcal{A}_2$ receives st and can continuously issue (Create, Response) except Response$(param, i_0^*, y_0^*)$ and Response$(param, i_1^*, y_1^*)$.

Guess. Finally, the adversary outputs a guess b'.

The adversary wins the indistinguishability game if $b' = b$ holds with probability more than $1/2$.

While the PUF is not a deterministic function, the adversary can estimate the challenger's coin if he can obtain $f_{i_0^*}(y_0^*)$ or $f_{i_1^*}(y_1^*)$ by checking the distance from z_b^*. Thus we cannot allow the adversary to issue Response$(param, i_0^*, y_0^*)$ nor Response$(param, i_1^*, y_1^*)$. Instead, $\mathcal{A}$ can choose $i_0^* = i_1^*$ to distinguish the output difference from one device or $y_0^* = y_1^*$ to consider the output variance between two devices with same input. The advantage of the adversary in the above indistinguishability-based game is defined by

$$\mathsf{Adv}_{\mathcal{A}}^{\mathsf{IND}}(\lambda) := |2 \cdot \Pr[b' = b] - 1|.$$

Definition 6. *A PUF satisfies* $(\mathcal{MP}, n, \ell, \epsilon)$-*indistinguishablility if for any PPT adversary* $\mathcal{A}$, $\mathsf{Adv}_{\mathcal{A}}^{\mathsf{IND}}(\lambda) \le \epsilon(\lambda)$ *holds.*

3.6 Pseudorandomness

Some protocols consider a PUF as a kind of physical pseudorandom function that cannot be shared simultaneously by two different parties (e.g., [29]). In fact, depending on how sensitive the PUF behavior is with respect to the physical state, such assumptions may be justified. In any case, a comprehensive model should cover a notion of pseudorandomness. Our definition is based on the pseudorandomness game described below:

Setup. The challenger proceeds as the setup phase in the one-wayness game and sends $(1^\lambda, \mathcal{MP}, param)$ to adversary $\mathcal{A}$. In addition, the challenger flips a coin $b \xleftarrow{\mathsf{U}} \{0, 1\}$, creates a list List which is initially empty and prepares counter (c_0, c_1) and truly random function RF, i.e., a random oracle.

Learning. The adversary can issue (Create and Response) queries as defined in the one-wayness game. When the challenger receives a Response$(param', i, y_j)$ query, the challenger performs the following :

  – If $param' \ne param$ or $b = 1$, performs as in the one-wayness game. When $param' = param$ and $i \le c_0$, responds with $z_{i,j} := f_i(y_j)$. When $param' \ne param$ and $i \le c_1$, respond $z_{i,j} := f'_i(y_j)$. In other cases, respond $\perp$.

  – If $param' = param$ and $b = 0$, the challenger inputs (i, y_j) to RF and obtains $z'_{i,j} \in \mathcal{R}$. Then he selects some random noise and applies it to $z'_{i,j}$ to derive $z_{i,j}$ which satisfies $\mathsf{Dist}(z_{i,j}, z'_{i,j}) \le \delta_1$. If $i \le c_0$, respond $z_{i,j}$. Otherwise, output $\perp$.

Guess. Finally, $\mathcal{A}$ outputs a guess b'.

The adversary wins the pseudorandomness game iff $b' = b$.

  The main difference from the canonical pseudorandom function is that the challenger does not directly hands outputs $z'_{i,j}$ which came from the truly random function but adds some noise bounded by δ_1. This additional procedure is critical to emulate the actual PUF's behavior from intra-distance perspective. Our description is more suitable to minimize the gap between the real output and ideal output. Even if $b = 0$, the challenger selects the same value $z'_{i,j}$ for a fixed input from RF and adds appropriate noise against $z'_{i,j}$. The advantage of the adversary in the above pseudorandomness game is defined by

$$\mathsf{Adv}_{\mathcal{A}}^{\mathsf{PR}}(\lambda, \delta_1) := |2 \cdot \Pr[b' = b] - 1|.$$

Definition 7. *A PUF has* $(\mathcal{MP}, n, \ell, \delta_1, \epsilon)$-*pseudorandomness if for any PPT adversary* $\mathcal{A}$, $\mathsf{Adv}^{\mathsf{PR}}_{\mathcal{A}}(\lambda, \delta_1) \leq \epsilon(\lambda)$ *holds.*

Sadeghi et al. [29] assumed an ideal PUF which achieves idealized behavior of PUFs and argued that the ideal PUF must satisfies the same notion. While the ideal PUF assumes no noise (i.e., $\delta_1 = 0$), we carefully defined this notion in a formal way to capture the intrinsic noise observed in real PUFs.

3.7 Tamper-Resilience

One of the motivations to employ a PUF in cryptographic schemes and protocols is to provide resilience to physical attacks at cheaper costs compared to other measures like using a Trusted Platform Module (TPM). Though the existing security models for PUFs do not formally define this property, physical attack against the PUF should not leak any internal structure of the device. We consider the following simulation based definition of tamper-resilience. That is, we consider two parties: an adversary $\mathcal{A}$ and a simulator $\mathcal{S}$. The adversary $\mathcal{A}$ can issue (Create, Response) queries as in the previous definitions. Moreover, whenever Create($param$) is launched, $\mathcal{A}$ receives the produced PUF f_i and can analyze it physically. That is, $\mathcal{A}$ can mount arbitrary physical attacks on the PUF (e.g., power analysis, probing attack, etc.). On the other hand, the algorithm $\mathcal{S}$ can only adaptively issue (Create, Response) but does not get physical access to the created PUFs. Both of them finally output internal state st. The idea is that if for any adversary $\mathcal{A}$ who has physical access to a PUF, there exists a simulator $\mathcal{S}$ which behaves practically the same but without physical access, then the consequence is that the physical access does not provide any advantage. In this case, we say that the PUF is tamper resilient. The advantage of $\mathcal{A}$ in the above experiment is defined by

$$\mathsf{Adv}^{\mathsf{Tamp}}_{\mathcal{A}, \mathcal{S}, \mathcal{B}}(\lambda) :=$$
$$\left| \begin{array}{l} \Pr[\mathcal{B}(1^\lambda, st) \to 1 \,|\, st \leftarrow \mathcal{A}^{\mathsf{Create}, \mathsf{Response}}(1^\lambda, \mathcal{MP}, param, f_1, f_2, \ldots)] \\ \quad - \Pr[\mathcal{B}(1^\lambda, st) \to 1 \,|\, st \leftarrow \mathcal{S}^{\mathsf{Create}, \mathsf{Response}}(1^\lambda, \mathcal{MP}, param)] \end{array} \right|$$

where $\mathcal{B}$ is a distinguisher who tries to distinguish st generated by $\mathcal{A}/\mathcal{S}$.

Definition 8. *A function* f *is a* $(\mathcal{MP}, n, \ell, \epsilon)$-*tamper resilient PUF if for any PPT adversary* $\mathcal{A}$, *there exists a PPT algorithm* $\mathcal{S}$, *for any PPT distinguisher* $\mathcal{B}$, $\mathsf{Adv}^{\mathsf{Tamp}}_{\mathcal{A}, \mathcal{S}, \mathcal{B}}(\lambda) \leq \epsilon(\lambda)$ *holds.*

As explained above, the intuition is that the adversary $\mathcal{A}$ actually receives PUFs themselves and hence can conduct different actions in principle, e.g., see the structure of the chip and gate-delay, and launch arbitrary side-channel analysis[1]. These results can be contained in st and $\mathcal{B}$ tries to distinguish whether st is

---

[1] We do not limit the number of physical attacks the adversary can mount as defined in [17]. Instead, the pamter-resilience assures there is no extra information is leaked by the physical attacks.

output from $\mathcal{A}$ or $\mathcal{S}$. Therefore, if $\mathcal{B}$ cannot distinguish $\mathcal{A}$'s output and $\mathcal{S}$'s output, this means that no additional information which is not trivially derived from challenge-response pairs is extracted by the physical attack (regardless of what they are).

3.8   Relationships Between the Security Properties

While each of the security properties had its own separate motivation, we show in the following that these are not completely independent. More precisely, we point out several relationships between these and show the following statements as described in Fig. 1 (full formal security proofs are in the full version):

- Restricted unclonability is equivalent to EUF-CMA security
- Indistinguishability implies EUF-CMA security and one-wayness
- No implication between one-wayness and EUF-CMA security
- Pseudorandomness implies indistinguishability
- $(\mathcal{MP}, n, |\mathcal{R}|, \lambda, \epsilon)$-min-entropy implies $(\mathcal{MP}, n, \ell, \delta_1, \epsilon)$-EUF-CMA security
- $(\mathcal{MP}, n, |\mathcal{R}|, \log|\mathcal{R}|, \epsilon)$-min-entropy implies $(\mathcal{MP}, n, \ell, \epsilon)$-pseudorandomness.

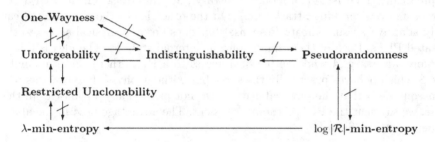

Fig. 1. Relationship among the security properties and min-entropy. For simplicity, we exclude several parameters corresponding to the number of devices, oracle queries and negligible fractions except the amount of min-entropy.

4   Comparison to Existing Security Models

In this section, we compare our model to previous models [1,2,6,12,13,20,26]. An overview is given in Tables 2 and 3. Due to the page limit, we provide the prior security definitions in the full version and discuss here only the differences with our definition.

In all previous models PUF outputs are noisy and hence they consider their intra-distance of outputs. However, the two metrics of inter-distance which refer to evaluations on either multiple inputs or multiple devices are not comprehensively discussed but have been considered in [12] and [20], respectively. This is somewhat surprising, since if the intra-distance is not smaller than the two

Table 2. Comparison of output distribution defined in the security models

	Intra-distance	Inter-distance I	Inter-distance II	Min-entropy	Number of PUFs	Number of queries
Pappu [26]	Yes[a]	-	-	-	1	1
Gassend et al. [12]	Yes	Yes	-	-	1	poly
Guajardo et al. [13]	Yes[a]	-	-	-	1	1
Armknecht et al. [2]	Yes	-	-	Yes[b]	1	poly
Armknecht et al. [1]	Yes	-	-	Yes	poly	poly
Brzuska et al. [6]	Yes	-	-	Yes	1	poly
Maes [20]	Yes	-	Yes	-	1	poly
Ours	Yes	Yes	Yes	Yes	poly	poly

[a] They do not formally define the intra-distance but their implementation results or arguments implicitly show the intra-distance.
[b] Their definition is not information-theoretical min-entropy but computational version of min-entropy called HILL entropy [15]

inter-distances (see discussion in Sect. 3.1), many security properties are trivially broken (including the unforgeability defined in each paper). In fact, the notions of intra-distance and inter-distance are widely known to implementation designers, but have not been formally captured, e.g., see [13,18,19,22].

As one can see from Table 3 (and as discussed in Sect. 1), our model covers more security properties than the previous models. This flexibility allows us to express more combinations of different security properties which, in turn, is advantageous for protocol designers to capture needed underlying security assumptions. A further difference is that previous work hardly discussed the relation between different security properties (and if, then often only in a heuristic

Table 3. Comparison of security properties proposed in the security models

	one-wayness	Unforge-ability	Unclon-ability	Indistin-guishability	Pseudo-randomness	Tamper-resilience	Evaluation
Pappu [26]	Yes	UUF-KOA	-	-	-	-	Equality
Gassend et al. [12]	-	UUF-KMA	-	-	-	-	Equality
Guajardo et al. [13]	-	UUF-OT-KMA	-	-	-	-	Equality
Armknecht et al. [2]	-	-	Yes	-	-	-	-
Armknecht et al. [1]	-	UUF-KMA	Yes	-	-	-	Equality[a]
		EUF-CMA					Equality
Brzuska et al. [6]	Yes	EUF-CMA	Yes	-	-	-[b]	Equality
Maes [20]	Yes	UUF-CMA	Yes	-	-	-	Distance
Ours	Yes	EUF-CMA	Yes	Yes	Yes	Yes	Distance

[a] As we noted in Sect. 3.3, this model concentrates on a combination of PUF and fuzzy extractor and the evaluation with equality is a natural result
[b] They argue the necessity of the tamper-resilience in the full version of [6], but no formal definition is described

sense, e.g., [6]) while, for reasoning about realization, it is crucial to prove which notion is stronger/weaker than another.

Another advantage of our definitions from a theoretical view point is that the intrinsic noise caused by the device is accurately reflected in the definition of an adversary's advantage. It is well known for implementation designers that PUFs output noisy data, and further how to efficiently derive a random but fixed output with a fuzzy extractor or other techniques; see [3,16,22]. On the other hand, the previous security models except [1] do not cover the noise in evaluating the advantage of the adversary in their security properties. Estimating the exact noise is intractable and their models cannot fairly evaluate the adversarial advantage. We argue that this neglects an important aspect of PUFs. For example, the higher the noise in the output distribution, the more likely it gets that two PUFs show indistinguishable behavior, and the easier it may become to create clones. Similar thoughts regarding noise apply to almost all security properties. Of course, one possible solution to the above specific issue would be to consider not the PUF alone but only in combination with an appropriate fuzzy extractor as in [1]. However, this approach does not capture the actual requirements for the PUF itself and may fail to cover cases where a PUF is not combined with a fuzzy extractor. Apart from this, a cryptographic protocol may require dedicated security properties of the deployed fuzzy extractor, e.g., see [5]. Hence, we think that the security for PUFs should be argued separately from its typically adjoined building blocks.

Somewhat surprising, we observed that even a seemingly straightforward notion of unforgeability has been treated differently in existing literature. To highlight these differences, we express them using the canonical terminology used for digital signatures and MACs (see Table 3). We specifically stress that our definition of unforgeability covers a stronger attack model compared to other models, since we allow the adversary to obtain direct PUF responses from multiple devices and oracle queries.

Finally, we want to point to the work of Delvaux et al. [9] where different security aspects of PUF-based protocols are discussed. Since their work does not treat security properties for PUFs formally, we do not compare our security model with their informal arguments.

5   Conclusion

In this paper, we proposed a new extended security model for PUFs motivated by existing models, typical demands of cryptographic protocols, but also based on our own considerations about the nature of PUFs. Compared to the existing works, our model is more comprehensive, and presents security definitions that are either new or stronger, (e.g., by allowing an adversary to query multiple devices). We also extended these definitions by taking PUF output distributions directly into account.

Formalizing security definitions with multiple properties, first, helps protocol designers to extract the actual requirements for PUF constructions, and, secondly, helps implementation designers to easily find which security properties the proposed PUF construction possesses. Moreover, having a unified security model allows to compare the security of different PUFs and different PUF models. We see our model as a significant step towards this goal.

In light of our methodology, various open questions remain. For example: Are all relevant security properties included in the model or are some missing? Furthermore, due to the physical nature of PUFs, it is often difficult to assess given a concrete PUF, if and what security properties are met. Thus, for the sake of applicability, a PUF security model should allow an engineer to evaluate for a PUF whether certain properties are fulfilled (at least to some extent). While our model follows common cryptographic considerations and models, one cannot rule out that adaptations of the definitions (within our methodology) would make them more applicable for engineers. This clear interdisciplinary task, is a natural open question.

References

1. Armknecht, F., Maes, R., Sadeghi, A., Standaert, F., Wachsmann, C.: A formalization of the security features of physical functions. In: IEEE S&P 2011, pp. 397–412. IEEE Computer Society (2011)
2. Armknecht, F., Maes, R., Sadeghi, A.-R., Sunar, B., Tuyls, P.: Memory leakage-resilient encryption based on physically unclonable functions. In: Matsui, M. (ed.) ASIACRYPT 2009. LNCS, vol. 5912, pp. 685–702. Springer, Heidelberg (2009)
3. Bösch, C., Guajardo, J., Sadeghi, A.-R., Shokrollahi, J., Tuyls, P.: Efficient helper data key extractor on FPGAs. In: Oswald, E., Rohatgi, P. (eds.) CHES 2008. LNCS, vol. 5154, pp. 181–197. Springer, Heidelberg (2008)
4. Boureanu, I., Ohkubo, M., Vaudenay, S.: The limits of composable crypto with transferable setup devices. In: Bao, F., Miller, S., Zhou, J., Ahn, G. (eds.) ASIACCS 2015, pp. 381–392. ACM (2015)
5. Boyen, X.: Reusable cryptographic fuzzy extractors. In: Atluri, V., Pfitzmann, B., McDaniel, P.D. (eds.) ACMCCS 2004, pp. 82–91. ACM (2004)
6. Brzuska, C., Fischlin, M., Schröder, H., Katzenbeisser, S.: Physically uncloneable functions in the universal composition framework. In: Rogaway, P. (ed.) CRYPTO 2011. LNCS, vol. 6841, pp. 51–70. Springer, Heidelberg (2011)
7. Busch, H., Katzenbeisser, S., Baecher, P.: PUF-based authentication protocols – revisited. In: Youm, H.Y., Yung, M. (eds.) WISA 2009. LNCS, vol. 5932, pp. 296–308. Springer, Heidelberg (2009)
8. Dachman-Soled, D., Fleischhacker, N., Katz, J., Lysyanskaya, A., Schröder, D.: Feasibility and infeasibility of secure computation with malicious PUFs. In: Garay, J.A., Gennaro, R. (eds.) CRYPTO 2014, Part II. LNCS, vol. 8617, pp. 405–420. Springer, Heidelberg (2014)
9. Delvaux, J., Gu, D., Peeters, R., Verbauwhede, I.: A survey on lightweight entity authentication with strong PUFs. IACR Cryptology ePrint Archive, p. 977 (2014)
10. van Dijk, M., Rührmair, U.: Physical unclonable functions in cryptographic protocols: security proofs and impossibility results. Cryptology ePrint Archive, Report 2012/228 (2012)
11. Dodis, Y., Ostrovsky, R., Reyzin, L., Smith, A.: Fuzzy extractors: how to generate strong keys from biometrics and other noisy data. SIAM J. Comput. 38(1), 97–139 (2008)

12. Gassend, B., Clarke, D.E., van Dijk, M., Devadas, S.: Silicon physical random functions. In: Atluri, V. (ed.) ACMCCS 2002, pp. 148–160. ACM (2002)
13. Guajardo, J., Kumar, S.S., Schrijen, G.-J., Tuyls, P.: FPGA intrinsic PUFs and their use for IP protection. In: Paillier, P., Verbauwhede, I. (eds.) CHES 2007. LNCS, vol. 4727, pp. 63–80. Springer, Heidelberg (2007)
14. Hammouri, G., Sunar, B.: PUF-HB: a tamper-resilient HB based authentication protocol. In: Bellovin, S.M., Gennaro, R., Keromytis, A.D., Yung, M. (eds.) ACNS 2008. LNCS, vol. 5037, pp. 346–365. Springer, Heidelberg (2008)
15. Håstad, J., Impagliazzo, R., Levin, L.A., Luby, M.: A pseudorandom generator from any one-way function. SIAM J. Comput. 28(4), 1364–1396 (1999)
16. Hofer, M., Boehm, C.: An alternative to error correction for SRAM-like PUFs. In: Mangard, S., Standaert, F.-X. (eds.) CHES 2010. LNCS, vol. 6225, pp. 335–350. Springer, Heidelberg (2010)
17. Kardas, S., Celik, S., Bingöl, M.A., Kiraz, M.S., Demirci, H., Levi, A.: k-strong privacy for radio frequency identification authentication protocols based on physically unclonable functions. Wire;. Commun. Mob. Comput 15, 2150–2166 (2013)
18. Katzenbeisser, S., Kocabaş, U., Rožić, V., Sadeghi, A.-R., Verbauwhede, I., Wachsmann, C.: PUFs: myth, fact or busted? A security evaluation of physically unclonable functions (PUFs) cast in silicon. In: Prouff, E., Schaumont, P. (eds.) CHES 2012. LNCS, vol. 7428, pp. 283–301. Springer, Heidelberg (2012)
19. Krishna, A.R., Narasimhan, S., Wang, X., Bhunia, S.: MECCA: a robust low-overhead PUF using embedded memory array. In: Preneel, B., Takagi, T. (eds.) CHES 2011. LNCS, vol. 6917, pp. 407–420. Springer, Heidelberg (2011)
20. Maes, R.: Physically Unclonable Functions - Constructions, Properties and Applications. Springer, Heidelberg (2013)
21. Maes, R., Van Herrewege, A., Verbauwhede, I.: PUFKY: a fully functional PUF-based cryptographic key generator. In: Prouff, E., Schaumont, P. (eds.) CHES 2012. LNCS, vol. 7428, pp. 302–319. Springer, Heidelberg (2012)
22. Maes, R., Tuyls, P., Verbauwhede, I.: Low-overhead implementation of a soft decision helper data algorithm for SRAM PUFs. In: Clavier, C., Gaj, K. (eds.) CHES 2009. LNCS, vol. 5747, pp. 332–347. Springer, Heidelberg (2009)
23. Majzoobi, M., Rostami, M., Koushanfar, F., Wallach, D.S., Devadas, S.: Slender PUF protocol: a lightweight, robust, and secure authentication by substring matching. In: IEEE S&P 2012, pp. 33–44. IEEE Computer Society (2012)
24. Oren, Y., Sadeghi, A.-R., Wachsmann, C.: On the effectiveness of the remanence decay side-channel to clone memory-based PUFs. In: Bertoni, G., Coron, J.-S. (eds.) CHES 2013. LNCS, vol. 8086, pp. 107–125. Springer, Heidelberg (2013)
25. Ostrovsky, R., Scafuro, A., Visconti, I., Wadia, A.: Universally composable secure computation with (malicious) physically uncloneable functions. In: Johansson, T., Nguyen, P.Q. (eds.) EUROCRYPT 2013. LNCS, vol. 7881, pp. 702–718. Springer, Heidelberg (2013)
26. Pappu, R.: Physical one-way functions. PhD thesis, MIT (2001)
27. Rührmair, U., van Dijk, M.: Pufs in security protocols: attack models and security evaluations. In: IEEE S&P 2013, pp. 286–300. IEEE Computer Society (2013)
28. Rührmair, U., Sehnke, F., Sölter, J., Dror, G., Devadas, S., Schmidhuber, J.: Modeling attacks on physical unclonable functions. In: Al-Shaer, E., Keromytis, A.D., Shmatikov, V. (eds.) ACMCCS 2010, pp. 237–249. ACM (2010)
29. Sadeghi, A., Visconti, I., Wachsmann, C.: PUF-enhanced RFID security and privacy. In: SECSI (2010), pp. 366–382 (2010)

30. Saha, I., Jeldi, R.R., Chakraborty, R.S.: Model building attacks on physically unclonable functions using genetic programming. In: HOST 2013, pp. 41–44. IEEE Computer Society (2013)
31. Tuyls, P., Skoric, B.: Strong authentication with physical unclonable functions. In: Petkovic, M., Jonker, W. (eds.) Security, Privacy, and Trust in Modern Data Management, pp. 133–148. Springer, Heidelberg (2007)

Structure-Preserving Signatures

Cryptanalysis of the Structure-Preserving Signature Scheme on Equivalence Classes from Asiacrypt 2014

Yanbin Pan[✉]

Key Laboratory of Mathematics Mechanization, NCMIS,
Academy of Mathematics and Systems Science,
Chinese Academy of Sciences, Beijing 100190, China
panyanbin@amss.ac.cn

Abstract. At Asiacrypt 2014, Hanser and Slamanig presented a new cryptographic primitive called structure-preserving signature scheme on equivalence classes in the message space $(\mathbb{G}_1^*)^\ell$, where $\mathbb{G}_1$ is some additive cyclic group. Based on the signature scheme, they constructed an efficient multi-show attribute-based anonymous credential system that allows to encode an arbitrary number of attributes. The signature scheme was claimed to be existentially unforgeable under the adaptive chosen message attacks in the generic group model. However, for $\ell = 2$, Fuchsbauer pointed out a valid existential forgery can be generated with overwhelming probability by using 4 adaptive chosen-message queries. Hence, the scheme is existentially forgeable under the adaptive chosen message attack at least when $\ell = 2$. In this paper, we show that even for the general case $\ell \geq 2$, the scheme is *existentially forgeable* under the *non-adaptive* chosen message attack and *universally forgeable* under the *adaptive* chosen message attack. It is surprising that our attacks will succeed all the time and need fewer queries, which give a better description of the scheme's security.

Keywords: Structure-preserving signature · Equivalence classes · EUF-CMA · UF-CMA

1 Introduction

Structure-preserving signatures introduced by Abe *et al.* [2] have many applications in cryptographic constructions, such as blind signatures [2,7], group signatures [2,7,13], homomorphic signatures [3,12], and tightly secure encryption [1,11]. Typically, the structure-preserving signatures are defined over some groups equipped with a bilinear map. The public key, the messages and the

Y. Pan—This work was supported in part by the NNSF of China (No. 11201458, No. 11471314 and No. 61572490), and in part by the National Center for Mathematics and Interdisciplinary Sciences, CAS.

K. Sako (Ed.): CT-RSA 2016, LNCS 9610, pp. 291–304, 2016.
DOI: 10.1007/978-3-319-29485-8_17

signatures in a structure-preserving signature scheme consist only of group elements, and the signature can be verified just by deciding group membership and by evaluating some pairing-product equations.

At Asiacrypt 2014, Hanser and Slamanig [9] proposed a new cryptographic primitive called structure-preserving signature scheme on equivalence classes (SPS-EQ), which allows to sign at one time an equivalence class of a group-element vector instead of just the vector itself. As shown in [9], the SPS-EQ scheme asks for some additional conditions to enable its applications to construct an efficient attribute-based multi-show anonymous credential systems. First, given a message-signature pair (here the message can be seen as a representative of some class), another valid signature for every other representative of the class can be efficiently produced, without knowing the secret key. Second, any two representatives of the same class with corresponding signatures seem unlinkable, which was called class hiding in [9].

Hanser and Slamanig [9] also presented a concrete SPS-EQ scheme on equivalence classes in the message space $(\mathbb{G}_1^*)^\ell$, where $\mathbb{G}_1$ is some additive cyclic group. Any two vectors in the same equivalence class are equal up to a scale factor. The scheme is claimed to be existentially unforgeable under adaptive chosen message attack (EUF-CMA) in the generic group model for SXDH groups [4]. However, Fuchsbauer [5] later pointed out their claim is flawed when $\ell = 2$ by showing how to generate a valid existential forgery with overwhelming probability with 4 chosen message queries. For $\ell \geq 3$, Fuchsbauer [5] did not give any discussion and it seems not trivial to generalize his attack to the case when $\ell \geq 3$. Hence, the signature scheme can not be EUF-CMA secure, at least when $\ell = 2$.

In this paper, we study its security further. Both of the cases when $\ell = 2$ and $\ell \geq 3$ are considered.

First, we show that the scheme is *existentially forgeable* under the *non-adaptive* chosen message attack. More precisely, we present a polynomial-time attack which can generate a valid existential forgery with just 2 (*resp.* 3) non-adaptive chosen message queries for $\ell = 2$ (*resp.* $\ell \geq 3$), which is half of the number of the queries needed in Fuchsbauer's adaptive chosen message attack.

Second, we show that the scheme is in fact *universally forgeable* under the *adaptive* chosen message attack. In our polynomial-time attack, we can forge the valid signature for any given message with 3 (*resp.* 4) chosen message queries for $\ell = 2$ (*resp.* $\ell \geq 3$), which is also less than the number of the queries needed in Fuchsbauer's attack.

Moreover, both of our attacks will always succeed, whereas Fuchsbauer's attack succeeds with overwhelming probability.

In a revised version [10], Hanser and Slamanig recently pointed out that the original security proof in [9] was incorrect since in it just the non-adaptive message queries were considered, but the adaptive message queries were neglected. They also proved the scheme can at least provide existential unforgeability under random message attacks (EUF-RMA). Together with our results, the security of this scheme is much more clear, which can be summarized as in Table 1.

Table 1. The security of the Hanser-Slamanig SPS-EQ scheme

Attack model	Security	ℓ
Random message attack	Existential unforgeability [10]	$\ell \geq 2$
Non-adaptive chosen message attack	Existential forgeability [this work]	$\ell \geq 2$
Adaptive chosen message attack	Existential forgeability [5]	$\ell = 2$
	Universal forgeability [this work]	$\ell \geq 2$

To fix the Hanser-Slamanig scheme, Fuchsbauer, Hanser and Slamanig [6] presented a new SPS-EQ scheme which is proved to be secure under adaptive chosen message attacks. We have to point out that the new scheme can resist our attack.

Roadmap. The remainder of the paper is organized as follows. In Sect. 2, we give some preliminaries needed. We describe the Hanser-Slamanig SPS-EQ scheme in Sect. 3, and present our attacks in Sect. 4. Finally, a short conclusion is given in Sect. 5.

2 Preliminaries

We denote by $\mathbb{Z}$ the integer ring, by $\mathbb{Z}_p$ the residue class ring $\mathbb{Z}/p\mathbb{Z}$ and by $\mathbb{Z}_p^*$ the group of all the invertible elements in $\mathbb{Z}_p$. Let $\mathbb{G}$ be the cyclic group and $\mathbb{G}^*$ be the set of all the non-zero elements in $\mathbb{G}$. Denote by $1_{\mathbb{G}}$ (*resp.* $\mathbf{0}$) the identity element when $\mathbb{G}$ is multiplicative (*resp.* additive). We denote by $\ker(\varphi)$ the kernel of map φ.

2.1 Bilinear Map

As in [9], we first give some definitions about bilinear map.

Definition 1 (Bilinear Map). *Let* $\mathbb{G}_1$, $\mathbb{G}_2$ *and* $\mathbb{G}_T$ *be cyclic groups of prime order* p, *where* $\mathbb{G}_1$ *and* $\mathbb{G}_2$ *are additive and* $\mathbb{G}_T$ *is multiplicative. Let* P *and* P' *generate* $\mathbb{G}_1$ *and* $\mathbb{G}_2$, *respectively. We call* $e : \mathbb{G}_1 \times \mathbb{G}_2 \to \mathbb{G}_T$ *a bilinear map if it is efficiently computable and satisfies*

- *For any* $a, b \in \mathbb{Z}_p$, $e(aP, bP') = e(P, P')^{ab} = e(bP, aP')$.
- $e(P, P') \neq 1_{\mathbb{G}_T}$.

Definition 2 (Bilinear Group Generator). *A bilinear-group generator is a probabilistic polynomial-time (PPT) algorithm BGGen that on input a security parameter* 1^κ *outputs a bilinear group description* $\mathbf{BG} = (p, \mathbb{G}_1, \mathbb{G}_2, \mathbb{G}_T, e, P, P')$ *which satisfies the definition of bilinear map and* p *is a* κ*-bit prime.*

2.2   Structure-Preserving Signature Scheme on Equivalence Classes

Given a cyclic group $\mathbb{G}$ of prime order p and an integer $\ell > 1$, we first define the equivalence relation $\mathcal{R}$ on length-ℓ vectors of nontrivial group elements as used in [9]:

$$\mathcal{R} = \{(M, N) \in (\mathbb{G}^*)^\ell \times (\mathbb{G}^*)^\ell : \exists \rho \in \mathbb{Z}_p^* \text{ s.t. } N = \rho M\}.$$

Then we denote by $[M]_\mathcal{R}$ all the elements in $(\mathbb{G}^*)^\ell$ equivalent to $M \in (\mathbb{G}^*)^\ell$ with relation $\mathcal{R}$, that is,

$$[M]_\mathcal{R} = \{N \in (\mathbb{G}^*)^\ell : \exists \rho \in \mathbb{Z}_p^* \text{ s.t. } N = \rho M\}.$$

We next give the definition of SPS-EQ as in [9].

Definition 3 (Structure-Preserving Signature Scheme for Equivalence Relation $\mathcal{R}$ (SPS-EQ-$\mathcal{R}$)). *An SPS-EQ-$\mathcal{R}$ scheme consists of the following polynomial-time algorithms:*

- **BGGen$_\mathcal{R}$$(1^\kappa)$:** *Given a security parameter κ, outputs a bilinear group description* **BG**.
- **KeyGen$_\mathcal{R}$(BG, ℓ):** *Given* **BG** *and vector length $\ell > 1$, outputs a key pair* (**sk**, **pk**).
- **Sign$_\mathcal{R}$(M, sk):** *On input a representative M of equivalence class $[M]_\mathcal{R}$ and secret key* **sk**, *outputs a signature σ for the equivalence class $[M]_\mathcal{R}$.*
- **ChgRep$_\mathcal{R}$(M, σ, ρ, pk):** *On input a representative M of an equivalence class $[M]_\mathcal{R}$, the corresponding signature σ, a scalar ρ and a public key* **pk**, *outputs $(\rho M, \hat{\sigma})$, where $\hat{\sigma}$ is the signature on ρM.*
- **Verify$_\mathcal{R}$(M, σ, pk):** *Given a representative M of equivalence class $[M]_\mathcal{R}$, a signature σ and public key* **pk**, *outputs true if σ is a valid signature for $[M]_\mathcal{R}$ and false otherwise.*

2.3   Security of Digital Signature Scheme

As in [8], the security of digital signature scheme can be considered under random message attack, non-adaptive chosen message attack, adaptive chosen message attack and so on. We just briefly introduce these three attacks.

- Random message attack: The polynomial-time adversary $\mathcal{A}$ has access to a signing oracle which on every call randomly chooses a message M from the message space, generates the signature σ on M and returns (M, σ).
- Non-adaptive chosen message attack (directed chosen message attack): The polynomial-time adversary $\mathcal{A}$ has access to a signing oracle and is allowed to obtain valid signatures for a chosen list of messages $M_1, M_2, \cdots, M_{poly(\kappa)}$ after seeing the public key but before knowing any signatures from the signing oracle.
- Adaptive chosen message attack: The polynomial-time adversary $\mathcal{A}$ has access to a signing oracle and can query it with any chosen message anytime.

A digital signature scheme is considered to be existentially unforgeable under some attack if any PPT adversary $\mathcal{A}$ will generate a valid message-signature pair with only negligible probability, where the message has not been queried to the signing oracle. To define the existentially unforgeability for the SPS-EQ-$\mathcal{R}$ scheme, a little adaption is needed, that is, not just the message but also the equivalence class of the message has not been queried. For example, we give the definition of EUF-CMA as in [9].

Definition 4 (EUF-CMA for SPS-EQ-$\mathcal{R}$ Scheme). *An SPS-EQ-$\mathcal{R}$ scheme on $(\mathbb{G}^*)^\ell$ is called existentially unforgeable under adaptive message chosen attack if for any PPT adversary $\mathcal{A}$ having access to a signing oracle $\mathcal{O}(sk, \cdot)$, there is a negligible function $\epsilon(\cdot)$ such that:*

$$Pr\left[\begin{array}{c} BG \leftarrow BGGen_\mathcal{R}(\kappa), (sk, pk) \leftarrow KeyGen_\mathcal{R}(BG, \ell), (M^*, \sigma^*) \leftarrow \mathcal{A}^{\mathcal{O}(sk, \cdot)}(pk) : \\ [M^*]_\mathcal{R} \neq [M]_\mathcal{R} \; \forall M \in Q \wedge Verify_\mathcal{R}(M^*, \sigma^*, pk) = true \end{array} \right]$$
$$\leq \epsilon(\kappa),$$

where Q is the set of queries which $\mathcal{A}$ has queried to the signing oracle $\mathcal{O}$.

Similarly we can also define the existentially unforgeability for non-adaptive chosen message attack and random message attack.

Under any attack model, the SPS-EQ-$\mathcal{R}$ scheme is called universal forgeable if there is a polynomial-time adversary $\mathcal{A}$ who can forge with overwhelming probability valid signature on any message, whose equivalence class has not been queried to the signing oracle.

3 The Hanser-Slamanig SPS-EQ Scheme

3.1 Description of the Hanser-Slamanig SPS-EQ Scheme

As follows we describe the SPS-EQ scheme proposed by Hanser and Slamanig.

- **BGGen$_\mathcal{R}$(1^κ)**: Given a security parameter κ, outputs

$$\mathbf{BG} = (p, \mathbb{G}_1, \mathbb{G}_2, \mathbb{G}_T, P, P', e),$$

  where prime p is the order of cyclic groups $\mathbb{G}_1$, $\mathbb{G}_2$, and $\mathbb{G}_T$, and $\mathbb{G}_1$ and $\mathbb{G}_2$ are additive but $\mathbb{G}_T$ is multiplicative where there is a bilinear map $e : \mathbb{G}_1 \times \mathbb{G}_2 \to \mathbb{G}_T$, P and P' generate $\mathbb{G}_1$ and $\mathbb{G}_2$ respectively.
- **KeyGen$_\mathcal{R}$(BG, ℓ)**: Given a bilinear group description **BG** and vector length $\ell > 1$, chooses $x \xleftarrow{R} \mathbb{Z}_p^*$ and $(x_i)_{i=1}^\ell \xleftarrow{R} (\mathbb{Z}_p^*)^\ell$, sets the secret key as

$$\mathbf{sk} \leftarrow (x, (x_i)_{i=1}^\ell),$$

  computes the public key

$$\mathbf{pk} \leftarrow (X', (X_i')_{i=1}^\ell) = (xP', (x_i x P')_{i=1}^\ell)$$

  and outputs $(\mathbf{sk}, \mathbf{pk})$.

- **Sign$_\mathcal{R}$**$(M, \mathbf{sk})$: On input a representative $M = (M_i)_{i=1}^\ell \in (\mathbb{G}_1^*)^\ell$ of equivalence class $[M]_\mathcal{R}$ and secret key $\mathbf{sk} = (x, (x_i)_{i=1}^\ell)$, chooses $y \xleftarrow{R} \mathbb{Z}_p^*$ and computes

$$Z \leftarrow x \sum_{i=1}^\ell x_i M_i, \quad V \leftarrow y \sum_{i=1}^\ell x_i M_i, \quad (Y, Y') \leftarrow y \cdot (P, P').$$

Then, outputs $\sigma = (Z, V, Y, Y')$ as signature for the equivalence class $[M]_\mathcal{R}$.

- **ChgRep$_\mathcal{R}$**$(M, \sigma, \rho, \mathbf{pk})$: On input a representative $M = (M_i)_{i=1}^\ell \in (\mathbb{G}_1^*)^\ell$ of an equivalence class $[M]_\mathcal{R}$, the corresponding signature $\sigma = (Z, V, Y, Y')$, a scalar $\rho \in \mathbb{Z}_p^*$ and a public key $\mathbf{pk}$, this algorithms picks $\hat{y} \xleftarrow{R} \mathbb{Z}_p^*$ and returns $(\hat{M}, \hat{\sigma})$ where $\hat{\sigma} \leftarrow (\rho Z, \hat{y} \rho V, \hat{y} Y, \hat{y} Y')$ is the update of signature σ for the new representative $\hat{M} \leftarrow \rho(M_i)_{i=1}^\ell$.

- **Verify$_\mathcal{R}$**$(M, \sigma, \mathbf{pk})$: Given a representative $M = (M_i)_{i=1}^\ell \in (\mathbb{G}_1^*)^\ell$ of equivalence class $[M]_\mathcal{R}$, a signature $\sigma = (Z, V, Y, Y')$ and public key $\mathbf{pk} = (X', (X_i')_{i=1}^\ell)$, checks whether

$$\prod_{i=1}^\ell e(M_i, X_i') \stackrel{?}{=} e(Z, P) \bigwedge e(Z, Y') \stackrel{?}{=} e(V, X') \bigwedge e(P, Y') \stackrel{?}{=} e(Y, P')$$

or not and outputs true if this holds and false otherwise.

3.2   Fuchsbauer's Attack to Break the EUF-CMA of the Scheme

For completeness, we describe Fuchsbauer's attack [5] for $l = 2$ briefly. Consider the following polynomial-time adversary $\mathcal{A}$:

1. $\mathcal{A}$ receives $\mathbf{pk}$ and has access to a signing oracle.
2. $\mathcal{A}$ makes a signing query (P, P) and receives the signature (Z_1, V_1, Y_1, Y_1').
3. $\mathcal{A}$ makes a signing query (Z_1, P) and receives the signature (Z_2, V_2, Y_2, Y_2').
4. $\mathcal{A}$ makes a signing query (P, Z_1) and receives the signature (Z_3, V_3, Y_3, Y_3').
5. $\mathcal{A}$ makes a signing query (Z_1, Z_2) and receives the signature (Z_4, V_4, Y_4, Y_4').
6. $\mathcal{A}$ outputs (Z_4, V_4, Y_4, Y_4') as a forgery for the equivalence class represented by (Z_3, Z_1).

Fuchsbauer showed that (Z_4, V_4, Y_4, Y_4') is a valid signature of (Z_3, Z_1) and with overwhelming probability the equivalence class of (Z_3, Z_1) has not been queried to the signing oracle. However, Fuchsbauer gave no discussions about the case when $\ell \geq 3$ and it seems not trivial to generalize his attack to the case when $\ell \geq 3$. Moreover, Fuchsbauer neglected to check whether (Z_3, Z_1) is in $(\mathbb{G}_1^*)^2$ or not in his proof.

4   Our Attacks

4.1   Key Observation of Our Attacks

We first give the key observation of our attacks:

Lemma 1. *Consider the following map:*

$$\varphi: \quad (\mathbb{G}_1)^\ell \to \mathbb{G}_1$$
$$(M_i)_{i=1}^\ell \mapsto \sum_{i=1}^\ell x_i M_i.$$

For any $K = (K_i)_{i=1}^\ell \in \ker(\varphi)$, *if* $\sigma = (Z, V, Y, Y')$ *is a valid signature on message* $M = (M_i)_{i=1}^\ell$, *then* σ *is also a valid signature on* $M + K = (M_i + K_i)_{i=1}^\ell$.

Proof. Notice that to verify the signature σ for $M + K$, the only thing we need check is $\prod_{i=1}^\ell e(M_i + K_i, X_i') \overset{?}{=} e(Z, P)$. Assume $M_i = m_i P$ and $K_i = k_i P$. Since $(K_i)_{i=1}^\ell \in \ker(\varphi)$, we have $(\sum_{i=1}^\ell x_i k_i)P = \mathbf{0}$ which yields $\sum_{i=1}^\ell x_i k_i = 0$ mod p. Then we have

$$\begin{aligned}
\prod_{i=1}^\ell e(M_i + K_i, X_i') &= e(P, P')^{\sum_{i=1}^\ell x x_i (m_i + k_i)} \mod p \\
&= e(P, P')^{\sum_{i=1}^\ell x x_i m_i + \sum_{i=1}^\ell x x_i k_i} \mod p \\
&= e(P, P')^{\sum_{i=1}^\ell x x_i m_i} \mod p \\
&= \prod_{i=1}^\ell e(M_i, X_i') \\
&= e(Z, P).
\end{aligned}$$

The last equation holds since σ is a valid signature on M.

By Lemma 1, if we can find any nontrivial $K \in \ker(\varphi)$, we can forge the signature on any message M by querying the signing oracle with $M - K$ and outputting the returned signature. Next we will show the nontrivial K can be obtained efficiently under the non-adaptive chosen message attack.

4.2   Procedure to Find Nontrivial Element in ker(φ)

We claim that

Lemma 2. *Under the non-adaptive chosen message attack, there is a polynomial time adversary* $\mathcal{A}$ *who can find a nontrivial element in* $\ker(\varphi)$. *Moreover,*

- *If* $\ell = 2$, $\mathcal{A}$ *needs two non-adaptive chosen message queries;*
- *If* $\ell \geq 3$, $\mathcal{A}$ *needs three non-adaptive chosen message queries.*

Proof. We present the polynomial-time procedures **FindKernel** for adversary $\mathcal{A}$ to obtain a nontrivial element in $\ker(\varphi)$ in two cases respectively.

i. Case $\ell = 2$

Consider the following procedure **FindKernel** for adversary $\mathcal{A}$:

1. $\mathcal{A}$ receives **pk** and has access to a signing oracle.

2. $\mathcal{A}$ first chooses any invertible matrix

$$\begin{pmatrix} a_1 \ a_2 \\ a_3 \ a_4 \end{pmatrix} \in \mathbb{Z}_p^{*2\times2}$$

and computes its inverse

$$\begin{pmatrix} b_1 \ b_2 \\ b_3 \ b_4 \end{pmatrix} \in \mathbb{Z}_p^{2\times2},$$

such that

$$\begin{pmatrix} b_1 \ b_2 \\ b_3 \ b_4 \end{pmatrix} \begin{pmatrix} a_1 \ a_2 \\ a_3 \ a_4 \end{pmatrix} = \begin{pmatrix} 1 \ 0 \\ 0 \ 1 \end{pmatrix} \quad \text{mod } p.$$

3. $\mathcal{A}$ makes a signing query with (a_1P, a_2P) and gets its signature (Z_1, V_1, Y_1, Y_1').
4. $\mathcal{A}$ makes a signing query with (a_3P, a_4P) and gets its signature (Z_2, V_2, Y_2, Y_2').
5. $\mathcal{A}$ computes $((b_3Z_1 + b_4Z_2), -(b_1Z_1 + b_2Z_2))$.

We claim that

$$((b_3Z_1 + b_4Z_2), -(b_1Z_1 + b_2Z_2)) = (xx_2P, -xx_1P) \in \ker(\varphi)\backslash(\mathbf{0},\mathbf{0}).$$

It is obvious that $(xx_2P, -xx_1P) \in \ker(\varphi)\backslash(\mathbf{0},\mathbf{0})$ since x, x_1, x_2 are not zero. It remains to prove $((b_3Z_1+b_4Z_2), -(b_1Z_1+b_2Z_2)) = (xx_2P, -xx_1P)$. Notice that

$$Z_1 = x(a_1x_1 + a_2x_2)P, \quad Z_2 = x(a_3x_1 + a_4x_2)P.$$

Hence

$$\begin{aligned} b_3Z_1 + b_4Z_2 &= b_3x(a_1x_1 + a_2x_2)P + b_4x(a_3x_1 + a_4x_2)P \\ &= x((b_3a_1 + b_4a_3)x_1 + (b_3a_2 + b_4a_4)x_2)P \\ &= xx_2P \end{aligned}$$

and

$$\begin{aligned} b_1Z_1 + b_2Z_2 &= b_1x(a_1x_1 + a_2x_2)P + b_2x(a_3x_1 + a_4x_2)P \\ &= x((b_1a_1 + b_2a_3)x_1 + (b_1a_2 + b_2a_4)x_2)P \\ &= xx_1P. \end{aligned}$$

ii. Case $l \geq 3$

We can generalize the procedure above for the case $\ell \geq 3$ by involving an l-by-l invertible matrix. However, notice that $(xx_2P, -xx_1P, \mathbf{0}, \mathbf{0}, \cdots, \mathbf{0})$ is a nontrivial element in the corresponding $\ker(\varphi)$. We have a more clever procedure **Find-Kernel** for adversary $\mathcal{A}$ to obtain $(xx_2P, -xx_1P, \mathbf{0}, \mathbf{0}, \cdots, \mathbf{0})$.

1. $\mathcal{A}$ receives **pk** and has access to a signing oracle.
2. $\mathcal{A}$ makes a signing query with $(P, P, P, \cdots, P)$ and gets (Z_1, V_1, Y_1, Y_1').
3. $\mathcal{A}$ makes a signing query with $(2P, P, P, \cdots, P)$ and gets (Z_2, V_2, Y_2, Y_2').
4. $\mathcal{A}$ makes a signing query with $(P, 2P, P, \cdots, P)$ and gets (Z_3, V_3, Y_3, Y_3').
5. $\mathcal{A}$ computes $(Z_3 - Z_1, Z_1 - Z_2, \mathbf{0}, \cdots, \mathbf{0})$.

We claim that

$$(Z_3 - Z_1, Z_1 - Z_2, \mathbf{0}, \cdots, \mathbf{0}) = (xx_2P, -xx_1P, \mathbf{0}, \cdots, \mathbf{0}) \in \ker(\varphi)\backslash(\mathbf{0}, \cdots, \mathbf{0}).$$

Notice that

$$Z_1 = x(x_1+x_2+\sum_{i=2}^{\ell} x_i)P, \; Z_2 = x(2x_1+x_2+\sum_{i=2}^{\ell} x_i)P, \; Z_3 = x(x_1+2x_2+\sum_{i=2}^{\ell} x_i)P,$$

which implies

$$Z_3 - Z_1 = xx_2P,$$
$$Z_1 - Z_2 = -xx_1P.$$

Hence the lemma follows.

Remark 1. For the **FindKernel** procedure when $\ell \geq 3$, notice that once the difference of two messages queried to the oracle is $(P, \mathbf{0}, \cdots, \mathbf{0})$, we can recover xx_1P. Similar results hold for xx_iP. In fact, we can get all the integer coefficient combination of the elements in the set $\{x^k x_{i_1} x_{i_2} \cdots x_{i_k}P | k = 1, 2, \cdots\}$ with only non-adaptive chosen message quries.

4.3 Breaking the EUF-Non-Adaptive-CMA of the Scheme

Notice that to find the nontrivial element in $\ker(\varphi)$, we just need the non-adaptive queries. To complete the non-adaptive chosen message attack, it remains to decide which message-signature pair should be outputted. Note that the outputted message should satisfy

- The equivalence class of the message has not been queried to the signing oracle;
- The message must be in $(\mathbb{G}_1^*)^\ell$, that is, every component of the message is not zero.

Before giving our attack, we first present some lemmas.

Lemma 3. *There is a polynomial time algorithm on input $(\alpha P, \beta P) \in (\mathbb{G}_1^*)^2$ and $a_i, a_j \in \mathbb{Z}_p^*$ that can decide whether $(\alpha P, \beta P)$ is equivalent to (a_iP, a_jP) or not without knowing α and β.*

Proof. Recall that $(\alpha P, \beta P)$ is equivalent to (a_iP, a_jP) if and only if there exits $\rho \in \mathbb{Z}_p^*$ such that $\rho(\alpha P, \beta P) = (a_iP, a_jP)$, which means that $(\alpha P, \beta P)$ is equivalent to (a_iP, a_jP) if and only if

$$\det \begin{pmatrix} \alpha & \beta \\ a_i & a_j \end{pmatrix} = 0 \mod p,$$

that is,

$$a_i\beta = a_j\alpha \mod p.$$

Hence we can decide the equivalence between $(\alpha P, \beta P)$ and (a_iP, a_jP) by checking if $a_i(\beta P) = a_j(\alpha P)$ in the group $\mathbb{G}_1$, which can be done in polynomial time.

Lemma 4. *For any $(\alpha P, \beta P) \in (\mathbb{G}_1^*)^2$ and $a_i, a_j \in \mathbb{Z}_p^*$, there must be at least one element Q in the set $\{(a_iP + \rho\alpha P, a_jP + \rho\beta P) : \rho = 1, 2, 3\}$, such that $Q \in (\mathbb{G}_1^*)^2$.*

Proof. For contradiction, suppose that every element in the set has at least one **0** as its component. Then there must be a $k \in \{1, 2\}$ such that there are at least two **0**'s in the k-th components of all the three elements. Without loss of generality, suppose $a_iP + \rho_s\alpha P = a_iP + \rho_t\alpha P = \mathbf{0}$, then it can be concluded that $\rho_s = \rho_t$, which contradicts the fact that $\rho_s \neq \rho_t$.

By the two lemmas above, we have

Theorem 1. *The Hanser-Slamanig SPS-EQ scheme is existentially forgeable under the non-adaptive chosen message attack. Moreover,*

- *If $\ell = 2$, two non-adaptive chosen message queries is needed;*
- *If $\ell \geq 3$, three non-adaptive chosen message queries is needed.*

Proof. We prove the theorem for two cases respectively.

i. Case $\ell = 2$

We give our non-adaptive chosen message attack as follows:

1. $\mathcal{A}$ runs **FindKernel** to get $(xx_2P, -xx_1P) \in (\mathbb{G}_1^*)^2 \bigcap \ker(\varphi)$, the signature (Z_1, V_1, Y_1, Y_1') for (a_1P, a_2P) and the signature (Z_2, V_2, Y_2, Y_2') for (a_3P, a_4P).
2. If $(xx_2P, -xx_1P)$ is equivalent to neither (a_1P, a_2P) nor (a_3P, a_4P), $\mathcal{A}$ can output the message $M = (xx_2P, -xx_1P)$ and the corresponding signature $\sigma = (\mathbf{0}, \mathbf{0}, yP, yP')$ for any $y \in \mathbb{Z}_p^*$.
3. If $(xx_2P, -xx_1P)$ is equivalent to (a_1P, a_2P), $\mathcal{A}$ can output the message $M = (a_3P + \rho xx_2P, a_4P - \rho xx_1P)$ and the corresponding signature $\sigma = (Z_2, V_2, Y_2, Y_2')$, where ρ is chosen as in Lemma 4 such that $M \in (\mathbb{G}_1^*)^2$.
4. If $(xx_2P, -xx_1P)$ is equivalent to (a_3P, a_4P), $\mathcal{A}$ can output the message $M = (a_1P + \rho xx_2P, a_2P - \rho xx_1P)$ and the corresponding signature $\sigma = (Z_1, V_1, Y_1, Y_1')$, where ρ is chosen as in Lemma 4 such that $M \in (\mathbb{G}_1^*)^2$.

It is obvious that $M \in (\mathbb{G}_1^*)^2$ and σ is indeed a valid signature on M by Lemma 1 since $(\rho xx_2P, -\rho xx_1P) \in \ker(\varphi)$.

By Lemma 3, the equivalence can be checked in polynomial time. It is easy to check the attack can be completed in polynomial time.

It remains to show $[M]_{\mathcal{R}}$ has not been queried.

If $(xx_2P, -xx_1P)$ is equivalent to neither (a_1P, a_2P) nor (a_3P, a_4P), $[M]_{\mathcal{R}}$ has not been queried obviously.

If $(xx_2P, -xx_1P)$ is equivalent to (a_1P, a_2P), we can write $xx_2 = ka_1$ and $-xx_1 = ka_2$ for some $k \in \mathbb{Z}_p^*$. We claim that now $(a_3P + \rho xx_2P, a_4P - \rho xx_1P)$ can not be equivalent to either (a_1P, a_2P) or (a_3P, a_4P), since

$$\det \begin{pmatrix} a_1 & a_2 \\ a_3 + \rho x x_2 & a_4 - \rho x x_1 \end{pmatrix}$$

$$= \det \begin{pmatrix} a_1 & a_2 \\ a_3 + k\rho a_1 & a_4 + k\rho a_2 \end{pmatrix}$$

$$= \det \begin{pmatrix} a_1 & a_2 \\ a_3 & a_4 \end{pmatrix}$$

$$\neq 0 \pmod p$$

and

$$\det \begin{pmatrix} a_3 + \rho x x_2 & a_4 - \rho x x_1 \\ a_3 & a_4 \end{pmatrix}$$

$$= \det \begin{pmatrix} a_3 + k\rho a_1 & a_4 + k\rho a_2 \\ a_3 & a_4 \end{pmatrix}$$

$$= k\rho \det \begin{pmatrix} a_1 & a_2 \\ a_3 & a_4 \end{pmatrix}$$

$$\neq 0 \pmod p.$$

If $(xx_2 P, -xx_1 P)$ is equivalent to $(a_3 P, a_4 P)$, the proof is similar as above.

ii. Case $l \geq 3$

Similarly, we give our non-adaptive chosen message attack as follows:

1. $\mathcal{A}$ runs **FindKernel** to get $(xx_2 P, -xx_1 P, 0, \cdots, 0) \in (\mathbb{G}_1^*)^\ell \bigcap \ker(\varphi)$ and the signature (Z_1, V_1, Y_1, Y_1') for $(P, P, P, \cdots, P)$.
2. $\mathcal{A}$ finds $\rho \in \{1, 2, 3\}$ such that $P + \rho x x_2 P \neq 0$ and $P - \rho x x_1 P \neq 0$.
3. $\mathcal{A}$ outputs $M = (P + \rho x x_2 P, P - \rho x x_1 P, P, \cdots, P)$ and the corresponding signature $\sigma = (Z_1, V_1, Y_1, Y_1')$.

It is easy to check that the attack can be completed in polynomial time, $M \in (\mathbb{G}_2^*)^\ell$ and σ is indeed a valid signature on M. It remains to show $[M]_\mathcal{R}$ has not been queried, which can be concluded from the fact that

- $(P + \rho x x_2 P, P - \rho x x_1 P, P, \cdots, P)$ is not equivalent to $(P, P, P, \cdots, P)$, since $\rho x x_1$ and $\rho x x_2$ are not 0;
- $(P + \rho x x_2 P, P - \rho x x_1 P, P, \cdots, P)$ is not equivalent to $(2P, P, P, \cdots, P)$, since $-\rho x x_1$ is not 0;
- $(P + \rho x x_2 P, P - \rho x x_1 P, P, \cdots, P)$ is not equivalent to $(P, 2P, P, \cdots, P)$, since $\rho x x_2$ is not 0.

4.4 The Universal Forgery Attack Against the Scheme

To commit a universal forgery attack, a natural idea is as follows. The adversary $\mathcal{A}$ runs **FindKernel** first to find a nontrivial K in $\ker(\varphi)$ and then runs the following **Forge** procedure to forge the valid signature on any given message M.

1. $\mathcal{A}$ first finds $\rho \in \{1, 2, 3\}$ such that $M - \rho K \in (\mathbb{G}_1^*)^\ell$.
2. $\mathcal{A}$ then makes a signing query with $M - \rho K$ and gets the signature $\sigma = (Z, V, Y, Y')$.

3. $\mathcal{A}$ outputs σ as the signature on M.

However, to avoid that the equivalence class of M has been queried, a little more attention should be paid. First notice that

Lemma 5. *If $M \notin \ker(\varphi)$, then M can not be equivalent to $M + K$ for any nontrivial $K \in \ker(\varphi)$.*

Proof. For contradiction, if M is equivalent to $M + K$ for some nontrivial $K \in \ker(\varphi)$, then it can be easily concluded that $M \in \ker(\varphi)$.

Then we can show that

Theorem 2. *The Hanser-Slamanig SPS-EQ scheme is universally forgeable under the adaptive chosen message attack. Moreover,*

- *If $\ell = 2$, three chosen message queries is needed;*
- *If $\ell \geq 3$, four chosen message queries is needed.*

Proof. We prove the theorem for two cases respectively.

i. Case $\ell = 2$

We give our universal forgery attack as follows:

1. $\mathcal{A}$ receives **pk** and has access to a signing oracle.
2. Given M, if $\sigma = (\mathbf{0}, \mathbf{0}, P, P')$ is a valid signature on M, then $\mathcal{A}$ outputs σ as the signature on M.
3. Otherwise, $M \notin \ker(\varphi)$. If M is equivalent to (P, P) or $(P, 2P)$, then $\mathcal{A}$ chooses the invertible matrix $\begin{pmatrix} a_1 & a_2 \\ a_3 & a_4 \end{pmatrix}$ to be $\begin{pmatrix} 1 & -1 \\ -1 & 2 \end{pmatrix}$, otherwise, $\mathcal{A}$ chooses the invertible matrix $\begin{pmatrix} a_1 & a_2 \\ a_3 & a_4 \end{pmatrix}$ to be $\begin{pmatrix} 1 & 1 \\ 1 & 2 \end{pmatrix}$.
4. $\mathcal{A}$ runs **FindKernel** to get a nontrivial $K \in \ker(\varphi)$.
5. $\mathcal{A}$ runs the **Forge** procedure to find a valid signature on M.

Notice that if M is equivalent to (P, P) or $(P, 2P)$, then M must be equivalent to neither $(P, -P)$ nor $(-P, 2P)$ since the order p of $\mathbb{G}_1$ is greater than 3. Together with Lemma 5, it can shown that $[M]_\mathcal{R}$ has not been queried.

ii. Case $\ell \geq 3$

We give our universal forgery attack as follows:

1. $\mathcal{A}$ receives **pk** and has access to a signing oracle.
2. Given M, if $\sigma = (\mathbf{0}, \mathbf{0}, P, P')$ is a valid signature on M, then $\mathcal{A}$ outputs σ as the signature on M.
3. Otherwise, we know that $M \notin \ker(\varphi)$. If M is equivalent to $(P, P, P, \cdots, P)$, or $(2P, P, P, \cdots, P)$, or $(P, 2P, P, \cdots, P)$, $\mathcal{A}$ runs the **FindKernel** algorithm with querying messages $(P, -P, P, \cdots, P)$, $(2P, -P, P, \cdots, P)$, and $(P, -2P, P, \cdots, P)$ to get $K = (Z_1 - Z_3, Z_1 - Z_2, \mathbf{0}, \cdots, \mathbf{0}) \in \ker(\varphi)$.

4. Otherwise, $\mathcal{A}$ runs **FindKernel** as before to get $K \in \ker(\varphi)$.
5. $\mathcal{A}$ runs the **Forge** procedure to find a valid signature.

Note that if the message M is equivalent to $(P, P, P, \cdots, P)$, or $(2P, P, P, \cdots, P)$, or $(P, 2P, P, \cdots, P)$, it must be equivalent to neither $(P, -P, P, \cdots, P)$, nor $(2P, -P, P, \cdots, P)$, nor $(P, -2P, P, \cdots, P)$. Together with Lemma 5, it can shown that $[M]_\mathcal{R}$ has not been queried.

For both of the two attacks, it is easy to check the correctness, the complexity.

4.5 Interesting Observations

By Lemma 1, we know that the signature is not only valid for the original message M, but also valid for any other message in another equivalent class $M + \ker(\varphi) \in \mathbb{G}_1^\ell / \ker(\varphi)$. Interestingly, we can conclude that

Proposition 1. *For any $M \notin \ker(\varphi)$,*

$$\bigcup_{\rho \in \mathbb{Z}_p} (\rho M + \ker(\varphi)) = \mathbb{G}_1^\ell.$$

Proof. Recall that

$$\varphi: \quad (\mathbb{G}_1)^\ell \to \mathbb{G}_1$$
$$(M_i)_{i=1}^\ell \mapsto \sum_{i=1}^\ell x_i M_i.$$

Assume that $M_i = \alpha_i P$ where $\alpha_i \in \mathbb{Z}_p$, we know that $\sum_{i=1}^\ell x_i M_i = \mathbf{0}$ if and only if $\sum_{i=1}^\ell x_i \alpha_i = 0 \mod p$. Hence $|\ker(\varphi)| = p^{\ell-1}$. Notice that φ is a group homomorphism, so we have

$$|\mathbb{G}_1^\ell / \ker(\varphi)| = p.$$

On the other hand, since $M \notin \ker(\varphi)$, then for any $i, j \in \mathbb{Z}_p$, $i \neq j$, iM and jM fall into different classes in $\mathbb{G}_1^\ell / \ker(\varphi)$. Therefore, $iM + \ker(\varphi)$'s ($i \in \mathbb{Z}_p$) are exactly the p different classes in $\mathbb{G}_1^\ell / \ker(\varphi)$, which yields the proposition.

By the proposition, given any message-signature pair (M, σ) where $M \notin \ker(\varphi)$, we can forge the signature on any message M', if we could find the unique ρ such that $M' \in \rho M + \ker(\varphi)$. What we need do is computing the signature on ρM with the algorithm **ChgRep**$_\mathcal{R}(M, \sigma, \rho, \mathbf{pk})$, and then outputting it.

Another discussion is about the leakage of the private keys. Although the private keys consist of $x_1, x_2, \cdots, x_\ell$, the scheme will be insecure when just x_i and x_j are leaked since from any two of $x_1, x_2, \cdots, x_\ell$ we can get a nontrivial element in $\ker(\varphi)$.

5 Conclusion

In this paper, we show that the Hanser-Slamanig SPS-EQ scheme is existentially forgeable under a non-adaptive chosen message attack and is universally forgeable under an adaptive chosen message attack. More precisely, we can produce a valid existential forgery with just 2 (*resp.* 3) non-adaptive chosen-message queries for $l = 2$ (*resp.* $l \geq 3$). Under the adaptive chosen message attack, we can forge the valid signature for any given message with just 3 (*resp.* 4) chosen-message queries for $l = 2$ (*resp.* $l \geq 3$). Both of the attacks need fewer queries, which give a better description of the scheme's security.

Acknowledgments. We very thank the anonymous referees for their valuable suggestions on how to improve the presentation of this paper.

References

1. Abe, M., David, B., Kohlweiss, M., Nishimaki, R., Ohkubo, M.: Tagged one-time signatures: tight security and optimal tag size. In: Kurosawa, K., Hanaoka, G. (eds.) PKC 2013. LNCS, vol. 7778, pp. 312–331. Springer, Heidelberg (2013)
2. Abe, M., Fuchsbauer, G., Groth, J., Haralambiev, K., Ohkubo, M.: Structure-preserving signatures and commitments to group elements. In: Rabin, T. (ed.) CRYPTO 2010. LNCS, vol. 6223, pp. 209–236. Springer, Heidelberg (2010)
3. Attrapadung, N., Libert, B., Peters, T.: Efficient completely context-hiding quotable and linearly homomorphic signatures. In: Kurosawa, K., Hanaoka, G. (eds.) PKC 2013. LNCS, vol. 7778, pp. 386–404. Springer, Heidelberg (2013)
4. Ballard, L., Green, M., Medeiros, B., Monrose, F.: Correlation- resistant storage via keyword-searchable encryption. IACR Cryptology ePrint Archive 2005: 417 (2005). http://eprint.iacr.org/2005/417
5. Fuchsbauer, G.: Breaking existential unforgeability of a signature scheme from asiacrypt 2014. IACR Cryptology ePrint Archive 2014: 892 (2014). http://eprint.iacr.org/2014/892
6. Fuchsbauer, G., Hanser, C., Slamanig, D.: EUF-CMA-secure structure-preserving signatures on equivalence classes. IACR Cryptology ePrint Archive 2014: 944 (2014). http://eprint.iacr.org/2014/944
7. Fuchsbauer, G., Vergnaud, D.: Fair blind signatures without random oracles. In: Bernstein, D.J., Lange, T. (eds.) AFRICACRYPT 2010. LNCS, vol. 6055, pp. 16–33. Springer, Heidelberg (2010)
8. Goldwasser, S., Micali, S., Rivest, R.: A digital signature scheme secure against adaptive chosen-message attacks. SIAM J. Comput. **17**(2), 281–308 (1988)
9. Hanser, C., Slamanig, D.: Structure-preserving signatures on equivalence classes and their application to anonymous credentials. In: Sarkar, P., Iwata, T. (eds.) ASIACRYPT 2014. LNCS, vol. 8873, pp. 491–511. Springer, Heidelberg (2014)
10. Hanser, C., Slamanig, D.: Structure-preserving signatures on equivalence classes and their application to anonymous credentials. Revised version, IACR Cryptology ePrint Archive 2014: 705 (2014). http://eprint.iacr.org/2014/705
11. Hofheinz, D., Jager, T.: Tightly secure signatures and public-key encryption. In: Safavi-Naini, R., Canetti, R. (eds.) CRYPTO 2012. LNCS, vol. 7417, pp. 590–607. Springer, Heidelberg (2012)
12. Libert, B., Peters, T., Joye, M., Yung, M.: Linearly homomorphic structure-preserving signatures and their applications. In: Canetti, R., Garay, J.A. (eds.) CRYPTO 2013, Part II. LNCS, vol. 8043, pp. 289–307. Springer, Heidelberg (2013)
13. Libert, B., Peters, T., Yung, M.: Group signatures with almost-for-free revocation. In: Safavi-Naini, R., Canetti, R. (eds.) CRYPTO 2012. LNCS, vol. 7417, pp. 571–589. Springer, Heidelberg (2012)

Short Structure-Preserving Signatures

Essam Ghadafi[(✉)]

University College London, London, UK
e.ghadafi@ucl.ac.uk

Abstract. We construct a new structure-preserving signature scheme
in the efficient Type-III asymmetric bilinear group setting with signatures shorter than all existing schemes. Our signatures consist of 3 group
elements from the first source group and therefore they are shorter than
those of existing schemes as existing ones have at least one component in
the second source group whose elements bit size is at least double that
of their first group counterparts.

Besides enjoying short signatures, our scheme is fully re-randomizable
which is a useful property for many applications. Our result also constitutes a proof that the impossibility of unilateral structure-preserving
signatures in the Type-III setting result of Abe et al. (Crypto 2011) does
not apply to constructions in which the message space is dual in both
source groups. Besides checking the well-formedness of the message, verifying a signature in our scheme requires checking 2 Pairing Product
Equations (PPE) and require the evaluation of only 5 pairings in total
which matches the best existing scheme and outperforms many other
existing ones. We give some examples of how using our scheme instead of
existing ones improves the efficiency of some existing cryptographic protocols such as direct anonymous attestation and group signature related
constructions.

Keywords: Structure-preserving · Digital signatures · Bilinear groups

1 Introduction

Structure-Preserving Signatures (SPS) [3] are digital signature schemes defined
over bilinear groups ($e : \mathbb{G} \times \tilde{\mathbb{G}} \rightarrow \mathbb{T}$). Their messages, verification key and
signatures are all group elements and signature verification involves evaluating
Pairing Product Equations (PPE). They are a useful tool for the design of modular cryptographic protocols since they compose nicely with existing popular tools
such as Groth-Sahai proofs [31] and ElGamal encryption scheme [20]. They are
prominently used in combination with Groth-Sahai proofs and other tools to
design cryptographic protocols that do not rely on heuristic assumptions such

The research leading to these results has received funding from the European Research Council under the European Union's Seventh Framework Programme (FP/2007–2013) / ERC Grant Agreement no. 307937 and EPSRC grant
EP/J009520/1.

© Springer International Publishing Switzerland 2016
K. Sako (Ed.): CT-RSA 2016, LNCS 9610, pp. 305–321, 2016.
DOI: 10.1007/978-3-319-29485-8_18

as random oracles [21]. They have numerous applications which include group signatures, e.g. [3,34,35], blind signatures, e.g. [3,23], tightly secure encryption schemes, e.g. [2,32], malleable signatures, e.g. [9], anonymous credentials, e.g. [23], network coding, e.g. [9], oblivious transfer, e.g. [28].

Related Work. The notion was formally defined by Abe et al. [3] but earlier schemes conforming to the definition were given by Groth [29] and Green and Hohenberger [28]. Because of its importance, the notion has received a significant amount of attention from the cryptographic community and many results relating to proving lower bounds for the design of such schemes as well as new schemes meeting those lower bounds have been published in the literature. Abe et al. [3] gave two constructions of structure-preserving signatures both relying on non-interactive intractability assumptions. Abe et al. [4] proved that any structure-preserving signature scheme in the most efficient Type-III bilinear group setting (cf. Sect. 2.1) must have at least 3 group elements and 2 pairing product verification equations. They also ruled out the existence of unilateral signatures and argued that the signature must contain elements from both source groups. They also gave constructions meeting the lower bound and proved them secure in the generic group model [40]. Abe et al. [5] proved the impossibility of the existence of a 3 group element structure-preserving signature in the Type-III setting that is based on non-interactive intractability assumptions. In essence, their result implies that in the Type-III setting, the only way to meet the 3 group element lower bound is to either employ interactive intractability assumptions or resort to direct proofs in the generic group model. Ghadafi [25] gave a structure-preserving variant of the Camenisch-Lysyanskaya signature scheme [15] that is secure under an interactive assumption in the Type-III setting. Abe et al. [7] constructed a scheme in the Type-II setting (where there is an efficiently computable isomorphism from the second source group to the first) which contains only 2 group elements. Chatterjee and Menezes [17] revisited the work of [7] and showed that Type-III constructions outperform their Type-II counterparts [17] also gave constructions in Type-III setting meeting the 3 group element lower bound. Barthe et al. [10] also gave optimal constructions of structure-preserving signatures in Type-II setting. Constructions relying on standard assumptions (such as DLIN and DDH) were given by [1,2,14,16,33,35]. Constructions based on standard assumptions are less efficient than those based on non-standard assumptions or proven directly in the generic group model. Recently, Abe et al. [8] and Groth [30] gave fully structure-preserving constructions where even the secret key consists of only group elements.

While by now there exist a number of schemes, e.g. [4,6,10,17,30], with signatures meeting the 3 group element lower bound in the Type-III setting proved by Abe et al. [4], all those schemes have at least one component of the signature in group $\tilde{\mathbb{G}}$ whose elements bit size is at least double that of those in $\mathbb{G}$. To the best of our knowledge, the only existing structure-preserving signature scheme in the Type-III setting whose all signature components are in $\mathbb{G}$ is that of Ghadafi [25]. However, signatures of latter consist of 4 group elements and require 3 pairing-product verification equations.

Our Contribution. We construct a (unilateral) structure-preserving signature scheme with signatures shorter than all existing structure-preserving signatures. Our scheme yields fully re-randomizable signatures consisting of 3 group elements from the first short source group.

Our results also serve as a proof that the impossibility of unilateral structure-preserving signature schemes in the Type-III setting result of Abe et al. [4] does not apply when the message space is dual in both source groups. We stress that Abe et al. never claimed that their Type-III lower bounds apply to this setting since their proofs only considered schemes with unilateral messages. As is the tradition with most existing structure-preserving schemes, we prove the security of our scheme directly in the generic group model. Our scheme can be viewed as an extension of the recent non-structure-preserving signature scheme of Pointcheval and Sanders [38].

We show that replacing some existing schemes used as building blocks in some protocols with ours improves the efficiency of those protocols which include direct anonymous attestation and group signature related constructions.

Paper Organization. In Sect. 2, we give some preliminary definitions. In Sect. 3, we present our signature scheme and prove its security. We give some applications of our signature scheme in Sect. 4.

Notation. We write $y = A(x; r)$ when the algorithm A on input x and randomness r outputs y. We write $y \leftarrow A(x)$ for the process of setting $y = A(x; r)$ where r is sampled at random. We also write $y \leftarrow S$ for sampling y uniformly at random from a set S. A function $\nu(.) : \mathbb{N} \to \mathbb{R}^+$ is negligible (in n) if for every polynomial $p(.)$ and all sufficiently large values of n, it holds that $\nu(n) < \frac{1}{p(n)}$. By PPT we mean running in probabilistic polynomial time in the relevant security parameter. By $[k]$, we denote the set $\{1, \ldots, k\}$.

2 Preliminaries

In this section we provide some preliminary definitions.

2.1 Bilinear Groups

A bilinear group is a tuple $\mathcal{P} := (\mathbb{G}, \tilde{\mathbb{G}}, \mathbb{T}, p, G, \tilde{G}, e)$ where $\mathbb{G}$, $\tilde{\mathbb{G}}$ and $\mathbb{T}$ are groups of a prime order p, and G and $\tilde{G}$ generate $\mathbb{G}$ and $\tilde{\mathbb{G}}$, respectively. The function e is a non-degenerate bilinear map $e : \mathbb{G} \times \tilde{\mathbb{G}} \longrightarrow \mathbb{T}$.

For clarity, elements of $\tilde{\mathbb{G}}$ will be accented with $\tilde{\ }$. We use multiplicative notation for all the groups. We let $\mathbb{G}^\times := \mathbb{G} \setminus \{1_{\mathbb{G}}\}$ and $\tilde{\mathbb{G}}^\times := \tilde{\mathbb{G}} \setminus \{1_{\tilde{\mathbb{G}}}\}$. In this paper, we work in the efficient Type-III setting [24], where $\mathbb{G} \neq \tilde{\mathbb{G}}$ and there is no efficiently computable isomorphism between the source groups in either direction. We assume there is an algorithm BGSetup that on input a security parameter λ, outputs a description of bilinear groups.

The message space of our signature scheme are elements of the subgroup $\hat{G}$ of $\mathbb{G} \times \tilde{\mathbb{G}}$ defined as the image of the map

$$\psi : \begin{cases} \mathbb{Z}_p \longrightarrow \mathbb{G} \times \tilde{\mathbb{G}} \\ x \longmapsto (G^x, \tilde{G}^x) \end{cases}$$

Given an element $(M, \tilde{N}) \in \mathbb{G} \times \tilde{\mathbb{G}}$, one can efficiently test whether $(M, \tilde{N}) \in \hat{G}$ by checking $e(M, \tilde{G}) = e(G, \tilde{N})$.[1]

2.2 Complexity Assumptions

Definition 1 (Decisional Diffie-Hellman (DDH) Assumption). *The DDH assumption holds relative to a group setup $\mathcal{G}$ if for all PPT adversaries $\mathcal{A}$*

$$\Pr \begin{bmatrix} (\mathbb{G}, G, p) \leftarrow \mathcal{G}(1^\lambda); \ r, s, t \leftarrow \mathbb{Z}_p; \ b \leftarrow \{0, 1\}; \\ R := G^r; \ S := G^s; \ T := G^{brs+(1-b)t} \ : \mathcal{A}(G, R, S, T) = b \end{bmatrix} \leq \frac{1}{2} + \nu(\lambda) .$$

Definition 2 (Symmetric External Diffie-Hellman (SXDH) Assumption). *Given a bilinear group $\mathcal{P} := (\mathbb{G}, \tilde{\mathbb{G}}, \mathbb{T}, p, G, \tilde{G}, e)$, the SXDH assumption requires that the DDH assumption holds in both groups $\mathbb{G}$ and $\tilde{\mathbb{G}}$.*

2.3 Digital Signatures

A digital signature scheme (over a bilinear group $\mathcal{P}$ generated by BGSetup) for a message space $\mathcal{M}$ is a tuple $\mathcal{DS} := (\mathsf{KeyGen}, \mathsf{Sign}, \mathsf{Verify})$ whose definitions are:

- $\mathsf{KeyGen}(\mathcal{P})$ this probabilistic algorithm takes as input a bilinear group $\mathcal{P}$ and outputs a pair of secret/verification keys $(\mathsf{sk}, \mathsf{vk})$.
- $\mathsf{Sign}(\mathsf{sk}, m)$ this probabilistic algorithm takes as input a secret key sk and a message $m \in \mathcal{M}$, and outputs a signature σ.
- $\mathsf{Verify}(\mathsf{vk}, m, \sigma)$ this deterministic algorithm outputs 1 if σ is a vlaid signature on m w.r.t. the verification key vk.

Definition 3 (Correctness). *A signature scheme $\mathcal{DS}$ over a bilinear group generator BGSetup is (perfectly) correct if for all $\lambda \in \mathbb{N}$*

$$\Pr \begin{bmatrix} \mathcal{P} \leftarrow \mathsf{BGSetup}(1^\lambda); (\mathsf{sk}, \mathsf{vk}) \leftarrow \mathsf{KeyGen}(\mathcal{P}); \\ m \leftarrow \mathcal{M}; \sigma \leftarrow \mathsf{Sign}(\mathsf{sk}, m) : \mathsf{Verify}(\mathsf{vk}, m, \sigma) = 1 \end{bmatrix} = 1.$$

Definition 4 (Existential Unforgeability). *A signature scheme $\mathcal{DS}$ over a bilinear group generator BGSetup is existentially unforgeable against adaptive chosen-message attack if for all $\lambda \in \mathbb{N}$ for all PPT adversaries $\mathcal{A}$*

$$\Pr \begin{bmatrix} \mathcal{P} \leftarrow \mathsf{BGSetup}(1^\lambda); (\mathsf{sk}, \mathsf{vk}) \leftarrow \mathsf{KeyGen}(\mathcal{P}); (\sigma^*, m^*) \leftarrow \mathcal{A}^{\mathsf{Sign}(\mathsf{sk}, \cdot)}(\mathcal{P}, \mathsf{vk}) \\ : \mathsf{Verify}(\mathsf{vk}, m^*, \sigma^*) = 1 \ and \ m^* \notin Q_{\mathsf{Sign}} \end{bmatrix} \leq \nu(\lambda),$$

where Q_{Sign} is the set of messages queried to Sign.

---

[1] The elements of this group are called Diffie-Hellman pairs in [3, 22].

We consider schemes which are re-randomizable (i.e. weakly unforgeable) in the sense that given a signature on a message m, anyone without knowledge of the signing key, can compute a fresh signature on the same message. A desirable property for such class of schemes is that randomized signatures are indistinguishable from fresh signatures on the same message. Thus, we define an algorithm Randomize which on input (vk, m, σ), where σ being a valid signature on m, outputs a new signature σ' on m.

Definition 5 (Randomizability). *A signature scheme $\mathcal{DS}$ over a bilinear group generator* BGSetup *is* randomizable *if for all $\lambda \in \mathbb{N}$ for all stateful adversaries $\mathcal{A}$*

$$\Pr \begin{bmatrix} \mathcal{P} \leftarrow \mathsf{BGSetup}(1^\lambda); (\mathsf{sk}, \mathsf{vk}) \leftarrow \mathsf{KeyGen}(\mathcal{P}); \\ (\sigma^*, m^*) \leftarrow \mathcal{A}(\mathcal{P}, \mathsf{sk}, \mathsf{vk}); b \leftarrow \{0, 1\}; \\ \sigma_0 \leftarrow \mathsf{Sign}(\mathsf{sk}, m^*); \sigma_1 \leftarrow \mathsf{Randomize}(\mathsf{vk}, m^*, \sigma^*); \\ : \mathsf{Verify}(\mathsf{vk}, m^*, \sigma^*) = 1 \ and \ \mathcal{A}(\sigma_b) = b \end{bmatrix} \leq \frac{1}{2} + \nu(\lambda).$$

We say the scheme has *Perfect Randomizability* when $\nu(\lambda) = 0$. Note that the above definition of randomizability is stronger than the variant where the signature σ^* is generated by the challenger rather than the adversary herself.

Structure-Preserving Signatures. Structure-preserving signatures [3] are signature schemes defined over bilinear groups where the messages, the verification key and signatures are all group elements and verifying signatures only involves deciding group membership of the signature components and evaluating Pairing Product Equations (PPE) of the form of Eq. 1.

$$\prod_i \prod_j e(A_i, \tilde{B}_j)^{c_{i,j}} = 1_{\mathbb{T}}, \tag{1}$$

where $A_i \in \mathbb{G}$ and $\tilde{B}_j \in \tilde{\mathbb{G}}$ are group elements appearing in $\mathcal{P}, m, \mathsf{vk}, \sigma$, whereas $c_{i,j} \in \mathbb{Z}_p$ are constants.

2.4 Randomizable Weakly Blind Signatures

A randomizable weakly blind signature scheme, as defined by Bernhard et al. [12], is similar to a standard blind signature scheme [18] but unlike the latter, in the former, the signer never gets to see the signed message. More precisely, in the blindness game of the former (referred to as *weak blindness*), the challenge messages are chosen by the challenger rather than the adversary and are never revealed to the adversary. Formally, a randomizable weakly blind signature scheme BS (with a two-move signature request phase) for a message space $\mathcal{M}_{\mathsf{BS}}$ consists of the following polynomial-time algorithms $\mathsf{BS} := (\mathsf{Setup}_{\mathsf{BS}}, \mathsf{KeyGen}_{\mathsf{BS}}, \mathsf{Request}_{\mathsf{BS}}, \mathsf{Issue}_{\mathsf{BS}}, \mathsf{Verify}_{\mathsf{BS}}, \mathsf{Randomize}_{\mathsf{BS}})$. All algorithms (bar $\mathsf{Setup}_{\mathsf{BS}}$) are assumed to take as (implicit) input a parameter set $\mathsf{param}_{\mathsf{BS}}$ output by $\mathsf{Setup}_{\mathsf{BS}}$.

- $\mathsf{Setup}_{\mathsf{BS}}(1^\lambda)$ outputs public parameters $\mathsf{param}_{\mathsf{BS}}$.
- $\mathsf{KeyGen}_{\mathsf{BS}}(\mathsf{param}_{\mathsf{BS}})$ outputs a public/secret key pair $(\mathsf{vk}_{\mathsf{BS}}, \mathsf{sk}_{\mathsf{BS}})$ for the signer.
- $(\mathsf{Request}^0_{\mathsf{BS}}, \mathsf{Issue}^1_{\mathsf{BS}}, \mathsf{Request}^1_{\mathsf{BS}})$ is an interactive protocol run between a user and a signer. The protocol is initiated by the user by calling $\mathsf{Request}^0_{\mathsf{BS}}(\mathsf{vk}_{\mathsf{BS}}, m)$ to obtain a value ρ_0 and some state information st^0_R (which is assumed to contain the message m). Then the signer and user execute, respectively,

$$(\beta_1, \mathsf{st}^1_I) \leftarrow \mathsf{Issue}^1_{\mathsf{BS}}(\mathsf{sk}_{\mathsf{BS}}, \rho_0) \quad \text{and} \quad \sigma \leftarrow \mathsf{Request}^1_{\mathsf{BS}}(\beta_1, \mathsf{st}^0_R),$$

where σ is a signature on the message m (or the reject symbol $\perp$). We write $\sigma \leftarrow \langle \mathsf{Request}_{\mathsf{BS}}(\mathsf{vk}_{\mathsf{BS}}, m), \mathsf{Issue}_{\mathsf{BS}}(\mathsf{sk}_{\mathsf{BS}}) \rangle$ for the output of correct running of this protocol on the given inputs.
- $\mathsf{Verify}_{\mathsf{BS}}(\mathsf{vk}_{\mathsf{BS}}, m, \sigma)$ outputs 1 if σ is a valid signature on m and 0 otherwise.
- $\mathsf{Randomize}_{\mathsf{BS}}(\mathsf{vk}_{\mathsf{BS}}, \sigma)$ given a signature σ on an unknown message m, produces another valid signature σ' on the same message.

Definition 6 (Correctness). *A randomizable weakly blind signature scheme is (perfectly) correct if for all $\lambda \in \mathbb{N}$*

$$\Pr \left[\begin{array}{l} \mathsf{param}_{\mathsf{BS}} \leftarrow \mathsf{Setup}_{\mathsf{BS}}(1^\lambda); (\mathsf{vk}_{\mathsf{BS}}, \mathsf{sk}_{\mathsf{BS}}) \leftarrow \mathsf{KeyGen}_{\mathsf{BS}}(\mathsf{param}_{\mathsf{BS}}); \\ m \leftarrow \mathcal{M}_{\mathsf{BS}}; \sigma \leftarrow \langle \mathsf{Request}_{\mathsf{BS}}(\mathsf{vk}_{\mathsf{BS}}, m), \mathsf{Issue}_{\mathsf{BS}}(\mathsf{sk}_{\mathsf{BS}}) \rangle; \\ \sigma' \leftarrow \mathsf{Randomize}_{\mathsf{BS}}(\mathsf{vk}_{\mathsf{BS}}, \sigma) \\ : \mathsf{Verify}_{\mathsf{BS}}(\mathsf{vk}_{\mathsf{BS}}, m, \sigma) = 1 \quad and \quad \mathsf{Verify}_{\mathsf{BS}}(\mathsf{vk}_{\mathsf{BS}}, m, \sigma') = 1 \end{array} \right] = 1.$$

Definition 7 (Unforgeability). *A randomizable weakly blind signature scheme is unforgeable if for all $\lambda \in \mathbb{N}$, all PPT adversaries $\mathcal{A}$ have a negligible advantage in the game in Fig. 1.*

Experiment: $\mathsf{Exp}^{\mathrm{Unforge}}_{\mathsf{BS}, \mathcal{A}}(\lambda)$:

- $\mathsf{param}_{\mathsf{BS}} \leftarrow \mathsf{Setup}_{\mathsf{BS}}(1^\lambda)$.
- $(\mathsf{vk}_{\mathsf{BS}}, \mathsf{sk}_{\mathsf{BS}}) \leftarrow \mathsf{KeyGen}_{\mathsf{BS}}(\mathsf{param}_{\mathsf{BS}})$.
- $\left((m_1, \sigma_1), \dots, (m_{n+1}, \sigma_{n+1}) \right) \leftarrow \mathcal{A}^{\mathsf{Issue}_{\mathsf{BS}}(\cdot, \cdot)}(\mathsf{vk}_{\mathsf{BS}}, \mathsf{param}_{\mathsf{BS}})$.
- Return 0 if any of the following holds. Otherwise, Return 1:
  - $\mathcal{A}$ called its oracle more than n times.
  - $\exists i, j \in \{1, \dots, n+1\}$ s.t. $i \neq j$, but $m_i = m_j$.
  - $\exists i \in \{1, \dots, n+1\}$ s.t. $\mathsf{Verify}_{\mathsf{BS}}(\mathsf{vk}_{\mathsf{BS}}, m_i, \sigma_i) = 0$.

Fig. 1. The unforgeability game for randomizable weakly blind signatures

Definition 8 (Weak Blindness). *A randomizable weakly blind signature scheme is weakly blind if for all $\lambda \in \mathbb{N}$, all PPT adversaries $\mathcal{A}$ have a negligible advantage in the game in Fig. 2.*

Experiment: $\mathsf{Exp}_{\mathsf{BS},\mathcal{A}}^{\mathsf{wBlind}}(\lambda)$:

- $\mathsf{param}_{\mathsf{BS}} \leftarrow \mathsf{Setup}_{\mathsf{BS}}(1^\lambda)$.
- $(\mathsf{vk}_{\mathsf{BS}}, \mathsf{sk}_{\mathsf{BS}}) \leftarrow \mathsf{KeyGen}_{\mathsf{BS}}(\mathsf{param}_{\mathsf{BS}})$.
- $m_0, m_1 \leftarrow \mathcal{M}_{\mathsf{BS}}$.
- $(\rho_0, \mathsf{st}_R^0) \leftarrow \mathsf{Request}_{\mathsf{BS}}^0(\mathsf{vk}_{\mathsf{BS}}, m_0)$.
- $(\beta_1, \mathsf{st}_\mathcal{A}) \leftarrow \mathcal{A}(\mathsf{param}_{\mathsf{BS}}, \mathsf{vk}_{\mathsf{BS}}, \mathsf{sk}_{\mathsf{BS}}, \rho_0)$.
- $\sigma_0 \leftarrow \mathsf{Request}_{\mathsf{BS}}^1(\beta_1, \mathsf{st}_R^0)$.
- If $\sigma_0 = \perp$ or $\mathsf{Verify}_{\mathsf{BS}}(\mathsf{vk}_{\mathsf{BS}}, m_0, \sigma_0) = 0$ Then Return 0.
- $b \leftarrow \{0, 1\}$.
- If $b = 0$ Then $\sigma_1 \leftarrow \mathsf{Randomize}_{\mathsf{BS}}(\mathsf{vk}_{\mathsf{BS}}, \sigma_0)$.
- Else $\sigma_1 \leftarrow \langle \mathsf{Request}_{\mathsf{BS}}(\mathsf{vk}_{\mathsf{BS}}, m_1), \mathsf{Issue}_{\mathsf{BS}}(\mathsf{sk}_{\mathsf{BS}}) \rangle$.
- $b^* \leftarrow \mathcal{A}(\mathsf{st}_\mathcal{A}, \sigma_0, \sigma_1)$.
- Return 1 If $b = b^*$ Else Return 0.

Fig. 2. The weak blindness game for randomizable weakly blind signatures

2.5 Groth-Sahai Proofs

Groth-Sahai (GS) proofs [31] are non-interactive proofs in the CRS model. We will use GS proofs that are secure under the SXDH assumption, which is the most efficient instantiation of the proof system [27], and that prove knowledge of witnesses to pairing-product equations of the form

$$\prod_{j=1}^{n} e(A_j, \underline{\tilde{Y}_j}) \prod_{i=1}^{m} e(\underline{X_i}, \tilde{B}_i) \prod_{i=1}^{m} \prod_{j=1}^{n} e(\underline{X_i}, \underline{\tilde{Y}_j})^{\gamma_{i,j}} = \prod_{\ell=1}^{k} e(G_\ell, \tilde{H}_\ell) \qquad (2)$$

All underlined variables are part of the witness whereas the rest of the values are public constants. The language for these proofs is of the form $\mathcal{L} :=$ {statement | ∃ witness : E(statement, witness) holds }, where E(statement, ·) is a set of pairing-product equations. The system is defined by a tuple of algorithms (GSSetup, GSProve, GSVerify, GSExtract, GSSimSetup, GSSimProve). GSSetup takes as input the description of a bilinear group $\mathcal{P}$ and outputs a *binding* reference string crs and an extraction key xk. GSProve takes as input the string crs, a set of equations statement and a witness, and outputs a proof Ω for the satisfiability of the equations. GSVerify takes as input a set of equations, a string crs and a proof Ω and outputs 1 if the proof is valid, and 0 otherwise. GSExtract takes as input a binding crs, the extraction key xk and a valid proof Ω, and outputs the witness used for the proof. GSSimSetup, on input a bilinear group $\mathcal{P}$, outputs a *hiding* string crs$_{\mathsf{Sim}}$ and a trapdoor key tr that allows to simulate proofs. GSSimProve takes as input crs$_{\mathsf{Sim}}$, a statement and the trapdoor tr and produces a simulated proof Ω_{Sim} without a witness. The distributions of strings crs and crs$_{\mathsf{Sim}}$ are computationally indistinguishable and simulated proofs are indistinguishable from proofs generated by an honest prover. The proof system has perfect completeness, (perfect) soundness, composable witness-indistinguishability/composable zero-knowledge. We refer to [31] for the formal definitions and the details of the instantiations.

3 Our Structure-Preserving Signature Scheme

Given the description of Type-III bilinear groups $\mathcal{P}$ output by $\mathsf{BGSetup}(1^\lambda)$, our scheme is given by the following four algorithms.

- $\mathsf{KeyGen}(\mathcal{P})$: Select $x, y \leftarrow \mathbb{Z}_p^\times$. Set $\mathsf{sk} := (x, y)$ and $\mathsf{vk} := (\tilde{X}, \tilde{Y}) := (\tilde{G}^x, \tilde{G}^y)$.
- $\mathsf{Sign}(\mathsf{sk}, (M, \tilde{N}))$: To sign a message $(M, \tilde{N}) \in \hat{G}$, (i.e. $(M, \tilde{N}) \in \mathbb{G} \times \tilde{\mathbb{G}}$ and $e(M, \tilde{G}) = e(G, \tilde{N})$), select $a \leftarrow \mathbb{Z}_p^\times$, and set $A := G^a$, $B := M^a$, $C := A^x \cdot B^y$. Return $\sigma := (A, B, C) \in \mathbb{G}^3$.
- $\mathsf{Verify}(\mathsf{vk}, (M, \tilde{N}), \sigma = (A, B, C))$: Return 1 iff $A \in \mathbb{G}^\times$ (i.e. $A \neq 1_\mathbb{G}$), $B, C \in \mathbb{G}$, $(M, \tilde{N}) \in \hat{G}$, and all of the following hold:

$$e(A, \tilde{N}) = e(B, \tilde{G})$$
$$e(C, \tilde{G}) = e(A, \tilde{X})e(B, \tilde{Y})$$

- $\mathsf{Randomize}(\mathsf{vk}, (M, \tilde{N}), \sigma = (A, B, C))$: Select $r \leftarrow \mathbb{Z}_p^\times$, and set $A' := A^r$, $B' := B^r$, $C' := C^r$. Return $\sigma' := (A', B', C')$.

Remark 1. Note that verifying the well-formedness of the message pair, i.e. that $(M, \tilde{N}) \in \hat{G}$, need only be done once when verifying multiple signatures on the same message. A similar argument applies to signature schemes with the same message space, e.g. [3,22,25].

Also, note that requiring checking that $A \neq 1_\mathbb{G}$ in the verification can in some sense be considered a slight deviation from the rigorous variant of the definition of structure-preserving signatures. However, since A is information-theoretically independent of the message, even when proving knowledge of a signature, one can reveal A after re-randomizing it which allows for verifying such a condition for free. We end by noting that Ghadafi [25] gave efficient Groth-Sahai proofs that a committed Groth-Sahai value is not the identity element.

Correctness of the scheme follows by inspection and is straightforward to verify. Also, that the signature is perfectly randomizable is straightforward. The distributions of valid signatures returned by the Randomize algorithm are identical to those returned by the Sign algorithm on the same message. Also, note that assuming the signature to be re-randomized is valid, one only needs the old signature to be able to produce a new one.

The following theorem proves that the scheme is unforgeable in the generic group model [37,40]. We note here that the unforgeability of the scheme could also be based on an interactive assumption.

Theorem 1. *The structure-preserving signature scheme is (weakly) existentially unforgeable against adaptive chosen-message attack in the generic group model.*

Proof. The proof follows from the proof of the following theorem:

Theorem 2. *Let $\mathcal{A}$ be an adversary in the generic group model against our scheme. Assume $\mathcal{A}$ makes q_G group operation queries, q_P pairing queries, and q_S sign queries. The probability ϵ of adversary $\mathcal{A}$ winning the game is bounded by $\epsilon \leq \frac{(q_G + q_P + 3q_S + 4)^2 \cdot 3}{p}$, where p is the (prime) order of the generic groups.*

Proof. We start by re-stating the following Schwartz Zippel lemma [39]:

Lemma 1. *Let p be a prime and $P(x_1, \ldots, x_n) \in \mathbb{F}_p[x_1, \ldots, x_n]$ be a non-zero polynomial with a total degree $\leq d$. Then the probability that $P(x_1, \ldots, x_n) = 0$ is $\leq \frac{d}{p}$.*

Adversary $\mathcal{A}$ interacts with those oracles via group handles. We define three random encoding functions $\xi_1 : \mathbb{G} \longrightarrow \{0,1\}^*$, $\xi_2 : \tilde{\mathbb{G}} \longrightarrow \{0,1\}^*$ and $\xi_3 : \mathbb{T} \longrightarrow \{0,1\}^*$ where ξ_i maps elements from the corresponding group into random strings. The challenger keeps three lists $\mathcal{L}_1, \mathcal{L}_2, \mathcal{L}_T$ which contain pairs of the form (τ, P) where τ is a "random" encoding of the group element (i.e. τ is an output of the map ξ_i) and P is some polynomial in $\mathbb{F}_p[X, Y, A_1, \ldots, A_{q_S}]$.

To each list we associate an Update algorithm, that takes as input the specific list $\mathcal{L}_i$ and a polynomial P. The algorithm $\mathsf{Update}(\mathcal{L}_i, P)$ searches the list in question for a pair whose second component is equal to P, if such a pair is found, the algorithm returns its first component as a result. Otherwise, a new random encoding τ, different from all other elements used so far, is chosen and the pair (τ, P) is added to the list $\mathcal{L}_i$. The value τ is then returned. Note that at no point $\mathcal{A}$ gets access to the second element in the pairs.

The challenger starts by calling: $\mathsf{Update}(\mathcal{L}_1, 1)$, $\mathsf{Update}(\mathcal{L}_2, 1)$, $\mathsf{Update}(\mathcal{L}_2, X)$ and $\mathsf{Update}(\mathcal{L}_2, Y)$. Those correspond to the group elements $G \in \mathbb{G}$ and $\tilde{G}, \tilde{X}, \tilde{Y} \in \tilde{\mathbb{G}}$ of the verification key and public elements the adversary gets in the scheme.

The oracles used in the game are defined as follows:

- Group Oracles: Oracles $\mathcal{O}_1$, $\mathcal{O}_2$ and $\mathcal{O}_T$ allow $\mathcal{A}$ access to the group operations in groups $\mathbb{G}$, $\tilde{\mathbb{G}}$ and $\mathbb{T}$, respectively, via subtraction/addition operations. On a call to $\mathcal{O}_i(\tau_1, \tau_2)$ $\mathcal{B}$ searches list $\mathcal{L}_i$ for pairs of the form (τ_1, P_1) and (τ_2, P_2). If both pairs exist, $\mathcal{B}$ returns the output of $\mathsf{Update}(\mathcal{L}_i, P_1 \pm P_2)$. Otherwise, it returns $\bot$. Note that exponentiation operations can be performed by calls to the group operation oracles.
- Pairing Oracle: Oracle $\mathcal{O}_P$ allows $\mathcal{A}$ to perform pairing operations. On a call to $\mathcal{O}_P(\tau_1, \tau_2)$, $\mathcal{B}$ searches the list $\mathcal{L}_1$ for the pair (τ_1, P_1), and the list $\mathcal{L}_2$ for the pair (τ_2, P_2). If both pairs exist, $\mathcal{B}$ returns the output of $\mathsf{Update}(\mathcal{L}_T, P_1 \cdot P_2)$. Otherwise, it returns $\bot$.
- Sign Oracle: The adversary may make up to q_S queries $\mathcal{O}_S(\tau_1, \tau_2)$. The challenger searches list $\mathcal{L}_1$ for a pair (τ_1, P_1) and list $\mathcal{L}_2$ for a pair (τ_2, P_2). If they do not exist or $P_1 \neq P_2$, $\mathcal{B}$ returns $\bot$. Otherwise, it executes the following operations, where A_i, X and Y are indeterminants:

$$\tau_{A_i} \leftarrow \mathsf{Update}(\mathcal{L}_1, A_i),$$
$$\tau_{B_i} \leftarrow \mathsf{Update}(\mathcal{L}_1, A_i \cdot P_1),$$
$$\tau_{C_i} \leftarrow \mathsf{Update}(\mathcal{L}_1, A_i \cdot (X + P_1 \cdot Y)).$$

Returning the tuple $(\tau_{A_i}, \tau_{B_i}, \tau_{C_i})$ to $\mathcal{A}$.

By using the above oracles, we can simulate the entire run of the adversary. At the end of the game, the total number of non-constant polynomials contained in the three lists $\mathcal{L}_1, \mathcal{L}_2$ and $\mathcal{L}_T$ is bounded from above by $t = q_G + q_P + 3q_S + 4$.

The Adversary Output. Eventually, $\mathcal{A}$ outputs a tuple $(\tau_{A^*}, \tau_{B^*}, \tau_{C^*}, \tau_{M^*}, \tau_{\tilde{N}^*})$, where τ_{A^*}, τ_{B^*}, τ_{C^*}, and τ_{M^*} are on list $\mathcal{L}_1$ while $\tau_{\tilde{N}^*}$ is on list $\mathcal{L}_2$. Let $P_{A^*}, P_{B^*}, P_{C^*}, P_{M^*}, P_{\tilde{N}^*}$ denote their associated polynomials. For $\mathcal{A}$'s output to be valid, those polynomials can be assumed to satisfy, for some assignment $(x, y, a_1, \ldots, a_{q_S}) \in \mathbb{F}_p^{2+q_S}$ to the variables $(X, Y, A_1, \ldots, A_{q_S})$, the equations:

$$P_{B^*} = P_{A^*} \cdot P_{\tilde{N}^*} \tag{3}$$
$$P_{C^*} = P_{A^*} \cdot X + P_{B^*} \cdot Y \tag{4}$$
$$P_{M^*} = P_{\tilde{N}^*} \tag{5}$$

From this we derive a contradiction, i.e. conclude that the adversary cannot win the game. To achieve this, we need to first ensure that these polynomial identities cannot hold identically, i.e. regardless of any particular assignment $(x, y, a_1, \ldots, a_{q_S}) \in \mathbb{F}_p^{2+q_S}$ to the variables $(X, Y, A_1, \ldots, A_{q_S})$.

Let $(M_i, \tilde{N}_i)$ denote the i-th signing query where we discount queries where $(M_i, \tilde{N}_i) \notin \hat{G}$. Note that $P_{\tilde{N}_i}$ can only be a linear combination of the terms $1, X$ and Y. Thus, we have $P_{\tilde{N}_i} = r_i + s_i \cdot X + t_i \cdot Y$. Since we must have $P_{M_i} = P_{\tilde{N}_i}$, this implies that the above polynomials must also appear on the list $\mathcal{L}_1$. However, there is no operation in $\mathbb{G}$ which creates a polynomial with a monomial term of X, nor one of Y. Thus, we conclude that all queries to the sign oracle correspond to elements whose polynomials are a constant term of the form $P_{M_i} = P_{\tilde{N}_i} = r_i$. By a similar argument, we can also deduce that the output of the adversary corresponds to polynomials with $P_{M^*} = P_{\tilde{N}^*} = r^*$. This is precisely where we use the property that the oracle will return $\perp$ unless the input query lies in $\hat{G}$.

Note that P_{A^*}, P_{B^*}, and P_{C^*} can only by a linear combination of the polynomials appearing on the list $\mathcal{L}_1$. Therefore, we have:

$$P_{A^*} = w_1 + \sum_{i=1}^{q} u_{1,i} \cdot A_i + \sum_{i=1}^{q} v_{1,i} \cdot A_i \cdot (X + r_i \cdot Y) \tag{6}$$

$$P_{B^*} = w_2 + \sum_{i=1}^{q} u_{2,i} \cdot A_i + \sum_{i=1}^{q} v_{2,i} \cdot A_i \cdot (X + r_i \cdot Y) \tag{7}$$

$$P_{C^*} = w_3 + \sum_{i=1}^{q} u_{3,i} \cdot A_i + \sum_{i=1}^{q} v_{3,i} \cdot A_i \cdot (X + r_i \cdot Y), \tag{8}$$

where $w_j, u_{j,i}, v_{j,i} \in \mathbb{F}_p$.

Note that P_{C^*}, i.e. Eq. (8), there is no monomial with a power > 1 of Y. Also, there is no monomial in $X \cdot Y$. Thus, by Eq. (4), we must have $v_{1,i} = v_{2,i} = 0$ for all i. Thus, we have

$$P_{A^*} = w_1 + \sum_{i=1}^{q} u_{1,i} \cdot A_i \qquad\qquad P_{B^*} = w_2 + \sum_{i=1}^{q} u_{2,i} \cdot A_i$$

Now by Eq. (3) we must have that

$$w_2 + \sum_{i=1}^{q} u_{2,i} \cdot A_i = r^* \cdot w_1 + \sum_{i=1}^{q} r^* \cdot u_{1,i} \cdot A_i$$

For the above to hold, we must have $w_2 = r^* \cdot w_1$ and $r^* \cdot u_{1,i} = u_{2,i}$ for all i.

By Eq. (4), we must have

$$w_3 + \sum_{i=1}^{q} u_{3,i} \cdot A_i + \sum_{i=1}^{q} v_{3,i} \cdot A_i \cdot (X + r_i \cdot Y)$$

$$= w_1 \cdot X + \sum_{i=1}^{q} u_{1,i} \cdot A_i \cdot X + r^* \cdot w_1 \cdot Y + \sum_{i=1}^{q} r^* \cdot u_{1,i} \cdot A_i \cdot Y$$

There is no term in X on the left-hand side so we must have $w_1 = 0$. Also, no constant terms or terms in A_i on the right-hand side so we must have $w_3 = 0$ and $u_{3,i} = 0$ for all i. Thus, we must have

$$\sum_{i=1}^{q} v_{3,i} \cdot A_i \cdot X + \sum_{i=1}^{q} v_{3,i} \cdot r_i \cdot A_i \cdot Y = \sum_{i=1}^{q} u_{1,i} \cdot A_i \cdot X + \sum_{i=1}^{q} r^* \cdot u_{1,i} \cdot A_i \cdot Y$$

By the monomial $A_i \cdot X$, we must have $u_{1,i} = v_{3,i}$ for all i. Since we must have $A^* \neq 1_{\mathbb{G}}$, we must have at least one pair $u_{1,i} = v_{3,i} \neq 0$ for some i. By the monomial $A_i \cdot Y$, we must have $v_{3,i} \cdot r_i = r^* \cdot u_{1,i}$. Since as we have seen we must have $u_{1,i} = v_{3,i}$, we have $r_i = r^*$ which contradicts the unforgeability requirement as the forgery is on a message pair that was queried to the sign oracle.

Thus, the adversary must win, or tell it is in a simulation, via a specific (random) assignment to the variables. We now turn to bounding the probability that the adversary wins (or detects the simulation) in this case.

The Simulation. Now the challenger chooses random values $x, y, a_i \in \mathbb{F}_p$ and evaluates the polynomials. We need to show that the challenger's simulation is sound. If $\mathcal{A}$ learned it was interacting in a simulated game, there would be two different polynomials $P_{i,j}(x, y, a_i) = P_{i,j'}(x, y, a_i)$ in list $\mathcal{L}_i$ where $P_{i,j} \neq P_{i,j'}$. The simulation will fail if any of the following is correct:

$$P_{1,j}(x, y, a_i) = P_{1,j'}(x, y, a_i) \tag{9}$$
$$P_{2,j}(x, y, a_i) = P_{2,j'}(x, y, a_i) \tag{10}$$
$$P_{T,j}(x, y, a_i) = P_{T,j'}(x, y, a_i) \tag{11}$$

Since the maximum degree of any polynomial in list $\mathcal{L}_1 \leq 2$, by applying [40][Lemma 1], we have that the probability of Eq. (9) holding is $\leq \frac{2}{p}$. Similarly, since the maximum degree of any polynomial in list $\mathcal{L}_2 \leq 1$, we have that the probability of Eq. (10) holding is $\leq \frac{1}{p}$. Finally, the probability of Eq. (11) holding is $\leq \frac{3}{p}$.

Summing over all possible values of j in each case, we have

$$\epsilon \leq \binom{|\mathcal{L}_1|}{2} \frac{2}{p} + \binom{|\mathcal{L}_2|}{2} \frac{1}{p} + \binom{|\mathcal{L}_T|}{2} \frac{3}{p},$$

where $|\mathcal{L}_i|$ denotes the size of list $\mathcal{L}_i$.

In conclusion, the probability that an adversary wins the unforgeability game is bounded by $\epsilon \leq \frac{(q_G + q_P + 3q_S + 4)^2 \cdot 3}{p}$. $\square$

3.1   Efficiency Comparison

We compare in Table 1 the efficiency of our scheme with that of existing schemes for a single a message in the Type-III setting. For concrete comparison, for instance, at 128-bit security, elements of $\mathbb{G}$ and $\tilde{\mathbb{G}}$ in Type-III are 256 and 512 bits long, respectively. Therefore, our signatures at this security level are at least 256 bits shorter than the best existing scheme. The efficiency gain is even better as the security level increases. Also, as can be seen, our scheme compares favorably to existing ones in terms of the efficiency of the verification equation. For the schemes whose message space is $\hat{G}$, the cost does not include checking membership of the message in the relevant group. As discussed earlier, such a check only needs to be performed once when verifying multiple signatures on the same message. Note that many applications require the signer to prove possession of/provide multiple signatures/credentials (possibly from different signers/issuers).

Also, our scheme works well in association with the (less efficient) automorphic structure-preserving signature scheme of [3,22] since the message and key spaces of the latter lie in the message space of our scheme.

It is obvious that structure-preserving signatures (on unilateral messages) in the Type-III setting have shorter messages than schemes, including ours, whose message space is $\hat{G}$. However, we stress that this is a small price to pay to get shorter signatures and more efficient verification while remaining in the most efficient Type-III bilinear group setting.

4   Applications of Our Scheme

In this section we give some examples of how using our signature scheme improves the efficiency of some existing cryptographic protocols.

Table 1. Efficiency comparison between our scheme and other schemes

Scheme	Size				Randomize?	Assumptions	Verification	
	σ	vk	Param	m			#PPE	#Pairings
[28][a]	$\mathbb{G}^4 \times \tilde{\mathbb{G}}$	$\tilde{\mathbb{G}}^2$	-	$\mathbb{G}$	Yes	q-HLRSW	4	8
[22]	$\mathbb{G}^3 \times \tilde{\mathbb{G}}^2$	$\mathbb{G} \times \tilde{\mathbb{G}}$	$\mathbb{G}^3$	$\hat{\mathbb{G}}$	No	q-ADHSDH + AWFCDH	3	7
[3] I	$\mathbb{G}^5 \times \tilde{\mathbb{G}}^2$	$\mathbb{G}^{10} \times \tilde{\mathbb{G}}^4$	-	$\mathbb{G}$	Partially	q-SFP	2	12
[3] II	$\mathbb{G}^2 \times \tilde{\mathbb{G}}^5$	$\mathbb{G}^{10} \times \tilde{\mathbb{G}}^4$	-	$\tilde{\mathbb{G}}$	Partially	q-SFP	2	12
[4] I	$\mathbb{G}^2 \times \tilde{\mathbb{G}}$	$\mathbb{G} \times \tilde{\mathbb{G}}^3$	-	$\mathbb{G} \times \tilde{\mathbb{G}}$	No	GGM	2	7
[4] II	$\mathbb{G}^2 \times \tilde{\mathbb{G}}$	$\mathbb{G} \times \tilde{\mathbb{G}}$	-	$\tilde{\mathbb{G}}$	Yes	GGM	2	5
[25]	$\mathbb{G}^4$	$\tilde{\mathbb{G}}^2$	-	$\hat{\mathbb{G}}$	Yes	DH-LRSW	3	6
[17] I	$\mathbb{G} \times \tilde{\mathbb{G}}^2$	$\mathbb{G}^2$	-	$\tilde{\mathbb{G}}$	No	GGM	2	5
[17] II	$\mathbb{G} \times \tilde{\mathbb{G}}^2$	$\mathbb{G}^2$	-	$\tilde{\mathbb{G}}$	Yes	GGM	2	6
[17] III	$\mathbb{G}^2 \times \tilde{\mathbb{G}}$	$\tilde{\mathbb{G}}^2$	-	$\mathbb{G}$	Yes	GGM	2	6
[6] I	$\mathbb{G}^3 \times \tilde{\mathbb{G}}$	$\tilde{\mathbb{G}}$	$\mathbb{G}$	$\mathbb{G}$	Yes	GGM	2	6
[6] II	$\mathbb{G}^2 \times \tilde{\mathbb{G}}$	$\tilde{\mathbb{G}}$	$\mathbb{G}$	$\mathbb{G}$	No	GGM	2	6
[10]	$\mathbb{G} \times \tilde{\mathbb{G}}^2$	$\mathbb{G}^2$	-	$\tilde{\mathbb{G}}$	Yes	GGM	2	5
[30] I	$\mathbb{G} \times \tilde{\mathbb{G}}^2$	$\mathbb{G}$	$\tilde{\mathbb{G}}$	$\tilde{\mathbb{G}}$	Yes	GGM	2	6
[30] II	$\mathbb{G} \times \tilde{\mathbb{G}}^2$	$\mathbb{G}$	$\tilde{\mathbb{G}}$	$\tilde{\mathbb{G}}$	No	GGM	2	7
Ours	$\mathbb{G}^3$	$\tilde{\mathbb{G}}^2$	-	$\hat{\mathbb{G}}$	Yes	GGM	2	5

[a]This scheme is only secure against a random message attack.

4.1 Direct Anonymous Attestation

Bernhard et al. [11] gave the first instantiations of Direct Anonymous Attestation (DAA) [13] which do not rely on random oracles. Their constructions are instantiations of Bernhard et al. [12] generic construction. Among other things, the generic construction of the latter requires a randomizable weakly blind signature. The weakly blind signature is used in the join protocol to issue a credential to the user without learning her secret key. Note that unlike in group signatures [19], in DAA users do not have public keys matching their secret keys.

To get an efficient instantiation of the notion and hence an efficient instantiation of DAA (without relying on random oracles), the efficient instantiation of Bernhard et al. [11] combined Ghadafi's structure-preserving signature scheme [25] with Groth-Sahai proofs [31] to construct an efficient weakly blind signature scheme. Their weakly blind signature instantiation yields signatures of size $\mathbb{G}^4$ and require 3 PPE equations (7 pairings or 6 pairings and 1 elliptic curve point addition in total) to verify. Exploiting the fact that our signature scheme has a similar structure to Ghadafi's scheme but yet has shorter signatures and the verification algorithm is more efficient, we get a more efficient instantiation of weakly blind signatures and hence DAA by using our scheme instead. The weakly blind signature (see Fig. 3) obtained by combining our signature scheme with Groth-Sahai proofs yields signatures of size $\mathbb{G}^3$ and require only 2 PPE equations (5 pairings in total) to verify. Also, the communication complexity of both the user and the signer in the signing protocol is the same as that in the instantiation in [11]. Thus, using our scheme one gets more efficient instantiations of DAA without relying on random oracles.

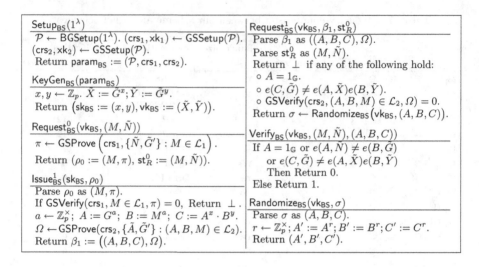

$\mathsf{Setup_{BS}}(1^\lambda)$	$\mathsf{Request}^1_{BS}(\mathsf{vk_{BS}}, \beta_1, \mathsf{st}^0_R)$
$\mathcal{P} \leftarrow \mathsf{BGSetup}(1^\lambda).\ (\mathsf{crs_1}, \mathsf{xk_1}) \leftarrow \mathsf{GSSetup}(\mathcal{P}).$	Parse β_1 as $((A, B, C), \Omega)$.
$(\mathsf{crs_2}, \mathsf{xk_2}) \leftarrow \mathsf{GSSetup}(\mathcal{P}).$	Parse st^0_R as $(M, \tilde{N})$.
Return $\mathsf{param_{BS}} := (\mathcal{P}, \mathsf{crs_1}, \mathsf{crs_2}).$	Return $\perp$ if any of the following hold:

$\mathsf{KeyGen_{BS}}(\mathsf{param_{BS}})$	$\circ\ A = 1_\mathbb{G}.$
$x, y \leftarrow \mathbb{Z}_p.\ \tilde{X} := \tilde{G}^x; \tilde{Y} := \tilde{G}^y.$	$\circ\ e(C, \tilde{G}) \neq e(A, \tilde{X})e(B, \tilde{Y}).$
Return $(\mathsf{sk_{BS}} := (x, y), \mathsf{vk_{BS}} := (\tilde{X}, \tilde{Y})).$	$\circ\ \mathsf{GSVerify}(\mathsf{crs_2}, (A, B, M) \in \mathcal{L}_2, \Omega) = 0.$

...

Fig. 3. Our weakly blind signature scheme

In the construction detailed in Fig. 3, we use the following languages for the zero-knowledge proofs for the user and signer respectively[2]:

$$\mathcal{L}_1 : \left\{ (M, (\tilde{N}, \tilde{G}')) : e(G, \underline{\tilde{N}}) = e(M, \underline{\tilde{G}'}) \wedge \underline{\tilde{G}'} \cdot \tilde{G}^{-1} = 1_{\tilde{\mathbb{G}}} \right\}$$

$$\mathcal{L}_2 : \left\{ ((A, B, M), (\tilde{A}, \tilde{G}')) : e(G, \underline{\tilde{A}}) = e(A, \underline{\tilde{G}'}) \wedge e(M, \underline{\tilde{A}}) = e(B, \underline{\tilde{G}'}) \wedge \underline{\tilde{G}'} \cdot \tilde{G}^{-1} = 1_{\tilde{\mathbb{G}}} \right\}$$

We prove following theorem in the full version of the paper [26].

Theorem 3. *If the SXDH assumption holds and the signature scheme is existentially unforgeable, the weakly blind signature scheme in Fig. 3 is secure.*

4.2 Group Signatures and Similar Primitives

In all constructions of group signatures [19], the issuer (the group manager) issues membership certificates by certifying users' verification keys. The message space of our scheme being the set of Diffie-Hellman pairs makes our scheme ideal to be combined with the automorphic structure-preserving signature scheme of Fuchsbauer [3, 22]. For instance, combining our signature scheme with Fuchsbauer's blind signature scheme [3, 22], we get more efficient instantiations of group blind signatures [25, 36] (without relying on random oracles) than those in [25]. An instantiation using our signature scheme yields group blind signatures of size $36 \cdot |\mathbb{G}| + 34 \cdot |\tilde{\mathbb{G}}|$ compared to $38 \cdot |\mathbb{G}| + 36 \cdot |\tilde{\mathbb{G}}|$ and $42 \cdot |\mathbb{G}| + 38 \cdot |\tilde{\mathbb{G}}|$ for the original constructions given in [25]. Also, since the final signature involves less

---

[2] The purpose of the two multi-scalar multiplication equations is to make the equations simulatable so that the proofs are zero-knowledge [31].

Groth-Sahai proofs, the verification algorithm is much more efficient as each Groth-Sahai proof requires a few pairings to verify.

Acknowledgments. We thank anonymous CT-RSA reviewers for their comments.

References

1. Abe, M., Chase, M., David, B., Kohlweiss, M., Nishimaki, R., Ohkubo, M.: Constant-size structure-preserving signatures: generic constructions and simple assumptions. In: Wang, X., Sako, K. (eds.) ASIACRYPT 2012. LNCS, vol. 7658, pp. 4–24. Springer, Heidelberg (2012)
2. Abe, M., David, B., Kohlweiss, M., Nishimaki, R., Ohkubo, M.: Tagged one-time signatures: tight security and optimal tag size. In: Kurosawa, K., Hanaoka, G. (eds.) PKC 2013. LNCS, vol. 7778, pp. 312–331. Springer, Heidelberg (2013)
3. Abe, M., Fuchsbauer, G., Groth, J., Haralambiev, K., Ohkubo, M.: Structure-preserving signatures and commitments to group elements. In: Rabin, T. (ed.) CRYPTO 2010. LNCS, vol. 6223, pp. 209–236. Springer, Heidelberg (2010)
4. Abe, M., Groth, J., Haralambiev, K., Ohkubo, M.: Optimal structure-preserving signatures in asymmetric bilinear groups. In: Rogaway, P. (ed.) CRYPTO 2011. LNCS, vol. 6841, pp. 649–666. Springer, Heidelberg (2011)
5. Abe, M., Groth, J., Ohkubo, M.: Separating short structure-preserving signatures from non-interactive assumptions. In: Lee, D.H., Wang, X. (eds.) ASIACRYPT 2011. LNCS, vol. 7073, pp. 628–646. Springer, Heidelberg (2011)
6. Abe, M., Groth, J., Ohkubo, M., Tibouchi, M.: Unified, minimal and selectively randomizable structure-preserving signatures. In: Lindell, Y. (ed.) TCC 2014. LNCS, vol. 8349, pp. 688–712. Springer, Heidelberg (2014)
7. Abe, M., Groth, J., Ohkubo, M., Tibouchi, M.: Structure-preserving signatures from Type II pairings. In: Garay, J.A., Gennaro, R. (eds.) CRYPTO 2014, Part I. LNCS, vol. 8616, pp. 390–407. Springer, Heidelberg (2014)
8. Abe, M., Kohlweiss, M., Ohkubo, M., Tibouchi, M.: Fully structure-preserving signatures and shrinking commitments. In: Oswald, E., Fischlin, M. (eds.) EURO-CRYPT 2015. LNCS, vol. 9057, pp. 35–65. Springer, Heidelberg (2015)
9. Attrapadung, N., Libert, B., Peters, T.: Computing on authenticated data: new privacy definitions and constructions. In: Wang, X., Sako, K. (eds.) ASIACRYPT 2012. LNCS, vol. 7658, pp. 367–385. Springer, Heidelberg (2012)
10. Barthe, G., Fagerholm, E., Fiore, D., Scedrov, A., Schmidt, B., Tibouchi, M.: Strongly-optimal structure preserving signatures from Type II pairings: synthesis and lower bounds. In: Katz, J. (ed.) PKC 2015. LNCS, vol. 9020, pp. 355–376. Springer, Heidelberg (2015)
11. Bernhard, D., Fuchsbauer, G., Ghadafi, E.: Efficient signatures of knowledge and DAA in the standard model. In: Jacobson, M., Locasto, M., Mohassel, P., Safavi-Naini, R. (eds.) ACNS 2013. LNCS, vol. 7954, pp. 518–533. Springer, Heidelberg (2013)
12. Bernhard, D., Fuchsbauer, G., Ghadafi, E., Smart, N.P., Warinschi, B.: Anonymous attestation with user-controlled linkability. Int. J. Inf. Secur. **12**(3), 219–249 (2013)
13. Brickell, E., Camenisch, J., Chen, L.: Direct anonymous attestation. In: CCS 2004, pp. 132–145. ACM (2004)

14. Camenisch, J., Dubovitskaya, M., Haralambiev, K.: Efficient structure-preserving signature scheme from standard assumptions. In: Visconti, I., De Prisco, R. (eds.) SCN 2012. LNCS, vol. 7485, pp. 76–94. Springer, Heidelberg (2012)

15. Camenisch, J.L., Lysyanskaya, A.: Signature schemes and anonymous credentials from bilinear maps. In: Franklin, M. (ed.) CRYPTO 2004. LNCS, vol. 3152, pp. 56–72. Springer, Heidelberg (2004)

16. Chase, M., Kohlweiss, M.: A new hash-and-sign approach and structure-preserving signatures from DLIN. In: Visconti, I., De Prisco, R. (eds.) SCN 2012. LNCS, vol. 7485, pp. 131–148. Springer, Heidelberg (2012)

17. Chatterjee, S., Menezes, A.: Typpe 2 Structure-Preserving Signature Schemes Revisited. Cryptology ePrint Archive, Report 2014/635 (2014)

18. Chaum, D.: Blind signatures for untraceable payments. In: Chaum, D., Rivest, R.L., Sherman, A.T. (eds.) Advances in Cryptology, pp. 199–203. Springer, Heidelberg (1983)

19. Chaum, D., van Heyst, E.: Group signatures. In: Davies, D.W. (ed.) EUROCRYPT 1991. LNCS, vol. 547, pp. 257–265. Springer, Heidelberg (1991)

20. ElGamal, T.: A public key cryptosystem and a signature scheme based on discrete logarithms. IEEE Trans. Inf. Theory $31(4)$, 469–472 (1985)

21. Fiat, A., Shamir, A.: How to prove yourself: practical solutions to identification and signature problems. In: Odlyzko, A.M. (ed.) CRYPTO 1986. LNCS, vol. 263, pp. 186–194. Springer, Heidelberg (1987)

22. Fuchsbauer, G.: Automorphic Signatures in Bilinear Groups and an Application to Round-Optimal Blind Signatures. Cryptology ePrint Archive, Report 2009/320 (2009)

23. Fuchsbauer, G.: Commuting signatures and verifiable encryption. In: Paterson, K.G. (ed.) EUROCRYPT 2011. LNCS, vol. 6632, pp. 224–245. Springer, Heidelberg (2011)

24. Galbraith, S., Paterson, K., Smart, N.P.: Pairings for cryptographers. Discrete Appl. Math. **156**, 3113–3121 (2008)

25. Ghadafi, E.: Formalizing group blind signatures and practical constructions without random oracles. In: Boyd, C., Simpson, L. (eds.) ACISP. LNCS, vol. 7959, pp. 330–346. Springer, Heidelberg (2013)

26. Ghadafi, E.: Short Structure-Preserving Signatures. Cryptology ePrint Archive, Report 2015/961 (2015). http://eprint.iacr.org/2015/961.pdf

27. Ghadafi, E., Smart, N.P., Warinschi, B.: Groth–sahai proofs revisited. In: Nguyen, P.Q., Pointcheval, D. (eds.) PKC 2010. LNCS, vol. 6056, pp. 177–192. Springer, Heidelberg (2010)

28. Green, M., Hohenberger, S.: Universally composable adaptive oblivious transfer. In: Pieprzyk, J. (ed.) ASIACRYPT 2008. LNCS, vol. 5350, pp. 179–197. Springer, Heidelberg (2008)

29. Groth, J.: Simulation-sound nizk proofs for a practical language and constant size group signatures. In: Lai, X., Chen, K. (eds.) ASIACRYPT 2006. LNCS, vol. 4284, pp. 444–459. Springer, Heidelberg (2006)

30. Groth, J.: Efficient Fully Structure-Preserving Signatures for Large Messages. Cryptology ePrint Archive, Report 2015/824 (2015)

31. Groth, J., Sahai, A.: Efficient non-interactive proof systems for bilinear groups. SIAM J. Comput. $41(5)$, 1193–1232 (2012)

32. Hofheinz, D., Jager, T.: Tightly secure signatures and public-key encryption. In: Safavi-Naini, R., Canetti, R. (eds.) CRYPTO 2012. LNCS, vol. 7417, pp. 590–607. Springer, Heidelberg (2012)

33. Kiltz, E., Pan, J., Wee, H.: Structure-preserving signatures from standard assumptions, revisited. In: Gennaro, R., Robshaw, M. (eds.) CRYPTO 2015. LNCS, vol. 9216, pp. 275–295. Springer, Heidelberg (2015)

34. Libert, B., Peters, T., Yung, M.: Scalable group signatures with revocation. In: Pointcheval, D., Johansson, T. (eds.) EUROCRYPT 2012. LNCS, vol. 7237, pp. 609–627. Springer, Heidelberg (2012)

35. Boneh, D., Boyen, X., Shacham, H.: Short group signatures. In: Franklin, M. (ed.) CRYPTO 2004. LNCS, vol. 3152, pp. 41–55. Springer, Heidelberg (2004)

36. Lysyanskaya, A., Ramzan, Z.: Group blind digital signatures: a scalable solution to electronic cash. In: Hirschfeld, R. (ed.) FC 1998. LNCS, vol. 1465, pp. 184–197. Springer, Heidelberg (1998)

37. Maurer, U.M.: Abstract models of computation in cryptography. In: Smart, N.P. (ed.) Cryptography and Coding 2005. LNCS, vol. 3796, pp. 1–12. Springer, Heidelberg (2005)

38. Pointcheval, D., Sanders, O.: Short Randomizable Signatures. Cryptology ePrint Archive, Report 2015/525 (2015)

39. Schwartz, J.T.: Fast probabilistic algorithms for verification of polynomial identities. J. ACM **27**, 701–717 (1980)

40. Shoup, V.: Lower bounds for discrete logarithms and related problems. In: Fumy, W. (ed.) EUROCRYPT 1997. LNCS, vol. 1233, pp. 256–266. Springer, Heidelberg (1997)

Lattice Cryptography

Which Ring Based Somewhat Homomorphic Encryption Scheme is Best?

Ana Costache and Nigel P. Smart[✉]

Department of Computer Science, University of Bristol, Bristol, UK
anamaria.costache@bristol.ac.uk, nigel@cs.bris.ac.uk

Abstract. The purpose of this paper is to compare side-by-side the NTRU and BGV schemes in their non-scale invariant (messages in the lower bits), and their scale invariant (message in the upper bits) forms. The scale invariant versions are often called the YASHE and FV schemes. As an additional optimization, we also investigate the ffect of modulus reduction on the scale-invariant schemes. We compare the schemes using the "average case" noise analysis presented by Gentry et al. In addition we unify notation and techniques so as to show commonalities between the schemes. We find that the BGV scheme appears to be more efficient for large plaintext moduli, whilst YASHE seems more efficient for small plaintext moduli (although the benefit is not as great as one would have expected).

1 Introduction

Some of the more spectacular advances in implementation improvements for Somewhat Homomorphic Encryption (SHE) schemes have come in the context of the ring based schemes such as BGV [3]. The main improvements here have come through the use of SIMD techniques (first introduced in the context of Gentry's original scheme [7] by Smart and Vercauteren [17], but then extended to the Ring-LWE based schemes by Gentry et al. [3]). SIMD techniques in the ring setting allow for a small overall asymptotic overhead in using SHE schemes [8] by exploiting the Galois group to move data between slots. The Galois group can also be used to perform cheap exponentiation via the Frobenius endomorphism [9]. Other improvements in the ring based setting come from the use of modulus switching to a larger modulus, so as to perform key switching [9], the use of scale invariant versions [1,6], and the use of NTRU to enable key homomorphic schemes [14].

The scale invariant schemes, originally introduced in [2], are particularly interesting, they place the message space in the "upper bits" of the decryption equation, as opposed to the lower bits. This enables a more effective noise control mechanism to be employed which does not on the face of it require modulus switching to keep the noise within bounds. However, the downside is that they require a more complex rounding operation to be performed in the multiplication procedure.

© Springer International Publishing Switzerland 2016
K. Sako (Ed.): CT-RSA 2016, LNCS 9610, pp. 325–340, 2016.
DOI: 10.1007/978-3-319-29485-8_19

However each paper which analyses the schemes uses a different methodology for deriving parameters, and examining the noise growth. In addition not all papers utilize all optimizations and improvements available. For example papers on the NTRU scheme [5,14], and its scale invariant version YASHE [1], rarely, if at all, make mention of the use of SIMD techniques. Papers working on scale invariant systems [1,6] usually focus on plaintext moduli of two, and discount larger moduli. But many applications, e.g. usage in the SPDZ [4] MPC system, require the use of large moduli.

We have therefore conducted a systematic study of the main ring-based SHE schemes with a view to producing a fair comparison over a range of possible application spaces, from low characteristic plaintext spaces through to large characteristic ones, from low depth circuits through to high depth ones. The schemes we have studied are BGV, whose details can be found in [3,8,9], and its scale-invariant version [6] (called FV in what follows), the basic NTRU scheme [5,14], and its scale-invariant version YASHE [1]. A previous study [12] only compared FV and YASHE, restricted to small plaintext spaces (in particular characteristic two), and did not consider the various variants in relation to key switching and modulus switching which we consider. Our results are broadly in line with [12] (where we have a direct comparison) for YASHE, but our estimates for FV appear slightly better.

On the face of it one expects that YASHE should be the most efficient, since it is scale invariant (which often leads to smaller parameters) and a ciphertext consists of only a single ring element, as opposed to two for the BGV style schemes. Yet this initial impression hides a number of details, wherein one can find a number of devils. It turns out that which is the most efficient scheme depends on the context (message characteristic and depth of admissible circuits).

To compare all four schemes fairly we apply the same API to all schemes, and the same optimizations. In particular we also investigate applying modulus switching to the scale invariant schemes (where its use is often discounted as not being needed). The use of modulus switching can be beneficial as it means ciphertexts become smaller as the function evaluation proceeds, resulting in increased performance. We also examine two forms of key switching (one based on the traditional decomposition technique and one based on raising the modulus to a larger value). For the decomposition technique we also examine the most efficient modulus to take in the modular decomposition, which turns out not to the two often seen in many treatments.

To compare the schemes we use the average distributional analysis first introduced in [9], which measures the noise in terms of the expected size in the canonical embedding norm. The use of the canonical embedding norm also deviates from some other treatments. For general rings the canonical embedding norm provides a more accurate measure of noise growth, over norms in the polynomial embedding, when analysed over a number of homomorphic operations. The noise growth of all of our schemes is analysed in the same way, and this is the first time (to our knowledge) that all schemes have been analysed on an equal footing.

The first question when performing such a comparison is how to compare security of differing schemes. On one hand one could take the standpoint of an exact security analysis and derive parameter sizes from the security theorems. However, even this is tricky when comparing schemes as the theorems may reduce security of different schemes to different hard problems. So instead we side-step this issue and select parameters according to an analysis of the best known attack on each scheme; which is luckily the same in all four cases. Thus we select parameters according to the Lindner-Peikert analysis [13]. To also afford a fair comparison we use similar distributions for the various parameters for each scheme; e.g. small Hamming weight for the secret key distributions etc.

The next question is how to measure what is "better". In the context of a given specific scheme we consider one set of parameters to be better than another, for a given plaintext modulus, level bound and security parameter, if the number of bits to represent a ring element is minimized. After all this corresponds directly to the computational overhead when implementing the scheme. When comparing schemes one has to be a little more careful, as ciphertexts in the BGV family consist of two ring elements and in the NTRU family they consist of one element, but still ciphertext size is a good crude measure of overall performance. In addition, the operations needed for the scale invariant schemes are not directly compatible with the efficient double-CRT representation of ring elements introduced in [9], thus even if ciphertext sizes for the scale invariant schemes are smaller than for the non-scale invariant schemes, the actual computation times might be much larger.

As one can appreciate much of the analysis is an intricate following through of various inequalities. The full derivations can be found in the full version of this paper. We find that the BGV scheme appears to be more efficient for large plaintext moduli, whilst YASHE seems more efficient for small plaintext moduli (although the benefit is not as great as one would have expected).

2   Preliminaries

In this section we outline the basic mathematical background which forms the basis of our four ring-based SHE schemes. Much of what follows can be found in [8,9], we recap on it here for convenience of the reader. We utilize rings defined by cyclotomic polynomials, $\mathbb{A} = \mathbb{Z}[X]/\Phi_m(X)$. We let $\mathbb{A}_q$ denote the set of elements of this ring reduced modulo various (possibly composite) moduli q. The ring $\mathbb{A}$ is the ring of integers of the mth cyclotomic number field $K = \mathbb{Q}(\zeta_m)$. We let $[a]_q$ for an element $a \in \mathbb{A}$ denote the reduction of a modulo q, with the set of representatives of coefficients lying in $(-q/2, \ldots, q/2]$, hence $[a]_q \in \mathbb{A}_q$. Assignment of variables will be denoted by $a \leftarrow b$, with equality being denoted by $=$ or $\equiv$.

Plaintext Slots: We will always use p for the plaintext modulus, and thus plaintexts will be elements of $\mathbb{A}_p$, and the polynomial $\Phi_m(X)$ factors modulo p into ℓ irreducible factors, $\Phi_m(X) = F_1(X) \cdot F_2(X) \cdots F_\ell(X) \pmod{p}$, all of degree $d = \phi(m)/\ell$. Just as in [3,8,9,17] each factor corresponds to a "plaintext slot". That is, we view a polynomial $a \in \mathbb{A}_p$ as representing an ℓ-vector $(a \bmod F_i)_{i=1}^{\ell}$. We assume that p does not divide m so as to enable the slots to exist. In a number of applications p is likely to split completely in $\mathbb{A}$, i.e. $p \equiv 1 \pmod{m}$. This is especially true in applications not requiring bootstrapping, and hence only requiring evaluation of low depth arithmetic circuits.

Canonical Embedding Norm: Following the work in [15], we use as the "size" of a polynomial $a \in \mathbb{A}$ the l_∞ norm of its canonical embedding. Recall that the canonical embedding of $a \in \mathbb{A}$ into $\mathbb{C}^{\phi(m)}$ is the $\phi(m)$-vector of complex numbers $\sigma(a) = (a(\zeta_m^i))_i$ where ζ_m is a complex primitive m-th root of unity and the indexes i range over all of $(\mathbb{Z}/m\mathbb{Z})^*$. We call the norm of $\sigma(a)$ the *canonical embedding norm* of a, and denote it by $\|a\|_\infty^{\mathsf{can}} = \|\sigma(a)\|_\infty$. We will make use of the following properties of $\|\cdot\|_\infty^{\mathsf{can}}$:

- For all $a, b \in \mathbb{A}$ we have $\|a \cdot b\|_\infty^{\mathsf{can}} \le \|a\|_\infty^{\mathsf{can}} \cdot \|b\|_\infty^{\mathsf{can}}$.
- For all $a \in \mathbb{A}$ we have $\|a\|_\infty^{\mathsf{can}} \le \|a\|_1$.
- There is a ring constant c_m (depending only on m) such that $\|a\|_\infty \le c_m \cdot \|a\|_\infty^{\mathsf{can}}$ for all $a \in \mathbb{A}$.

where $\|a\|_\infty$ and $\|a\|_1$ refer to the relevant norms on the coefficient vectors of a in the power basis. The ring constant c_m is defined by $c_m = \|\mathsf{CRT}_m^{-1}\|_\infty$ where CRT_m is the CRT matrix for m, i.e. the Vandermonde matrix over the complex primitive m-th roots of unity. Asymptotically the value c_m can grow super-polynomially with m, but for the "small" values of m one would use in practice values of c_m can be evaluated directly. See [4] for a discussion of c_m.

Sampling From $\mathbb{A}_q$: At various points we will need to sample from $\mathbb{A}_q$ with different distributions, as described below. We denote choosing the element $a \in \mathbb{A}$ according to distribution $\mathcal{D}$ by $a \leftarrow \mathcal{D}$. The distributions below are described as over $\phi(m)$-vectors, but we always consider them as distributions over the ring $\mathbb{A}$, by identifying a polynomial $a \in \mathbb{A}$ with its coefficient vector.

The uniform distribution $\mathcal{U}_q$: This is just the uniform distribution over $(\mathbb{Z}/q\mathbb{Z})^{\phi(m)}$, which we identify with $(\mathbb{Z} \cap (-q/2, q/2])^{\phi(m)}$.

The "rounded Gaussian" $\mathcal{DG}_q(\sigma^2)$: Let $\mathcal{N}(0, \sigma^2)$ denote the normal (Gaussian) distribution on real numbers with zero-mean and variance σ^2, we use drawing from $\mathcal{N}(0, \sigma^2)$ and rounding to the nearest integer as an approximation to the discrete Gaussian distribution. The distribution $\mathcal{DG}_{q_t}(\sigma^2)$ draws a real ϕ-vector according to $\mathcal{N}(0, \sigma^2)^{\phi(m)}$, rounds it to the nearest integer vector, and outputs that integer vector reduced modulo q (into the interval $(-q/2, q/2]$).

Sampling small polynomials, $\mathcal{ZO}(p)$ and $\mathcal{HWT}(h)$: These distributions produce vectors in $\{0, \pm 1\}^{\phi(m)}$.

- For a real parameter $\rho \in [0,1]$, $\mathcal{ZO}(p)$ draws each entry in the vector from $\{0, \pm 1\}$, with probability $\rho/2$ for each of -1 and $+1$, and probability of being zero $1 - \rho$.
- For an integer parameter $h \leq \phi(m)$, the distribution $\mathcal{HWT}(h)$ chooses a vector uniformly at random from $\{0, \pm 1\}^{\phi(m)}$, subject to the condition that it has exactly h nonzero entries.

Canonical Embedding Norm of Random Polynomials: In the coming sections we will need to bound the canonical embedding norm of polynomials that are produced by the distributions above, as well as products of such polynomials. Following the work in [9] we use a heuristic approach, which we now recap on.

Let $a \in A$ be a polynomial that was chosen by one of the distributions above, hence all the (nonzero) coefficients in a are independently identically distributed. For a complex primitive m-th root of unity ζ_m, the evaluation $a(\zeta_m)$ is the inner product between the coefficient vector of a and the fixed vector $\mathbf{z}_m = (1, \zeta_m, \zeta_m^2, \ldots)$, which has Euclidean norm exactly $\sqrt{\phi(m)}$. Hence the random variable $a(\zeta_m)$ has variance $V = \sigma^2 \phi(m)$, where σ^2 is the variance of each coefficient of a. Specifically, when $a \leftarrow \mathcal{U}_q$ then each coefficient has variance $(q-1)^2/12 \approx q^2/12$, so we get variance $V_U = q^2 \cdot \phi(m)/12$. When $a \leftarrow \mathcal{DG}_q(\sigma^2)$ we get variance $V_G \approx \sigma^2 \cdot \phi(m)$, and when $a \leftarrow \mathcal{ZO}(\rho)$ we get variance $V_Z = \rho \cdot \phi(m)$. When choosing $a \leftarrow \mathcal{HWT}(h)$ we get a variance of $V_H = h$ (but not $\phi(m)$, since a has only h nonzero coefficients).

Moreover, the random variable $a(\zeta_m)$ is a sum of many independent identically distributed random variables, hence by the law of large numbers it is distributed similarly to a complex Gaussian random variable of the specified variance.[1] We therefore use $6\sqrt{V}$ (i.e. six standard deviations) as a high-probability bound on the size of $a(\zeta_m)$. Since the evaluation of a at all the roots of unity obeys the same bound, we use six standard deviations as our bound on the canonical embedding norm of a. (We chose six standard deviations since $\mathrm{erfc}(6) \approx 2^{-55}$, which is good enough for us even when using the union bound and multiplying it by $\phi(m) \approx 2^{16}$.)

In this paper we model all canonical embedding norms as if from a random distribution. In [9] the messages were always given a norm of $\|m\|_\infty^{\mathrm{can}} \leq p \cdot \phi(m)/2$, i.e. a worst case bound. We shall assume that messages, and similar quantities, behave as if selected uniformly at random and hence estimate $\|m\|_\infty^{\mathrm{can}} \leq 6 \cdot p \cdot \sqrt{\phi(m)/12} = p \cdot \sqrt{3 \cdot \phi(m)}$. This makes our bounds better, and does not materially affect the decryption ability due to the larger effect of other terms. However, this simplification makes the formulae somewhat easier to parse.

In many cases we need to bound the canonical embedding norm of a product of two or more such "random polynomials". In this case our task is to bound the magnitude of the product of two random variables, both are distributed close to

---

[1] The mean of $a(\zeta_m)$ is zero, since the coefficients of a are chosen from a zero-mean distribution.

Gaussians, with variances σ_a^2, σ_b^2, respectively. For this case we use $16 \cdot \sigma_a \cdot \sigma_b$ as our bound, since $\mathrm{erfc}(4) \approx 2^{-25}$, so the probability that both variables exceed their standard deviation by more than a factor of four is roughly 2^{-50}. For a product of three variables we use $40 \cdot \sigma_a \cdot \sigma_b \cdot \sigma_c$, since $\mathrm{erfc}(3.4) \approx 2^{-19}$, and $3.4^3 \approx 40$.

3   Ring Based SHE Schemes

We refer to our four schemes as BGV, FV, NTRU and YASHE. The various schemes have been used/defined in various papers: for example one can find BGV in [3,8,9], FV in [6], NTRU in [5,14] and YASHE in [1]. In all four schemes we shall use a chain of moduli for our homomorphic evaluation[2] by choosing L "small primes" $p_0, p_1, \ldots, p_{L-1}$ and the tth modulus in our chain is defined as $q_t = \prod_{j=0}^{t} p_j$. A chain of L primes allows us to perform $L-1$ multiplications. The primes p_i's are chosen so that for all i, $\mathbb{Z}/p_i\mathbb{Z}$ contains a primitive m-th root of unity, i.e. $p_i \equiv 1 \pmod{m}$. Hence we can use the double-CRT representation, see [9], for all $\mathbb{A}_{q_t}$.

For the BGV and NTRU schemes we additionally assume that $p_i \equiv 1 \pmod{p}$. This is to enable the Scaling operation to work without having to additionally scale by $p_i \pmod{p}$, which would result in slightly more noise growth. A disadvantage of this is that the moduli p_i will need to be slightly larger than would otherwise be the case. The two scale invariant schemes (FV and YASHE) will make use of a scaling factor Δ_q defined by $\Delta_q = \left\lfloor \frac{q}{p} \right\rfloor = \frac{q}{p} - \epsilon_q$, where $0 \le \epsilon_q < 1$.

3.1   Key Generation

We utilize the following methods for key generation, they sample the secret key in all cases, from a sparse distribution, this follows the choices made in [9]. This leads to more efficient homomorphic operations (since noise growth depends on the size of the secret key in many situations). However, such choices might lead to security weaknesses, which would need to be considered in any commercial deployment.

$\mathsf{KeyGen}^{\mathsf{BGV}}()$: Sample $\mathfrak{st} \leftarrow \mathcal{HWT}(h)$, $a \leftarrow \mathcal{U}_{q_{L-1}}$, and $e \leftarrow \mathcal{DG}_{q_{L-1}}(\sigma^2)$. Then set the secret key as $\mathfrak{st}$ and the public key as $\mathfrak{pt} \leftarrow (a, b)$ where $b \leftarrow [a \cdot \mathfrak{st} + p \cdot e]_{q_{L-1}}$.

$\mathsf{KeyGen}^{\mathsf{FV}}()$: Sample $\mathfrak{st} \leftarrow \mathcal{HWT}(h)$, $a \leftarrow \mathcal{U}_{q_{L-1}}$, and $e \leftarrow \mathcal{DG}_{q_{L-1}}(\sigma^2)$. Then set the secret key as $\mathfrak{st}$ and the public key as $\mathfrak{pt} \leftarrow (a, b)$ where $b \leftarrow [a \cdot \mathfrak{st} + e]_{q_{L-1}}$.

$\mathsf{KeyGen}^{\mathsf{NTRU}}()$: Sample $f, g \leftarrow \mathcal{HWT}(h)$. Then set the secret key as $\mathfrak{st} \leftarrow p \cdot f + 1$ and the public key as $\mathfrak{pt} \leftarrow [p \cdot g/\mathfrak{st}]_{q_{L-1}}$. Note, if $p \cdot f + 1$ is not invertible in $\mathbb{A}_{q_{L-1}}$ we repeat the sampling again until it is.

---

[2] This is not strictly needed for the Scale invariant version if modulus switching is not performed.

$\underline{\text{KeyGen}^{\text{YASHE}}()}$: Sample $f, g \leftarrow \mathcal{HWT}(h)$. Then set the secret key as $\mathfrak{sk} \leftarrow p \cdot f + 1$ and the public key as $\mathfrak{pk} \leftarrow [p \cdot g/\mathfrak{sk}]_{q_{L-1}}$. Again, if $p \cdot f + 1$ is not invertible in $\mathbb{A}_{q_{L-1}}$ we repeat the sampling until it is.

3.2 Encryption and Decryption

The encryption algorithms for all four schemes are given in Fig. 1. As for key generation we select slightly simpler distributions than the theory would imply so as to ensure noise growth is not as bad as it would otherwise be. The output of each algorithm is a tuple $\mathfrak{c}$ consisting of the ciphertext data, the current level, plus a bound on the current "noise" B^*_{clean}. This bound is on the canonical embedding norm of a particular critical quantity which comes up in the decryption process; a different critical quantity depending on which scheme we are using. If the critical quantity has canonical embedding norm less than a specific value then decryption will work, otherwise decryption will likely fail. Thus having each ciphertext carry around an upper bound on the norm of this quantity allows us to analyse noise growth dynamically.

$\underline{\text{Enc}^{\text{BGV}}_{\mathfrak{pk}}(m)}$:
  - $v \leftarrow \mathcal{ZO}(0.5)$.
  - $e_0, e_1 \leftarrow \mathcal{DG}_{q_{L-1}}(\sigma^2)$.
  - $c_0 \leftarrow [b \cdot v + p \cdot e_0 + m]_{q_{L-1}}$,
  - $c_1 \leftarrow [a \cdot v + p \cdot e_1]_{q_{L-1}}$,
  - Output $\mathfrak{c} \leftarrow (c_0, c_1, L - 1, B^{\text{BGV}}_{\text{clean}})$.

$\underline{\text{Enc}^{\text{FV}}_{\mathfrak{pk}}(m)}$:
  - $v \leftarrow \mathcal{ZO}(0.5)$.
  - $e_0, e_1 \leftarrow \mathcal{DG}_{q_{L-1}}(\sigma^2)$.
  - $c_0 \leftarrow [b \cdot v + e_0 + \Delta_{q_{L-1}} \cdot m]_{q_{L-1}}$,
  - $c_1 \leftarrow [a \cdot v + e_1]_{q_{L-1}}$,
  - Output $\mathfrak{c} \leftarrow (c_0, c_1, L - 1, B^{\text{FV}}_{\text{clean}})$.

$\underline{\text{Enc}^{\text{NTRU}}_{\mathfrak{pk}}(m)}$:
  - $e_0, e_1 \leftarrow \mathcal{DG}_{q_{L-1}}(\sigma^2)$.
  - $c \leftarrow [e_1 \cdot \mathfrak{pk} + p \cdot e_0 + m]_{q_{L-1}}$,
  - Output $\mathfrak{c} \leftarrow (c, L - 1, B^{\text{NTRU}}_{\text{clean}})$.

$\underline{\text{Enc}^{\text{YASHE}}_{\mathfrak{pk}}(m)}$:
  - $e_0, e_1 \leftarrow \mathcal{DG}_{q_{L-1}}(\sigma^2)$.
  - $c \leftarrow [e_1 \cdot \mathfrak{pk} + e_0 + \Delta_{q_{L-1}} \cdot m]_{q_{L-1}}$,
  - Output $\mathfrak{c} \leftarrow (c, L - 1, B^{\text{YASHE}}_{\text{clean}})$.

Fig. 1. Encryption algorithms for BGV, FV, NTRU and YASHE

To understand the critical quantity we have to first look at the decryption procedure in each case. Then we can apply our heuristic noise analysis to obtain an upper bound on the canonical embedding norm of the critical quantity for a fresh ciphertext, and so obtain B^*_{clean}; a process which is done in the full version of this paper.

$\underline{\text{Dec}^{\text{BGV}}_{\mathfrak{pk}}(\mathfrak{c})}$: Decryption of a ciphertext (c_0, c_1, t, ν) at level t is performed by setting $m' \leftarrow [c_0 - \mathfrak{sk} \cdot c_1]_{q_t}$, and outputting $m' \mod p$. If we define the critical quantity to be $c_0 - \mathfrak{sk} \cdot c_1 \pmod{q_t}$, then this procedure will work when ν is an upper bound on the canonical embedding norm of this quantity and $c_m \cdot \nu < q_t/2$. If ν satisfies this inequality then the value of $c_0 - \mathfrak{sk} \cdot c_1 \pmod{q_t}$ will be produced exactly with no wrap-around, and will hence be equal to $m + p \cdot v$, if $c_0 = \mathfrak{s}\mathfrak{k} \cdot c_1 + p \cdot v + m \pmod{q_t}$. Thus we must pick the smallest prime $q_0 = p_0$ large enough to ensure that this always holds.

$\underline{\mathsf{Dec}^{\mathsf{FV}}_{\mathfrak{p}\mathfrak{k}}(\mathfrak{c})}$: Decryption of a ciphertext (c_0, c_1, t, ν) at level t is performed by setting

$$m' \leftarrow \left[\frac{p}{q_t} \cdot [c_0 - \mathfrak{s}\mathfrak{k} \cdot c_1]_{q_t} \right],$$

and outputting $m' \bmod p$. Consider the value of $[c_0 - \mathfrak{s}\mathfrak{k} \cdot c_1]_{q_t}$ computed during decryption, suppose this is equal to (over the integers before reduction mod q_t) $m \cdot \Delta_{q_t} + w + r \cdot q_t$. Then another way of looking at decryption is that we perform rounding on the value

$$\frac{p \cdot \Delta_{q_t} \cdot m}{q_t} + \frac{p \cdot w}{q_t} + \frac{p \cdot r \cdot q_t}{q_t} = \frac{p \cdot (\frac{q_t}{p} - \epsilon_{q_t}) \cdot m}{q_t} + \frac{p \cdot w}{q_t} + p \cdot r$$

$$= m + p \cdot \frac{w - \epsilon_{q_t} \cdot m}{q_t} + p \cdot r$$

and then take the result modulo p. Thus the critical quantity in this case is the value of $w - \epsilon_{q_t} \cdot m$. So that the rounding is correct we require that ν is an upper bound on $\|w - \epsilon_{q_t} \cdot m\|_\infty^{\mathsf{can}}$. The decryption procedure will then work when $c_m \cdot \nu < \Delta_{q_t}/2$, since in this case we have

$$\left\| p \cdot \frac{w - \epsilon_{q_t} \cdot m}{q_t} \right\|_\infty \leq \frac{c_m \cdot p}{q_t} \cdot \|w - \epsilon_{q_t} \cdot m\|_\infty^{\mathsf{can}} \leq \frac{\Delta_{q_t} \cdot p}{2 \cdot q_t} < \frac{1}{2}.$$

Thus again we must pick the smallest prime $q_0 = p_0$ large enough, to ensure that $c_m \cdot \nu < \Delta_{q_t}/2$.

$\underline{\mathsf{Dec}^{\mathsf{NTRU}}_{\mathfrak{p}\mathfrak{k}}(\mathfrak{c})}$: Decryption of a ciphertext (c, t, ν) at level t is performed by setting $m' \leftarrow [c \cdot \mathfrak{s}\mathfrak{k}]_{q_t}$, and outputting $m' \bmod p$. Much as with BGV the critical quantity is $[c \cdot \mathfrak{s}\mathfrak{k}]_{q_t}$. If ν is an upper bound on the canonical embedding norm of $c \cdot \mathfrak{s}\mathfrak{k}$, and we have $c = a \cdot \mathfrak{p}\mathfrak{k} + p \cdot e + m$ modulo q_t, for some values of a and e, then over the integers we have

$$[c \cdot \mathfrak{s}\mathfrak{k}]_{q_t} = m + p \cdot (a \cdot g + e + f \cdot m) + p^2 \cdot e \cdot f,$$

which will decrypt to m. Thus for decryption to work we require that $c_m \cdot \nu < q_t/2$.

$\underline{\mathsf{Dec}^{\mathsf{YASHE}}_{\mathfrak{p}\mathfrak{k}}(\mathfrak{c})}$: Decryption of a ciphertext (c, t, ν) at level t is performed by setting

$$m' \leftarrow \left[\frac{p}{q_t} \cdot [c \cdot \mathfrak{s}\mathfrak{k}]_{q_t} \right],$$

and outputting $m' \bmod p$. Following the same reasoning as for the FV scheme, suppose $c \cdot \mathfrak{s}\mathfrak{k}$ is equal to (again over the integers before reduction mod q_t) $m \cdot \Delta_{q_t} + w + r \cdot q_t$. Then for decryption to work we require ν to be an upper bound on $\|w - \epsilon_{q_t} \cdot m\|_\infty^{\mathsf{can}}$ and $c_m \cdot \nu < q_t/2$.

3.3 Scale

These operations scale a ciphertext, reducing the corresponding level and more importantly scaling the noise. The syntax is $\mathsf{Scale}^*(\mathfrak{c}, t_{out})$ where $\mathfrak{c}$ is at level t_{in} and the output ciphertext is at level t_{out} with $t_{out} \leq t_{in}$. The noise is scaled by a factor of approximately $q_{t_{in}}/q_{t_{out}}$, however an additive term of B^*_{scale} is added. For each of our variants see the full version of this paper for a justification of the proposed method and an estimate on B^*_{scale}.

For use in one of the $\mathsf{SwitchKey}^*$ variants we also use a Scale which takes a ciphertext with respect to modulus Q and produces a ciphertext with respect to modulus q, where $q|Q$. The syntax for this is $\mathsf{Scale}^*(\mathfrak{c}, Q)$; the idea here is that Q is a "temporary" modulus unrelated to the actual level t of the ciphertext, and we aim to reduce Q down to q_t. The former scale function can be defined in terms of the latter via

$\underline{\mathsf{Scale}^*(\mathfrak{c}, t_{out})}$:

- Write $\mathfrak{c} = (c, t, \nu)$.
- $\mathfrak{c}' \leftarrow \mathsf{Scale}^*((c, t_{out}, \nu), q_t)$.
- Output $\mathfrak{c}'$.

The Scale^* function was originally presented in [3] as a form of noise control for the non-scale invariant schemes. However, the use of such a function within the scale invariant schemes can also provide more efficient schemes, as alluded to in [6]. This is due to the modulus one is working with which decreases as homomorphic operations are applied. It is also needed for our second key switching variant. We thus present a Scale^* function for all our four schemes in Fig. 2.

$\mathsf{Scale}^{\mathsf{BGV}}(\mathfrak{c}, Q)$:
- Write $\mathfrak{c} = ((c_0, c_1), t, \nu)$.
- Fix δ_i such that $\delta_i \equiv -c_i \pmod{P}$ and $\delta_i \equiv 0 \pmod{p}$.
- Write $c'_i \leftarrow (c_i + \delta_i)/P$.
- $\nu' \leftarrow \nu/P + B^{\mathsf{BGV}}_{\mathsf{scale}}$.
- Output $((c'_0, c'_1), t, \nu')$.

$\mathsf{Scale}^{\mathsf{NTRU}}(\mathfrak{c}, Q)$:
- Write $\mathfrak{c} = (c, t, \nu)$.
- Fix δ such that $\delta \equiv -c \pmod{P}$ and $\delta \equiv 0 \pmod{p}$.
- Write $c' \leftarrow (c + \delta)/P$.
- $\nu' \leftarrow \nu/P + B^{\mathsf{NTRU}}_{\mathsf{scale}}$.
- Output (c', t, ν').

$\mathsf{Scale}^{\mathsf{FV}}(\mathfrak{c}, Q)$:
- Write $\mathfrak{c} = ((c_0, c_1), t, \nu)$.
- Fix δ_i such that $\delta_i \equiv -c_i \pmod{P}$.
- Write $c'_i \leftarrow (c_i + \delta_i)/P$.
- $\nu' \leftarrow \nu/P + B^{\mathsf{FV}}_{\mathsf{scale}}$.
- Output $((c'_0, c'_1), t, \nu')$.

$\mathsf{Scale}^{\mathsf{YASHE}}(\mathfrak{c}, Q)$:
- Write $\mathfrak{c} = (c, t, \nu)$.
- Fix δ such that $\delta \equiv -c \pmod{P}$.
- Write $c' \leftarrow (c + \delta)/P$.
- $\nu' \leftarrow \nu/P + B^{\mathsf{YASHE}}_{\mathsf{Scale}}$.
- Output (c', t, ν').

Fig. 2. Scale algorithms for BGV, FV, NTRU and YASHE. In all methods $Q = q_t \cdot P$, and for the BGV and NTRU schemes we assume that $P \equiv 1 \pmod{p}$.

3.4 Reduce Level

For all schemes we can define a ReduceLevel* operation which reduces a cipher-text level from level t' to level t where $t' \geq t$. For the non-scale invariant schemes when we reduce a level we only perform a scaling (which could be an expensive operation) if the noise is above some global bound B. This is because for small noise we can easily reduce the level by just dropping terms off the modulus, since the modulus is a product of primes. For the scale invariant schemes we actually need to perform a Scale operation since we need to modify the Δ_{q_t} term. See the full version of this paper for details. In our parameter estimation evaluation we examine the case, for FV and YASHE, of applying modulus switching to reduce levels and not applying it. In the case of not applying it all ciphertexts remain at level $L - 1$, and ReduceLevel* becomes a NOP.

3.5 Switch Key

The switch key operation is needed to relinearize after a multiplication, or after the application of a Galois automorphism (see [8] for more details on the latter). For all schemes we present two switch key operations:

- One based on decomposition modulo a general modulus T. See [11] for this method explained in the case of the BGV scheme. Unlike prior work we do not take $T = 2$, as we treat T as a parameter to be optimized to achieve the most efficient scheme. Although to ease parameter search we restrict to T being a power of two.
- Our second method is based on the raising the modulus idea from [9], where it was applied to the BGV scheme. Here we adopt a more complex switching operation, and a potentially larger parameter set, but we gain by reducing the size of the switching "matrices".

For each variant we require algorithms SwitchKeyGen and SwitchKey; the first generates the public switching "matrix", whilst the second performs the actual switch key. In the BGV and FV schemes we perform a general key switch of the underlying decryption equation of the form $d_0 - \mathfrak{s}\mathfrak{k} \cdot d_1 + \mathfrak{s}\mathfrak{k}' \cdot d_2 \longrightarrow c_0 - \mathfrak{s}\mathfrak{k} \cdot c_1$. For the NTRU and YASHE schemes the underlying key switch is of the form $c \cdot \mathfrak{s}\mathfrak{k}' \longrightarrow c' \cdot \mathfrak{s}\mathfrak{k}$. In Fig. 3 we present the key switching methods for the BGV algorithm. See the full version of this paper for the methods for the other schemes, plus derivations of upper bounds on the constants $B_{\mathsf{Ks},*} * (*)$.

In the context of BGV the first method requires us to store $\log_T(q_{L-1})$ "encryptions" of $\mathfrak{s}\mathfrak{k}'$, each of which is an element in $R^2_{q_{L-1}}$. The second method requires us to store a single "encryption" of $P \cdot \mathfrak{s}\mathfrak{k}'$, but this time as an element in $R^2_{P \cdot q_{L-1}}$. The former will require more space than the latter as soon as $\log_2 P < \log_T(q_{L-1})$. In terms of noise the output noise of the first method is modified by an additive constant of

$$B^{\mathsf{BGV}}_{\mathsf{Ks},1}(t) = \frac{8}{\sqrt{3}} \cdot p \cdot \left\lceil \log_T q_t \right\rceil \cdot \sigma \cdot \phi(m) \cdot T.$$

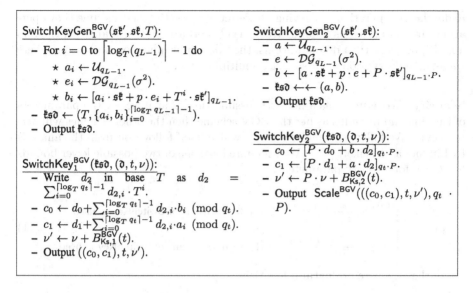

Fig. 3. The two variants of Key Switching for BGV.

whilst the output noise of the second method is modified by the additive constant

$$\frac{B_{\mathsf{Ks},2}^{\mathsf{BGV}}(t)}{P} + B_{\mathrm{scale}}^* = \frac{8 \cdot p \cdot q_t \cdot \sigma \cdot \phi(m)}{\sqrt{3} \cdot P} + B_{\mathrm{scale}}^*.$$

As the level decreases this becomes closer and closer to B_{scale}^*, as the P in the denominator will wipe out the numerator term. Thus the noise will grow of the order of $O(\sqrt{\phi(m)})$ using the second method and as $O(\phi(m))$ using the first method. A similar outcomes arises when comparing the two methods with respect to the other three schemes.

3.6   Addition and Multiplication

We can now turn to presenting the homomorphic addition and multiplication operations. For reasons of space we give the addition and multiplication methods in the full version of this paper. In all methods the input ciphertexts c_i have level t_i, and recall our parameters are such that we can evaluate circuits with multiplicative depth $L - 1$.

3.7   Security and Parameters

In this section we outline how we select parameters in the case where ReduceLevel* is not a NOP (a no-operation). An analysis, for the FV and YASHE schemes, where ReduceLevel* is a NOP we defer the analysis to the full version of this paper. We let B denote an upper bound on ν at the output of any

ReduceLevel* operation. Following [9] we set $B = 2 \cdot B^*_{\text{scale}}$. We assume that operations are performed as follows. We encrypt, perform up to ζ additions, then do a multiplication, then do ζ additions, then do a multiplication and so on, where we assume decryption occurs after a multiplication.

Security: We assume, as a heuristic assumption, that if we set the parameters of the ring and modulus as per the BGV scheme then the other schemes will also be secure. We follow the analysis in [9], which itself follows on from the analysis by Lindner and Peikert [13][3]. We therefore have one of two possible lower bounds for $\phi(m)$, for security parameter k

$$\phi(m) \geq \begin{cases} \frac{\log(q_{L-1}/\sigma) \cdot (k+110)}{7.2} & \text{If the first variant of SwitchKey is used,} \\[3mm] \frac{\log(P \cdot q_{L-1}/\sigma) \cdot (k+110)}{7.2} & \text{If the second variant of SwitchKey is used.} \end{cases} \tag{1}$$

Note the logs here are natural logarithms.

Bottom Modulus: To ensure decryption correctness at level zero we require that

$$4 \cdot c_m \cdot B^*_{\text{scale}} = 2 \cdot c_m \cdot B < \begin{cases} p_0 & \text{For BGV and NTRU} \\[3mm] \left\lfloor \frac{p_0}{p} \right\rfloor & \text{For FV and YASHE.} \end{cases} \tag{2}$$

Top Modulus: At the top level we take as input a ciphertext with noise B^*_{clean}, perform ζ additions to produce a ciphertext with noise $B_1 = \zeta \cdot B^*_{\text{clean}}$. We then perform a multiplication to produce something with noise

$$B_2 = \begin{cases} F^*(B_1, B_1) + B^*_{\text{Ks},1}(L-1) & \text{If the first variant of SwitchKey is used,} \\[3mm] F^*(B_1, B_1) + \frac{B^*_{\text{Ks},2}(L-1)}{P} + B^*_{\text{scale}} & \text{If the second variant of SwitchKey is used.} \end{cases}$$

We then scale down a level to obtain something at the next level down. Thus we obtain something with noise bounded by $B_3 = \frac{B_2}{p_{L-1}} + B^*_{\text{scale}}$. We require, for our invariant, $B_3 \leq B = 2 \cdot B^*_{\text{scale}}$. Thus we require,

$$p_{L-1} \geq \frac{B_2}{B^*_{\text{scale}}}. \tag{3}$$

---

[3] One could take into account a more elaborate analysis here, for example looking at BKW style attacks e.g. [10]. But for simplicity we follow the same analysis as in [9].

Middle Moduli: A similar argument applies for the middle moduli, but now we start off with a ciphertext with bound $B = 2 \cdot B^*_{\text{scale}}$ as opposed to B^*_{clean}. Thus we form

$$B'(t) = \begin{cases} F^*(\zeta \cdot B, \zeta \cdot B) + B^*_{\text{Ks},1}(t) & \text{First variant of SwitchKey,} \\[2mm] F^*(\zeta \cdot B, \zeta \cdot B) + \dfrac{B^*_{\text{Ks},2}(t)}{P} + B^*_{\text{scale}} & \text{Second variant of SwitchKey.} \end{cases}$$

after which a Scale operation is performed. Hence, the modulus p_t for $t \neq 0, L-1$ needs to be selected so that

$$p_t \geq \frac{B'(t)}{B^*_{\text{scale}}}. \tag{4}$$

Note, in practice we can do a bit better in the second variant of SwitchKey by merging the final two final scalings into one.

Putting it All Together: We are looking for parameters which satisfy Eqs. (1), (2), (3) and (4), and which also minimize the size of data being processed, which is

$$\phi(m) \cdot \left(\sum_{t=0}^{L-1} p_t \right).$$

To do this we iterate through all possible values of $\log_2 q_{L-1}$ and $\log_2 T$ (resp. $\log_2 P$). We then determine $\phi(m)$, as the smallest value which satisfies Eq. (1). Here, we might need to take a larger value than the right hand side of Eq. (1) due to application requirements on p or the amount of packing required.

We then determine the size of p_{L-1} from Eq. (3), via

$$p_{L-1} \approx \left\lceil \frac{B_2}{B^*_{\text{scale}}} \right\rceil.$$

We can now iterate downwards for $t = L - 2, \dots, 1$ by determining the size of $\log_2 q_t$, via

$$\log_2 q_t = \log_2 q_{t+1} - \log_2 p_{t+1}.$$

If we obtain $\log_2 q_t < 0$ then we abort, and pass to the next pair of $(\log_2 q_{L-1}, T)$ (resp. $(\log_2 q_{L-1}, \log_2 P)$) values. The value of p_t being determined by Eq. (4), via

$$p_t \approx \left\lceil \frac{B'(t)}{B^*_{\text{scale}}} \right\rceil.$$

Finally we check whether a prime p_0 the size of $\log_2 q_0$, will satisify Eq. (2), if so we accept this set of values as a valid set of parameters, otherwise we pass to the next pair of $(\log_2 q_{L-1}, T)$ (resp. $(\log_2 q_{L-1}, \log_2 P)$) values.

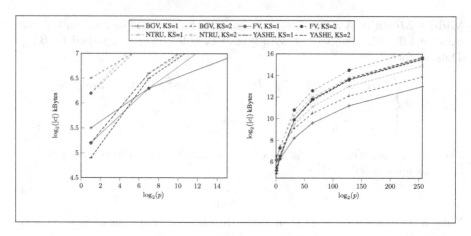

Fig. 4. Size of required ciphertext for various sizes of plaintext modulus when $L = 5$. The graph on the left zooms into the portion of the right graph for small values of $\log_2 p$ (Color figure online).

4   Results

In the full version of this paper one can find a full set of parameters for each scheme, and variant of key switching, for various values of the plaintext modulus p and the number of levels L. In this section we summarize the overall conclusion. As a measure of efficiency we examine the size of a ciphertext in kBytes; this is a very crude measure but it will capture both the size of any data needed to be transmitted as well as the computational cost of dealing with a single ciphertext element within a calculation. In the full version of this paper we also examine the size of the associated key switching matrices, which is significantly smaller for the case of our second key switching method. In a given application this additional cost of holding key switching data may impact on the overall choices, but for this section we ignore this fact.

For all schemes we used a Hamming weight of $h = 64$ to generate the secret key data, we used a security level of $k = 80$ bits of security, a standard deviation of $\sigma = 3.2$ for the rounded Gaussians, a tolerance factor of $\zeta = 8$ and a ring constant of $c_m = 1.3$. These are all consistent with the prior estimates for parameters given in [9]. The use of a small ring constant can be justified by either selecting $\phi(m)$ to be a power of two, or selecting m to be prime, as explained in [4]. As a general conclusion we find that for FV and YASHE the use of modulus switching to lower levels results in slightly bigger parameters to start for large values of L; approximately a factor of two for $L = 20$ or 30. But as a homomorphic calculation progresses this benefit will drop away, leaving, for most calculations, the variant in which modulus switching is applied the most efficient. Thus in what follows we assume that modulus switching is applied in all schemes.

Firstly examine the graphs in Figs. 4 and 5. We see that for a fixed number of levels and very small plaintext moduli the most efficient scheme seems to be

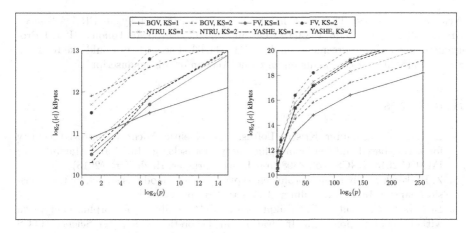

Fig. 5. Size of required ciphertext for various sizes of plaintext modulus when $L = 30$. The graph on the left zooms into the portion of the right graph for small values of $\log_2 p$ (Color figure online).

YASHE. However, quite rapidly, as the plaintext modulus increases the BGV scheme quickly outperforms all other schemes. In particular for the important case of the SPDZ MPC system [4] which requires an SHE scheme supporting circuits of multiplicative depth one, i.e. $L = 2$, for a large plaintext modulus p, the BGV scheme is seen to be the most efficient.

Examining Fig. 6 we see that if we fix the prime and just increase the number of levels then the choice of which is the better scheme is be very consistent. Thus one is led to conclude that the main choice of which scheme to adopt depends on the plaintext modulus, where one selects YASHE for very small plaintext moduli and BGV for larger plaintext moduli.

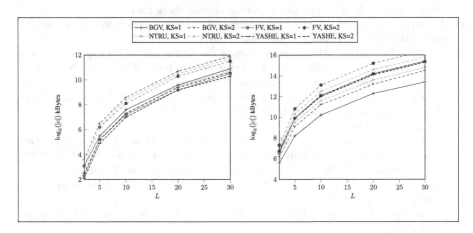

Fig. 6. Size of required ciphertext for various values of L when $p = 2$ and $p \approx 2^{32}$ (Color figure online).

Acknowledgments. This work has been supported in part by an ERC Advanced Grant ERC-2010-AdG-267188-CRIPTO and by the European Union's H2020 Programme under grant agreement number ICT-644209. The authors would like to thank Steven Galbraith for comments on an earlier version of this manuscript.

References

1. Bos, Joppe W., Lauter, Kristin, Loftus, Jake, Naehrig, Michael: Improved security for a ring-based fully homomorphic encryption scheme. In: Stam, Martijn (ed.) IMACC 2013. LNCS, vol. 8308, pp. 45–64. Springer, Heidelberg (2013)
2. Z. Brakerski. Fully homomorphic encryption without modulus switching from classical gapsvp. In: Safavi-Naini and Canetti [16], pp. 868–886
3. Brakerski, Z., Gentry, C., Vaikuntanathan, V.: Fully homomorphic encryption without bootstrapping. In: Innovations in Theoretical Computer Science (ITCS 2012) (2012). http://eprint.iacr.org/2011/277
4. Damgård, I., Pastro, V., Smart, N.P., Zakarias, S.: Multiparty computation from somewhat homomorphic encryption. In: Safavi-Naini and Canetti [16], pp. 643–662
5. Doröz, Y., Hu, Y., Sunar, B.: Homomorphic AES evaluation using the modified LTV scheme. Des. Codes, Cryptography (2015, to appear). https://eprint.iacr.org/2014/039
6. Fan, J., Vercauteren, F.: Somewhat practical fully homomorphic encryption. IACR Cryptology ePrint Archive **2012**, 144 (2012)
7. C. Gentry. A fully homomorphic encryption scheme. Ph.D thesis, Stanford University (2009). http://crypto.stanford.edu/craig
8. Gentry, C., Halevi, S., Smart, N.P.: Fully homomorphic encryption with polylog overhead. In: Pointcheval, D., Johansson, T. (eds.) EUROCRYPT 2012. LNCS, vol. 7237, pp. 465–482. Springer, Heidelberg (2012)
9. Gentry, C., Halevi, S., Smart, N.P.: Homomorphic evaluation of the AES circuit. In: Safavi-Naini and Canetti [16], pp. 850–867
10. Kirchner, P., Fouque, P.: An improved BKW algorithm for LWE with applications to cryptography and lattices. In: Gennaro, R., Robshaw, M. (eds.) CRYPTO – 2015. LNCS, vol. 9215, pp. 43–62. Springer, Heidelberg (2015)
11. Lauter, K., Naehrig, M., Vaikuntanathan, V.: Can homomorphic encryption be practical? In: CCSW, pp. 113–124. ACM (2011)
12. Lepoint, T., Naehrig, M.: A comparison of the homomorphic encryption schemes FV and YASHE. In: Pointcheval, D., Vergnaud, D. (eds.) AFRICACRYPT 2014. LNCS, vol. 8469, pp. 318–335. Springer, Heidelberg (2014)
13. Lindner, R., Peikert, C.: Better key sizes (and attacks) for LWE-based encryption. In: Kiayias, A. (ed.) CT-RSA 2011. LNCS, vol. 6558, pp. 319–339. Springer, Heidelberg (2011)
14. Lòpez-Alt, A., Tromer, E., Vaikuntanathan, V.: On-the-fly multiparty computation on the cloud via multikey fully homomorphic encryption. In: STOC, ACM (2012)
15. Lyubashevsky, V., Peikert, C., Regev, O.: On ideal lattices and learning with errors over rings. In: Gilbert, H. (ed.) EUROCRYPT 2010. LNCS, vol. 6110, pp. 1–23. Springer, Heidelberg (2010)
16. Safavi-Naini, R., Canetti, R. (eds): Cryptogr. – 2015. LNCS, vol. 7417, Springer, Heidelberg (2012)
17. Smart, N.P., Vercauteren, F.: Fully homomorphic SIMD operations. Des. Codes Cryptogr. **71**(1), 57–81 (2014)

NFLlib: NTT-Based Fast Lattice Library

Carlos Aguilar-Melchor[1], Joris Barrier[2], Serge Guelton[3], Adrien Guinet[3],
Marc-Olivier Killijian[2], and Tancrède Lepoint[4(✉)]

[1] INP-ENSEEIHT, CNRS, IRIT, Université de Toulouse, Toulouse, France
`carlos.aguilar@enseeiht.fr`
[2] CNRS, LAAS, Université de Toulouse, Toulouse, France
`{joris.barrier,marco.killijian}@laas.fr`
[3] Quarkslab, Paris, France
`{sguelton,aguinet}@quarkslab.com`
[4] CryptoExperts, Paris, France
`tancrede.lepoint@cryptoexperts.com`

Abstract. Recent years have witnessed an increased interest in lattice cryptography. Besides its strong security guarantees, its simplicity and versatility make this powerful theoretical tool a promising competitive alternative to classical cryptographic schemes.

In this paper, we introduce NFLLIB, an efficient and open-source C++ library dedicated to ideal lattice cryptography in the widely-spread polynomial ring $\mathbb{Z}_p[x]/(x^n + 1)$ for n a power of 2. The library combines algorithmic optimizations (Chinese Remainder Theorem, optimized Number Theoretic Transform) together with programming optimization techniques (SSE and AVX2 specializations, C++ expression templates, etc.), and will be fully available under an open source license.

The library compares very favorably to other libraries used in ideal lattice cryptography implementations (namely the generic number theory libraries NTL and FLINT implementing polynomial arithmetic, and the optimized library for lattice homomorphic encryption HELIB): restricting the library to the aforementioned polynomial ring allows to gain several orders of magnitude in efficiency.

Keywords: C++ library · Implementation · Ideal lattice cryptography · Number theoretic transform · Chinese remainder theorem · SEE specializations

Note: NFLlib is available under an open source license at https://github.com/quarkslab/NFLlib

1 Introduction

Lattice cryptography is often praised for its simplicity, its versatility and its possible resistance to quantum attacks. However, its large memory requirements makes its practical use strenuous. The introduction of ideal lattice cryptography

© Springer International Publishing Switzerland 2016
K. Sako (Ed.): CT-RSA 2016, LNCS 9610, pp. 341–356, 2016.
DOI: 10.1007/978-3-319-29485-8_20

completely reshaped this belief [24,27]. In ideal lattice cryptography, primitives rely on the hardness of problems involving polynomial rings in which lattices can be represented by a few polynomials. In recent years, several hardware and software implementations of lattice signatures and encryption have been developed. These implementations show performances competitive with (or even surpassing) those of currently used primitives such as RSA or elliptic curves (see e.g. [9,26]). Due to its efficiency and security arguments, ideal lattice cryptography starts to be deployed in products[1] and is promised a bright future.

Besides signature and encryption, lattice cryptography has shown to be amazingly versatile. In particular, most of the homomorphic encryption (HE) schemes rely on lattices. The latter research area is really active, and recent years have seen loads of HE implementations using polynomial rings. Lattices are also used to instantiate schemes with advanced properties, such as identity-based encryption (IBE), functional encryption or multilinear maps.

To work efficiently over polynomials rings in software, we are aware of three main approaches:

(1) Use the *generic* number theory library NTL [30]. This is the approach used in lots of HE implementations (and in particular HELIB [16,17]), and in the IBE implementation of [10].
(2) Use the *generic* number theory library FLINT [18]. This is the approach used in [22] to implement two HE schemes, and in [1] for multilinear maps.
(3) Use *home-made* libraries that implement operations in the polynomial ring $\mathbb{Z}_p[x]/(x^n + 1)$.
    This is the approach used in the open-source VPN implementation [31], Microsoft homomorphic encryption implementation [4], SIMD-optimized implementations [12,15], GPU implementations [7,21] and also [9,26].

Note that *all* the aforementioned implementations consider uniquely (or may be instantiated with) the polynomial ring

$$R_p \stackrel{\text{def}}{=} \mathbb{Z}_p[x]/(x^n + 1)$$

for a modulus $p \equiv 1 \pmod{2n}$ and n some power of 2. This setting is *widespread* in ideal lattice cryptography because of its simplicity of exposition and of implementation. Among other advantages, in that setting, polynomials can be multiplied in quasi-linear time using the Number Theoretic Transform (NTT), a Fast Fourier Transform on finite rings [28]. Now, home-made implementations (*i.e.* item (3)) of polynomial operations in the latter setting have shown to achieve better performances than using the generic libraries NTL or FLINT (see e.g. [22, Table 4]).[2] This leads us to the following question:

---

[1] The open-source IPsec-based VPN solution strongSwan [31] includes the BLISS lattice signature [9] as an IKEv2 public key authentication method starting from version 5.2.2.

[2] This is also hinted at in the HELIB library [16,17] which modifies the internal routines of NTL to achieve better performances — although for any cyclotomic polynomial ring $\mathbb{Z}_p[x]/(\Phi)$.

How fast can a specialized polynomial library dedicated to lattice cryptography over R_p be?

1.1   Our Contribution: NFLlib

In this work, we present NFLLIB, an efficient and scalable C++ library specialized for cryptography over $R_p = \mathbb{Z}_p[x]/(x^n + 1)$. NFLLIB includes optimized subroutines to perform arithmetic operations over polynomials and allows to easily implement ideal lattice cryptography.[3] The library contains algorithmic optimizations (Double-CRT representation, Number-Theoretic Transform, lazy modular reduction), and programming optimizations (Streaming SIMD Extensions, Advanced Vector Extensions, C++ expression templates).

We benchmarked the library's arithmetic operations over R_p against the generic libraries NTL, FLINT, and against the HE library HELIB. Our results show that focusing on a setting widely used in ideal lattice cryptography allowed to gain several orders of magnitude of efficiency compared to generic libraries.

NFLLIB will be open-source and available under the GNU General Public License v3.0. It is designed for ideal lattice cryptography, provides a complete set of operations, and minimizes the amount of new code needed to add new features. In short, one of our hopes is that making this library open-source (and thus seeking for contributions) spurs on the development of ideal lattice cryptography in prototypes in the very near future.

1.2   Related Work

Libraries. The NFLLIB library is *specialized* for a particular polynomial ring and therefore differs completely from the *generic* libraries NTL [30] and FLINT [18]. These latter libraries allow to perform powerful number theory, while NFLLIB focus on a particular polynomial ring. This specialization allowed us to optimize the underlying operations while being designed to be used for ideal lattice cryptography. Another library that implements lattice cryptography is HELIB [16,17], which uses NTL. HELIB has become a reference to benchmark HE because it implements a full-fledged HE scheme [5] and features efficient packing techniques and other optimizations. Note that NFLLIB does not compare to HELIB in term of functionality, but NFLLIB could replace NTL in HELIB when working over R_p, and would yield a much more efficient implementation.

Double-CRT Representation. Using moduli that split completely to store the polynomial coefficients in CRT form (first layer of CRT), and using the NTT representation of the polynomials (second layer of CRT) is a technique that has been used previously in lattice cryptography. In particular, it is used in the

---

[3] Even though architecture-optimized implementations will always outperform generic libraries, this paper tackles the issue of designing an *efficient* library that can be used on a large range of architecture. Also, NFLLIB includes state-of-the-art SSE and AVX2 optimizations for the NTT and the modular multiplication operation.

HELIB library [13,16,17] and in the GPU implementation [7]. However, NFLLIB features specific primes in the moduli decomposition, chosen to optimize the NTT and allow lazy modular multiplication.

1.3   Outline

In Sect. 2 we describe the basic cryptographic and mathematical notions needed in our paper. In Sect. 3 we present our library, its main components and how these allowed us to get our performance results. In Sect. 4 we compare the performance of our library with other libraries on different algorithms (NTT, multiplications, additions, etc.). Finally, in Sect. 5, we describe some implementations of lattice cryptographic algorithms and highlight the performance results obtained.

2   Preliminaries

Throughout the paper, we let n be a power of 2 and $p > 0$ be a modulus (not necessarily prime as we will see later). Define R to be the ring $R_p \overset{\text{def}}{=} \mathbb{Z}_p[x]/(x^n+1)$, i.e. the ring of polynomials having integer coefficients, modulo $x^n + 1$. For any integer p, define $R_p \overset{\text{def}}{=} \mathbb{Z}_p[x]/(x^n + 1)$ the ring R modulo p, i.e. polynomials modulo $x^n + 1$ with coefficients modulo p. We denote by $a \bmod b$ the remainder of the euclidean division of a by b, and $c \equiv a \pmod{b}$ represents any number such that $c \bmod b = a$. We use the classical Landau notation.

Ideal Lattice Cryptography. In most of existing implementations, the structured lattices used in ideal lattice cryptography have an interpretation in terms of arithmetic in the ring $\mathbb{Z}_p[x]/(x^n + 1)$, for n a power of 2. Jumping ahead, note that we will chose particular values for p in order to optimize the polynomial multiplications when using the Number Theoretic Transform (see also [9,15,29]) in combination with the Chinese Remainder Theorem.

The Chinese Remainder Theorem (CRT). Throughout the paper, the modulus p will be composite and square-free, and its factorization is denoted $p = p_1 \cdots p_\ell$. The CRT yields an isomorphism $\mathbb{Z}_p \simeq \mathbb{Z}_{p_1} \times \cdots \times \mathbb{Z}_{p_\ell}$, which extends directly to polynomials rings. In particular, we have that $R_p \simeq R_{p_1} \times \cdots \times R_{p_\ell}$. Jumping ahead of Sect. 3.1, the latter equivalence shows that, instead of working with a polynomial $a(x) \in R_p$, we will choose $p = p_1 \cdots p_\ell$ with particular p_i's and work with ℓ polynomials $a_i(x) \in R_{p_i}$.

The Number Theoretic Transform (NTT). To multiply polynomials efficiently, we use the quasi-linear polynomial multiplication algorithm called the NTT [28]. The advantages of using NTT for ideal lattice cryptography were recently demonstrated in hardware and software implementations [9,14,15,29].

3   NFLlib: A Library for Ideal-Lattice Cryptography

In this section, we introduce NFLLIB, a C++ library for ideal-lattice cryptography, *i.e.* for manipulating polynomials of $R_p = \mathbb{Z}_p[x]/(x^n + 1)$. The entry point to our library is a templated class `poly < class T, size_t degree, size_t sizeModulus >`.

To obtain a usable class, one must define three parameters before compilation: the word type (`uint16_t`, `uint32_t` or `uint64_t`), the degree n of the polynomial $x^n + 1$ that defines R_p (which must be a power of two), and the bit-size of the modulus p, which will be internally constructed as a product of ℓ fixed-size primes: $p = p_1 \times \cdots \times p_\ell$.

The `poly` class features: overloaded operators for modular arithmetic and data manipulation (and the associated static functions); C++ template expressions to minimize the inherent performance degradation of overloaded operator; functions to sample polynomials in R_p with different distributions for the coefficients (uniform distribution modulo p, uniformly bounded distribution, discrete Gaussian distribution); transformation-related functions (NTT, CRT, export, import); SSE and AVX2 optimizations for compatible architectures.

The word type `T` is the most critical parameter. It defines which (and how many) primes p_i's are available, what is the maximal polynomial degree n possible, and which underlying code is used. Indeed, the code is specialized and might feature SIMD optimizations (especially when using 32-bit and 16-bit words).

All the functions provided by the `poly` class have been developed from scratch, and are based on the native (scalar or vectorial) instructions of a modern CPU. Only exceptions, the Salsa20-based pseudo-random number generator, and the CRT inversion function which uses GMP if the modulus used is too large for native instructions.

NFLLIB is a specialized polynomial library dedicated to ideal-lattice cryptography. It is well known that in this setting representing polynomials by their values instead of their coefficients (*i.e.* representing them in NTT form) and using the CRT to represent values is very beneficial for performance. We therefore use such a representation.

NFLLIB's performance results are mainly due to the fact that most of the functions have been developed directly based on native operations, and to four major choices that have proven to be very efficient. These choices are:

– the fixed-size CRT representation — see Sect. 3.1;
– the modular multiplication for scalars — see Sect. 3.2;
– the NTT algorithm — see Sect. 3.3.
– the SSE and AVX2 optimizations — see Sect. 4.

In the aforementioned sections, we describe the particular choices we made in NFLLIB, and discuss their respective impacts.

3.1 Fixed-Size CRT Representation

For efficiency reasons, we selected the moduli p used in our ideal lattice setting as a product of ℓ fixed-size primes p_i's fitting on one word.[4] Thus, one can work with the CRT representation $(a_1(x), \dots, a_\ell(x)) \in R_{p_1} \times \cdots \times R_{p_\ell}$ of a polynomial $a(x) \in R_p$, where $a_i(x) = a(x) \mod p_i$. All the $a_i(x)$ can then be processed independently.

The primes forming the moduli are chosen with the following constraints:

Constraint 1. Their size must be at most the word size minus two bits, so that we can do lazy modular reductions in the NTT algorithm (which gives roughly a 30 % speedup);

Constraint 2. They must satisfy Eq. (1) for a given parameter s_0, in order to use the modular multiplication algorithm of Sect. 3.2;

Constraint 3. For any possible value of n — the degree of the quotient polynomial in R_p — they must be congruent to 1 (mod $2n$), so that we can find n-th roots of -1 to use the NTT algorithm of Sect. 3.3 and do polynomial multiplications modulo $x^n + 1$.

Constraint 2 will ensure that Constraint 1 is satisfied when $s_0 \geq 2$. By default, NFLLIB sets $s_0 = 2$. In order to satisfy Constraint 3, we had to arbitrarily select a maximal polynomial degree $n_{\max}$ in NFLLIB. (Note that the constraint is then satisfied for any degree $n \leq n_{\max}$). The higher $n_{\max}$ is, the less primes verify Constraint 3. When the word size is 16 bits, these constraints are stronger than for larger words. For example for $n_{\max} = 2048$, only one 14-bit prime verifies Constraint 3 (supposing $s_0 = 2$). For 64-bit words on the other hand, it is possible to find thousands of primes verifying the constraints even for very large polynomial degrees such as $n_{\max} = 2^{20}$. Algorithm 1 returns the primes satisfying Contraints 1–3.

Defining these primes statically is beneficial for performance, and therefore they have been included in a parameter file params.hpp with $n_{\max} = 512$ when $s = 16$ (2 primes), $n_{\max} = 2^{15}$ when $s = 32$ (291 primes), and $n_{\max} = 2^{20}$ when $s = 64$ (primes limited voluntarily to one thousand). All of these have been chosen with $s_0 = 2$ as explained before. Of course other values of s_0 and $n_{\max}$ may be defined by the user of NFLLIB.[5]

---

[4] At the heart of many kinds of ideal-lattice schemes (ranging from classical encryption to fully homomorphic encryption and multilinear maps) is the decision-Ring-Learning-With-Errors (dRLWE) assumption. Working with cyclotomic polynomials $\Phi(x) = x^n + 1$ implies that we have *provable worst-case hardness* for dRLWE with essentially **any** large enough p — splitting, inert, or anywhere in between [6]. In NFLLIB, we therefore chose a p that splits completely for efficiency reasons.

[5] NFLLIB has been designed to work with a wide range of parameters: polynomial degrees $2 \leq n \leq 2^{20}$ and moduli $2^{13} < p < 2^{1000 \cdot 62}$. However, the users of NFLLIB are responsible for selecting parameters (n, p) that ensure κ bits of security for the specific application they are developing. We refer to [2,3,23] for selecting concrete security parameters of lattice encryption schemes.

Algorithm 1. Prime selection algorithm

Input: s word size, s_0 margin bits, n_{max} maximum polynomial degree
Output: $(p_1, \ldots, p_t)$ a list of primes satisfying Constraints 1-3
1 $\beta = 2^s, i = 1, \texttt{outputList} = ()$
2 **do**
3    $\quad c = \beta/2^{s_0} - i \cdot 2^{n_{max}+1} + 1$
4    $\quad$ **if** $\texttt{isPrime}(c)$ *and* $c > (1 + 1/2^{3s_0}) \cdot \beta/(2^{s_0} + 1)$ **then**
5      $\quad\quad |$ Add c to $\texttt{outputList}$
6    $\quad$ **end**
7    $\quad i = i{+}1$
8 **while** $c > (1 + 1/2^{3s_0}) \cdot \beta/(2^{s_0} + 1)$
9 **return** $\texttt{outputList}$

3.2 Optimizing the Modular Multiplication

As explained in Sect. 3.1, NFLLIB includes invariant primes of 14, 30 and 62 bits, and computations are performed independently over these primes. However — as already emphasized in [25] — computing modular reductions with an invariant integer using a well-tuned Newton reciprocal followed by multiplications and adjustments wins over the hardware division instructions.

During the library construction, we observed that the gcc compiler automatically optimized the modular multiplications when working with 16-bit or 32-bit words (*i.e.* for 14- and 30-bit primes), but not with 64-bit words. In this section, we consider the problem of dividing a two-word integer by a single word integer. This problem was extensively studied in [25] which proposed a new algorithm (Algorithm 4 in the latter paper) giving a speedup of roughly 30 % over the Newton reciprocal algorithm [25, Algorithm 1]. The former algorithm was included in the version 4.3 of the GMP library.

However, in NFLLIB, the primes are feature so that their (two) most significant bits equal to 0, and the algorithms in [25] are optimized for numbers with their most significant bit equal to 1. In the rest of the section, we describe a new algorithm which significantly improves over [25] for numbers p smaller than the word base $\beta = 2^s$, as illustrated in Table 1.

Table 1. Time per componentwise multiplication of polynomials of degree 1024 modulo a 62-bit prime (average over 100,000 polynomial multiplications on an Intel Xeon CPU E5-2666 v3 at 2.90GHz). We implemented Algorithms 1 and 4 of [25] (with $4p$ instead of p and two conditional subtractions at the end), but they perform one order of magnitude slower than our improved algorithm.

Algorithm	Naive	[25]	[25]	Ours
	(*i.e.* using %)	Algorithm 1	Algorithm 4	Algorithm 2
Polynomial Modular Mult. (μs)	29.8 μs	15.5 μs	12.9 μs	**2.90 μs**

Algorithm 2. Modular reduction with a modulus verifying Eq. (1)

Input: $u = \langle u_1, u_0 \rangle \in [0, p^2)$, p verifying Eq. (1), $v_0 = \lfloor \beta^2/p \rfloor \mod \beta$,
    $1 \leqslant s_0 \leqslant s - 1$ margin bits
Output: $r = u \mod p$
1 $q \leftarrow v_0 \cdot u_1 + 2^{s_0} \cdot u \mod \beta^2$
2 $r \leftarrow u - \lfloor q/\beta \rfloor \cdot p \mod \beta$
3 **if** $r \geqslant p$ **then** $r \leftarrow r - p$
4 **return** r

Assume that one wants to compute a modular reduction with a modulus p such that

$$(1 + 1/2^{3s_0}) \cdot \beta/(2^{s_0} + 1) \; < \; p \; < \; \beta/2^{s_0}, \tag{1}$$

for an integer $1 \leqslant s_0 \leqslant s - 1$ (note that all our 62-bit primes verify Eq. (1)). For any number $u \in [0, \beta^2)$, denote $\langle u_1, u_0 \rangle$ its decomposition in words smaller than β, so that $u = u_1 \cdot \beta + u_0$. We describe our new modular reduction in Algorithm 2.

We have the following theorem. For space constraints, we defer its proof to the final version of the paper.

Theorem 1. *Assume* $1 \leqslant s_0 \leqslant s - 1$ *and* p *verifies Eq. (1) and* $u = \langle u_1, u_0 \rangle \in [0, p^2)$. *Let* $v = \langle v_1, v_0 \rangle = \lfloor \beta^2/p \rfloor$. *Then Algorithm 2 with input* (u, p, v_0, s_0) *outputs* $(u \mod p)$.

3.3 A Lazy NTT Algorithm

We use Harvey's NTT algorithm [14]. This algorithm uses two techniques to reduce its computational costs: pre-computed quotients to accelerate modular multiplications, and lazy reductions (*i.e.* inputs and outputs can be up to twice the modulus). Quotient pre-computations in the NTT was already performed by NTL [30] but Harvey proves elegantly that the NTT butterflies can be modified so that the output is in $[0, 2p)$ when the input is in $[0, p)$, using only one conditional subtraction (instead of three in the initial algorithm). This gives a very nice performance boost of about 30 %, as shown in [14]. Note that this justifies to select primes ad in Sect. 3.2.

As usual, before applying the NTT we multiply the i-th coordinate of the polynomial we are going to transform by ψ^i, where ψ is an n-th root of -1 which allows us to have negatively wrapped convolutions when we multiply two elements (*i.e.* reductions modulo $x^n + 1$). After the NTT, we reduce the coefficients to $[0, p)$ but we do not apply the bit-reverse permutation by default. The reason for this is that, in lattice based cryptography, we often want to offload work from the NTT to the inverse NTT. For example in an LWE encryption scheme, at encryption time one needs to: (1) generate multiple noise polynomials, (2) convert each of them with an NTT, and (3) multiply/add them. In the decryption phase, on the other hand, there is no noise polynomials to generate and there is just one multiplication, one addition and a single inverse NTT. If in a given case, such as the one described in Sect. 5.1 we want to balance both transformations, such a change can be activated with a compilation option.

Our library has no particular contribution concerning the NTT, we just show in this paper that it is a lot more efficient than the Bluestein FFT used in HElib (see Sect. 4). Our implementation does not use assembly language, but it is quite efficient, scalable and general.

4   Performances Evaluation and Comparison with NTL, FLINT and HElib

In this section we analyze the performance of our library and report comparative benchmarks with the NTL [30], FLINT [18] and HELIB [16] libraries.

Recall that NTL and FLINT are generic libraries that allow to work with polynomials in any modular rings, and HELIB is a software library (based on NTL) that implement an optimized version of the Brakerski-Gentry-Vaikuntanathan [5] (BGV) homomorphic encryption scheme. We chose to compare to these libraries because they are widely used in the literature on lattice cryptography implementations. We restricted them to the same settings as NFLLIB, i.e. to work over $R_p = \mathbb{Z}_p[x]/(x^n + 1)$ with moduli p as in Sect. 3.1.

Setting. We benchmarked NFLLIB against NTL, FLINT and HELIB on random polynomial generation, NTT and inverse NTT, modular addition and multiplication in NTT representation. All the benchmarks were made using the following fixed parameter sets:

(1) $n = 256$ with a modulus p of 14 bits,
(2) $n = 512$ with a modulus p of 30 bits,
(3) $n = 1024$ with a modulus p of 62 bits,
(4) $n = 1024$ with a modulus p of about 6200 bits (product of 100 62-bit moduli).

As expected, NFLLIB has been instantiated with 16-bit words and 32-bit words respectively for the parameters sets 1 and 2. For NTL, we used the zz_pX objects for the parameters sets 1 and 2, and ZZ_pX otherwise. For FLINT, we used the type fmpz_mod_poly_t. Finally, HELIB includes a DoubleCRT class with the same representation as NFLLIB.[6]

We performed all our benchmarks on a c4.2xlarge instance of Amazon Web Services with an Intel Xeon CPU E5-2666 v3 (Haswell) at 2900 Mhz and 15 GB of RAM with gcc 4.9, GMP 6.0, NTL 8.1, FLINT 2.5.[7]

---

[6] In HELIB, the instantiation of a FHEContext — storing the modulus decomposition — is needed to use DoubleCRT objects. Now, this constructor try to produced primes of a size close to 44 bits and this size is hard-coded in the value FHE_p2Size (maybe to fit largely the long primitive type and be able to do specific homomorphic operations?).

For the sake of comparison, we kept this hardcoded value. Therefore the benchmarks of HELIB are with a 44-bit prime for parameters (1) and (2), with two 44-bit primes for parameters (3) and 141 44-bit primes for parameters (4).

[7] TurboBoost and Hyperthreading were disabled during the benchmarks. We chose an AWS machine as a typical cloud environment which allows reproductibility of the results.

Remark 1. To demonstrate the performance of our library on different architectures, we also benchmarked the NTT transformation on a MacBook Air (called `macbookair`) with an Intel Core i7-4650U Processor at 1700 Mhz and 8 GB of RAM, using the native `clang++` (Apple LLVM version 6.0), GMP 6.0, NTL 8.1, FLINT 2.5. (We restricted ourselves to the benchmark of the NTT transform to be concise.)

Random Polynomial Generation. To benchmark random generation, we used the `ntl::random` function of NTL, the `fmpz_mod_poly_randtest` function of FLINT and the default random generator of NFLLIB (described only in the full version due to space constraints). We present our results in Table 2. Note that the FLINT library implements the Mersenne Twister algorithm that is unsuitable for a cryptographic use.

Table 2. Timings to generate random polynomials in $\mathbb{Z}_p[x]/(x^n + 1)$ using the built-in functions of different libraries on `c4.2xlarge`.

Library	NTL random	FLINT fmpz_mod_poly_randtest	HELIB	NFLLIB nfl::uniform
$(1) = (256, 14)$	$9.2\,\mu s$	$4.8\,\mu s$	$69\,\mu s$	$\mathbf{0.6\,\mu s}$
$(2) = (512, 30)$	$23.2\,\mu s$	$9.1\,\mu s$	$135.5\,\mu s$	$\mathbf{2.6\,\mu s}$
$(3) = (1024, 62)$	$173.0\,\mu s$	$18.3\,\mu s$	$540.0\,\mu s$	$\mathbf{9.7\,\mu s}$
$(4) = (1024, 6200)$	$8675\,\mu s$	$1082\,\mu s$	$37929\,\mu s$	$\mathbf{1029.6\,\mu s}$

NTT and iNTT. Working with the NTT representation of polynomials (after the negative wrapped convolution) is a cornerstone of our optimization, since additions and multiplications become essentially linear in the number of coefficients. We report in Table 3 the benchmarks of the NTT (*including* the negative wrapped convolution). Note that NTL provides an NTT functions thanks to `TofftRep` and to `toFFTRep` (resp. for `zz_pX` and `ZZ_pX`); no such functions seem to be available in the FLINT library.[8] In HELIB, the `DoubleCRT` class has two functions to convert from (via negative wrapped convolution and NTT) and to (via inverse NTT and inverse of the convolution) a polynomial `ZZX`. (For space constraints, the timings of the inverse NTT are provided in the full version of the paper).

SEE and AVX2 Optimizations. Because of the highly parallel nature of operations over polynomials (the same operations are to be performed on multiple data objects), using Streaming SIMD Extensions (SSE) and Advanced Vector Extensions (AVX) instructions might greatly increase performance. This has been shown in [12,15] respectively for lattice signature and encryption.

---

[8] We neglected the cost of the (linear) negative wrapped convolution computation in NTL to mitigate the impact of a non highly-optimized hand-made implementation; one would therefore have to expect slightly worse timings when working over R_p.

Table 3. Timings to compute the Number Theoretic Transform of a polynomial in $\mathbb{Z}_p[x]/(x^n + 1)$ using (when possible) the built-in functions of different libraries.

(a) NTT on c4.2xlarge using gcc				
Library	NTL toFFT/ToFFT	FLINT	HELIB conv(DoubleCRT,ZZX)	NFLLIB
$(1) = (256, 14)$	7.2 μs	–	33.7 μs	**2.5 μs**
$(2) = (512, 30)$	14.7 μs	–	70.7 μs	**4.5 μs**
$(3) = (1024, 62)$	45.7 μs	–	317.7 μs	**13.9 μs**
$(4) = (1024, 6200)$	33921 μs	–	23240 μs	**1341.0 μs**
(b) NTT on macbookair using clang				
Library	NTL	FLINT	HELIB	NFLLIB
$(1) = (256, 14)$	7.7 μs	–	37.6 μs	**1.7 μs**
$(2) = (512, 30)$	16.0 μs	–	74.9 μs	**5.7 μs**
$(3) = (1024, 62)$	47.5 μs	–	333.8 μs	**15.3 μs**
$(4) = (1024, 6200)$	34799 μs	–	24713 μs	**1163.4 μs**

NFLLIB includes SSE and AVX2 specializations of the NTT algorithm and of the modular operations for 16-bit and 32-bit words. We compared NFLLIB's NTT to Güneysu et al. AVX-optimized NTT [15] (where once again the NTT includes the negative wrapped convolution Ψ) on c4.2xlarge.

The GOPS implementation works with the double type for a 23-bit modulus p (lazy-reduction) and takes 5030 cycles. NFLLIB can be instantiated with 14-bit primes or 30-bit primes and takes respectively 3324 and 7334 cycles when using SSE4 instructions, and 2767 and 5956 cycles when using AVX2 instructions. As a comparison, the 62-bit version (i.e. non-SIMD) of the NTT takes 10020 cycles.

5   Implementing Ideal Lattice Cryptography with NFLlib

5.1   High Performance Key Exchange

In this section, we consider an equivalent of the key transport protocol RSASVE of NIST SP 800 56B, using [23] encryption scheme, to illustrate the performances of our library in a concrete setting. The client chooses a random message and encrypts it with the server public key then, the server decrypts this random value that is used to derivate (with a hashing function) a common secret.

Server-Side Focus. As a server usually has to handle many clients, the main issue is how costly is the server-side computation. Thus, we focus on the server cost.

Server Authentication and Forward Secrecy. The public key sent by the server may be a certificate signed by any algorithm (*e.g.* DSA) so that the client is able to be convinced of the server's identity. Since this has no cost for the server we do not focus on which signature scheme is used. We note that as suggested in [20], the server can send two keys: one signed to prove his identity, and one ephemeral key generated to ensure forward secrecy. Then the client sends two secrets and the common secret is derived from both initial secrets with a key derivation function (*e.g.* a hash function). Due to the signature of one of the public keys, the client knows that only the server can get the common secret and if the ephemeral key is destroyed at the end of the key exchange, forward secrecy is ensured. This means that from the server side multiplying the communication and computational costs just by two, allows to have a forward secrecy property.

The algorithm we implemented is the RLWE encryption scheme of [23].[9] The code for the encryption and decryption functions (see [23]) is presented in Algorithms 3 and 4. This code highlights how simple is to implement algorithms with NFLLIB: the encryption function and decryption functions are very readable, and have respectively 9 and 4 lines of code.

Algorithm 3. Ring-LWE based public key encryption function

Input: P a polynomial type, g_prng Gaussian generator, pka, pkb public key, m the message
Output: resa, resb an encryption of m

```
using value_t = typename P::value_type;
P tmpu = nfl::gaussian<value_t>(g_prng);       // no noise multiplier
P tmpe1 = nfl::gaussian<value_t>(g_prng, 2); // noise multiplier: 2
P tmpe2 = nfl::gaussian<value_t>(g_prng, 2); // noise multiplier: 2
tmpe2 += m;

tmpu.ntt_pow_phi();
tmpe1.ntt_pow_phi();
tmpe2.ntt_pow_phi();

resa = tmpu * pka + tmpe1;
resb = tmpu * pkb + tmpe2;
```

Table 4 shows the performances of the protocols for 80, 128 and 256 bits of security. In RSA and NFLLIB, the server needs to do a decryption, while in ECDH it performs a modular exponentiation. NFLLIB allows to deal with more clients or to use less CPU time for the same amount of clients. The gap is around a factor 200, so it is possible to process 10 times more clients with 10 times less CPU time and to increase by a factor two the security with respect to ECDH (or maintain the security level and add forward secrecy).

---

[9] We choose two parameter sets from [23], a 14-bit modulus with polynomials of degree 256, and the same modulus with polynomials of degree 512. These two parameter sets correspond roughly to 128 and 256 bits of security. Note that if these estimates are too low it is possible to choose parameters such as $(14, 1024)$ and the performance presented in Table 4 is just divided by two.

Algorithm 4. Ring-LWE based public key decryption function

Input: P a polynomial type, resa, resb a ciphertext, s a secret key, p a modulus
Output: A polynomial m

```
m = resb - resa * s;
m.invntt_pow_invphi();
for(auto & v : m)
    v = (v<modulus/2) ? v%2 : 1-v%2;
```

Table 4. Number of key exchanges per second on a server with an i7-4770 processor using only one core. When the four cores are used, performance are multiplied by a factor four. There is no standard implementation of RSA15360 and our library does not work with 80 bits of security for this application (hence the input N/A). RSA and ECDH (p curves) results have been obtained with the speed test of openssl 1.0.1f. The results noted NFLLIB correspond to the amount of decryptions per second with our implementation of the RLWE scheme of [23].

Protocol	80 bits	128 bits	256 bits
RSA	7.95 Kops/s	0.31 Kops/s	N/A
ECDH	7.01 Kops/s	5.93 Kops/s	1.61 Kops/s
NFLLIB	N/A	1020 Kops/s	508 Kops/s

5.2 Using NFLlib for Homomorphic Encryption

A trending application of ideal lattice cryptography is homomorphic encryption; a fully homomorphic encryption (FHE) scheme enables one to process any function on encrypted data. The first implementations of FHE were quite inefficient, but in six years the landscape has considerably changed and recent implementations run in reasonable time [11,17]. However, the bootstrapping procedure — necessary to achieve *fully* homomorphic encryption — remains a bottleneck.

To overcome thereof, the cryptographic community focused on somewhat homomorphic encryption (SHE) schemes, *i.e.* schemes only able to handle a *bounded* number of homomorphic operations (and especially of homomorphic multiplications). However, even for this simplified setting, to homomorphically evaluate non trivial functions the parameter sizes remain very large (see *e.g.* [8, 22]); to handle around 40 levels, one usually works with parameters such that $2^{10} \leqslant n, \log q \leqslant 2^{20}$.

These large parameters explain why the static parameters in NFLLIB were selected to handle polynomials up to degree 2^{20} and modulus up to 62,000 bits. Now, from the results of Sect. 4, we estimate that implementations using NTL or FLINT with R_p should immediately gain a factor 15 to 50 in performances by using NFLLIB. As an example, we modified the open-source implementation of the somewhat homomorphic encryption scheme FV of [22] and directly replaced FLINT by NFLLIB— we obtained the improvements described in Table 5.

Table 5. Using NFLLIB in the FV implementation of [22], instead of FLINT. The polynomial degree is $n = 4096$ and the modulus p has 124 bits. The relatively small gain on the homomorphic multiplication can be explained by the fact that the scale-invariant procedure is essentially constituted of operations independent of NFLLIB, such as divisions and rounding.

	Encrypt	Decrypt	Hom. Add.	Hom. Mult.
[22] with FLINT	26.7 ms	13.3 ms	1.1 ms	91.2 ms
[22] with NFLLIB	0.9 ms	0.9 ms	0.01 ms	17.2 ms
Gain	×30	×15	×110	×5.5

6   Conclusion

This work introduces NFLLIB, an optimized open-source C++ library designed to handle polynomials over $\mathbb{Z}_p[x]/(x^n+1)$, a widespread setting in ideal lattice cryptography. Because of its algorithmic and programming optimizations, NFLLIB is much faster than NTL and FLINT, and as fast as AVX-optimized implementations of the literature. We hope the library will help building efficient prototypes using lattice cryptography in the very near future.

Acknowledgements. This work has been supported in part by the European Union's H2020 Programme under grant agreement number ICT-644209 and by French's FUI project CRYPTOCOMP.

References

1. Albrecht, M.R., Cocis, C., Laguillaumie, F., Langlois, A.: Implementing candidate graded encoding schemes from ideal lattices. Cryptology ePrint Archive, Report 2014/928 (2014). http://eprint.iacr.org/2014/928
2. Albrecht, M.R., Fitzpatrick, R., Göpfert, F.: On the efficacy of solving LWE by reduction to unique-SVP. In: Lee, H.-S., Han, D.-G. (eds.) ICISC 2013. LNCS, vol. 8565, pp. 293–310. Springer, Heidelberg (2014)
3. Albrecht, M.R., Player, R., Scott, S.: On the concrete hardness of learning with errors. Cryptology ePrint Archive, Report 2015/046 (2015). http://eprint.iacr.org/2015/046
4. Bos, J.W., Lauter, K., Loftus, J., Naehrig, M.: Improved security for a ring-based fully homomorphic encryption scheme. In: Stam, M. (ed.) IMACC 2013. LNCS, vol. 8308, pp. 45–64. Springer, Heidelberg (2013)
5. Brakerski, Z., Gentry, C., Vaikuntanathan, V.: (Leveled) fully homomorphic encryption without bootstrapping. In: Goldwasser, S. (ed.) ITCS 2012, pp. 309–325. ACM, January 2012
6. Brakerski, Z., Langlois, A., Peikert, C., Regev, O., Stehlé, D.: Classical hardness of learning with errors. In: Boneh, D., Roughgarden, T., Feigenbaum, J. (eds.) 45th ACM STOC, pp. 575–584. ACM Press, June 2013

7. Dai, W., Doröz, Y., Sunar, B.: Accelerating NTRU based homomorphic encryption using GPUs. In: IEEE High Performance Extreme Computing Conference, HPEC 2014, Waltham, MA, USA, 9–11 September 2014, pp. 1–6. IEEE (2014)
8. Doröz, Y., Shahverdi, A., Eisenbarth, T., Sunar, B.: Toward practical homomorphic evaluation of block ciphers using prince. In: Böhme, R., Brenner, M., Moore, T., Smith, M. (eds.) FC 2014 Workshops. LNCS, vol. 8438, pp. 208–220. Springer, Heidelberg (2014)
9. Ducas, L., Durmus, A., Lepoint, T., Lyubashevsky, V.: Lattice signatures and bimodal Gaussians. In: Canetti, R., Garay, J.A. (eds.) CRYPTO 2013, Part I. LNCS, vol. 8042, pp. 40–56. Springer, Heidelberg (2013)
10. Ducas, L., Lyubashevsky, V., Prest, T.: Efficient identity-based encryption over NTRU lattices. In: Sarkar, P., Iwata, T. (eds.) ASIACRYPT 2014, Part II. LNCS, vol. 8874, pp. 22–41. Springer, Heidelberg (2014)
11. Ducas, L., Micciancio, D.: FHEW: bootstrapping homomorphic encryption in less than a second. In: Oswald, E., Fischlin, M. (eds.) EUROCRYPT 2015. LNCS, vol. 9056, pp. 617–640. Springer, Heidelberg (2015)
12. El Bansarkhani, R., Buchmann, J.: High performance lattice-based CCA-secure encryption. Cryptology ePrint Archive, Report 2015/042 (2015). http://eprint.iacr.org/2015/042
13. Gentry, C., Halevi, S., Smart, N.P.: Homomorphic evaluation of the AES circuit. In: Safavi-Naini, R., Canetti, R. (eds.) CRYPTO 2012. LNCS, vol. 7417, pp. 850–867. Springer, Heidelberg (2012)
14. Göttert, N., Feller, T., Schneider, M., Buchmann, J., Huss, S.: On the design of hardware building blocks for modern lattice-based encryption schemes. In: Prouff, E., Schaumont, P. (eds.) CHES 2012. LNCS, vol. 7428, pp. 512–529. Springer, Heidelberg (2012)
15. Güneysu, T., Oder, T., Pöppelmann, T., Schwabe, P.: Software speed records for lattice-based signatures. In: Gaborit, P. (ed.) PQCrypto 2013. LNCS, vol. 7932, pp. 67–82. Springer, Heidelberg (2013)
16. Halevi, S., Shoup, V.: Algorithms in HElib. In: Garay, J.A., Gennaro, R. (eds.) CRYPTO 2014, Part I. LNCS, vol. 8616, pp. 554–571. Springer, Heidelberg (2014)
17. Halevi, S., Shoup, V.: Bootstrapping for HElib. In: Oswald, E., Fischlin, M. (eds.) EUROCRYPT 2015. LNCS, vol. 9056, pp. 641–670. Springer, Heidelberg (2015)
18. Hart, W., et al.: Fast library for number theory (Version 2.5) (2015). http://www.flintlib.org
19. Harvey, D.: Faster arithmetic for number-theoretic transforms. J. Symb. Comput. **60**, 113–119 (2014)
20. Itkis, G.: Forward security, adaptive cryptography: time evolution (2004). http://www.cs.bu.edu/fac/itkis/pap/forward-secure-survey.pdf
21. Khedr, A., Gulak, G., Vaikuntanathan, V.: SHIELD: scalable homomorphic implementation of encrypted data-classifiers. Cryptology ePrint Archive, Report 2014/838 (2014). http://eprint.iacr.org/2014/838
22. Lepoint, T., Naehrig, M.: A comparison of the homomorphic encryption schemes FV and YASHE. In: Pointcheval, D., Vergnaud, D. (eds.) AFRICACRYPT. LNCS, vol. 8469, pp. 318–335. Springer, Heidelberg (2014)
23. Lindner, R., Peikert, C.: Better key sizes (and attacks) for LWE-based encryption. In: Kiayias, A. (ed.) CT-RSA 2011. LNCS, vol. 6558, pp. 319–339. Springer, Heidelberg (2011)
24. Lyubashevsky, V., Micciancio, D.: Generalized compact knapsacks are collision resistant. In: Bugliesi, M., Preneel, B., Sassone, V., Wegener, I. (eds.) ICALP 2006. LNCS, vol. 4052, pp. 144–155. Springer, Heidelberg (2006)

25. Moller, N., Granlund, T.: Improved division by invariant integers. IEEE Trans. Comput. **60**(2), 165–175 (2011)
26. Oder, T., Pöppelmann, T., Güneysu, T.: Beyond ECDSA and RSA: lattice-based digital signatures on constrained devices. In: The 51st Annual Design Automation Conference 2014, DAC 2014, San Francisco, CA, USA, 1–5 June 2014, pp. 1–6 (2014)
27. Peikert, C., Rosen, A.: Efficient collision-resistant hashing from worst-case assumptions on cyclic lattices. In: Halevi, S., Rabin, T. (eds.) TCC 2006. LNCS, vol. 3876, pp. 145–166. Springer, Heidelberg (2006)
28. Pollard, J.M.: The fast Fourier transform in a finite field. Math. Comput. **25**(114), 365–374 (1971)
29. Pöppelmann, T., Güneysu, T.: Towards efficient arithmetic for lattice-based cryptography on reconfigurable hardware. In: Hevia, A., Neven, G. (eds.) LatinCrypt 2012. LNCS, vol. 7533, pp. 139–158. Springer, Heidelberg (2012)
30. Shoup, V.: Number theory library (Version 8.1) (2015). http://www.shoup.net/ntl
31. Steffen, A., et al.: strongSwan (Version 5.2.2) (2015). https://www.strongswan.org/

Cryptanalysis of Symmetric Key Encryption

Optimization of Rainbow Tables
for Practically Cracking GSM A5/1
Based on Validated Success Rate Modeling

Zhen Li[(⊠)]

Infocomm Security Department, Institute for Infocomm Research,
Agency for Science, Technology and Research,
1 Fusionopolis Way, #11-01, Connexis 138632, Singapore
liz@i2r.a-star.edu.sg

Abstract. GSM (Global System for Mobile Communications) communication is a ubiquitous technology developed by European Telecommu-
nications Standards Institute for cellular network. To ensure the confidentiality of the user communication, it is protected against eaves-
droppers by the A5/1 cryptographic algorithm. Various time-memory
trade-off (TMTO) techniques have been proposed to crack A5/1. These
techniques map the keystreams to the initial states of the algorithm at a
reasonable success rate. Among TMTO techniques, rainbow table is an
efficient method that allows a good trade-off between run-time and storage. The link between rainbow table parameters and the success rate is
not well established yet. In view of this, a statistical success rate model is
proposed in this paper, which takes various parameters of a given TMTO
structure into consideration. The developed success rate model can be
used to optimize the TMTO parameters for the best performance. Comprehensive experiments show that A5/1 can be broken with 43 % success
rate in 9 s using 1.29 TB rainbow tables, which is consistent with the
theoretically predicted success rate. When using 3.84 TB rainbow tables,
the extrapolated success rate is 81 %.

Keywords: GSM · Rainbow table · Keystream space · Success rate
model

1 Introduction

The A5/1 cryptography algorithm in the GSM protocol, used by many cell-
phones, protects user communication. GSM is also used for text messaging and
some other wireless communications. The first information about the design of
A5/1 appeared in 1994 [1], accompanied by an attack on alleged A5/1 [10], and
the algorithm was reverse engineered from actual GSM equipment by Briceno
et al. [7].

  The general idea of the attack is to determine the encryption key for a sample
of encoded information bits (keystream). Some practical methods of breaking the

© Springer International Publishing Switzerland 2016
K. Sako (Ed.): CT-RSA 2016, LNCS 9610, pp. 359–377, 2016.
DOI: 10.1007/978-3-319-29485-8_21

encryption for a keystream involve the inversion of the one-way function used in the cryptography algorithm. Brute force (no storage, long attack time) and dictionary attacks (large storage, instantaneous) are two extremes of generic cryptographic attacks. A space-time trade-off exists between the two extremes. Hellman [11] was the first to explore this trade-off. In 1982, Rivest et al. suggested using distinguished points (DPs) as endpoints (EPs) for the generated chains [18]. In 2003, Oechslin [2,17] proposed the Rainbow Table technique, as an extension of the Hellman Table technique. It applies XOR operations to different columns to reduce collision rates of EPs. A more detailed survey of TMTO techniques is available in [14].

Amongst the most successful GSM attacks, a rainbow table structure is used to map the keystream to the initial state of the algorithm [16]. The cracking rate of A5/1 algorithm is 87 % in about 10 s, using eight 114-bit keystreams, showing that A5/1 encryption is not secure. The implementation details of the project were not revealed, and parameters of the rainbow table are not optimized in theory. Recently, Lu et al. reconstructed the technique, and revealed the implementation details for the first time [14]. A variation of rainbow table structure is used, achieving similar performance. However, the underlying mechanics that a rainbow table with given TMTO parameters can produce a certain success rate is not well established yet, making it experimentally instead of theoretically guided.

In view of this aspect, both a comprehensive insight in the A5/1 encryption algorithm and the rainbow table statistics are presented in this work. Through the theoretical analysis, the success rate can be predicted based on given parameters and a given rainbow table structure, which is perfectly validated by the experimental results. Thus the optimal rainbow table parameters can be automatically selected. The proposed method is believed to be able to further adapt to break other ciphers based on TMTO techniques.

This paper is organized as follows: Sect. 2 shows the related work in cracking GSM A5/1. In Sect. 3 the characteristics of applying TMTO to A5/1 is analyzed based on statistical models. Section 4 briefs the implementation details of A5/1 TMTO and shows the experimental results of the success rate and speed when using the optimal parameters to crack GSM A5/1. The experimental results validate that the theoretical model predicts the success rate accurately. Section 5 sums up this paper and gives a brief view of future work.

2 GSM and Related Work

A5/1 is a commonly used symmetric cipher for encrypting over-the-air transmissions in the GSM standard. Although A5/3 and GEA3, which are more secure key stream generators built around the KASUMI core block cipher, have been standardized for use in GSM and GPRS, most over-the-air conversations are still protected by A5/1 encryption. A5/1 is a synchronous stream cipher based on linear feedback shift registers (LFSRs), and has a 64-bit secret key. A GSM conversation is transmitted as a sequence of 228-bit frames. Each frame is XORed

(Exclusive OR operation) with a 228-bit keystream produced by the A5/1 function. Phone calls and text messages can be encrypted between a phone and a base station. The first 114 bits of keystream constitute the downlink keystream and the second half the uplink keystream.

The initial state IS of this A5/1 encryption depends on the 64-bit secret key, denoted by Kc and a 22-bit public frame counter, denoted by Fn. Kc is derived from a unique SIM card number and a unique network random number generated by the $A8$ hash function. It is fixed during the conversation. Fn is assigned in every frame, and the frame counter is changed approximately every 4.615 ms. After the conversation is encrypted by the keystream, the ciphertext is transmitted over the GSM channel. In order to obtain the keystream from ciphertext using TMTO, some of the corresponding plaintext must be known. In typical settings, several chunks of consecutive 64 bits of keystreams are required, relying on knowing some formatting in encrypted control messages, or guessing the content. Commercial A5/1 crackers leverage the Cipher Mode Complete message, which is the first encrypted message in an encrypted transaction and usually contains constant data, mostly empty padding bytes. Empty dummy frames are also encrypted even though they carry zero information, making them a prime target for key crackers. After obtaining at least a chunk of 64-bit keystream, software can be used to map the keystream to the corresponding 64-bit session key, which is bijection of the initial state, based on TMTO.

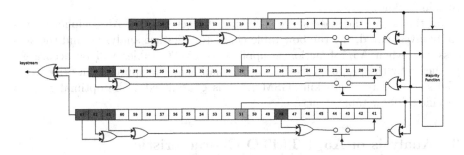

Fig. 1. A5/1 algorithm diagram

The principle of A5/1 cipher is shown in Fig. 1. Internally the generator consists of three Linear Feedback Shift Registers (LFSR): $R1$, $R2$ and $R3$, which are clocked according to the majority rule. The 64-bit initial state IS is initialized by Kc and Fn in the three registers. The clocking rule of the LFSRs works as follows: The clocking bits of each LFSR $R1$, $R2$ and $R3$ are the bits 8, 29 and 51, respectively. The values of these bits are compared and the LFSRs where the clocking bit agrees with the majority are clocked. Therefore at each clock cycle either two or three of the LFSRs are clocked. Each keystream bit is generated by XORing the most significant bits of the three LFSRs at each clock cycle. A5/1 encryption includes 100 clocks for bit-mixing without output and 64 clocks for outputting keystream bits.

Since A5/1 algorithm was revealed, a number of attacks have been published [5,6,8,9,12,16,19]. The work [8] exploits some weaknesses of the key initialization procedure. The attack needs a few minutes of computation time with a data requirement of two to five minutes of conversation plaintext. The work [9] requires at least a few seconds of conversation and run very fast. However, it needs both huge precomputation time and huge memory. More practical results are achieved by TMTO attacks, e.g. Biham and Dunkelman [5], by Biryukov et al. [6], and Nohl [16], "A5/1 Security Project". In the last work, the rainbow table structure is integrated with DPs, and the implementation is carried out using specialized processors such as GPUs and PS3 cells, with about 4 Terabytes pre-computation data (about 2 TB after compression). However, the theoretical aspects are not revealed. Hong et al. proposed theoretical TMTO success rate models [13,15], which are complete and sophisticated. However, it is generic analysis not customized for a specific cipher algorithm and of insufficient accuracy to optimize TMTO parameters in practical scenarios. In 2015, Lu et al. analyzed the computational complexity of several TMTO table structures, worked out the detailed GSM cracking procedure, and carried out a commodity GPGPU implementation [14]. Based on a combination of the rainbow table structures proposed in [3] and the DP technique [18] as well as an optimized implementation, the GSM A5/1 cracking efficiency is slightly better than that reported in [16]. However, the statistical analysis of the success model is still not well established, and thus the link between the TMTO parameters and the cracking success rate remains unknown.

In this work, the state space shrinking characteristic of A5/1 cipher is specially investigated, the rainbow table characteristics are analyzed, and the success rate when A5/1 function is applied to TMTO tables will be accurately predicted by the proposed models rather than heuristic approach in prior work. The success rate of cracking GSM A5/1 is guaranteed to be optimal given a specific rainbow table structure.

3   Analysis of A5/1 TMTO Characteristics

In TMTO, a subset of the keyspace is pre-computed, which limits subsequent search operations. The whole search space exists because the encryption function is applied iteratively from the keystream forward through the keyspace. The larger the subset of keyspace pre-computed, the shorter the time needed for online computation. An effective technique to further reduce search operations is the distinguished point, which is a value that satisfies some easily tested criteria, e.g. the LSBs of a keystream are all zeros. Given a keystream to be cracked, a chain of intermediate keystreams is calculated iteratively until a DP is generated. Only then it is looked up as in endpoint (EP) stored in a TMTO table. This establishes which chain of the TMTO table the keystream was found in, and then the corresponding startpoint (SP) of that chain is obtained. Finally the chain is regenerated from the SP to check if the keystream to be cracked can be reached. If successful, the initial state of the keystream of the encryption algorithm is obtained. Otherwise it is a false alarm. Using DP, the number of the slow TMTO table lookup operations will be reduced. Typically, each keystream in the chain is XORed with its color, i.e. the number of DPs the chain has generated from its SP. In this way, the collision rates of TMTO can be greatly reduced.

3.1 Chain Characteristics

Now we consider the chain length of TMTO when combining the standard rainbow table structure and the DP technique [18]. During pre-computation of the rainbow tables, the chains that costs too many A5/1 functions, such as an infinite loop, are discarded. The threshold is set to $r = 16$ in this work, so that $1 \leqslant t \leqslant r \cdot D$ A5/1 functions are applied to each intermediate point until it reaches a DP. The probability that a DP is reached after at most t operations of the A5/1 function is clearly $p_{DP}(t) = 1 - (1 - \frac{1}{D})^t$, where $D = 2^d$ and d is length of zero-bit mask in DP. Then the probability that a SP can successfully generate an EP is $P_{DP}(r) = (p_{DP}(r \cdot D))^S = \left(1 - (1 - \frac{1}{D})^{r \cdot D}\right)^S$, where $S = 256$ is a typical number of DPs in a chain in rainbow tables. The expected number of chains that are not discarded is $M = M_0 \cdot P_{DP} = \left(1 - (1 - \frac{1}{D})^{r \cdot D}\right)^S$, where M_0 and M are total number and the valid number of SPs, respectively. When $M_0 = 2^{36.678}$ (which corresponds to 1.6 TB), we have $P_{DP} = 0.9999721$, then $M_0 - M = 2^{21.55}$ SPs that cannot successfully generate EPs will be discarded. This perfectly matches the experimental result that $2^{21.55}$ startpoints are actually discarded, thus $M \approx 2^{36.678} \approx M_0$. The average number of A5/1 function operations T required for the M valid chains can be approximated by $T \approx \frac{1}{M} \sum_{t=1}^{r} M_0 (P_{DP}(t) - P_{DP}(t-1)) t \approx D \cdot S$ which can be interpreted as each DP section is on average about $D = 2^d = 256$ and there are $S = 256$ such DP sections in each chain in this work. This corresponds to chain length of $T = 2^{16}$ in standard rainbow table without DP.

3.2 Keystream Space Shrinking

Due to imperfect non-linear behavior of A5/1, multiple initial states can be mapped to the same internal state, thereby decreasing the number of valid internal states for each added clock. As a result, the 100 bit-mixing clocks of each A5/1 operation shrinks the Kc state to 15.3 % of the original size, effectively reducing key size by 2.71 bits. Here we investigate how the initial state of A5/1 encryption can be reversed from an internal state after multiple bit-mixing clocks.

First consider one reverse clocking, which is well studied in [10]. By reversing an internal state by 1 clock, we have up to 4 previous states, and the probabilities are: $P_1(0) = C_2^1 C_3^1 (\frac{1}{2})^4 = \frac{3}{8}$, $P_1(1) = C_2^1 C_3^1 (\frac{1}{2})^4 + C_2^1 (\frac{1}{2})^6 = \frac{13}{32}$, $P_1(2) = C_2^1 C_3^1 (\frac{1}{2})^6 = \frac{3}{32}$, $P_1(3) = C_2^1 C_3^1 (\frac{1}{2})^6 = \frac{3}{32}$, $P_1(4) = C_2^1 (\frac{1}{2})^6 = \frac{1}{32}$, where $P_1(k) = P(\#solution = k)$. See Appendix A for more details. These $P_1(0)$ randomly distributed states which have no ancestors are called illegal states, and others are legal states. As such, the keystream space is shrunk to $1 - P_1(0) = 62.5 \%$ of the original Kc space.

In this work, we consider the reverse (backward) clocking by more than 1 clock, which is not shown in previous literature. The calculation is based on

Table 8 in Appendix A, which is iterated for each reverse clocking. The calculation becomes much more tedious when reverse clocking by more than 3 clocks since each reverse clocking can produce multiple solutions, because the current reverse clocking depends on all previous reverse clockings and the solutions by the current reverse clocking are also dependent upon each other.

Since 1-clock reverse can generate up to 4 solutions, it is intuitive that 2-clock reverse generates up to $4^2 = 16$ solutions, so on and so forth. However, it is not the case because some states die out in the procedure of reverse clocking. $\frac{3}{8}$ of the states have no ancestors after 1-clock reverse, and the obtained backward solutions may also have no ancestors. As a result, the summations of distributions of 1-clock, 2-clock and 3-clock reverse are 1.0, 0.625 and 0.578125, respectively. The distributions of number of solutions when reverse clocking by 1 to 3 clocks are shown in Table 1. Note that the discrete distribution cannot be exactly represented by continuous distribution as in [10]. For example, it is impossible for 3-clock reverse to generate 8 or 9 solutions, but 10-solutions is possible.

Table 1. Conditional distribution of #solutions

#reverse\#solution	0	1	2	3	4	5	6	7	8	9	10
1	$\frac{12}{32}$	$\frac{13}{32}$	$\frac{3}{32}$	$\frac{3}{32}$	$\frac{1}{32}$	0	0	0	0	0	0
2	$\frac{12}{256}$	$\frac{97}{256}$	$\frac{12}{256}$	$\frac{27}{256}$	$\frac{8}{256}$	$\frac{3}{256}$	0	$\frac{1}{256}$	0	0	0
3	$\frac{36}{2048}$	$\frac{733}{2048}$	$\frac{108}{2048}$	$\frac{204}{2048}$	$\frac{60}{2048}$	$\frac{27}{2048}$	$\frac{3}{2048}$	$\frac{12}{2048}$	0	0	$\frac{1}{2048}$

Consider the mapping between initial states and the internal space with one backward clocking. On average, $\frac{12}{32}$ states of internal space are illegal and have no corresponding initial states, $\frac{13}{32}$ internal states have one-to-one mapping, $\frac{3}{32}$ internal states reverses to 2 states each, another $\frac{3}{32}$ states reverses to 3 each, and $\frac{1}{32}$ states will be reversed to 4 states each. When the internal states are randomly chosen by uniform distribution, the average number of solutions in the initial state space is $\frac{12}{32} \times 0 + \frac{13}{32} \times 1 + \frac{3}{32} \times 2 + \frac{3}{32} \times 3 + \frac{1}{32} \times 4 = 1.0$, which means backward clocking will not produce more states on average. However, the internal states are not chosen by uniform distribution in real scenario, but generated by forward clocking from initial states following uniform distribution instead. As a result, $\frac{13}{32}$ states have one-to-one mapping, $\frac{3 \times 2}{32}$ states reproduce 2 states each, $\frac{3 \times 3}{32}$ states reproduce 3 states each, and $\frac{1 \times 4}{32}$ states reproduce 4 states each. The expectation of the backward clocking solutions is $\frac{13}{32} \times 1 + \frac{6}{32} \times 2 + \frac{9}{32} \times 3 + \frac{4}{32} \times 4 = \frac{17}{8} = 2.125$, which means 1-clock forward-backward clocking will reproduce 2.125 times states on average. Note that although it seems the internal state space is $\frac{1}{2.125} = \frac{8}{17}$ of the initial state space, the fact is that the internal state space is $\frac{5}{8}$ of the initial state space. This seemingly inconsistency is due to the fact that A5/1 cipher has a preference towards a smaller group of favored states instead of a perfect uniform mapping.

Since 1 more reverse clock will increase the maximum number of solutions by 3 (see Appendix A), the expected number of solutions after r-clock reverse can be represented as $\sum_{i=1}^{3r+1} P_r(i) \cdot i^2$, where $P_r(i)$ is the probability of number of solutions, and the square operation comes from the non-uniform mapping between the states before and after the clocking. For up to 3-clock reverse, the expectations are calculated as $\sum_{i=1}^{4} P_1(i) \cdot i^2 = \frac{17}{8} = 2.1250$, $\sum_{i=1}^{7} P_2(i) \cdot i^2 = \frac{160}{2^6} = 2.5000$, $\sum_{i=1}^{10} P_3(i) \cdot i^2 = \frac{1358}{2^9} = 2.6523$, which perfectly match experimental results. As the calculation of $P_r(i)$ becomes tedious for more clocks, the expectations are obtained by experiments: $\sum_{i=1}^{13} P_4(i) \cdot i^2 \approx 2.78$, $\sum_{i=1}^{31} P_{10}(i) \cdot i^2 \approx 3.54$, and $\sum_{i=1}^{301} P_{100}(i) \cdot i^2 \approx 13.04$. The internal state space after the 100-clock bit-mixing in A5/1 function $1 - P_{100}(0) \approx 0.153 = 15.3\%$ of the initial state space, instead of $\frac{1}{13.04} \approx 7.7\%$. An example of 15 clocks forward and backward clocking is illustrated in Fig. 5 in Appendix B, where all connected states can be revisited from any internal or initial state by traversing the paths, and the number along with each path indicates its index.

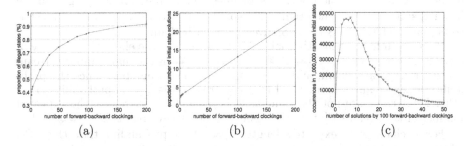

Fig. 2. Forward-backward clockings (a) proportion of illegal internal states (b) expected number of initial state solutions (c) occurrence of solution numbers

To verify the above space shrink theory, we simulate the reverse clocking by randomly choosing 1 million legal states in the internal state space. It is achieved by forward clocking from initial states to generate legal states and then backward clocking by the same number of clocks. Figure 2(a) shows the proportion of illegal states by reverse clocking, which is close to an exponential function. It indicates that proportion of illegal states of the 100-clocked internal states is $P_{100}(0) \approx \frac{847435}{1000000} \approx 84.7\%$, which is consistent to the theoretical prediction. The expected number of initial state solutions by reverse clocking from legal internal states is shown in Fig. 2(b). It is noticed that the expected number of solutions is approximately exponential within 10 clocks and linearly proportional to a larger number of bit-mixing clocks. Figure 2(c) simulates the distribution of number of initial states by 100-clock reverse from a legal state, which is close to a Gamma-distribution. By assuming a uniform mapping between the initial state space and the internal state space, one would expect the number of solutions to be $\frac{1}{1-0.847} = 6.538$ which is around the peak in Fig. 2(c). However, the assumption does not hold true. Instead, the expected number of solutions for reverse clocking from legal states is 13.04. For reverse clocking from random states, including legal and illegal ones, the expected number of initial state solutions is exactly 1.00 in obvious. Since the keystream space shrinks to only 15.3% after 100 forward clockings, the effective keystream space of A5/1 is no bigger than $2^{64} \times 0.153 = 2^{61.29}$. Thus an ideal TMTO technique will need $2^{61.29}$ pre-computation of A5/1 functions. However, redundancy is inevitable in TMTO due to the imperfect mapping of A5/1 cipher, resulting in collisions among different chains.

3.3 Intermediate Space and Chain Collisions

We have the parameter (M, S, D), where M is the number of SPs to generate each rainbow table, S is the expected number of DP sections in each chain, and $D = 2^d$ is the average length of DPs. In rainbow table, at first the M distinct initial states are bit-mixed by 100 clocks of A5/1, which shrinks the state space to $N = \frac{2^{64}}{K}$, where $K \approx 6.538$ is the space shrink rate for each f. Then these internal states are mapped to keystreams, XORed with colors and used as input of the next A5/1 operation, which is assumed to be a random mapping from the internal state space to the original 2^{64} space again. This procedure is expected to be repeated $T = D \cdot S$ times on average in each chain.

It can be inferred that, through t A5/1 operations, the effective space size of a DP is approximately $S_t = \frac{N}{D \cdot t} = \frac{2^{64}}{K \cdot D \cdot t}$, where $N = \frac{2^{64}}{K}$ is the maximum keystream space for A5/1 algorithm, and $1 \leq t \leq T$ is the column number. Since the probability a keystream A is identical to a keystream B is $\frac{1}{N}$, the probability $M - 1$ other keystreams are not the same as A is $\left(1 - \frac{1}{N}\right)^{M-1}$. Therefore, the expected number of keystreams that do not appear in other keystreams is $M\left(1 - \frac{1}{N}\right)^{M-1}$.

For a chain with expected length $T = D \cdot S$ probability that the EPs, which are also DPs, having zero, one and two collision(s) are calculated $P_0 = \left(\left(1 - \frac{D}{N}\right)^{M-1}\right)^T \approx \frac{D \cdot K \cdot T \cdot M}{2^{64}}$, $P_1 \approx \frac{D(M-1)}{N\left(1 - \frac{D}{N}\right)}\left(1 - \frac{2D}{N}\right)^{(M-3)T} \sum_{t=1}^{T}\left(\frac{N-D}{N-2D}\right)^{(M-3)t}\left(1 - \frac{D}{N}\right)^{2t}$, and $P_2 \approx \frac{D(M-1)}{N}\left(1 - \frac{D}{N}\right)^{M-2} \sum_{t=1}^{T}\left(1 - \frac{D}{N}\right)^{(M-1)(t-1)}$, respectively. According to experiments with $M = 2^{36.678}$ and $T = 2^{16}$, the actual ratio of EP redundancy is about 40%, which is close to the estimation $1 - \frac{P_0}{1} - \frac{P_1}{2} - \frac{P_2}{3} \approx 36\%$. The difference is partially because we appended new EPs to the rainbow table by several times instead of one time generation with distinct SPs, thus more collisions occurred. However, the difference is not large. Theoretical probability of non-collision points is shown in Fig. 3. It is noted the rate of non-collisions in EPs can be as low as 64%. After removing the duplicate EPs to generate the perfect TMTO table, the actual rainbow table size is $1.6\,\text{TB} \times (1 - 40\%) \approx 0.96\,\text{TB}$.

3.4 Success Rate

An accurate statistical model for predicting the success rate of rainbow table $P_{rainbow}$ has been an open problem. Existing success probability formula for rainbow table cryptanalysis is not validated by experiments on real data, including some descriptive models that are not computationally feasible [14]. Prior work [13, 15] has not considered the A5/1 internal space characteristics when computing success rate for rainbow table cryptanalysis while the cryptographic primitive

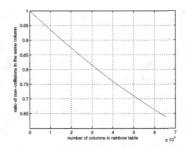

Fig. 3. Theoretical probability of non-collision points after A5/1 operations

is actually A5/1. In this work, we accurately predict the success rate of rainbow tables with A5/1 as the cryptographic primitive.

In standard rainbow tables with DPs [16], the keystreams differ by applying different colors, and will unlikely to generate identical A5/1 output since their effective space size is 2^{64} instead of $\frac{2^{64}}{K}$. We are only concerned with the collisions that occur in the same DP section with the same color, i.e. the columns $\lfloor \frac{t}{D} \rfloor \cdot D + 1, \lfloor \frac{t}{D} \rfloor \cdot D + 2, \ldots, t - 1, t$. Let M_t denote the expected number of distinct intermediate points in column t of the standard rainbow table with DP. The points are called "distinct" in the sense that, each of the M_t points is different from other points in t-th column and also does not appear in any previous columns. Obviously the initial condition is $M_1 = M$. The numbers $M_t, t = 2, 3, \ldots, T$, are determined iteratively: after $(t-1)$-th A5/1 operations have be calculated, there are $Pool_R = \sum_{j=\lfloor \frac{t}{D} \rfloor \cdot D + 1}^{t-1} M_j$ distinct points in all chains. Therefore the probability that a point in the t-th column is distinct from $Pool_R$ is $p_{pre}(t) = 1 - \frac{Pool_R}{N}$, where $N = \frac{2^{64}}{K}$ is the shrunk space due to one operation of A5/1. In addition, the probability that the points in the t-th column are distinct from each other is $p_{cur}(t) = \left(1 - \frac{1}{N}\right)^{M_{t-1}}$ since M_t is derived from M_{t-1}. As a result, the probability that a point in t-th column is a distinct one is as follow:

$$P_{dist}(t) = p_{pre}(t) \cdot p_{cur}(t) = \left(1 - \frac{1}{N} \sum_{j=\lfloor \frac{t}{D} \rfloor \cdot D + 1}^{t-1} M_j\right)\left(1 - \frac{1}{N}\right)^{M_{t-1}} \quad (1)$$

The expected number that a point in space N does not occur in columns $1, 2, \ldots, t$ is $N \cdot P_{distinct}(t)$. Therefore, we can calculate the number of new distinct points in column t as

$$M_t = N - N \cdot P_{dist}(t) - \sum_{j=\lfloor \frac{t}{D} \rfloor \cdot D + 1}^{t-1} M_j \approx \left(N - \sum_{j=\lfloor \frac{t}{D} \rfloor \cdot D + 1}^{t-1} m_j\right)\left(1 - e^{-\frac{M_{t-1}}{N}}\right) \quad (2)$$

Hence the expected coverage rate (ECR) of all the distinct points generated by rainbow tables over all the possible keystreams is estimated as $ECR = \frac{1}{S \cdot D \cdot M} \sum_{t=1}^{S \cdot D} M_t$, where $M_1 = M$ and M_t can be obtained iteratively for $t > 1$ based on Eq. (2). Note that a 114-bit keystream is comprised of fifty-one 64-bit overlapping but independent samples, each having a chance p to obtain the initial state by reverse clocking. By utilizing all the 51 samples upon the rainbow tables, the probability that at least one sample of the 114-bit keystream is contained in a standard rainbow table is $P_{hit} = 1 - (1 - \frac{M \cdot S \cdot D}{N} \cdot ECR)^{51}$. This is one crucial technique worked out to enhance the success rate by about 51 times.

Note that although about 13 candidates of initial states (one-to-one mapping to Kc) can be obtained by forward clocking from a pre-image of the keystream to a legal internal state and then reverse clocking, exactly only one of them corresponds to the ground-truth Kc that was really used for generating the keystream to be cracked. Thus the success rate will be only $\frac{P_{hit}}{13.04}$ in terms of finding out the ground-truth Kc, which is the ultimate goal of cracking. In this regard, at least two 114-bit keystreams of two frames (different Fn) are used in order to find out the ground-truth Kc, as in [14]. The Kc candidates obtained from one frame will be verified: they are initialized with the Fn of the other frame and, most probably only one of them can produce the other keystream. In the rare case more than one Kc remain, an additional frame will be used to further verify, which never occurred in a real scenario. This is the second crucial technique that enhances the success rate to P_{hit} by about 13 times. Finally, the success rate is similar to that of [16], indicating the two crucial techniques are correctly worked out. The final success rate by utilizing 4 keystreams is

$$P_{rainbow} = 1 - \left(1 - \frac{1}{N} \cdot \sum_{t=1}^{S \cdot D} M_t\right)^{51 \times 4} \tag{3}$$

and the success rate based on 4 rainbow tables with different color configurations will be approximated as $P_{rainbow}^4 = 1 - \left(1 - \left(1 - \frac{1}{N} \cdot \sum_{t=1}^{S \cdot D} M_t\right)^{51 \times 4}\right)^4$.

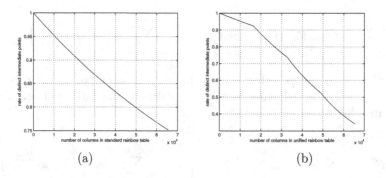

(a)   (b)

Fig. 4. Ratio of new distinct points in rainbow table (a) standard (b) unified

When considering the success rate of the unified rainbow table structure proposed in [14], the case is similar since unified rainbow table is essentially repetitions of standard rainbow table horizontally. The difference is the color configuration. Given the column number t, the number of the repeated color patterns in previous columns is $u = \lceil \frac{(\lfloor \frac{t}{D} \rfloor \cdot D + 1) \cdot U}{S \cdot D} \rceil$, where U is the total number of color pattern repetition. Then distinct points in all chains are

$$Pool_U = \sum_{j=\lfloor \frac{t}{D} \rfloor \cdot D + 1}^{t-1} M_j + \sum_{i=1}^{u-1} \sum_{j=\lfloor \frac{t}{D} \rfloor \cdot D + 1 - i \cdot \frac{S \cdot D}{U}}^{t-1-i \cdot \frac{S \cdot D}{U}} M_j \qquad (4)$$

which is larger than that of standard rainbow table $Pool_U > Pool_R$. Accordingly, $P_{distinct}(t)$ decreases, and the final success rate $P_{rainbow}$ also decreases. The ratio of new distinct intermediate points in each column, i.e. $\frac{M_t}{M}$, $t = 1, 2, \ldots, S \cdot D$, is shown in Fig. 4, where more distinct points are generated by standard rainbow tables.

Table 2. Theoretical success rate of standard rainbow table with DP with $T = 2^{16}$

$M \backslash (S, D)$	$(2^6, 2^{10})$	$(2^7, 2^9)$	$(2^8, 2^8)$	$(2^9, 2^7)$	Precomputation
$2^{37.678}$	89.3 %	94.6 %	97.0 %	98.1 %	$2^{53.678}$
$2^{36.678}$	76.7 %	82.7 %	**86.1 %**	87.9 %	$2^{52.678}$
$2^{35.678}$	58.4 %	62.6 %	65.2 %	66.5 %	$2^{51.678}$
$2^{34.678}$	38.9 %	41.0 %	42.1 %	42.8 %	$2^{50.678}$

Basically, the success rate is $P_{hit}(M, S, D)$ and it is also constrained by storage size and table lookup time, false alarm, etc. Provided the same precomputation time, when the chain length $T = S \cdot D$ decreases, the number of chains M has to be increased, resulting in more storage size of the rainbow tables. It is a four-dimensional space curve which cannot be visualized. Now we try some reasonable parameters. Table 2 lists the theoretical success rates with average chain length of 2^{16}. When M or S increases, the success rates increase, which is obvious. However, the penalty of the increase of success rate is more offline pre-computation time and more online lookup time. As a compromise, we choose the setting $(M, S, D) = (2^{36.678}, 2^8, 2^8)$.

Table 3. Theoretical success rate of standard rainbow table with DP with $D \cdot S = 2^{15}$

$M \backslash (S, D)$	$(2^5, 2^{10})$	$(2^6, 2^9)$	$(2^7, 2^8)$	$(2^8, 2^7)$	$(2^9, 2^6)$	Precomputation
$2^{38.678}$	94.6 %	97.0 %	98.1 %	98.5 %	98.7 %	$2^{53.678}$
$2^{37.678}$	82.7 %	86.1 %	**87.9 %**	88.8 %	89.3 %	$2^{52.678}$
$2^{36.678}$	62.7 %	65.2 %	66.5 %	67.2 %	67.6 %	$2^{51.678}$
$2^{35.678}$	41.0 %	42.1 %	42.8 %	43.1 %	43.2 %	$2^{50.678}$

Table 4. Theoretical success rate of unified rainbow table with DP with $D \cdot S \cdot U = 2^{16}$

$M \backslash (S \cdot U, D)$	$(2^6, 2^{10})$	$(2^7, 2^9)$	$(2^8, 2^8)$	$(2^9, 2^7)$	Precomputation
$2^{37.678}$	74.5 %	85.4 %	92.4 %	96.0 %	$2^{53.678}$
$2^{36.678}$	61.7 %	72.4 %	**80.0 %**	84.7 %	$2^{52.678}$
$2^{35.678}$	47.5 %	55.4 %	60.8 %	64.2 %	$2^{51.678}$
$2^{34.678}$	33.2 %	37.4 %	40.1 %	41.7 %	$2^{50.678}$

Table 3 lists the theoretical success rates of standard rainbow table with average chain length of 2^{15}. Theoretical success rates of unified rainbow table with DP with 4 repetitions and chain length of $T = S \cdot D \cdot U = 2^{16}$ are listed in Fig. 4. By comparing with Table 2, unified rainbow table is inferior than standard rainbow tables in terms of success rate. However, it allows less online computation with the same table lookup, as shown in [14]. It is a trade-off of rainbow table structure between success rate and online cracking time.

Based on experimental results, using 4 keystreams on a 0.96 TB rainbow table with parameters $(M, S, D, U) = (2^{36.678}, 2^6, 2^8, 4)$, the success rate of cracking A5/1 cipher is 33.85 %, which corresponds to $1 - (1 - 33.85\%)^4 = 80.85\%$ success rate by using four 0.96 TB rainbow tables with different color configurations (zero-bit masks are at different bit positions). This is consistent with the 80.0 % theoretical success rate in Table 4. Note that according to Hong's model in [13], in every of the U color pattern section in rainbow table, $M_t = 2M_{t-1} / \left(1 + \sqrt{1 + \frac{2 M_t t^2}{N_0}}\right)$, where t is the column index in its section, and $N_0 = 2^{64}$ without considering the state space shrinking in Sect. 3.2. Although it is an elegant close form model, its theoretical success rate is about 12 % for unified rainbow table, which is not accurate compared to the experimental result 81 %. As such, a generic analysis of rainbow table success rate without considering the specific characteristic of the actual cipher is insufficient for parameter optimization. In this work, the optimal configuration (M, S, D, U) of rainbow tables can be automatically set in minutes by searching in the limited discrete space, e.g. $M \in (2^{34.678}, 2^{35.678}, 2^{36.678}, 2^{37.678}, 2^{38.678})$, $S \in (2^5, 2^6, 2^7, 2^8, 2^9)$, $D \in (2^6, 2^7, 2^8, 2^9, 2^{10})$ and $U \in (1, 2, 4, 8)$.

3.5   False Alarms

In actual online cracking, each keystream Ks will generate $S \cdot D \cdot U = 256$ DPs by assuming Ks to be in various positions in its chain. These 256 DPs are all potential endpoints, and on average around 90 DPs can be found in EPs stored in unified rainbow tables. Unfortunately, Ks may not be reproduced from the SPs that correspond to the 90 EPs stored in tables. This is called false alarm since the keystream is found in rainbow tables but its pre-image cannot be retrieved. Essentially the false alarm is caused by the duplication of the EP in the previous intermediate DPs in a chain. False alarm rate based on Rainbow tables can be estimated as $FalseAlarm \approx \frac{K \cdot M \cdot T^2}{2^{64} \cdot D}$. With a fixed pre-computation task, a longer DP section will reduce the false alarm. When using unified rainbow table with parameters $(M, S, D, U) = (2^{36.678}, 2^6, 2^8, 4)$, theoretical false alarm rate is about 36 %, which is close to the experimental false alarm rate $\frac{90}{256} = 35.2\,\%$.

4 System Evaluation

4.1 Implementation and Settings

The workstation setup consists of a host system of a dual XEON CPU at 2.0 GHz with 32 GB ECC RAM, 1 Quadro 600 GPU for the display and 3 GeForce GTX690 (equivalent to 6 GTX680 cards) for parallel computation. The NVidia GTX690 chip was launched as a high-end member of GeForce family in 2012. GTX690 is equivalent to fitting two GTX680 chips onto the same circuit board, and contains 8 graphic processing clusters (GPCs), 16 streaming multiprocessors (SMs), each of which contains 192 streaming processors (SPs). There are in total 3072 cores with processor clock of 915 MHz, and the on-chip memory is 2×2 GB GDDR5 with 2×256 bit width.

A pedagogical implementation of A5/1 is available in [7]. It is further optimized on the host side first, and then migrated to the GPU side using Compute Unified Device Architecture (CUDA). The implementation mainly consists of A5/1 computation and the TMTO table access time. The computation consists of an offline table generation phase and an online cracking phase. For offline generation of the unified tables, we used bitslice optimization [4] to process multiple data simultaneously. As a result, the throughput for generating rainbow tables of A5/1 is about 3247 Megabytes per second using all GPUs.

The online computational cost when cracking A5/1 cipher includes table lookup time and chain regeneration time. For rainbow table structures, table lookup is much more time consuming than online computation and is thus the bottleneck for computational cost. To address the hard disk bottleneck, several table lookup acceleration strategies are used:

1. Distinguished points can reduce the harddisk access chance to $\frac{1}{D}$ (typically $D = 256$);
2. We set up 10×447 GB Solid State Disks (SSDs) to store the rainbow tables;
3. Several multi-threading techniques are used to reduce access time, including cached binary search, endpoint indexing, and thread pool, speeding up 3 times, 8 times, and 9 times, respectively;
4. Designing an fast harddisk I/O method to access only one of the L small table files of a single TMTO table (typically $L = 512$), reducing the access time to $\frac{1}{L}$ of the full search.

To carry out 256 lookups for 51 keystream samples on 512 rainbow tables of 1 TB, the final optimized speed by using all the four optimization techniques is $\frac{256 \times 51}{0.43} \approx 30,000$ searches per second, which is higher than 20,000 searches per second reported in the "A51 security project" [16]. To speed up online computation, three strategies are used:

1. 4-bit patterns of A5/1 registers are pre-computed and a tabular method is implemented for speeding up the online computation.
2. A unified rainbow table structure [14] is used in this work. A unified rainbow table structure reduces online chain regeneration computation to approximately $\frac{1}{U}$ of the rainbow table with DP, where U is a positive integer.

Setting up the workstation following up the above configurations needs less than 10,000USD in 2015. Besides the standard workstation, the extra expense includes 3 NVidia GTX690 chips each worth 1,000USD and ten 447 GB SSDs each worth 200USD. We will show that the GSM conversation can be cracked in several seconds using this low cost setting. For the task of pre-computation of rainbow tables, the SPs can be processed by 6 GTX680s in parallel, which needs 6 CPU threads to control 6 GPUs respectively. An additional thread is used to store the rainbow tables. Since a GPU can modify the host memory via Direct Memory Access (DMA), the host can check the generated DPs in real time before the whole DP computation task in GPU is finished. Because optimized lookup time is shorter than DP computation time, it has virtually no time cost. The total online crack time is approximately the summation of online DP computation time and the online regeneration time of the false alarms. For more details of the GSM A5/1 crack procedure, one can refer to [14].

4.2   Performance Evaluation of the Project

At first, a standard rainbow table and a unified rainbow table, both 95 GB, are generated for comparison in small scale. The performance is shown in Table 5, using 1, 4, and 16 114-bit keystreams for cracking. The results are reported on an average of 20,000 experiments. The success rates based on unified rainbow table is slightly lower than those of standard rainbow table. However, the online cracking phase for the unified rainbow table is lower. Note that the experimental success rates match the theoretical predictions by Eq. (2) perfectly.

Table 5. Success rate of standard and unified rainbow tables

95 GB\#keystream	1	4	16
Unified rainbow tables	1.26 %	5.0 %	18.5 %
Standard rainbow tables	1.28 %	5.0 %	18.6 %
"Unified" online time	6.3 s	9.0 s	17.5 s
"Standard" online time	7.1 s	9.5 s	18.5 s

Table 6. Success rate of finding the correct Kc on 0.9612 TB unified table

#keystream	1	4	8	16
Success rate	9.8 %	33.8 %	56.2 %	80.8 %
Computation time in GPU	4.1 s	5.0 s	9.0 s	18 s
False alarm time in CPU	2.0 s	4.0 s	7.5 s	15 s
Lookup time in CPU	0.7 s	1.4 s	2.8 s	5.8 s
Total online time	6.1 s	9.0 s	16.5 s	33 s

Based on the theoretical model of success rate, the success rate of unified rainbow table ($U = 4$) will be about 6 % less than that of the standard rainbow table ($U = 1$). Therefore it is believed that when rainbow table structure is changed to the standard rainbow table, the success rate will be 87 % in about 10 s, the same as [16], indicating that the implementation is correctly worked out. As we select unified table method for a higher efficiency, a large unified table (0.9612 TB) is generated for further verification of the proposed theoretical success rate model.

According to careful parameter selection based on the success rate model, a reasonable setting is $(M, D, S, U) = (2^{36.68}, 2^8, 2^6, 4)$ of unified rainbow table. The performance using 1 GTX680 GPU is shown in Table 6, where the total online time is decomposed to online computation time, false alarm removal time, and table lookup time. By utilizing 4, 8, and 16 114-bit known keystreams of different frames, the success rate is 33.8 %, 56 % and 81 %, in 9 s, 16.5 s, and 33 s, respectively. The experimental success rates perfectly match the theoretical predictions.

In order to increase the scale of unified tables, 3 additional unified tables are generated. The 4 unified tables differ in color configurations of the A5/1 function variations, in order to avoid the substantial collisions when increasing startpoints in a single unified table. Finally, four unified tables (0.961 TB, 0.093 TB, 0.093 TB, 0.140 TB, respectively) are generated in 75 days. Using 4 GTX680 GPUs in parallel, the success rate of finding the correct Kc based on the 1.29 TB unified rainbow tables is 43 % in 9 s, as shown in Table 7. The extrapolated results when increasing each unified table to 0.961 TB are also shown in Table 7. The success rate will increase to 56 % and 81 % based on 1.92 TB and 3.84 TB, using 2 and 4 unified rainbow tables, respectively, with the same online crack time. By extrapolating our results on four 0.96 TB tables and 8 keystreams, the success rate will be 96 %, but the online time will also increase to 16.5 s.

Table 7. Time and success rate using 4 keystreams and 4 unified tables

Table sizes	Time				Success rate
	DP comp	False alarm	Lookup	Online	
0.961+0.093+0.093+0.140=1.29 TB	5 s	4 s	2 s	9 s	43 %
0.961+0.961=1.922 TB	5 s	4 s	2.8 s	9 s	56 %
0.961+0.961+0.961+0.961=3.84 TB	5 s	4 s	4 s	9 s	81 %

According to Nohl [16], $129\,\text{GB} \times 30 = 3.78\,\text{TB}$ and 8 keystreams are used to achieve final success rate of 87 % in about 10 s. Their GPU device is AMD ATI5970, similar to our Nvidia GTX 690 in terms of total computation power. Considering that online cracking time has a constraint in practical operations and the availability of 8 known keystreams is limited in certain GSM modes, we only use 4 keystreams on unified rainbow tables. The success rate in this work will be 81 % in 9 s on 3.84 TB tables using 4 GPUs by extrapolation.

5   Conclusions and Future Work

This paper presents a study of statistical characteristics of A5/1 encryption algorithms of GSM and the rainbow table time-memory trade-off, and established an accurate link between the TMTO parameters and the success rate of the cracking procedure. The experiments show consistent performance with the theoretical model proposed in this paper. They show that the characteristics of the targeted cipher needs to be carefully analyzed when applying the TMTO techniques, instead of the general assumption as used in existing cryptanalysis. The proposed framework can be extended to practically breaking other ciphers using TMTO techniques in future.

A   Appendix

Refer to A5/1 algorithm flowchart in Fig. 1. Denote the clock-bits as $c_1 = R(8)$, $c_2 = R(29)$ and $c_3 = R(51)$, where $R(l)$ is the l-th bit of the initial state after the frame number Fn is mixed in Ks. The bits previous to them are $c_1' = IS(9)$, $c_2' = IS(30)$ and $c_3' = IS(52)$. When reversing one clock in LFSR registers in A5/1, the following six cases can occur [10]:

1 For any k, if $c_i' = c_j' \neq c_k' = c_k$, then the i-th and j-th LFSRs clocked;
2 For any k, if $c_i' = c_j' \neq c_k' \neq c_k$, then this state has no reverse clocking result;
3 If $c_i' = c_j' = c_k' = c_i = c_j = c_k$, then all the LFSRs clocked;
4 For any k, if $c_i' = c_j' = c_k' = c_i = c_j \neq c_k$, then there are 2 possibilities: the i-th and j-th LFSRs clocked, or all the LFSRs clocked;

5 For any i, if $c_i' = c_j' = c_k' = c_i \neq c_j = c_k$, then there are 3 possibilities: the i-th and j-th LFSRs clocked, or the i-th and k-th LFSRs clocked, or all the LFSRs clocked.

6 If $c_i' = c_j' = c_k' \neq c_i = c_j = c_k$, then there are 4 possibilities: every pair among the 3 LFSRs clocked or all the LFSRs clocked;

Table 8. Number of previous states (solutions) for reverse clocking

$\left(c_i' c_j' c_k'\right) \setminus (c_i c_j c_k)$	(000)	(001)	(010)	(011)	(100)	(101)	(110)	(111)
(000)	1	2	2	3	2	3	3	4
(001)	0	1	0	1	0	1	0	1
(010)	0	0	1	1	0	0	1	1
(011)	1	1	1	1	0	0	0	0
(100)	0	0	0	0	1	1	1	1
(101)	1	1	0	0	1	1	0	0
(110)	1	0	1	0	1	0	1	0
(111)	4	3	3	2	3	2	2	1

Suppose that c_1, c_2 and c_3 are randomly chosen under uniform distribution (which is the case keystreams are randomly chosen), then the number of the solutions for c_1', c_2' and c_3' follow a probability distribution: $P_1(0) = C_2^1 C_3^1 \left(\frac{1}{2}\right)^4 = \frac{3}{8}$, $P_1(1) = C_2^1 C_3^1 \left(\frac{1}{2}\right)^4 + C_2^1 \left(\frac{1}{2}\right)^6 = \frac{13}{32}$, $P_1(2) = C_2^1 C_3^1 \left(\frac{1}{2}\right)^6 = \frac{3}{32}$, $P_1(3) = C_2^1 C_3^1 \left(\frac{1}{2}\right)^6 = \frac{3}{32}$, $P_1(4) = C_2^1 \left(\frac{1}{2}\right)^6 = \frac{1}{32}$, where $P_1(k) = P(\#solution = k)$. When $c_1 = 0$, $c_2 = 1$, $c_3 = 1$ and $c_1' = 1$, $c_2' = 0$, $c_3' = 1$, it is easy to observe that this is an illegal state because of a contradiction when the majority clocking function is performed after the inverse clocking step is applied. The calculation is based on Table 8. After a solution is guessed in the current reverse clocking, (c_i, c_j, c_k) are replaced by (c_i', c_j', c_k'), and (c_i', c_j', c_k') are replaced by the previous bits (c_i'', c_j'', c_k''), where $c_1'' = IS(10)$, $c_2'' = IS(31)$ and $c_3'' = IS(53)$. This procedure repeats for every reverse clocking. When reversing one more clock, each pair among the 3 LFSRs in the abovementioned case 6 can produce 2 solutions, and the 3 LFSRs can produce 1 solutions, according to Table 8. Consequently, the 4-solution case grows to 7-solution case with a certain probability, and each reverse clock will constantly increase the maximum number of solutions by 3.

B Appendix

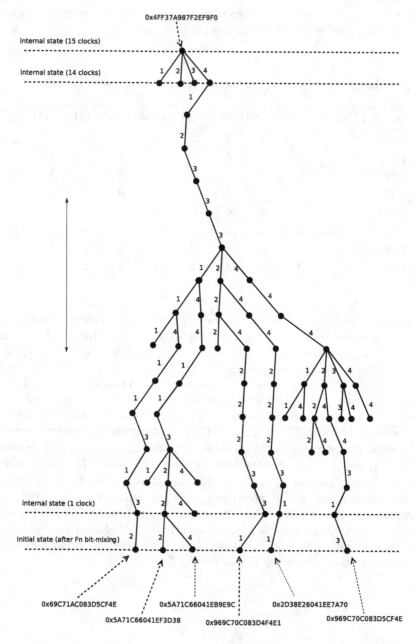

Fig. 5. An example of the paths of forward and backward clocking

References

1. Anderson, R.: A5 (was: Hacking digital phones). Newsgroup Communication (1994)
2. Avoine, G., Junod, P., Oechslin, P.: Characterization and improvement of time-memory trade-off based on perfect tables. ACM Trans. Inf. Syst. Secur. **11**(4), 17 (2008)
3. Barkan, E., Biham, E., Shamir, A.: Rigorous bounds on cryptanalytic time/memory tradeoffs. In: Dwork, C. (ed.) CRYPTO 2006. LNCS, vol. 4117, pp. 1–21. Springer, Heidelberg (2006)
4. Biham, E.: A fast new DES implementation in software. In: Biham, E. (ed.) FSE 1997. LNCS, vol. 1267, pp. 260–272. Springer, Heidelberg (1997)
5. Biham, E., Dunkelman, O.: Cryptanalysis of the A5/1 GSM stream cipher. In: Roy, B., Okamoto, E. (eds.) INDOCRYPT 2000. LNCS, vol. 1977, pp. 43–51. Springer, Heidelberg (2000)
6. Biryukov, A., Shamir, A., Wagner, D.: Real time cryptanalysis of A5/1 on a PC. In: Schneier, B. (ed.) FSE 2000. LNCS, vol. 1978, pp. 1–18. Springer, Heidelberg (2001)
7. Briceno, M., Goldberg, I., Wagner, D.: A pedagogical implementation of the GSM A5/1 and A5/2 'voice privacy' encryption algorithms (1999). www.scard.org/gsm/a51.html
8. Ekdahl, P., Johansson, T.: Another attack on A5/1. IEEE Trans. Inf. Theor. **49**(1), 284–289 (2003)
9. Gendrullis, T., Novotný, M., Rupp, A.: A real-world attack breaking A5/1 within hours. In: Oswald, E., Rohatgi, P. (eds.) CHES 2008. LNCS, vol. 5154, pp. 266–282. Springer, Heidelberg (2008)
10. Golić, J.D.: Cryptanalysis of alleged A5 stream cipher. In: Fumy, W. (ed.) EURO-CRYPT 1997. LNCS, vol. 1233, pp. 239–255. Springer, Heidelberg (1997)
11. Hellman, M.: A cryptanalytic time-memory trade-off. IEEE Trans. Inf. Theor. **26**(4), 401–406 (1980)
12. Keller, J., Seitz, B.: A hardware-based attack on the A5/1 stream cipher. In: ITG FACHBERICHT, pp. 155–158 (2001)
13. Kim, B.-I., Hong, J.: Analysis of the non-perfect table fuzzy rainbow tradeoff. In: Boyd, C., Simpson, L. (eds.) ACISP 2013. LNCS, vol. 7959, pp. 347–362. Springer, Heidelberg (2013)
14. Lu, J., Li, Z., Henricksen, M.: Time–memory trade-off attack on the GSM A5/1 stream cipher using commodity GPGPU. In: Malkin, T., et al. (eds.) ACNS 2015. LNCS, vol. 9092, pp. 350–369. Springer, Heidelberg (2015)
15. Ma, D., Hong, J.: Success probability of the Hellman trade-off. Inf. Process. Lett. **109**(7), 347–351 (2009)
16. Nohl, K.: Attacking phone privacy. In: BlackHat 2010 Lecture Notes USA (2010). https://srlabs.de/decrypting_gsm
17. Oechslin, P.: Making a Faster cryptanalytic time-memory trade-off. In: Boneh, D. (ed.) CRYPTO 2003. LNCS, vol. 2729, pp. 617–630. Springer, Heidelberg (2003)
18. Robling Denning, D.E.: Cryptography and Data Security. Addison-Wesley Longman Publishing Co., Inc., Boston (1982)
19. Sykes, E.R., Skoczen, W.: An improved parallel implementation of RainbowCrack using MPI. J. Comput. Sci. **5**(3), 536–541 (2014). Elsevier

New Observations on Piccolo Block Cipher

Yanfeng Wang[1,2,3]([✉]) and Wenling Wu[1,2,3]

[1] TCA, SKLCS, ISCAS, Beijing 100190, People's Republic of China
[2] State Key Laboratory of Cryptology,
P.O.Box 5159, Beijing 100878, People's Republic of China
[3] University of Chinese Academy of Sciences,
Beijing 100049, People's Republic of China
{wangyanfeng,wwl}@tca.iscas.ac.cn

Abstract. To reduce the cost in hardware, key schedules of lightweight block ciphers are usually simple and some even are direct linear transformations on master keys. Designers always add some asymmetry round-dependent constants to prevent the well-known slide attack. For linear key schedules, the choice of round constants becomes important but lacks principles. In this paper, we aim at evaluating the robustness of the key schedule algorithm and summarizing some design principles for simple key schedules. We define a special kind of weak keys named linear-reflection weak keys and their existence breaks the independence between different keys. For one weak key k, we can find another related weak key k' such that the decryption under k' can be linearly represented by the encryption under k. For a block cipher, the number of rounds that exhibits linear-reflection weak keys should be as small as possible. Besides, an automatic searching algorithm is designed to find weak keys for Piccolo ciphers. Results show that 7-round Piccolo-80 and 10-round Piccolo-128 both have many weak keys. Furthermore, we also find some special features for the key schedule of Piccolo-128. One of them is used to extract that the round permutation RP in Piccolo-128 should not be allowed to be self-inverse. Another is applied to show an efficient pseudo-preimage attack on hash function based on full-round Piccolo-128. The results do not threaten the application of Piccolo in secret-key setting but reveal the weakness of Piccolo-128's key schedule algorithm to some extent. We expect the results of our paper may guide the design of key schedules for block ciphers especially for the design of round constants for simple key schedules.

Keywords: Lightweight block cipher · Key schedule · Round constants · Piccolo · Hash function

1 Introduction

With the large development of communication and electronic applications, the low resource devices such as RFID tags and sensor nodes have been used in many aspects of our life such as access control, parking management, eHealth and so

© Springer International Publishing Switzerland 2016
K. Sako (Ed.): CT-RSA 2016, LNCS 9610, pp. 378–393, 2016.
DOI: 10.1007/978-3-319-29485-8_22

on. This kind of new cryptography environment is ubiquitous but constrained. Traditional block ciphers are not suitable for this extremely constrained environment. The new cipher should provide the best security possible while under tight constraints. New innovative and unconventional designs pose new challenges. For instance, to reduce the power consumption of the encryption algorithm, new lightweight block ciphers, such as KATAN & KTANTAN [1], Piccolo [2], PRINTcipher [3], LED [4] and Zorro [5] with very simple key-schedules or even without key-schedule, have been proposed.

Avoiding MITM (Meet-in-the-Middle) attacks [6–8], related-key differential attack [9] and key bits leakage [10] are three main goals in the design of key schedules. Designers tend to exploit relatively fast diffusion or avalanche to achieve these goals, which is infeasible for lightweight key schedules. The resistent to MITM attacks is usually claimed by ensuring that all master key bits are used within several rounds. Huang et al. proposed a measure called actual key information(AKI) to evaluate the effective speed of diffusing key bits and claimed that a computation path should have as high AKI as possible [11,12]. For related-key attack, designers usually search for the largest probability related-key differential trail or the minimum differential active s-boxes for a given cipher to illustrate the security against related-key attack [13]. Besides, a formulated necessary criterion for key schedule design is proposed to guide to avoid key bits leakage within a given number of rounds [12]. However, the choice of round constants makes no influence on the security of block ciphers against the above three attacks. That is to say, the security against them does not guide the design of round constants.

Slide cryptanalysis [14,15] is a well-known attack method on block ciphers and it utilizes the symmetry properties of the cipher to show a related-key attack. The condition for a block cipher to be vulnerable to the slide attack is that the sliding of all subkeys derived from a given key by one round (or eventually more) gives rise to a sequence or subkeys that can be derived from another key. To resist the slide attack, designers usually add some asymmetry round-dependent constants to the data input at each round to make the rounds different. At FSE 2014 [16], a probabilistic slide cryptanalysis is proposed and it takes advantage of the round constant differences to slide the partial function with a high probability. The slide and probability slide attacks both utilize the similarity properties to attack the ciphers. Differently, Leander et al. proposed a new attack technique named invariant subspace attack in Crypto 2011, which breaks the PRINTcipher in a practical setting [17]. As the following work, they presented a generic algorithm to detect invariant subspaces and improved the general understanding of invariant subspace [18]. Their attacks showed the existence of weak keys in some block ciphers, including Zorro block cipher. However, as mentioned by the authors, all attacks can be prevented by a careful choice of round constants, which reflects the significant role of round constants.

In this paper, we take the Piccolo block cipher as a target cipher to reveal some new design principles on round constants. For one key k, if there exists another related key k' such that the decryption with k' can be linearly determined by the encryption under k, then two keys k and k' are called linear-reflection weak keys. The linear-reflection property reveals that the key schedule algorithm is lack of robustness. We also design a specific algorithm to search weak keys for both Piccolo-80 and Piccolo-128. The searching results show that 7-round Piccolo-80 and 10-round Piccolo-128 both have linear-reflection weak keys. Besides, the searching algorithm can also be modified and extended to arbitrary given block cipher to check the existence of linear-reflection weak keys. Furthermore, we find some interesting characteristics on the key schedule algorithm of Piccolo-128. Generally speaking, there exist several key pairs (k and k') such that round keys under k' for 30 rounds among total 31 rounds are equal to that under k. Among them, two special features are respectively used to extract the design principle of encryption process and reveal the weakness of Piccolo-128 from the hash function respective. Firstly, if we replace the RP in Piccolo-128 by a self-inverse permutation RP', there exist 2^{32} weak keys for the full-round new cipher. They can be parted into 2^{31} pairs (k, k') such that the decryption under k' can be represented by a non-linear function of the encryption under k and the degree of the non-linear function is equal to the degree of F function in Piccolo. Secondly, we find an efficient pseudo-preimage attack on the hash function constructed from Piccolo-128 by using DM mode [19], which extracts the weakness of key schedule of Piccolo-128. We hope our analysis contributes some insight for the choice of round constants in cryptographic permutations.

This paper is organized as follows. Section 2 provides a detailed description of Piccolo. Section 3 describes the linear-reflection weak keys for Piccolo ciphers. Section 4 presents two observations on Piccolo-128. Finally, Sect. 5 concludes the whole paper.

2   Description of Piccolo

Piccolo is a 64-bit blockcipher supporting 80 and 128-bit keys. Two different key modes are referred as Piccolo-80 and Piccolo-128, respectively. Both ciphers consist of an encryption algorithm and a key schedule algorithm.

2.1   Encryption Algorithm

The general structure of Piccolo is a variant of Generalized Feistel Network, which is depicted in Fig. 1. The number of iterative rounds is 25 for Piccolo-80 and is 31 for Piccolo-128. Each round is made up of two functions $F : \{0,1\}^{16} \to \{0,1\}^{16}$ and one round permutation $RP : \{0,1\}^{64} \to \{0,1\}^{64}$. F consists of two S-box layers separated by a diffusion matrix M. RP divides a 64-bit input into eight bytes and then permutes them.

2.2   Key Schedule Algorithm

To reduce the cost of hardware and to decrease key set-up time, key schedules of Piccolo, denoted by KS_r^{80} and KS_r^{128}, are rather simple. Firstly, a series of

16-bit constants, con_i^{80} and con_i^{128}, are generated as follows:

$$\begin{cases} (con_{2i}^{80}||con_{2i+1}^{80}) \leftarrow (c_{i+1}||c_0||c_{i+1}||\{00\}_{(2)}||c_{i+1}||c_0||c_{i+1}) \oplus 0x0f1e2d3c \\ (con_{2i}^{128}||con_{2i+1}^{128}) \leftarrow (c_{i+1}||c_0||c_{i+1}||\{00\}_{(2)}||c_{i+1}||c_0||c_{i+1}) \oplus 0x6547a98b \end{cases}$$

where b denotes the bit length of a in $a_{(b)}$ and c_i is a 5-bit representation of i in binary, e.g., $c_{11} = \{01011\}_{(5)}$.

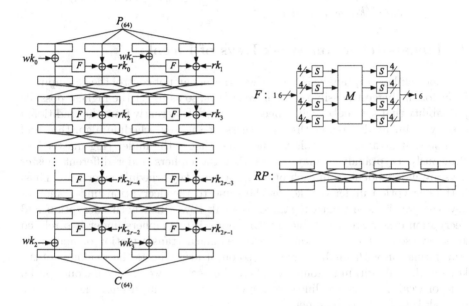

Fig. 1. Description of the block cipher Piccolo

Key Schedule for 80-Bit Key Mode: The key scheduling function divides an 80-bit master key $k_{(80)}$ into five 16-bit words k_i $(0 \leq i < 5)$ and provides the subkeys as follows:

Algorithm $KS_r^{80}(k_{(80)})$:
$wk_0 \leftarrow k_0^L|k_1^R, \; wk_1 \leftarrow k_1^L|k_0^R, \; wk_2 \leftarrow k_4^L|k_3^R, \; wk_3 \leftarrow k_3^L|k_4^R$
for $i \leftarrow 0$ to $(r-1)$ do

$$(rk_{2i}, rk_{2i+1}) \leftarrow (con_{2i}^{80}, con_{2i+1}^{80}) \oplus \begin{cases} (k_2, k_3) & \text{if } i \bmod 5 = 0 \text{ or } 2 \\ (k_0, k_1) & \text{if } i \bmod 5 = 1 \text{ or } 4 \\ (k_4, k_4) & \text{if } i \bmod 5 = 3 \end{cases}$$

The notations k_i^L and k_i^R stand for the left and right 8-bit values of k_i respectively.

Key Schedule for 128-Bit Key Mode: It divides the 128-bit master key $k_{(128)}$ into eight 16-bit words $k_i(0 \le i < 8)$ and provides subkeys as follows:

$$\text{Algorithm } KS_r^{128}(k_{(128)}):$$
$$wk_0 \leftarrow k_0^L | k_1^R, \ wk_1 \leftarrow k_1^L | k_0^R, \ wk_2 \leftarrow k_4^L | k_7^R, \ wk_3 \leftarrow k_7^L | k_4^R$$
$$\text{for } i \leftarrow 0 \text{ to } (2r-1) \text{ do}$$
$$\text{if } (i+2) \bmod 8 = 0 \text{ then}$$
$$(k_0, k_1, k_2, k_3, k_4, k_5, k_6, k_7) \leftarrow (k_2, k_1, k_6, k_7, k_0, k_3, k_4, k_5)$$
$$rk_i \leftarrow k_{(i+2) \bmod 8} \oplus con_i^{128}$$

3   Linear-Reflection Weak Keys of Piccolo

For block cipher cryptanalysis, since the attacker can not control the key input he looks for the biggest possible class of weak keys, so as to get the highest possible probability that a weak key will indeed be chosen. Differently from the traditional case, we aim at discussing the robustness of the key schedule algorithm and assume that attackers are able to know and choose the underlying master key. Previously, cryptanalysts may expect that the ciphers under different master keys are independent from each other for a good key schedule algorithm. Thus, if the encryption under one key is the same to the decryption under another key, the two keys are both regarded as weak keys when both encryption and decryption oracle are accessible. Furthermore, if two ciphers under two related keys have some simple relationship, such as linear transformation or non-linear transformation with small degree and so on, it also reflects the weakness of the key schedule algorithm to some extent. In this section, we first define one special kind of weak keys named linear-reflection weak keys and discuss the existence of weak keys for Piccolo cipher.

3.1   Definition of Weak Key

As mentioned above, if two ciphers under two related keys have linear relationship, then the keys may be regarded weak because the linear correlation breaks the rule of independence and only one key leakages the information for two related keys. If the linear relationship is built between both encryption ciphers or both decryption ciphers, it results a related-key differential trail with probability 1. In this paper, we default that the cipher is secure against related-key differential attacks and we focus on the cases for which the linear relationship is built between the encryption under one key and the decryption under another key. Thus, the weak keys are named linear-reflection weak keys and defined as follows:

Definition 1 (Weak Key). *Let k and k' are two different master keys of cipher E. Given arbitrary (P, C) with $C = E_k(P)$, we can obtain a corresponding pair (P', C') such that $C' = E_{k'}(P')$. Furthermore, $\{(P', C')\}$ is a linear transformation of $\{(P, C)\}$ and P' can be linearly represented by C while C' can be linearly represented by P. Then, the key k and k' are both linear-reflection weak keys.*

The fact that the encryption algorithm under some weak key is completely determined by the decryption under the related key reflects the weakness of the key schedule algorithm. If there exist linear-reflection weak keys for a given cipher, we can easily distinguish the cipher from random permutations in the chosen-key setting. Furthermore, the maximum number of rounds that exhibit weak keys should be as small as possible because the linear transformation implies a reflective differential trail with probability 1 and the number of rounds with non-random property can be extended based on the completely non-random part. Up to now, readers may wonder how to determine the maximum number of rounds that exhibit linear-reflection weak keys. We will take the Piccolo block cipher as an example to show the searching process. For convenience, we first describe the property of permutation RP used in Piccolo and use 4-round Piccolo to explain the condition for existing linear-reflection weak keys.

Observation 1 (Property of RP). *The permutation RP used in Piccolo has some relationships with its inverse RP^{-1}:*

1. *If the input of permutation RP is $X_{(64)}$ and the corresponding output is denoted by $(Y_{1(32)}, Y_{2(32)})$, then the output of RP^{-1} with the same input will be $(Y_{2(32)}, Y_{1(32)})$.*
2. *$RP^2 = (RP^{-1})^2 = (RP^2)^{-1}$. The fact reveals that RP^2 is self-inverse and the period of permutation RP is 4.*

Combining the property of RP with the variant of Generalized Feistel Network, we obtain some interesting results between the encryption and decryption of 4-round Piccolo block cipher (Fig. 2).

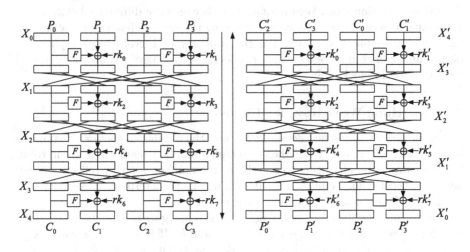

Fig. 2. Weak keys for 4-round Piccolo

Weak Key for 4-round Piccolo For 4-round Piccolo block cipher without whitening keys,

1. if there are two keys k and k' such that: $rk_0 = rk'_6, rk_1 = rk'_7, rk_2 = rk'_5, rk_3 = rk'_4, rk_4 = rk'_2, rk_5 = rk'_3, rk_6 = rk'_1, rk_7 = rk'_0$, then the keys k and k' are both linear-reflection weak keys. Meanwhile, an arbitrary plaintext-ciphertext pair (P, C) under key k results in a right pair $(C \ggg 32, P)$ under k'.
2. if there are two master keys k and k' such that $rk_2 = rk'_5, rk_3 = rk'_4, rk_4 = rk'_2, rk_5 = rk'_3$, then k and k' are also linear-reflection weak keys. Specifically, when (P, C) is a plaintext-ciphertext pair under key k, $((C \ggg 32) \oplus (0, \triangle_3, 0, \triangle_4), P \oplus (0, \triangle_1, 0, \triangle_2))$ is a plaintext-ciphertext pair under k', where $\triangle_1 = rk_0 \oplus rk'_6$, $\triangle_2 = rk_1 \oplus rk'_7$, $\triangle_3 = rk_7 \oplus rk'_0$ and $\triangle_4 = rk_6 \oplus rk'_1$.

Proof. The proof for above two cases are similar, we will describe the proof of the first one in detail and that of the second case in simple.

1. We input the same P to the encryption cipher with k and the decryption algorithm with k', the outputs of the first nonlinear function are the same value because $rk_0 = rk'_6$ and $rk_1 = rk'_7$. Meanwhile, $X_1 = (X'_1) \ggg 32$ because of the first property of Observation 1. Next, the equations $rk_2 = rk'_5$ and $rk_3 = rk'_4$, the same 16-bit F functions and the special RP result in $X_2 = X'_2$. Similarly, $X_3 = (X'_3) \ggg 32$ and $X_4 = (X'_4) \ggg 32$ are obtained due to the equations of round keys. Therefore, $(C \ggg 32, P)$ is a right plaintext-ciphertext pair under k' when P is encrypted to C under k.
2. Compared with the above case, the differences between the related keys for the first and last rounds are not restricted to be zero. We use the differences of plaintexts and ciphertexts to eliminate the influence of the non-zero differences and obtain the similar conclusion.   □

Note that if we add the pre- and post-whitening keys to the 4-round cipher, the linear-reflection weak keys remain weak because the difference between the whitening keys can also be canceled by adding the same difference to the related plaintext and ciphertext. To reveal the property of Piccolo block cipher, we design an algorithm to search linear-reflection weak keys for arbitrary round reduced Piccolo block cipher.

3.2   Searching Weak Keys for Piccolo

Given the specific key schedule algorithm and the number of rounds, we want to know if there are weak keys for the given cipher and how many there are in total. Thus, we design an algorithm to search out the number of linear-reflection weak keys for Piccolo block cipher. The algorithm can be described as Algorithm 1, where r, KS and n are all positive integers.

Firstly, process the corresponding key schedule algorithm for the given value of KS and two master keys are denoted by k and k'. If $KS = 80$, the round keys $rk_{\{0,1,\cdots,2r-1\}}$ are represented by five unknown 16-bit variables $k_{\{0,1,2,3,4\}}$ and determined constants $con^{80}_{\{0,1,\cdots,2r-1\}}$. Meanwhile, all $2r$ rk's are also described with $k'_{\{0,1,2,3,4\}}$ and constants. In total, there are 10 unknown 16-bit variables for Piccolo-80. Similarly, all round keys under k and k' for Piccolo-128 can be represented by 16 unknown variables $k_{\{0,1,\cdots,7\}}$ and $k'_{\{0,1,\cdots,7\}}$.

Secondly, construct the system of linear equations between corresponding rk and rk' to guarantee that the keys are linear-reflection weak keys. Avoiding the whitening keys and the first and last rounds, there are $2(r-2)$ equations for a r-round Piccolo cipher.

Finally, use the method of Gaussian Elimination to solve the linear equations and denote the dimension of solutions as n. As the size of each variable is 16-bit, thus the number of pairs of weak keys is 2^{16n}.

Algorithm 1. $SearchWK(r, KS)$

Require: Number of rounds r, key schedule algorithm KS
Ensure: Dimension of solutions n
1: **if** $(KS{=}80)$ **then**
2:     $KS_r^{80}(k_{80})$;
3:     $KS_r^{80}(k'_{80})$;
4:     Set the number of variables to 10: $lenC = 10$;
5: **else**
6:     $KS_r^{128}(k_{128})$;
7:     $KS_r^{128}(k'_{128})$;
8:     Set the number of variables to 16: $lenC = 16$;
9: **end if**
10: Set the number of equations: $lenR = 2 \times (r-2)$;
11: Construct the system of linear equations with $lenR$ equations and $lenC$ variables
12: **for** $(i = 1; i < r - 1; i++)$ **do**
13:     **if** $(i \bmod 2{=}0)$ **then**
14:         $rk_{2i} \oplus rk'_{2(r-1-i)} = 0$;
15:         $rk_{2i+1} \oplus rk'_{2(r-1-i)+1} = 0$;
16:     **else**
17:         $rk_{2i} \oplus rk'_{2(r-1-i)+1} = 0$;
18:         $rk_{2i+1} \oplus rk'_{2(r-1-i)} = 0$;
19:     **end if**
20: **end for**
21: Solve the system of linear equations using the Gaussian Elimination method and record the dimension of solutions as n
22: **return** n;

For completeness, we will show the specific linear relationships between two ciphers under the related weak keys k and k'. The influence of whitening keys is avoided due to the complex expression. To present the detailed correlation, we first assume that $(P_0, P_1, P_2, P_3) \xrightarrow{k} (C_0, C_1, C_2, C_3)$. The values of corresponding pair under the related key k' differ to the clarity of the number of rounds r.

1. For odd r, $(C_0, C_1, C_2, C_3) \oplus (0, \Delta_3, 0, \Delta_4) \xrightarrow{k'} (P_0, P_1, P_2, P_3) \oplus (0, \Delta_1, 0, \Delta_2)$, where $\Delta_1 = rk_0 \oplus rk'_{2(r-1)}$, $\Delta_2 = rk_1 \oplus rk'_{(2r-1)}$, $\Delta_3 = rk_{2(r-1)} \oplus rk'_0$ and $\Delta_4 = rk_{(2r-1)} \oplus rk'_1$.

2. For even r, $(C_0, C_1, C_2, C_3) \ggg 32 \oplus (0, \Delta_3, 0, \Delta_4) \xrightarrow{k'} (P_0, P_1, P_2, P_3) \oplus (0, \Delta_1, 0, \Delta_2)$, where $\Delta_1 = rk_0 \oplus rk'_{2(r-1)}$, $\Delta_2 = rk_1 \oplus rk'_{(2r-1)}$, $\Delta_3 = rk_{(2r-1)} \oplus rk'_0$ and $\Delta_4 = rk_{2(r-1)} \oplus rk'_1$.

The above algorithm can also be modified to search linear-reflection weak keys for some other ciphers and we can set the starting round be arbitrary internal round to find the maximum number of rounds that exhibit weak keys.

3.3 Weak Keys of Piccolo

After searching all possible reduced and starting rounds for both Piccolo-80 and Piccolo-128, we conclude two interesting results.

Observation 2. *There are 2^{49} linear-reflection weak keys for 6-round Piccolo-80 cipher. Besides, if we change the starting of cipher to the first round, there are 2^{49} weak keys for 7-round Piccolo-80.*

Proof. To illustrate the correctness of the above statement, we will show the process to find linear-reflection weak keys for 6-round original Piccolo-80 in detail. The detailed proof for the second conclusion is avoided due to the similar process. In the system of linear equations, the number of unknown variables is 10 and the number of linear equations is 8.

$$\begin{cases} k_0 \oplus k'_1 = 0x2623 \\ k_1 \oplus k'_0 = 0x022a \\ k_2 \oplus k'_4 = 0x380e \\ k_3 \oplus k'_4 = 0x1c07 \\ k_4 \oplus k'_3 = 0x0e29 \\ k_4 \oplus k'_2 = 0x2a20 \\ k_0 \oplus k'_0 = 0x380e \\ k_1 \oplus k'_1 = 0x1c07 \end{cases}$$

The dimension of solutions for the above system of linear equations is 3 and we denote the bases as x, y and z. Correspondingly, the 2^{48} pairs of master keys can be represented as $k = (x, x \oplus 0x3a24, y \oplus 0x380e, y \oplus 0x1c07, z)$ and $k' = (x \oplus 0x380e, x \oplus 0x2623, z \oplus 0x2a20, z \oplus 0x0e29, y)$. The number of whole weak keys is 2^{49} because $k \neq k'$ is always true. At the same time, if $P = (P_0, P_1, P_2, P_3)$ and $C = (C_0, C_1, C_2, C_3)$ is a right plaintext-ciphertext pair of 6-round Piccolo-80 under master key k, then (P', C') is the corresponding pair under the related key k', where

$$\begin{aligned} P' &= (C_2, C_3 \oplus k_3 \oplus 0x353a \oplus k'_2 \oplus 0x071c, C_0, C_1 \oplus k_2 \oplus 0x3f12 \oplus k'_3 \oplus 0x293d) \\ &= (C_2, C_3 \oplus y \oplus z \oplus 0x0401, C_0, C_1 \oplus y \oplus z \oplus 0x2008), \end{aligned}$$

$$\begin{aligned} C' &= (P_0, P_1 \oplus k_2 \oplus 0x071c \oplus k'_2 \oplus 0x3f12, P_2, P_3 \oplus k_3 \oplus 0x293d \oplus k'_3 \oplus 0x353a) \\ &= (P_0, P_1 \oplus y \oplus z \oplus 0x2a20, P_2, P_3 \oplus y \oplus z \oplus 0x0e29). \end{aligned}$$ $\square$

Observation 3. *There are 2^{17} weak keys for 10-round Piccolo-128 cipher.*

Proof. There are 16 unknown variables and 16 linear equations in the system of linear equations.

$$\begin{cases}
k_4 \oplus k'_5 = 0xf8c1 \\
k_5 \oplus k'_4 = 0x8cdc \\
k_6 \oplus k'_6 = 0x5816 \\
k_7 \oplus k'_1 = 0x2c0b \\
k_2 \oplus k'_5 = 0xf0c3 \\
k_1 \oplus k'_4 = 0xe4c6 \\
k_6 \oplus k'_0 = 0x1806 \\
k_7 \oplus k'_3 = 0x0c03 \\
k_0 \oplus k'_7 = 0xe8c5 \\
k_3 \oplus k'_6 = 0xfcc0 \\
k_4 \oplus k'_2 = 0x1806 \\
k_5 \oplus k'_1 = 0x0c03 \\
k_6 \oplus k'_7 = 0x80df \\
k_1 \oplus k'_6 = 0xf4c2 \\
k_4 \oplus k'_4 = 0x5816 \\
k_5 \oplus k'_5 = 0x2c0b
\end{cases}$$

The dimension of solutions for the system of linear equations is only 1 and the base is denoted by x. Correspondingly, $k = (x\oplus0x781e, x\oplus0xbcd0, x\oplus0x0802, x\oplus 0xb4d2, x, x\oplus0xd4ca, x\oplus0x1004, x\oplus0xf4c2)$ and $k' = (x\oplus0x0802, x\oplus0xd8c9, x\oplus 0x1806, x \oplus 0xf8c1, x \oplus 0x5816, x \oplus 0xf8c1, x \oplus 0x4812, x \oplus 0x90db)$. If $P = (P_0, P_1, P_2, P_3)$ and $C = (C_0, C_1, C_2, C_3)$ is a right plaintext-ciphertext pair of 10-round Piccolo-128 under master key k, then (P', C') is the corresponding pair under the related key k', where

$$P' = (C_2, C_3 \oplus k_7 \oplus 0x8181 \oplus k'_2 \oplus 0x6d45, C_0, C_1 \oplus k_2 \oplus 0x3553 \oplus k'_3 \oplus 0xad8a)$$
$$= (C_2, C_3, C_0, C_1 \oplus 0x681a),$$

$$C' = (P_0, P_1 \oplus k_2 \oplus 0x6d45 \oplus k'_2 \oplus 0x3553, P_2, P_3 \oplus k_3 \oplus 0xad8a \oplus k'_7 \oplus 0x8181)$$
$$= (P_0, P_1 \oplus 0x4812, P_2, P_3 \oplus 0x0802).$$

Note that the values of k and k' are always different and the length of the base x is 16-bit, the number of weak keys for 10-round Piccolo-128 is 2^{17}.   □

The existence of linear-reflection weak keys reflects the weakness of design of block ciphers obviously and the maximum number of rounds that exhibit weak keys should be as small as possible. This property should be evaluated for new designed block ciphers especially for ciphers with simple key schedules.

4   New Observations on Piccolo-128

In this section, we show two surprising observations on Piccolo-128 cipher and they are largely due to the property of key schedule algorithm.

Table 1. Property of key schedule of Piccolo-128

(Δ_0, Δ_1)	Permutation																														
	0	1	2	3	4	5	6	7	8	9	10	11	12	13	14	15	16	17	18	19	20	21	22	23	24	25	26	27	28	29	30
(0000,0000)	0	1	2	3	4	5	6	7	8	9	10	11	12	13	14	15	16	17	18	19	20	21	22	23	24	25	26	27	28	29	30
(1806,0c03)	1	0	*	6	5	4	3	10	9	8	7	14	13	12	11	18	17	16	15	22	21	20	19	26	25	24	23	30	29	28	27
(1004,0802)	2	*	0	5	6	3	4	9	10	7	8	13	14	11	12	17	18	15	16	21	22	19	20	25	26	23	24	29	30	27	28
(280a,1405)	3	6	5	0	*	2	1	12	11	14	13	8	7	10	9	20	19	22	21	16	15	18	17	28	27	30	29	24	23	26	25
(2008,1004)	4	5	6	*	0	1	2	11	12	13	14	7	8	9	10	19	20	21	22	15	16	17	18	27	28	29	30	23	24	25	26
(380c,1c07)	5	4	3	2	1	0	*	14	13	12	11	10	9	8	7	22	21	20	19	18	17	16	15	30	29	28	27	26	25	24	23
(300c,1806)	6	3	4	1	2	*	0	13	14	11	12	9	10	7	8	21	22	19	20	17	18	15	16	29	30	27	28	25	26	23	24
(4812,2409)	7	10	9	12	11	14	13	0	*	2	1	4	3	6	5	24	23	26	25	28	27	30	29	16	15	18	17	20	19	22	21
(4010,2008)	8	9	10	11	12	13	14	*	0	1	2	3	4	5	6	23	24	25	26	27	28	29	30	15	16	17	18	19	20	21	22
(5816,2c0b)	9	8	7	14	13	12	11	2	1	0	*	6	5	4	3	26	25	24	23	30	29	28	27	18	17	16	15	22	21	20	19
(5014,280a)	10	7	8	13	14	11	12	1	2	*	0	5	6	3	4	25	26	23	24	29	30	27	28	17	18	15	16	21	22	19	20
(681a,340d)	11	14	13	8	7	10	9	4	3	6	5	0	*	2	1	28	27	30	29	24	23	26	25	20	19	22	21	16	15	18	17
(6018,300c)	12	13	14	7	8	9	10	3	4	5	6	*	0	1	2	27	28	29	30	23	24	25	26	19	20	21	22	15	16	17	18
(781e,3c0f)	13	12	11	10	9	8	7	6	5	4	3	2	1	0	*	30	29	28	27	26	25	24	23	22	21	20	19	18	17	16	15
(701c,380e)	14	11	12	9	10	7	8	5	6	3	4	1	2	*	0	29	30	27	28	25	26	23	24	21	22	19	20	17	18	15	16
(8822,4411)	15	18	17	20	19	22	21	24	23	26	25	28	27	30	29	0	*	2	1	4	3	6	5	8	7	10	9	12	11	14	13
(8020,4010)	16	17	18	19	20	21	22	23	24	25	26	27	28	29	30	*	0	1	2	3	4	5	6	7	8	9	10	11	12	13	14
(9826,4c13)	17	16	15	22	21	20	19	26	25	24	23	30	29	28	27	2	1	0	*	6	5	4	3	10	9	8	7	14	13	12	11
(9024,4812)	18	15	16	21	22	19	20	25	26	23	24	29	30	27	28	1	2	*	0	5	6	3	4	9	10	7	8	13	14	11	12
(a82a,5415)	19	22	21	16	15	18	17	28	27	30	29	24	23	26	25	4	3	6	5	0	*	2	1	12	11	14	13	8	7	10	9
(a028,5014)	20	21	22	15	16	17	18	27	28	29	30	23	24	25	26	3	4	5	6	*	0	1	2	11	12	13	14	7	8	9	10
(b82e,5c17)	21	20	19	18	17	16	15	30	29	28	27	26	25	24	23	6	5	4	3	2	1	0	*	14	13	12	11	10	9	8	7
(b02c,5816)	22	19	20	17	18	15	16	29	30	27	28	25	26	23	24	5	6	3	4	1	2	*	0	13	14	11	12	9	10	7	8
(c832,6419)	23	26	25	28	27	30	29	16	15	18	17	20	19	22	21	8	7	10	9	12	11	14	13	0	*	2	1	4	3	6	5
(c030,6018)	24	25	26	27	28	29	30	15	16	17	18	19	20	21	22	7	8	9	10	11	12	13	14	*	0	1	2	3	4	5	6
(d836,6c1b)	25	24	23	30	29	28	27	18	17	16	15	22	21	20	19	10	9	8	7	14	13	12	11	2	1	0	*	6	5	4	3
(d034,681a)	26	23	24	29	30	27	28	17	18	15	16	21	22	19	20	9	10	7	8	13	14	11	12	1	2	*	0	5	6	3	4
(e83a,741d)	27	30	29	24	23	26	25	20	19	22	21	16	15	18	17	12	11	14	13	8	7	10	9	4	3	6	5	0	*	2	1
(e038,701c)	28	29	30	23	24	25	26	19	20	21	22	15	16	17	18	11	12	13	14	7	8	9	10	3	4	5	6	*	0	1	2
(f83e,7c1f)	29	28	27	26	25	24	23	22	21	20	19	18	17	16	15	14	13	12	11	10	9	8	7	6	5	4	3	2	1	0	*
(f03c,781e)	30	27	28	25	26	23	24	21	22	19	20	17	18	15	16	13	14	11	12	9	10	7	8	5	6	3	4	1	2	*	0

† *: the 32-bit key of the corresponding round i can not be obtained from the original round subkeys but the difference of subkey in i-th round under two different master keys is fixed to be (Δ_0, Δ_1).

† The values of differences shown in this table are all represented in hexadecimal

4.1   Property of Key Schedule of Piccolo-128

From the key schedule of Piccolo-128, we observe that rk_{2i} are only influenced by the even-th 16-bit blocks of the master key and rk_{2i+1} are only influenced by the odd-th blocks for all i. Thus, we fix the values of the even-th blocks of the master key including (k_0, k_2, k_4, k_6) to be $even_{(16)}$ and the values of the odd-th blocks (k_1, k_3, k_5, k_7) are fixed to be $odd_{(16)}$. For simplicity, the 128-bit master keys is also denoted by $(even, odd)$. Interestingly, for a fixed $(even, odd)$, there exist 31 different $(even', odd')$s such that the round keys for 30 rounds under $(even', odd')$ are equal to that under $(even, odd)$. The total number of rounds for Piccolo-128 is 31 and we use a permutation including 30 integers and one signal $'*'$ to present the corresponding relation, where $'*'$ means that the subkey is not equal to all 31 subkeys under $(even, odd)$. We denote the difference between $(even, odd)$ and $(even', odd')$ as $(\triangle_0, \triangle_1)$, and the relationships are described as Table 1.

We will take $(\triangle_0, \triangle_1) = (0x1806, 0x0c03)$ as an example to explain the specific meaningless of Table 1. We denote the original master key as $k = (even, odd)$, and the related key is $k' = (even', odd') = (even \oplus 0x1806, odd \oplus 0x0c03)$. As shown in the table, the permutation is $(1, 0, *, \cdots)$. The first two values mean that the 0-th round key under k' is equal to the 1-st round key under k and 1-st round key with k' is the 0-th round key with k. Beside, the position of the 2-nd round is filled with $'*'$. It is impossible to find a round key under k which is equal to the 2-nd round key under k'. However, the difference between two different 2-nd round keys under k and k' is equal to $(\triangle_0, \triangle_1) = (0x1806, 0x0c03)$.

4.2   Observations on Piccolo-128

We focus on two rows where the differences between two keys are respectively $(0x8020, 0x4010)$ and $(0xf83e, 0x7c1f)$. For $(0x8020, 0x4010)$, the round keys in the former continuous 15 rounds under the related key are equal to the keys in the last continuous 15 rounds under the original key. For $(0xf83e, 0x7c1f)$, the first 30 values in the corresponding permutation is a reverse order of $0 - 29$. Two interesting or surprising results are observed based on these two special cases.

Observation 4. *If we replace the RP in Piccolo-128 by a self-inverse permutation RP', there exists 2^{32} weak keys for the full round new cipher and they can be parted into 2^{31} pairs (k, k') such that the decryption under k' can be represented by a non-linear function of the encryption under k and the degree of the non-linear function is equal to the degree of F function in Piccolo.*

Proof. Note that the full-round cipher consists of all the whitening keys before and after the 31-round encryption. One of the weak key can be represented by $k = (e, o)$ and the related weak key is $k' = (e', o') = (e \oplus 0xf83e, o \oplus 0x7c1f)$. The relationship between the encryption under k and the decryption under k' is shown in Fig. 3.

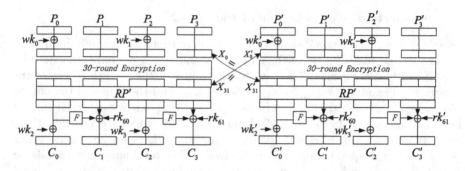

Fig. 3. Weak keys for modified Piccolo-128

Assume that (P, C) is a plaintext-ciphertext pair under (e, o) and the related plaintext-ciphertext pair under related key (e', o') is denoted by (P', C'). As shown in Table 1, the round keys of first 30 rounds under k' is the inverse order of round keys under k. Besides, the new round permutation RP' is self-inverse and the iterative structure of Piccolo cipher is the Generalized Feistel Structure. Thus, the encryption from X_0 to X_{31} is the same transformation as the decryption from X'_{31} to X'_0. To obtain the relationship between (P, C) and (P', C'), we try to guarantee that $X_0 = X'_{31}$ and $X_{31} = X'_0$ and obtain the following equations:

$P' = RP'(C_0 \oplus (e^L||o^R), F(C_0 \oplus (e^L||o^R)) \oplus C_1 \oplus e \oplus 0x9d79, C_2 \oplus (o^L||e^R), F(C_2 \oplus (o^L||e^R)) \oplus C_3 \oplus o \oplus 0xd594) \oplus (e'^L||o'^R, 0, o'^L||e'^R, 0),$

$C' = (P_0^* \oplus (e'^L||o'^R), F(P_0^* \oplus (e'^L||o'^R)) \oplus P_1^* \oplus e' \oplus 0x9d79, P_2^* \oplus (o'^L||e'^R), F(P_2^* \oplus (o'^L||e'^R)) \oplus P_3^* \oplus o' \oplus 0xd594),$

where $P^* = RP'((P_0, P_1, P_2, P_3) \oplus (e^L||o^R, 0, o^L||e^R, 0))$.

As a result, the set $\{(P', C')\}$ can be described as a non-linear transformation on set $\{(P, C)\}$ and the only non-linear function is the F function, which is a known permutation on $\{0, 1\}^{16}$. The low degree of F function results in an efficient distinguisher between full-round modified Piccolo-128 and random permutations in the chosen-key setting.   □

In summary, this simple non-linear relationship between two related ciphers also reflects the weakness of key schedule algorithm. Luckily, the round permutation RP used in Piccolo block cipher is not self-inverse. The fact may also reveal the design principle of the round permutation of RP from one aspect.

Observation 5. *The time complexity of pseudo-preimage attack on the hash function constructed from Piccolo-128 by using DM (Davies-Meyer) mode is less than the brute-force attack.*

Proof. DM (Davies-Meyer) is the most usual simple-length mode among all 12 secure PGV modes [19]. Let M_{i-1}, H_{i-1} and H_i be the input message block, the input chaining value, and the output, respectively. E denotes a block cipher,

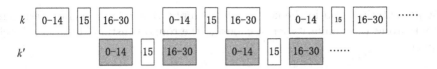

Fig. 4. Pseudo-preimage attack on hash function based on Piccolo-128

and E_K denotes its encryption algorithm with a key K. The new chaining value H_i under the DM mode is computed as:

$$H_i = E_{M_{i-1}}(H_{i-1}) \oplus H_{i-1}.$$

The target of pseudo-preimage attack is to find right (H_{i-1}, M_{i-1}) for arbitrary given H_i. We can see that the message M is regarded as the underlying key of the block cipher and it can be chosen and known. We mainly use the relationship between two master keys $k = (e, o)$ and $k' = (e', o') = (e \oplus 0x8020, o \oplus 0x4010)$ to show an efficient pseudo-preimage attack on the hash function based on the full-round Piccolo-128. The full-round cipher consists of all the whitening keys before and after the 31-round encryption. The main idea can be described as Fig. 4 and the time complexity of the attack is mainly computed based on the number of non-linear F functions.

Firstly, choose an arbitrary 64-bit value of H_{i-1} and encrypt it for 31 rounds under the key $k = (e, o)$. During the computation to the corresponding cipher-text, record the value of the internal state after 16 rounds because the xorring of the state and new pre-whitening key is chosen as the new input(H_{i-1}) to the next Piccolo-128 cipher under $k' = (e', o')$. If the difference $k \oplus k' = (0x8020, 0x4010)$, the computation of first 15 rounds under k' is the similar process as the previous last 15 rounds under k and the difference only occurs in the linear computation of the last round. The time for xorring with the whitening keys and processing the round permutation RP can be avoided because they are largely less than the time for computing the nonlinear F function. Thus, the computation for the first 15 rounds can be avoided which is denoted in gray. Similarly, the last 15 round encryption can also be reused for the next full-round computation. Let us focus on the example shown in Fig. 4, 5 (H_{i-1}, M_{i-1})s are tested to verify if they are the right pseudo-preimages. It only costs 3 full-round encryptions and two round encryptions to obtain the 5 candidates. If we want to obtain n candidates, it spends $(n/2+1)$ full-round encryptions and $(n/2-1)$ round encryptions, which is about $(n/2+1)$ full-round encryptions for large n. In average, there is one right solution among 2^{64} candidates. Thus, the time for finding one pseudo-preimage solution is about 2^{63} full-round encryption, which is half time of the brute force attack. □

The last observation reveals that the security of the hash function based on the full-round Piccolo-128 is insufficient. It also extracts some weakness of the key schedule algorithm of Piccolo-128 as it is a security evaluation in the chosen-key setting. This weakness can be avoided by changing the round constants or the permutation used in the key schedule simply. Generally speaking, designers should avoid this similarity when choosing the round constants for a new block cipher.

5   Conclusion

We have evaluated the security of Piccolo block cipher from the known and chosen key respective. To clarify the property of key schedule, we defined the linear-reflection weak keys. For one weak key k, we can find another related weak key k' such that the cipher with k' can be completely determined by the cipher under k. The existence of weak keys reveals that the key schedule algorithm is lack of independence and the maximum number of rounds that exhibit linear-reflection weak keys should be as small as possible. We also designed an algorithm to search linear-reflection weak keys for Piccolo ciphers. The results show that 7-round Piccolo-80 and 10-round Piccolo-128 both exist this kind of weak keys (Observation 2 and Observation 3). Furthermore, some interesting characteristics of key schedule algorithm for Piccolo-128 are summarized. Two of them are respectively used to extract the design principle of Piccolo block ciphers and reveal the weakness of Piccolo-128 from the hash function respective (Observation 4 and Observation 5). One is that the round permutation RP should not be allowed to be self-inverse. The other is that the security of hash function based on full-round Piccolo-128 is insufficient. It does not threaten the application of Piccolo-128 in secret-key setting but reveals the weakness of key schedule algorithm of Piccolo-128 to some extent.

We have evaluated the property of key schedule algorithm from a new specific aspect. In future, the similar method can also be applied to some other block ciphers with simple key schedules. We expect that the results of our paper may guide the design of round constants for some simple key schedules.

Acknowledgments. We would like to thank anonymous referees for their helpful comments and suggestions. The research presented in this paper is supported by the National Basic Research Program of China (No. 2013CB338002) and National Natural Science Foundation of China (No. 61272476, No.61232009 and No. 61202420).

References

1. De Cannière, C., Dunkelman, O., Knežević, M.: KATAN and KTANTAN — a family of small and efficient hardware-oriented block ciphers. In: Clavier, C., Gaj, K. (eds.) CHES 2009. LNCS, vol. 5747, pp. 272–288. Springer, Heidelberg (2009)
2. Shibutani, K., Isobe, T., Hiwatari, H., Mitsuda, A., Akishita, T., Shirai, T.: *Piccolo*: an ultra-lightweight blockcipher. In: Preneel, B., Takagi, T. (eds.) CHES 2011. LNCS, vol. 6917, pp. 342–357. Springer, Heidelberg (2011)
3. Knudsen, L., Leander, G., Poschmann, A., Robshaw, M.J.B.: PRINTCIPHER: a block cipher for IC-printing. In: Mangard, S., Standaert, F.-X. (eds.) CHES 2010. LNCS, vol. 6225, pp. 16–32. Springer, Heidelberg (2010)

4. Guo, J., Peyrin, T., Poschmann, A., Robshaw, M.: The LED block cipher. In: Preneel, B., Takagi, T. (eds.) CHES 2011. LNCS, vol. 6917, pp. 326–341. Springer, Heidelberg (2011)

5. Gérard, B., Grosso, V., Naya-Plasencia, M., Standaert, F.X.: Block ciphers that are easier to mask: how far can we go? In: Bertoni, G., Coron, J.S. (eds.) CHES 2013. LNCS, vol. 8086, pp. 383–399. Springer, Heidelberg (2013)

6. Isobe, T., Shibutani, K.: Security analysis of the lightweight block ciphers XTEA, LED and Piccolo. In: Susilo, W., Mu, Y., Seberry, J. (eds.) ACISP 2012. LNCS, vol. 7372, pp. 71–86. Springer, Heidelberg (2012)

7. Zhu, B., Gong, G.: Multidimensional meet-in-the-middle attack and its applications to KATAN32/48/64. Cryptogr. Commun. **6**(4), 313–333 (2014)

8. Derbez, P., Fouque, P.-A.: Exhausting Demirci-Selçuk meet-in-the-middle attacks against reduced-round AES. In: Moriai, S. (ed.) FSE 2013. LNCS, vol. 8424, pp. 541–560. Springer, Heidelberg (2014)

9. Biham, E.: New types of cryptanalytic attacks using related keys. J. Cryptol. **7**(4), 229–246 (1994)

10. May, L., Henricksen, M., Millan, W.L., Carter, G., Dawson, E.: Strengthening the key schedule of the AES. In: Batten, L.M., Seberry, J. (eds.) ACISP 2002. LNCS, vol. 2384, p. 226. Springer, Heidelberg (2002)

11. Huang, J., Lai, X.: Revisiting key schedule's diffusion in relation with round function's diffusion. Des. Codes Crypt. **73**(1), 85–103 (2014)

12. Huang, J., Vaudenay, S., Lai, X.: On the key schedule of lightweight block ciphers. In: Meler, W., Mukhopadhyay, D. (eds.) INDOCRYPT 2014. LNCS, vol. 8885, pp. 124–142. Springer, Heidelberg (2014)

13. Biryukov, A., Nikolić, I.: Automatic search for related-key differential characteristics in byte-oriented block ciphers: application to AES, Camellia, Khazad and others. In: Gilbert, H. (ed.) EUROCRYPT 2010. LNCS, vol. 6110, pp. 322–344. Springer, Heidelberg (2010)

14. Biryukov, A., Wagner, D.: Slide attacks. In: Knudsen, L.R. (ed.) FSE 1999. LNCS, vol. 1636, p. 245. Springer, Heidelberg (1999)

15. Biryukov, A., Wagner, D.: Advanced slide attacks. In: Preneel, B. (ed.) EUROCRYPT 2000. LNCS, vol. 1807, p. 589. Springer, Heidelberg (2000)

16. Soleimany, H.: Probabilistic slide cryptanalysis and its applications to LED-64 and Zorro. In: Cid, C., Rechberger, C. (eds.) FSE 2014. LNCS, vol. 8540, pp. 373–389. Springer, Heidelberg (2015)

17. Leander, G., Abdelraheem, M.A., AlKhzaimi, H., Zenner, E.: A cryptanalysis of PRINTCIPHER: the invariant subspace attack. In: Rogaway, P. (ed.) CRYPTO 2011. LNCS, vol. 6841, pp. 206–221. Springer, Heidelberg (2011)

18. Leander, G., Minaud, B., Rønjom, S.: A generic approach to invariant subspace attacks: cryptanalysis of Robin, iSCREAM and Zorro. In: Oswald, E., Fischlin, M. (eds.) EUROCRYPT 2015. LNCS, vol. 9056, pp. 254–283. Springer, Heidelberg (2015)

19. Preneel, B., Govaerts, R., Vandewalle, J.: Hash functions based on block ciphers: a synthetic approach. In: Stinson, D.R. (ed.) CRYPTO 1993. LNCS, vol. 773, pp. 368–378. Springer, Heidelberg (1994)

Message Authentication Code and PRF-Security

Replacing SHA-2 with SHA-3 Enhances Generic Security of HMAC

Yusuke Naito[1]([✉]) and Lei Wang[2]

[1] Mitsubishi Electric Corporation, Kanagawa, Japan
Naito.Yusuke@ce.MitsubishiElectric.co.jp
[2] Shanghai Jiao Tong University, Shanghai, China
wanglei@cs.sjtu.edu.cn

Abstract. In this paper, we study the MAC- and the PRF-security of HMAC in the sense of generic security when replacing SHA-2 with SHA-3. We first consider the generic security of the SHA-3-based HMAC construction: Sponge-based HMAC. We provide (nearly) tight upper-bounds on the MAC- and the PRF-security of Sponge-based HMAC, which are $O(\frac{nq}{2^n})$ and $O(\frac{q^2}{2^n})$, respectively. Here, q is the number of queries to HMAC and n is the output length of the hash function.

We then compare the MAC- and the PRF-security of Sponge-based HMAC with those of the SHA-2-based HMAC constructions: MD- (Merkle-Damgård) or ChopMD-based HMAC. It was proven that the upper-bounds on the MAC- and the PRF-security of MD-based HMAC are both $O(\frac{\ell q^2}{2^n})$, and those for ChopMD-based HMAC are both $O(\frac{q^2}{2^n} + \frac{\ell q^2}{2^{n+t}})$. Here, q is the number of queries to HMAC, ℓ is the maximum query length, n is the output length of the hash function, and t is the number of truncated bits in ChopMD. Hence, replacing SHA-2 with SHA-3 enhances the MAC-security of HMAC. Replacing SHA-2 having the MD construction with SHA-3 enhances the PRF-security of HMAC, and if $\ell > 2^t$ then replacing SHA-2 having the ChopMD construction with SHA-3 enhances the PRF-security of HMAC.

Keywords: HMAC · Replacing SHA-2 with SHA-3 · MD · ChopMD · Sponge · MAC-security · PRF-security

1 Introduction

HMAC [3] is a very popular message authentication code (MAC) that is based on a cryptographic hash function. It is standardized by NIST [18], IETF RFC [14], etc., and has been widely used, being implemented in various worldwide security protocols such as SSL, SSH, IPSec, TLS, etc. HMAC is used as a pseudo-random function (PRF) in addition to a MAC function. This is the case for example when used for key-derivation in TLS and IKE (the Internet Key Exchange protocol of IPSec). Hence HMAC is required to have MAC-security (unforgeability under chosen message attack) and PRF-security.

© Springer International Publishing Switzerland 2016
K. Sako (Ed.): CT-RSA 2016, LNCS 9610, pp. 397–412, 2016.
DOI: 10.1007/978-3-319-29485-8_23

Hereafter, we assume that hash functions have n-bit outputs and r-bit blocks. We then briefly explain the HMAC construction using a hash function H, where for an input m, the response HMAC(m) is defined as follows. If a secret key $K \in \{0,1\}^k$ is such that $k > r$ then refine $K \leftarrow H(K)$. Then, let K' be the padded key where the sufficiently many zeros are appended to the suffix of K to get a r bit string. Finally, compute the response as HMAC(m) := $H(K' \oplus \text{opad} \| H(K' \oplus \text{ipad} \| m))$, where ipad and opad are distinct r-bit constant values.

So far, hash functions with the Merkle-Damgård MD construction [9,17] or the ChopMD construction have been implemented as the underlying hash functions of HMAC. Especially, SHA-2 family [19] has been mainly implemented. The members of SHA-2 family are SHA-n ($n = 224, 256, 384, 512$) and SHA-$n/512$ ($n = 224, 256$), where SHA-n ($n = 256, 512$) use the MD construction, and SHA-n ($n = 224, 384$) and SHA-$n/512$ ($n = 224, 256$) use the ChopMD construction. MD is the construction of iterating a compression function with n-bit outputs, and ChopMD has the MD construction with output truncation. By t, we denote the number of the truncated bits. Namely, the output length of the compression function used in ChopMD is $n+t$ bits. It was proven that the upper-bounds on the PRF- and the MAC-security of MD-based HMAC (HMAC_MD) are both $O(\frac{\ell q^2}{2^n})$, and those for the ChopMD-based HMAC (HMAC_ChopMD) are both $O(\frac{q^2}{2^n} + \frac{\ell q^2}{2^{n+t}})$ [2,3,11].[1] Here, q is the total number of online queries (queries to HMAC), ℓ is the maximum number of message blocks by an online query. Note that these upper-bounds hold under the assumption that compression functions are PRFs.

Recently, variants of Keccak [6] were selected as the new hash function standard SHA-3, and they were standardized by NIST in FIPS202 [20], where the following sentences are written.

> Page 20: SHA3-224, SHA3-256, SHA3-384, and SHA3-512 are approved cryptographic hash functions. One of the approved uses of cryptographic hash functions occurs within the Keyed-Hash Message Authentication Code (HMAC).
> Page 24: The four SHA-3 hash functions are alternatives to the SHA-2 functions, ...

Hence, SHA-2 hash functions may be replaced with SHA-3 hash functions in the several systems. The standardization motivates us to study the MAC- and the PRF-security of HMAC corresponding with the replacement. In this paper, we first provide (nearly) tight upper-bounds on the MAC- and the PRF-security of the SHA-3 based HMAC construction in the sense of generic security. Namely, this paper considers the security of HMAC using the Sponge function [7]. By HMAC_Sponge, we denote Sponge-based HMAC. Then, by using the upper-bounds for HMAC_MD, HMAC_ChopMD, and HMAC_Sponge, we compare the MAC- and the PRF-security of HMAC-SHA-3 with those of HMAC-SHA-2.

---

[1] Although the proofs in [2,3,11] deal with only HMAC_MD, these can be applied to HMAC_ChopMD. Their proofs only depend on ℓ and the output length of a compression function. The upper-bounds for HMAC_ChopMD are obtained by adding the probability corresponding with the truncated output length.

PREVIOUS RESULTS OF HMAC_Sponge. The Sponge function is a permutation-based hash construction. By P, we denote the underlying permutation. We assume that the size of P is b bits with $b \geq r$. Then, for an input m, the output Sponge(m) is defined as follows. Firstly, the (padded) message is partitioned into r-bit message blocks $m_1, \ldots, m_l$, and let $s_0 \leftarrow 0^b$. Then, for $i = 1, \ldots, l$, compute $s_i \leftarrow P((m_i \| 0^c) \oplus s_{i-1})$. Finally return the first n bits of s_l as the output. Hereafter, we assume that $3n \leq b$ and $c \, (= b - r) = 2n$. Note that SHA-3 hash functions satisfy the conditions.

Sponge was designed with the goal of behaving as a random oracle (in the sense of indifferentiability [15]). It was proven that the upper-bound on the indifferentiability of Sponge is $O(\frac{\sigma^2}{2^c})$ [7] when P is a random permutation. Here, σ is the total number of P calls. Note that when the underlying hash function of HMAC is a random oracle, the upper-bounds on the MAC- and PRF-security of HMAC are both $O(\frac{q^2}{2^n})$ [2,3,10]. Hence, by combining these upper-bounds, we obtain the upper-bounds on the MAC- and PRF-security of HMAC_Sponge: $O(\frac{\sigma^2}{2^c} + \frac{q^2}{2^n})$. Here q is the number of online queries, ℓ is the maximum length of message blocks, Q is the number of offline queries (queries to P), and $\sigma = \ell q + Q$.[2]

However, these upper-bounds are not tight. For the lower-bound on the MAC-security, one can forge a tag by guessing a tag randomly, and thus the lower-bound is $\Omega(\frac{q}{2^n})$. For the lower-bound on the PRF-security, by using a collision in outputs of the "inner" function $H(K' \oplus \text{ipad} \| \cdot)$, one can distinguish HMAC from a random function, and thus the lower-bound is $\Omega(\frac{q^2}{2^n})$.

OUR RESULTS. In this paper, we give more strict upper-bounds on the MAC- and PRF-security of HMAC_Sponge. In Sects. 3, 4, and 5, we prove that the upper-bounds on the MAC- and the PRF-security are $O(\frac{\ell q Q + \ell^2 q^2}{2^b} + \frac{nQ}{2^{b-n}} + (\frac{qQ}{2^b})^{1/2} + \frac{nq}{2^n} + \frac{q}{2^n})$ and $O(\frac{\ell q Q + \ell^2 q^2}{2^b} + \frac{nQ}{2^{b-n}} + (\frac{qQ}{2^b})^{1/2} + \frac{q^2}{2^n})$, respectively. In SHA-3 hash functions, b is large enough ($b = 1600$) and $3n \leq b$. So it seems reasonable to suppose that $Q \leq 2^{b/2}$ and $\ell q \leq 2^{b/2}$.[3] Then the bounds on the MAC- and PRF-security become $O(\frac{nq}{2^n})$ and $O(\frac{q^2}{2^n})$, respectively. Hence, the upper-bound on the MAC-security is nearly tight, and that on the PRF-security is tight.

SHA-3 VS. SHA-2 FOR HMAC. In Table 1, we summarize the MAC- and the PRF-security of HMAC-SHA-3 and of HMAC-SHA-2 in the sense of generic security. The table compares q's such that the security bounds become constants.

SHA-3 family has SHA3-n ($n = 224, 256, 384, 512$). We put n's to the upper-bounds for HMAC_Sponge. Then the results are shown in the column for HMAC-SHA3-n, where the left (resp., right) side shows q's for the MAC-security (resp., the PRF-security). For SHA-2 family, the truncated bits of SHA-n ($n = 224, 384$) and SHA-$n/512$ ($n = 224, 256$) are $t = 32$, $t = 128$, $t = 288$, and $t = 256$,

---

[2] Note that for the sake of simplicity, we omit the discussion for the probability of recovering a secret key that is $O(\frac{Q}{2^k})$.

[3] Note that $|K'| = r$ holds. Hence one can recover K' with $Q \leq 2^r$. In the case of SHA3-512 ($c = 1024$, $r = 574$ and $n = 512$), $2^r \leq 2^{b/2}$ holds, thereby, in order to obtain the bounds, we require the assumption that $Q \leq 2^{574}$.

Table 1. Comparisons security of HMAC_Sponge with security of HMAC_MD and HMAC_ChopMD

Size	HMAC-SHA3-n		HMAC-SHA-n	HMAC-SHA-n/512
n	q (MAC)	q (PRF)	q (MAC,PRF)	q (MAC,PRF)
224	$2^{216.192...}$	2^{112}	$\min\{2^{112}, 2^{128}/\ell^{1/2}\}$	2^{112}
256	2^{248}	2^{128}	$2^{128}/\ell^{1/2}$	2^{128}
384	$2^{375.415...}$	2^{192}	$\min\{2^{192}, 2^{256}/\ell^{1/2}\}$	–
512	2^{503}	2^{256}	$2^{256}/\ell^{1/2}$	–

respectively. We put n's and t's of SHA-2 family to the upper-bounds for HMAC_MD $(O(\frac{\ell q^2}{2^n}))$ and HMAC_ChopMD $(O(\frac{q^2}{2^n} + \frac{\ell q^2}{2^{n+t}}))$. The results are shown in the columns for HMAC-SHA-n and HMAC-SHA-n/512. Since the upper-bounds on the MAC- and PRF-security are the same, we group q's of the MAC- and PRF-security together. Note that the exact values of q's for HMAC-SHA-224/512 and HMAC-SHA-256/512 are $\min\{2^{112}, 2^{256}/\ell^{1/2}\}$ and $\min\{2^{128}, 2^{256}/\ell^{1/2}\}$, respectively. In the table, we assume that $\ell \leq 2^{256}$.

From the table, when fixing the output length $n \in \{224, 256, 384, 512\}$, replacing the SHA-2 hash function with the SHA-3 hash function enhances the MAC-security of HMAC. For $n \in \{256, 512\}$, replacing SHA-n with SHA3-n enhances the PRF-security of HMAC. Replacing SHA-256 with SHA3-256 enhances the PRF-security of HMAC if $\ell > 2^{64}$, and does not otherwise. Replacing SHA-384 with SHA3-384 enhances the PRF-security of HMAC if $\ell > 2^{128}$, and does not otherwise. For $n \in \{224, 256\}$, replacing SHA-n/512 with SHA3-n does not enhance the PRF-security of HMAC.

Finally, we remark that the above discussion relies on the *known* upper-bounds for HMAC_MD and HMAC_ChopMD. The upper-bounds on the PRF-security of HMAC_MD and HMAC_ChopMD are tight, since a collision on internal states offers a distinguishing attack. The upper-bound on the MAC-security of HMAC_MD is also tight, since a collision on internal states of the *inner function* offers a forgery attack. On the other hand, the upper-bound on the MAC-security of HMAC_ChopMD may not be tight, since ChopMD has the wide size internal state which ensures that the collision probability in the internal states is smaller than the known upper-bound. We conjecture that our proof of HMAC_Sponge (Proof of Theorem 1) is applicable to HMAC_ChopMD, and thus the upper-bound on the MAC-security becomes $O(\frac{nq}{2^n} + \frac{\ell q^2}{2^{n+t}})$.

PREVIOUS WORKS FOR OTHER SHA-3 BASED MACs. Bertoni et al. [7] suggested the use of the keyed Sponge construction with the structure Sponge($K\|m$), which we denote by PrefixMAC. PrefixMAC calls Sponge one time, while HMAC calls it twice. Hence PrefixMAC is more efficient than HMAC_Sponge. At CRYPTO 2015, Gaži et al. [12] proved the tight upper-bound on the PRF-security of PrefixMAC, where the upper-bound is $O(\frac{q^2}{2^{b-d}} + \frac{Qq}{2^{b-n}})$, assuming $\ell q \leq 2^{b/2}$ and $Q \leq 2^{b/2}$. Since the PRF-security is carried over into the

MAC-security, the bound on the MAC-security is $O(\frac{q}{2^n} + \frac{q^2}{2^{b-n}} + \frac{Qq}{2^{b-n}})$. When $3n \leq b$, PrefixMAC has higher security than HMAC_Sponge. We note that our goal is to study the security of HMAC when replacing SHA-2 with SHA-3 and is not to study the advantage of HMAC_Sponge over PrefixMAC.

Several papers have studied the generic security proofs of keyed Sponge constructions [1,5,13,16], which consider the single-user or the multi-user settings (not related key setting). We note that HMAC uses related keys $K' \oplus$ ipad and $K' \oplus$ opad and these proofs don't cover the related key setting. Hence, these generic security proofs cannot be applied to HMAC_Sponge.

2 Preliminaries

Notation. For a bit string x of b bits, $x[i,j]$ is its substring between the left i-th bit to the left j-th one, where $1 \leq i \leq j \leq b$. For a finite set X, $x \xleftarrow{\$} X$ means that an element is randomly drawn from X and assigned to x. For a set X, let Perm(X) be the set of all permutations on X. For sets X and Y, let Func(X,Y) be the set of all functions: $X \to Y$.

Security Definitions. Through this paper, an adversary $\mathbf{A}$ is a computationally unbounded probabilistic algorithm. It is given query access to one or more oracles $\mathcal{O}$, denoted $\mathbf{A}^{\mathcal{O}}$. Its complexity is solely measured by the number of queries made to its oracles. Let $\mathcal{F}_K : \{0,1\}^* \to \{0,1\}^d$ be a keyed function based on a permutation having keys $K \in \{0,1\}^k$. Let $\mathcal{V}_K : \{0,1\}^* \times \{0,1\}^d \to \{\text{accept, reject}\}$ be a verification function. $\mathcal{V}_K(m, tag)$ returns accept if $\mathcal{F}_K(m) = tag$, and reject otherwise. The security proofs will be done in the ideal model, regarding the underlying permutation as a random permutation $\mathcal{P} \xleftarrow{\$} \text{Perm}(\{0,1\}^b)$. We denote by $\mathcal{P}^{-1}$ its inverse.

▶ Indistinguishability: In this paper, we use the security in terms of indistinguishability between the real world and the ideal world. Let $\mathcal{O}_R$ be the oracle in the real world, and let $\mathcal{O}_I$ be the oracle in the ideal world. The indistinguishability considers the case where an adversary $\mathbf{A}$ has query access to $(\mathcal{O}_R, \mathcal{P}, \mathcal{P}^{-1})$ in the real world and $(\mathcal{O}_I, \mathcal{P}, \mathcal{P}^{-1})$ in the ideal world, and after $\mathbf{A}$'s interaction, it outputs a result $y \in \{0,1\}$. We call queries to $\mathcal{O}_R/\mathcal{O}_I$ "online queries" and queries to $(\mathcal{P}, \mathcal{P}^{-1})$ "offline queries." We define the advantage function as

$$\mathbf{Adv}^{\text{ind}}_{\mathcal{O}_R,\mathcal{O}_I}(\mathbf{A}) := \Pr[\mathbf{A}^{\mathcal{O}_R,\mathcal{P},\mathcal{P}^{-1}} \Rightarrow 1] - \Pr[\mathbf{A}^{\mathcal{O}_I,\mathcal{P},\mathcal{P}^{-1}} \Rightarrow 1] .$$

▶ PRF-Security: The PRF-security of $\mathcal{F}_K$ is the indistinguishability between the real world and the ideal world, where $\mathcal{O}_R = \mathcal{F}_K$ for $K \xleftarrow{\$} \{0,1\}^k$ and $\mathcal{O}_I = \mathcal{R}$ for a random function $\mathcal{R} \xleftarrow{\$} \text{Func}(\{0,1\}^*, \{0,1\}^d)$. By q and Q, we denote the numbers of online queries and offline queries, respectively. We define the advantage function as

$$\mathbf{Adv}^{\text{prf}}_{\mathcal{F}_K}(\mathbf{A}) := \mathbf{Adv}^{\text{ind}}_{\mathcal{F}_K,\mathcal{R}}(\mathbf{A}) .$$

▶ MAC-Security: The standard MAC-security is unforgeability under chosen message attack. In this game, an adversary $\mathbf{A}$ has query access to $(\mathcal{F}_K, \mathcal{V}_K, \mathcal{P}, \mathcal{P}^{-1})$ for $K \xleftarrow{\$} \{0,1\}^k$ and $\mathcal{P} \xleftarrow{\$} \mathsf{Perm}(\{0,1\}^b)$. We call queries to $\mathcal{F}_K$ "MAC queries" and queries to $\mathcal{V}_K$ "verification queries." By q_M, q_V, and Q, we denote the numbers of MAC queries, verification queries, and queries to $\mathcal{P}$ and $\mathcal{P}^{-1}$, respectively. We let $q := q_M + q_V$. We define the advantage function as

$$\mathbf{Adv}^{mac}_{\mathcal{F}_K}(\mathbf{A}) = \Pr[\mathbf{A}^{\mathcal{F}_K, \mathcal{V}_K, \mathcal{P}, \mathcal{P}^{-1}} \text{ forges}]$$

where by "forges" we mean the event that $\mathcal{V}_K$ returns accept. We forbid $\mathbf{A}$ to make a trivial verification query (m, tag), where $\mathbf{A}$ already made m to $\mathcal{F}_K$ and obtained the response tag.

3   Specification of HMAC_Sponge and Security Results

In this section, we give the specification of the HMAC_Sponge construction, and show the security results for the MAC- and the PRF-security.

3.1   Specification of HMAC_Sponge

The Sponge function is a permutation-based one. We assume that the underlying permutation has b-bit blocks. Then the size of the internal states Sponge becomes b bits, where the first r bits ($0 < r \leq b$) are assigned to be the so-called rate bits and the remaining c ($= b - r$) bits are assigned to be the so-called capacity bits. Let $P \in \mathsf{Perm}(\{0,1\}^b)$ be the underlying permutation, and by Sponge^P we denote Sponge using P. In Sponge^P, by using the rate part, input message blocks are absorbed, and after message blocks are absorbed, output blocks are squeezed. In this paper, we assume that the output length of Sponge is n bits with $n \leq r$. Note that SHA-3 hash functions satisfy the condition $n \leq r$.

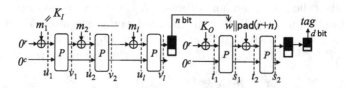

Fig. 1. The procedure of $\mathsf{HMAC\_Sponge}^P_K$ with $\ell_{\mathrm{out}} = 2$

Let HMAC_Sponge be the Sponge-based HMAC construction. We assume that the output length of HMAC_Sponge is d bits with $d \leq n$. By $\mathsf{HMAC\_Sponge}^P_K$, we denote HMAC using Sponge^P and having a key $K \in \{0,1\}^k$. For the sake of simplicity, we assume that $k \leq r$. For a message m, the response $\mathsf{HMAC\_Sponge}^P_K(m) = tag$ is defined as follows. Here, let $K_I := (K \| 0^{r-k}) \oplus \mathsf{ipad}$ be the inner key and

$K_O := (K\|0^{r-k}) \oplus$ opad the outer key where ipad and opad are distinct r-bit constant values, and let pad the padding function, where for a bit string x, pad($|x|$) is a bit string such that the bit length of $x\|$pad($|x|$) becomes a multiple of r and the last r bits are not zeros.

1. Partition $K_I\|m\|$pad($|K_I\|m|$) into r-bit blocks $m_1, m_2, \ldots, m_l$
2. $v_0 \leftarrow 0^b$; For $i = 1, \ldots, l$ do $u_i \leftarrow (m_i\|0^c) \oplus v_{i-1}$; $v_i \leftarrow P(u_i)$
3. $w \leftarrow v_l[1, n]$
4. Partition $K_O\|w\|$pad($|K_O\|w|$) into r-bit blocks $w_1, \ldots, w_{\ell_{out}}$
5. $s_0 \leftarrow 0^b$; For $i = 1, \ldots, \ell_{out}$ do $t_i \leftarrow (w_i\|0^c) \oplus s_{i-1}$; $s_i \leftarrow P(t_i)$
6. $tag \leftarrow s_{\ell_{out}}[1, d]$; Return tag

The Fig. 1 shows the HMAC_Sponge construction with $\ell_{out} = 2$. Thought this paper, assume that number of message blocks is at most $\ell_{in} - 1$ blocks, that is, $l \leq \ell_{in}$. We let $\ell := \ell_{in} + \ell_{out}$.

3.2 Security Results

The following theorem shows the MAC-security of HMAC_Sponge$_K^{\mathcal{P}}$ in the random permutation model, where $e = 2.71\ldots$ is the base of the natural logarithm.

Theorem 1. *Let* $\mathbf{A}$ *be an adversary. Then we have* $\mathbf{Adv}_{HMAC\_Sponge_K^{\mathcal{P}}}^{mac}(\mathbf{A})$

$$\leq \frac{2Q}{2^k} + \frac{4\ell qQ + 2\ell^2 q^2}{2^b} + \frac{2dQ}{2^{b-d}} + \left(\frac{16eqQ}{2^b}\right)^{1/2} + \frac{dq_V}{2^n} + \frac{q_V}{2^d} + \left(\frac{q_M}{2^{d-1}}\right)^d.$$

The following theorem shows the PRF-security of HMAC_Sponge$_K^{\mathcal{P}}$ in the random permutation model.

Theorem 2. *Let* $\mathbf{A}$ *be an adversary. Then we have* $\mathbf{Adv}_{HMAC\_Sponge_K^{\mathcal{P}}}^{prf}(\mathbf{A})$

$$\leq \frac{2Q}{2^k} + \frac{4\ell qQ + 2\ell^2 q^2}{2^b} + \frac{2dQ}{2^{b-d}} + \left(\frac{16eqQ}{2^b}\right)^{1/2} + \frac{q^2}{2^{n+1}}.$$

4   Proof of Theorem 1

This proof uses a function $\mathcal{H} := \mathcal{R}_O \circ \mathcal{R}_I$ where $\mathcal{R}_I \xleftarrow{\$} \mathsf{Func}(\{0,1\}^*, \{0,1\}^n)$ and $\mathcal{R}_O \xleftarrow{\$} \mathsf{Func}(\{0,1\}^*, \{0,1\}^d)$ are random functions. In the proof, firstly, we show that HMAC_Sponge$_K^{\mathcal{P}}$ is indistinguishable from $\mathcal{H}$ (Lemma 1). Secondly, we show that $\mathcal{H}$ is a secure MAC (Lemma 4). Finally, we combine the two results. Since the first result ensures that HMAC_Sponge$_K^{\mathcal{P}}$ behaves like $\mathcal{H}$, the second result is carried over into the MAC-security of HMAC_Sponge$_K^{\mathcal{P}}$. Hence, by Lemmas 1 and 4, we can conclude that HMAC_Sponge$_K^{\mathcal{P}}$ is a secure MAC.

Lemma 1. *Let* $\mathbf{A}$ *be an adversary. Then we have*

$$\mathbf{Adv}_{HMAC\_Sponge_K^{\mathcal{P}}, \mathcal{H}}^{ind} \leq \frac{2Q}{2^k} + \frac{4\ell qQ + 2\ell^2 q^2}{2^b} + \frac{2dQ}{2^{b-d}} + \left(\frac{16eqQ}{2^b}\right)^{1/2}.$$

Proof of Lemma 1. We prove Lemma 1 via four games. We denote these games by Game 1, Game 2, Game 3, and Game 4. In each game, $\mathbf{A}$ has query access to $(L_i, \mathcal{P}, \mathcal{P}^{-1})$ for $\mathcal{P} \xleftarrow{\$} \text{Perm}(\{0,1\}^b)$. We let $L_1 := \text{HMAC\_Sponge}_K^{\mathcal{P}}$ and $L_4 := \mathcal{H}$. Note that L_2 and L_3 will be defined later. For $i \in \{1,2,3,4\}$, we let $G_i := (L_i, \mathcal{P}, \mathcal{P}^{-1})$. Note that in each game, $\mathcal{P}$ is independently chosen. Then we have

$$\mathbf{Adv}_{\text{HMAC\_Sponge}_K^{\mathcal{P}}, \mathcal{H}}^{\text{ind}} = \sum_{i=1}^{3} \left(\Pr[\mathbf{A}^{G_i} \Rightarrow 1] - \Pr[\mathbf{A}^{G_{i+1}} \Rightarrow 1] \right) .$$

Hereafter, for $i \in \{1,2,3\}$ we upper-bound $\Pr[\mathbf{A}^{G_i} \Rightarrow 1] - \Pr[\mathbf{A}^{G_{i+1}} \Rightarrow 1]$.

For $\alpha \in \{1, \ldots, Q\}$, we denote an α-th offline query by x^α or y^α, and the response by y^α or x^α, where $y^\alpha = \mathcal{P}(x^\alpha)$ or $x^\alpha = \mathcal{P}^{-1}(y^\alpha)$. For $\alpha \in \{1, \ldots, q\}$, we denote an α-th online query by m^α and the response by tag^α. We also use superscripts for internal values e.g., v_2^1, u_2^1, etc.

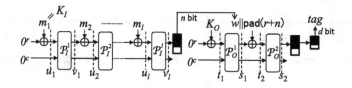

Fig. 2. The procedure of L_2

Upper-Bound of $\Pr[\mathbf{A}^{G_1} \Rightarrow 1] - \Pr[\mathbf{A}^{G_2} \Rightarrow 1]$. We start by defining L_2. Let $\mathcal{P}_I^1, \mathcal{P}_I^2, \ldots, \mathcal{P}_I^{\ell_{\text{in}}}, \mathcal{P}_O^1, \mathcal{P}_O^2, \ldots, \mathcal{P}_O^{\ell_{\text{out}}} \xleftarrow{\$} \text{Perm}(\{0,1\}^b)$ be random permutations. Let $K \xleftarrow{\$} \{0,1\}^k$ be a secret key. Let $K_I = (K\|0^{r-k}) \oplus \text{ipad}$ and $K_O = (K\|0^{r-k}) \oplus \text{opad}$. For a message $m \in \{0,1\}^*$, the response $L_2(m) = tag$ is defined as follows, and the Fig. 2 shows the procedure of L_2 with $\ell_{\text{out}} = 2$.

1. Partition $K_I\|m\|\text{pad}(|K_I\|m|)$ into r-bit blocks $m_1, m_2, \ldots, m_l$
2. $v_0 \leftarrow 0^b$; For $i = 1, \ldots, l$ do $u_i \leftarrow (m_i\|0^c) \oplus v_{i-1}$; $v_i \leftarrow \mathcal{P}_I^i(u_i)$
3. $w \leftarrow v_l[1, n]$
4. Partition $K_O\|w\|\text{pad}(|K_O\|w|)$ into r-bit blocks $w_1, \ldots, w_{\ell_{\text{out}}}$
5. $s_0 \leftarrow 0^b$; For $i = 1, \ldots, \ell_{\text{out}}$ do $t_i \leftarrow (w_i\|0^c) \oplus s_{i-1}$; $s_i \leftarrow \mathcal{P}_O^i(t_i)$
6. $tag \leftarrow s_{\ell_{\text{out}}}[1, d]$; Return tag

Transcript. Let $\tau_L = \{(m^1, tag^1), \ldots, (m^q, tag^q)\}$ be online query-response pairs and $\tau_{\mathcal{P}} = \{(x^1, y^1), \ldots, (x^Q, y^Q)\}$ be offline query-response pairs. Additionally we define the following sets. $\tau_I[1] := \{(u_1, v_1)\}$, $\tau_I[i] := \{(u_i^1, v_i^1), \ldots, (u_i^q, v_i^q)\}$ for $i \in \{2, \ldots, \ell_{\text{in}}\}$, $\tau_O[1] := \{(t_1, s_1)\}$, and $\tau_O[i] := \{(t_i^1, s_i^1), \ldots, (t_i^q, s_i^q)\}$ for $i \in \{2, \ldots, \ell_{\text{out}}\}$. We let $\tau_I = \bigcup_{i=1}^{\ell_{\text{in}}} \tau_I[i]$ be all input-output pairs in the inner function, and let $\tau_O = \bigcup_{i=1}^{\ell_{\text{out}}} \tau_O[i]$ all input-output pairs in the outer function. In this proof, $\mathbf{A}$ is permitted obtaining τ_I, τ_O, and K after $\mathbf{A}$'s interaction but before it outputs a result. Then $\mathbf{A}$'s interaction is summarized into the transcript $\tau = (K, \tau_L, \tau_I, \tau_O, \tau_P)$.

Let T_1 be the transcript in Game 1 obtained by sampling $K \xleftarrow{\$} \{0,1\}^k$ and $\mathcal{P} \xleftarrow{\$} \mathsf{Perm}(\{0,1\}^b)$. Let T_2 be the transcript in Game 2 obtained by sampling $K \xleftarrow{\$} \{0,1\}^k$ and $\mathcal{P}, \mathcal{P}_I^1, \ldots, \mathcal{P}_I^{\ell_{\mathrm{in}}}, \mathcal{P}_O^1, \ldots, \mathcal{P}_O^{\ell_{\mathrm{out}}} \xleftarrow{\$} \mathsf{Perm}(\{0,1\}^b)$. We call τ *valid* if an interaction with their oracles could render this transcript, namely, $\Pr[\mathsf{T}_i = \tau] > 0$. Then $\Pr[\mathbf{A}^{G_1} \Rightarrow 1] - \Pr[\mathbf{A}^{G_2} \Rightarrow 1]$ is upper-bounded by the statistical distance of transcripts, i.e.,

$$\Pr[\mathbf{A}^{G_1} \Rightarrow 1] - \Pr[\mathbf{A}^{G_2} \Rightarrow 1] \leq \mathsf{SD}(\mathsf{T}_1, \mathsf{T}_2) = \frac{1}{2} \sum_{\tau} |\Pr[\mathsf{T}_1 = \tau] - \Pr[\mathsf{T}_2 = \tau]|,$$

where the sum is over all valid transcripts.

H-coefficient Technique. We upper-bound the statistical distance by using H-coefficient technique [8,21]. In this technique, firstly, we need to partition the set of valid transcripts into good transcripts $\mathcal{T}_{\mathrm{good}}$ and bad transcripts $\mathcal{T}_{\mathrm{bad}}$. Then we can bound the statistical distance by the following lemma.

Lemma 2 (H-coefficient Technique). *Let* $0 \leq \varepsilon \leq 1$ *be such that for all* $\tau \in \mathcal{T}_{\mathrm{good}}$, $\frac{\Pr[\mathsf{T}_1 = \tau]}{\Pr[\mathsf{T}_2 = \tau]} \geq 1 - \varepsilon$. *Then,* $\mathsf{SD}(\mathsf{T}_1, \mathsf{T}_2) \leq \varepsilon + \Pr[\mathsf{T}_2 \in \mathcal{T}_{\mathrm{bad}}]$.

We refer the proof of the lemma to [8]. Hence, we can upper-bound the statistical distance by defining good and bad transcripts and evaluating ε and $\Pr[\mathsf{T}_2 \in \mathcal{T}_{\mathrm{bad}}]$.

Good and Bad Transcripts. We define $\mathcal{T}_{\mathrm{bad}}$ that satisfy one of the following conditions.

- $\mathsf{hit}_{\mathsf{ux,vy}}$: $\exists (u,v) \in \tau_I, (x,y) \in \tau_P$ s.t. $u = x \vee v = y$.
- $\mathsf{hit}_{\mathsf{tx,sy}}$: $\exists (t,s) \in \tau_O, (x,y) \in \tau_P$ s.t. $t = x \vee s = y$.
- $\mathsf{hit}_{\mathsf{ut}}$: $\exists (u,v) \in \tau_I, (t,s) \in \tau_O$ s.t. $u = t$.
- $\mathsf{hit}_{\mathsf{uu}}$: $\exists i,j \in \{1, \ldots, \ell_{\mathrm{in}}\}$ with $i \neq j$ s.t. $\exists (u_i, v_i) \in \tau_I[i], (u_j, v_j) \in \tau_I[j]$ s.t. $u_i = u_j$.
- $\mathsf{hit}_{\mathsf{tt}}$: $\exists i,j \in \{1, \ldots, \ell_{\mathrm{out}}\}$ with $i \neq j$ s.t. $\exists (t_i, s_i) \in \tau_O[i], (t_j, s_j) \in \tau_O[j]$ s.t. $t_i = t_j$.

Hence, in $\mathcal{T}_{\mathrm{bad}}$, these sets does not overlap each other. $\mathcal{T}_{\mathrm{good}}$ is defined such that the above conditions are not satisfied.

Upper-Bound of $\Pr[\mathbf{T}_2 \in \mathcal{T}_{\mathbf{bad}}]$. Note that the following inequation holds.

$$\Pr[\mathsf{T}_2 \in \mathcal{T}_{bad}] = \Pr[\mathsf{hit}_{\mathsf{ux,vy}} \vee \mathsf{hit}_{\mathsf{tx,sy}} \vee \mathsf{hit}_{\mathsf{ut}} \vee \mathsf{hit}_{\mathsf{uu}} \vee \mathsf{hit}_{\mathsf{tt}}]$$
$$\leq \Pr[\mathsf{hit}_{\mathsf{ux,vy}}] + \Pr[\mathsf{hit}_{\mathsf{tx,sy}}] + \Pr[\mathsf{hit}_{\mathsf{ut}}] + \Pr[\mathsf{hit}_{\mathsf{uu}}] + \Pr[\mathsf{hit}_{\mathsf{tt}}].$$

▶ We upper-bound $\Pr[\mathsf{hit}_{\mathsf{ux,vy}}]$. We note that $\mathsf{hit}_{\mathsf{ux,vy}}$ implies that $\exists \alpha \in \{1, \ldots, q\}, i \in \{1, \ldots, l^{\alpha}\}, \beta \in \{1, \ldots, Q\}$ s.t. $u_i^{\alpha} = x^{\beta} \vee v_i^{\alpha} = y^{\beta}$. We consider the following cases.

- $\mathsf{hit}_{\mathsf{ux,vy}} \wedge u_i^\alpha = x^\beta \wedge i = 1$: Since $u_1^\alpha = (K_I\|0^c) \oplus 0^b$, $K_I = (K\|0^{r-k}) \oplus \mathsf{ipad}$ and $K \xleftarrow{\$} \{0,1\}^k$, the probability that the case holds is at most $Q/2^k$.
- $\mathsf{hit}_{\mathsf{ux,vy}} \wedge u_i^\alpha = x^\beta \wedge i \neq 1$: Since $u_i^\alpha = (m_i^\alpha\|0^c) \oplus v_{i-1}^\alpha$ holds and v_{i-1}^α is randomly drawn from at least $2^b - q$ values, the probability that the case holds is at most $(\ell_{\mathsf{in}} - 1)q \times Q/(2^b - q)$.
- $\mathsf{hit}_{\mathsf{ux,vy}} \wedge v_i^\alpha = y^\beta$: Since v_i^α is randomly drawn from at least $2^b - q$ values in b bits, the probability that the case holds is at most $\ell_{\mathsf{in}}q \times Q/(2^b - q)$.

Hence we have

$$\Pr[\mathsf{hit}_{\mathsf{ux,vy}}] \leq \frac{Q}{2^k} + \frac{2(2\ell_{\mathsf{in}} - 1)qQ}{2^b}, \text{ assuming } q \leq 2^{b-1}.$$

▶ We upper-bound $\Pr[\mathsf{hit}_{\mathsf{tx,sy}}]$. First we define a ρ-multi-collision event which is defined as follows. Let $S := \bigcup_{\alpha=1}^q \{s_{\ell_{\mathsf{out}}}^\alpha\}$. Note that S does not include duplex elements.

- $\mathsf{mcoll} \Leftrightarrow \exists s^{(1)}, s^{(2)}, \dots, s^{(\rho)} \in S \text{ s.t. } s^{(1)}[1, d] = \dots = s^{(\rho)}[1, d]$,

where ρ is a free parameter which will be defined later. Then we have

$$\Pr[\mathsf{hit}_{\mathsf{tx,sy}}] \leq \Pr[\mathsf{mcoll}] + \Pr[\mathsf{hit}_{\mathsf{tx,sy}}|\neg\mathsf{mcoll}] .$$

We first upper-bound $\Pr[\mathsf{mcoll}]$. Since for all $s \in S$, s is randomly drawn from at least $2^b - q$ values, we have $\Pr[\mathsf{mcoll}] \leq 2^d \times \binom{q}{\rho} \times \left(\frac{2^{b-d}}{2^b - q}\right)^\rho \leq 2^d \times \left(\frac{2eq}{2^d \rho}\right)^\rho$, using Stirling's approximation ($x! \geq (x/e)^x$ for any x) and assuming $q \leq 2^{b-1}$.

We next upper-bound $\Pr[\mathsf{hit}_{\mathsf{tx,sy}}|\neg\mathsf{mcoll}]$. Note that $\mathsf{hit}_{\mathsf{tx,sy}}$ implies that $\exists \alpha \in \{1, \dots, q\}, i \in \{1, \dots, \ell_{\mathsf{out}}\}, \beta \in \{1, \dots, Q\} \text{ s.t. } t_i^\alpha = x^\beta \vee s_i^\alpha = y^\beta$. We consider the following cases.

- $\mathsf{hit}_{\mathsf{tx,sy}} \wedge t_i^\alpha = x^\beta \wedge i = 1$: Since $t_1^\alpha = (K_O\|0^c) \oplus 0^b$, $K_O = (K\|0^{r-k}) \oplus \mathsf{opad}$, and $K \xleftarrow{\$} \{0,1\}^k$, the probability that the case holds is at most $Q/2^k$.
- $\mathsf{hit}_{\mathsf{tx,sy}} \wedge t_i^\alpha = x^\beta \wedge i \neq 1$: Note that t_i^α has the form $t_i^\alpha = (w_i^\alpha\|0^c) \oplus s_{i-1}^\alpha$, where s_{i-1}^α is randomly drawn from at least $2^b - q$ values. Hence, the probability that the case holds is at most $(\ell_{\mathsf{out}} - 1)q \times Q/(2^b - q)$.
- $\mathsf{hit}_{\mathsf{tx,sy}} \wedge s_i^\alpha = y^\beta \wedge i \neq \ell_{\mathsf{out}}$: Since s_i^α is randomly drawn from at least $2^b - q$ values, the probability that the case holds is at most $(\ell_{\mathsf{out}} - 1)q \times Q/(2^b - q)$.
- $\mathsf{hit}_{\mathsf{tx,sy}} \wedge s_i^\alpha = y^\beta \wedge i = \ell_{\mathsf{out}}$: By $\neg\mathsf{mcoll}$, the number of elements whose first d bits are equal to $y^\beta[1, d]$ is at most ρ. Since $s_{\ell_{\mathsf{out}}}^\alpha$ is randomly drawn from at least $2^b - q$ values, the probability that the case holds is at most $Q \times \rho 2^d/(2^b - q)$.

Hence we have $\Pr[\mathsf{hit}_{\mathsf{tx,sy}}|\neg\mathsf{mcoll}] \leq \frac{Q}{2^k} + \frac{4(\ell_{\mathsf{out}}-1)qQ}{2^b} + \frac{2\rho Q}{2^{b-d}}$, assuming $q \leq 2^{b-1}$. We put $\rho = \max\left\{d, \left(\frac{2^{b-d}eq}{2^d Q}\right)^{1/2}\right\}$. Then we have

$$\Pr[\mathsf{hit}_{\mathsf{tx,sy}}] \leq \frac{Q}{2^k} + \frac{4(\ell_{\mathsf{out}} - 1)qQ}{2^b} + \frac{2dQ}{2^{b-d}} + \left(\frac{16eqQ}{2^b}\right)^{1/2} .$$

▶ We upper-bound $\Pr[\mathsf{hit}_{\mathsf{ut}}]$. Note that $\mathsf{hit}_{\mathsf{ut}}$ implies that $\exists \alpha, \beta \in \{1, \ldots, q\}$, $i \in \{1, \ldots, \ell_{\mathsf{in}}\}$, $j \in \{1, \ldots, \ell_{\mathsf{out}}\}$ s.t. $u_i^\alpha = t_j^\beta$. We consider the case $i = 1$. Note that in this case, $j \neq 1$ holds. Since t_j^β has the form $t_j^\beta = w_j \| 0^c \oplus s_{j-1}^\beta$ and s_{j-1}^β is randomly drawn from at least $2^b - q$ values, the probability that $u_1^\alpha = t_j^\beta$ holds is at most $(\ell_{\mathsf{out}} - 1)q/(2^b - q)$. Next we consider the case $i \neq 1$. Note that u_i^α has the form $u_i^\alpha = (m_i^\alpha \| 0^c) \oplus v_{i-1}^\alpha$, where v_{i-1}^α is randomly drawn from at least $2^b - q$ values. Hence, the probability that $u_i^\alpha = t_j^\beta$ holds is at most $(\ell_{\mathsf{in}} - 1)q \times \ell_{\mathsf{out}} q/(2^b - q)$. We thus have

$$\Pr[\mathsf{hit}_{\mathsf{ut}}] \leq \frac{2\ell_{\mathsf{in}}\ell_{\mathsf{out}}q^2}{2^b}, \text{ assuming } q \leq 2^{b-1}.$$

▶ We upper-bound $\Pr[\mathsf{hit}_{\mathsf{uu}}]$. Note that $\mathsf{hit}_{\mathsf{uu}}$ implies that $\exists i, j \in \{1, \ldots, \ell_{\mathsf{in}}\}$ with $i \neq j$ and $\exists \alpha, \beta \in \{1, \ldots, q\}$ s.t. $u_i^\alpha = u_j^\beta$. Without loss of generality, assume that $i \neq 1$. Note that u_i^α has the form $u_i^\alpha = (m_i^\alpha \| 0^c) \oplus v_{i-1}^\alpha$, where v_{i-1}^α is randomly drawn from at least $2^b - q$ values. Hence, we have

$$\Pr[\mathsf{hit}_{\mathsf{uu}}] \leq \binom{\ell_{\mathsf{in}}}{2} \times q^2 \times \frac{1}{2^b - q} \leq \frac{(\ell_{\mathsf{in}}q)^2}{2^b}, \text{ assuming } q \leq 2^{b-1}.$$

▶ We upper-bound $\Pr[\mathsf{hit}_{\mathsf{tt}}]$. Note that $\mathsf{hit}_{\mathsf{tt}}$ implies that $\exists i, j \in \{1, \ldots, \ell_{\mathsf{out}}\}$ with $i \neq j$ and $\exists \alpha, \beta \in \{1, \ldots, q\}$ s.t. $t_i^\alpha = t_j^\beta$. Without loss of generality, assume that $i \neq 1$. Note that t_i^α has the form $t_i^\alpha = (w_i^\alpha \| 0^c) \oplus s_{i-1}^\alpha$, where s_{i-1}^α is randomly drawn from at least $2^b - q$ values in b bits. Hence we have

$$\Pr[\mathsf{hit}_{\mathsf{tt}}] \leq \binom{\ell_{\mathsf{out}}}{2} \times q^2 \times \frac{1}{2^b - q} \leq \frac{(\ell_{\mathsf{out}}q)^2}{2^b}, \text{ assuming } q \leq 2^{b-1}.$$

▷ From the above bounds, we have

$$\Pr[\mathsf{T}_2 \in \mathcal{T}_{bad}] \leq \frac{2Q}{2^k} + \frac{4\ell qQ + \ell^2 q^2}{2^b} + \frac{2dQ}{2^{b-d}} + \left(\frac{16eqQ}{2^b}\right)^{1/2}.$$

Upper-Bound of ε. Let $\tau \in \mathcal{T}_{\mathsf{good}}$. For $i \in \{1, 2\}$, let all_i be the set of all oracles in Game i. For $i \in \{1, 2\}$, let $\mathsf{comp}_i(\tau)$ be the set of oracles compatible with τ in Game i. Then $\Pr[\mathsf{T}_1 = \tau] = \frac{|\mathsf{comp}_1(\tau)|}{|\mathsf{all}_1|}$ and $\Pr[\mathsf{T}_2 = \tau] = \frac{|\mathsf{comp}_2(\tau)|}{|\mathsf{all}_2|}$.

First we evaluate $|\mathsf{all}_1|$ and $|\mathsf{all}_2|$. Since $K \in \{0, 1\}^k$ and $\mathcal{P} \in \mathsf{Perm}(\{0, 1\}^b)$, we have $|\mathsf{all}_1| = 2^k \cdot 2^n!$. Since $K \in \{0, 1\}^k$ and $\mathcal{P}, \mathcal{P}_I^1, \ldots, \mathcal{P}_I^{\ell_{\mathsf{in}}}, \mathcal{P}_O^1, \ldots, \mathcal{P}_O^{\ell_{\mathsf{out}}} \in \mathsf{Perm}(\{0, 1\}^b)$, we have $|\mathsf{all}_2| = 2^k \cdot (2^n!)^{\ell_{\mathsf{in}} + \ell_{\mathsf{out}} + 1}$.

Next we evaluate $|\mathsf{comp}_1(\tau)|$. Let $\gamma_I[i]$ ($i = 1, \ldots, \ell_{\mathsf{in}}$) be the number of pairs in $\tau_I[i]$. Let $\gamma_O[i]$ ($i = 1, \ldots, \ell_{\mathsf{out}}$) be the number of pairs in $\tau_O[i]$. Let $\gamma_{\mathcal{P}}$ be the number of pairs in $\tau_{\mathcal{P}}$. Let $\gamma = \sum_{i=1}^{\ell_{\mathsf{in}}} \gamma_I[i] + \sum_{j=1}^{\ell_{\mathsf{out}}} \gamma_O[j] + \gamma_{\mathcal{P}}$. We note that $\mathcal{T}_{\mathsf{good}}$ is defined so that $\tau_I[1], \ldots, \tau_I[\ell_{\mathsf{in}}]$, $\tau_O[1], \ldots, \tau_O[\ell_{\mathsf{out}}]$, and $\tau_{\mathcal{P}}$ do not overlap with each other. Moreover, K is uniquely determined. Hence we have $|\mathsf{comp}_1(\tau)| = (2^n - \gamma)!$.

Finally we evaluate $|\text{comp}_2(\tau)|$. Here, $\gamma_I[i]$ $(i = 1, \ldots, \ell_{\text{in}})$, $\gamma_O[i]$ $(i = 1, \ldots, \ell_{\text{out}})$, $\gamma_{\mathcal{P}}$ and γ are analogously defined. Then we have

$$|\text{comp}_2(\tau)| = (2^n - \gamma_{\mathcal{P}})! \prod_{i=1}^{\ell_{\text{in}}} (2^n - \gamma_I[i])! \prod_{j=1}^{\ell_{\text{out}}} (2^n - \gamma_O[j])! \geq (2^n - \gamma)! (2^n!)^{\ell_{\text{in}} + \ell_{\text{out}}}$$

where we use the fact that $(2^n - a)! \cdot (2^n - b)! \geq (2^n - a - b)! \cdot 2^n!$ for any a, b.

Hence we have

$$\frac{\Pr[T_1 = \tau]}{\Pr[T_2 = \tau]} = \frac{|\text{comp}_1(\tau)|}{|\text{all}_1|} \cdot \frac{|\text{all}_2|}{|\text{comp}_2(\tau)|} \geq \frac{(2^n - \gamma)!}{2^k \cdot 2^n!} \cdot \frac{2^k \cdot (2^n!)^{\ell_{\text{in}} + \ell_{\text{out}} + 1}}{(2^n - \gamma)! \cdot (2^n!)^{\ell_{\text{in}} + \ell_{\text{out}}}} = 1.$$

We thus have $\varepsilon = 0$.

Bound of $\Pr[A^{G_1} \Rightarrow 1] - \Pr[A^{G_2} \Rightarrow 1]$. From the upper-bound of $\Pr[T_2 \in \mathcal{T}_{bad}]$ and ε, we have

$$\Pr[A^{G_1} \Rightarrow 1] - \Pr[A^{G_2} \Rightarrow 1] \leq \frac{2Q}{2^k} + \frac{4\ell q Q + \ell^2 q^2}{2^b} + \frac{2dQ}{2^{b-d}} + \left(\frac{16eqQ}{2^b}\right)^{1/2}.$$

Upper-Bound of $\Pr[A^{G_2} \Rightarrow 1] - \Pr[A^{G_3} \Rightarrow 1]$. We start by defining L_3. Let $\mathcal{G}_I^1, \ldots, \mathcal{G}_I^{\ell_{\text{in}}}, \mathcal{G}_O^1, \ldots, \mathcal{G}_O^{\ell_{\text{out}}} \xleftarrow{\$} \text{Func}(\{0,1\}^b, \{0,1\}^b)$ be random functions. L_3 has the same structure as L_2 except for the underling functions: for $i = 1, \ldots, \ell_{\text{in}}$, $\mathcal{P}_I^i$ is replaced with $\mathcal{G}_I^i$, and for $i = 1, \ldots, \ell_{\text{out}}$, $\mathcal{P}_O^i$ is replaced with $\mathcal{G}_O^i$. By PRF/PRP switching lemma [4], we have $\Pr[A^{G_2} \Rightarrow 1] - \Pr[A^{G_3} \Rightarrow 1] \leq \frac{\ell q^2}{2^{b+1}}$.

Upper-Bound of $\Pr[A^{G_3} \Rightarrow 1] - \Pr[A^{G_4} \Rightarrow 1]$. In Game 4, $L_4 = \mathcal{H}$, where $\mathcal{H} = \mathcal{R}_O \circ \mathcal{R}_I$. We show the following lemma.

Lemma 3. L_3 *and* L_4 *are indistinguishable unless the following conditions hold in Game 3.*

- $\text{coll}_I \Leftrightarrow \exists \alpha, \beta \in \{1, \ldots, q\}$ *with* $\alpha \neq \beta$ *s.t.* $l^\alpha = l^\beta$ *and* $u_{l^\alpha}^\alpha = u_{l^\beta}^\beta$.
- $\text{coll}_O \Leftrightarrow \exists \alpha, \beta \in \{1, \ldots, q\}$ *with* $\alpha \neq \beta$ *s.t.* $w^\alpha \neq w^\beta$ *and* $t_{\ell_{\text{out}}}^\alpha = t_{\ell_{\text{out}}}^\beta$.

Note that coll_I is the collision event in the last input blocks of the inner function. coll_O is the collision event in the last input blocks of the outer function.

Proof. We assume that $\text{coll}_I \vee \text{coll}_O$ does not hold. We consider the following cases.

- $\forall \alpha, \beta \in \{1, \ldots, q\}$ with $\alpha \neq \beta$ s.t. $w^\alpha \neq w^\beta$:
  Since coll_O does not hold, all inputs to $\mathcal{G}_O^{\ell_{\text{out}}}$ are fresh, thereby, all outputs of L_3 are randomly and independently chosen from $\{0,1\}^d$. Hence in this case, L_3 and L_4 are indistinguishable.
- $\exists \alpha, \beta \in \{1, \ldots, q\}$ with $\alpha \neq \beta$ s.t. $w^\alpha = w^\beta$:

If $l^\alpha \neq l^\beta$ holds, then since $\mathcal{G}_I^{l^\alpha}$ and $\mathcal{G}_I^{l^\beta}$ are independent random functions, the outputs $v_{l^\alpha}^\alpha$ and $v_{l^\beta}^\beta$ are randomly and independently drawn from $\{0,1\}^b$. If $l^\alpha = l^\beta$ holds, then since coll_I does not hold, the inputs to $\mathcal{G}_I^{l^\alpha}$, $u_{l^\alpha}^\alpha$ and $u_{l^\beta}^\beta$, are distinct, thereby, the outputs $v_{l^\alpha}^\alpha$ and $v_{l^\beta}^\beta$ are randomly and independently drawn from $\{0,1\}^b$. Hence in this case, L_3 and L_4 are indistinguishable.

From above discussions, L_3 and L_4 are indistinguishable unless $\mathsf{coll}_I \vee \mathsf{coll}_O$ does not hold. □

From the above lemma, $\Pr[\mathbf{A}^{G_3} \Rightarrow 1 | \neg(\mathsf{coll}_I \vee \mathsf{coll}_O)] = \Pr[\mathbf{A}^{G_4} \Rightarrow 1]$ holds. Hence we have

$$\Pr[\mathbf{A}^{G_3} \Rightarrow 1] - \Pr[\mathbf{A}^{G_4} \Rightarrow 1] \leq \Pr[\mathsf{coll}_I \vee \mathsf{coll}_O] \leq \Pr[\mathsf{coll}_I] + \Pr[\mathsf{coll}_O] \ .$$

We next upper-bound $\Pr[\mathsf{coll}_I]$. Since $\mathbf{A}$ makes no repeated query, coll_I implies that there exists $j \in \{2, \ldots, l^\alpha - 1\}$ such that $u_{l^\alpha - j}^\alpha \neq u_{l^\beta - j}^\beta$ and $u_{l^\alpha - j+1}^\alpha = u_{l^\beta - j+1}^\beta$, where $l^\alpha = l^\beta$. Note that for some b-bit block M^α, $u_{l^\alpha - j+1}^\alpha = v_{l^\alpha - j}^\alpha \oplus (M^\alpha \| 0^c)$ holds, and for some b-bit block M^β, $u_{l^\beta - j+1}^\beta = v_{l^\beta - j}^\alpha \oplus (M^\beta \| 0^c)$ holds. Since $u_{l^\alpha - j}^\alpha \neq u_{l^\beta - j}^\beta$ holds, $v_{l^\alpha - j}^\alpha$ and $v_{l^\beta - j}^\alpha$ are independently and randomly drawn from $\{0,1\}^b$. Hence we have $\Pr[\mathsf{coll}_I] \leq \binom{q}{2} \times \ell_{\mathrm{in}} \times \frac{1}{2^b} \leq \frac{\ell_{\mathrm{in}} q^2}{2^{b+1}}$.

We next upper-bound $\Pr[\mathsf{coll}_O]$. Since $w^\alpha \neq w^\beta$ and $t_{\ell_{\mathrm{out}}}^\alpha = t_{\ell_{\mathrm{out}}}^\beta$ hold, there exists $j \in \{2, \ldots, \ell_{\mathrm{out}} - 1\}$ such that $u_{\ell_{\mathrm{out}} - j}^\alpha \neq u_{\ell_{\mathrm{out}} - j}^\beta$ and $u_{\ell_{\mathrm{out}} - j+1}^\alpha = u_{\ell_{\mathrm{out}} - j+1}^\beta$. From the same analysis as $\Pr[\mathsf{coll}_I]$, we have $\Pr[\mathsf{coll}_O] \leq \binom{q}{2} \times \ell_{\mathrm{out}} \times \frac{1}{2^b} \leq \frac{\ell_{\mathrm{out}} q^2}{2^{b+1}}$.

Hence we have

$$\Pr[\mathbf{A}^{G_3} \Rightarrow 1] - \Pr[\mathbf{A}^{G_4} \Rightarrow 1] \leq \frac{\ell q^2}{2^{b+1}} \ .$$

Upper-Bound of the Advantage. Finally, the sum of the above bounds offers the following upper-bound.

$$\mathbf{Adv}_{\mathsf{HMAC\_Sponge}_K^{\mathcal{P}}, \mathcal{H}}^{\mathrm{ind}} \leq \frac{2Q}{2^k} + \frac{4\ell q Q + 2\ell^2 q^2}{2^b} + \frac{2dQ}{2^{b-d}} + \left(\frac{16 e q Q}{2^b} \right)^{1/2} \ .$$

□

Lemma 4. *Let $\mathbf{A}$ be an adversary which interacts with $(\mathcal{H}, \mathcal{V})$. We have*

$$\mathbf{Adv}_{\mathcal{H}}^{\mathrm{mac}}(\mathbf{A}) \leq \frac{d q_V}{2^n} + \frac{q_V}{2^d} + \left(\frac{q_M}{2^{d-1}} \right)^d \ .$$

Proof of Lemma 4. We first define the following conditions. Here $\mathcal{T}$ is the set of query-response pairs by MAC queries.

- forge $\Leftrightarrow$ $\mathbf{A}$ makes a verification query (m, tag) s.t. accept is returned,
- mcoll $\Leftrightarrow$ $\exists (m_1, tag_1), \ldots, (m_\xi, tag_\xi) \in \mathcal{T}$ s.t. $tag_1 = \cdots = tag_\xi$

where ξ is a free parameter which will be defined later. Then we have

$$\Pr[\text{forge}] \leq \Pr[\text{forge} \wedge \neg\text{mcoll}] + \Pr[\text{mcoll}] .$$

▶We first upper-bound $\Pr[\text{forge} \wedge \neg\text{mcoll}]$. Fix $\rho \in \{1, \ldots, q_V\}$. Let forge^ρ be an event that forge holds at the ρ-th verification query. Let (m^ρ, tag^ρ) be the ρ-th verification query-response pair. Let $\mathcal{T}^\rho$ be the set $\mathcal{T}$ before the ρ-th query. We define a collision condition

$$\text{coll}^\rho \Leftrightarrow \exists (m, tag) \in \mathcal{T}^\rho \text{ s.t. } \mathcal{R}_I(m) = \mathcal{R}_I(m^\rho).$$

Then we have

$$\Pr[\text{forge}^\rho \wedge \neg\text{mcoll}] \leq \Pr[\text{forge}^\rho \wedge \neg\text{mcoll} \wedge \neg\text{coll}^\rho] + \Pr[\text{forge}^\rho \wedge \neg\text{mcoll} \wedge \text{coll}^\rho]$$
$$\leq \Pr[\text{forge}^\rho | \neg\text{coll}^\rho] + \Pr[\text{forge}^\rho \wedge \text{coll}^\rho | \neg\text{mcoll}]$$

We upper-bound $\Pr[\text{forge}^\rho | \neg\text{coll}^\rho]$. Since $\forall (m, tag) \in \mathcal{T}^\rho: \mathcal{R}_I(m) \neq \mathcal{R}_I(m^\rho)$ holds due to $\neg\text{coll}^\rho$, $\mathcal{H}(m^\rho)$ is randomly drawn from $\{0,1\}^d$ and is independent of $\mathcal{T}^\rho$. Thus we have $\Pr[\text{forge}^\rho | \neg\text{coll}^\rho] \leq 1/2^d$.

We upper-bound $\Pr[\text{forge}^\rho \wedge \text{coll}^\rho | \neg\text{mcoll}]$. We note that $\text{forge}^\rho \wedge \text{coll}^\rho$ implies that

$$\big(\mathcal{H}(m^\rho) = tag^\rho\big) \wedge \big(\exists (m, tag) \in \mathcal{T}^\rho \text{ s.t. } \mathcal{R}_I(m) = \mathcal{R}_I(m^\rho)\big).$$

In this case, $tag = tag^\rho$ holds. Since $\mathcal{R}_I(m^\rho)$ is randomly drawn from $\{0,1\}^n$, the probability that $\exists (m, tag) \in \mathcal{T}^\rho$ s.t. $\mathcal{R}_I(m) = \mathcal{R}_I(m^\rho)$ is at most $\rho/2^n$. Since $\mathcal{R}_I(m)$ is enveloped by $\mathcal{R}_O$, $\mathbf{A}$ cannot find $\mathcal{R}_I(m)$. Thus, $\mathbf{A}$ must choose tag^ρ such that $tag = tag^\rho$ without knowing the equality. By $\neg\text{mcoll}$, the number of tags in $\mathcal{T}^\rho$ is at least ρ/ξ, thereby the probability that $tag = tag^\rho$ is at most ξ/ρ. Hence we have $\Pr[\text{forge}^\rho \wedge \text{coll}^\rho | \neg\text{mcoll}] \leq \rho/2^n \times \xi/\rho = \xi/2^n$.

We thus have

$$\Pr[\text{forge} \wedge \neg\text{mcoll}] \leq \sum_{\rho=1}^{q_V} \Pr[\text{forge}^\rho \wedge \neg\text{mcoll}] \leq \sum_{\rho=1}^{q_V} \left(\frac{1}{2^d} + \frac{\xi}{2^n}\right) \leq \frac{q_V}{2^d} + \frac{\xi q_V}{2^n} .$$

▶We next upper-bound $\Pr[\text{mcoll}]$. Fix a value $tag \in \{0,1\}^d$. Then the probability that for distinct ξ values $m_1, \ldots, m_\xi$, $\mathcal{H}(m_1) = \cdots = \mathcal{H}(m_\xi) = tag$ holds is at most

$$\frac{1}{2^d} \times \left(\frac{1}{2^d} + \frac{1}{2^n}\right) \times \left(\frac{1}{2^d} + \frac{2}{2^n}\right) \times \cdots \times \left(\frac{1}{2^d} + \frac{\xi-1}{2^n}\right) \leq \frac{\xi!}{(2^d)^\xi}.$$

Since $tag \in \{0,1\}^d$ and the number of mac queries is at most q_M, we have

$$\Pr[\text{mcoll}] \leq 2^d \cdot \binom{q_M}{\xi} \cdot \frac{\xi!}{(2^d)^\xi} \leq 2^d \cdot \left(\frac{q_M}{2^d}\right)^\xi, \text{ using Stirling's approximation.}$$

▷Finally, we put $\xi := d$. Then we have

$$\mathbf{Adv}_{\mathcal{H}}^{\text{mac}}(\mathbf{A}) = \Pr[\text{forge}] \leq \frac{dq_V}{2^n} + \frac{q_V}{2^d} + \left(\frac{q_M}{2^{d-1}}\right)^d. \qquad \square$$

Finally, by combining Lemma 4 with Lemma 1, we have $\mathbf{Adv}^{mac}_{\mathtt{HMAC\_Sponge}^{\mathcal{P}}_K}(\mathbf{A})$

$$\leq \frac{2Q}{2^k} + \frac{4\ell qQ + 2\ell^2 q^2}{2^b} + \frac{2dQ}{2^{b-d}} + \left(\frac{16eqQ}{2^b}\right)^{1/2} + \frac{dq_V}{2^n} + \frac{q_V}{2^d} + \left(\frac{q_M}{2^{d-1}}\right)^d. \quad \Box$$

5 Proof of Theorem 2

As the proof of Theorem 1, the proof uses a function $\mathcal{H} = \mathcal{R}_O \circ \mathcal{R}_I$, where $\mathcal{R}_I \xleftarrow{\$}$ Func$(\{0,1\}^*, \{0,1\}^n)$ and $\mathcal{R}_O \xleftarrow{\$}$ Func$(\{0,1\}^*, \{0,1\}^d)$ are random functions. In this proof, firstly, we prove that $\mathcal{H}$ is a PRF (Lemma 5). We then combine Lemma 1 with Lemma 5. Since Lemma 1 ensures that $\mathtt{HMAC\_Sponge}^{\mathcal{P}}_K$ behaves like $\mathcal{H}$, Lemma 5 is carried over into the PRF-security of $\mathtt{HMAC\_Sponge}^{\mathcal{P}}_K$. Then we can conclude that $\mathtt{HMAC\_Sponge}^{\mathcal{P}}_K$ is a secure PRF.

Lemma 5. *Let $\mathbf{A}$ be an adversary. Then we have* $\mathbf{Adv}^{prf}_{\mathcal{H}}(\mathbf{A}) \leq \frac{q^2}{2^{n+1}}$.

Proof. Let coll_I be an event that a collision occurs on outputs of $\mathcal{R}_I$. For any query, the output is randomly drawn from $\{0,1\}^d$ as long as $\mathsf{coll}_I = \mathsf{false}$. Hence $\Pr[\mathbf{A}^{\mathcal{H},\mathcal{P},\mathcal{P}^{-1}} \Rightarrow 1|\neg\mathsf{coll}_I] = \Pr[\mathbf{A}^{\mathcal{R},\mathcal{P},\mathcal{P}^{-1}} \Rightarrow 1]$ holds. We thus have $\mathbf{Adv}^{prf}_{\mathcal{H}}(\mathbf{A}) \leq \Pr[\mathsf{coll}_I]$. By the birthday analysis, we have $\Pr[\mathsf{coll}_I] \leq q^2/2^{n+1}$. $\Box$

We combine Lemma 5 with Lemma 1. Then we have $\mathbf{Adv}^{prf}_{\mathtt{HMAC\_Sponge}^{\mathcal{P}}_K}(\mathbf{A})$

$$\leq \frac{2Q}{2^k} + \frac{4\ell qQ + 2\ell^2 q^2}{2^b} + \frac{2dQ}{2^{b-d}} + \left(\frac{16eqQ}{2^b}\right)^{1/2} + \frac{q^2}{2^{n+1}}.$$

$\Box$

Acknowledgements. Lei Wang is supported by Major State Basic Research Development Program (973 Plan) (2013CB338004), National Natural Science Foundation of China (61472250), Innovation Plan of Science and Technology of Shanghai (14511100300), Doctoral Fund of Ministry of Education of China (20120073110094), and National Natural Science Foundation of China (NO. 61402288).

References

1. Andreeva, E., Daemen, J., Mennink, B., Van Assche, G.: Security of keyed sponge constructions using a modular proof approach. In: Leander, G. (ed.) FSE 2015. LNCS, vol. 9054, pp. 364–384. Springer, Heidelberg (2015)
2. Bellare, M.: New proofs for NMAC and HMAC: security without collision-resistance. In: Dwork, C. (ed.) CRYPTO 2006. LNCS, vol. 4117, pp. 602–619. Springer, Heidelberg (2006)
3. Bellare, M., Canetti, R., Krawczyk, H.: Keying hash functions for message authentication. In: Koblitz, N. (ed.) CRYPTO 1996. LNCS, vol. 1109, pp. 1–15. Springer, Heidelberg (1996)

4. Bellare, M., Rogaway, P.: The security of triple encryption and a framework for code-based game-playing proofs. In: Vaudenay, S. (ed.) EUROCRYPT 2006. LNCS, vol. 4004, pp. 409–426. Springer, Heidelberg (2006)
5. Bertoni, G., Daemen, J., Peeters, M., Van Assche, G.: Duplexing the sponge: single-pass authenticated encryption and other applications. In: Miri, A., Vaudenay, S. (eds.) SAC 2011. LNCS, vol. 7118, pp. 320–337. Springer, Heidelberg (2012)
6. Bertoni, G., Daemen, J., Peeters, M., Van Assche, G.: Keccak. In: Johansson, T., Nguyen, P.Q. (eds.) EUROCRYPT 2013. LNCS, vol. 7881, pp. 313–314. Springer, Heidelberg (2013)
7. Bertoni, G., Daemen, J., Peeters, M., Van Assche, G.: On the indifferentiability of the sponge construction. In: Smart, N.P. (ed.) EUROCRYPT 2008. LNCS, vol. 4965, pp. 181–197. Springer, Heidelberg (2008)
8. Chen, S., Steinberger, J.: Tight security bounds for key-alternating ciphers. In: Nguyen, P.Q., Oswald, E. (eds.) EUROCRYPT 2014. LNCS, vol. 8441, pp. 327–350. Springer, Heidelberg (2014)
9. Damgård, I.B.: A design principle for hash functions. In: Brassard, G. (ed.) CRYPTO 1989. LNCS, vol. 435, pp. 416–427. Springer, Heidelberg (1990)
10. Dodis, Y., Ristenpart, T., Steinberger, J., Tessaro, S.: To hash or not to hash again? (In)Differentiability results for H^2 and HMAC. In: Safavi-Naini, R., Canetti, R. (eds.) CRYPTO 2012. LNCS, vol. 7417, pp. 348–366. Springer, Heidelberg (2012)
11. Gaži, P., Pietrzak, K., Rybár, M.: The exact PRF-security of NMAC and HMAC. In: Garay, J.A., Gennaro, R. (eds.) CRYPTO 2014, Part I. LNCS, vol. 8616, pp. 113–130. Springer, Heidelberg (2014)
12. Gaži, P., Pietrzak, K., Tessaro, S.: The exact PRF security of truncation: tight bounds for keyed sponges and truncated CBC. In: Gennaro, R., Robshaw, M. (eds.) CRYPTO 2015. LNCS, vol. 9215, pp. 368–387. Springer, Heidelberg (2015)
13. Jovanovic, P., Luykx, A., Mennink, B.: Beyond $2^{c/2}$ security in sponge-based authenticated encryption modes. In: Sarkar, P., Iwata, T. (eds.) ASIACRYPT 2014. LNCS, vol. 8873, pp. 85–104. Springer, Heidelberg (2014)
14. Krawczyk, H., Bellare, M., Canetti, R.: HMAC: Keyed-Hashing for Message Authentication. Internet RFC 2104 (1997)
15. Maurer, U.M., Renner, R.S., Holenstein, C.: Indifferentiability, impossibility results on reductions, and applications to the random oracle methodology. In: Naor, M. (ed.) TCC 2004. LNCS, vol. 2951, pp. 21–39. Springer, Heidelberg (2004)
16. Mennink, B., Reyhanitabar, R., Vizár, D.: Security of full-state keyed and duplex sponge: applications to authenticated encryption. IACR Cryptology ePrint Archive 2015/541
17. Merkle, R.C.: One way hash functions and DES. In: Brassard, G. (ed.) CRYPTO 1989. LNCS, vol. 435, pp. 428–446. Springer, Heidelberg (1990)
18. NIST: The keyed-hash message authentication code (HMAC). In: FIPS PUB 198-1 (2008)
19. NIST: Secure hash standard (SHS). In: DFIPS PUB 180-4 (2012)
20. NIST: SHA-3 standard: permutation-based hash and extendable-output functions. In: FIPS PUB 202 (2015)
21. Patarin, J.: The "Coefficients H" technique. In: Avanzi, R.M., Keliher, L., Sica, F. (eds.) SAC 2008. LNCS, vol. 5381, pp. 328–345. Springer, Heidelberg (2009)

Constrained PRFs for Unbounded Inputs

Hamza Abusalah$^{(\boxtimes)}$, Georg Fuchsbauer, and Krzysztof Pietrzak

Institute of Science and Technology Austria, Klosterneuburg, Austria
{habusalah,gfuchsbauer,pietrzak}@ist.ac.at

Abstract. A constrained pseudorandom function $F \colon \mathcal{K} \times \mathcal{X} \to \mathcal{Y}$ for a family $\mathcal{T} \subseteq 2^{\mathcal{X}}$ of subsets of $\mathcal{X}$ is a function where for any key $k \in \mathcal{K}$ and set $S \in \mathcal{T}$ one can efficiently compute a constrained key k_S which allows to evaluate $F(k, \cdot)$ on all inputs $x \in S$, while even given this key, the outputs on all inputs $x \notin S$ look random. At Asiacrypt'13 Boneh and Waters gave a construction which supports the most general set family so far. Its keys k_C are defined for sets decided by boolean circuits C and enable evaluation of the PRF on any $x \in \mathcal{X}$ where $C(x) = 1$. In their construction the PRF input length and the size of the circuits C for which constrained keys can be computed must be fixed beforehand during key generation.

We construct a constrained PRF that has an unbounded input length and whose constrained keys can be defined for any set recognized by a Turing machine. The only a priori bound we make is on the description size of the machines. We prove our construction secure assuming public-coin differing-input obfuscation.

As applications of our constrained PRF we build a broadcast encryption scheme where the number of potential receivers need not be fixed at setup (in particular, the length of the keys is independent of the number of parties) and the first identity-based non-interactive key exchange protocol with no bound on the number of parties that can agree on a shared key.

Keywords: Constrained PRFs · Broadcast encryption · Identity-based non-interactive key exchange

1 Introduction

Constrained PRFs. A pseudorandom function (PRF) [23] is a keyed function $F \colon \mathcal{K} \times \mathcal{X} \to \mathcal{Y}$ for which no efficient adversary, given access to an oracle $\mathcal{O}(\cdot)$, can distinguish the case where $\mathcal{O}(\cdot)$ is $F(k, \cdot)$ with a random key $k \in \mathcal{K}$ from the case where $\mathcal{O}(\cdot)$ is a uniformly random function $\mathcal{X} \to \mathcal{Y}$.

Three papers [10,14,28] independently introduce the concept of a *constrained* PRF. Consider a set $\mathcal{P}$, where each $v \in \mathcal{P}$ specifies some predicate $p_v \colon \mathcal{X} \to \{0, 1\}$ that defines a (potentially exponential-size) subset $S_v = \{x \in \mathcal{X} \mid p_v(x) = 1\}$. A constrained PRF for a predicate family $\mathcal{P}$ is a PRF F with an additional constrain

Supported by the European Research Council, ERC Starting Grant (259668-PSPC).

© Springer International Publishing Switzerland 2016
K. Sako (Ed.): CT-RSA 2016, LNCS 9610, pp. 413–428, 2016.
DOI: 10.1007/978-3-319-29485-8_24

algorithm $k_v \leftarrow \mathsf{F.Constr}(k, v)$ that on input a key $k \in \mathcal{K}$ and a predicate $v \in \mathcal{P}$ outputs a constrained key k_v that can be used to compute $\mathsf{F}(k, x)$ on all $x \in S_v$, while, given this key, all values $\mathsf{F}(k, x)$ for $x \notin S_v$ still look random.

Constrained PRFs (CPRF) have been constructed for several interesting predicates. All three papers [10, 14, 28] show that the classical GGM construction [23] of a PRF with input domain $\{0, 1\}^n$ yields a *prefix*-constrained PRF. This means $\mathcal{P} = \{0, 1\}^{\leq n}$ and for any $v \in \mathcal{P}$ the derived key k_v allows to compute $\mathsf{F}(k, x)$ for all x with prefix v, i.e., $x = v \| x' \in \{0, 1\}^n$ for some x'. Assuming (leveled) multilinear maps [15, 19, 30], Boneh and Waters [10] construct CPRFs for much more general set systems. They present a bit-fixing PRF, where $\mathcal{P} = \{0, 1, ?\}^n$ and for $v \in \mathcal{P}$ we have $p_v(x) = 1$ if x agrees with v on all indices different from '?', i.e., for all $i = 1, \ldots, n$, either $v[i] = ?$ or $v[i] = x[i]$. They moreover construct a circuit-constrained PRF, where the predicates are arbitrary circuits $C \colon \{0, 1\}^n \to \{0, 1\}$ of some fixed depth.

CPRFs have already found many interesting applications. From a prefix CPRF, one can construct a puncturable PRF [33], which is a constrained PRF for predicates $\mathcal{P} = \{0, 1\}^n$ where for $v \in \mathcal{P}$, the key k_v lets one compute $\mathsf{F}(k, x)$ on all $x \neq v$. The GGM construction yields a puncturable PRF with punctured keys whose length is linear in the PRF input length. Puncturable PRFs play a crucial role in the security proofs of most of the recent constructions based on indistinguishability obfuscation [4, 20], and we will also use them in this paper.

The more general bit-fixing and circuit-constrained PRFs can be used to construct a variety of sophisticated cryptographic tools including broadcast encryption (BE) and identity-based non-interactive key-exchange, as outlined next.

BROADCAST ENCRYPTION. In a BE scheme [8, 9, 11, 16, 32, 35] there is a set of n users, and for any given subset $S \subseteq \{1, \ldots, n\}$ of users, we want to be able to encrypt a message (as a short ciphertext) that can be decrypted only by the users included in S. This can be achieved using a bit-fixing PRF with domain $\{0, 1\}^n$: Sample a random key k, and give a constrained key k_{v_i} to user i where $v_i[i] = 1$ and $v_i[j] = ?$ for any $j \neq i$. Thus, k_{v_i} allows to evaluate the PRF on exactly those inputs with a '1' in position i.

To broadcast a message m to a set S of users, we simply send a symmetric encryption of m under the key $\mathsf{F}(k, x_S)$, where $x_S[i] = 1$ if $i \in S$ and $x_S[i] = 0$ otherwise. Note that user i can compute $\mathsf{F}(k, x_S)$ (and thus decrypt) iff her key k_{v_i} satisfies $v_i[i] = x_S[i]$, which by construction holds iff $i \in S$.

NON-INTERACTIVE KEY EXCHANGE. In an identity-based non-interactive key exchange (ID-NIKE) [10, 12, 17, 34] scheme there are parties that each have some identity $id \in \{0, 1\}^\ell$. For any set S of at most n parties we want the parties in S to be able to locally compute a shared key K_S which is indistinguishable from random for all parties outside of S. Such a scheme can be constructed from a bit-fixing PRF F with domain $\{0, 1\}^{n \cdot \ell}$. At setup, sample a key k for F and give to party $id \in \{0, 1\}^\ell$ a set of n constrained keys $k_{id}^{(1)}, \ldots, k_{id}^{(n)}$, where $k_{id}^{(i)}$ is a key for the set $?^{(i-1)\ell} \| id \| ?^{(n-i)\ell}$. Now, only parties $id_1, \ldots, id_n$ can compute the joint key $K_S := \mathsf{F}(k, id_1 \| id_2 \| \ldots \| id_n)$.

CPRFs with unbounded input length. The disadvantage of the BE and ID-NIKE constructions just outlined is that the number n of possible recipients (for BE) or parties agreeing on a key (for ID-NIKE) must be fixed when setting up the system. Moreover, the length of the constrained keys given to every user is at least linear in n.

In this paper we construct a constrained PRF for which there is no a priori bound on the input length. The constraints on keys are given by Turing machines (TM), that is, given a key k and a machine M, we can derive a constrained key k_M that allows to compute $F(k, x)$ for any input x for which $M(x) = 1$. The only thing that must be bounded beforehand is the *size* of the TMs that we want to support. In our construction a constrained key for a machine M will be an obfuscated circuit whose size only depends on the size of M.

ADAPTIVE VS. SELECTIVE SECURITY. Security of constrained PRFs is defined via a game in which a challenger picks a random key k and the adversary chooses $x^* \in \mathcal{X}$ and must distinguish $F(k, x^*)$ from random. The adversary has also access to oracles to query constrained keys for sets $S \not\ni x^*$. We prove *selective* security of our CPRF where the adversary must choose x^* before it can query constrained keys. From a selectively secure CPRF we can get an *adaptively* secure CPRF (where the adversary can decide on x^* after its key queries) via "complexity leveraging"—but this reduction loses a factor that is exponential in the input length. Proving adaptive security for CPRFs without an exponential security loss is generally hard and Fuchsbauer et al. [18] show that for the bit-fixing CPRF from [10] any "simple" security reduction must lose an exponential factor.

Adaptive security of CPRFs was proved for the GGM-based prefix-constrained PRF in [18] losing only a quasi-polynomial (rather than an exponential) factor. Moreover, Hohenberger et al. [25] construct an adaptively secure puncturable PRF with polynomial security loss using indistinguishability obfuscation $(i\mathcal{O})$ [20,31,33]. Hofheinz et al. [24] construct an adaptively secure bit-fixing PRF, also using $i\mathcal{O}$, and additionally relying on the random-oracle model. We leave the construction of adaptively secure constrained unbounded-length PRFs (for any interesting set of constraints) as a challenging open problem.

Applications. As two applications of our constrained PRFs we show that they directly yield broadcast encryption and ID-NIKE for an unbounded number of parties. In particular, all parameters (private/public key size and for BE also ciphertext overhead) are poly-logarithmic in the number of potential parties (or equivalently, polynomial in the length of the identities). For BE, this has only recently been achieved by Boneh et al. [11], who construct a BE scheme supporting n parties directly from $O(\log(n))$-way multilinear maps. For ID-NIKE, our construction is the first to achieve this; all previous schemes require the maximum size of the group of users agreeing on a key to be fixed at setup, and they have parameters that depend at least linearly on this size.

Due to space constraints, we detail the applications in the full version [1].

A circuit-constrained PRF. A first idea for constructing a constrained PRF is to start with a standard PRF F; given a key k and a set S, we can define a constrained key as a program P_S which on input x checks whether $x \in S$, and if so, outputs $\mathsf{F}(k, x)$. We cannot define the constrained key as the program P_S as such, since an adversary could extract the key k from P_S, and hence $\mathsf{F}(k, \cdot)$ would not be pseudorandom for $x \notin S$ given P_S.

When S is decided by a circuit, the above issue can be avoided by *obfuscating* P_S before outputting it. The strong notion of *virtual black-box obfuscation*, which requires that an obfuscated program leaks nothing about the program apart from its input/output behavior, is not achievable for general functionalities [4]. We therefore use *indistinguishability obfuscation* ($i\mathcal{O}$), which only guarantees that obfuscations of two circuits (of the same size) that output the same on any input are indistinguishable. A candidate $i\mathcal{O}$ scheme was proposed by Garg et al. [20]. Although the notion seems weak, it has proven to be surprisingly useful.

Consider a CPRF derived from a puncturable PRF F for which a constrained key k_C for a circuit C is defined as an $i\mathcal{O}$ obfuscation of the circuit P_C, which on input x returns $\mathsf{F}(k, x)$ if $C(x) = 1$ and $\bot$ otherwise. In the selective-security game an adversary $\mathcal{A}$ chooses an input x^*, can then ask for constrained keys for circuits C with $C(x^*) = 0$ and must distinguish $\mathsf{F}(k, x^*)$ from random. In the security proof we first define a modified game where $\mathcal{A}$, when asking for a constrained key for a circuit C, is given an $i\mathcal{O}$ obfuscation of a circuit P'_C that outputs $\mathsf{F}(k_{x^*}, x)$ if $C(x) = 1$ and $\bot$ otherwise. The difference between P_C and P'_C is that in the latter F is evaluated using a key k_{x^*} that is punctured at x^*.

Recall that the adversary can only submit circuits C with $C(x^*) = 0$ to its oracle. For every such C we have $P_C(x^*) = P'_C(x^*) = \bot$, and on any other input x, P_C and P'_C also return the same output (namely $\mathsf{F}(k, x)$ if $C(x) = 1$ and $\bot$ otherwise). By security of $i\mathcal{O}$, obfuscations of P_C and P'_C are thus indistinguishable, which means that the modified game is indistinguishable from the original game. From an adversary $\mathcal{A}$ winning the modified game we obtain an adversary $\mathcal{B}$ that breaks the puncturable PRF F: When $\mathcal{A}$ commits to x^*, $\mathcal{B}$ asks for a punctured key k_{x^*}, which allows $\mathcal{B}$ to answer $\mathcal{A}$'s constrained-key queries in the modified game. If $\mathcal{A}$ distinguishes $\mathsf{F}(k, x^*)$ from random then so does $\mathcal{B}$.

A TM-constrained PRF. The above construction uses $i\mathcal{O}$ for circuits. Recently, Koppula et al. [29] constructed $i\mathcal{O}$ for Turing machines. However, we cannot simply replace circuits by TMs in the construction just sketched. In the security proof we need to upper-bound the size of the TM to be obfuscated when we switch from a TM using k to a TM using k_{x^*}. This is however impossible because the size of the underlying punctured key k_{x^*} cannot be a priori bounded for unbounded inputs x^*.

To overcome this problem, we use a collision-resistant hash function H to map long inputs to inputs of fixed length. Concretely, we define our CPRF as $\mathsf{F}(k, x) := \mathsf{PF}(k, H(x))$, where PF is a puncturable PRF. Consequently, a constrained key would be an obfuscation of the TM P_M that checks the input legitimacy of x, i.e., whether $M(x) = 1$, and evaluates PF on $H(x)$. In order to give a reduction of security to the puncturable PRF PF, we would, as before, replace the obfuscation of P_M by one of P'_M, which uses $k_{H(x^*)}$ instead of k.

While this solves the size-bounding problem, it poses new challenges. Namely, $i\mathcal{O}$ is not sufficient as P_M and P'_M are in general not functionally equivalent: consider a machine M with $M(x^*) = 0$ and $M(x) = 1$ for some x with $H(x) = H(x^*)$; then $P_M(x) = \mathsf{F}(k, x)$, whereas $P'_M(x) = \bot$.

DIFFERING-INPUT OBFUSCATION. Instead of $i\mathcal{O}$, we resort to a stronger form of obfuscation. Whereas $i\mathcal{O}$ yields indistinguishable obfuscations of programs that are functionally equivalent, differing-input obfuscation ($di\mathcal{O}$, a.k.a. extractability obfuscation) introduced by [4,5] for circuits and later by [2,13] for TMs, guarantees that from an adversary that distinguishes obfuscations of two circuits (or TMs), one can extract an input on which they differ. $di\mathcal{O}$ is a strong assumption and in fact was shown to be implausible to exist [21]. We will use a weaker assumption suggested by Ishai et al. [27] and called public-coin $di\mathcal{O}$, for which no such implausibility results are known. Informally, this notion only implies indistinguishability for pairs of programs if it is hard to find an input on which the two programs differ *even when given the randomness used to sample this pair of circuits.*

We replace $i\mathcal{O}$ in our CPRF construction by public-coin $di\mathcal{O}$ for TMs with unbounded inputs from [27] and define a constrained key for M as a $di\mathcal{O}$ obfuscation of P_M. This solution is not without limitations; a constrained key is now a $di\mathcal{O}$-obfuscated TM and therefore keys are large and their size depends on the running time of the constraining TM M, which we show how to avoid next.

SNARKs. We "outsource" the check of input legitimacy (whether x satisfies $M(x) = 1$) to the party that evaluates the PRF. The latter first computes a succinct non-interactive argument of knowledge (SNARK) of a legitimate x and passes this SNARK to the obfuscated program. A SNARK system is a computationally sound non-interactive proof of knowledge for which proofs are universally succinct. That is, the length of a proof π for a statement η as well as its verification time are bounded by an a-priori-fixed polynomial in the length $|\eta|$ of the statement. In particular, we use a SNARK system for the language $L_{legit} := \{(H, M, h) \mid \exists x : M(x) = 1 \wedge H(x) = h\}$.

Instead of running M, the program P_M now only needs to verify a SNARK, which can be implemented by a *circuit*; we thus only require obfuscation of circuits. Let P_M be the circuit that on input (h, π) outputs $\mathsf{PF}(k, h)$ iff π is a valid SNARK for (H, M, h). A constrained key is then a public-coin $di\mathcal{O}$ obfuscation of P_M, whose size only depends on the size of M but not on its running time.

As we use public-coin $di\mathcal{O}$, we require the hash function H to be public-coin [26], that is, collision-resistance (CR) must hold when the adversary is given the randomness used to sample a hash function from the family; moreover, the SNARK must be in the common random string model. Such hash functions and SNARKs exist as discussed in [27]. Assuming puncturable PRFs, public-coin CR hash functions, a SNARK for the language L_{legit} and public-coin $di\mathcal{O}$ for circuits, our construction is a TM-constrained PRF for inputs of unbounded length.

$\mathbf{Exp}_{\mathcal{F},\mathcal{A}}^{\mathcal{O},b}(\lambda)$	**Oracle** $\mathrm{CONSTR}(S)$	**Oracle** $\mathrm{EVAL}(x)$
$k \leftarrow \mathsf{F.Smp}(1^\lambda); C, E := \emptyset$	If $S \notin \mathcal{S}_\lambda \vee S \cap C \neq \emptyset$	If $x \notin \mathcal{X} \vee x \in C$
$(x^*, st) \leftarrow \mathcal{A}_1^{\mathcal{O}_1}(1^\lambda)$	Return $\perp$	Return $\perp$
If $x^* \in E$ then abort	$E := E \cup S$	$E := E \cup \{x\}$
If $b = 1$ then $y := \mathsf{F.Eval}(k, x^*)$	$k_S \leftarrow \mathsf{F.Constr}(k, S)$	$y = \mathsf{F.Eval}(k, x)$
Else $y \leftarrow \mathcal{Y}$	Return k_S	Return y
$C := C \cup \{x^*\}$		
Return $b' \leftarrow \mathcal{A}_2^{\mathcal{O}_2}(st, y)$		

Fig. 1. The security game for constrained PRFs.

2 Preliminaries

2.1 Constrained and Puncturable PRFs

Definition 1 (Constrained Functions). *A family of keyed functions* $\mathcal{F}_\lambda = \{F \colon \mathcal{K} \times \mathcal{X} \to \mathcal{Y}\}$ *over a key space* $\mathcal{K}$, *a domain* $\mathcal{X}$ *and a range* $\mathcal{Y}$ *is efficiently computable if there exist a PPT sampler* $\mathsf{F.Smp}$ *and a deterministic polynomial-time (PT) evaluator* $\mathsf{F.Eval}$ *such that:*

- $k \leftarrow \mathsf{F.Smp}(1^\lambda)$: *On input a security parameter* λ, $\mathsf{F.Smp}$ *outputs a key* $k \in \mathcal{K}$.
- $F(k, x) := \mathsf{F.Eval}(k, x)$, *for* $k \in \mathcal{K}$ *and* $x \in \mathcal{X}$.

We say $\mathcal{F}_\lambda$ *is* constrained *w.r.t. a family* $\mathcal{S}_\lambda$ *of subsets of* $\mathcal{X}$, *with constrained key space* $\mathcal{K}_S$ *such that* $\mathcal{K}_S \cap \mathcal{K} = \emptyset$, *if* $\mathsf{F.Eval}$ *accepts inputs from* $(\mathcal{K} \cup \mathcal{K}_S) \times \mathcal{X}$ *and there exists the following PPT algorithm:*

- $k_S \leftarrow \mathsf{F.Constr}(k, S)$: *On input a key* $k \in \mathcal{K}$ *and a description[1] of a set* $S \in \mathcal{S}_\lambda$, $\mathsf{F.Constr}$ *outputs a constrained key* $k_S \in \mathcal{K}_S$ *such that*

$$\mathsf{F.Eval}(k_S, x) = \begin{cases} F(k, x) & \text{if } x \in S \\ \perp & \text{otherwise} \end{cases}.$$

Definition 2 (Security of Constrained PRFs). *A family of (efficiently computable) constrained functions* $\mathcal{F}_\lambda = \{F \colon \mathcal{K} \times \mathcal{X} \to \mathcal{Y}\}$ *is* selectively *pseudorandom, if for every PPT adversary* $\mathcal{A} = (\mathcal{A}_1, \mathcal{A}_2)$ *in* $\mathbf{Exp}_{\mathcal{F},\mathcal{A}}^{\mathcal{O},b}$, *defined in Fig. 1, with* $\mathcal{O}_1 = \emptyset$ *and* $\mathcal{O}_2 = \{\mathrm{CONSTR}(\cdot), \mathrm{EVAL}(\cdot)\}$, *it holds that*

$$\mathsf{Adv}_{\mathcal{F},\mathcal{A}}^{\mathcal{O}}(\lambda) := \left| \Pr\left[\mathbf{Exp}_{\mathcal{F},\mathcal{A}}^{\mathcal{O},0}(\lambda) = 1\right] - \Pr\left[\mathbf{Exp}_{\mathcal{F},\mathcal{A}}^{\mathcal{O},1}(\lambda) = 1\right] \right| = \mathsf{negl}(\lambda) . \quad (1)$$

$\mathcal{F}_\lambda$ *is* adaptively *pseudorandom if the same holds for* $\mathcal{O}_1 = \mathcal{O}_2 = \{\mathrm{CONSTR}(\cdot), \mathrm{EVAL}(\cdot)\}$.

---

[1] As outlined in the introduction, we assume that every set in $\mathcal{S}$ can be specified by a short and efficiently computable predicate.

$\mathbf{Exp}_{\mathcal{F},\mathcal{A}}^{\text{PCT-}b}(\lambda)$	Oracle $\text{EVAL}(x)$
$(x^*, T, st) \leftarrow \mathcal{A}_1(1^\lambda)$; If $x^* \notin T$, then abort	If $x = x^*$, return $\perp$
$k \leftarrow \mathsf{F.Smp}(1^\lambda)$; $k_{\overline{T}} \leftarrow \mathsf{F.Constr}(k, \{0,1\}^n \setminus T)$	Return $\mathsf{F.Eval}(k, x)$
If $b = 1$ then $y := \mathsf{F.Eval}(k, x^*)$; else $y \leftarrow \mathcal{Y}$	
Return $b' \leftarrow \mathcal{A}_2^{\text{EVAL}(\cdot)}(st, k_{\overline{T}}, y)$	

Fig. 2. The selective-security game for puncturable PRFs.

Puncturable PRFs [33] are a simple type of constrained PRFs whose domain is $\{0,1\}^n$ for some n, and constrained keys can only be derived for the sets $\{\{0,1\}^n \setminus \{x_1,\ldots,x_m\} \mid x_1,\ldots,x_m \in \{0,1\}^n, m = \mathsf{poly}(\lambda)\}$, i.e., a punctured key $k_{x_1\ldots x_m}$ can evaluate the PRF on all inputs *except* on polynomially many $x_1,\ldots,x_m$. We only require pseudorandomness to hold against selective adversaries.

Definition 3 (Puncturable PRFs [33]). *A family of PRFs* $\mathcal{F}_\lambda = \{\mathsf{F}\colon \mathcal{K} \times \{0,1\}^n \to \mathcal{Y}\}$ *is* puncturable *if it is constrainable for sets* $\{0,1\}^n \setminus T$, *where* $T \subseteq \{0,1\}^n$ *is of polynomial size.* $\mathcal{F}_\lambda$ *is (selectively) pseudorandom if for every PPT adversary* $\mathcal{A} = (\mathcal{A}_1, \mathcal{A}_2)$ *in* $\mathbf{Exp}_{\mathcal{F},\mathcal{A}}^{\text{PCT-}b}(\lambda)$, *defined in Fig. 2, we have*

$$\mathsf{Adv}_{\mathcal{F},\mathcal{A}}^{\text{PCT}}(\lambda) := \big| \Pr\big[\mathbf{Exp}_{\mathcal{F},\mathcal{A}}^{\text{PCT-}0}(\lambda) = 1\big] - \Pr\big[\mathbf{Exp}_{\mathcal{F},\mathcal{A}}^{\text{PCT-}1}(\lambda) = 1\big]\big| = \mathsf{negl}(\lambda).$$

Puncturable PRFs are easily obtained from prefix-constrained PRFs, which were constructed from the GGM PRF [23] in [10, 14, 28].

2.2 Collision-Resistant Hash Functions

A family of hash functions is collision-resistant (CR) if given a uniformly sampled function, it is hard to find inputs on which it collides. It is called public-coin CR if this is hard even when given the coins used to sample the function.

Definition 4 (Public-Coin CR Hash Functions [26]). *A family of (efficiently computable) functions* $\mathcal{H}_\lambda = \{H\colon \{0,1\}^* \to \{0,1\}^n\}$, *for which* Smp *samples a random function, is* public-coin collision-resistant *if for every PPT adversary* $\mathcal{A}$ *it holds that*

$$\Pr\left[\begin{matrix} r \leftarrow \{0,1\}^{\mathsf{poly}(\lambda)}; H := \mathsf{Smp}(1^\lambda, r); \\ (x_1, x_2) \leftarrow \mathcal{A}(1^\lambda, r) \end{matrix} : \begin{matrix} H(x_1) = H(x_2) \\ \wedge\ x_1 \neq x_2 \end{matrix}\right] = \mathsf{negl}(\lambda)\ .$$

2.3 Indistinguishability and Differing-Input Obfuscation

As a consequence of the impossibility of virtual black-box obfuscation, Barak et al. [4], proposed two weaker notions: *indistinguishability obfuscation* ($i\mathcal{O}$) and *differing-input obfuscation* ($di\mathcal{O}$). The first, $i\mathcal{O}$, guarantees that obfuscations of equivalent functionalities are computationally indistinguishable.

Definition 5 (iO [20]). *A uniform PPT algorithm* iO *is an indistinguishability obfuscator for a family of polynomial-size circuits* $\mathcal{C}_\lambda$, *if the following hold:*

- *For all* $\lambda \in \mathbb{N}$, $C \in \mathcal{C}_\lambda$, *and* x: $\Pr\left[\widetilde{C} \leftarrow \mathsf{iO}(1^\lambda, C) : C(x) = \widetilde{C}(x)\right] = 1$.
- *For every PPT adversary* $\mathcal{A}$ *and all* $C_0, C_1 \in \mathcal{C}_\lambda$ *s.t.* $\forall x, C_0(x) = C_1(x)$:

$$\left| \Pr\left[\mathcal{A}(\mathsf{iO}(1^\lambda, C_0)) = 1\right] - \Pr\left[\mathcal{A}(\mathsf{iO}(1^\lambda, C_1)) = 1\right] \right| = \mathsf{negl}(\lambda) \ .$$

Differing-input obfuscation is a stronger notion which requires that for any efficient adversary that distinguishes obfuscations of two functionalities, there exists an efficient *extractor* $\mathcal{E}$ that extracts a point on which the functionalities differ. Ishai et al. [27] weaken this to *public-coin diO*, where the extractor is given the coins used to sample the functionalities. We will use this concept for circuits, which is formalized by requiring that indistinguishability only holds for circuits output by a sampler Samp for which no differing-input extractor exists.

Definition 6 (Public-Coin Differing-Input Sampler [27]). *A non-uniform PPT sampler* Samp *is a public-coin differing-input sampler for a polynomial-size family of circuits* $\mathcal{C}_\lambda$ *if the output of* Samp *is in* $\mathcal{C}_\lambda \times \mathcal{C}_\lambda$ *and for every non-uniform PPT extractor* $\mathcal{E}$ *it holds that*

$$\Pr\left[\begin{array}{l} r \leftarrow \{0,1\}^{\mathsf{poly}(\lambda)}; \\ (C_0, C_1) := \mathsf{Samp}(1^\lambda, r); x \leftarrow \mathcal{E}(1^\lambda, r) \end{array} : C_0(x) \neq C_1(x) \right] = \mathsf{negl}(\lambda) \ . \quad (2)$$

Definition 7 (Public-Coin diO [27]). *A uniform PPT algorithm* diO *is a public-coin differing-input obfuscator for a family of polynomial-size circuits* $\mathcal{C}_\lambda$ *if the following hold:*

- *For all* $\lambda \in \mathbb{N}$, $C \in \mathcal{C}_\lambda$ *and* x: $\Pr\left[\widetilde{C} \leftarrow \mathsf{diO}(1^\lambda, C) : C(x) = \widetilde{C}(x)\right] = 1$.
- *For every public-coin differing-input sampler* Samp *for a family of polynomial-size circuits* $\mathcal{C}_\lambda$, *every non-uniform PPT distinguisher* $\mathcal{D}$ *and every* $\lambda \in \mathbb{N}$:

$$\left| \Pr\left[\begin{array}{l} r \leftarrow \{0,1\}^{\mathsf{poly}(\lambda)}; (C_0, C_1) := \mathsf{Samp}(1^\lambda, r); \\ \widetilde{C} \leftarrow \mathsf{diO}(1^\lambda, C_0) \end{array} : 1 \leftarrow \mathcal{D}(r, \widetilde{C}) \right] - \right. \quad (3)$$

$$\left. \Pr\left[\begin{array}{l} r \leftarrow \{0,1\}^{\mathsf{poly}(\lambda)}; (C_0, C_1) := \mathsf{Samp}(1^\lambda, r); \\ \widetilde{C} \leftarrow \mathsf{diO}(1^\lambda, C_1) \end{array} : 1 \leftarrow \mathcal{D}(r, \widetilde{C}) \right] \right| = \mathsf{negl}(\lambda) \ .$$

A candidate $i\mathcal{O}$ was constructed based on a simplified variant of multilinear maps and proven secure in an idealized model [20]. The candidate was conjectured to be a $di\mathcal{O}$ for NC^1 [13]. Unfortunately, Garg et al. [21] present an implausibility result for $di\mathcal{O}$ for arbitrary distributions. However, Ishai et al. [27] argue that current candidate constructions for $i\mathcal{O}$ satisfy their notion of public-coin $di\mathcal{O}$.

2.4 Succinct Non-interactive Arguments of Knowledge

A succinct non-interactive argument of knowledge (SNARK) is a computationally sound non-interactive proof-of-knowledge system for which proofs are universally succinct. A proof π of knowledge of a witness w to a statement η is succinct if the proof length and its verification time are bounded by an a priori fixed polynomial in the statement length $|\eta|$.

Definition 8 (The Universal Relation $\mathcal{R}_{\mathcal{U}}$ [3]). *The universal relation $\mathcal{R}_{\mathcal{U}}$ is the set of instance/witness pairs of the form $((M, m, t), w)$ where M is a TM accepting an input/witness pair (m, w) within t steps. In particular $|w| \leq t$.*

We define SNARK systems in the common-random-string model following Bitansky et al. [6,7,27] as follows.

Definition 9 (SNARK). *A pair of PPT algorithms (Prove, Verify) is a succinct non-interactive argument of knowledge (SNARK) in the common-random-string model for a language $\mathcal{L}$ with witness relation $\mathcal{R} \subseteq \mathcal{R}_{\mathcal{U}}$ if there exist polynomials p, ℓ, q independent of $\mathcal{R}$ such that the following hold:*

1. *Completeness: For every $(\eta = (M, m, t), w) \in \mathcal{R}$ the following holds:*
   $\Pr\left[\text{crs} \leftarrow \{0,1\}^{\text{poly}(\lambda)};\ \pi \leftarrow \text{Prove}(\text{crs}, \eta, w) : \text{Verify}(\text{crs}, \eta, \pi) = 1\right] = 1$. *Moreover, Prove runs in time $q(\lambda, |\eta|, t)$.*

2. *(Adaptive) Soundness: For every PPT adversary $\mathcal{A}$:*

$$\Pr\left[\begin{array}{c} \text{crs} \leftarrow \{0,1\}^{\text{poly}(\lambda)}; \\ (\eta, \pi) \leftarrow \mathcal{A}(\text{crs}) \end{array} : \text{Verify}(\text{crs}, \eta, \pi) = 1 \ \wedge \ \eta \notin \mathcal{L}\right] = \text{negl}(\lambda) \ .$$

3. *(Adaptive) Argument of knowledge: For every PPT adversary $\mathcal{A}$ there exists a PPT extractor $\mathcal{E}_{\mathcal{A}}$ such that*

$$\Pr\left[\begin{array}{c} \text{crs} \leftarrow \{0,1\}^{\text{poly}(\lambda)}; r \leftarrow \{0,1\}^{\text{poly}(\lambda)} \\ (\eta, \pi) := \mathcal{A}(\text{crs}; r); w \leftarrow \mathcal{E}_{\mathcal{A}}(1^\lambda, \text{crs}, r) \end{array} : \begin{array}{c} \text{Verify}(\text{crs}, \eta, \pi) = 1 \\ \wedge (\eta, w) \notin \mathcal{R} \end{array}\right] = \text{negl}(\lambda).$$

4. *Succinctness: For all $(\text{crs}, \eta, w) \in \{0,1\}^{\text{poly}(\lambda)} \times \mathcal{R}$, the length of a proof $\pi \leftarrow \text{Prove}(\text{crs}, \eta, w)$ is bounded by $\ell(\lambda, \log t)$; moreover, the running time of $\text{Verify}(\text{crs}, \eta, \pi)$ is bounded by $p(\lambda + |\eta|) = p(\lambda + |M| + |m| + \log t)$.*

Bitansky et al. [6] construct SNARKs for $\mathcal{R}_c \subset \mathcal{R}_{\mathcal{U}}$ where $t = |m|^c$ and c is a constant, based on knowledge-of-exponent assumptions [7] and extractable collision-resistant hash functions (ECRHF) [6]. These are both non-falsifiable assumptions, but Gentry and Wichs [22] prove that SNARKs cannot be built from falsifiable assumptions via black-box reductions. Relying on exponentially hard one-way functions and ECRHF, [6] construct SNARKs for $\mathcal{R}_{\mathcal{U}}$.

3 Constrained PRFs for Unbounded Inputs

As a warm-up we first construct a constrained PRF for sets decided by polynomial-size circuits and show how to extend it to Turing machines in Sect. 3.2.

3.1 A Circuit-Constrained PRF

Our circuit-constrained PRF F uses a puncturable PRF PF with input space $\mathcal{X} = \{0,1\}^n$. The output of $F(k, x)$ is simply $PF(k, x)$. To constrain F w.r.t. a circuit C, we construct a circuit $P_{k,C}$, which on input x runs C on x and outputs $PF(k, x)$ if $C(x) = 1$, and $\bot$ otherwise. A constrained key k_C for C is then an indistinguishability obfuscation of $P_{k,C}$, i.e., $k_C \leftarrow iO(1^\lambda, P_{k,C})$.

Construction 1 (Circuit-Constrained PRF). Let $\mathcal{C}_\lambda = \{C \colon \{0,1\}^n \to \{0,1\}\}$ be a family of polynomial-size circuits, $\mathcal{PF}_\lambda = \{\mathsf{PF} \colon \mathcal{K} \times \{0,1\}^n \to \mathcal{Y}\}$ a family of selectively secure puncturable PRFs, and $i\mathcal{O}$ an indistinguishability obfuscator for a family of poly-size circuits $\mathcal{P}_\lambda$ that contains all circuits defined in (4) for all $C \in \mathcal{C}_\lambda$. We construct a family of PRFs $\mathcal{F}_\lambda = \{\mathsf{F} \colon \mathcal{K} \times \{0,1\}^n \to \mathcal{Y}\}$ constrained w.r.t. $\mathcal{C}_\lambda$ with a constrained-key space $\mathcal{K}_\mathcal{C}$ such that $\mathcal{K}_\mathcal{C} \cap \mathcal{K} = \emptyset$.[2]

$\underline{k \leftarrow \mathsf{F.Smp}(1^\lambda)}$: Given security parameter λ, output $k \in \mathcal{K}$ as $k \leftarrow \mathsf{PF.Smp}(1^\lambda)$.

$\underline{k_C \leftarrow \mathsf{F.Constr}(k, C)}$: On input a secret key $k \in \mathcal{K}$ and a description of a circuit $C \in \mathcal{C}_\lambda$, output $k_C \in \mathcal{K}_\mathcal{C}$ as $k_C \leftarrow i\mathsf{O}(1^\lambda, P_{k,C})$, with $P_{k,C} \in \mathcal{P}_\lambda$ defined as:

$$P_{k,C}(x) := \begin{cases} \mathsf{PF}(k, x) & \text{if } |x| = n \wedge C(x) = 1 \\ \bot & \text{otherwise} \end{cases} . \tag{4}$$

$\underline{y := \mathsf{F.Eval}(\kappa, x)}$: On input $\kappa \in \mathcal{K} \cup \mathcal{K}_\mathcal{C}$ and $x \in \{0,1\}^n$, do the following:
  – If $\kappa \in \mathcal{K}$, output $\mathsf{PF.Eval}(\kappa, x)$.
  – If $\kappa \in \mathcal{K}_\mathcal{C}$, interpret κ as a circuit and output $\kappa(x)$.

The proof of selective security of $\mathcal{F}$, as just constructed, is relatively straightforward. Recall that in the selective-security game the adversary $\mathcal{A}$ outputs x^*, then the challenger chooses $k \leftarrow \mathsf{F.Smp}$ and gives $\mathcal{A}$ access to a constrained-key oracle $\textsc{Constr}$, which can be queried on any C with $C(x^*) = 0$. $\mathcal{A}$ must then distinguish $\mathsf{F}(k, x^*)$ from random. We modify this game by deriving from k a key k_{x^*} which is punctured at x^* and computing constrained keys as obfuscations of $P_{k_{x^*}, C}$ (defined like $P_{k,C}$ but using k_{x^*} instead of k). Since $\mathsf{PF}(k, x) = \mathsf{PF}(k_{x^*}, x)$ for all $x \neq x^*$, and since for any circuit C that the adversary can query we have $P_{k,C}(x^*) = P_{k_{x^*}, C}(x^*) = \bot$, the circuits $P_{k_{x^*}, C}$ and $P_{k,C}$ are functionally equivalent, and thus by Definition 5 the two games are indistinguishable. Note that we also need to ensure that these circuits are of the same size, which can be achieved by appropriate padding.

An adversary $\mathcal{A}$ winning the modified game can be translated into an adversary $\mathcal{B}$ against $\mathcal{PF}$. In the security game for $\mathcal{PF}$ (Fig. 2), $\mathcal{B}$ runs $(x^*, st) \leftarrow \mathcal{A}$ and outputs $(x^*, \{x^*\}, st)$. Given k_{x^*} and y, $\mathcal{B}$ can simulate the modified game and output whatever $\mathcal{A}$ outputs. $\mathcal{B}$'s probability of breaking the security of $\mathcal{PF}$ is the same as that of $\mathcal{A}$ winning the modified game.

3.2 A TM-Constrained PRF

In this section we construct a family of constrained PRFs for unbounded inputs whose keys can be constrained to sets decided by Turing machines (TM). As a first attempt, in Construction 1 we could replace C in $P_{k,C}$ with a TM M, yielding a TM $P_{k,M}$. We would thus have to use obfuscation for Turing machines rather than just circuits. However, the problem with this construction is that in the proof we would have to replace the underlying PRF key k with a punctured

---

[2] W.l.o.g. we assume from now on that $\mathcal{K} \cap \mathcal{K}_\mathcal{C} = \emptyset$, as this can always be achieved by simply prepending a '0' to elements from $\mathcal{K}$ and a '1' to elements from $\mathcal{K}_\mathcal{C}$.

key k_{x^*} for some x^* whose length is not a priori bounded. It is thus not clear how to pad the original key, which could be done in our previous construction.

To overcome this problem we compress the unbounded input to a fixed length by applying a collision-resistant hash function H to it, that is, we evaluate the PRF on hashed inputs. Moreover, we outsource the check of input legitimacy outside the program $P_{k,M}$ by using a SNARK. In particular, when evaluating the PRF, the user computes a SNARK proving that a given hash is the hash value of a legitimate input. The program $P_{k,M}$ is then only given the *hash* of the input to the PRF and a SNARK proof confirming the legitimacy of a preimage, and evaluates the PRF on the hash if the proof verifies.

Note that $P_{k,M}$ can now be implemented by a circuit, which means that we can avoid obfuscation of Turing machines altogether. In our construction a constrained key k_M for a TM M is a public-coin $di\mathcal{O}$ obfuscation of a circuit $P_{k,M}$ which is given (h, π) and checks whether π proves knowledge of an x such that $H(x) = h$ and $M(x) = 1$, and if so, evaluates PF on h.

Let us justify the use of (public-coin) $di\mathcal{O}$ and SNARKs. As for our circuit-constrained PRF, we want to reduce the selective security of the TM-constrained PRF F to the selective security of the underlying puncturable PRF PF. In a first game hop we replace $P_{k,M}$ with $P_{k_{h^*},M}$, which is identical to $P_{k,M}$ except that the key k is replaced with a key k_{h^*} that punctures out $h^* := H(x^*)$. Unfortunately, the two circuits $P_{k,M}$ and $P_{k_{h^*},M}$ are not equivalent: there exists $x \neq x^*$ such that $H(x) = H(x^*)$, and on input $H(x)$, $P_{k,M}$ outputs $\mathsf{PF}(k, H(x)) = \mathsf{PF}(k, h^*)$ and $P_{k_{h^*},M}$ outputs $\perp$. We thus cannot use $i\mathcal{O}$ and hence we use $di\mathcal{O}$ instead. This requires that it be hard to find an input (h, π) on which the two circuits differ, which means that either π proves a wrong statement or it proves knowledge of some x with $H(x) = H(x^*)$. That is, finding a differing input amounts to either breaking soundness of the SNARK or breaking collision-resistance of H. Since both are hard even for adversaries that know the coins used to sample the hash function or the common random string for the SNARK, it suffices to use public-coin $di\mathcal{O}$.

Finally, hash-function collisions are also the reason we need to use SNARKs rather than SNARGs: if an adversary can distinguish obfuscations of $P_{k,M}$ and $P_{k_{h^*},M}$ by finding a collision for H then we need to extract this collision in the security proof, which SNARKs (arguments of *knowledge*) allow us to do.

Definition 10 (R_{legit}). *We define the relation $R_{legit} \subset \mathcal{R}_\mathcal{U}$, with $\mathcal{R}_\mathcal{U}$ defined in Definition 8, to be the set of instance/witness pairs $(((H, M), h, t), x)$ such that $M(x) = 1$ and $H(x) = h$ within t steps, and M is a TM and H is a hash function. We let L_{legit} be the language corresponding to R_{legit}. For notational convenience, we abuse the notation and write $((H, M, h), x) \in R_{legit}$ to mean $(((H, M), h, t), x) \in R_{legit}$ while implicitly setting $t = 2^\lambda$.*

Remark 1. Let $t = 2^\lambda$ in the definition of R_{legit}; then by succinctness of SNARKs (Definition 9), the length of a SNARK proof is bounded by $\ell(\lambda)$ and its verification time is bounded by $p(\lambda + |M| + |H| + |h|)$, where p, ℓ are a priori fixed polynomials that do not depend on R_{legit}.

Construction 2 (TM-Constrained PRF). *Let* $\mathcal{PF}_\lambda = \{\mathsf{PF}: \mathcal{K} \times \{0,1\}^n \to \mathcal{Y}\}$ *be a selectively secure puncturable PRF,* $\mathcal{H}_\lambda = \{H: \{0,1\}^* \to \{0,1\}^n\}_\lambda$ *a family of public-coin CR hash functions,* diO *a public-coin diO obfuscator for a family of polynomial-size circuits* $\mathcal{P}_\lambda$, *and* SNARK *a SNARK system for* R_{legit} *(cf. Definition 10). We construct a family of PRFs* $\mathcal{F}_\lambda = \{\mathsf{F}: \mathcal{K} \times \{0,1\}^* \to \mathcal{Y}\}$ *constrained w.r.t. to any polynomial-size family of TMs* $\mathcal{M}_\lambda$ *as follows:*

$\underline{K \leftarrow \mathsf{F.Smp}(1^\lambda)}$: *On input a security parameter* λ, *sample* $H \leftarrow \mathsf{H.Smp}(1^\lambda)$, $\mathrm{crs} \leftarrow \{0,1\}^{\mathsf{poly}(\lambda)}$ *and* $k \leftarrow \mathsf{PF.Smp}(1^\lambda)$, *set* $\mathrm{pp} := (H, \mathrm{crs}))$ *and return* $K := (k, \mathrm{pp})$.

$\underline{k_M \leftarrow \mathsf{F.Constr}(K, M)}$: *On input* $K = (k, \mathrm{pp} = (H, \mathrm{crs}))$ *and* $M \in \mathcal{M}_\lambda$, *set*

$$P_{M,H,\mathrm{crs},k}(h, \pi) := \begin{cases} \mathsf{PF.Eval}(k, h) & \textit{if } \mathsf{SNARK.Verify}(\mathrm{crs}, (H, M, h), \pi) = 1 \\ \perp & \textit{otherwise} \end{cases} \quad (5)$$

and compute $\widetilde{P} \leftarrow \mathsf{diO}(1^\lambda, P_{M,H,\mathrm{crs},k})$. *Return* $k_M := (M, \widetilde{P}, (H, \mathrm{crs}))$.

$\underline{y := \mathsf{F.Eval}(\kappa, x)}$: *On input* $\kappa \in \mathcal{K} \cup \mathcal{K_M}$ *and* $x \in \{0,1\}^*$, *do the following:*

- *If* $\kappa \in \mathcal{K}$, $\kappa = (k, (H, \mathrm{crs}))$: *return* $\mathsf{PF.Eval}(k, H(x))$.
- *If* $\kappa \in \mathcal{K_M}$, $\kappa = (M, \widetilde{P}, (H, \mathrm{crs}))$: *if* $M(x) = 1$, *let* $h := H(x)$ *(thus* $((H, M, h), x) \in R_{legit})$, *compute* $\pi \leftarrow \mathsf{SNARK.Prove}(\mathrm{crs}, (H, M, h), x)$, *interpret* $\widetilde{P}$ *as a circuit and return* $\widetilde{P}(h, \pi)$.

Remark 2. Note that $\mathcal{P}_\lambda$ is in fact a family of circuits with an input length $n + |\pi|$ where $|\pi|$ is upper bounded by $\ell(\lambda)$ even for an exponentially long x (cf. Remark 1).

Theorem 1. $\mathcal{F}_\lambda$ *of Construction 2 is a selectively secure family of constrained PRFs with input space* $\{0,1\}^*$ *for which constrained keys can be derived for any set that can be decided by a polynomial-size Turing machine.*

Proof. Let $\mathcal{A}$ be an arbitrary PPT adversary for game $\mathbf{Exp}_{\mathcal{F}, \mathcal{A}}^{(\emptyset, \{\text{CONSTR}, \text{EVAL}\}), b}(\lambda)$, as defined in Fig. 3, which we abbreviate as $\mathbf{Exp}^b$ for simplicity. We need to show that $\mathbf{Exp}^0$ and $\mathbf{Exp}^1$ are indistinguishable. Our proof will be by game hopping and we define a series of hybrid games $\mathbf{Exp}^{b,(0)} := \mathbf{Exp}^b$, $\mathbf{Exp}^{b,(1)}$ and $\mathbf{Exp}^{b,(2)}$, which are all defined in Fig. 3. We show that for $b = 0, 1$ and $c = 0, 1$ the games $\mathbf{Exp}^{b,(c)}$ and $\mathbf{Exp}^{b,(c+1)}$ are indistinguishable and that $\mathbf{Exp}^{0,(2)}$ and $\mathbf{Exp}^{1,(2)}$ are also indistinguishable, which concludes the proof.

$\mathbf{Exp}^{b,(0)}$ is the original game $\mathbf{Exp}_{\mathcal{F}, \mathcal{A}}^{b,(\emptyset, \{\text{CONSTR}, \text{EVAL}\})}(\lambda)$ for Construction 2.

$\mathbf{Exp}^{b,(1)}$ differs from $\mathbf{Exp}^{b,(0)}$ by replacing the full key of the puncturable PRF PF, with one that is punctured at $H(x^*)$ in the definition of P.

$\mathbf{Exp}^{b,(2)}$ differs from $\mathbf{Exp}^{b,(1)}$ by answering EVAL queries using the punctured key k_{h^*} and aborting whenever the query is a collision with x^* for H.

$\underline{\mathbf{Exp}_{\mathcal{F},\mathcal{A}}^{(\emptyset,\{\text{Constr},\text{Eval}\}),b}(\lambda)}$

$(x^*, st) \leftarrow \mathcal{A}_1(1^\lambda)$
$K \leftarrow \mathsf{F.Smp}(1^\lambda)$
If $b = 1$
$\quad y^* := \mathsf{F.Eval}(K, x^*)$
Else
$\quad y^* \leftarrow \mathcal{Y}$
$b' \leftarrow \mathcal{A}_2^{\text{Constr}(\cdot),\text{Eval}(\cdot)}(st, y^*)$
Return b'

Oracle $\text{Constr}(M)$

If $M \notin \mathcal{M}_\lambda \vee M(x^*) = 1$
$\quad$ Return $\perp$
$k_M \leftarrow \mathsf{F.Constr}(K, M)$
Return k_M

Oracle $\text{Eval}(x)$

If $x = x^*$
$\quad$ Return $\perp$
$y = \mathsf{F.Eval}(K, x)$
Return y

$\underline{\mathbf{Exp}_{\mathcal{F},\mathcal{A}}^{b,(c)}(\lambda)} \quad /\!/ \ c \in \{0, 1, 2\}$

$(x^*, st) \leftarrow \mathcal{A}_1(1^\lambda)$
$H \leftarrow \mathsf{H.Smp}(1^\lambda)$
$crs \leftarrow \{0,1\}^{\mathsf{poly}(\lambda)}$
$k \leftarrow \mathsf{PF.Smp}(1^\lambda)$
$k_{h^*} \leftarrow \mathsf{PF.Constr}(k, \{0,1\}^n \setminus \{H(x^*)\})$
$pp := (H, crs)$
If $b = 1$, $y^* := \mathsf{PF.Eval}(k, H(x^*))$, else $y^* \leftarrow \mathcal{Y}$
$b' \leftarrow \mathcal{A}_2^{\text{Constr}(\cdot),\text{Eval}(\cdot)}(st, y^*)$
Return b'

Oracle $\text{Constr}(M)$ **Oracle** $\text{Eval}(x)$

If $M \notin \mathcal{M}_\lambda \vee M(x^*) = 1$ If $x = x^*$
$\quad$ Return $\perp$ $\quad$ Return $\perp$
If $c = 0$ If $c \leq 1$
$\quad P := P_{M,H,crs,k}$ $\quad y := \mathsf{PF.Eval}(k, H(x))$
$\quad$ (as defined in (5))   Else
Else $\quad$ If $H(x) = H(x^*)$, abort
$\quad P := P_{M,H,crs,k_{h^*}}$ $\quad$ Else $y :=$
$\widetilde{P} \leftarrow \mathsf{diO}(1^\lambda, P)$ $\qquad \mathsf{PF.Eval}(k_{h^*}, H(x))$
Return $k_M := (M, \widetilde{P}, pp)$ Return y

Fig. 3. The original security game and hybrids used in the proof of Theorem 1.

The only difference between $\mathbf{Exp}^{b,(0)}$ and $\mathbf{Exp}^{b,(1)}$ is the definition of the circuits P that are obfuscated when the Constr oracle is queried. In $\mathbf{Exp}^{b,(0)}$ the circuit P is defined as in (5), with $k \leftarrow \mathsf{PF.Smp}(1^\lambda)$. In $\mathbf{Exp}^{b,(1)}$, the key k is replaced by $k_{h^*} \leftarrow \mathsf{ConstrPF}(k, \{0,1\}^n \setminus \{H(x^*)\})$, a key that punctures out $H(x^*)$. By a hybrid argument there must exist some query (say the ith for M_i) where the adversary distinguishes a diO obfuscation of $P_{M_i,H,crs,k}$ from one of $P_{M_i,H,crs,k_{h^*}}$. Thus, there exists a diO extractor that extracts an input $(\hat{h}, \hat{\pi})$ on which $P_{M_i,H,crs,k}$ and $P_{M_i,H,crs,k_{h^*}}$ differ.

By correctness of PF, the circuits only differ on inputs $(\hat{h}, \hat{\pi})$, where

$$\hat{h} = H(x^*) \ , \tag{6}$$

as that is where the punctured key behaves differently. Moreover, the extracted proof $\hat{\pi}$ must be valid for $(H, M_i, \hat{h})$, as otherwise both circuits output $\perp$. By SNARK extractability, we can extract a witness $\hat{x}$ for $(H, M_i, \hat{h}) \in L_{legit}$, that is, (i) $M_i(\hat{x}) = 1$ and (ii) $H(\hat{x}) = \hat{h}$. Since M_i is a legitimate query, we have $M_i(x^*) = 0$, which together with (i) implies $\hat{x} \neq x^*$. On the other hand, (ii) and (6) imply $H(\hat{x}) = H(x^*)$. Together, this means $(\hat{x}, x^*)$ is a collision for H.

Proposition 1. *For $b = 0, 1$, $\mathbf{Exp}^{b,(0)}$ and $\mathbf{Exp}^{b,(1)}$ are computationally indistinguishable if* diO *is a public-coin differing-input obfuscator and $\mathcal{H}$ is public-coin collision-resistant.*

For the game hop from games $\mathbf{Exp}^{b,(1)}$ to $\mathbf{Exp}^{b,(2)}$, indistinguishability follows directly from collision resistance of $\mathcal{H}$, as the only difference is that $\mathbf{Exp}^{b,(2)}$ aborts when $\mathcal{A}$ finds a collision.

Proposition 2. *For $b = 0, 1$, $\mathbf{Exp}^{b,(1)}$ and $\mathbf{Exp}^{b,(2)}$ are computationally indistinguishable for if $\mathcal{H}$ is collision-resistant.*

We have now reached a game, $\mathbf{Exp}^{b,(2)}$, in which the key k is only used to create a punctured key k_{h^*}. The experiment can thus be simulated by an adversary $\mathcal{B}$ against selective security of $\mathcal{PF}$, which first asks for a key for the set $\{0, 1\}^n \setminus \{H(x^*)\}$ and then uses $\mathcal{A}$ to distinguish $y^* = \mathsf{PF.Eval}(k, H(x^*))$ from random.

Proposition 3. $\mathbf{Exp}^{0,(2)}$ *and* $\mathbf{Exp}^{1,(2)}$ *are indistinguishable if $\mathcal{PF}$ is a selectively secure family of puncturable PRFs.*

Theorem 1 now follows from Propositions 1, 2 and 3. Proofs of the propositions can be found in the full version [1]. $\qquad\qquad\qquad\qquad\qquad\qquad\qquad\qquad\qquad$ $\square$

We refer to the full version for applications of our TM-constrained PRF.

References

1. Abusalah, H., Fuchsbauer, G., Pietrzak, K.: Constrained PRFs for unbounded inputs. In: Cryptology ePrint Archive, Report /840 (2014)
2. Ananth, P., Boneh, D., Garg, S., Sahai, A., Zhandry, M.: Differing-inputs obfuscation and applications. In: Cryptology ePrint Archive, Report 2013/689 (2013). http://eprint.iacr.org/2013/689
3. Barak, B., Goldreich, O.: Universal arguments and their applications. SIAM J. Comput. **38**(5), 1661–1694 (2008)
4. Barak, B., Goldreich, O., Impagliazzo, R., Rudich, S., Sahai, A., Vadhan, S., Yang, K.: On the (im)possibility of obfuscating programs. J. ACM **59**(2), 6:1–6:48 (2012)
5. Bellare, M., Stepanovs, I., Tessaro, S.: Poly-many hardcore bits for any one-way function and a framework for differing-inputs obfuscation. In: Sarkar, P., Iwata, T. (eds.) ASIACRYPT 2014, Part II. LNCS, vol. 8874, pp. 102–121. Springer, Heidelberg (2014)
6. Bitansky, N., Canetti, R., Chiesa, A., Goldwasser, S., Lin, H., Rubinstein, A., Tromer, E.: The hunting of the SNARK. IACR Cryptology ePrint Archive, 2014:580 (2014)
7. Bitansky, N., Canetti, R., Chiesa, A., Tromer, E.: Recursive composition and bootstrapping for SNARKS and proof-carrying data. In: Boneh, D., Roughgarden, T., Feigenbaum, J. (eds.) 45th ACM STOC, pp. 111–120. ACM Press, June 2013
8. Boneh, D., Gentry, C., Waters, B.: Collusion resistant broadcast encryption with short ciphertexts and private keys. In: Shoup, V. (ed.) CRYPTO 2005. LNCS, vol. 3621, pp. 258–275. Springer, Heidelberg (2005)
9. Boneh, D., Hamburg, M.: Generalized identity based and broadcast encryption schemes. In: Pieprzyk, J. (ed.) ASIACRYPT 2008. LNCS, vol. 5350, pp. 455–470. Springer, Heidelberg (2008)

10. Boneh, D., Waters, B.: Constrained pseudorandom functions and their applications. In: Sako, K., Sarkar, P. (eds.) ASIACRYPT 2013, Part II. LNCS, vol. 8270, pp. 280–300. Springer, Heidelberg (2013)
11. Boneh, D., Waters, B., Zhandry, M.: Low overhead broadcast encryption from multilinear maps. In: Garay, J.A., Gennaro, R. (eds.) CRYPTO 2014, Part I. LNCS, vol. 8616, pp. 206–223. Springer, Heidelberg (2014)
12. Boneh, D., Zhandry, M.: Multiparty key exchange, efficient traitor tracing, and more from indistinguishability obfuscation. In: Garay, J.A., Gennaro, R. (eds.) CRYPTO 2014, Part I. LNCS, vol. 8616, pp. 480–499. Springer, Heidelberg (2014)
13. Boyle, E., Chung, K.-M., Pass, R.: On extractability obfuscation. In: Lindell, Y. (ed.) TCC 2014. LNCS, vol. 8349, pp. 52–73. Springer, Heidelberg (2014)
14. Boyle, E., Goldwasser, S., Ivan, I.: Functional signatures and pseudorandom functions. In: Krawczyk, H. (ed.) PKC 2014. LNCS, vol. 8383, pp. 501–519. Springer, Heidelberg (2014)
15. Coron, J.-S., Lepoint, T., Tibouchi, M.: Practical multilinear maps over the integers. In: Canetti, R., Garay, J.A. (eds.) CRYPTO 2013, Part I. LNCS, vol. 8042, pp. 476–493. Springer, Heidelberg (2013)
16. Fiat, A., Naor, M.: Broadcast encryption. In: Stinson, D.R. (ed.) CRYPTO 1993. LNCS, vol. 773, pp. 480–491. Springer, Heidelberg (1994)
17. Freire, E.S.V., Hofheinz, D., Paterson, K.G., Striecks, C.: Programmable hash functions in the multilinear setting. In: Canetti, R., Garay, J.A. (eds.) CRYPTO 2013, Part I. LNCS, vol. 8042, pp. 513–530. Springer, Heidelberg (2013)
18. Fuchsbauer, G., Konstantinov, M., Pietrzak, K., Rao, V.: Adaptive security of constrained PRFs. In: Sarkar, P., Iwata, T. (eds.) ASIACRYPT 2014, Part II. LNCS, vol. 8874, pp. 82–101. Springer, Heidelberg (2014)
19. Garg, S., Gentry, C., Halevi, S.: Candidate multilinear maps from ideal lattices. In: Johansson, T., Nguyen, P.Q. (eds.) EUROCRYPT 2013. LNCS, vol. 7881, pp. 1–17. Springer, Heidelberg (2013)
20. Garg, S., Gentry, C., Halevi, S., Raykova, M., Sahai, A., Waters, B.: Candidate indistinguishability obfuscation and functional encryption for all circuits. In: 54th FOCS, pp. 40–49. IEEE Computer Society Press, October 2013
21. Garg, S., Gentry, C., Halevi, S., Wichs, D.: On the implausibility of differing-inputs obfuscation and extractable witness encryption with auxiliary input. In: Garay, J.A., Gennaro, R. (eds.) CRYPTO 2014, Part I. LNCS, vol. 8616, pp. 518–535. Springer, Heidelberg (2014)
22. Gentry, C., Wichs, D.: Separating succinct non-interactive arguments from all falsifiable assumptions. In: Fortnow, L., Vadhan, S.P. (eds.) 43rd ACM STOC, pp. 99–108. ACM Press, June 2011
23. Goldreich, O., Goldwasser, S., Micali, S.: How to construct random functions. J. ACM 33(4), 792–807 (1986)
24. Hofheinz, D., Kamath, A., Koppula, V., Waters, B.: Adaptively secure constrained pseudorandom functions. In: Cryptology ePrint Archive, Report 2014/720 (2014). http://eprint.iacr.org/
25. Hohenberger, S., Koppula, V., Waters, B.: Adaptively secure puncturable pseudorandom functions in the standard model. In: Cryptology ePrint Archive, Report 2014/521 (2014). http://eprint.iacr.org/2014/521
26. Hsiao, C.-Y., Reyzin, L.: Finding collisions on a public road, or do secure hash functions need secret coins? In: Franklin, M. (ed.) CRYPTO 2004. LNCS, vol. 3152, pp. 92–105. Springer, Heidelberg (2004)

27. Ishai, Y., Pandey, O., Sahai, A.: Public-coin differing-inputs obfuscation and its applications. In: Dodis, Y., Nielsen, J.B. (eds.) TCC 2015, Part II. LNCS, vol. 9015, pp. 668–697. Springer, Heidelberg (2015)

28. Kiayias, A., Papadopoulos, S., Triandopoulos, N., Zacharias, T.: Delegatable pseudorandom functions and applications. In: Sadeghi, A.-R., Gligor, V.D., Yung, M. (eds.) ACM CCS 2013, pp. 669–684. ACM Press, November 2013

29. Koppula, V., Lewko, A.B., Waters, B.: Indistinguishability obfuscation for turing machines with unbounded memory. In: Servedio, R.A., Rubinfeld, R. (eds.) 47th ACM STOC, pp. 419–428. ACM Press, June 2015

30. Langlois, A., Stehlé, D., Steinfeld, R.: GGHLite: more efficient multilinear maps from ideal lattices. In: Nguyen, P.Q., Oswald, E. (eds.) EUROCRYPT 2014. LNCS, vol. 8441, pp. 239–256. Springer, Heidelberg (2014)

31. Pass, R., Seth, K., Telang, S.: Indistinguishability obfuscation from semantically-secure multilinear encodings. In: Garay, J.A., Gennaro, R. (eds.) CRYPTO 2014, Part I. LNCS, vol. 8616, pp. 500–517. Springer, Heidelberg (2014)

32. Phan, D.H., Pointcheval, D., Strefler, M.: Security notions for broadcast encryption. In: Lopez, J., Tsudik, G. (eds.) ACNS 2011. LNCS, vol. 6715, pp. 377–394. Springer, Heidelberg (2011)

33. Sahai, A., Waters, B.: How to use indistinguishability obfuscation: deniable encryption, and more. In: Shmoys, D.B. (ed.) 46th ACM STOC, pp. 475–484. ACM Press, May/June 2014

34. Sakai, R., Ohgishi, K., Kasahara, M.: Cryptosystems based on pairing. In: SCIS 2000, Okinawa, Japan, January 2000

35. Yao, D., Fazio, N., Dodis, Y., Lysyanskaya, A.: ID-based encryption for complex hierarchies with applications to forward security and broadcast encryption. In: Atluri, V., Pfitzmann, B., McDaniel, P. (eds.) ACM CCS 2004, pp. 354–363. ACM Press, October 2004

Security of Public Key Encryption

Construction of Fully CCA-Secure Predicate Encryptions from Pair Encoding Schemes

Johannes Blömer and Gennadij Liske[(✉)]

Paderborn University, Paderborn, Germany
{bloemer,gennadij.liske}@upb.de

Abstract. This paper presents a new framework for constructing fully CCA-secure predicate encryption schemes from pair encoding schemes. Our construction is the first in the context of predicate encryption which uses the technique of well-formedness proofs known from public key encryption. The resulting constructions are simpler and more efficient compared to the schemes achieved using known generic transformations from CPA-secure to CCA-secure schemes. The reduction costs of our framework are comparable to the reduction costs of the underlying CPA-secure framework. We achieve this last result by applying the dual system encryption methodology in a novel way.

Keywords: Predicate encryption schemes · Chosen-ciphertext security · Full security · Key-encapsulation mechanisms · Pair encoding schemes

1 Introduction

Predicate encryption (PE) with public index, as a subclass of functional encryption [7], is a powerful generalization of traditional public-key encryption (PKE). In a PE system for a predicate R, data are encrypted under so-called ciphertext indices cInd, which are public. A user can decrypt such a ciphertext if she holds a secret key with a key index kInd, such that R (kInd, cInd) = 1. Identity-based encryption (IBE) schemes realize the equality relation and are the simplest example of PE. In general, predicate encryption schemes provide a powerful tool for achieving fine-grained access control on confidential data.

Except for IBE, constructions of fully (also called adaptively) secure PEs have been missing for a long time. The dual system encryption methodology, introduced and extended by Waters and Lewko [15,19], provides fundamental techniques to achieve fully secure PE schemes which withstand chosen-plaintext attacks (CPA). Based on this methodology, schemes for various predicates such as (hierarchical) identity-based encryption [15,19], attribute-based encryption [14,16], inner-product encryption [4,17], spatial encryption [4,11], and schemes for regular languages [3], to name just a few, have been constructed.

The authors were partially supported by the German Research Foundation (DFG) within the Collaborative Research Centre "On-The-Fly Computing" (SFB 901).

© Springer International Publishing Switzerland 2016
K. Sako (Ed.): CT-RSA 2016, LNCS 9610, pp. 431–447, 2016.
DOI: 10.1007/978-3-319-29485-8_25

Although many PE schemes have been presented, constructions for new predicates have each been built from the ground up until the following results were published. Attrapadung [3] and Wee [20] independently introduced generic frameworks for the design and analysis of PE schemes with public index from composite-order bilinear groups. These frameworks are based on the dual system encryption methodology and define new cryptographic primitives called pair encoding and predicate encoding. Attrapadung and Wee showed that fully CPA-secure PEs can be constructed from encoding schemes in a generic fashion. This approach simplifies the development of new schemes, since the complexity of security proofs is reduced. Furthermore, the properties required to achieve secure constructions are better understood, structured, and defined in terms of security properties of encodings. Recently, both frameworks were adapted to prime-order groups in [1,2] and in [8], respectively. Overall, the research on encodings resulted in new and efficient CPA-secure schemes for various predicates. In this paper, we extend the framework of Attrapadung [3] to achieve fully CCA-secure PE schemes. We chose this framework because of its powerful computational (rather than information theoretic) security notion which allows to capture involved predicates. Although this will be a non-trivial task, we believe that our techniques can be applied to the pair encoding framework in prime order groups [2].

Related Work. Although there exist many adaptively CPA-secure PE schemes for various predicates, only a few papers consider the realization of fully secure schemes which withstand chosen-ciphertext attacks (CCA), the most desirable security notion in practice. Comparing this situation with PKE schemes and IBE schemes, we identify the following gap. Mainly two different approaches are known to achieve *efficient* CCA-secure schemes *without random oracle model* in the context of PKE and IBE (cf. discussion in [6]). The first approach goes back to the CCA-secure PKE schemes introduced in [10]. Schemes following this approach achieve CCA-security using a kind of *well-formedness proofs*, exploit specific properties of the underlying CPA-secure schemes, and sacrifice generality for efficiency. The second approach goes back to the generic transformations presented in [6] and uses one-time signatures or message authentication codes as building blocks. Whereas both approaches are well studied for PKE [6,9,10] and (hierarchical) IBE [6,12,13] this is not the case for PE with more involved predicates.

Generic transformations of CPA-secure PE schemes into CCA-secure schemes presented in [21,22] pursue the second approach from above and use one-time signatures as a building block. However, the first approach of well-formedness proofs has not been taken into account for PEs. Indeed, only a few PE schemes are proven to be fully CCA-secure without applying the generic transformations from [21,22]. To the best of our knowledge these are the broadcast-encryption scheme from [18] and the (index hiding) encryption for relations that are specified by non-monotone access structures combined with inner product relations [17]. The techniques from [18] are closely related to the techniques used for adaptively secure IBE schemes. The schemes from [17] achieve CCA-security using one-time signature schemes and their techniques are closely related to [22].

We can only speculate why the non-generic approach of well-formedness proofs from [10] has not been considered for fully secure predicate encryption schemes. Probably because of the complex structure of the ciphertexts in PE schemes well-formedness proofs have been assumed to be inefficient. Furthermore, the consistency checks for the ciphertexts seem to be in conflict with the dual system encryption methodology, since an essential part of this technique is based on incorrectly formed ciphertexts, i.e. semi-functional ciphertexts. In this work we show that these assumptions are premature. We show that the dual system encryption techniques can be combined with well-formedness proofs and that the resulting fully CCA-secure PE schemes require computational overhead, which is comparable to the additional overhead required by the generic transformations.

Our Contribution. In this work we take a significant step to close the gap between PKE/IBE and PE w.r.t. non-generic CCA-secure constructions. Namely, given any pair encoding scheme (with natural restrictions) secure in terms of [3], we construct a fully CCA-secure key-encapsulation mechanism (KEM) for the corresponding predicate using a kind of well-formedness proofs. Surprisingly, due to the pair encoding abstraction, we achieve a semi-generic transformation and still exploit structural properties of the underlying CPA-secure schemes. Since the underlying framework of [3] is defined on composite-order groups, our construction is also build on these groups. Combined with an appropriate symmetric encryption, our framework leads to various new fully CCA-secure PE schemes through the usual hybrid construction. In fact, for efficiency reasons hybrid schemes are preferred to plain encryption schemes in practice.

Although our extensions of CPA-secure schemes are similar to those used in PKE schemes, the application to complex predicates as well as the generic nature of our construction are novel for the underlying techniques. We achieve simpler and usually more efficient constructions than those obtained from CPA-secure schemes and the generic transformations based on one-time signatures [21,22]. Furthermore, we keep the advantage of tight reductions from the original framework of Attrapadung [3], and the reduction costs of our CCA-secure construction are comparable to the reduction costs of the underlying CPA-secure construction. This is indeed surprising and is due to our extension of the dual system encryption methodology which we describe below. The only additional cryptographic primitive required by our construction is a collision-resistant hash function, which is used to add a single redundant group element to the ciphertext. Apart from that, we add two group elements to the public parameters of the underlying CPA-secure scheme. The security of our framework is based on the same security assumptions as the security of the original CPA-secure framework.

Moving Beyond the Dual System Encryption Methodology. Security proofs in cryptography often consist of a sequence of probability experiments (or games) with small differences. The first experiment is the target security experiment

(CCA-security experiment in our case) whereas the last experiment is constructed in such a way, that the adversaries cannot achieve any advantage. The task of the proof is to show that consecutive experiments are computationally indistinguishable. This proof structure is also used in dual system encryption methodology [19], but the changes between the experiments are quite special. The main idea of this technique is to define so-called semi-functional keys and semi-functional ciphertexts, which are indistinguishable from their normal counterparts. In the proof sequence, the challenge ciphertext and all generated keys are transformed from normal to semi-functional one by one. In the last experiment, when all elements are modified, the challenge can be changed to the ciphertext of a randomly chosen message.

The obvious way to apply dual system encryption methodology in the context of CCA-security is to treat keys used to answer decryption queries in the same way as keys queried by the adversary. This strategy was followed in [17] (see discussion of this work below), but our proof strategy diverges from it. We deal with decryption queries in a novel and surprisingly simple manner. As an additional advantage, the reductions of the original CPA-security proof require only a few and simple modifications. The main idea is to answer decryption queries in *all* games using separately generated *normal* keys. Our well-formedness checks ensure that this modification cannot be noticed. Moreover, we ensure that normal and semi-functional ciphertexts both pass our well-formedness checks. Mainly because of this approach, we can keep the basic structure of the original CPA-security proof of Attrapadung. We only have to add four additional experiments: three at the beginning and one before the last game. In our last game we show that by using the redundant element added to the ciphertext we can answer all decryption queries without the user secret keys. The indistinguishability for this experiment is again based on our well-formedness checks.

The main advantage of our construction and our proof strategy becomes obvious if compared to the techniques in [17], where *all keys* are changed and the security guarantees decrease linearly in the number of decryption queries and the number of corrupted keys. In our approach, the number of decryption queries influences the security guarantees only negligibly. In a realistic scenario, the number of decryption queries must be assumed to be much larger than the number of corrupted keys. Hence, our approach results in smaller security parameters, which also increases efficiency.

Organization. In Sect. 2 we present the preliminaries including security definitions and assumptions. Section 3 contains our formal requirements on pair encoding schemes and our fully CCA-secure framework. In Sect. 4 we present our main theorem and explain our proof strategy. Finally, in Sect. 5 we compare our resulting schemes with generic constructions and conclude.

2   Background

We denote by $\alpha := a$ the algorithmic action of assigning the value a to the variable α. For $n \in \mathbb{N}$, we denote by $[n]$ the set $\{i \in \mathbb{N} \mid 1 \leq i \leq n\}$ and by $[n]_0$ the set $[n] \cup \{0\}$. Let X be a random variable on a finite set S. We denote by $[X]$ the support of X, that is $[X] = \{s \in S \mid \Pr[X = s] > 0\}$. We write $\alpha \leftarrow X$ to denote the algorithmic action of sampling an element of S according to the distribution defined by X. We also write $\alpha \leftarrow S$ when sampling an element from S according to the uniform distribution. Furthermore, $\alpha_1, \ldots, \alpha_n \leftarrow X$ is a shortcut for $\alpha_1 \leftarrow X, \ldots, \alpha_n \leftarrow X$. This notation can be extended to probabilistic polynomial time (ppt) algorithms, since every ppt algorithm $\mathcal{A}$ on input x defines a finite output probability space denoted by $\mathcal{A}(x)$. Finally, vectors are written in bold and we do not distinguish between row and column vectors. It will be obvious from context what we mean. We usually denote the components of a vector $\boldsymbol{v}$ by $(v_1, \ldots, v_n)$, where $n = |\boldsymbol{v}|$.

2.1   Predicate Families

In this work, a predicate family is a set of relations $\mathcal{R}_{\Omega, \Sigma} = \{R_\kappa\}_{\kappa \in \Omega \times \Sigma}$, where each R_κ maps pairs $(\text{kInd}, \text{cInd}) \in \mathbb{X}_\kappa \times \mathbb{Y}_\kappa$ of a key index kInd and a ciphertext index cInd to $\{0, 1\}$. Predicate indices des $\in \Omega$ specify some general description properties of the corresponding predicates (e.g. maximal number of attributes), and indices dom $\in \Sigma$ specify domain properties which will depend on the security parameter (e.g. domain of computation $\mathbb{Z}_p$). Our framework is defined over composite order groups and hence, we have to take care of zero-divisors in $\mathbb{Z}_N$ for composite $N \in \mathbb{N}$. The following definition is adapted from [3] to our notation and specifies the required property of the predicate families.

Definition 2.1. *A predicate family $\mathcal{R}_{\Omega, \Sigma}$ is called* domain-transferable *if $\Sigma \subset \mathbb{N}$ and there exists a ppt algorithm* Factor *such that for every $\kappa = (\text{des}, N) \in \Omega \times \Sigma$, every $p \in \mathbb{N}^{>1}$ with $p \mid N$ it holds $\kappa' = (\text{des}, p) \in \Omega \times \Sigma$, and $\mathbb{X}_{\kappa'} \subseteq \mathbb{X}_\kappa$, $\mathbb{Y}_{\kappa'} \subseteq \mathbb{Y}_\kappa$. Furthermore, there must exist projection maps $f_1 : \mathbb{X}_\kappa \mapsto \mathbb{X}_{\kappa'}$ and $f_2 : \mathbb{Y}_\kappa \mapsto \mathbb{Y}_{\kappa'}$ such that for all kInd $\in \mathbb{X}_\kappa$ and cInd $\in \mathbb{Y}_\kappa$ it holds:*

Completeness: *If $R_\kappa(\text{kInd}, \text{cInd}) = 1$, then $R_{\kappa'}(f_1(\text{kInd}), f_2(\text{cInd})) = 1$.*
Soundness: *If $R_\kappa(\text{kInd}, \text{cInd}) = 0$ but $R_{\kappa'}(f_1(\text{kInd}), f_2(\text{cInd})) = 1$, then a nontrivial factor F of N can be computed by $F := \text{Factor}(\kappa, \text{kInd}, \text{cInd})$.*

2.2   Predicate Key-Encapsulation Mechanisms

In this subsection we present the definition of predicate key-encapsulation mechanisms (P-KEMs) and the definition of full security against adaptively chosen-ciphertext attacks (also called CCA2 attacks) for these schemes. P-KEMs combined with appropriate symmetric encryption schemes lead to fully functional predicate encryptions through the usual hybrid construction (see the full version). Let $\mathcal{K} = \{\mathbb{K}_\lambda\}$ be a family of finite sets indexed by security parameter λ and possibly some further parameters. A P-KEM Π for predicate family $\mathcal{R}_{\Omega, \Sigma}$ and a family of key spaces $\mathcal{K}$ consists of four ppt algorithms:

Setup $(1^\lambda, \text{des}) \rightarrow (\text{msk}, \text{pp}_\kappa)$: takes as input security parameter λ, des $\in \Omega$, and outputs a master secret key and public parameters. The algorithm also chooses dom $\in \Sigma$ and $\kappa = (\text{des}, \text{dom})$ is (implicitly) included in pp_κ.

KeyGen$_{\mathrm{msk}}\left(1^\lambda, \mathrm{pp}_\kappa, \mathrm{kInd}\right) \to \mathrm{sk}$: takes as input the master secret key msk and a key index $\mathrm{kInd} \in \mathbb{X}_\kappa$. It generates a secret key sk for kInd.

Encaps$\left(1^\lambda, \mathrm{pp}_\kappa, \mathrm{cInd}\right) \to (\mathrm{K}, \mathrm{CT})$: takes as input a ciphertext index $\mathrm{cInd} \in \mathbb{Y}_\kappa$ and outputs a key $\mathrm{K} \in \mathbb{K}_\lambda$, and an encapsulation CT of this key.

Decaps$_{\mathrm{sk}}\left(1^\lambda, \mathrm{pp}_\kappa, \mathrm{CT}\right) \to \mathrm{K}$: takes as input a secret key sk and an encapsulation. It outputs a key $\mathrm{K} \in \mathbb{K}_\lambda$ or an error symbol $\perp \notin \mathbb{K}_\lambda$.

Correctness: For every security parameter λ, every des $\in \Omega$, every $(\mathrm{msk}, \mathrm{pp}_\kappa) \in$ $\left[\mathrm{Setup}\left(1^\lambda, \mathrm{des}\right)\right]$, every $\mathrm{kInd} \in \mathbb{X}_\kappa$ and $\mathrm{cInd} \in \mathbb{Y}_\kappa$ with $\mathrm{R}_\kappa\left(\mathrm{kInd}, \mathrm{cInd}\right) = 1$, every $\mathrm{sk} \in \left[\mathrm{KeyGen}_{\mathrm{msk}}\left(1^\lambda, \mathrm{pp}_\kappa, \mathrm{kInd}\right)\right]$ and $(\mathrm{K}, \mathrm{CT}) \in \left[\mathrm{Encaps}\left(1^\lambda, \mathrm{pp}_\kappa, \mathrm{cInd}\right)\right]$ it must hold that $\Pr\left[\mathrm{Decaps}_{\mathrm{sk}}\left(1^\lambda, \mathrm{pp}_\kappa, \mathrm{CT}\right) = \mathrm{K}\right] = 1$.

We will leave out 1^λ and pp_κ from the input of the algorithms, if these are obvious from the context. Furthermore, for every $\mathrm{kInd} \in \mathbb{X}_\kappa$ and every $\mathrm{cInd} \in \mathbb{Y}_\kappa$ we denote by $\mathbb{SK}_{\mathrm{kInd}}$ and by $\mathbb{C}_{\mathrm{cInd}}$ the sets of syntactically correct secret keys and encapsulations, respectively. These sets are certain supersets of corresponding correctly generated elements and represent their syntactic structure, which can be easily checked (e.g. the correct number of group elements).

CCA Security Definition for P-KEMs. Whereas in the context of traditional PKE there is only a single secret key in question, in PE schemes there are many user secret keys generated from the master secret key. Actually, several users may have different keys for the same key index. In order to model this issue, we have to give the adversary the possibility to specify not only the key index, but also the keys which have to be used for answering decapsulation queries. Similar to [18], we model this using so-called covered key generation queries.

Let Π be a P-KEM for predicate family $\mathcal{R}_{\Omega,\Sigma}$ and family $\mathcal{K} = \{\mathbb{K}_\lambda\}$ of key spaces. The CCA-security experiment $\mathrm{aP\text{-}KEM}_{\Pi,\mathcal{A}}^{\mathrm{aCCA}}\left(\lambda, \mathrm{des}\right)$ between challenger $\mathcal{C}$ and adversary $\mathcal{A}$ is defined next. In this experiment, index i denotes the number of a covered key generation query and kInd_i denotes the key index used in the query with number i. W.l.o.g. we assume, that $\mathcal{A}$ uses index i in the oracle queries only after the i'th query to the covered key generation oracle. In the security proof we will change this experiment step by step. The parts of the experiment, which will be changed later, are framed and numbered.

aP-KEM$_{\Pi,\mathcal{A}}^{\mathrm{aCCA}}\left(\lambda, \mathrm{des}\right)$:

Setup : $\mathcal{C}$ generates $^{\langle 1 \rangle}$ $\boxed{(\mathrm{msk}, \mathrm{pp}_\kappa) \leftarrow \mathrm{Setup}\left(1^\lambda, \mathrm{des}\right)}$ and starts $\mathcal{A}\left(1^\lambda, \mathrm{pp}_\kappa\right)$.

Phase I : $\mathcal{A}$ has access to the following oracles:

    CoveredKeyGen (kInd_i) with $\mathrm{kInd}_i \in \mathbb{X}_\kappa$: $\mathcal{C}$ generates and stores a secret key $^{\langle 2 \rangle}$ $\boxed{\mathrm{sk}_i \leftarrow \mathrm{KeyGen}_{\mathrm{msk}}\left(\mathrm{kInd}_i\right)}$, but returns nothing.

    Open (i) with $i \in \mathbb{N}$: $\mathcal{C}$ returns $^{\langle 3 \rangle}$ $\boxed{\mathrm{sk}_i}$. We call the corresponding key index kInd_i a corrupted key index.

    Decapsulate (CT, i) with $\mathrm{CT} \in \mathbb{C}_{\mathrm{cInd}}$ for some $\mathrm{cInd} \in \mathbb{Y}_\kappa$, and $i \in \mathbb{N}$: $\mathcal{C}$ returns the decapsulation $^{\langle 4 \rangle}$ $\boxed{\mathrm{Decaps}_{\mathrm{sk}_i}\left(\mathrm{CT}\right)}$.[1]

---

[1] For schemes, where cInd is not efficiently computable from CT, the decapsulation oracle requires the ciphertext index as additional input.

Challenge : $\mathcal{A}$ submits a target ciphertext index $\text{cInd}^* \in \mathbb{Y}_\kappa$ under the restriction that for every corrupted key index kInd it holds $\text{R}_\kappa(\text{kInd}, \text{cInd}^*) = 0$.
$\mathcal{C}$ computes $^{\langle 5 \rangle}$ $\boxed{(\text{K}_0, \text{CT}^*) \leftarrow \text{Encaps}(\text{cInd}^*)}$, chooses $\text{K}_1 \leftarrow \mathbb{K}_\lambda$, flips a bit $b \leftarrow \{0, 1\}$, sets $^{\langle 6 \rangle}$ $\boxed{\text{K}^* := \text{K}_b}$, and returns the challenge $(\text{K}^*, \text{CT}^*)$.

Phase II : $\mathcal{A}$ has access to the following oracles:

CoveredKeyGen (kInd_i) with $\text{kInd}_i \in \mathbb{X}_\kappa$: $\mathcal{C}$ generates a stores a secret key $^{\langle 7 \rangle}$ $\boxed{\text{sk}_i \leftarrow \text{KeyGen}_{\text{msk}}(\text{kInd}_i)}$, but returns nothing.

Open (i) with $i \in \mathbb{N}$: Under the restriction that $\text{R}_\kappa(\text{kInd}_i, \text{cInd}^*) = 0$, $\mathcal{C}$ returns $^{\langle 8 \rangle}$ $\boxed{\text{sk}_i}$.

Decapsulate (CT, i) with $\text{CT} \in \mathbb{C}_{\text{cInd}}$ for some $\text{cInd} \in \mathbb{Y}_\kappa$, and $i \in \mathbb{N}$: $\mathcal{C}$ returns the error symbol $\bot$ if $\text{CT} = \text{CT}^*$ and $\text{R}_\kappa(\text{kInd}_i, \text{cInd}^*) = 1$. Otherwise, $\mathcal{C}$ returns $^{\langle 9 \rangle}$ $\boxed{\text{Decaps}_{\text{sk}_i}(\text{CT})}$.

Guess : $\mathcal{A}$ outputs a guess $b' \in \{0, 1\}$.

$^{\langle 10 \rangle}$ $\boxed{\text{The output of the experiment is 1 iff } b' = b}$.

The advantage of $\mathcal{A}$ in security experiment $\text{aP-KEM}_{\Pi,\mathcal{A}}^{\text{aCCA}}(\lambda, \text{des})$ is defined as
$$\text{Adv-aP-KEM}_{\Pi,\mathcal{A}}^{\text{aCCA}}(\lambda, \text{des}) := \left| \Pr\left[\text{aP-KEM}_{\Pi,\mathcal{A}}^{\text{aCCA}}(\lambda, \text{des}) = 1 \right] - \tfrac{1}{2} \right|.$$

Definition 2.2. *A predicate key encapsulation mechanism Π for predicate family $\mathcal{R}_{\Omega,\Sigma}$ is called* fully *(or adaptively)* secure against adaptively chosen-ciphertext attacks *if for every* $\text{des} \in \Omega$ *and every ppt adversary $\mathcal{A}$ the function* $\text{Adv-aP-KEM}_{\Pi,\mathcal{A}}^{\text{aCCA}}(\lambda, \text{des})$ *is negligible in λ.*

2.3   Composite Order Bilinear Groups

In this section we briefly recall the main properties of composite order bilinear groups (cf. [15]). We define these groups using a group generation algorithm $\mathcal{G}$, a ppt algorithm which takes as input a security parameter 1^λ and outputs a description $\mathbb{GD}$ of bilinear groups. We require that $\mathcal{G}$ outputs

$$\mathbb{GD} = (p_1, p_2, p_3, (g, \mathbb{G}), \mathbb{G}_T, e : \mathbb{G} \times \mathbb{G} \to \mathbb{G}_T) ,$$

where p_1, p_2, p_3 are distinct primes of length λ, $\mathbb{G}$ and $\mathbb{G}_T$ are cyclic groups of order $N = p_1 p_2 p_3$, g is a generator of $\mathbb{G}$, and function e is a non-degenerate bilinear map: i.e., $e\left(g^a, g^b\right) = e(g, g)^{a \cdot b}$ and $e(g, g) \neq 1_{\mathbb{G}_T}$. We require that the group operations as well as the bilinear map e are computable in polynomial time with respect to λ. We denote by $\mathbb{GD}_N$ the same group description but with N instead of the corresponding prime numbers. We require that $\mathbb{GD}_N$ is sufficient to perform group operations and to evaluate e.

$\mathbb{G}$ can be decomposed as $\mathbb{G}_{p_1} \times \mathbb{G}_{p_2} \times \mathbb{G}_{p_3}$, where for every $p_i \mid N$ we denote by $\mathbb{G}_{p_i}$ the unique subgroup of $\mathbb{G}$ of order p_i and by g_i a generator of $\mathbb{G}_{p_i}$. Every $h \in \mathbb{G}$ can be expressed as $g_1^{a_1} g_2^{a_2} g_3^{a_3}$, where a_i are uniquely defined modulo p_i. Hence, we will call $g_i^{a_i}$ the $\mathbb{G}_{p_i}$ component of h. Note that, e.g., $g^{p_1 p_2}$ generates $\mathbb{G}_{p_3}$ and hence, given the factorization of N, we can pick random elements from every subgroup. An important property of composite order bilinear groups is that for $p_i \neq p_j$ and $g_i \in \mathbb{G}_{p_i}$, $g_j \in \mathbb{G}_{p_j}$ it holds $e(g_i, g_j) = 1_{\mathbb{G}_T}$.

We will also use the following common shortcuts for vectors of group elements. Let $g, h, r \in \mathbb{G}$, $\boldsymbol{v}, \boldsymbol{w}, \boldsymbol{u} \in \mathbb{Z}_N^k$, and $\boldsymbol{E} \in \mathbb{Z}_N^{k \times d}$ for $k, d \in \mathbb{N}$. We denote by $g^{\boldsymbol{v}}$ the vector $(g^{v_1}, g^{v_2}, \ldots, g^{v_k}) \in \mathbb{G}^k$. Furthermore, we define $g^{\boldsymbol{v}} \cdot g^{\boldsymbol{w}} := g^{\boldsymbol{v}+\boldsymbol{w}}$, $(g^{\boldsymbol{v}})^{\boldsymbol{E}} := g^{\boldsymbol{v} \cdot \boldsymbol{E}}$, and $e(g^{\boldsymbol{v}}, h^{\boldsymbol{w}}) := \prod_{i=1}^{k} e(g^{v_i}, h^{w_i})$. Hence, it also holds $e(g^{\boldsymbol{v}}, h^{\boldsymbol{w}} \cdot r^{\boldsymbol{u}}) = e(g^{\boldsymbol{v}}, h^{\boldsymbol{w}}) \cdot e(g^{\boldsymbol{v}}, r^{\boldsymbol{u}})$. Furthermore, given $g^{\boldsymbol{v}}$ and $\boldsymbol{E}$ one can efficiently compute components of $(g^{\boldsymbol{v}})^{\boldsymbol{E}} \in \mathbb{Z}_N^d$.

2.4 Security Assumptions

In this subsection we define the Subgroup Decision Assumptions used to prove the security of our construction. We use exactly the same assumptions as the original CPA-secure framework [3]. See also [15] for validity of these assumptions in the generic group model. Let $\mathcal{G}$ be a group generation algorithm. Each of the following probability experiments starts with $\mathbb{GD} \leftarrow \mathcal{G}(1^\lambda)$.

SD1 (λ): $\quad g_1 \leftarrow \mathbb{G}_{p_1}, \quad g_3 \leftarrow \mathbb{G}_{p_3}$,
$\qquad D := (\mathbb{GD}_N, g_1, g_3), \quad Z_0 \leftarrow \mathbb{G}_{p_1}, \quad Z_1 \leftarrow \mathbb{G}_{p_1 p_2}$.

SD2 (λ): $\quad g_1, X_1 \leftarrow \mathbb{G}_{p_1}, \quad X_2, Y_2 \leftarrow \mathbb{G}_{p_2}, \quad g_3, Y_3 \leftarrow \mathbb{G}_{p_3}$,
$\qquad D := (\mathbb{GD}_N, g_1, X_1 X_2, Y_2 Y_3, g_3), \quad Z_0 \leftarrow \mathbb{G}_{p_1 p_3}, \quad Z_1 \leftarrow \mathbb{G}$.

SD3 (λ): $\quad g_1 \leftarrow \mathbb{G}_{p_1}, \quad g_2, X_2, Y_2 \leftarrow \mathbb{G}_{p_2}, \quad g_3 \leftarrow \mathbb{G}_{p_3}, \quad \alpha, s \leftarrow \mathbb{Z}_N$
$\qquad D := (\mathbb{GD}_N, g_1, g_1^\alpha X_2, g_1^s Y_2, g_2, g_3), \quad Z_0 \leftarrow \mathbb{G}_T, \quad Z_1 := e(g_1, g_1)^{\alpha s}$.

The advantage of $\mathcal{A}$ in breaking experiment SDi (λ) is defined as $\mathrm{Adv}_{\mathcal{A}}^{\mathrm{SD}i}(\lambda) := |\Pr[\mathcal{A}(D, Z_0) = 1] - \Pr[\mathcal{A}(D, Z_1) = 1]|$. We say that $\mathcal{G}$ satisfies Assumption i if for every ppt algorithm $\mathcal{A}$ the function $\mathrm{Adv}_{\mathcal{A}}^{\mathrm{SD}i}(\lambda)$ is negligible.

The following lemma was implicitly proven in [15] (see the proof of Lemma 5). This lemma implies, that under Assumption SD2, it is computationally infeasible to compute a non-trivial factor of N (see the full version).

Lemma 2.1. *There exists a ppt algorithm $\mathcal{A}$ with $\mathrm{Adv}_{\mathcal{A}}^{\mathrm{SD}2}(\lambda) \approx 1$ if $\mathcal{A}$ is given a non-trivial factor F of N.*

3 Framework for CCA-Secure P-KEMs

In this section we recall the definition of pair encoding schemes and define two additional properties, which are required for our CCA-secure framework. Our framework is presented in Subsect. 3.3.

3.1 Pair Encoding Schemes

In this subsection we first recall the formal definition of *pair encodings* presented by Attrapadung [3] and slightly adapted to our notation. This cryptographic primitive is used to construct PE schemes. Let $\mathcal{R}_{\Omega,\Sigma}$ be a domain-transferable predicate family, $\kappa = (\mathrm{des}, N) \in \Omega \times \Sigma$, kInd $\in \mathbb{X}_\kappa$ and cInd $\in \mathbb{Y}_\kappa$.

A *pair encoding scheme* P for $\mathcal{R}_{\Omega,\Sigma}$ consists of four ppt algorithms:

Param $(\kappa) =: n$: outputs $n \in \mathbb{N}$, which defines the number of so-called common variables denoted by $\mathbf{X}_h = (X_{h_1}, \ldots, X_{h_n})$.

Enc1 $(\kappa, \mathrm{kInd}) =: (\boldsymbol{k}, m_2)$: outputs $m_2 \in \mathbb{N}$ and a vector $\boldsymbol{k} = (k_1, \ldots, k_{m_1})$ of m_1 multivariate polynomials $k_1, \ldots, k_{m_1} \in \mathbb{Z}_N[X_\alpha, \mathbf{X}_r, \mathbf{X}_h]$. The variables X_α and $\mathbf{X}_r = (X_{r_1}, \ldots, X_{r_{m_2}})$ are called key-specific. The k_i's are restricted to linear combinations of monomials $\{X_\alpha, X_{r_i}, X_{h_j}X_{r_i}\}_{i \in [m_2], j \in [n]}$.

Enc2 $(\kappa, \mathrm{cInd}) =: (\boldsymbol{c}, w_2)$: outputs $w_2 \in \mathbb{N}$ and a vector $\boldsymbol{c} = (c_1, \ldots, c_{w_1})$ of w_1 multivariate polynomials $c_1, \ldots, c_{w_1} \in \mathbb{Z}_N[X_s, \mathbf{X}_s, \mathbf{X}_h]$. The variables X_s and $\mathbf{X}_s = (X_{s_1}, \ldots, X_{s_{w_2}})$ are called ciphertext-specific. The c_i's are restricted to linear combinations of monomials $\{X_s, X_{s_i}, X_{h_j}X_s, X_{h_j}X_{s_i}\}_{i \in [w_2], j \in [n]}$.

Pair $(\kappa, \mathrm{kInd}, \mathrm{cInd}) \to \boldsymbol{E}$: outputs a matrix $\boldsymbol{E} \in \mathbb{Z}_N^{m_1 \times w_1}$, where m_1 and w_1 are defined by Enc1 (κ, kInd) and Enc2 (κ, cInd), respectively.

Correctness: For formal definition we refer to [3]. Informally, if $R_\kappa(\mathrm{kInd}, \mathrm{cInd}) = 1$, $(\boldsymbol{k}, m_2) \in [\mathrm{Enc1}(\kappa, \mathrm{kInd})]$, and $(\boldsymbol{c}, w_2) \in [\mathrm{Enc2}(\kappa, \mathrm{cInd})]$, then it holds symbolically $\boldsymbol{k} \cdot \boldsymbol{E} \cdot \boldsymbol{c} = X_\alpha X_s$. Additionally, the encoding must be compatible with the domain transferability property to a certain extent.

As a notational convention, whenever a particular relation index κ, a key index kInd $\in \mathbb{X}_\kappa$, and a ciphertext index cInd $\in \mathbb{Y}_\kappa$ are under consideration, the following values are also implicitly defined: $n = \mathrm{Param}(\kappa)$, $(\boldsymbol{k}, m_2) = \mathrm{Enc1}(\kappa, \mathrm{kInd})$, $m_1 = |\boldsymbol{k}|$, and $(\boldsymbol{c}, w_2) = \mathrm{Enc2}(\kappa, \mathrm{cInd})$, $w_1 = |\boldsymbol{c}|$. Note that differently from [3] we allow the algorithm Pair to be probabilistic. The results from [3] still hold with our definition.

Security Notions for Pair Encoding Schemes. We prove the security of our framework based on the computational security notions of pair encoding schemes presented in [3], i.e. selectively master-key hiding (SMH) and co-selectively master-key hiding (CMH). These security notions make the pair encoding framework so powerful.

3.2 Additional Requirements of CCA-Secure Framework

In this subsection we formalize properties of the pair encoding scheme, which are required to achieve CCA-secure P-KEMs. As in [5] we require *normality* of pair encoding P, a very natural restriction (this is also one of the restrictions of regular encodings from [2]). A pair encoding P for $\mathcal{R}_{\Omega,\Sigma}$ is normal, if for every $\kappa \in \Omega \times \Sigma$ and every cInd $\in \mathbb{Y}_\kappa$ one of the polynomials in $\boldsymbol{c}(X_s, \mathbf{X}_s, \mathbf{X}_h)$ is X_s, where $(\boldsymbol{c}, w_2) = \mathrm{Enc2}(\kappa, \mathrm{cInd})$. W.l.o.g, we will assume that $c_1 = X_s$.

Next, we formally define the verifiability property. For the intuition behind this property we refer to the discussion in the next subsection. Let $\mathcal{R}_{\Omega,\Sigma}$ be a domain-transferable predicate family, $\mathcal{G}$ be a group generator and λ be a security parameter. Let $\mathbb{GD} \in [\mathcal{G}(1^\lambda)]$ and $\mathbb{GD}_N$ be the same group description with $N = p_1 p_2 p_3$ instead of the prime numbers. Furthermore, let des $\in \Omega$, kInd $\in \mathbb{X}_\kappa$, and cInd $\in \mathbb{Y}_\kappa$ be arbitrary but fixed ($\kappa = (\text{des}, N)$).

Definition 3.1 (Verifiability). P *is called* verifiable with respect to $\mathcal{G}$ *if it is normal and there exists a deterministic polynomial-time algorithm* Vrfy, *which given* des, $\mathbb{GD}_N$, $g_1 \in \mathbb{G}_{p_1}$, $g_1^h \in \mathbb{G}_{p_1}^n$, kInd, cInd, $\boldsymbol{E} \in [\text{Pair}(\kappa, \text{kInd}, \text{cInd})]$, *and* $\boldsymbol{C} = (C_1, \ldots, C_{w_1}) \in \mathbb{G}^{w_1}$ *outputs 0 or 1 such that:*

Completeness: *If there exist* $s \in \mathbb{Z}_N$ *and* $\boldsymbol{s} \in \mathbb{Z}_N^{w_2}$ *such that the* $\mathbb{G}_{p_1}$ *components of* $\boldsymbol{C}$ *are equal to* $g_1^{c(s,\boldsymbol{s},h)}$ *for* $(\boldsymbol{c}, w_2) = \text{Enc2}(\kappa, \text{cInd})$, *then the output is 1.*
Soundness: *If the output is 1, then for every* $\alpha \in \mathbb{Z}_N$, $\boldsymbol{r} \in \mathbb{Z}_N^{m_2}$ *it holds:*

$$\text{e}\left(g_1^{k(\alpha, \boldsymbol{r}, h) \cdot \boldsymbol{E}}, \boldsymbol{C}\right) = \text{e}(g_1, C_1)^\alpha , \tag{1}$$

where $(\boldsymbol{k}, m_2) = \text{Enc1}(\kappa, \text{kInd})$.

Remark 3.1. Suppose that the verification algorithm outputs 1 *if and only if* there exist $s \in \mathbb{Z}_N$ and $\boldsymbol{s} \in \mathbb{Z}_N^{w_2}$ such that the $\mathbb{G}_{p_1}$ components of $\boldsymbol{C}$ are equal to $g_1^{c(s,\boldsymbol{s},h)}$. Then, both required properties are satisfied due to the correctness of the pair encoding scheme, which ensures that for every $\boldsymbol{E} \in [\text{Pair}(\kappa, \text{kInd}, \text{cInd})]$ it holds $\boldsymbol{k}(\alpha, \boldsymbol{r}, h) \cdot \boldsymbol{E} \cdot \boldsymbol{c}(s, \boldsymbol{s}, h) = \alpha \cdot s$.

Collision-Resistant Hash Functions. Our construction requires a collision-resistant hash function in order to hash elements from $\mathbb{Y}_\kappa$ and a restricted number of elements from $\mathbb{G}_T$ into $\mathbb{Z}_N$. Such a function can be realized using an appropriate injective encoding function and a cryptographic hash function (see the full version). We denote by $\text{H} \leftarrow \mathcal{H}_\kappa$ the random choice of such a function.

3.3   Fully CCA-Secure Framework

In this section we present our framework for constructing fully CCA-secure P-KEMs from pair encoding schemes. Let P be a verifiable pair encoding scheme for predicate family $\mathcal{R}_{\Omega, \mathbb{N}}$ and Vrfy be the algorithm from Definition 3.1. Let $\mathcal{G}$ be a composite order group generator, and $\mathcal{H}$ be a family of appropriate collision-resistant hash functions. A P-KEM Π for $\mathcal{R}$ is defined as follows:

Setup $(1^\lambda, \text{des})$: If des $\in \Omega$, generate $\mathbb{GD} \leftarrow \mathcal{G}(1^\lambda)$, $g_1 \leftarrow \mathbb{G}_{p_1}$ and $g_3 \leftarrow \mathbb{G}_{p_3}$. Set $\kappa := (\text{des}, N)$, compute $n := \text{Param}(\kappa)$ and pick $\boldsymbol{h} \leftarrow \mathbb{Z}_N^n$. Choose $\alpha, u, v \leftarrow \mathbb{Z}_N$ and set $Y := \text{e}(g_1, g_1)^\alpha$, $U_1 := g_1^u$, and $V_1 := g_1^v$. Choose $\text{H} \leftarrow \mathcal{H}_\kappa$ and output msk $:= \alpha$ and $\text{pp}_\kappa := (\text{des}, \mathbb{GD}_N, g_1, g_1^h, U_1, V_1, g_3, Y, \text{H})$.
KeyGen$_{\text{msk}}$ (kInd) : If kInd $\in \mathbb{X}_\kappa$, compute $(\boldsymbol{k}, m_2) := \text{Enc1}(\kappa, \text{kInd})$ (let $m_1 = |\boldsymbol{k}|$). Pick $\boldsymbol{r} \leftarrow \mathbb{Z}_N^{m_2}$, $\boldsymbol{R}_3 \leftarrow \mathbb{G}_{p_3}^{m_1}$, compute $\boldsymbol{K} := g_1^{k(\text{msk}, \boldsymbol{r}, h)} \cdot \boldsymbol{R}_3$ and output sk $:= (\text{kInd}, \boldsymbol{K})$. The key space for kInd $\in \mathbb{X}_\kappa$ is $\mathbb{SK}_{\text{kInd}} := \{\text{kInd}\} \times \mathbb{G}^{m_1}$.

Encaps (cInd) : If cInd $\in \mathbb{Y}_\kappa$, compute $(c, w_2) := \text{Enc2}(\kappa, \text{cInd})$ (let $w_1 = |c|$). Pick $s \leftarrow \mathbb{Z}_N$, $\boldsymbol{s} \leftarrow \mathbb{Z}_N^{w_2}$ and compute $\boldsymbol{C} := g_1^{c(s,\boldsymbol{s},h)} = (C_1, \ldots, C_{w_1})$. Compute

$$t := \text{H}(\text{cInd}, \text{e}(g_1, C_1), \ldots, \text{e}(g_1, C_{w_1})) \tag{2}$$

and $C'' := (U_1^t \cdot V_1)^s$. Set CT $:= (\text{cInd}, \boldsymbol{C}, C'')$, K $:= Y^s$ and output (K, CT). The ciphertext space for cInd $\in \mathbb{Y}_\kappa$ is $\mathbb{C}_{\text{cInd}} := \{\text{cInd}\} \times \mathbb{G}^{w_1+1}$. Note that, given CT $\in \mathbb{C}_{\text{cInd}}$, the corresponding hash value can be computed efficiently. We denote by HInput (CT) the input of the hash function as defined in (2).

Decaps$_{\text{sk}}$ (CT) : It must hold CT $\in \mathbb{C}_{\text{cInd}}$ for cInd $\in \mathbb{Y}_\kappa$ and sk $\in \mathbb{SK}_{\text{kInd}}$ for kInd $\in \mathbb{X}_\kappa$. If $\text{R}_N(\text{kInd}, \text{cInd}) \neq 1$, output $\bot$. Compute $t := \text{H}(\text{HInput}(\text{CT}))$ and $\boldsymbol{E} \leftarrow \text{Pair}(\kappa, \text{kInd}, \text{cInd})$. Output $\bot$, if one of the following checks fails:

$$\text{e}(C'', g_1) \stackrel{?}{=} \text{e}(C_1, U_1^t \cdot V_1) \ , \tag{3}$$

$$\text{e}(C'', g_3) \stackrel{?}{=} 1 \text{ and } \forall_{i \in [w_1]} : \text{e}(C_i, g_3) \stackrel{?}{=} 1 \ , \tag{4}$$

$$\text{Vrfy}(\text{des}, \mathbb{GD}_N, g_1, g_1^h, \text{kInd}, \text{cInd}, \boldsymbol{E}, \boldsymbol{C}) \stackrel{?}{=} 1 \ . \tag{5}$$

Output K $:= \text{e}(\boldsymbol{K}^{\boldsymbol{E}}, \boldsymbol{C})$.

Correctness is based mainly on the correctness of pair encoding and the completeness of the verification algorithm (see the full version). Compared to the original CPA-secure framework of [3] we add only the hash function H and the group elements $U_1, V_1 \in \mathbb{G}$ to the public parameter. The user secret keys are not changed at all. The encapsulation is extended by a single group element $C'' \in \mathbb{G}$. The checks in (3), (4) and (5) are new. We call them *consistency checks* and explain them in more detail below.

Semi-functional Algorithms. The following semi-functional algorithms are basically from [3] and are essential to prove adaptive security of the original and our extended framework. The main idea is to extend the keys and the ciphertexts with components from $\mathbb{G}_{p_2}$ subgroup. Due to the subgroup decision assumptions these modifications cannot be noticed by a ppt adversary. We extended the algorithms from [3] by semi-functional components for our additional elements $\hat{u}_2$, $\hat{v}_2$, and $\widehat{C''}$.

SFSetup $(1^\lambda, \text{des})$: Generate $(\text{msk}, \text{pp}_\kappa) \leftarrow \text{Setup}(1^\lambda, \text{des})$, $g_2 \leftarrow \mathbb{G}_{p_2}$, $\hat{\boldsymbol{h}} \leftarrow \mathbb{Z}_N^n$ and $\hat{u}_2, \hat{v}_2 \leftarrow \mathbb{Z}_N$. Output $(\text{msk}, \text{pp}_\kappa, g_2, \hat{\boldsymbol{h}}, \hat{u}_2, \hat{v}_2)$.

SFKeyGen$_{\text{msk}}$ $(1^\lambda, \text{pp}_\kappa, \text{kInd}, \text{type}, \hat{\alpha}, g_2, \hat{\boldsymbol{h}})$: Let $\hat{\alpha} \in \mathbb{Z}_N$. Generate a normal key $(\text{kInd}, \boldsymbol{K}) \leftarrow \text{KeyGen}_{\text{msk}}(\text{kInd})$, $\hat{\boldsymbol{r}} = (\hat{r}_1, \ldots, \hat{r}_{m_2}) \leftarrow \mathbb{Z}_N^{m_2}$, and compute $\widehat{\boldsymbol{K}} := g_2^{k(0,\hat{r},\hat{h})}$ if type $= 1$, $\widehat{\boldsymbol{K}} := g_2^{k(\hat{\alpha},\hat{r},\hat{h})}$ if type $= 2$ or $\widehat{\boldsymbol{K}} := g_2^{k(\hat{\alpha},0,0)}$ if type $= 3$.
Output the semi-functional key sk $:= (\text{kInd}, \boldsymbol{K} \cdot \widehat{\boldsymbol{K}})$.

SFEncaps $\left(1^\lambda, \mathrm{pp}_\kappa, \mathrm{cInd}, g_2, \hat{h}, \hat{u}_2, \hat{v}_2\right)$: Generate normal encapsulation components $(\mathrm{K}, (\mathrm{cInd}, \boldsymbol{C}, C'')) \leftarrow \mathrm{Encaps}\,(\mathrm{cInd})$. Let t be the corresponding hash value. Pick random elements $\hat{s} \leftarrow \mathbb{Z}_N$ and $\hat{\boldsymbol{s}} \leftarrow \mathbb{Z}_N^{w_2}$, compute $\widehat{\boldsymbol{C}} := g_2^{c(\hat{s}, \hat{s}, \hat{h})}$ and $\widehat{C''} := \left(g_2^{\hat{u}_2 t} \cdot g_2^{\hat{v}_2}\right)^{\hat{s}}$. Output key K and semi-functional encapsulation $\mathrm{CT} = \left(\mathrm{cInd}, \boldsymbol{C} \cdot \widehat{\boldsymbol{C}}, C'' \cdot \widehat{C''}\right)$.

Intuition Behind the Consistency Checks. In this subsection we provide a high-level explanation of why the consistency checks render the decapsulation oracle useless to any ppt adversary. Our explanation leaves out many important details of the formal proof.

Assume that $\mathcal{A}$ queries the decapsulation oracle with $\mathrm{CT} = (\mathrm{cInd}, \boldsymbol{C}, C'') \in \mathbb{C}_{\mathrm{cInd}}$ such that the group elements of CT contain only $\mathbb{G}_{p_1}$ components. If CT passes (5), then by the verifiability property $\mathrm{e}\left(\boldsymbol{K}^E, \boldsymbol{C}\right) = \mathrm{e}(g_1, C_1)^{\mathrm{msk}}$. Next, our additional element C'' and the check in (3) guarantee that the $\mathbb{G}_{p_1}$ component of C_1 is of the form g_1^s and s is known to $\mathcal{A}$. Hence, the output of the decapsulation is $\mathrm{e}(g_1, C_1)^{\mathrm{msk}} = Y^s$. Since $\mathcal{A}$ knows Y and s anyway, this can be computed by $\mathcal{A}$ itself and the decapsulation oracle is useless for $\mathcal{A}$.

We still have to justify the assumption that the elements in CT contain only the $\mathbb{G}_{p_1}$ components. The checks in (4) guarantee that the elements of CT contain no $\mathbb{G}_{p_3}$ components. Then, the subgroup decision assumptions ensures that CT does not also contain $\mathbb{G}_{p_2}$ components.

Extension of Our Construction. Our framework requires additional computational overhead during the computation of the hash value. Namely, a pairing is computed for every group element in the ciphertext. We can avoid this computation by hashing the original ciphertext (see the full version). Then, our last reduction must be adapted in order to prove the security for this variant. We decided to present the given less efficient construction in order to explicitly show which parts of the ciphertext are important for the well-formedness proofs, when the dual system encryption methodology is used to achieve CCA-secure schemes.

4   Main Theorem and Extended Proof Technique

In this section we present our main theorem and explain the proof technique. We also state that all known pair encodings satisfy our verifiability property.

Theorem 4.1. *Let Π be the P-KEM from Sect. 3.3. Suppose that the subgroup decision assumptions from Sect. 2.4 are correct, the underlying pair encoding scheme P is selectively and co-selectively master key hiding, and the family of collision-resistant hash functions $\mathcal{H}$ is secure. Then, Π is fully CCA-secure with respect to Definition 2.2. Furthermore, for every ppt algorithm $\mathcal{A}$, there exist ppt* *algorithms $\mathcal{B}_1, \ldots, \mathcal{B}_6$ with essentially the same running time as $\mathcal{A}$ such that*

$$\text{Adv-aP-KEM}_{\Pi,\mathcal{A}}^{\text{aCCA}}(\lambda, \text{des}) \leq \text{Adv}_{\mathcal{H},\mathcal{B}_1}^{\text{CR}}(\lambda, \text{des}) + \text{Adv}_{\mathcal{B}_2}^{\text{SD1}}(\lambda) + \text{Adv}_{\mathcal{B}_4}^{\text{SD3}}(\lambda)$$
$$+ (2q_1 + 4) \cdot \text{Adv}_{\mathcal{B}_3}^{\text{SD2}}(\lambda) + \text{Adv}_{\text{P},\mathcal{B}_6}^{\text{SMH}}(\lambda, \text{des})$$
$$+ q_1 \cdot \text{Adv}_{\text{P},\mathcal{B}5}^{\text{CMH}}(\lambda, \text{des}) + q_{\text{dec1}}/p_1 + \text{negl}(\lambda) ,$$

where q_1 is the number of keys that are corrupted in Phase 1 and q_{dec1} is the number of decapsulation queries in Phase 1 of experiment aP-KEM$_{\Pi,\mathcal{A}}^{\text{aCCA}}(\lambda, \text{des})$.

For simplicity, we collected some negligible terms such as $1/p_1$ in negl (λ). It is important to notice that the number of decapsulation queries from Phase 1 only appears in the term q_{dec1}/p_1 and decreases the security guarantees only negligibly. Furthermore, compared to the CPA-secure framework of [3] we only loose the additional terms $\text{Adv}_{\mathcal{H},\mathcal{B}_1}^{\text{CR}}(\lambda, \text{des})$ and $\text{Adv}_{\mathcal{B}_3}^{\text{SD2}}(\lambda)$.

The structure for the proof of Theorem 4.1 is presented in Fig. 1. The nodes represent different probability experiments. In Table 1 the modifications between the probability experiments are defined. The first experiment is the target experiment aP-KEM$_{\Pi,\mathcal{A}}^{\text{aCCA}}(\lambda, \text{des})$ from page 6 and the last experiment is constructed in such a way, that the advantage of every adversary is zero. The edges represent reduction steps and their labels the underlying security assumptions, except for the edge labeled with Vrfy. The corresponding proof is based on the verifiability property of the pair encoding scheme. In the proof we show that no ppt algorithm can distinguish between any pair of consecutive experiments (see the full version). Here, we explain the main steps of the proof and the proof technique.

$$G_{\text{Real}} \quad G_{\text{resH}} \quad G_{\text{resQ}} \quad G_0' \quad G_{0,3} \quad G_{k-1,3} \quad G_{k,1} \quad G_{k,2} \quad G_{k,3} \quad G_{q_1,3} \quad G_{q_1+1} \quad G_{q_1+2} \quad G_{q_1+3} \quad G_{q_1+3}' \quad G_{\text{Final}}$$

$$\circ \xrightarrow{} \circ \xrightarrow{} \circ \xrightarrow{} \circ \xrightarrow{} \circ \cdots \cdots \dashrightarrow \circ \xrightarrow{} \circ \xrightarrow{} \circ \xrightarrow{} \circ \cdots \cdots \dashrightarrow \circ \xrightarrow{} \circ \xrightarrow{} \circ \xrightarrow{} \circ \xrightarrow{} \circ$$
$$\text{CR}_{\mathcal{H}} \quad \text{SD2} \quad \text{SD1} \quad \text{Vrfy} \quad\quad\quad \text{SD2} \quad \text{CMH} \quad \text{SD2} \quad\quad\quad \text{SD2} \quad \text{SMH} \quad \text{SD2} \quad \text{SD2} \quad \text{SD3}$$

Fig. 1. Proof structure

The structure of the proof for our CCA-secure construction is similar to the structure of the proof for the CPA-secure construction of [3]. Experiments G_{resH}, G_{resQ}, G_0', and G_{q_1+3}' as well as the four reduction steps denoted by bold edges in Fig. 1 are new. The remaining experiments and reductions are from the original CPA-security proof from [3] and require only simple extensions.

Our first reduction $G_{\text{Real}} \rightarrow G_{\text{resH}}$ is based on the security of the family of collision-resistant hash functions. In the second reduction $G_{\text{resH}} \rightarrow G_{\text{resQ}}$ we separate failure events which enable us to find a non-trivial factor of N, which violates Assumption SD2 by Lemma 2.1. This reduction is an extension of the first reduction step from [3]. These two steps are of a standard technical nature. Our additional games G_0' and G_{q_1+3}' and the corresponding new reductions $G_0' \rightarrow G_{0,3}$ and $G_{q_1+3} \rightarrow G_{q_1+3}'$ are the most important parts of the CCA-security proof and enable us to deal with decapsulation queries in an elegant way. The major modification in $G_{0,3}$ is that the decapsulation queries are answered using separately generated *normal keys* which we denote by sk'_i. We do not change these keys to semi-functional in the following games. In particular, using consistency check (5) we show that for every (unconditional) $\mathcal{A}$, experiments G'_0 and $G_{0,3}$ are indistinguishable. The next important observation is that in all reductions between $G_{0,3}$ and G_{q_1+3}, the master secret key is known to the reduction algorithm. Hence, the normal keys for the decapsulation queries can be generated by the key generation algorithm. The final challenge is to answer decapsulation queries without the user secret keys in the last experiment G_{Final}. Experiment G'_{q_1+3} and the corresponding new reduction step $G_{q_1+3} \rightarrow G'_{q_1+3}$ allow us to deal with this problem. In the proof of this reduction step we use our additional group element from the encapsulation in order to answer the decapsulation queries. To prove that this modification can not be noticed, again the consistency checks are crucial. See the full version for the formal proof.

Table 1. The probability experiments from security proof.

G_{resH}:	Modify [10]	Output is 0 if there is a collision for H
G_{resQ}:	Modify [10]	Output 0 if $\mathcal{A}$ implicitly found a factor of N.
G'_0:	Modify [1]	$\left(\text{msk}, \text{pp}, g_2, \hat{\boldsymbol{h}}, \hat{u}_2, \hat{v}_2\right) \leftarrow \text{SFSetup}\left(1^\lambda, \text{des}\right)$
	Modify [5]	$(K_0, \text{CT}^*) \leftarrow \text{SFEncaps}\left(\text{cInd}^*, g_2, \hat{\boldsymbol{h}}, \hat{u}_2, \hat{v}_2\right)$
$G_{0,3}$:	Modify [4], [9]	$\text{sk}'_i \leftarrow \text{KeyGen}_{\text{msk}}(\text{kInd}_i), \text{Decaps}_{\text{sk}'_i}(\text{CT})$
	Change	Generate keys in Open oracle.
$G_{k,1}$:	Modify [3]	$\begin{aligned}&\hat{\alpha}_j \leftarrow \mathbb{Z}_N,\\ \text{sk}_j \leftarrow &\begin{cases} \text{SFKeyGen}_{\text{msk}}(\text{kInd}, 3, \hat{\alpha}_j, g_2, \_) & \text{if } j < k\\ \text{SFKeyGen}_{\text{msk}}\left(\text{kInd}, 1, \_, g_2, \hat{\boldsymbol{h}}\right) & \text{if } j = k\\ \text{KeyGen}_{\text{msk}}(\text{kInd}) & \text{if } j > k \end{cases}\end{aligned}$
$G_{k,2}$:	Modify [3]	$\begin{aligned}&\hat{\alpha}_j \leftarrow \mathbb{Z}_N,\\ \text{sk}_j \leftarrow &\begin{cases} \text{SFKeyGen}_{\text{msk}}(\text{kInd}, 3, \hat{\alpha}_j, g_2, \_) & \text{if } j < k\\ \text{SFKeyGen}_{\text{msk}}\left(\text{kInd}, 2, \hat{\alpha}_j, g_2, \hat{\boldsymbol{h}}\right) & \text{if } j = k\\ \text{KeyGen}_{\text{msk}}(\text{kInd}) & \text{if } j > k \end{cases}\end{aligned}$
$G_{k,3}$:	Modify [3]	$\begin{aligned}&\hat{\alpha}_j \leftarrow \mathbb{Z}_N,\\ \text{sk}_j \leftarrow &\begin{cases} \text{SFKeyGen}_{\text{msk}}(\text{kInd}, 3, \hat{\alpha}_j, g_2, \_) & \text{if } j \leq k\\ \text{KeyGen}_{\text{msk}}(\text{kInd}) & \text{if } j > k \end{cases}\end{aligned}$
G_{q_1+1}:	Modify [8]	$\text{SFKeyGen}_{\text{msk}}\left(\text{kInd}, 1, \_, g_2, \hat{\boldsymbol{h}}\right)$
G_{q_1+2}:	Insert	$\hat{\alpha} \leftarrow \mathbb{Z}_N$ at the beginning of Phase 2
	Modify [8]	$\text{SFKeyGen}_{\text{msk}}\left(\text{kInd}, 2, \hat{\alpha}, g_2, \hat{\boldsymbol{h}}\right)$
G_{q_1+3}:	Modify [8]	$\text{SFKeyGen}_{\text{msk}}(\text{kInd}, 3, \hat{\alpha}, g_2, \_)$
G'_{q_1+3}:	Insert	$X_2 \leftarrow \mathbb{G}_{p_2}$ in the Setup phase
	Modify [4], [9]	Check consistency, return $e\left(g_1^{\text{msk}} \cdot X_2, C_1\right)$
G_{Final}:	Modify [6]	$K^* \leftarrow \mathbb{G}_T$

Verifiability of Pair Encoding Schemes. All (nineteen) pair encoding schemes from [3,5] satisfy the verifiability property according to Definition 3.1. We refer to the full version for the constructive proof of this statement.

5   Comparison with Generic Constructions and Conclusion

In this section we compare the efficiency of our construction to the efficiency of generic constructions for fully CCA-secure PEs from [21,22]. On the one hand we look at the size of public parameters, user secret keys and ciphertexts. On the other hand we look at the efficiency of the encapsulation (encryption) and the decapsulation (decryption) algorithms.

All generic transformations from above use one-time signature schemes as a building block and integrate the verification key vk into the ciphertexts. This results in non-trivial extensions of public parameters, user secret keys and ciphertexts. For example, keys and ciphertexts of PE for the dual of regular languages are extended by $6 \cdot |vk|$ and by $2 \cdot |vk|$ group elements. In contrast to this, we only add two group elements to the public parameters and a single group element to the ciphertext independently of the predicate. Hence, with respect to the size of public parameters, secret keys, and ciphertexts our construction is more efficient.

Considering the efficiency of the encapsulation and the decapsulation, we further need to distinguish two types of generic transformations of CPA-secure schemes into CCA-secure schemes: schemes based on verifiability, and schemes based on key delegation. CCA-secure attribute-based schemes achieved from key delegation [21] require derandomization and delegation of the user secret keys in every decryption. Depending on the predicate, on kInd and on cInd this can be more efficient or more costly compared to the schemes achieved using our construction. Generic constructions based on verifiability require a verification algorithm which ensures that decryption of a ciphertext under every secret key for kInd and every secret key corresponding to vk will be the same. In our construction we require that decapsulation using every secret key for kInd will be the same. Hence, schemes from generic constructions have to check in addition those parts of the ciphertext, that correspond to the verification key included in the ciphertext ($2 \cdot |vk|$ group elements in the example from above). This results in more costly verification algorithms compared to ours. Furthermore, these additional elements have to be computed in the encryption algorithm together with the one-time signature, whereas we only use a hash function and have to compute a single group element in addition.

Summarizing, we presented a semi-generic framework to construct fully CCA-secure PEs in composite-order groups from any verifiable pair encoding schemes including regular pair encoding schemes. From this point of view our framework is as generic as the underlying CPA-secure framework of [3]. Our security proofs are based on a small but significant modification of the dual system encryption methodology, i.e. we do not change decryption keys to semi-functional. This results in a reduction of CCA-security to the security of pair encodings which is almost as tight as the reduction of CPA-security to the security of pair encodings given by Attrapadung [3].

References

1. Agrawal, S., Chase, M.: A study of pair encodings: predicate encryption in prime order groups. In: Kushilevitz, E., Malkin, T. (eds.) TCC 2016-A. LNCS, vol. 9563, pp. 259–288. Springer, Heidelberg (2016). doi:10.1007/978-3-662-49099-0_10
2. Attrapadung, N.: Dual system encryption framework in prime-order groups. Cryptology ePrint Archive, Report 2015/390
3. Attrapadung, N.: Dual system encryption via doubly selective security: framework, fully secure functional encryption for regular languages, and more. In: Nguyen, P.Q., Oswald, E. (eds.) EUROCRYPT 2014. LNCS, vol. 8441, pp. 557–577. Springer, Heidelberg (2014)
4. Attrapadung, N., Libert, B.: Functional encryption for public-attribute inner products: achieving constant-size ciphertexts with adaptive security or support for negation. J. Math. Cryptology $5(2)$, 115–158 (2012)
5. Attrapadung, N., Yamada, S.: Duality in ABE: converting attribute based encryption for dual predicate and dual policy via computational encodings. In: Nyberg, K. (ed.) CT-RSA 2015. LNCS, vol. 9048, pp. 87–105. Springer, Heidelberg (2015)
6. Boneh, D., Canetti, R., Halevi, S., Katz, J.: Chosen-ciphertext security from identity-based encryption. SIAM J. Comput. $36(5)$, 1301–1328 (2007)
7. Boneh, D., Sahai, A., Waters, B.: Functional encryption: definitions and challenges. In: Ishai, Y. (ed.) TCC 2011. LNCS, vol. 6597, pp. 253–273. Springer, Heidelberg (2011)
8. Chen, J., Gay, R., Wee, H.: Improved dual system ABE in prime-order groups via predicate encodings. In: Oswald, E., Fischlin, M. (eds.) EUROCRYPT 2015. LNCS, vol. 9057, pp. 595–624. Springer, Heidelberg (2015)
9. Cramer, R., Shoup, V.: Universal hash proofs and a paradigm for adaptive chosen ciphertext secure public-key encryption. In: Knudsen, L.R. (ed.) EUROCRYPT 2002. LNCS, vol. 2332, pp. 45–64. Springer, Heidelberg (2002)
10. Cramer, R., Shoup, V.: Design and analysis of practical public-key encryption schemes secure against adaptive chosen ciphertext attack. SIAM J. Comput. $33(1)$, 167–226 (2003)
11. Hamburg, M.: Spatial encryption. Cryptology ePrint Archive, Report 2011/389
12. Kiltz, E., Galindo, D.: Direct chosen-ciphertext secure identity-based key encapsulation without random oracles. Theor. Comput. Sci. $410(47–49)$, 5093–5111 (2009)
13. Kiltz, E., Vahlis, Y.: CCA2 secure IBE: standard model efficiency through authenticated symmetric encryption. In: Malkin, T. (ed.) CT-RSA 2008. LNCS, vol. 4964, pp. 221–238. Springer, Heidelberg (2008)
14. Lewko, A., Okamoto, T., Sahai, A., Takashima, K., Waters, B.: Fully secure functional encryption: attribute-based encryption and (Hierarchical) inner product encryption. In: Gilbert, H. (ed.) EUROCRYPT 2010. LNCS, vol. 6110, pp. 62–91. Springer, Heidelberg (2010)
15. Lewko, A., Waters, B.: New techniques for dual system encryption and fully secure HIBE with short ciphertexts. In: Micciancio, D. (ed.) TCC 2010. LNCS, vol. 5978, pp. 455–479. Springer, Heidelberg (2010)
16. Lewko, A., Waters, B.: Unbounded HIBE and attribute-based encryption. In: Paterson, K.G. (ed.) EUROCRYPT 2011. LNCS, vol. 6632, pp. 547–567. Springer, Heidelberg (2011)

17. Okamoto, T., Takashima, K.: Fully secure functional encryption with general relations from the decisional linear assumption. In: Rabin, T. (ed.) CRYPTO 2010. LNCS, vol. 6223, pp. 191–208. Springer, Heidelberg (2010)

18. Phan, D.H., Pointcheval, D., Shahandashti, S.F., Strefler, M.: Adaptive CCA broadcast encryption with constant-size secret keys and ciphertexts. Int. J. Inf. Secur. **12**(4), 251–265 (2013)

19. Waters, B.: Dual system encryption: realizing fully secure IBE and HIBE under simple assumptions. In: Halevi, S. (ed.) CRYPTO 2009. LNCS, vol. 5677, pp. 619–636. Springer, Heidelberg (2009)

20. Wee, H.: Dual system encryption via predicate encodings. In: Lindell, Y. (ed.) TCC 2014. LNCS, vol. 8349, pp. 616–637. Springer, Heidelberg (2014)

21. Yamada, S., Attrapadung, N., Hanaoka, G., Kunihiro, N.: Generic constructions for chosen-ciphertext secure attribute based encryption. In: Catalano, D., Fazio, N., Gennaro, R., Nicolosi, A. (eds.) PKC 2011. LNCS, vol. 6571, pp. 71–89. Springer, Heidelberg (2011)

22. Yamada, S., Attrapadung, N., Santoso, B., Schuldt, J.C.N., Hanaoka, G., Kunihiro, N.: Verifiable predicate encryption and applications to CCA security and anonymous predicate authentication. In: Fischlin, M., Buchmann, J., Manulis, M. (eds.) PKC 2012. LNCS, vol. 7293, pp. 243–261. Springer, Heidelberg (2012)

Factoring $N = p^r q^s$ for Large r and s

Jean-Sébastien Coron[1]([✉]), Jean-Charles Faugère[2,3,4],
Guénaël Renault[2,3,4], and Rina Zeitoun[5]

[1] University of Luxembourg, Luxembourg City, Luxembourg
jean-sebastien.coron@uni.lu
[2] INRIA, POLSYS, Centre Paris-Rocquencourt, 78153 Le Chesnay, France
[3] Sorbonne Universités, UPMC Univ Paris 06,
Équipe POLSYS, LIP6 UPMC, 75005 Paris, France
[4] CNRS, UMR 7606, LIP6 UPMC, 75005 Paris, France
jean-charles.faugere@inria.fr
guenael.renault@lip6.fr
[5] Oberthur Technologies, 420 rue d'Estienne d'Orves,
CS 40008, 92705 Colombes, France
r.zeitoun@oberthur.com

Abstract. Boneh *et al.* showed at Crypto 99 that moduli of the form $N = p^r q$ can be factored in polynomial time when $r \simeq \log p$. Their algorithm is based on Coppersmith's technique for finding small roots of polynomial equations. In this paper we show that $N = p^r q^s$ can also be factored in polynomial time when r or s is at least $(\log p)^3$; therefore we identify a new class of integers that can be efficiently factored.

We also generalize our algorithm to moduli with k prime factors $N = \prod_{i=1}^{k} p_i^{r_i}$; we show that a non-trivial factor of N can be extracted in polynomial-time if one of the exponents r_i is large enough.

1 Introduction

At Crypto 98, Takagi [Tak98] showed that RSA decryption can be performed significantly faster with a modulus of the form $N = p^r q$, by using a p-adic expansion technique [Tak97]. However, at Crypto 99, Boneh, Durfee and Howgrave-Graham (BDH) showed that $N = p^r q$ can be factored in polynomial time for large r, when $r \simeq \log p$ [BDHG99]. Their algorithm is based on Coppersmith's technique for finding small roots of polynomial equations [Cop97], based on lattice reduction. This implies that Takagi's cryptosystem should not be used with a large r.

In light of the BDH attack, Takagi's cryptosystem was later extended by Lim *et al.* in [LKYL00] to moduli of the form $N = p^r q^s$. Namely the authors describe a public-key cryptosystem with modulus $N = p^r q^s$, and obtain even faster decryption than in Takagi's cryptosystem. In particular, for a 8192-bit RSA modulus of the form $N = p^2 q^3$, decryption becomes 15 times faster than for a standard RSA modulus of the same size.

In the BDH paper, the generalization of factoring moduli of the form $N = p^r q^s$ was explicitly left as an open problem. Therefore one could be tempted to use the

© Springer International Publishing Switzerland 2016
K. Sako (Ed.): CT-RSA 2016, LNCS 9610, pp. 448–464, 2016.
DOI: 10.1007/978-3-319-29485-8_26

Lim *et al.* cryptosystem [LKYL00], since no attack is known and it offers a significant speed-up compared to standard RSA. In this paper we show that moduli of the form $N = p^r q^s$ can also be factored in polynomial time for large r and/or s; this gives a new class of integers that can be factored efficiently. Our result implies that the Lim *et al.* cryptosystem should not be used for large r or s.

Factoring $N = p^r q$ with Coppersmith. Coppersmith's technique for finding small roots of polynomial equations [Cop97] has found numerous applications in cryptography, for example cryptanalysis of RSA with $d < N^{0.29}$ [BD00] (see also [DN00] for an extension), cryptanalysis of RSA with small secret CRT-exponents [JM07], and deterministic equivalence between recovering the private exponent d and factoring N [May04].

Coppersmith also showed that $N = pq$ can be factored in polynomial time when half of the bits of p are known [Cop97]. The BDH paper is actually an extension of this result for moduli $N = p^r q$, using a simplification by Howgrave-Graham [HG97]; namely the authors showed that knowing a fraction $1/(r+1)$ of the bits of p is enough for polynomial-time factorization of $N = p^r q$. Therefore when $r \simeq \log p$ only a constant number of bits of p must be known, hence those bits can be recovered by exhaustive search, and factoring $N = p^r q$ becomes polynomial-time [BDHG99].

As mentioned previously, in the BDH paper the generalization to moduli of the form $N = p^r q^s$ (where r and s can have the same size), is explicitly left as an open problem. To factor such N one could let $Q := q^s$ and try to apply BDH on $N = p^r Q$; however the condition for polynomial-time factorization becomes $r \simeq \log Q \simeq s \log q$; therefore this can only work if r is much larger than s. Alternatively a natural approach to factor $N = p^r q^s$ would be to write $N = (P+x)^r (Q+y)^s$ and apply Coppersmith's second theorem for finding small roots of bivariate polynomials over $\mathbb{Z}$; however from Coppersmith's bound this does not seem to give a polynomial-time factorization (see Appendix A).

Factoring $N = p^r q^s$. In this paper we solve this open problem and describe a new algorithm to factor $N = p^r q^s$ in deterministic polynomial time when r and/or s is greater than $(\log p)^3$.

We first illustrate our technique with a particular case. Let consider a modulus of the form $N = p^{r+1} q^r$. As observed in [LKYL00], we can rewrite $N = (pq)^r p = P^r Q$ with $P := pq$ and $Q := p$ and apply BDH to $N = P^r Q$ to recover P and Q, which gives p and q. In that case the condition for polynomial-time factorization becomes $r = \Omega(\log Q) = \Omega(\log p)$, the same condition as BDH. This shows that $N = p^{r+1} q^r$ can also be factored in polynomial time for large r. We note that in [LKYL00] only moduli of the form $N = p^{r+1} q^r$ were considered for lattice-based factorisation.

However it is easy to generalize the previous observation to any modulus of the form $N = p^{\alpha \cdot r + a} q^{\beta \cdot r + b}$ for small integers α, β, a and b. Namely as previously one can let $P := p^\alpha q^\beta$ and $Q := p^a q^b$ and apply BDH on $N = P^r Q$ to recover P and Q, which gives p and q. The condition for polynomial-time factorization is again $r = \Omega(\log Q)$, which for small a, b gives the same condition $r = \Omega(\log p)$ as previously (assuming that p and q have similar bitsize).

Now it is natural to ask whether we can generalize the above method to any modulus $N = p^r q^s$. More precisely, we should determine which class of integers (r, s) can be written as:

$$\begin{cases} r = u \cdot \alpha + a \\ s = u \cdot \beta + b \end{cases} \tag{1}$$

with large enough integer u, and small enough integers α, β, a, b, so that we can apply the above method; namely rewrite $N = p^r q^s$ as $N = P^u Q$ where $P := p^\alpha q^\beta$ and $Q := p^a q^b$, and apply BDH on $N = P^u Q$ to recover P and Q and eventually p and q. In this paper we show that it is enough that the max of r and s is $\Omega(\log^3 \max(p, q))$; namely in that case we are guaranteed to find a "good" decomposition of r and s according to (1), leading to a polynomial-time factorization of $N = p^r q^s$. Hence we identify a new class of integers that can be efficiently factored, namely $N = p^r q^s$ for large enough r or s (or both).

Extension to $N = \prod_{i=1}^{k} p_i^{r_i}$. We extend the above technique to moduli with k prime factors $N = \prod_{i=1}^{k} p_i^{r_i}$. Note that with 3 prime factors or more (instead of only 2) we cannot hope to obtain a complete factorization of N. Namely starting from an RSA modulus $N_1 = pq$ one could artificially embed N_1 into a larger modulus $N = (pq)^r q'$ for some known prime q', and hope to recover the factorization of N_1 by factoring N; clearly this cannot work. For the same reason we cannot hope to extract even a single prime factor of N; namely given two RSA moduli $N_1 = p_1 q_1$ and $N_2 = p_2 q_2$ and using $N = (N_1)^r N_2$, extracting a prime factor of N would factor either N_1 or N_2. Instead we show that we can always extract a non-trivial factor of N, if one of the exponents r_i is large enough. More precisely we can extract a non-trivial (not necessarily prime) factor of N in polynomial-time if one of the k exponents r_i is at least $(\log p)^{\theta_k}$, with $\theta_3 = 17$, $\theta_4 = 61$, $\theta_5 = 257$ and $\theta_k \sim 4e \cdot (k-1)!$ for large k. Note that the exponent θ_k grows exponentially with the number of prime factors k; however for a fixed value of k extracting a non-trivial factor of N is always polynomial-time in $\log N$.

Practical Experiments. It is well known that the BDH algorithm for factoring $N = p^r q$ is unpractical. Namely the experiments from [BDHG99] show that the BDH algorithm is practical only for relatively small primes p and q, namely 96 bits in [BDHG99], but for such small primes factors the ECM method [Len87] performs much better. However ECM is subexponential whereas BDH is polynomial-time, so at some point the BDH algorithm must beat ECM; the authors conjecture that BDH should become faster than ECM in practice when p and q are roughly 400 bits.

Needless to say, our algorithm for factoring $N = p^r q^s$ should be even less practical, since for $N = p^r q^s$ we need much larger exponents r or s than in BDH for $N = p^r q$. However we have performed some practical experiments, in order to estimate the running time of our algorithm for factoring a modulus of the form $N = p^r q^s$. We describe the results in Sect. 5; unsurprisingly we observed that for relatively small primes p and q, namely 128 bits, our algorithm performs much worse than ECM. However as for BDH our algorithm scales polynomially whereas ECM scales exponentially, so our algorithm must also beat ECM for large enough p and q.

2 Background

We first recall the following Landau notations: we write $f(n) = \mathcal{O}(g(n))$ if there exists constants n_0 and $c > 0$ such that $|f(n)| \leq c|g(n)|$ for all $n \geq n_0$. We write $f(n) = \Omega(g(n))$ if $g(n) = \mathcal{O}(f(n))$. Therefore $f(n) = \Omega(g(n))$ if and only if there exists constants n_0 and $c > 0$ such that $|f(n)| \geq c|g(n)|$ for all $n \geq n_0$.

2.1 LLL and Simultaneous Diophantine Approximation

Let $b_1, \ldots, b_d \in \mathbb{Z}^n$ be linearly independent vectors with $d \leqslant n$. A lattice L spanned by $\langle b_1, \ldots, b_d \rangle$ is the set of all integer linear combinations of $b_1, \ldots, b_d$. Here we consider full-rank lattices, *i.e.* $d = n$. The $d \times d$ matrix $M = (b_1, \ldots, b_d)$ is called a *basis* of L. The algorithms described in this paper require the ability to find short vectors in a lattice. This can be achieved by the celebrated LLL algorithm [LLL82].

Theorem 1 (LLL). *Let L be a lattice spanned by $\langle b_1, \ldots, b_d \rangle \in \mathbb{Z}^n$. The LLL algorithm, given $\langle b_1, \ldots, b_d \rangle$, finds in time polynomial in the size of the entries, a vector v such that:*
$$\|v\| \leq 2^{(d-1)/4} \det(L)^{1/d}.$$

In this paper we also use an application of LLL for simultaneous Diophantine approximation; we recall the theorem from [LLL82].

Theorem 2. *There exists a polynomial time algorithm that, given a positive integer n and rational numbers $e_1, e_2, \ldots, e_n, \varepsilon$ satisfying $0 < \varepsilon < 1$, finds integers $p_1, p_2, \ldots, p_n, q$ for which*

$$|p_i - qe_i| \leqslant \varepsilon \text{ for } 1 \leqslant i \leqslant n, \text{ and } 1 \leqslant q \leqslant 2^{\frac{n(n+1)}{4}} \varepsilon^{-n}.$$

2.2 Coppersmith's Algorithm

We recall Coppersmith's first theorem [Cop97] for finding small roots of univariate modular polynomial equations.

Theorem 3 (Coppersmith). *Let $f(x)$ be a monic polynomial of degree r in one variable, modulo an integer N of unknown factorization. Let X be such that $X < N^{1/r}$. One can find all integers x_0 with $f(x_0) \equiv 0 \pmod{N}$ and $|x_0| < X$ in time polynomial in $(\log N, r)$.*

In the original Coppersmith paper the complexity is stated as polynomial in $(\log N, 2^r)$ where r is the degree of the polynomial equation, but it is well known that the 2^r is a typo and the complexity is polynomial in r only; see for example

[BM05, Theorem 11]. We recall the main steps of Coppersmith's algorithm in Appendix B.

The following variant of Coppersmith's first theorem was obtained by Blömer and May [BM05], using Coppersmith's technique for finding small roots of bivariate integer equations.

Theorem 4 ([BM05, **Corollary 14**]). *Let N be a composite integer of unknown factorization with divisor $b \geq N^\beta$. Let $f(x) = \sum_i f_i x^i \in \mathbb{Z}[x]$ be a polynomial of degree δ with $\gcd(f_1, \ldots, f_\delta, N) = 1$. Then we can find all points $x_0 \in \mathbb{Z}$ satisfying $f(x_0) = b$ in time polynomial in $\log N$ and δ provided that $|x_0| \leq N^{\beta^2/\delta}$.*

2.3   The Boneh-Durfee-Howgrave-Graham Algorithm

At Crypto 99, Boneh, Durfee and Howgrave-Graham [BDHG99] showed that moduli of the form $N = p^r q$ can be factored in polynomial time for large r, when $r \simeq \log p$. We recall their main theorem.

Theorem 5 (BDH). *Let $N = p^r q$ where $q < p^c$ for some c. The factor p can be recovered from N, r, and c by an algorithm with a running time of:*

$$exp\left(\frac{c+1}{r+c} \cdot \log p\right) \cdot \mathcal{O}(\gamma),$$

where γ is the time it takes to run LLL on a lattice of dimension $\mathcal{O}(r^2)$ with entries of size $\mathcal{O}(r \log N)$. The algorithm is deterministic, and runs in polynomial space.

Their algorithm is based on Coppersmith's technique for finding small roots of polynomial equations. We recall the main steps of the proof in Appendix C. When p and q have similar bitsize we can take $c = 1$; in that case we have $(c+1)/(r+c) = \mathcal{O}(1/r)$ and therefore the algorithm is polynomial time when $r = \Omega(\log p)$. More generally one can take $c = \log q/\log p$, which gives:

$$\frac{c+1}{r+c} \cdot \log p \leq \frac{c+1}{r} \cdot \log p \leq \frac{\frac{\log q}{\log p}+1}{r} \cdot \log p \leq \frac{\log q + \log p}{r}$$

Therefore a sufficient condition for polynomial-time factorization is $r = \Omega(\log q + \log p)$.

Actually by simple inspection of the proof of Theorem 5 in [BDHG99] one can obtain the slightly simpler condition $r = \Omega(\log q)$. We use the following theorem for the rest of the paper.

Theorem 6 (BDH). *Let p and q be two integers with $p \geq 2$ and $q \geq 2$, and let $N = p^r q$. The factors p and q can be recovered in polynomial time in $\log N$ if $r = \Omega(\log q)$.*

We provide the proof of Theorem 6 in Appendix D, based on Lemma 3.3 from [BDHG99]. Note that p and q can be any integers, not necessarily primes.

We can also obtain a proof of Theorem 6 directly from [BM05, Corollary 14], as recalled in Theorem 4. Namely given $N = p^r q$ we let the divisor $b := p^r$ and:

$$f(x) = (V + x)^r$$

where V is an integer such that $p = V + x_0$ and the high-order bits of V are the same as the high-order bits of p. One must then solve $f(x_0) = b$, and applying [BM05, Corollary 14] this can be done in time polynomial in $\log N$ and r provided that $|x_0| < N^{\beta^2/r}$. We can take β such that $b = p^r = N^\beta$. This gives the condition:

$$|x_0| < p^\beta \tag{2}$$

From $p^r = N^\beta = (p^r q)^\beta$ we get:

$$\beta = \frac{r \log p}{r \log p + \log q} = \frac{1}{1 + \frac{\log q}{r \log p}} \geq 1 - \frac{\log q}{r \log p}$$

Therefore from (2) a sufficient condition for applying [BM05, Corollary 14] is:

$$|x_0| < p \cdot q^{-1/r}$$

Therefore one can perform exhaustive search on the high-order bits of p under the previous condition $r = \Omega(\log q)$, and eventually recover the factors p and q, still in time polynomial in $\log N$.

3   Factoring $N = p^r q^s$ for Large r

We prove the following theorem; this is the main theorem of our paper.

Theorem 7. *Let $N = p^r q^s$ be an integer of unknown factorization with $r > s$ and $\gcd(r, s) = 1$. Given N as input one can recover the prime factors p and q in polynomial time in $\log N$ under the condition $r = \Omega(\log^3 \max(p, q))$.*

We first provide a proof intuition. Note that given $N = p^r q^s$ as input we can assume that the exponents r and s are known, since otherwise they can be recovered by exhaustive search in time $\mathcal{O}(\log^2 N)$.

As explained in introduction, given as input $N = p^r q^s$ and assuming that r and s are known, our technique consists in representing r and s as:

$$\begin{cases} r = u \cdot \alpha + a \\ s = u \cdot \beta + b \end{cases} \tag{3}$$

with large enough integer u, and small enough integers α, β, a, b, so that N can be rewritten as:

$$N = p^r q^s = p^{u \cdot \alpha + a} \cdot q^{u \cdot \beta + b} = (p^\alpha q^\beta)^u \cdot p^a q^b = P^u \cdot Q$$

where $P := p^\alpha q^\beta$ and $Q := p^a q^b$. One can then apply BDH on $N = P^u Q$ to recover P and Q and eventually p and q.

Observe that from (3) we obtain:

$$r \cdot \beta - s \cdot \alpha = \gamma \tag{4}$$

where $\gamma := a \cdot \beta - b \cdot \alpha$ must be a small integer, since α, β, a and b must be small. This gives:

$$\alpha \cdot s \equiv -\gamma \pmod{r} \tag{5}$$

Using LLL in dimension 2 (or equivalently the Gauss-Lagrange algorithm), we can find two small integers α and γ satisfying (5) with $|\alpha| \cdot |\gamma| \simeq r$. We then recover β from (4); for integers r and s of similar bitsize, we get $|\beta| \simeq |\alpha|$. The integer u is then defined as $u := \lfloor r/\alpha \rfloor$, and we let a be the remainder of the division of r by α. We obtain $|a|, |\beta| \simeq |\alpha|$ and $|b| \simeq |\gamma|/|\alpha| \simeq r/|\alpha|^2$.

Recall that the condition for BDH factorization is $u = \Omega(\log Q)$; assuming for simplicity that p and q have similar bitsize, from $Q = p^a q^b$ we get the condition:

$$u \simeq \left(|\alpha| + \frac{r}{|\alpha|^2} \right) \log p$$

It is therefore optimal to take $|\alpha| \simeq r^{1/3}$, which gives $u \simeq r^{1/3} \log p$, and with $u := \lfloor r/\alpha \rfloor \simeq r^{2/3}$ we obtain $r^{1/3} \simeq \log p$. This gives the condition $r \simeq \log^3 p$; therefore we recover the condition from Theorem 7 for prime factors p and q of similar bitsize.

We now provide a rigorous analysis. The proof of Theorem 7 is based on the following lemma.

Lemma 1. *Let r and s be two integers such that $r > s > 0$. One can compute in polynomial time integers u, α, β, a, b such that*

$$\begin{cases} r = u \cdot \alpha + a \\ s = u \cdot \beta + b \end{cases} \tag{6}$$

with $0 < \alpha \le 2r^{1/3}$, $0 \le \beta \le \alpha$, $|a| < \alpha$, $|b| \le 6r^{2/3}/\alpha$, $u > r/\alpha - 1$, where the integers a and b are either both ≥ 0 (Case 1), or both ≤ 0 (Case 2).

Proof. We first generate two small integers $\alpha > 0$ and β such that:

$$r \cdot \beta - s \cdot \alpha = \gamma, \tag{7}$$

for some small integer γ. For this we apply LLL on the following matrix M of row vectors:

$$M = \begin{pmatrix} \lfloor r^{1/3} \rfloor & -s \\ 0 & r \end{pmatrix}.$$

We obtain a short non-zero vector $\boldsymbol{v} = (\lfloor r^{1/3} \rfloor \cdot \alpha, \gamma)$, where $\gamma = -s \cdot \alpha + r \cdot \beta$ for some $\beta \in \mathbb{Z}$; hence we obtain integers α, β and γ satisfying (7). From Theorem 1 we must have

$$\|\boldsymbol{v}\| \le 2^{1/4} \cdot (\det M)^{1/2} \le 2^{1/4} \cdot (\lfloor r^{1/3} \rfloor \cdot r)^{1/2} \le 2^{1/4} \cdot r^{2/3} \tag{8}$$

Note that by applying the Gauss-Lagrange algorithm instead of LLL one can obtain a slightly better bound for $\|v\|$, corresponding to Minkowski bound.

From (8) we obtain $|\alpha| \leq 2r^{1/3}$ and $|\gamma| \leq 2r^{2/3}$. We can take $\alpha \geq 0$. Moreover we must have $\alpha \neq 0$ since otherwise we would have $v = (0, \beta r)$ for some integer $\beta \neq 0$, which would give $\|v\| \geq r$, which would contradict the previous bound. Therefore we must have $0 < \alpha \leq 2r^{1/3}$.

From (7) we have $\beta = (\gamma + \alpha \cdot s)/r$ and moreover using $-1 < \gamma/r < 1$ and $0 < s < r$ we obtain:

$$-1 < \frac{\gamma}{r} < \frac{\gamma + \alpha \cdot s}{r} < \frac{\gamma}{r} + \alpha < 1 + \alpha$$

Since α and β are integers this implies $0 \leq \beta \leq \alpha$. We now show how to generate the integers u, a and b. We distinguish two cases.

Case 1: $\beta = 0$ or ($\beta \neq 0$ and $\lfloor r/\alpha \rfloor \leq s/\beta$). In that case we let:

$$u := \left\lfloor \frac{r}{\alpha} \right\rfloor$$

and we let $a := r - u \cdot \alpha$ and $b := s - u \cdot \beta$; this gives (6) as required. Since a is the remainder of the division of r by α we must have $0 \leq a < \alpha$. If $\beta = 0$ we then have $b = s > 0$. If $\beta \neq 0$ we have using $\lfloor r/\alpha \rfloor \leq s/\beta$:

$$b = s - u \cdot \beta = s - \left\lfloor \frac{r}{\alpha} \right\rfloor \cdot \beta \geq s - \frac{s}{\beta} \cdot \beta = 0$$

so in both cases $b \geq 0$. Therefore in Case 1 we have that the integers a and b are both ≥ 0. Moreover combining (6) and (7) we obtain $a \cdot \beta - b \cdot \alpha = \gamma$, which gives using $0 \leq \beta \leq \alpha$ and $0 \leq a < \alpha$:

$$0 \leq b = \frac{a \cdot \beta - \gamma}{\alpha} < \alpha + \frac{2r^{2/3}}{\alpha}$$

Since $0 < \alpha \leq 2r^{1/3}$ we have $4r^{2/3}/\alpha \geq 2r^{1/3} \geq \alpha$, therefore we obtain as required:

$$0 \leq b < \frac{6r^{2/3}}{\alpha}$$

Case 2: $\beta \neq 0$ and $\lfloor r/\alpha \rfloor > s/\beta$. In that case we let:

$$u := \left\lceil \frac{r}{\alpha} \right\rceil$$

As previously we let $a := r - u \cdot \alpha$ and $b := s - u \cdot \beta$, which gives again (6); moreover we have $-\alpha < a \leq 0$. As previously using $\lceil r/\alpha \rceil \geq \lfloor r/\alpha \rfloor > s/\beta$ we obtain:

$$b = s - u \cdot \beta = s - \left\lceil \frac{r}{\alpha} \right\rceil \cdot \beta < s - \frac{s}{\beta} \cdot \beta = 0$$

Therefore in Case 2 we have that the integers a and b are both ≤ 0. As previously using $0 \leq \beta \leq \alpha$, $-\alpha < a \leq 0$ and $\alpha \leq 4r^{2/3}/\alpha$ we obtain as required:

$$|b| \leq \left| \frac{a \cdot \beta - \gamma}{\alpha} \right| < \alpha + \frac{2r^{2/3}}{\alpha} \leq \frac{6r^{2/3}}{\alpha}$$

This terminates the proof of Lemma 1.   □

3.1   Proof of Theorem 7

We now proceed with the proof of Theorem 7. We are given as input $N = p^r q^s$ with $r > s > 0$ and $\gcd(r, s) = 1$. We can assume that the exponents r and s are known, otherwise they can be recovered by exhaustive search in time $\mathcal{O}(\log^2 N)$. We apply Lemma 1 with r, s and obtain u, α, β, a and b such that:

$$\begin{cases} r = u \cdot \alpha + a \\ s = u \cdot \beta + b \end{cases}$$

We first consider Case 1 of Lemma 1 with $a \geq 0$ and $b \geq 0$. In that case the modulus $N = p^r q^s$ can be rewritten as follows:

$$N = p^r q^s = p^{u \cdot \alpha + a} q^{u \cdot \beta + b} = (p^\alpha q^\beta)^u p^a q^b = P^u Q,$$

where $P := p^\alpha q^\beta$ and $Q := p^a q^b$. One can then apply Theorem 6 on $N = P^u Q$ to recover P and Q in polynomial time in $\log N$ under the condition $u = \Omega(\log Q)$. Since $u > r/\alpha - 1$, we get the sufficient condition $r = \Omega(\alpha \cdot \log Q)$. We have from the bounds of Lemma 1:

$$\alpha \cdot \log Q = \alpha \cdot (a \log p + b \log q) \leq \alpha \cdot \left(\alpha \cdot \log p + \frac{6r^{2/3}}{\alpha} \cdot \log q \right)$$

$$\leq \alpha^2 \cdot \log p + 6r^{2/3} \cdot \log q \leq 10 \cdot r^{2/3} \cdot \log \max(p, q)$$

which gives the sufficient condition $r = \Omega(r^{2/3} \cdot \log \max(p, q))$. Therefore one can recover P and Q in polynomial time under the condition:

$$r = \Omega(\log^3 \max(p, q))$$

Alternatively the factors P and Q can be recovered by applying the variant of Coppersmith's theorem from [BM05, Corollary 14], i.e. Theorem 4. Namely as explained in Sect. 2.3, given $N = P^u q$ we can let $b := P^u$ and let:

$$f(x) := (V + x)^u$$

where V is an integer such that $P = V + x_0$ and the high-order bits of V are the same as the high-order bits of p. One must then solve $f(x_0) = b$, and applying [BM05, Corollary 14] this can be done in time polynomial in $\log N$ and u provided that $|x_0| < N^{\beta^2/u}$. As in Sect. 2.3, we can take $b = P^u = N^\beta$, and we obtain the sufficient condition:

$$|x_0| < P \cdot Q^{-1/u}$$

Therefore one can perform exhaustive search on the high-order bits of P in polynomial time in $\log N$ under the same condition as previously, namely $u = \Omega(\log Q)$. As previously one recovers P and Q in polynomial time under the condition $r = \Omega(\log^3 \max(p, q))$.

Finally the prime factors p and q can easily be recovered from $P = p^\alpha q^\beta$ and $Q = p^a q^b$. Namely the matrix $\begin{pmatrix} a & b \\ \alpha & \beta \end{pmatrix}$ whose determinant is $a\beta - b\alpha = \gamma$, is invertible with inverse $\begin{pmatrix} \beta/\gamma & -b/\gamma \\ -\alpha/\gamma & a/\gamma \end{pmatrix}$. Namely we must have $\gamma \neq 0$, since otherwise we would have $\beta \cdot r = \alpha \cdot s$; since we have $\gcd(r, s) = 1$, the integer α would be a non-zero multiple of r, which would contradict the bound from Lemma 1. Therefore one can retrieve p and q by computing:

$$\begin{cases} Q^{\frac{\beta}{\gamma}} \cdot P^{\frac{-b}{\gamma}} = (p^a q^b)^{\frac{\beta}{\gamma}} \cdot (p^\alpha q^\beta)^{\frac{-b}{\gamma}} = p^{\frac{a\beta - b\alpha}{\gamma}} \cdot q^{\frac{b\beta - b\beta}{\gamma}} = p^1 \cdot q^0 = p \\ Q^{\frac{-\alpha}{\gamma}} \cdot P^{\frac{a}{\gamma}} = (p^a q^b)^{\frac{-\alpha}{\gamma}} \cdot (p^\alpha q^\beta)^{\frac{a}{\gamma}} = p^{\frac{a\alpha - a\alpha}{\gamma}} \cdot q^{\frac{a\beta - b\alpha}{\gamma}} = p^0 \cdot q^1 = q \end{cases}.$$

We now consider Case 2 from Lemma 1, that is $a \leq 0$ and $b \leq 0$. In that case we can write:

$$N = p^r q^s = p^{u \cdot \alpha + a} q^{u \cdot \beta + b} = (p^\alpha q^\beta)^u p^a q^b = P^u / Q$$

for $P := p^\alpha q^\beta$ and $Q := p^{-a} q^{-b}$. Note that Q is an integer because $a \leq 0$ and $b \leq 0$. We obtain $P^u = Q \cdot N$ which implies:

$$P^u \equiv 0 \pmod{N}$$

Therefore P is a small root of a univariate polynomial equation of degree u modulo N; hence we can apply Coppersmith's first theorem; the condition from Theorem 3 is $P \leq N^{1/u} = P/Q^{1/u}$. Although the condition is not directly satisfied, it can be met by doing exhaustive search on the high-order $(\log Q)/u$ bits of P, which is still polynomial time under the condition $u = \Omega(\log Q)$; this is the same condition as in Case 1 for BDH.

More precisely, we write $P = X \cdot t + x_0$ where $X = \lfloor N^{1/u} \rfloor$ and $|x_0| \leq X$. We obtain the polynomial equation:

$$(X \cdot t + x_0)^u \equiv 0 \mod N$$

For a fixed t this is a univariate modular polynomial equation of degree u and small unknown x_0. We have $X < N^{1/u}$; therefore we can apply Theorem 3 and recover x_0 in polynomial time in $\log N$, since the degree u satisfies $u \leq r \leq \log N$. We do exhaustive search on t, where:

$$0 \leq t \leq P/X \leq 2P/N^{1/u} = 2Q^{1/u}$$

Therefore the algorithm is still polynomial time under the same condition as in Case 1, namely $u = \Omega(\log Q)$. Since in Lemma 1 the bounds on u, a and b are the same in both Case 1 and Case 2, we obtain that in Case 2 recovering P and Q is polynomial-time under the same condition $r = \Omega(\log^3 \max(p, q))$. As previously given P and Q one can easily recover the prime factors p and q. This terminates the proof of Theorem 7.

4   Generalization to $N = \prod_{i=1}^{k} p_i^{r_i}$ for Large r_i's

We prove the following theorem, which is a generalization of Theorem 7 to moduli $N = \prod_{i=1}^{k} p_i^{r_i}$ with more than two prime factors. As explained in introduction, in that case we cannot hope to obtain a complete factorization of N; however we show that we can always recover a non-trivial factor of N in polynomial time if the largest r_i is at least $\Omega(\log^{\theta_k} \max p_i)$, for some sequence θ_k with $\theta_3 = 17$, $\theta_4 = 61$, $\theta_5 = 257$ and $\theta_k \sim 4e \cdot (k-1)!$ for large k. We provide the proof of Theorem 8 in the full version of this paper [CFRZ15].

Theorem 8. *Let $k \geq 2$ be fixed and let $N = \prod_{i=1}^{k} p_i^{r_i}$ where $r_1 = \max(r_i)$. Let $p := \max\{p_i, 1 \leqslant i \leqslant k\}$. Given N as input one can recover a non-trivial factor of N in time polynomial in $\log N$ if $r_1 = \Omega(\log^{\theta_k} p)$, where $\theta_2 = 5$ and:*

$$\theta_k = 4(k-1)\left(1 + \sum_{i=1}^{k-2}\prod_{j=i}^{k-2} j\right) + 1,$$

with $\theta_k = 4e \cdot (k-1)! - 3 - \circ(1)$ for large k.

5   Experiments

We have implemented our algorithm using Magma Software V2.19-5. We considered four moduli $N = p^r q^s$ with $r = 8$, and $s = 1, 3, 5, 7$, with 128-bit primes p and q. Since in Sect. 3 a fraction $1/u$ of the bits of Q is guessed by exhaustive search, for each modulus N we have determined the values of α, β, a and b that minimize the quantity $\log(Q)/u$; such minimum is reached either by the BDH method (Case 1), or by the Coppersmith method (Case 2). To speed up the LLL computation we have implemented the Rounding and Chaining methods from [BCF+14]. This consists in applying LLL on a matrix with truncated coefficients (Rounding), and using partially LLL-reduced matrices when doing the exhaustive search (Chaining); the first LLL reduction is then costlier than the subsequent ones.

In Table 1 we give the optimal decomposition of N, using either the BDH method (Case 1) or the Coppersmith method (Case 2), with number of bits given, lattice dimension, running time LLL_f of the first LLL reduction, and running time LLL_c of subsequent LLL reductions; finally we also estimate the total running time of the factorization, by multiplying LLL_c by 2^n where n is the number of bits given.

Table 1. Number of bits given, lattice dimension, running time LLL_f of the first LLL, running time LLL_c of subsequent LLLs, and estimated total running time.

	Method	$(p^\alpha q^\beta)^u p^a q^b$	Bits given	Dim.	LLL_f	LLL_c	Est. time
$\mathbf{N = p^8 q}$	BDH	$p^8 q$	29	68	142 s	8.6 s	146 years
$\mathbf{N = p^8 q^3}$	Copp	$(p^2 q)^4 q^{-1}$	51	61	86 s	4.2 s	$3 \cdot 10^8$ years
$\mathbf{N = p^8 q^5}$	BDH	$(p^2 q)^4 q$	55	105	115 s	1.3 s	$2 \cdot 10^9$ years
$\mathbf{N = p^8 q^7}$	Copp	$(pq)^8 q^{-1}$	38	81	676 s	26 s	$2 \cdot 10^5$ years

As observed in [BDHG99] the BDH algorithm is unpractical compared to the ECM factorization algorithm [Len87]. Namely for 128-bit primes p and q and $N = p^{10}q$ the predicted runtime of ECM from [BDHG99] is only 7000 h [BDHG99], instead of 146 years for BDH for $N = p^8 q$. As illustrated in Table 1 for integers $N = p^r q^s$ our algorithm performs even worse. However the ECM scales exponentially[1], whereas our algorithm scales polynomially. Hence for large enough primes p and q our algorithm (like BDH) must outpace ECM.

A   Coppersmith's Second Theorem for Factoring $N = p^r q^s$

A natural approach to factor $N = p^r q^s$ would be to write $N = (P+x)^r (Q+y)^s$ and apply Coppersmith's second theorem for finding small roots of bivariate polynomials over $\mathbb{Z}$. Here we show that this approach does not work. We first recall Coppersmith's second theorem.

Theorem 9 (Coppersmith [Cop97]). *Let $f(x, y)$ be an irreducible polynomial in two variables over $\mathbb{Z}$, of maximum degree δ in each variable separately. Let X and Y be upper bounds on the desired integer solution (x_0, y_0), and let $W = \max_{i,j} |f_{ij}| X^i Y^j$. If $XY < W^{2/(3\delta)}$, then in time polynomial in $(\log W, 2^\delta)$, one can find all integer pairs (x_0, y_0) such that $f(x_0, y_0) = 0$, $|x_0| \leq X$, and $|y_0| \leq Y$.*

For $N = p^r q^s$ we write $p = P + x_0$ and $q = Q + y_0$ where $|x_0| \leq X$ and $|y_0| \leq Y$ for some y, and we assume that P and Q are given. Therefore (x_0, y_0) is a small root over $\mathbb{Z}$ of the bivariate polynomial:

$$f(x, y) = (P+x)^r (Q+y)^s$$

Assuming that $r > s$, the degree of $f(x, y)$ is at most r separately in x and y. Therefore we must have:

$$XY < W^{2/(3r)}$$

where $W = P^r Q^s \simeq N$. Assuming $r \simeq s$, we have:

$$W^{2/(3r)} \simeq N^{2/(3r)} = p^{2/3} q^{2s/(3r)} \simeq (pq)^{2/3}$$

Therefore one should take the bounds $X \simeq p^{2/3}$ and $Y \simeq q^{2/3}$. This implies that to recover p and q in polynomial time we must know at least $1/3$ of the high-order bits of p and $1/3$ of the high-order bits of q. Since this is a constant fraction of the bits of p and q, Coppersmith's second theorem does not enable to factor $N = p^r q^s$ in polynomial-time.

We stress that the above reasoning does not prove that Coppersmith's bivariate technique will not work. Namely as shown in [BM05] to obtain the optimal bound one must use the right construction corresponding to $f(x, y)$'s Newton polygon. However for $r \simeq s$ the polynomial $f(x, y)$ has (almost) the same degree in x and y separately, so it is natural to use the bounds from Coppersmith's original bivariate theorem (Theorem 9) as above; this corresponds to the Rectangle construction in [BM05].

---

[1] The complexity of the ECM factorization algorithm for extracting a prime factor p is $\exp\left((\sqrt{2} + o(1))\sqrt{\log p \log \log p}\right)$.

B   Coppersmith's First Theorem

In this section we recall the main steps of Coppersmith's algorithm for finding small roots of univariate modular equations modulo N, corresponding to Theorem 3. We follow the classical approach by Howgrave-Graham [HG97].

Let $f(x)$ be a polynomial of degree r, with small unknown x_0 such that

$$f(x_0) \equiv 0 \pmod{N}.$$

One considers the following polynomials $g_{i,j}(x)$, where $m \geq 1$ is a given parameter:

$$g_{i,j}(x) = x^j \cdot N^{m-i} f^i(x)$$

for all i and j such that $0 \leq i < m$ and $0 \leq j < r$, and $j = 0$ for $i = m$. We have:

$$g_{i,j}(x_0) \equiv 0 \pmod{N^m}$$

Let $h(x)$ be a linear combination of the $g_{i,j}(x)$; therefore we must have

$$h(x_0) \equiv 0 \pmod{N^m} \tag{9}$$

Let X be such that $|x_0| < X$. If the coefficients of $h(x)$ are sufficiently small, since x_0 is small we will have $|h(x_0)| < N^m$ and therefore Eq. (9) will hold over $\mathbb{Z}$. The root x_0 of $h(x_0) = 0$ can then be recovered using a classical root-finding algorithm. The condition is formalized by the following lemma due to Howgrave-Graham [HG97]. Given a polynomial $h(x) = \sum_i h_i x^i$ we define $\|h(x)\|^2 = \sum_i |h_i|^2$.

Lemma 2 (Howgrave-Graham). *Let $h(x) \in \mathbb{Z}[x]$ be the sum of at most d monomials. Assume that $h(x_0) \equiv 0 \pmod{N^m}$ where $|x_0| \leq X$ and $\|h(xX)\| < N^m/\sqrt{d}$. Then $h(x_0) = 0$ over the integers.*

Proof. We have:

$$|h(x_0)| = \left| \sum h_i x_0^i \right| = \left| \sum h_i X^i \left(\frac{x_0}{X} \right)^i \right| \leq \sum \left| h_i X^i \left(\frac{x_0}{X} \right)^i \right|$$

$$\leq \sum |h_i X^i| \leq \sqrt{d} \|h(xX)\| < N^m.$$

Since $h(x_0) \equiv 0 \pmod{N^m}$, this gives $h(x_0) = 0$. □

It remains to show how to obtain $h(x)$ such that $\|h(xX)\| < N^m/\sqrt{d}$. We consider the matrix M of dimension $d = rm + 1$ whose row vectors are the coefficients of the polynomials $g_{i,j}(xX)$. This matrix is reduced using the well-known LLL algorithm [LLL82] or an analogous algorithm with improved complexity [NS09, NSV11]. Since the matrix M is triangular, the determinant of M is the product of its diagonal elements:

$$\det M = N^{(m+1)(d-1)/2} X^{d(d-1)/2}.$$

From Theorem 1, the first resulting polynomial $v(xX)$ of the reduced matrix is such that $\|v(xX)\| \leq 2^{(d-1)/4}(\det M)^{1/d}$. As a consequence, we get:

$$\|v(xX)\| \leq 2^{(d-1)/4} N^{(m+1)(d-1)/2d} X^{(d-1)/2}.$$

In order to fulfill the condition $\|v(xX)\| < N^m/\sqrt{d}$, we get the following condition on the upper-bound X, under which the solution $|x_0| < X$ can be retrieved:

$$X < \frac{1}{4} \cdot N^{\frac{1}{r} - \frac{1}{rd}}.$$

Eventually by using a dimension $d = \mathcal{O}(\log N)$ and performing exhaustive search on a constant number of high-order bits of x_0, one obtains the sufficient condition $X < N^{1/r}$; this proves Theorem 3.

C   The BDH Method for Factoring $N = p^r q$

In this section we recall the main steps of the BDH method from Theorem 6; we refer to [BDHG99] for more details. Let $N = p^r q$. Assume that we are also given an integer V such that $p = V + x_0$ where the high-order bits of V are the same as the high-order bits of p, and x_0 is a small unknown. One considers the polynomial $f(x) = (V + x)^r$ which satisfies:

$$f(x_0) \equiv (V + x_0)^r \equiv 0 \pmod{p^r}$$

Moreover we also have:

$$N \equiv 0 \pmod{p^r}$$

Therefore for a given integer m one considers the polynomials

$$g_{ik}(x) = N^{m-k} x^i f^k(x)$$

for $0 \leq k \leq m$ and $i \geq 0$, and we have for all k, i:

$$g_{ik}(x_0) \equiv N^{m-k} \cdot x_0^i \cdot f^k(x_0) \equiv 0 \pmod{p^{rm}}$$

Let X be a bound on x_0. One considers the lattice L spanned by the coefficient vectors of $g_{ik}(xX)$ for $0 \leq k \leq m-1$ and $0 \leq i \leq r-1$, and also $g_{ik}(xX)$ for $k = m$ and $0 \leq i \leq d-mr-1$, where d is a parameter which is actually the lattice dimension. Since the matrix basis of the lattice is triangular, the determinant of the lattice is the product of the diagonal entries, which gives:

$$\det L = \left(\prod_{k=0}^{m-1} \prod_{i=0}^{r-1} N^{m-k} \right) \left(\prod_{j=0}^{d-1} X^j \right) < N^{rm(m+1)/2} X^{d^2/2}$$

By applying the LLL algorithm on the previous matrix, we obtain a short vector $v(xX)$ such that:

$$\|v(xX)\|^d \leq 2^{d^2/2} \det L \leq N^{rm(m+1)/2} (2X)^{d^2/2}$$

From Lemma 2 and omitting the $\sqrt{d}$ factor, we must have $\|v(xX)\| \leq p^{rm}$, which gives the condition:

$$(2X)^{d^2/2} < p^{rmd} N^{-rm(m+1)/2}$$

We assume that $q < p^c$ for some $c > 0$. This gives $N < p^{r+c}$, which gives the condition:

$$(2X)^{d^2/2} < p^{rmd - r(r+c)m(m+1)/2}.$$

We wish to maximize the value $md - (r + c)m(m + 1)/2$. Working through tedious arithmetic allows to find that the maximum is well approximated by $\frac{d^2}{2(r+c)}\left(1 - \frac{r+c}{d}\right)$, which is reached for $m = \frac{d}{r+c} - \frac{1}{2}$ (we assume that $m \in \mathbb{N}$ by an appropriate choice of r and d). Therefore, this results in the following condition on X:

$$X < p^{1 - \frac{c}{r+c} - 2\frac{r}{d}},$$

which proves Lemma 3.3 from [BDHG99].

Lemma 3 [BDHG99]. *Let $N = p^r q$ be given, and assume $q < p^c$ for some c. Furthermore assume that P is an integer satisfying*

$$|P - p| < p^{1 - \frac{c}{r+c} - 2\frac{r}{d}}$$

Then the factor p may be computed from N, r, c and P by an algorithm whose running time is dominated by the time it takes to run LLL on a lattice of dimension d.

In [BDHG99] the authors take $d = 2r(r + c)$, which gives:

$$|P - p| < p^{1 - \frac{c+1}{r+c}}$$

and therefore to factor $N = p^r q$ it suffices to perform exhaustive search on a fraction $(c + 1)/(r + c)$ of the bits of p, and the running time becomes:

$$\exp\left(\frac{c+1}{r+c} \cdot \log p\right) \cdot \mathrm{poly}(\log N)$$

which proves Theorem 5.

D   Proof of Theorem 6

We start from Lemma 3 from [BDHG99] whose proof is briefly recalled in the previous section. Note that in Lemma 3 the integers p and q can be any integers ≥ 2, not necessarily primes; namely the proof of Lemma 3 does not depend on p and q being primes.

Instead of taking $d = 2r(r + c)$ as in the previous section, we now take $d = 2\lceil r \cdot \log p \rceil$, which gives:

$$|P - p| < p^{1 - \frac{c}{r+c} - \frac{1}{\log p}}$$

and therefore to factor $N = p^r q$ it suffices to perform exhaustive search on a fraction $c/(r + c) < c/r$ of the bits of p, which gives a running time:

$$\exp\left(\frac{c}{r} \cdot \log p\right) \cdot \mathsf{poly}(\log N)$$

Moreover we can take c such that $(p^c)/2 < q < p^c$, which gives $p^c < 2q$, which gives $c \log p < \log q + \log 2$. Therefore the running time is:

$$\exp\left(\frac{\log q}{r}\right) \cdot \mathsf{poly}(\log N)$$

and therefore a sufficient condition for polynomial-time factorization of $N = p^r q$ is $r = \Omega(\log q)$; this proves Theorem 6.

References

[BCF+14] Bi, J., Coron, J.-S., Faugère, J.-C., Nguyen, P.Q., Renault, G., Zeitoun, R.: Rounding and chaining lll: finding faster small roots of univariate polynomial congruences. IACR Cryptology ePrint Archive, 2014 (2014)

[BD00] Boneh, D., Durfee, G.: Cryptanalysis of RSA with private key d less than $N^{0.292}$. IEEE Trans. Inf. Theory **46**(4), 1339 (2000)

[BDHG99] Boneh, D., Durfee, G., Howgrave-Graham, N.: Factoring tex $n = p^r q$ for large r. In: Wiener, M. (ed.) CRYPTO 1999. LNCS, vol. 1666, pp. 326–337. Springer, Heidelberg (1999)

[BM05] Blömer, J., May, A.: A tool kit for finding small roots of bivariate polynomials over the integers. In: Cramer, R. (ed.) EUROCRYPT 2005. LNCS, vol. 3494, pp. 251–267. Springer, Heidelberg (2005)

[CFRZ15] Coron, J.-S., Faugere, J.-C., Renault, G., Zeitoun, R.: Factoring $N = p^r q^s$ for large r and s. Cryptology ePrint Archive, Report 2015/071 (2015). http://eprint.iacr.org/. Full version of this paper

[Co96a] Coppersmith, D.: Finding a small root of a bivariate integer equation; factoring with high bits known. In: Maurer, U.M. (ed.) EUROCRYPT 1996. LNCS, vol. 1070, pp. 178–189. Springer, Heidelberg (1996)

[Co96b] Coppersmith, D.: Finding a small root of a univariate modular equation. In: Maurer, U.M. (ed.) EUROCRYPT 1996. LNCS, vol. 1070, pp. 155–165. Springer, Heidelberg (1996)

[Cop97] Coppersmith, D.: Small solutions to polynomial equations, and low exponent RSA vulnerabilities. J. Cryptology **10**(4), 233–260 (1997). Journal version of [Co96b, Co96a]

[DN00] Durfee, G., Nguyên, P.Q.: Cryptanalysis of the RSA schemes with short secret exponent from asiacrypt '99. In: Okamoto, T. (ed.) ASIACRYPT 2000. LNCS, vol. 1976, pp. 14–29. Springer, Heidelberg (2000)

[HG97] Howgrave-Graham, N.: Finding small roots of univariate modular equations revisited. In: Darnell, M. (ed.) Cryptography and Coding. LNCS, vol. 1355, pp. 131–142. Springer, Heidelberg (1997)

[JM07] Jochemsz, E., May, A.: A polynomial time attack on RSA with private CRT-exponents smaller than $N^{0.073}$. In: Menezes, A. (ed.) CRYPTO 2007. LNCS, vol. 4622, pp. 395–411. Springer, Heidelberg (2007)

[Len87] Lenstra, H.W.: Factoring integers with elliptic curves. Ann. Math. **126**, 649–673 (1987)

[LKYL00] Lim, S., Kim, S., Yie, I., Lee, H.: A generalized takagi-cryptosystem with a modulus of the form $p^r q^s$. In: Roy, B., Okamoto, E. (eds.) INDOCRYPT 2000. LNCS, vol. 1977, pp. 283–294. Springer, Heidelberg (2000)

[LLL82] Lenstra, A.K., Lenstra Jr., H.W., Lovász, L.: Factoring polynomials with rational coefficients. Math. Ann. **261**, 513–534 (1982)

[May04] May, A.: Computing the RSA secret key is deterministic polynomial time equivalent to factoring. In: Franklin, M. (ed.) CRYPTO 2004. LNCS, vol. 3152, pp. 213–219. Springer, Heidelberg (2004)

[NS09] Nguyen, P.Q., Stehlé, D.: An LLL algorithm with quadratic complexity. SIAM J. Comput. **39**(3), 874–903 (2009)

[NSV11] Novocin, A., Stehlé, D., Villard, G.: An LLL-reduction algorithm with quasi-linear time complexity: extended abstract. In: Proceedings of the STOC 2011, pp. 403–412. ACM (2011)

[Tak97] Takagi, T.: Fast RSA-type cryptosystems using n-adic expansion. In: Kaliski Jr., B.S. (ed.) CRYPTO 1997. LNCS, vol. 1294, pp. 372–384. Springer, Heidelberg (1997)

[Tak98] Takagi, T.: Fast RSA-type cryptosystem modulo $p^k q$. In: Krawczyk, H. (ed.) CRYPTO 1998. LNCS, vol. 1462, pp. 318–326. Springer, Heidelberg (1998)

Author Index

Printed in the United States
By Bookmasters